# SpringBoard®

## English Language Arts

### California Edition

**Grade 10**

 **CollegeBoard**

## ABOUT THE COLLEGE BOARD

The College Board is a mission-driven not-for-profit organization that connects students to college success and opportunity. Founded in 1900, the College Board was created to expand access to higher education. Today, the membership association is made up of more than 6,000 of the world's leading educational institutions and is dedicated to promoting excellence and equity in education. Each year, the College Board helps more than seven million students prepare for a successful transition to college through programs and services in college readiness and college success—including the SAT® and the Advanced Placement Program®. The organization also serves the education community through research and advocacy on behalf of students, educators and schools. For further information, visit www.collegeboard.com.

ISBN: 978-1-4573-0466-8

1 2 3 4 5 6 7 8    16 17 18 19 20 21 22
Printed in the United States of America

## ACKNOWLEDGMENTS

The College Board gratefully acknowledges the outstanding work of the classroom teachers and writers who have been integral to the development of this revised program. The end product is testimony to their expertise, understanding of student learning needs, and dedication to rigorous and accessible English Language Arts instruction.

**Colleen Ancrile**
English Teacher
Los Angeles Unified School District
Sun Valley, California

**Alli Bennett**
Assistant Principal
Bethel School District 403
Spanaway, Washington

**Kirstin A. Daniels**
English Teacher
Sunnyside Unified School District
Tucson, Arizona

**Paul DeMaret**
SpringBoard/AP English Teacher
Poudre School District
Fort Collins, Colorado

**Allison Fonseca**
English Teacher
Hillsborough County Public Schools
Tampa, Florida

**Karen Fullam**
Advanced Academics Coordinator
Hillsborough County Public Schools
Tampa, Florida

**Ron Lybarger**
English Teacher/Department Head
Decatur Public School District #61
Decatur, Illinois

**Glenn Morgan**
English Teacher
San Diego Unified School District
San Diego, California

**Michelle Nellon**
English Teacher
Los Angeles Unified School District
Sun Valley, California

**Carmen P. Padilla, M.Ed.**
English Teacher
Los Angeles Unified School District
Los Angeles, California

**Stephanie Sharpe**
English Teacher
Hillsborough County Public Schools
Tampa, Florida

**Susan Van Doren**
English/AP English Language/AP
Computer Science Teacher
Douglas County School District
Zephyr Cove, Nevada

**Rebecca Wenrich**
English Teacher
Peninsula School District 401
Gig Harbor, Washington

**Tom Wilkins**
English Teacher
Fayette County Public Schools
Lexington, Kentucky

## SPRINGBOARD ENGLISH LANGUAGE ARTS

**Lori O'Dea**
Executive Director
Content Development

**Doug Waugh**
Executive Director
Product Management

**Joely Negedly**
Senior Director
Humanities Curriculum and Instruction

**JoEllen Victoreen**
Senior Product Manager
English Language Arts

**Julie Manley**
Senior Director
Professional Learning

**Sarah Balistreri**
Director
ELA Content Development

**Eden Orlando**
SpringBoard District Coach

**Jennifer Duva**
English Language Arts Editor

**Rebecca Grudzina**
English Language Arts Editor

**Spencer Gonçalves**
Assistant ELA Editor

**Jessica Pippin**
Assistant ELA Editor

## RESEARCH AND PLANNING ADVISORS

We also wish to thank the members of our SpringBoard Advisory Council and the many educators who gave generously of their time and their ideas as we conducted research for both the print and online programs. Your suggestions and reactions to ideas helped immeasurably as we planned the revisions. We gratefully acknowledge the teachers and administrators in the following districts.

ABC Unified School District
Cerritos, California

Bellevue School District 405
Bellevue, Washington

Charleston County School District
Charleston, South Carolina

Clark County School District
Las Vegas, Nevada

Denver Public Schools
Denver, Colorado

Hillsborough County Public Schools
Tampa, Florida

Kenton County School District
Fort Wright, Kentucky

Los Angeles Unified School District
Los Angeles, California

Milwaukee Public Schools
Milwaukee, Wisconsin

Newton County Schools
Covington, Georgia

Noblesville Schools
Noblesville, Indiana

Oakland Unified School District
Oakland, California

Orange County Public Schools
Orlando, Florida

Peninsula School District
Gig Harbor, Washington

Quakertown Community School District
Quakertown, Pennsylvania

St. Vrain School District
Longmont, Colorado

Scottsdale Public Schools
Phoenix, Arizona

Seminole County Public Schools
Sanford, Florida

Spokane Public Schools
Spokane, Washington

# Contents

## Unit 1   Cultural Conversations

### Activities

## Unit 2  Cultural Perspectives

### Activities

**Unit 3** Cultures in Conflict

**Activities**

## Unit 4 Dramatic Justice

**Activities**

## Unit 5  Building Cultural Bridges

### Activities

# To the Student

## WELCOME TO SPRINGBOARD!

Dear Student,

Welcome to the SpringBoard program! This program has been created with you in mind: it contains the English Language Arts content you need to learn, the tools to help you learn, and tasks to strengthen the critical thinking skills that will help you succeed in high school and beyond.

In SpringBoard, you will explore compelling themes through reading, writing, discussions, performances, and research. You will closely read short stories, novels, poems, historical texts, and articles. You'll also view and interpret films, plays, and audio texts while comparing them to their related print versions. With frequent opportunities to write creatively and analytically throughout the program, you will develop fluency, research skills, and an understanding of how to craft your writing based on audience and purpose. Through collaborative discussions, presentations, performances, and debates with your peers, you will deepen your understanding of the texts you've read and viewed and learn how to convey your ideas with clarity and voice.

Tools to help you learn are built into every lesson. At the beginning of each activity, you will see suggested learning strategies, each of which is explained in full in the Resources section of your book. These strategies will help you deeply analyze text, collect evidence for your writing, and critically think about and discuss issues and ideas. Within the activities, you'll also notice explanations about essential vocabulary and grammar concepts that will enrich your ability to read and write effectively.

High school is the time to challenge yourself to develop skills and habits you need to be successful throughout your academic life and career. The SpringBoard program provides you with meaningful and engaging activities built on the rigorous standards that lead to college and career success. Your participation in SpringBoard will help you advance your reading, writing, language, and speaking and listening skills, all while helping you build confidence in your ability to succeed academically.

We hope you enjoy learning with the SpringBoard program. It will give you many opportunities to explore ideas and issues collaboratively and independently and to cultivate new skills as you prepare for your future.

Sincerely,

SpringBoard

## AP CONNECTIONS

When you reach high school, you may have an opportunity to take Advanced Placement (AP) classes or other rigorous courses. When the time comes to make that decision, we want you to be equipped with the kind of higher-order thinking skills, knowledge, and behaviors necessary to be successful in AP classes and beyond. You will see connections to AP in the texts that you read, the strategies you use, and the writing tasks you encounter throughout the course.

Connections to AP Language and Literature will help you

- Read closely and analyze both literary and nonfiction texts

- Analyze relationships among author's purpose, literary/stylistic devices, rhetorical appeals, and desired effects for intended audiences

- Write with attention to selecting textual evidence and organizational patterns according to purpose and audience

- Write to interpret and evaluate multiple perspectives in literature

- Develop the control of language and command of conventions required for academic writing

## THE SPRINGBOARD DIFFERENCE

SpringBoard is different because it provides instruction with hands-on participation that involves you and your classmates in daily discussions and analysis of what you're reading and learning. You will have an opportunity to

- Discuss and collaborate with your peers to explore and express your ideas

- Explore multiple perspectives by reading a variety of texts—both fiction and nonfiction—that introduce you to different ways of thinking, writing, and communicating

- Examine writing from the perspective of a reader and writer and learn techniques that good writers use to communicate their message effectively

- Gain a deep understanding of topics, enabling you to apply your learning to new and varied situations

- Take ownership of your learning by practicing and selecting strategies that work for you

- Reflect on your growth and showcase your best work as a reader, writer, speaker, and listener in a working Portfolio

## HIGH SCHOOL AT A GLANCE
### Grade 9

Investigating the thematic concept of **coming of age**, you will read Harper Lee's novel *To Kill a Mockingbird*; informational articles about college; short stories by Poe and Collier; historical articles about segregation; poetry by Wordsworth, Neruda, Lorde, and Silko; and Shakespeare's *Romeo and Juliet*. From your reading, you will gather evidence from texts and incorporate it in written and oral responses, including a presentation using multiple forms of media.

You will encounter more varied and complex writing in this grade as you write in a variety of modes including argumentative, explanatory, and narrative writing. Film texts are a large part of Grade 9 activities. In Unit 2, you will study film director's style and analyze how style is evident in the transformation of print texts to films. In Unit 5, you will study *Romeo and Juliet* and analyze how key scenes are represented in multiple film versions as well as the print text.

### Grade 10

In this grade, you will explore the thematic concept of culture. Texts include Chinua Achebe's *Things Fall Apart*, Sophocles' *Antigone*, Susan B. Anthony's "On Women's Right to Vote," and the Nobel Prize acceptance speeches of Alexander Solzhenitsyn and Elie Wiesel. You will be challenged to use evidence from these texts in both your written and oral responses. For example, you will study the extent to which one's culture influences one's worldview, and incorporate textual evidence in a written argument. Research plays a role as you investigate the Ibo culture represented in *Things Fall Apart* and present your findings in a collaborative presentation using digital media.

Film texts play a role when you analyze the degree of objectivity and subjectivity present in documentary films while also gathering evidence about environmental issues.

## Grade 11

In this grade, you will explore concepts that have shaped American thought and discourse since its revolution through the study of American literature and rhetoric. You will read foundational U.S. documents such as Lincoln's Second Inaugural Address and The Declaration of Independence, essays by Ralph Waldo Emerson and Henry David Thoreau, and poetry by Langston Hughes and Walt Whitman. You will also read full-length works from the 20th century: Arthur Miller's drama *The Crucible*, Jon Krakauer's *Into the Wild*, and Zora Neale Hurston's *Their Eyes Were Watching God*. These texts will help you gather evidence to incorporate in writing, speeches, performances, and presentations about the American Dream, what it means to be an American, the freedom of speech, the role of media in a democracy, and literary movements like Transcendentalism and the Harlem Renaissance.

You will compare print and film versions of *Their Eyes Were Watching God*, and study various features of news outlets while working collaboratively to create your own news collection of news pieces.

## Grade 12

Your SpringBoard journey culminates in Grade 12 with a year-long focus on using literary theory to analyze complex texts through multiple perspectives. You will encounter James Baldwin's "Stranger in the Village," George Orwell's "Shooting an Elephant," Shakespeare's *Othello*, and George Bernard Shaw's *Pygmalion*. Throughout the level, you will learn about and apply Archetypal, Cultural, Feminist, Historical, Marxist, and Reader Response Criticism to both literary and informational texts. You will also use your knowledge of these theories to shed new light on film, photography, and media coverage of newsworthy events, including Hurricane Katrina.

Senior English offers many opportunities for you to synthesize your learning through rigorous writing and speaking tasks. Independent research, film study, and presentations go hand in hand with your study of print texts, and allow you to develop complex and nuanced understandings of the texts, films, and issues in the course.

## CLASSROOM TOOLS

As you move through each SpringBoard unit, your teacher will guide you to use tools that will help you develop strong study habits, keep your work organized, and track your learning progress.

### Reader/Writer Notebook

Your **Reader/Writer Notebook** is a place to record and keep track of vocabulary words, grammar practice, notes and reflections on readings, some writing assignments, brainstorms, and other items as determined by your teacher. You will use your Reader/Writer Notebook often, so think of it as an extension of the main SpringBoard book.

### Word Wall

Your teacher will regularly add new vocabulary words to the class **Word Wall**. The Word Wall gives you and your classmates a visual reminder of the words you are learning throughout the unit of study. Also, you can use the Word Wall to easily check the spelling of new words.

### Performance Portfolio

Your **Performance Portfolio** is a place to keep your assignments organized so that you can see your growth and learning across the school year. Keeping a portfolio will make it easier to share your work with others, reflect on what you are learning, revise certain pieces of work, and set goals for future learning.

Your teacher will guide you to include items in your portfolio that illustrate a wide range of work, such as first drafts, final drafts, quickwrites, notes, reading logs, graphic organizers, audio and video examples, and graphics that represent a variety of genres, forms, and media created for a multitude of purposes. As you progress through the course, you will have opportunities to revisit prior work, revise it based on new learning, and reflect on the learning strategies and activities that help you be successful.

### Independent Reading

Based on your personal interests and preferences, you will be encouraged to select books, articles, and other texts to read independently. Reading independently not only reinforces the learning you're doing in class, but it also gives you a chance to expand your knowledge about topics that fascinate you.

You can find **Independent Reading Lists** in the Resources section at the back of your book. The lists provide ideas for texts that complement the reading you're doing in each SpringBoard unit. These are suggestions to get you started, but you may also choose other readings with input from your teacher, family, and peers.

While you work your way through each SpringBoard unit, your teacher will give you time to read independently. You can record general thoughts or reactions to your independent reading in the **Independent Reading Log** in the Resources section of your book. You may also use the Independent Reading Log to respond to the occasional **Independent Reading Links** that you'll encounter in each SpringBoard unit. These links prompt you to think about your independent reading by responding to questions, doing research, making connections between texts and themes, discussing ideas in book groups, and recommending titles to your classmates.

We hope you enjoy exploring the texts, topics, and themes in SpringBoard and that you feel inspired to deepen your reading, writing, speaking, and analytic skills through the program.

## Reading Standards for Literature

| | | |
|---|---|---|
| **Key Ideas and Details** | RL.9–10.1 | Cite strong and thorough textual evidence to support analysis of what the text says explicitly as well as inferences drawn from the text. |
| | RL.9–10.2 | Determine a theme or central idea of a text and analyze in detail its development over the course of the text, including how it emerges and is shaped and refined by specific details; provide an objective summary of the text. |
| | RL.9–10.3 | Analyze how complex characters (e.g., those with multiple or conflicting motivations) develop over the course of a text, interact with other characters, and advance the plot or develop the theme. |
| **Craft and Structure** | RL.9–10.4 | Determine the meaning of words and phrases as they are used in the text, including figurative and connotative meanings; analyze the cumulative impact of specific word choices on meaning and tone (e.g., how the language evokes a sense of time and place; how it sets a formal or informal tone). **(See grade 9–10 Language standards 4–6 for additional expectations.) CA** |
| | RL.9–10.5 | Analyze how an author's choices concerning how to structure a text, order events within it (e.g., parallel plots), and manipulate time (e.g., pacing, flashbacks) create such effects as mystery, tension, or surprise. |
| | RL.9–10.6 | Analyze a particular point of view or cultural experience reflected in a work of literature from outside the United States, drawing on a wide reading of world literature. |
| **Integration of Knowledge and Ideas** | RL.9–10.7 | Analyze the representation of a subject or a key scene in two different artistic mediums, including what is emphasized or absent in each treatment (e.g., Auden's "Musée des Beaux Arts" and Breughel's *Landscape with the Fall of Icarus*). |
| | RL.9–10.8 | (Not applicable to literature) |
| | RL.9–10.9 | Analyze how an author draws on and transforms source material in a specific work (e.g., how Shakespeare treats a theme or topic from Ovid or the Bible or how a later author draws on a play by Shakespeare). |
| **Range of Reading and Level of Text Complexity** | RL.9–10.10 | By the end of grade 9, read and comprehend literature, including stories, dramas, and poems, in the grades 9–10 text complexity band proficiently, with scaffolding as needed at the high end of the range.<br><br>By the end of grade 10, read and comprehend literature, including stories, dramas, and poems, at the high end of the grades 9–10 text complexity band independently and proficiently. |

## Reading Standards for Informational Text

| | | |
|---|---|---|
| **Key Ideas and Details** | RI.9–10.1 | Cite strong and thorough textual evidence to support analysis of what the text says explicitly as well as inferences drawn from the text. |
| | RI.9–10.2 | Determine a central idea of a text and analyze its development over the course of the text, including how it emerges and is shaped and refined by specific details; provide an objective summary of the text. |
| | RI.9–10.3 | Analyze how the author unfolds an analysis or series of ideas or events, including the order in which the points are made, how they are introduced and developed, and the connections that are drawn between them. |
| **Craft and Structure** | RI.9–10.4 | Determine the meaning of words and phrases as they are used in a text, including figurative, connotative, and technical meanings; analyze the cumulative impact of specific word choices on meaning and tone (e.g., how the language of a court opinion differs from that of a newspaper). **(See grade 9–10 Language standards 4–6 for additional expectations.) CA** |
| | RI.9–10.5 | Analyze in detail how an author's ideas or claims are developed and refined by particular sentences, paragraphs, or larger portions of a text (e.g., a section or chapter). |
| | **RI.9–10.5a** | **Analyze the use of text features (e.g., graphics, headers, captions) in functional workplace documents. CA** |
| | RI.9–10.6 | Determine an author's point of view or purpose in a text and analyze how an author uses rhetoric to advance that point of view or purpose. |
| **Integration of Knowledge and Ideas** | RI.9–10.7 | Analyze various accounts of a subject told in different mediums (e.g., a person's life story in both print and multimedia), determining which details are emphasized in each account. |
| | RI.9–10.8 | Delineate and evaluate the argument and specific claims in a text, assessing whether the reasoning is valid and the evidence is relevant and sufficient; identify false statements and fallacious reasoning. |
| | RI.9–10.9 | Analyze seminal U.S. documents of historical and literary significance (e.g., Washington's Farewell Address, the Gettysburg Address, Roosevelt's Four Freedoms speech, King's "Letter from Birmingham Jail"), including how they address related themes and concepts. |
| **Range of Reading and Level of Text Complexity** | RI.9–10.10 | By the end of grade 9, read and comprehend literary nonfiction in the grades 9–10 text complexity band proficiently, with scaffolding as needed at the high end of the range. <br> By the end of grade 10, read and comprehend literary nonfiction at the high end of the grades 9–10 text complexity band independently and proficiently. |

## Writing Standards

| | | |
|---|---|---|
| **Text Types and Purposes** | W.9–10.1 | Write arguments to support claims in an analysis of substantive topics or texts, using valid reasoning and relevant and sufficient evidence. |
| | W.9–10.1a | Introduce precise claim(s), distinguish the claim(s) from alternate or opposing claims, and create an organization that establishes clear relationships among claim(s), counterclaims, reasons, and evidence. |
| | W.9–10.1b | Develop claim(s) and counterclaims fairly, supplying evidence for each while pointing out the strengths and limitations of both in a manner that anticipates the audience's knowledge level and concerns. |
| | W.9–10.1c | Use words, phrases, and clauses to link the major sections of the text, create cohesion, and clarify the relationships between claim(s) and reasons, between reasons and evidence, and between claim(s) and counterclaims. |
| | W.9–10.1d | Establish and maintain a formal style and objective tone while attending to the norms and conventions of the discipline in which they are writing. |
| | W.9–10.1e | Provide a concluding statement or section that follows from and supports the argument presented. |
| | W.9–10.2 | Write informative/explanatory texts to examine and convey complex ideas, concepts, and information clearly and accurately through the effective selection, organization, and analysis of content. |
| | W.9–10.2a | Introduce a topic **or thesis statement**; organize complex ideas, concepts, and information to make important connections and distinctions; include formatting (e.g., headings), graphics (e.g., figures, tables), and multimedia when useful to aiding comprehension. **CA** |
| | W.9–10.2b | Develop the topic with well-chosen, relevant, and sufficient facts, extended definitions, concrete details, quotations, or other information and examples appropriate to the audience's knowledge of the topic. |
| | W.9–10.2c | Use appropriate and varied transitions to link the major sections of the text, create cohesion, and clarify the relationships among complex ideas and concepts. |
| | W.9–10.2d | Use precise language and domain-specific vocabulary to manage the complexity of the topic. |
| | W.9–10.2e | Establish and maintain a formal style and objective tone while attending to the norms and conventions of the discipline in which they are writing. |

## Writing Standards

| Text Types and Purposes | W.9–10.2f | Provide a concluding statement or section that follows from and supports the information or explanation presented (e.g., articulating implications or the significance of the topic). |
| --- | --- | --- |
| | W.9–10.3 | Write narratives to develop real or imagined experiences or events using effective technique, well-chosen details, and well-structured event sequences. |
| | W.9–10.3a | Engage and orient the reader by setting out a problem, situation, or observation, establishing one or multiple point(s) of view, and introducing a narrator and/or characters; create a smooth progression of experiences or events. |
| | W.9–10.3b | Use narrative techniques, such as dialogue, pacing, description, reflection, and multiple plot lines, to develop experiences, events, and/or characters. |
| | W.9–10.3c | Use a variety of techniques to sequence events so that they build on one another to create a coherent whole. |
| | W.9–10.3d | Use precise words and phrases, telling details, and sensory language to convey a vivid picture of the experiences, events, setting, and/or characters. |
| | W.9–10.3e | Provide a conclusion that follows from and reflects on what is experienced, observed, or resolved over the course of the narrative. |
| Production and Distribution of Writing | W.9–10.4 | Produce clear and coherent writing in which the development, organization, and style are appropriate to task, purpose, and audience. (Grade-specific expectations for writing types are defined in standards 1–3 above.) |
| | W.9–10.5 | Develop and strengthen writing as needed by planning, revising, editing, rewriting, or trying a new approach, focusing on addressing what is most significant for a specific purpose and audience. (Editing for conventions should demonstrate command of Language standards 1–3 up to and including grades 9–10.) |
| | W.9–10.6 | Use technology, including the Internet, to produce, publish, and update individual or shared writing products, taking advantage of technology's capacity to link to other information and to display information flexibly and dynamically. |
| Research to Build and Present Knowledge | W.9–10.7 | Conduct short as well as more sustained research projects to answer a question (including a self-generated question) or solve a problem; narrow or broaden the inquiry when appropriate; synthesize multiple sources on the subject, demonstrating understanding of the subject under investigation. |

## Writing Standards

| | | |
|---|---|---|
| **Research to Build and Present Knowledge** | W.9–10.8 | Gather relevant information from multiple authoritative print and digital sources, using advanced searches effectively; assess the usefulness of each source in answering the research question; integrate information into the text selectively to maintain the flow of ideas, avoiding plagiarism and following a standard format for citation **including footnotes and endnotes. CA** |
| | W.9–10.9 | Draw evidence from literary or informational texts to support analysis, reflection, and research. |
| | W.9–10.9a | Apply *grades 9–10 Reading standards* to literature (e.g., "Analyze how an author draws on and transforms source material in a specific work [e.g., how Shakespeare treats a theme or topic from Ovid or the Bible or how a later author draws on a play by Shakespeare]"). |
| | W.9–10.9b | Apply *grades 9–10 Reading standards* to literary nonfiction (e.g., "Delineate and evaluate the argument and specific claims in a text, assessing whether the reasoning is valid and the evidence is relevant and sufficient; identify false statements and fallacious reasoning"). |
| **Range of Writing** | W.9–10.10 | Write routinely over extended time frames (time for research, reflection, and revision) and shorter time frames (a single sitting or a day or two) for a range of tasks, purposes, and audiences. |

## Speaking and Listening Standards

| Comprehension and Collaboration | SL.9–10.1 | Initiate and participate effectively in a range of collaborative discussions (one-on-one, in groups, and teacher-led) with diverse partners on *grades 9–10 topics, texts, and issues*, building on others' ideas and expressing their own clearly and persuasively. |
|---|---|---|
| | SL.9–10.1a | Come to discussions prepared, having read and researched material under study; explicitly draw on that preparation by referring to evidence from texts and other research on the topic or issue to stimulate a thoughtful, well-reasoned exchange of ideas. |
| | SL.9–10.1b | Work with peers to set rules for collegial discussions and decision-making (e.g., informal consensus, taking votes on key issues, presentation of alternate views), clear goals and deadlines, and individual roles as needed. |
| | SL.9–10.1c | Propel conversations by posing and responding to questions that relate the current discussion to broader themes or larger ideas; actively incorporate others into the discussion; and clarify, verify, or challenge ideas and conclusions. |
| | SL.9–10.1d | Respond thoughtfully to diverse perspectives, summarize points of agreement and disagreement, and, when warranted, qualify or justify their own views and understanding and make new connections in light of the evidence and reasoning presented. |
| | SL.9–10.2 | Integrate multiple sources of information presented in diverse media or formats (e.g., visually, quantitatively, orally) evaluating the credibility and accuracy of each source. |
| | SL.9–10.3 | Evaluate a speaker's point of view, reasoning, and use of evidence and rhetoric, identifying any fallacious reasoning or exaggerated or distorted evidence. |
| Presentation of Knowledge and Ideas | SL.9–10.4 | Present information, findings, and supporting evidence clearly, concisely, and logically **(using appropriate eye contact, adequate volume, and clear pronunciation)** such that listeners can follow the line of reasoning and the organization, development, substance, and style are appropriate to purpose **(e.g., argument, narrative, informative, response to literature presentations)**, audience, and task. **CA** |
| | SL.9–10.4a | **Plan and deliver an informative/explanatory presentation that: presents evidence in support of a thesis, conveys information from primary and secondary sources coherently, uses domain specific vocabulary, and provides a conclusion that summarizes the main points. (9th or 10th grade) CA** |
| | SL.9–10.4b | **Plan, memorize, and present a recitation (e.g., poem, selection from a speech or dramatic soliloquy) that: conveys the meaning of the selection and includes appropriate performance techniques (e.g., tone, rate, voice modulation) to achieve the desired aesthetic effect. (9th or 10th grade) CA** |
| | SL.9–10.5 | Make strategic use of digital media (e.g., textual, graphical, audio, visual, and interactive elements) in presentations to enhance understanding of findings, reasoning, and evidence and to add interest. |
| | SL.9–10.6 | Adapt speech to a variety of contexts and tasks, demonstrating command of formal English when indicated or appropriate. (See grades 9–10 Language standards 1 and 3 for specific expectations.) |

## Language Standards

| | | |
|---|---|---|
| **Conventions of Standard English** | L.9–10.1 | Demonstrate command of the conventions of standard English grammar and usage when writing or speaking. |
| | L.9–10.1a | Use parallel structure.* |
| | L.9–10.1b | Use various types of phrases (noun, verb, adjectival, adverbial, participial, prepositional, absolute) and clauses (independent, dependent; noun, relative, adverbial) to convey specific meanings and add variety and interest to writing or presentations. |
| | L.9–10.2 | Demonstrate command of the conventions of standard English capitalization, punctuation, and spelling when writing. |
| | L.9–10.2a | Use a semicolon (and perhaps a conjunctive adverb) to link two or more closely related independent clauses. |
| | L.9–10.2b | Use a colon to introduce a list or quotation. |
| | L.9–10.2c | Spell correctly. |
| **Knowledge of Language** | L.9–10.3 | Apply knowledge of language to understand how language functions in different contexts, to make effective choices for meaning or style, and to comprehend more fully when reading or listening. |
| | L.9–10.3a | Write and edit work so that it conforms to the guidelines in a style manual (e.g., *MLA Handbook*, Turabian's *Manual for Writers*) appropriate for the discipline and writing type. |
| **Vocabulary Acquisition and Use** | L.9–10.4 | Determine or clarify the meaning of unknown and multiple-meaning words and phrases based on *grades 9–10 reading and content*, choosing flexibly from a range of strategies. |
| | L.9–10.4a | Use context (e.g., the overall meaning of a sentence, paragraph, or text; a word's position or function in a sentence) as a clue to the meaning of a word or phrase. |
| | L.9–10.4b | Identify and correctly use patterns of word changes that indicate different meanings or parts of speech (e.g., *analyze, analysis, analytical; advocate, advocacy*) **and continue to apply knowledge of Greek and Latin roots and affixes. CA** |
| | L.9–10.4c | Consult general and specialized reference materials (e.g., **college-level** dictionaries, **rhyming dictionaries, bilingual dictionaries**, glossaries, thesauruses), both print and digital, to find the pronunciation of a word or determine or clarify its precise meaning, its part of speech, or its etymology. **CA** |
| | L.9–10.4d | Verify the preliminary determination of the meaning of a word or phrase (e.g., by checking the inferred meaning in context or in a dictionary). |

## Language Standards

| Vocabulary Acquisition and Use | L.9–10.5 | Demonstrate understanding of figurative language, word relationships, and nuances in word meanings. |
| --- | --- | --- |
| | L.9–10.5a | Interpret figures of speech (e.g., euphemism, oxymoron) in context and analyze their role in the text. |
| | L.9–10.5b | Analyze nuances in the meaning of words with similar denotations. |
| | L.9–10.6 | Acquire and use accurately general academic and domain-specific words and phrases, sufficient for reading, writing, speaking, and listening at the college and career readiness level; demonstrate independence in gathering vocabulary knowledge when considering a word or phrase important to comprehension or expression. |

# California English Language Development Standards

## Part I: Interacting in Meaningful Ways

| Communicative Modes | Standard Code | Emerging | Expanding | Bridging |
| --- | --- | --- | --- | --- |
| Collaborative | PI.9–10.1 | **Exchanging information/ideas**<br><br>Engage in conversational exchanges and express ideas on familiar current events and academic topics by asking and answering *yes-no* questions and *wh-* questions and responding using phrases and short sentences. | **Exchanging information/ideas**<br><br>Contribute to class, group, and partner discussions, sustaining conversations on a variety of age and grade-appropriate academic topics by following turn-taking rules, asking and answering relevant, on-topic questions, affirming others, providing additional, relevant information, and paraphrasing key ideas. | **Exchanging information/ideas**<br><br>Contribute to class, group, and partner discussions, sustaining conversations on a variety of age and grade-appropriate academic topics by following turn-taking rules, asking and answering relevant, on-topic questions, affirming others, and providing coherent and well-articulated comments and additional information. |
| | PI.9–10.2 | **Interacting via written English**<br><br>Collaborate with peers to engage in short, grade-appropriate written exchanges and writing projects, using technology as appropriate. | **Interacting via written English**<br><br>Collaborate with peers to engage in increasingly complex grade-appropriate written exchanges and writing projects, using technology as appropriate. | **Interacting via written English**<br><br>Collaborate with peers to engage in a variety of extended written exchanges and complex grade-appropriate writing projects, using technology as appropriate. |
| | PI.9–10.3 | **Supporting opinions and persuading others**<br><br>Negotiate with or persuade others in conversations using learned phrases (e.g., *Would you say that again? I think ...* ), as well as open responses to express and defend opinions. | **Supporting opinions and persuading others**<br><br>Negotiate with or persuade others in conversations (e.g., to provide counter-arguments) using a growing number of learned phrases (*I see your point, but ...* ) and open responses to express and defend nuanced opinions. | **Supporting opinions and persuading others**<br><br>Negotiate with or persuade others in conversations in appropriate registers (e.g., to acknowledge new information in an academic conversation but then politely offer a counterpoint) using a variety of learned phrases, indirect reported speech (e.g., *I heard you say X, and I haven' t thought about that before. However ...* ), and open responses to express and defend nuanced opinions. |
| | PI.9–10.4 | **Adapting language choices**<br><br>Adjust language choices according to the context (e.g., classroom, community) and audience (e.g., peers, teachers). | **Adapting language choices**<br><br>Adjust language choices according to the context (e.g., classroom, community), purpose (e.g., to persuade, to provide arguments or counterarguments), task, and audience (e.g., peers, teachers, guest lecturer). | **Adapting language choices**<br><br>Adjust language choices according to the task (e.g., group presentation of research project), context (e.g., classroom, community), purpose (e.g., to persuade, to provide arguments or counterarguments), and audience (e.g., peers, teachers, college recruiter). |

| Communicative Modes | Standard Code | Emerging | Expanding | Bridging |
|---|---|---|---|---|
| **Interpretive** | PI.9–10.5 | **Listening actively**<br><br>Demonstrate comprehension of oral presentations and discussions on familiar social and academic topics by asking and answering questions, with prompting and substantial support. | **Listening actively**<br><br>Demonstrate comprehension of oral presentations and discussions on a variety of social and academic topics by asking and answering questions that show thoughtful consideration of the ideas or arguments, with moderate support. | **Listening actively**<br><br>Demonstrate comprehension of oral presentations and discussions on a variety of social and academic topics by asking and answering detailed and complex questions that show thoughtful consideration of the ideas or arguments, with light support. |
| | PI.9–10.6a | **Reading/viewing closely**<br><br>Explain ideas, phenomena, processes, and text relationships (e.g., compare/contrast, cause/effect, evidence-based argument) based on close reading of a variety of grade-appropriate texts, presented in various print and multi-media formats, using short sentences and a select set of general academic and domain-specific words. | **Reading/viewing closely**<br><br>Explain ideas, phenomena, processes, and relationships within and across texts (e.g., compare/contrast, cause/effect, themes, evidence-based argument) based on close reading of a variety of grade-appropriate texts, presented in various print and multimedia formats, using increasingly detailed sentences, and an increasing variety of general academic and domain-specific words. | **Reading/viewing closely**<br><br>Explain ideas, phenomena, processes, and relationships within and across texts (e.g., compare/contrast, cause/effect, themes, evidence-based argument) based on close reading of a variety of grade-level texts, presented in various print and multimedia formats, using a variety of detailed sentences and a range of general academic and domain-specific words. |
| | PI.9–10.6b | **Reading/viewing closely**<br><br>Explain inferences and conclusions drawn from close reading of grade-appropriate texts and viewing of multimedia using familiar verbs (e.g., *seems that*). | **Reading/viewing closely**<br><br>Explain inferences and conclusions drawn from close reading of grade-appropriate texts and viewing of multimedia using an increasing variety of verbs and adverbials (e.g., *indicates that, suggests, as a result*). | **Reading/viewing closely**<br><br>Explain inferences and conclusions drawn from close reading of grade-level texts and viewing of multimedia using a variety of verbs and adverbials (e.g., *creates the impression that, consequently*). |
| | PI.9–10.6c | **Reading/viewing closely**<br><br>Use knowledge of morphology (e.g., common prefixes and suffixes), context, reference materials, and visual cues to determine the meaning of unknown and multiple-meaning words on familiar topics. | **Reading/viewing closely**<br><br>Use knowledge of morphology (e.g., affixes, Greek and Latin roots), context, reference materials, and visual cues to determine the meaning of unknown and multiple-meaning words on familiar and new topics. | **Reading/viewing closely**<br><br>Use knowledge of morphology (e.g., derivational suffixes), context, reference materials, and visual cues to determine the meaning, including figurative and connotative meanings, of unknown and multiple-meaning words on a variety of new topics. |

| Communicative Modes | Standard Code | Emerging | Expanding | Bridging |
|---|---|---|---|---|
| **Interpretive** | PI.9–10.7 | **Evaluating language choices**<br><br>Explain how successfully writers and speakers structure texts and use language (e.g., specific word or phrasing choices) to persuade the reader (e.g., by providing evidence to support claims or connecting points in an argument) or create other specific effects, with substantial support. | **Evaluating language choices**<br><br>Explain how successfully writers and speakers structure texts and use language (e.g., specific word or phrasing choices) to persuade the reader (e.g., by providing well-worded evidence to support claims or connecting points in an argument in specific ways) or create other specific effects, with moderate support. | **Evaluating language choices**<br><br>Explain how successfully writers and speakers structure texts and use language (e.g., specific word or phrasing choices) to persuade the reader (e.g., by providing well-worded evidence to support claims or connecting points in an argument in specific ways) or create other specific effects, with light support. |
| | PI.9–10.8 | **Analyzing language choices**<br><br>Explain how a writer's or speaker's choice of phrasing or specific words (e.g., describing a character or action as *aggressive* versus *bold*) produces nuances and different effects on the audience. | **Analyzing language choices**<br><br>Explain how a writer's or speaker's choice of phrasing or specific words (e.g., using figurative language or words with multiple meanings to describe an event or character) produces nuances and different effects on the audience. | **Analyzing language choices**<br><br>Explain how a writer's or speaker's choice of a variety of different types of phrasing or words (e.g., hyperbole, varying connotations, the cumulative impact of word choices) produces nuances and different effects on the audience. |
| **Productive** | PI.9–10.9 | **Presenting**<br><br>Plan and deliver brief oral presentations and reports on grade-appropriate topics that present evidence and facts to support ideas. | **Presenting**<br><br>Plan and deliver a variety of oral presentations and reports on grade-appropriate topics that present evidence and facts to support ideas by using growing understanding of register. | **Presenting**<br><br>Plan and deliver a variety of oral presentations and reports on grade-appropriate topics that express complex and abstract ideas well supported by evidence and sound reasoning, and are delivered using an appropriate level of formality and understanding of register. |
| | PI.9–10.10a | **Writing**<br><br>Write short literary and informational texts (e.g., an argument about water rights) collaboratively (e.g., with peers) and independently. | **Writing**<br><br>Write longer literary and informational texts (e.g., an argument about water rights) collaboratively (e.g., with peers) and independently by using appropriate text organization and growing understanding of register. | **Writing**<br><br>Write longer and more detailed literary and informational texts (e.g., an argument about water rights) collaboratively (e.g., with peers) and independently using appropriate text organization and register. |

| Communicative Modes | Standard Code | Emerging | Expanding | Bridging |
|---|---|---|---|---|
| **Productive** | PI.9–10.10b | **Writing**<br><br>Write brief summaries of texts and experiences by using complete sentences and key words (e.g., from notes or graphic organizers). | **Writing**<br><br>Write increasingly concise summaries of texts and experiences by using complete sentences and key words (e.g., from notes or graphic organizers). | **Writing**<br><br>Write clear and coherent summaries of texts and experiences by using complete and concise sentences and key words (e.g., from notes or graphic organizers). |
| | PI.9–10.11a | **Justifying/arguing**<br><br>Justify opinions by articulating some relevant textual evidence or background knowledge, with visual support. | **Justifying/arguing**<br><br>Justify opinions and positions or persuade others by making connections between ideas and articulating relevant textual evidence or background knowledge. | **Justifying/arguing**<br><br>Justify opinions or persuade others by making connections and distinctions between ideas and texts and articulating sufficient, detailed, and relevant textual evidence or background knowledge, using appropriate register. |
| | PI.9–10.11b | **Justifying/arguing**<br><br>Express attitude and opinions or temper statements with familiar modal expressions (e.g., *can, may*). | **Justifying/arguing**<br><br>Express attitude and opinions or temper statements with a variety of familiar modal expressions (e.g., *possibly/likely, could/would*). | **Justifying/arguing**<br><br>Express attitude and opinions or temper statements with nuanced modal expressions (e.g., *possibly/potentially/certainly/absolutely, should/might*). |
| | PI.9–10.12a | **Selecting language resources**<br><br>Use familiar general academic (e.g., *temperature, document*) and domain-specific (e.g., *characterization, photosynthesis, society, quadratic functions*) words to create clear spoken and written texts. | **Selecting language resources**<br><br>Use an increasing variety of grade-appropriate general academic (e.g., *dominate, environment*) and domain-specific (e.g., *characterization, photosynthesis, society, quadratic functions*) academic words accurately and appropriately when producing increasingly complex written and spoken texts. | **Selecting language resources**<br><br>Use a variety of grade-appropriate general (e.g., *anticipate, transaction*) and domain-specific (e.g., *characterization, photosynthesis, society, quadratic functions*) academic words and phrases, including persuasive language, accurately and appropriately when producing complex written and spoken texts. |
| | PI.9–10.12b | **Selecting language resources**<br><br>Use knowledge of morphology to appropriately select basic affixes (e.g., The skull protects the brain). | **Selecting language resources**<br><br>Use knowledge of morphology to appropriately select affixes in a growing number of ways to manipulate language (e.g., diplomatic, stems are branch*ed* or unbranch*ed*). | **Selecting language resources**<br><br>Use knowledge of morphology to appropriately select affixes in a variety of ways to manipulate language (e.g., changing *humiliate* to *humiliation* or *incredible* to *incredibly*). |

California English Language Development Standards  **xxv**

# Part II: Learning About How English Works

| Language Processes | Standard Code | Emerging | Expanding | Bridging |
|---|---|---|---|---|
| **Structuring Cohesive Texts** | PII.9–10.1 | **Understanding text structure**<br><br>Apply analysis of the organizational structure of different text types (e.g., how arguments are organized by establishing clear relationships among claims, counterclaims, reasons, and evidence) to comprehending texts and to writing brief arguments, informative/explanatory texts and narratives. | **Understanding text structure**<br><br>Apply analysis of the organizational structure of different text types (e.g., how arguments are organized by establishing clear relationships among claims, counterclaims, reasons, and evidence) to comprehending texts and to writing increasingly clear and cohesive arguments, informative/explanatory texts and narratives. | **Understanding text structure**<br><br>Apply analysis of the organizational structure of different text types (e.g., how arguments are organized by establishing clear relationships among claims, counterclaims, reasons, and evidence) to comprehending texts and to writing clear and cohesive arguments, informative/explanatory texts and narratives. |
| | PII.9–10.2a | **Understanding cohesion**<br><br>Apply knowledge of familiar language resources for referring to make texts more cohesive (e.g., using pronouns to refer back to nouns in text) to comprehending and writing brief texts. | **Understanding cohesion**<br><br>Apply knowledge of a growing number of language resources for referring to make texts more cohesive (e.g., using nominalizations to refer back to an action or activity described earlier) to comprehending texts and to writing increasingly cohesive texts for specific purposes and audiences. | **Understanding cohesion**<br><br>Apply knowledge of a variety of language resources for referring to make texts more cohesive (e.g., using nominalization, paraphrasing, or summaries to reference or recap an idea or explanation provided earlier) to comprehending grade-level texts and to writing clear and cohesive grade-level texts for specific purposes and audiences. |
| | PII.9–10.2b | **Understanding cohesion**<br><br>Apply knowledge of familiar language resources for linking ideas, events, or reasons throughout a text (e.g., using connecting/transition words and phrases, such as *first, second, third*) to comprehending and writing brief texts. | **Understanding cohesion**<br><br>Apply knowledge of familiar language resources for linking ideas, events, or reasons throughout a text (e.g., using connecting/transition words and phrases, such as *meanwhile, however, on the other hand*) to comprehending texts and to writing increasingly cohesive texts for specific purposes and audiences. | **Understanding cohesion**<br><br>Apply knowledge of familiar language resources for linking ideas, events, or reasons throughout a text (e.g., using connecting/transition words and phrases, such as *on the contrary, in addition, moreover*) to comprehending grade-level texts and to writing cohesive texts for specific purposes and audiences. |

| Language Processes | Standard Code | Emerging | Expanding | Bridging |
|---|---|---|---|---|
| **Expanding and Enriching Ideas** | PII.9–10.3 | **Using verbs and verb phrases**<br><br>Use a variety of verbs in different tenses (e.g., past, present, future, simple, progressive) appropriate to the text type and discipline to create short texts on familiar academic topics. | **Using verbs and verb phrases**<br><br>Use a variety of verbs in different tenses (e.g., past, present, future, simple, progressive, perfect) appropriate to the text type and discipline to create a variety of texts that explain, describe, and summarize concrete and abstract thoughts and ideas. | **Using verbs and verb phrases**<br><br>Use a variety of verbs in different tenses (e.g., past, present, future, simple, progressive, perfect), and mood (e.g., subjunctive) appropriate to the text type and discipline to create a variety of texts that describe concrete and abstract ideas, explain procedures and sequences, summarize texts and ideas, and present and critique points of view. |
| | PII.9–10.4 | **Using nouns and noun phrases**<br><br>Expand noun phrases to create increasingly detailed sentences (e.g., adding adjectives for precision) about personal and familiar academic topics. | **Using nouns and noun phrases**<br><br>Expand noun phrases in a growing number of ways (e.g., adding adjectives to nouns; simple clause embedding) to create detailed sentences that accurately describe, explain, and summarize information and ideas on a variety of personal and academic topics. | **Using nouns and noun phrases**<br><br>Expand noun phrases in a variety of ways (e.g., more complex clause embedding) to create detailed sentences that accurately describe concrete and abstract ideas, explain procedures and sequences, summarize texts and ideas, and present and critique points of view on a variety of academic topics. |
| | PII.9–10.5 | **Modifying to add details**<br><br>Expand sentences with simple adverbials (e.g., adverbs, adverb phrases, prepositional phrases) to provide details (e.g., time, manner, place, cause) about familiar activities or processes. | **Modifying to add details**<br><br>Expand sentences with a growing variety of adverbials (e.g., adverbs, adverb phrases, prepositional phrases) to provide details (e.g., time, manner, place, cause) about familiar or new activities or processes. | **Modifying to add details**<br><br>Expand sentences with a variety of adverbials (e.g., adverbs, adverb phrases and clauses, prepositional phrases) to provide details (e.g., time, manner, place, cause) about a variety of familiar and new activities and processes. |

| Language Processes | Standard Code | Emerging | Expanding | Bridging |
|---|---|---|---|---|
| **Connecting and Condensing Ideas** | PII.9–10.6 | **Connecting ideas**<br><br>Combine clauses in a few basic ways (e.g., creating compound sentences using *and, but, so*; creating complex sentences using *because*) to make connections between and to join ideas (e.g., *I want to read this book because it describes the solar system*). | **Connecting ideas**<br><br>Combine clauses in a growing number of ways to create compound and complex sentences that make connections between and link concrete and abstract ideas, for example, to express a reason (e.g., *He stayed at home on Sunday in order to study for Monday's exam*) or to make a concession (e.g., *She studied all night even though she wasn't feeling well*). | **Connecting ideas**<br><br>Combine clauses in a variety of ways to create compound and complex sentences that make connections between and link concrete and abstract ideas, for example, to make a concession (e.g., *While both characters strive for success, they each take different approaches through which to reach their goals.*), or to establish cause (e.g., *Women's lives were changed forever after World War II as a result of joining the workforce*). |
| | PII.9–10.7 | **Condensing ideas**<br><br>Condense ideas in a few basic ways (e.g., by compounding verb or prepositional phrases) to create precise and detailed simple, compound, and complex sentences (e.g., *The students asked survey questions and recorded the responses*). | **Condensing ideas**<br><br>Condense ideas in a growing number of ways (e.g., through embedded clauses or by compounding verbs or prepositional phrases) to create more precise and detailed simple, compound, and complex sentences (e.g., *Species that could not adapt to the changing climate eventually disappeared*). | **Condensing ideas**<br><br>Condense ideas in a variety of ways (e.g., through a variety of embedded clauses, or by compounding verbs or prepositional phrases, nominalization) to create precise simple, compound, and complex sentences that condense concrete and abstract ideas (e.g., *Another issue that people may be concerned with is the amount of money that it will cost to construct the new building*). |
| **Foundational Literacy Skills:**<br><br>**Literacy in an Alphabetic Writing System**<br><br>• Print concepts<br>• Phonological awareness<br>• Phonics and word recognition<br>• Fluency | PIII.9–10 | **See Chapter 6 [of the California ELD Standards] for information on teaching reading foundational skills to English learners of various profiles based on age, native language, native language writing system, schooling experience, and literacy experience and proficiency. Some considerations are as follows:**<br><br>• Native language and literacy (e.g., phoneme awareness or print concept skills in native language) should be assessed for potential transference to English language and literacy.<br>• Similarities between the native language and English should be highlighted (e.g., phonemes or letters that are the same in both languages).<br>• Differences between native language and English should be highlighted (e.g., some phonemes in English may not exist in the student's native language; native language syntax may be different from English syntax). | | |

# Cultural Conversations

**Visual Prompt:** How does this image express a culture to you?

## Unit Overview

Culture is often difficult to define, but it influences everything from who you are as an individual to how you relate to other people at home and around the world. In this unit, you will explore different cultures by reading texts in a variety of genres that reflect on the connection between one's cultural heritage and his or her sense of identity. Using your own experiences and information in texts, you will write a reflection about cultural identity, as well as create an argument about the extent to which culture shapes an individual's perceptions of the world.

# Cultural Conversations

**GOALS:**

- To analyze how culture affects identity and perceptions
- To practice effective speaking and listening skills that build capacity for collaboration and communication
- To analyze the concept of voice in reading and writing
- To examine and apply the elements of argument
- To analyze and apply syntactic structures in writing

**ACADEMIC VOCABULARY**

synthesis
argument
claim
counterclaim
concession
refutation

**Literary Terms**

voice
syntax
conflict
theme
thematic statement
symbol
allusion
imagery
figurative language

## Contents

**Activities**

**Language and Writer's Craft**
- Formal and Informal Voice (1.3)
- Syntax (1.4)
- Colon and Semicolon (1.10)
- Phrases and Clauses (1.12)

**MY INDEPENDENT READING LIST**

_____

_____

_____

_____

_____

_____

_____

_____

_____

_____

_____

_____

_____

_____

_____

_____

_____

# Previewing the Unit

**My Notes**

## Learning Targets

- Preview the big ideas and the vocabulary for the unit.
- Identify and analyze the skills and knowledge required to complete Embedded Assessment 1 successfully.

## Making Connections

In this unit, you will read poetry, short stories, and essays—all focusing on some element of cultural identity. What is your personal cultural identity, and how does it affect the way you see the world? Cultural perspectives are shaped by family, life experiences, and perceptions about the world around you. You will explore all of these as you prepare to write your reflective essay about your cultural identity.

## Essential Questions

Based on your current knowledge, write your answers to these questions.

1. What is my cultural identity?

2. How do cultural experiences shape, impact, or influence our identity and perceptions?

## Vocabulary Development

Go back to the Contents page and use a QHT strategy to analyze and evaluate your knowledge of the Academic Vocabulary and Literary Terms for the unit.

## Unpacking Embedded Assessment 1

Read the following assignment for Embedded Assessment 1:

Your assignment is to write a reflective essay explaining your cultural identity.

Summarize in your own words what you will need to know to complete this assessment successfully. With your class, create a graphic organizer to represent the skills and knowledge you will need to complete the tasks identified in the Embedded Assessment. To help you complete your graphic organizer, be sure to review the criteria in the Scoring Guide on page 56.

# Exploring Culture and Communication

## Learning Targets
- Explore the concept of culture and the role it plays in personal perceptions.
- Analyze the communication process to develop collaborative discussion norms.

## Defining Culture

1. When you see the word *culture*, what are your thoughts about what it means? Write your definition in the space below.

   Culture is

2. Discuss your definition with a small group of peers. In the space below, record any new ideas you have about culture after your discussion.

3. What are some examples of culture? Create a word web around the word *Culture*, writing words or phrases that you associate with culture.

> **LEARNING STRATEGIES:**
> graphic organizer,
> Discussion Groups,
> Quickwrite, Word Sort,
> Sharing and Responding

**My Notes**

# Exploring Culture and Communication

My Notes

4. With these ideas about culture in mind, write down the impressions and associations evoked by the images your teacher shares with you.

| Object/Image | My First Associations | Responses from Peers |
|---|---|---|
| | | |
| | | |
| | | |
| | | |

5. Why did other students share some of your perceptions but differ with others?

6. In the box below, write five items you could bring to class tomorrow that would express something about your cultural identity. In the second column, write a description of what each item represents to you and your cultural connection (e.g., heritage, values, practices, experiences). Share some of your examples and how they connect to your culture in a class discussion.

| Object | What do the objects reveal about you and your culture? |
|---|---|
| | |
| | |
| | |
| | |

## Explanatory Writing Prompt

Choose one of the five items from your list as the focus of a brief essay that explains the object to an audience that is unfamiliar with what it is, how it is used, and how it connects to your culture (and personally to you). Be sure to:

- Describe the object clearly using vivid and concrete language.
- Explain how the object connects to your culture.
- Explain the significance of the object to you.

## Communicating Effectively

Our individual cultures affect the way we communicate. During this course, you will participate in discussions with partners and in groups. To make collaborative discussion groups productive, all members of a group need to communicate effectively as speakers and listeners.

7. What are the characteristics of effective communication?

8. What obstacles get in the way of effective communication, and how can we remove some of the barriers identified?

9. George Bernard Shaw once said, "The problem with communication ... is the *illusion* that it has been accomplished." One of the goals of this unit is "to develop speaking and listening skills to communicate effectively" in collegial discussions. Identify two to three norms (set rules) you and your fellow classmates can follow to communicate effectively.

**Class Norms**

1.

2.

3.

# Exploring Culture and Communication

**INDEPENDENT READING LINK**

**Read and Respond**

In this unit, you will be exploring cultural identity. For your independent reading, find texts by authors who share your cultural ideas and make comparisons about shared experiences and experiences that are different.

**My Notes**

## Check Your Understanding

Explain why classroom communication norms are important for productive discussion.

 **Independent Reading Plan**

Reading independently gives you a chance to expand your knowledge about topics that fascinate you while also reinforcing and deepening the learning you are doing in class. Each of the selections that you will read in this course can help you analyze and understand your independent reading texts in new and enlightening ways.

Discuss your independent reading plan with a partner by responding to these questions:

- How do you go about choosing what to read independently? Where can you find advice on which books or articles to read?
- What genre of texts do you most enjoy reading outside of class?
- How can you make time in your schedule to read independently?
- How do you think learning about new cultures might change your perspective of the texts you read independently?
- Look at the Independent Reading Link on this page and think about which text or author you plan on reading during the first half of Unit 1.

## Learning Targets
- Compare and contrast how a central idea of a text is developed in an informational text and a personal essay.

## Preview
In this activity, you will read an informational text and a personal essay to compare and contrast how the main idea is developed through the authors' distinct **voices**.

## Setting a Purpose for Reading
- Underline or highlight information that helps you define the concept of cultural identity.
- Circle unknown words and phrases. Try to determine the meaning of the words by using context clues, word parts, or a dictionary.

---

### Informational Text

# What Is Cultural Identity?

*by* Elise Trumbull and Maria Pacheco, Brown University

1  Children begin to develop a sense of identity as individuals and as members of groups from their earliest interactions with others (McAdoo, 1993; Sheets, 1999a). One of the most basic types of identity is ethnic identity, which **entails** an awareness of one's membership in a social group that has a common culture. The common culture may be marked by a shared language, history, geography, and (frequently) physical characteristics (Fishman, 1989; Sheets, 1999a).

2  Not all of these aspects need to be shared, however, for people to psychologically identify with a particular ethnic group. Cultural identity is a broader term: people from multiple ethnic backgrounds may identify as belonging to the same culture. For example, in the Caribbean and South America, several ethnic groups may share a broader, common, Latin culture. Social groups existing within one nation may share a common language and a broad cultural identity but have distinct ethnic identities associated with a different language and history. Ethnic groups in the United States are examples of this....

**Definitions of Culture and the Invisibility of One's Own Culture**

3  Anthropologists and other scholars continue to debate the meaning of this term. García (1994) refers to culture as

> [T]he system of understanding characteristics of that individual's society, or of some subgroup within that society. This system of understanding includes values, beliefs, notions about acceptable and unacceptable behavior, and other socially constructed ideas that members of the society are taught are "true." (p. 51)

---

**LEARNING STRATEGIES:**
Think-Pair-Share, Marking the Text, Word Maps, Discussion Groups

**My Notes**

**Literary Terms**
**Voice** is the way a writer or speaker uses words and tone to express ideas as well as the writer's persona or personality.

**entails:** involves; includes

# Exploring Cultural Identity

**My Notes**

manifest: show; display

phenomenon: occurrence
distributive: spreading out
posits: suggests

attributes: characteristics

4  Geertz (1973) asserts that members of cultures go about their daily lives within shared webs of meaning. If we link García and Geertz's definitions, we can imagine culture as invisible webs composed of values, beliefs, ideas about appropriate behavior, and socially constructed truths.

5  One may ask, why is culture made up of invisible webs? Most of the time, our own cultures are invisible to us (Greenfield, Raeff, & Quiroz, 1996; Philips, 1983), yet they are the context within which we operate and make sense of the world. When we encounter a culture that is different from our own, one of the things we are faced with is a set of beliefs that **manifest** themselves in behaviors that differ from our own.

6  In this way, we often talk about other people's cultures, and not so much about our own. Our own culture is often hidden from us, and we frequently describe it as "the way things are." Nonetheless, one's beliefs and actions are not any more natural or biologically predetermined than any other group's set of beliefs and actions; they have emerged from the ways one's own group has dealt with and interpreted the particular conditions it has faced. As conditions change, so do cultures; thus, cultures are considered to be dynamic.

**Individual Differences Within Cultures and the Dynamic Nature of Culture**

7  Individual cultural identity presents yet another layer of complexity. Members of the same culture vary widely in their beliefs and actions. How can we explain this **phenomenon**? The argument for a "**distributive** model" of culture addresses the relationship between culture and personality (García, 1994; Schwartz, 1978). This argument **posits** that individuals select beliefs, values, and ideas that guide their actions from a larger set of cultural beliefs, values, and ideas. In most cases, we do not consciously pick and choose **attributes** from the total set; rather, the conditions and events in our individual lives lead us to favor some over others. In summarizing Spiro's concept of "cultural heritage," García (1994) draws a distinction between "cultural heritage" and "cultural inheritance." Cultural heritage refers to what society as a whole possesses, and a cultural inheritance is what each individual possesses. In other words, each individual inherits some (but not all) of the cultural heritage of the group.

8  We all have unique identities that we develop within our cultures, but these identities are not fixed or static. This is the reason that stereotypes do not hold up: no two individuals from any culture are exactly alike. While living inside a culture allows members to become familiar with the total cultural heritage of that society, no individual actually internalizes the entire cultural heritage. In fact, it would be impossible for any one person to possess a society's entire cultural heritage; there are inevitably complex and contradictory values, beliefs, and ideas within that heritage, a result of the conditions and events that individuals and groups experience. For example, arranged marriage has long been a cultural practice in India based on the belief that the families of potential spouses best know who would make a desirable match. More and more frequently, however, individuals reject the practice of arranged marriage; this is partly due to the sense of independence from family brought on by both men's and women's participation in a rapidly developing job market. The changing experience of work is shifting cultural attitudes towards family and marriage. These different experiences and the new values, beliefs, and ideas they produce contribute to the dynamic nature of culture.

## References

Fishman, J. (1989). *Language and ethnicity in minority sociolinguistic perspective.* Clevedon, England: Multilingual Matters.

García, E. (1994). *Understanding and meeting the challenge of student cultural diversity.* Boston: Houghton Mifflin.

Geertz, C. (1973). Thick description: Toward an interpretive theory of culture. *The interpretation of cultures: Selected essays by Clifford Geertz.* New York: Basic Books.

Greenfield, P. M., Raeff, C., & Quiroz, B. (1996). Cultural values in learning and education. In B. Williams (Ed.), *Closing the achievement gap: A vision for changing beliefs and practices* (pp. 37–55). Alexandria, VA: Association for Supervision and Curriculum Development.

McAdoo, H. P. (Ed.). (1993). *Family ethnicity, strength in diversity.* Thousand Oaks, CA: Sage.

Philips, S. (1983). *Cultural differences among students: Communication in the classroom and community in the Warm Springs Indian Reservation.* White Plains, NY: Longman.

Sheets, R. H. (1999a). Human development and ethnic identity. In R. H. Sheets & E. R. Hollins (Eds.), *Racial and ethnic identity in school practices: Aspects of human development* (pp. 91–105). Mahwah, NJ: Lawrence Erlbaum Associates.

Schwartz, T. (1978). Where is the culture? Personality as the distributive locus of culture. In G. Spindler (Ed.), *The making of psychological anthropology* (pp. 429–441). Berkeley, CA: University of California Press.

## Second Read

- Reread the informational text to answer these text-dependent questions.
- Write any additional questions you have about the text in your Reader/Writer Notebook.

1. **Key Ideas and Details:** What is the purpose of beginning the selection with the individual's sense of identity and then moving to shared webs of meaning?

2. **Key Ideas and Details:** What is meant by the "invisibility of one's own culture"? Cite details from the text to support your answer.

**My Notes**

# Exploring Cultural Identity

3. **Key Ideas and Details:** Based on the information given in the text, explain the difference between "cultural heritage" and "cultural inheritance."

4. **Craft and Structure:** What is the meaning of *stereotype* in paragraph 8?

5. **Craft and Structure:** Consider the authors' use of the words "static" and "dynamic" in paragraph 8 to explain the concept of cultural identity. What can the reader conclude about the author's point, and how does that relate to cultural identity?

## Working from the Text

6. Using the My Notes space, write an objective summary of each section of this text. How does each section contribute to the development of ideas about cultural identity? Be sure to note how ideas are developed and refined throughout the text.

7. What is your understanding of cultural identity based on this text?

8. Reflect on invisible aspects of your culture. What differences exist between you and your culture?

9. What are some examples of your culture? Explain how these aspects are dynamic.

**INDEPENDENT READING LINK**

Read and Discuss

From your independent reading, select an example that illustrates a character's cultural experience. The character may be part of a smaller cultural group within a larger and much different culture. Discuss the text with your peers, sharing how characters experience cultural identity.

## Setting a Purpose for Reading

- Underline or highlight information that helps you define the concept of cultural identity.
- Circle unknown words and phrases. Try to determine the meaning of the words by using context clues, word parts, or a dictionary.

**WORD CONNECTIONS**

Etymology

*Hors d' oeuvre* (awr DURV) is a French term that refers to appetizers—small food portions served before a main meal. The word can be traced back to 1714 and a meaning of "outside the ordinary courses of a meal." It comes from *fors* ("outside"), *de* ("from") and *ouvre* ("work"), which in turn is from Latin *opera*.

## Personal Essay

# Ethnic Hash

*by* Patricia J. Williams from *Transition*

1   Recently, I was invited to a book party. The book was about **pluralism**. "Bring an hors d'oeuvre representing your ethnic heritage," said the hostess, innocently enough. Her request threw me into a panic. Do I even have an ethnicity? I wondered. It was like suddenly discovering you might not have a belly button. I tell you, I had to go to the dictionary. What were the flavors, accents, and **linguistic** trills that were passed down to me over the ages? What are the habits, customs, and common traits of the social group by which I have been guided in life—and how do I cook them?

2   My last name is from a presumably Welsh plantation owner. My mother chose my first name from a dictionary of girls' names. "It didn't sound like Edna or Myrtle," she says, as though that explains anything. I have two mostly Cherokee grandparents. There's a Scottish great-grandfather, a French-Canadian great uncle, and a bunch of other relations no one ever talks about. Not one of them left recipes. Of course the ancestors who have had the most tangible influence on my place in the world were probably the West Africans, and I can tell you right off that I haven't the faintest idea what they do for hors d'oeuvres in West Africa (although I have this Senegalese friend who always serves the loveliest, poufiest little fish mousse things in puff pastries that look, well, totally French).

3   Ethnic recipes throw me into the same sort of **quandary** as that proposed "interracial" box on the census form: the concept seems so historically vague, so cheerfully open-ended, as to be virtually meaningless. Everyone I know has at least three different kinds of cheese in their fondue. I suppose I could serve myself up as something like Tragic Mulatta Souffle, except that I've never gotten the hang of souffles. (Too much fussing, too little reward.) So as far as this world's concerned, I've always thought of myself as just plain black. Let's face it: however much my categories get jumbled when I hang out at my favorite kosher sushi spot, it's the little black core of me that moves through the brave new world of Manhattan as I hail a cab, rent an apartment, and apply for a job.

4   Although it's true, I never have tried hailing a cab as an *ethnic*....

5   So let me see. My father is from the state of Georgia. When he cooks, which is not often, the results are distinctly Southern. His specialties are pork chops and pies; he makes the good-luck black-eyed peas on New Year's. His recipes are definitely black in a regional sense, since most blacks in the United States until recently lived in the Southeast. He loves pig. He uses lard.

6   My mother's family is also black, but relentlessly steeped in the New England tradition of hard-winter cuisine. One of my earliest memories is of my mother

**pluralism:** state in which people of different backgrounds live in society together but hold on to their unique traditions and customs

**linguistic:** relating to language

### My Notes

_____

_____

_____

**quandary:** dilemma; difficulty

_____

_____

_____

_____

_____

_____

_____

_____

_____

**My Notes**

**piccalilli:** relish of pickled vegetables

**primeval:** ancient or old

**faux:** fake

**culmination:** conclusion

**gastronomic:** relating to cooking
**palate:** appetite

borrowing my father's screwdriver so she could pry open a box of salt cod. In those days, cod came in wooden boxes, nailed shut, and you really had to hack around the edges to loosen the lid. Cod-from-a-box had to be soaked overnight. The next day you mixed it with boiled potatoes and fried it in Crisco. Then you served it with baked beans in a little brown pot, with salt pork and molasses. There was usually some shredded cabbage as well, with carrots for color. And of course there was **piccalilli**—every good homemaker had piccalilli on hand. Oh, and hot rolls served with homemade Concord grape jelly. Or maybe just brown bread and butter. These were the staples of Saturday night supper.

7  We had baked chicken on Sundays, boiled chicken other days. My mother has recipes for how to boil a chicken: a whole range of them, with and without bay leaf, onions, potatoes, carrots. With boiled chicken, life can never be dull.

8  The truth is we liked watermelon in our family. But the only times we ate it—well, those were secret moments, private moments, guilty, even shameful moments, never unburdened by the thought of what might happen if our white neighbors saw us enjoying the **primeval** fruit. We were always on display when it came to things stereotypical. Fortunately, my mother was never handier in the kitchen than when under political pressure. She would take that odd, thin-necked implement known as a melon-baller and gouge out innocent pink circlets and serve them to us, like little mounds of **faux** sorbet, in fluted crystal goblets. The only time we used those goblets was to disguise watermelon, in case someone was peering idly through the windows, lurking about in racial judgment.

9  I don't remember my parents having many dinner parties, but for those special occasions requiring actual hors d'oeuvres, there were crackers and cream cheese, small sandwiches with the crusts cut off, Red Devil deviled ham with mayonnaise and chopped dill pickles. And where there were hors d'oeuvres, there had to be dessert on the other end to balance things out. Slices of home-made cake and punch. "Will you take coffee or tea?" my mother would ask shyly, at the proud **culmination** of such a meal. . . .

**QUADROON SURPRISE**

10  Some have said that too much salt cod too early in life hobbles the culinary senses forever. I have faith that this is not the case, and that any disadvantage can be overcome with time and a little help from Williams-Sonoma. Having grown up and learned that you are what you eat, I have worked to broaden my horizons and cultivate my tastes. I entertain global **gastronomic** aspirations, and my **palate** knows no bounds. After all, if Aunt Jemima and Uncle Ben[1] can Just Get Over It, who am I to cling to the limitations of the past? Yes, I have learned to love my inner ethnic child. And so, I leave you with a recipe for the Twenty-first Century:

*Chicken with Spanish Rice and Not-Just-Black Beans*
  • *Boil the chicken*
  • *Boil the rice*
  • *Boil the beans*

11  Throw in as many exotic-sounding spices and mysterious roots as you can lay your hands on—go on, use your imagination!—and garnish with those fashionable little wedges of lime that make everything look vaguely Thai. Watch those taxis screech to a halt! A guaranteed crowd-pleaser that can be reheated or rehashed generation after generation.

12  Coffee? Tea?

---

[1] African American advertising icons that some consider to be offensive.

## Second Read

- Reread the personal essay to answer these text-dependent questions.
- Write any additional questions you have about the text in your Reader/Writer Notebook.

10. **Key Ideas and Details:** What does the metaphorical title suggest about Williams's cultural identity?

11. **Craft and Structure:** What do you think the term *mulatta* means, based on the way the author uses it in paragraph 3?

12. **Craft and Structure:** How does the author use food to develop her ideas about ethnicity?

# Exploring Cultural Identity

My Notes

## Working from the Text

### Language & Writer's Craft: Formal and Informal Voice

Though formal and informal voice are both effective and correct writing styles, each is characterized differently.

**Formal (academic) voice:** main point(s) are clearly introduced in logical order with obvious transitions; uses limited emotion and depicts confidence and expertise; avoids contractions, abbreviations, and slang; arguments are supported by evidence; longer and more complex sentences are preferred; may contain technical language and cited facts or statistics

> **Example:** "Children begin to develop a sense of identity as individuals and as members of groups from their earliest interactions with others (McAdoo, 1993; Sheets, 1999a). One of the most basic types of identity is ethnic identity, which entails an awareness of one's membership in a social group that has a common culture. The common culture may be marked by a shared language, history, geography, and (frequently) physical characteristics (Fishman, 1989; Sheets, 1999a)."

**Informal voice:** similar to spoken conversation in structure; displays emotion and acknowledges difficulty of subject; may use contractions, abbreviations, or slang; arguments are supported by personal example; may use short and simple sentences; vocabulary is conversational more than technical

> **Example:** "My last name is from a presumably Welsh plantation owner. My mother chose my first name from a dictionary of girls' names. 'It didn't sound like Edna or Myrtle,' she says, as though that explains anything. I have two mostly Cherokee grandparents. There's a Scottish great-grandfather, a French-Canadian great uncle, and a bunch of other relations no one ever talks about. Not one of them left recipes. Of course the ancestors who have had the most tangible influence on my place in the world were probably the West Africans, and I can tell you right off that I haven't the faintest idea what they do for hors d'oeuvres in West Africa (although I have this Senegalese friend who always serves the loveliest, poufiest little fish mousse things in puff pastries that look, well, totally French)."

**PRACTICE** Referencing the characteristics of formal and informal voice, use the My Notes space to notate the characteristics of formal voice found in the first example and the characteristics of informal voice found in the second example. Choose one of the above examples, and rewrite it using the opposite voice.

## Check Your Understanding

In your Reader/Writer Notebook create a Venn Diagram to compare and contrast the two passages in this activity. What does each text say about cultural identity? How does each text convey that message?

### Writing to Sources: Explanatory Text

Use your notes as the basis of an essay that examines the similarities and differences between the formation of cultural identity as analyzed by academics and as experienced by individuals. Draw on both selections as you explore this issue. Be sure to:

- Use a formal, academic voice to examine the issues.
- Begin with a clear thesis that states your position; include clear transitions between points; and include a concluding statement.
- Effectively incorporate multiple direct quotations from both texts, introducing and punctuating them correctly.

**Group Discussion:** This is the first of many opportunities you will have to participate in a collaborative discussion with your peers about the concept of cultural identity. Choose a characteristic of culture and use it to explain your cultural identity to your group. Remember to follow the Class Norms during the discussion.

**INDEPENDENT READING LINK**

**Read and Respond**

In your independent reading, consider people's awareness of how their cultural identity is shaped—through ethnicity, family history, and/or geographical location. Note in your journal specific texts that cause you to reflect on how your own cultural identity has been shaped.

**My Notes**

# Language and Writer's Craft: Syntax

**LEARNING STRATEGIES:**
Think-Pair-Share

## Literary Terms
**Syntax** refers to the arrangement of words and the order of grammatical elements in a sentence or the way in which words are put together to make meaningful elements, such as phrases, clauses, and sentences.

**My Notes**

## Learning Targets
- Identify different types of phrases and use them in writing.
- Revise writing to include phrases and parenthetical expressions.

## Understanding Phrases

Consider sounds as the building blocks of language. Combined, they create words, or diction. When writers move those words around, they are playing with **syntax**. One essential element of syntax is the phrase. Understanding what a phrase is, how to punctuate it, and when to use this tool in your writing will help you make informed decisions about your syntax.

*Phrases* clarify meaning by adding information or by describing the subject, the action, or other nouns in the sentence. Standing alone, a phrase is not a complete sentence. Three types of phrases include *gerund phrases*, *participial phrases*, and *infinitive phrases*. Review their definitions in your Grammar Handbook, marking the text to highlight their function and the proper method of punctuating them within a sentence.

Highlight the gerund, participial, or infinitive phrases in the following sentences from the texts from this unit. Note the punctuation of each phrase. Then label the type of phrase.

1. "able to sit in a paneled office/drafting memos in smooth English,/able to order in fluent Spanish/at a Mexican restaurant …"—Pat Mora, "Legal Alien"

2. "They rode away through our large garden, still bright green from the rains, and we turned back into the twilight of the house and the sound of fans whispering in every room."—Santha Rau, "By Any Other Name"

3. "It felt like worms and toads and slimy things were crawling out of my chest, but it also felt good, that this awful side of me had surfaced, at last."—Amy Tan, "Two Kinds"

4. "Impressed with her, they worshiped the well-turned phrase, the cute shape, the scalding humor that erupted like bubbles in lye."—Alice Walker, "Everyday Use"

5. "The lessons were mostly concerned with reading and writing…."—Santha Rau, "By Any Other Name"

The beauty of recognizing types of phrases in writing rests in your ability to incorporate those syntactic structures in your own writing. Choose three of the previous sentences and use them as models to write original sentences using gerund, participle, and infinitive phrases.

1.

2.

3.

## Prepositional and Appositive Phrases

Phrases come in more shapes and sizes than gerunds, participles, and infinitives. Prepositional phrases and appositives also add precision to writing; in fact, they provide critical information that helps us combine sentences rather than depend on multiple simple sentences.

**Example:** Sophomores take English. They study world cultures.
Revised with prepositional phrases: Sophomores study world cultures *in English class.*

**Example:** The study of grammar remains a critical skill. It is a lost art.
Revised with appositive phrase: The study of grammar, *a lost art,* remains a critical skill.

Find prepositional and appositive phrases in the following sentences, and then, using the mentor sentence as a model, practice writing sentences with those types of phrases.

1. "She seemed entranced by the music, a frenzied little piano piece with a mesmerizing quality, which alternated between quick, playful passages and teasing, lilting ones."
   —Amy Tan, "Two Kinds"

   Practice:

2. "I looked briefly at the children's drawings pinned to the wall, and then concentrated on a lizard clinging to the ledge of the high, barred window behind the teacher's head."—Santha Rau, "By Any Other Name"

   Practice:

My Notes

# Language and Writer's Craft: Syntax

## Parenthetical Expressions

Parenthetical expressions can be effectively used to add voice to writing as they add editorial comments to the text. When you incorporate parenthetical expressions in your writing, set them apart from the rest of the sentence by placing commas around them. Practice writing your own sentences by emulating the style of the examples below.

1. "The headmistress had been in India, *I suppose*, fifteen years or so, but she still smiled her helpless inability to cope with Indian names." —Santha Rau, "By Any Other Name"
   Practice:

2. "I tell you, I had to go to the dictionary." —Patricia Williams, "Ethnic Hash"
   Practice:

## Check Your Understanding

Revisit a piece of your writing from this unit and revise it to include various types of phrases, or revisit a reading passage from this unit to identify phrases that might be present. Highlight and label the phrases you find.

# "Two Kinds" of Cultural Identity

## Learning Target
- Analyze how two characters interact and develop over the course of a text to explain how conflict is used to advance the theme.

## Preview
In this activity, you will read an excerpt from a novel and analyze the **conflict** between two characters.

## Setting a Purpose for Reading
- As you read Amy Tan's "Two Kinds," look for evidence of conflict. Mark the text for the reasons for the conflict and how it is resolved.
- Circle unknown words and phrases. Try to determine the meaning of the words by using context clues, word parts, or a dictionary.

### ABOUT THE AUTHOR
Amy Tan was born in California in 1952, several years after her parents left their native China. A writer from a very young age, Tan experienced difficulty early in life resulting from the untimely deaths of her father and brother, a rebellious adolescence, and the expectations of others. Educated at a Switzerland boarding school as well as at San Jose State and Berkeley, Tan ultimately became a writer of fiction. She has written numerous award-winning novels, including her most famous *The Joy Luck Club*, from which "Two Kinds" is an excerpt. Tan resides in San Francisco with her husband and two dogs, Bubba and Lilli.

> **LEARNING STRATEGIES:**
> Discussion Groups, Marking the Text, Brainstorming, graphic organizer, Questioning the Text

> **Literary Terms**
> A **conflict** is a struggle or problem in a story. The central conflict of a fictional text sets the story in motion. An *internal conflict* occurs when a character struggles between opposing needs or desires or emotions within his or her own mind. An *external conflict* occurs when a character struggles against an outside force. This force may be another character, a societal expectation, or something in the physical world.

> **My Notes**

## Novel Excerpt

# Two Kinds

*by* Amy Tan

**Chunk 1**

1  My mother believed you could be anything you wanted to be in America. You could open a restaurant. You could work for the government and get good retirement. You could buy a house with almost no money down. You could become rich. You could become instantly famous.

2  "Of course, you can be a prodigy, too," my mother told me when I was nine. "You can be best anything. What does Auntie Lindo know? Her daughter, she is only best tricky."

# "Two Kinds" of Cultural Identity

## My Notes

**indignity:** something that happens that causes insult or embarrassment

**reproach:** criticism

3  America was where all my mother's hopes lay. She had come to San Francisco in 1949 after losing everything in China: her mother and father, her home, her first husband, and two daughters, twin baby girls. But she never looked back with regret. Things could get better in so many ways.

4  We didn't immediately pick the right kind of prodigy. At first my mother thought I could be a Chinese Shirley Temple. We'd watch Shirley's old movies on TV as though they were training films. My mother would poke my arm and say, "*Ni kan*. You watch." And I would see Shirley tapping her feet, or singing a sailor song, or pursing her lips into a very round O while saying "Oh, my goodness." "*Ni kan*," my mother said, as Shirley's eyes flooded with tears. "You already know how. Don't need talent for crying!"

5  Soon after my mother got this idea about Shirley Temple, she took me to the beauty training school in the Mission District and put me in the hands of a student who could barely hold the scissors without shaking. Instead of getting big fat curls, I emerged with an uneven mass of crinkly black fuzz. My mother dragged me off to the bathroom and tried to wet down my hair.

6  "You look like a Negro Chinese," she lamented, as if I had done this on purpose.

7  The instructor of the beauty training school had to lop off these soggy clumps to make my hair even again. "Peter Pan is very popular these days" the instructor assured my mother. I now had bad hair the length of a boy's, with curly bangs that hung at a slant two inches above my eyebrows. I liked the haircut, and it made me actually look forward to my future fame.

8  In fact, in the beginning I was just as excited as my mother, maybe even more so. I pictured this prodigy part of me as many different images, and I tried each one on for size. I was a dainty ballerina girl standing by the curtain, waiting to hear the music that would send me floating on my tiptoes. I was like the Christ child lifted out of the straw manger, crying with holy **indignity**. I was Cinderella stepping from her pumpkin carriage with sparkly cartoon music filling the air.

9  In all of my imaginings I was filled with a sense that I would soon become perfect: My mother and father would adore me. I would be beyond **reproach**. I would never feel the need to sulk, or to clamor for anything. But sometimes the prodigy in me became impatient. "If you don't hurry up and get me out of here, I'm disappearing for good," it warned. "And then you'll always be nothing."

### Chunk 2

10  Every night after dinner my mother and I would sit at the Formica topped kitchen table. She would present new tests, taking her examples from stories of amazing children that she read in *Ripley's Believe It or Not* or *Good Housekeeping, Reader's Digest*, or any of a dozen other magazines she kept in a pile in our bathroom. My mother got these magazines from people whose houses she cleaned. And since she cleaned many houses each week, we had a great assortment. She would look through them all, searching for stories about remarkable children.

11  The first night she brought out a story about a three-year-old boy who knew the capitals of all the states and even most of the European countries. A teacher was quoted as saying that the little boy could also pronounce the names of the foreign cities correctly. "What's the capital of Finland?" my mother asked me, looking at the story.

12 All I knew was the capital of California, because Sacramento was the name of the street we lived on in Chinatown. "Nairobi!" I guessed, saying the most foreign word I could think of. She checked to see if that might be one way to pronounce *Helsinki* before showing me the answer.

13 The tests got harder—multiplying numbers in my head, finding the queen of hearts in a deck of cards, trying to stand on my head without using my hands, predicting the daily temperatures in Los Angeles, New York, and London. One night I had to look at a page from the Bible for three minutes and then report everything I could remember. "Now Jehoshaphat had riches and honor in abundance and … that's all I remember, Ma," I said.

14 And after seeing, once again, my mother's disappointed face, something inside me began to die. I hated the tests, the raised hopes and failed expectations. Before going to bed that night I looked in the mirror above the bathroom sink, and I saw only my face staring back—and understood that it would always be this ordinary face—I began to cry. Such a sad, ugly girl! I made high-pitched noises like a crazed animal, trying to scratch out the face in the mirror.

15 And then I saw what seemed to be the prodigy side of me—a face I had never seen before. I looked at my reflection, blinking so that I could see more clearly. The girl staring back at me was angry, powerful. She and I were the same. I had new thoughts, willful thoughts—or, rather, thoughts filled with lots of won'ts. I won't let her change me, I promised myself. I won't be what I'm not.

16 So now when my mother presented her tests, I performed **listlessly**, my head propped on one arm. I pretended to be bored. And I was. I got so bored that I started counting the **bellows** of the foghorns out on the bay while my mother drilled me in other areas. The sound was comforting and reminded me of the cow jumping over the moon. And the next day I played a game with myself, seeing if my mother would give up on me before eight bellows. After a while I usually counted only one bellow, maybe two at most. At last she was beginning to give up hope.

**Chunk 3**

17 Two or three months went by without any mention of my being a prodigy. And then one day my mother was watching the *Ed Sullivan Show* on TV. The TV was old and the sound kept shorting out. Every time my mother got halfway up from the sofa to adjust the set, the sound would come back on and Sullivan would be talking. As soon as she sat down, Sullivan would go silent again. She got up—the TV broke into loud piano music. She sat down—silence. Up and down, back and forth, quiet and loud. It was like a stiff, embraceless dance between her and the TV set. Finally, she stood by the set with her hand on the sound dial.

18 She seemed entranced by the music, a frenzied little piano piece with a **mesmerizing** quality, which alternated between quick, playful passages and teasing, lilting ones.

19 "*Ni kan,*" my mother said, calling me over with hurried hand gestures. "Look here."

## My Notes

**listlessly:** without energy or enthusiasm
**bellows:** deep, low sounds
**mesmerizing:** spellbinding

### GRAMMAR &USAGE
Syntax
Effective syntax enhances the meaning and contributes to the tone of a piece of writing.

Notice the arrangement of words in the sentences beginning with "She got up …" through the rest of the first paragraph in Chunk 3. The short, abrupt sentences affect the reader's perception of the mother. She appears comical, almost like a mechanical toy.

Now look back at the underlined sentence in Chunk 2. What feeling or attitude does this syntax convey? Look for other longer, moare complex sentences in the story. Describe how the syntax helps the author express more complicated ideas and feelings.

## My Notes

20 I could see why my mother was fascinated by the music. It was being pounded out by a little Chinese girl, about nine years old, with a Peter Pan haircut. The girl had the sauciness of a Shirley Temple. She was proudly modest, like a proper Chinese Child. And she also did a fancy sweep of a curtsy, so that the fluffy skirt of her white dress cascaded to the floor like petals of a large carnation.

21 In spite of these warning signs, I wasn't worried. Our family had no piano and we couldn't afford to buy one, let alone reams of sheet music and piano lessons. So I could be generous in my comments when my mother badmouthed the little girl on TV.

22 "Play note right, but doesn't sound good!" my mother complained. "No singing sound."

23 "What are you picking on her for?" I said carelessly. "She's pretty good. Maybe she's not the best, but she's trying hard." I knew almost immediately that I would be sorry I had said that.

24 "Just like you," she said. "Not the best. Because you not trying." She gave a little huff as she let go of the sound dial and sat down on the sofa.

25 The little Chinese girl sat down also, to play an encore of "Anitra's Tanz," by Grieg. I remember the song, because later on I had to learn how to play it.

26 Three days after watching the *Ed Sullivan Show* my mother told me what my schedule would be for piano lessons and piano practice. She had talked to Mr. Chong, who lived on the first floor of our apartment building. Mr. Chong was a retired piano teacher, and my mother had traded housecleaning services for weekly lessons and a piano for me to practice on every day, two hours a day, from four until six.

27 When my mother told me this, I felt as though I had been sent to hell. I whined, and then kicked my foot a little when I couldn't stand it anymore.

28 "Why don't you like me the way I am?" I cried. "I'm *not* a genius! I can't play the piano. And even if I could, I wouldn't go on TV if you paid me a million dollars!"

29 My mother slapped me. "Who ask you to be genius?" she shouted. "Only ask you be your best. For you sake. You think I want you to be genius? Hnnh! What for! Who ask you!"

30 "So ungrateful," I heard her mutter in Chinese, "If she had as much talent as she has temper, she'd be famous now."

### Chunk 4

31 Mr. Chong, whom I secretly nicknamed Old Chong, was very strange, always tapping his fingers to the silent music of an invisible orchestra. He looked ancient in my eyes. He had lost most of the hair on the top of his head, and he wore thick glasses and had eyes that always looked tired. But he must have been younger than I thought, since he lived with his mother and was not yet married.

32 I met Old Lady Chong once, and that was enough. She had a peculiar smell, like a baby that had done something in its pants, and her fingers felt like a dead person's, like an old peach I once found in the back of the refrigerator: its skin just slid off the flesh when I picked it up.

33  I soon found out why Old Chong had retired from teaching piano. He was deaf. "Like Beethoven!" he shouted to me: We're both listening only in our head!" And he would start to conduct his frantic silent sonatas.

34  Our lessons went like this. He would open the book and point to different things, explaining their purpose: "Key! Treble! Bass! No sharps or flats! So this is C major! Listen now and play after me!"

35  And then he would play the C scale a few times, a simple chord, and then, as if inspired by an old unreachable itch, he would gradually add more notes and running **trills** and a pounding bass until the music was really something quite grand.

36  I would play after him, the simple scale, the simple chord, and then just play some nonsense that sounded like a rat running up and down on top of garbage cans. Old Chong would smile and applaud and say "Very good! But now you must learn to keep time!"

37  So that's how I discovered that Old Chong's eyes were too slow to keep up with the wrong notes I was playing. He went through the motions in half time. To help me keep rhythm, he stood behind me and pushed down on my right shoulder for every beat. He balanced pennies on top of my wrists so that I would keep them still as I slowly played scales and **arpeggios**. He had me curve my hand around an apple and keep that shape when playing chords. He marched stiffly to show me how to make each finger dance up and down, staccato, like an obedient little soldier.

38  He taught me all these things, and that was how I also learned I could be lazy and get away with mistakes, lots of mistakes. If I hit the wrong notes because I hadn't practiced enough, I never corrected myself, I just kept playing in rhythm. And Old Chong kept conducting his own private **reverie**.

39  So maybe I never really gave myself a fair chance. I did pick up the basics pretty quickly, and I might have become a good pianist at the young age. But I was so determined not to try, not to be anybody different, and I learned to play only the most ear-splitting preludes, the most discordant hymns.

40  Over the next year I practiced like this, dutifully in my own way. And then one day I heard my mother and her friend Lindo Jong both after church, and I was leaning against a brick wall, wearing a dress with stiff white petticoats. Auntie Lindo's daughter, Waverly, who was my age, was standing farther down the wall, about five feet away. We had grown up together and shared all the closeness of two sisters, squabbling over crayons and dolls. In other words, for the most part, we hated each other. I thought she was snotty. Waverly Jong had gained a certain amount of fame as "Chinatown's Littlest Chinese Chess Champion."

41  "She bring home too many trophy." Auntie Lindo lamented that Sunday. "All day she play chess. All day I have no time do nothing but dust off her winnings." She threw a scolding look at Waverly, who pretended not to see her.

42  "You lucky you don't have this problem," Auntie Lindo said with a sigh to my mother.

43  And my mother squared her shoulders and bragged: "Our problem worser than yours. If we ask Jing-mei wash dish, she hear nothing but music. It's like you can't stop this natural talent." And right then I was determined to put a stop to her foolish pride.

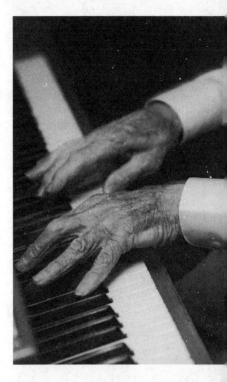

**trills:** the sound produced when two notes that are close together are pressed

**arpeggio:** a chord in which notes are played individually instead of simultaneously

**reverie:** daydream

My Notes

_____
_____
_____
_____
_____
_____
_____
_____
_____
_____

# "Two Kinds" of Cultural Identity

## WORD CONNECTIONS

### Cognates

Many words in English are the same in Spanish, such as *piano, honor,* and *natural.* Other words are similar, such as *fame-fama, purpose-propósito, music-música, reflection-reflexión,* and *talent-talento.* Look for these cognates as you read.

### My Notes

**Chunk 5**

44  A few weeks later Old Chong and my mother conspired to have me play in a talent show that was to be held in the church hall. By then my parents had saved up enough to buy me a secondhand piano, a black Wurlitzer spinet with a scarred bench. It was the showpiece of our living room.

45  For the talent show I was to play a piece called "Pleading Child," from Schumann's *Scenes From Childhood.* It was a simple, moody piece that sounded more difficult than it was. I was supposed to memorize the whole thing. But I dawdled over it, playing a few bars and then cheating, looking up to see what notes followed. I never really listened to what I was playing. I daydreamed about being somewhere else, about being someone else.

46  The part I liked to practice best was the fancy curtsy: right foot out, touch the rose on the carpet with a pointed foot, sweep to the side, bend left leg, look up, and smile.

47  My parents invited all the couples from their social club to witness my debut. Auntie Lindo and Uncle Tin were there. Waverly and her two older brothers had also come. The first two rows were filled with children either younger or older than I was. The littlest ones got to go first. They recited simple nursery rhymes, squawked out tunes on miniature violins, and twirled hula hoops in pink ballet tutus, and when they bowed or curtsied, the audience would sigh in unison, "Awww," and then clap enthusiastically.

48  When my turn came, I was very confident. I remember my childish excitement. It was as if I knew, without a doubt, that the prodigy side of me really did exist. I had no fear whatsoever, no nervousness. I remember thinking, This is it! This is it! I looked out over the audience, at my mother's blank face, my father's yawn, Auntie Lindo's stiff-lipped smile, Waverly's sulky expression. I had on a white dress, layered with sheets of lace, and a pink bow in my Peter Pan haircut. As I sat down, I envisioned people jumping to their feet and Ed Sullivan rushing up to introduce me to everyone on TV.

49  And I started to play. Everything was so beautiful. I was so caught up in how lovely I looked that I wasn't worried about how I would sound. So I was surprised when I hit the first wrong note. And then I hit another and another. A chill started at the top of my head and began to trickle down. Yet I couldn't stop playing, as though my hands were bewitched. I kept thinking my fingers would adjust themselves back, like a train switching to the right track. I played this strange jumble through to the end, the sour notes staying with me all the way.

50  When I stood up, I discovered my legs were shaking. Maybe I had just been nervous, and the audience, like Old Chong had seen me go through the right motions and had not heard anything wrong at all. I swept my right foot out, went down on my knee, looked up, and smiled. The room was quiet, except for Old Chong, who was beaming and shouting "Bravo! Bravo! Well done!" By then I saw my mother's face, her stricken face. The audience clapped weakly, and I walked back to my chair, with my whole face quivering as I tried not to cry. I heard a little boy whisper loudly to his mother, "That was awful," and the mother whispered, "Well, she certainly tried."

51  And now I realized how many people were in the audience—the whole world, it seemed. I was aware of eyes burning into my back. I felt the shame of my mother and father as they sat stiffly through the rest of the show.

52  We could have escaped during intermission. Pride and some strange sense of honor must have anchored my parents to their chairs. And so we watched it all: the eighteen-year-old boy with a fake moustache who did a magic show and juggled flaming hoops while riding a unicycle. The breasted girl with white makeup who sang an aria from *Madama Butterfly* and got an honorable mention. And the eleven-year-old boy who won first prize playing a tricky violin song that sounded like a busy bee.

53  After the show the Hsus, the Jongs, and the St. Clairs from the Joy Luck Club, came up to my mother and father.

54  "Lots of talented kids," Auntie Lindo said vaguely, smiling broadly. "That was somethin' else," my father said, and I wondered if he was referring to me in a humorous way, or whether he even remembered what I had done.

55  Waverly looked at me and shrugged her shoulders. "You aren't a genius like me," she said matter-of-factly. And if I hadn't felt so bad, I would have pulled her braids and punched her stomach.

56  But my mother's expression was what devastated me: a quiet, blank look that said she had lost everything. I felt the same way, and everybody seemed now to be coming up, like gawkers at the scene of an accident to see what parts were actually missing.

**Chunk 6**

57  When we got on the bus to go home, my father was humming the busy-bee tune and my mother kept silent. I kept thinking she wanted to wait until we got home before shouting at me. But when my father unlocked the door to our apartment, my mother walked in and went straight to the back, into the bedroom. No accusations. No blame. And in a way, I felt disappointed. I had been waiting for her to start shouting, so that I could shout back and cry and blame her for all my misery.

58  I had assumed that my talent-show **fiasco** meant that I would never have to play the piano again. But two days later, after school, my mother came out of the kitchen and saw me watching TV.

59  "Four clock," she reminded me, as if it were any other day. I was stunned, as though she were asking me to go through the talent-show torture again. I planted myself more squarely in front of the TV.

60  "Turn off TV," she called from the kitchen five minutes later. I didn't budge. And then I decided, I didn't have to do what mother said anymore. I wasn't her slave. This wasn't China. I had listened to her before, and look what happened. She was the stupid one.

61  She came out of the kitchen and stood in the arched entryway of the living room. "Four clock," she said once again, louder.

62  "I'm not going to play anymore," I said **nonchalantly**. "Why should I? I'm not a genius."

63  She stood in front of the TV. I saw that her chest was heaving up and down in an angry way.

64  "No!" I said, and I now felt stronger, as if my true self had finally emerged. So this was what had been inside me all along.

**GRAMMAR & USAGE**
Syntax
Skilled writers take poetic license and break rules of proper syntax. Why do you think Tan uses fragments to describe the acts in the show?

**My Notes**

fiasco: disaster
nonchalantly: calmly

## My Notes

65 "No! I won't!" I screamed. She snapped off the TV, yanked me by the arm and pulled me off the floor. She was frighteningly strong, half pulling, half carrying me towards the piano as I kicked the throw rugs under my feet. She lifted me up onto the hard bench. I was sobbing by now, looking at her bitterly. Her chest was heaving even more and her mouth was open, smiling crazily as if she were pleased that I was crying.

66 "You want me to be something that I'm not!" I sobbed. "I'll never be the kind of daughter you want me to be!"

67 "Only two kinds of daughters," she shouted in Chinese. "Those who are obedient and those who follow their own mind! Only one kind of daughter can live in this house. Obedient daughter!"

68 "Then I wish I weren't your daughter, I wish you weren't my mother," I shouted. As I said these things I got scared. It felt like worms and toads and slimy things were crawling out of my chest, but it also felt good, that this awful side of me had surfaced, at last.

69 "Too late to change this," my mother said shrilly.

70 And I could sense her anger rising to its breaking point. I wanted to see it spill over. And that's when I remembered the babies she had lost in China, the ones we never talked about. "Then I wish I'd never been born!" I shouted. "I wish I were dead! Like them."

71 It was as if I had said magic words. Alakazam!—her face went blank, her mouth closed, her arms went slack, and she backed out of the room, stunned, as if she were blowing away like a small brown leaf, thin, brittle, lifeless.

**Chunk 7**

72 It was not the only disappointment my mother felt in me. In the years that followed, I failed her many times, each time asserting my will, my right to fall short of expectations. I didn't get straight As. I didn't become class president. I didn't get into Stanford. I dropped out of college.

73 For unlike my mother, I did not believe I could be anything I wanted to be, I could only be me.

74 And for all those years we never talked about the disaster at the recital or my terrible declarations afterward at the piano bench. Neither of us talked about it again, as if it were a betrayal that was now unspeakable. So I never found a way to ask her why she had hoped for something so large that failure was inevitable.

75 And even worse, I never asked her about what frightened me the most: Why had she given up hope? For after our struggle at the piano, she never mentioned my playing again. The lessons stopped. The lid to the piano was closed, shutting out the dust, my misery, and her dreams.

76 So she surprised me. A few years ago she offered to give me the piano, for my thirtieth birthday. I had not played in all those years. I saw the offer as a sign of forgiveness, a tremendous burden removed. "Are you sure?" I asked shyly. "I mean, won't you and Dad miss it?" "No, this your piano," she said firmly. "Always your piano. You only one can play."

77 "Well, I probably can't play anymore," I said. "It's been years." "You pick up fast," my mother said, as if she knew this was certain. "You have natural talent. You could be a genius if you want to." "No, I couldn't." "You just not trying," my mother said. And she was neither angry nor sad. She said it as if announcing a fact that could never be disproved. "Take it," she said.

78 But I didn't at first. It was enough that she had offered it to me. And after that, every time I saw it in my parents' living room, standing in front of the bay window, it made me feel proud, as if it were a shiny trophy that I had won back.

**Chunk 8**

79 Last week I sent a tuner over to my parent's apartment and had the piano reconditioned, for purely sentimental reasons. My mother had died a few months before and I had been getting things in order for my father a little bit at a time. I put the jewelry in special silk pouches. The sweaters I put in mothproof boxes. I found some old Chinese silk dresses, the kind with little slits up the sides. I rubbed the old silk against my skin, and then wrapped them in tissue and decided to take them home with me.

80 After I had the piano tuned, I opened the lid and touched the keys. It sounded even richer than I remembered. Really, it was a very good piano. Inside the bench were the same exercise notes with handwritten scales, the same secondhand music books with their covers held together with yellow tape.

81 I opened up the Schumann book to the dark little pieces I had played at the recital. It was on the left-hand page, "Pleading Child." It looked more difficult than I remembered. I played a few bars, surprised at how easily the notes came back to me.

82 And for the first time, or so it seemed, I noticed the piece on the right-hand side, It was called "Perfectly Contented." I tried to play this one as well. It had a lighter melody but with the same flowing rhythm and turned out to be quite easy. "Pleading Child" was shorter but slower; "Perfectly Contented" was longer but faster. And after I had played them both a few times, I realized they were two halves of the same song.

**My Notes**

**INDEPENDENT READING LINK**

**Read and Respond**

In your independent reading look for evidence of generational conflicts in defining cultural identity. You may want to focus on the experiences of a younger generation in an immigrant family. Prepare a summary of your findings on how young people deal with family versus cultural expectations.

# "Two Kinds" of Cultural Identity

**My Notes**

## Second Read

- Reread the novel excerpt to answer these text-dependent questions.
- Write any additional questions you have about the text in your Reader/Writer Notebook.

1. **Key Ideas and Details:** What is the relationship between Jing-mei and her mother at the start of the narrative? Cite textual evidence that supports your response.

2. **Key Ideas and Details:** In paragraph 15, what does Jing-mei discover about herself? How does this help develop the theme of the selection?

3. **Key Ideas and Details:** What conflicts are apparent in chunk 3? What are the reasons for the conflicts?

4. **Key Ideas and Details:** In chunk 4, how does the relationship between Jing-mei's mother and Auntie Lindo contribute to the conflict between Jing-mei and her mother in the story?

5. **Key Ideas and Details:** How does the narrator's tone shift during chunk 5?

6. **Key Ideas and Details:** Reread the last paragraph of chunk 5. Colons and the word *but* often signal a shift in literature. What shift is happening here? How is it related to the central conflict in the story?

7. **Key Ideas and Details:** To what is "Two Kinds" referring to in paragraph 67? What conflicting perspectives on cultural identity are evident in this scene?

8. **Craft and Structure:** How does the sentence beginning "For unlike my mother, I did not ..." connect to the first paragraph of the story? Does this suggest that the conflict in the story is primarily internal or external?

9. **Key Ideas and Details:** What is significant about Jing-mei's discovery in the final paragraphs? What does it reveal about her perspective now? Does this bring resolution to the conflict(s) in the story or not?

**My Notes**

# "Two Kinds" of Cultural Identity

*pick*
*fo*

## Working from the Text

10. Review your notes about the conflicts in "Two Kinds." Complete the following graphic organizer analyzing Jing-mei's internal conflict and her external conflict with her mother.

| | |
|---|---|
| Mother's perspective on cultural identity | |
| Jing-mei's perspective on cultural identity | |
| The contrast with Waverly and Auntie Lindo | |
| How do the conflicts connect with the meaning of the work as a whole? | |

### Literary Terms
The **theme** of a work is the writer's central idea or main message about life. The theme may be either implicit or explicit. A **thematic statement** is an interpretive statement articulating the central meaning of the text.

## Check Your Understanding

How can the conflict between characters develop the **theme** of a work? With your group members, generate a list of possible themes and then craft a **thematic statement** for the theme you think is most central to the story.

### Writing to Sources: Explanatory Text

Explain how Tan uses the central conflict between mother and daughter to develop the theme of the work. Be sure to:

- Build your essay around a clear focus (her perspective toward her cultural identity, toward her mother, toward America).
- Support your response with quotes and details from the text.
- Use an academic voice and vary your syntax by incorporating a variety of phrases in your writing.

## Learning Targets

- Analyze a particular point of view regarding a cultural experience expressed in literature and art.
- Compare and contrast the representation of a subject in different media.

LEARNING STRATEGIES:
Close Reading,
Metacognitive Markers,
Discussion Groups, OPTIC

## Preview

In this activity, you will analyze multiple media—a flim clip, a biography, a painting, and a poem—to compare and contrast perceptions of cultural identity.

## Viewing a Film

In preparation for a discussion on the life, art, and culture of Frida Kahlo, watch a short PBS film clip, *The Life and Times of Frida*. Take notes on the key ideas and details that help you understand Kahlo's life, art, and cultural identity.

## Setting a Purpose for Reading

- As you read a brief introductory excerpt from Hayden Herrera's biography, *Frida, a Biography of Frida Kahlo,* use metacognative markers to mark the text. As you mark the text, focus on the details emphasized that help you understand Kahlo's life, art, and cultural identity.
- Circle unknown words and phrases. Try to determine the meaning of the words by using context clues, word parts, or a dictionary.

**My Notes**

## Biography

From *Frida, a Biography of*

## Frida Kahlo

*by* Hayden Herrera

1   In April, 1953, less than a year before her death at the age of forty-seven, Frida Kahlo had her first major exhibition of paintings in her native Mexico. By that time her health had so deteriorated that no one expected her to attend. But at 8:00 P.M., just after the doors of Mexico City's Gallery of Contemporary Art opened to the public, an ambulance drew up. The artist, dressed in her favorite Mexican costume, was carried on a hospital stretcher to her four-poster bed, which had been installed in the gallery that afternoon. The bed was bedecked as she liked it, with photographs of her husband, the great muralist Diego Rivera, and of her political heroes. Papier-mache skeletons dangled from the canopy, and a mirror affixed to the underside of the canopy reflected her joyful though ravaged face. One by one, two hundred friends and admirers greeted Frida Kahlo, then formed a circle around the bed and sang Mexican ballads with her until well past midnight.

**encapsulates:** sums up

**gallantry:** courage

**haute couture:** high fashion; expensive and fashionable clothing

## My Notes

**transmuted:** transformed
**tempered:** made less severe

**rhetoric:** language

2  The occasion **encapsulates** as much as it culminates this extraordinary woman's career. It testifies, in fact, to many of the qualities that marked Kahlo as a person and as a painter: her **gallantry** and indomitable *alegria* in the face of physical suffering; her insistence on surprise and specificity; her peculiar love of spectacle as a mask to preserve privacy and personal dignity. Above all, the opening of her exhibition dramatized Frida Kahlo's central subject—herself. Most of the some two hundred paintings she produced in her abbreviated career were self-portraits....

3  She dressed in flamboyant clothes, greatly preferring floor-length native Mexican costumes to **haute couture**. Wherever she went she caused a sensation. One New Yorker remembers that children used to follow her in the streets. "Where's the circus?" they would ask; Frida Kahlo did not mind a bit.... Frida flaunted her *alegria* the way a peacock spreads its tail, but it camouflaged a deep sadness and inwardness, even self-obsession.

4  "I paint my own reality," she said. "The only thing I know is that I paint because I need to, and I paint always whatever passes through my head, without any other consideration." What passed through Frida Kahlo's head and into her art was some of the most original and dramatic imagery of the twentieth century. Painting herself bleeding, weeping, cracked open, she **transmuted** her pain into art with remarkable frankness **tempered** by humor and fantasy. Always specific and personal, deep-probing rather than comprehensive in scope, Frida's autobiography in paint has peculiar intensity and strength—a strength that can hold the viewer in an uncomfortably tight grip.

5  The majority of her paintings are small—twelve by fifteen inches is not unusual; their scale suits the intimacy of her subject matter. With very small sable brushes, which she kept immaculately clean, she would carefully lay down delicate strokes of color, bringing the image into precise focus, making fantasy persuasive through the **rhetoric** of realism....

6  In the fall of 1977, the Mexican government turned over the largest and most prestigious galleries in the Palace of Fine Arts to a retrospective exhibition of Frida Kahlo's works. It was a strange sort of homage, for it seemed to celebrate the exotic personality and story of the artist rather more than it honored her art. The grand, high-ceilinged rooms were dominated by huge blow-up photographs of incidents in Frida's life, which made the jewel-like paintings look almost like punctuation points.

7  The art—the legend Frida herself had created—won out in the end, however. Because her paintings were so tiny in relation to the photographs and to the exhibition space, the spectator had to stand within a few feet of each one to focus on it at all. And at that proximity their strange magnetism exerted its pull. Taken from separate, poignant moments in her life, each was like a smothered cry, a nugget of emotion so dense that one felt it might explode....

## Second Read

- Reread the biography to answer these text-dependent questions.
- Write any additional questions you have about the text in your Reader/Writer Notebook.

1. **Key Ideas and Details:** Based on details in paragraph 1, what inference can you make about Frida Kahlo's character and personality?

2. **Craft and Structure:** Using context clues from paragraphs 2 and 3, determine the meaning of the word *alegria* as it applies to Kahlo's personality.

3. **Craft and Structure:** Choose a line of text that best characterizes the biographer's opinion of Kahlo's art and explain your understanding of the opinion.

4. **Key Ideas and Details:** In paragraph 6, the author describes an exhibition of Kahlo's work as "a strange sort of homage, for it seemed to celebrate the exotic personality and story of the artist rather more than it honored her art." How does this statement help develop the central idea of the text?

5. **Key Ideas and Details:** What connection does the author make between the outer Frida and the inner one of her art?

6. **Craft and Structure:** How does the author develop her ideas about Frida Kahlo and her art?

**My Notes**

# Two Perspectives on Cultural Identity

## Working from the Text

7. Organize your notes from both texts (the film clip and the informational text) so that you can come to the discussion prepared with well-reasoned, text-based responses to address Kalho's life, art, and cultural identity.

**Group Discussion:** What did you learn about Frida Kahlo's life, art, and cultural identity? What details are emphasized in each text to support your interpretation of this artist and how she depicts her cultural identity in her work? In your discussion, be sure to:

- Adhere to the class norms for discussions.
- Present thoughtful, well-reasoned ideas.
- Use textual evidence to support responses to questions or statements.

## Writing to Sources: Explanatory Text

Explain how Kahlo expresses her cultural identity in her art, drawing on examples from both sources. In your writing, be sure to do the following:

- Begin with a clear thesis that states your position. Include a clear definition of Kahlo's cultural identity, as you understand it.
- Include direct quotations and specific examples from the texts to support your claims. Introduce and punctuate all quotations correctly.
- Include transitions between points and a concluding statement.
- Vary your syntax, using a variety of sentence types.

**Group Discussion:** Exchange your response to the Writing Prompt with a peer. Consider the syntactical choices they have made in their writing. What is the effect they are trying to achieve? Were they successful? What suggestions do you have for improvement?

## ABOUT THE ARTIST

In 1930 Frida Kahlo's husband, Diego Rivera, received several commissions to paint murals in the United States, causing them to move from Mexico to this country. After three years in the United States, Frida was homesick and longed to return to Mexico. This tension between living in one world and longing to be in another inspired her painting *Self-Portrait on the Borderline Between Mexico and the United States.*

WORD CONNECTIONS

**Content Connections**

The word *medium* has different meanings in art, communication, science, and math. In art, *medium* refers to the mode or material used to communicate artistic expression, such as watercolor or sculpture. In communication, medium is the system of communication, such as newspapers or television. In science, *medium* can be a substance placed in a habitat, such as a petri dish, to help organisms grow. In math, *medium* is used to describe a middle degree or mean.

Like literature, art is a medium that intends to communicate to an audience. Just as every literary work is a conversation waiting to happen, so is a work of art waiting for a listening audience. As a viewer and reader of art, you must consider the elements of the art before making an interpretation.

## Introducing the Strategy: OPTIC

OPTIC is an acronym for overview, parts, title, interrelationships, and conclusion. OPTIC is a strategy for analyzing visual texts—including paintings, photographs, advertisements, maps, charts, or graphs—and developing an interpretation regarding the meaning or theme(s) of the text.

8. Use the OPTIC graphic organizer on the next page to analyze this painting.

**My Notes**

# Two Perspectives on Cultural Identity

**Title of Piece:** _____

_____          _____

| | |
|---|---|
| **Overview** | Look at the artwork for at least 10 seconds. Generate questions that you have about the artwork, such as the following: What is the subject? What strikes you as interesting, odd, etc.? What is happening? |
| **Parts** | Look closely at the artwork, making note of important elements and details. Ask additional questions, such as the following: Who are the figures? What is the setting and time period? What symbols are present? What historical information would aid understanding of this piece? |
| **Title** | Consider what the title and any written elements of the text suggest about meaning. How does the title relate to what is portrayed? |
| **Interrelationships** | Look for connections between and among the title, caption, and the parts of the art. How are the different elements related? |
| **Conclusion** | Form a conclusion about the meaning/theme of the text. Remember the questions you asked when you first examined it. Be prepared to support your conclusions with evidence. |

9. How did the information about the artist's life help you to understand the artwork?

10. What is the conflict presented in the artwork? Provide examples from the text to support your analysis.

**Literary Terms**

A **symbol** is anything (object, animal, event, person, or place) that represents itself but also stands for something else on a figurative level.

## Check Your Understanding

How does Frida Kahlo's painting *Self-Portrait on the Borderline Between Mexico and the United States* represent her cultural identity? Write an interpretive response and provide examples from the text, including Kahlo's **symbolism**, to support your analysis.

## Setting a Purpose for Reading

- Every writer has a unique voice. You have learned that voice is the distinctive use of a writer's language, achieved in part through diction and syntax, to convey persona or personality. The term *voice* is also used to express cultural identity. Read the poem several times and use metacognitive markers to examine the voice used in the text.

- Circle unknown words and phrases. Try to determine the meaning of the words by using context clues, word parts, or a dictionary.

**My Notes**

# Two Perspectives on Cultural Identity

## WORD CONNECTIONS

### Roots and Affixes

The prefix *bi-* comes from Latin and means "both" or "in two parts." Why does the author begin and end the poem with words that use the prefix *bi-*? What is she saying about her cultural identity?

## My Notes

hyphenated: connected

**ABOUT THE AUTHOR**

Pat Mora is a poet, writer, and social activist whose works explore issues of heritage and social inequality. An avid traveler, Mora wrote *Communion* (1991) about her experiences traveling in Cuba, India, and Pakistan. A year later, she published her first children's book about a beloved aunt who taught her to appreciate her own Mexican American heritage.

Poetry

# Legal Alien

*by* Pat Mora

Bi-lingual, Bi-cultural,
able to slip from "How's life?"
to "Me'stan volviendo loca,"
able to sit in a paneled office
5   drafting memos in smooth English,
able to order in fluent Spanish
at a Mexican restaurant,
American but **hyphenated**,
viewed by Anglos as perhaps exotic,
10   perhaps inferior, definitely different,
viewed by Mexicans as alien,
(their eyes say, "You may speak
Spanish but you're not like me")
an American to Mexicans
15   a Mexican to Americans
a handy token
sliding back and forth
between the fringes of both worlds
by smiling
20   by masking the discomfort
of being pre-judged
Bi-laterally.

## Second Read

- Reread the poem to answer these text-dependent questions.
- Write any additional questions you have about the text in your Reader/Writer Notebook.

11. **Craft and Structure:** What is the meaning of the word *alien* as it is used in the title of the poem? What is the meaning as it is used in line 11?

12. **Key Ideas and Details:** What is implied in lines 5–7 by the different activities performed in English and Spanish?

13. **Craft and Structure:** As you saw in Frida Kahlo's artwork, *juxtaposition* is the arrangement of two or more things for the purpose of comparison. Identify places where Mora juxtaposes two contrasting views, situations, or actions. How does she use this technique throughout the poem to create a sense of the speaker's conflict with others—or her conflicted sense of self?

14. **Key Ideas and Details:** How does Pat Mora represent cultural identity in this poem?

My Notes

# Two Perspectives on Cultural Identity

© 2017 College Board. All rights reserved.

## INDEPENDENT READING LINK

### Read and Recommend

As you learn how people express their cultural identity in your independent reading, pay close attention to photographs and artwork as well as text. Use the OPTIC strategy to analyze how effective these images are in helping you understand cultural identity. Use your analysis to recommend a text to your peers.

### My Notes

## Working from the Text

15. **Group Discussion:** Share your annotated poem within your small group and address the following questions. Remember to follow the class norms for meaningful group discussions.

    Create a diagram to synthesize information about the art and the poem as you answer these questions:

    - What is emphasized in the art?
    - What is emphasized in the poem?
    - What ideas and images are present in the poem but absent from the art?
    - What ideas and images are present in the art but absent from the poem?

## Writing to Sources: Explanatory Text

Write an explanatory essay that explores the similarities and differences in the cultural identity of the artist Frida Kahlo and the poet Pat Mora, as expressed in the painting and the poem. Be sure to:

- Begin with a clear thesis that states your view of the overall similarities and differences between the cultural identities of the two.
- Include direct quotations and specific examples from both the painting and the poem. Introduce and punctuate all quotations correctly.
- Use a coherent organizational structure and employ transitions effectively to highlight similarities and differences.
- Use an appropriate voice and a variety of phrases to add interest to your writing.

## Check Your Understanding

**Group Discussion:** Now that you have studied art and poetry, choose a medium of interest to you and respond to one of the prompts below. After you complete the prompt, you will participate in a small group discussion and present your piece to the group.

**Artistic Prompt:** What would a self-portrait say about your perspective on your own cultural identity? Create an artistic work that portrays aspects of this identity. You might revisit your Perception Box work from Activity 1.2 as you consider objects to include in your self-portrait. Also, consider techniques and specific images you can use as evidence to depict and/or symbolize potential conflicts that arise when various aspects of your culture collide. Because artwork, like literature, speaks to an audience, keep in mind the message you want your audience to "read" as they view your work.

**Creative Writing Prompt:** Write a poem emulating the style of Pat Mora and exploring your perspective on a key component of your cultural identity. Be sure to:

- Focus on a specific culturally based conflict, which may be internal, external, or both.
- Structure the poem to use juxtaposition for effect at least once.
- Use diction, syntax, and imagery to present your own voice.

## Learning Target

- Analyze cultural elements in a memoir in order to infer how cultural identity is central to the meaning of a work.
- Evaluate the effect of an author's use of parallel structure and use it in your own writing.

## Preview

In this activity, you will read a memoir and analyze the cultural elements the author uses to describe her cultural identity.

## Setting a Purpose for Reading

- As you read the memoir "By Any Other Name" by Santha Rama Rau, mark the text for cultural elements that reveal a sense of the narrator's cultural identity.
- Circle unknown words and phrases. Try to determine the meaning of the words by using context clues, word parts, or a dictionary.

**LEARNING STRATEGIES:**
Predicting, Think-Pair-Share, Questioning the Text, Discussing, graphic organizer

**My Notes**

### ABOUT THE AUTHOR

Santha Rama Rau was born in 1923 in Madras, British India (now Chennai, India) and died in Armenia, New York in April 2009. She was an author and journalist who was best-known for her travel books, but all of her work was characterized by a strong autobiographical element and the examination of the tension between Western and Indian traditions. In 1944, Rama Rau graduated from Wellesley College in the United States, but returned to India where she wrote her first novel, *Home to India*. While traveling throughout Africa, Asia, and Russia, Rama Rau published travel essays and short stories in such periodicals as *The New Yorker* and *Vogue*, completed her third novel, and wrote a screen adaptation of E.M. Forster's novel *A Passage to India*. The following short memoir was published in *The New Yorker* on March 17, 1951.

### Memoir

# By Any Other Name

*by* Santha Rama Rau

1    At the Anglo-Indian day school[1] in Zorinabad[2] to which my sister and I were sent when she was eight and I was five and a half, they changed our names. On the first day of school, a hot, windless morning of a north Indian September, we stood in the headmistress's study and she said, "Now you're the *new* girls. What are your names?"

2    My sister answered for us. "I am Premila, and she"—nodding in my direction—"is Santha."

---

[1] The *Anglo-Indian day school* was a non-boarding school with British administrators
[2] *Zorinabad* is a village in northern India.

# Connecting Cultural Identity to Theme

**precarious:** unstable or shaky

**intimidated:** frightened

**provincial:** unsophisticated

**monsoon:** rainy season that occurs twice per year in South Asia

**insular:** limited and narrow

## GRAMMAR & USAGE
### Parallel Structure

Sentences have *parallel structure* when two or more sentence elements of equal rank or importance are expressed in a similar way, as in Julius Caesar's famous quote "I came; I saw; I conquered." Stating equal and closely related ideas in parallel constructions adds clarity and smoothness to writing. Notice the parallel structure in the underlined sentence in paragraph 7. The clauses sound like steps (1, 2, 3) that the girls need to take to start school. They have a "matter of fact" tone to them, which belies the importance of leaving behind their language and religion.

What other examples of parallel structure do you see in the text?

3 The headmistress had been in India, I suppose, fifteen years or so, but she still smiled her helpless inability to cope with Indian names. Her rimless half-glasses glittered, and the **precarious** bun on the top of her head trembled as she shook her head. "Oh, my dears, those are much too hard for me. Suppose we give you pretty English names.

4 "Wouldn't that be more jolly? Let's see, now—Pamela for you, I think." She shrugged in a baffled way at my sister. "That's as close as I can get. And for *you*," she said to me, "how about Cynthia? Isn't that nice?"

5 My sister was always less easily **intimidated** than I was, and while she kept a stubborn silence, I said, "Thank you," in a very tiny voice.

6 We had been sent to that school because my father, among his responsibilities as an officer of the civil service, had a tour of duty to perform in the villages around that steamy little **provincial** town, where he had his headquarters at that time. He used to make his shorter inspection tours on horseback, and a week before, in the stale heat of a typically post-**monsoon** day, we had waved good-by to him and a little procession—an assistant, a secretary, two bearers[3], and the man to look after the bedding rolls and luggage. They rode away through our large garden, still bright green from the rains, and we turned back into the twilight of the house and the sound of fans whispering in every room.

7 Up to then, my mother had refused to send Premila to school in the British-run establishments of that time, because, she used to say, "You can bury a dog's tail for seven years and it still comes out curly, and you can take a Britisher away from his home for a lifetime and he still remains **insular**." The examinations and degrees from entirely Indian schools were not, in those days, considered valid. In my case, the question had never come up, and probably never would have come up if Mother's extraordinary good health had not broken down. For the first time in my life, she was not able to continue the lessons she had been giving us every morning. So our Hindi[4] books were put away, the stories of the Lord Krishna as a little boy were left in mid-air, and we were sent to the Anglo-Indian school.

8 That first day at school is still, when I think of it, a remarkable one. At that age, if one's name is changed, one develops a curious form of dual personality. Accordingly, I followed the thin, erect back of the headmistress down the veranda to my classroom feeling, at most, a passing interest in what was going to happen to me in this strange, new atmosphere of School.

9 The building was Indian in design, with wide verandas opening onto a central courtyard, but Indian verandas are usually whitewashed, with stone floors. These, in the tradition of British schools, were painted dark brown and had matting on the floors. It gave a feeling of extra intensity to the heat.

10 I suppose there were about a dozen Indian children in the school—which contained perhaps forty children in all—and four of them were in my class. They were all sitting at the back of the room, and I went to join them. I sat next to a small, solemn girl who didn't smile at me. She had long, glossy black braids and wore a cotton dress, but she still kept on her Indian jewelry—a gold chain around her neck, thin gold bracelets, and tiny ruby studs in her ears. Like most Indian children, she had a rim of black kohl[5] around her eyes. The cotton dress should have looked strange, but all I could think of was that I should ask my mother if I couldn't wear a dress to school, too, instead of my Indian clothes.

---

[3] *Bearers* carry heavy loads of materials and supplies.
[4] *Hindi* is the official language of India.
[5] *Kohl* is a dark powder used as eye makeup in the Middle East and India.

11  I can't remember too much about the proceedings in class that day, except for the beginning. The teacher pointed to me and asked me to stand up. "Now, dear, tell the class your name."

12  I said nothing. "Come along," she said, frowning slightly. "What's your name, dear?" "I don't know," I said, finally.

13  The English children in the front of the class—there were about eight or ten of them—giggled and twisted around in their chairs to look at me. I sat down quickly and opened my eyes very wide, hoping in that way to dry them off. The little girl with the braids put out her hand and very lightly touched my arm. She still didn't smile.

14  Most of that morning I was rather bored. I looked briefly at the children's drawings pinned to the wall, and then concentrated on a lizard clinging to the ledge of the high, barred window behind the teacher's head. Occasionally it would shoot out its long yellow tongue for a fly, and then it would rest, with its eyes closed and its belly **palpitating** as though it were swallowing several times quickly. The lessons were mostly concerned with reading and writing and simple numbers—things that my mother had already taught me—and I paid very little attention. The teacher wrote on the easel blackboard words like "bat" and "cat," which seemed babyish to me; only "apple" was new and incomprehensible.

15  When it was time for the lunch recess, I followed the girl with braids out onto the **veranda**. There the children from the other classes were assembled. I saw Premila at once and ran over to her, as she had charge of our lunchbox. The children were all opening packages and sitting down to eat sandwiches. Premila and I were the only ones who had Indian food—thin wheat chapatis,[6] some vegetable curry,[7] and a bottle of buttermilk. Premila thrust half of it into my hand and whispered fiercely that I should go and sit with my class, because that was what the others seemed to be doing.

---

[6] *Chapatis* are thin griddlecakes of unleavened bread eaten in northern India.
[7] *Vegetable curry* is a pungent dish of vegetables cooked in a sauce with curry powder.

**My Notes**

**palpitating:** beating, throbbing

**veranda:** an open area outside of a building that has a roof

## My Notes

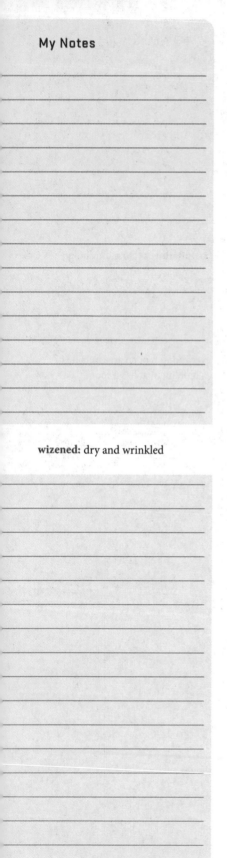

wizened: dry and wrinkled

16  The enormous black eyes of the little Indian girl from my class looked at my food longingly, so I offered her some. But she only shook her head and plowed her way solemnly through her sandwiches.

17  I was very sleepy after lunch, because at home we always took a siesta. It was usually a pleasant time of day, with the bedroom darkened against the harsh afternoon sun, the drifting off into sleep with the sound of Mother's voice reading a story in one's mind, and, finally, the shrill, fussy voice of the ayah[8] waking one for tea.

18  At school, we rested for a short time on low, folding cots on the veranda, and then we were expected to play games. During the hot part of the afternoon we played indoors, and after the shadows had begun to lengthen and the slight breeze of the evening had come up we moved outside to the wide courtyard.

19  I had never really grasped the system of competitive games. At home, whenever we played tag or guessing games, I was always allowed to "win"—"because," Mother used to tell Premila, "she is the youngest, and we have to allow for that." I had often heard her say it, and it seemed quite reasonable to me, but the result was that I had no clear idea of what "winning" meant.

20  When we played twos-and-threes[9] that afternoon at school, in accordance with my training, I let one of the small English boys catch me, but was naturally rather puzzled when the other children did not return the courtesy. I ran about for what seemed like hours without ever catching anyone, until it was time for school to close. Much later I learned that my attitude was called "not being a good sport," and I stopped allowing myself to be caught, but it was not for years that I really learned the spirit of the thing.

21  When I saw our car come up to the school gate, I broke away from my classmates and rushed toward it yelling, "Ayah! Ayah!" It seemed like an eternity since I had seen her that morning—a **wizened**, affectionate figure in her white cotton sari,[10] giving me dozens of urgent and useless instructions on how to be a good girl at school. Premila followed more sedately, and she told me on the way home never to do that again in front of the other children.

22  When we got home we went straight to Mother's high, white room to have tea with her, and I immediately climbed onto the bed and bounced gently up and down on the springs. Mother asked how we had liked our first day in school. I was so pleased to be home and to have left that peculiar Cynthia behind that I had nothing whatever to say about school, except to ask what "apple" meant. But Premila told Mother about the classes, and added that in her class they had weekly tests to see if they had learned their lessons well.

23  I asked, "What's a test?"

24  Premila said, "You're too small to have them. You won't have them in your class for donkey's years." She had learned the expression that day and was using it for the first time. We all laughed enormously at her wit. She also told Mother, in an aside, that we should take sandwiches to school the next day. Not, she said, that *she* minded. But they would be simpler for me to handle.

---

[8] In India, an *ayah* is a native maid or nanny.

[9] *Twos-and-threes* is a game similar to tag.

[10] A *sari* is a garment worn by Indian women. It consists of a long cloth wrapped around the body with one end draped over one shoulder or over the head.

25 That whole lovely evening I didn't think about school at all. I sprinted barefoot across the lawns with my favorite playmate, the cook's son, to the stream at the end of the garden. We quarreled in our usual way, waded in the tepid water under the lime trees, and waited for the night to bring out the smell of the jasmine. I listened with fascination to his stories of ghosts and demons, until I was too frightened to cross the garden alone in the semidarkness. The ayah found me, shouted at the cook's son, scolded me, hurried me in to supper—it was an entirely usual, wonderful evening.

26 It was a week later, the day of Premila's first test, that our lives changed rather abruptly. I was sitting at the back of my class, in my usual inattentive way, only half listening to the teacher. I had started a rather guarded friendship with the girl with the braids, whose name turned out to be Nalini (Nancy, in school). The three other children were already fast friends. Even at that age it was apparent to all of us that friendship with the English or Anglo-Indian children was out of the question. Occasionally, during the class, my new friend and I would draw pictures and show them to each other secretly.

27 The door opened sharply and Premila marched in. At first, the teacher smiled at her in a kindly and encouraging way and said, "Now, you're little Cynthia's sister?"

28 Premila didn't even look at her. She stood with her feet planted firmly apart and her shoulders rigid, and addressed herself directly to me. "Get up," she said. "We're going home."

29 I didn't know what had happened, but I was aware that it was a crisis of some sort. I rose obediently and started to walk toward my sister.

30 "Bring your pencils and your notebook," she said.

31 I went back for them, and together we left the room. The teacher started to say something just as Premila closed the door, but we didn't wait to hear what it was.

32 In complete silence we left the school grounds and started to walk home. Then I asked Premila what the matter was. All she would say was "We're going home for good."

33 It was a very tiring walk for a child of five and a half, and I dragged along behind Premila with my pencils growing sticky in my hand. I can still remember looking at the dusty hedges, and the tangles of thorns in the ditches by the side of the road, smelling the faint fragrance from the eucalyptus trees and wondering whether we would ever reach home. Occasionally a horse-drawn tonga[11] passed us, and the women, in their pink or green silks, stared at Premila and me trudging along on the side of the road. A few coolies[12] and a line of women carrying baskets of vegetables on their heads smiled at us. But it was nearing the hottest time of day, and the road was almost deserted. I walked more and more slowly, and shouted to Premila, from time to time, "Wait for me!" with increasing peevishness. She spoke to me only once, and that was to tell me to carry my notebook on my head, because of the sun.

34 When we got to our house the ayah was just taking a tray of lunch into Mother's room. She immediately started a long, worried questioning about what are you children doing back here at this hour of the day.

35 Mother looked very startled and very concerned, and asked Premila what had happened.

---

[11] A *tonga* is a two-wheeled, horse-drawn vehicle.
[12] *Coolies* are workers hired at low wages for unskilled work.

## GRAMMAR & USAGE
### Parallel Structure
Focus your attention on paragraph 25. Identify the author's use of parallel structure. What is its effect?

### My Notes

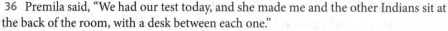

36  Premila said, "We had our test today, and she made me and the other Indians sit at the back of the room, with a desk between each one."

37  Mother said, "Why was that, darling?"

38  "She said it was because Indians cheat," Premila added. "So I don't think we should go back to that school."

39  Mother looked very distant, and was silent a long time. At last she said, "Of course not, darling." She sounded displeased.

40  We all shared the curry she was having for lunch, and afterward I was sent off to the beautifully familiar bedroom for my siesta. I could hear Mother and Premila talking through the open door.

41  Mother said, "Do you suppose she understood all that?" Premila said, "I shouldn't think so. She's a baby." Mother said, "Well, I hope it won't bother her."

42  Of course, they were both wrong. I understood it perfectly, and I remember it all very clearly. But I put it happily away, because it had all happened to a girl called Cynthia, and I never was really particularly interested in her.

## My Notes

_____
_____
_____
_____
_____
_____
_____
_____
_____
_____
_____
_____
_____
_____
_____
_____
_____
_____
_____
_____
_____

## Second Read

- Reread the memoir to answer these text-dependent questions.
- Write any additional questions you have about the text in your Reader/Writer Notebook.

1. **Craft and Structure:** Identify the diction that gives evidence of a developing conflict between the girls and the headmistress in the first scene?

2. **Craft and Structure:** What mood is created by the participle phrase "whispering in every room" in paragraph 6?

3. **Key Ideas and Details:** After reading the text, what can you infer about the social structure in India during British rule?

4. **Key Ideas and Details:** Reread paragraphs 15, 16, and 24. How do you think "the little Indian girl from my class" feels about Indian food as compared to sandwiches? Why does Premila suggest that they take sandwiches in the future?

5. **Craft and Structure:** How does the author's tone change in paragraphs 27 and 28?

6. **Craft and Structure:** Based on the way it is used in paragraph 33, what is the most likely meaning of *peevishness*?

7. **Key Ideas and Details:** Identify the conflicts in the story. How does the resolution at the end of the story address those conflicts?

8. **Key Ideas and Details:** How is the idea of the importance of names developed in this selection?

**My Notes**

## My Notes

## Working from the Text

9. Rau uses a variety of different approaches to draw attention to culture in this narrative. Using the culture web you generated in Activity 1.2 with your peers, map out specific cultural elements Rau describes, placing them into categories, such as clothing, food, language, and values.

# Culture

10. Once you have mapped out the various cultural elements from the story, rank which ones seem most important to establishing the characters' cultural identity in a way that sets up the story's conclusion and resulting theme.

11. Which cultural elements do you think would best allow you to describe your own cultural identity to a reader? Why?

## Check Your Understanding

Revisit a piece of your writing from this unit and revise it to include parallel structure.

## Learning Target
- Analyze a mentor text to determine how a writer describes a multiethnic, multicultural heritage.

## Preview
In this activity, you will read a mentor text and think about how the writer describes her cultural identity.

## Setting a Purpose for Reading
- Read the following interview/essay to discover the thesis or central idea. Mark the text to locate supporting information (well-chosen, relevant details that support the thesis).
- Circle unknown words and phrases. Try to determine the meaning of the words by using context clues, word parts, or a dictionary.

LEARNING STRATEGIES:
Quickwrite, SOAPSTone, Marking the Text, Discussion Groups, Jigsaw

My Notes

---

Interview/Essay

# Multiculturalism Explained in One Word: HAPA

1 In a guest commentary, the [Tell Me More radio] program's outgoing intern, Kristen Lee, describes how she explains her multicultural roots, and why she embraces the term *HAPA* to describe her heritage.

2 LYNN NEARY, host:

Well, being a part of the Tell Me More team is a real workout for any young journalist. Our summer intern, Kristen Lee, could tell you that. She just recently ended her time with us and as part of our program's tradition, she finished her tenure with a commentary. And what's on Kristen's mind? Dealing with the curiosity and occasional ignorance of people confused by her multiethnic background.

3 KRISTEN LEE: What are you? People say this to me as a pickup line in a bar or a question to prove their own assumptions about my race. I answer with a formula. I'm a quarter Chinese and the rest is Swedish.

4 From my appearance, people assume I am Asian, but how could a quarter measurement define who I am? So can I just tell you? I am a hip-hop-loving piano-playing dancing diva who grew up on a ranch in rural Michigan with some horses, dogs and every kind of hand-sized pet imaginable.

5 I flaunt all of my cultural mix but so many people want me to pick a label. So if I have to choose, I'd choose "HAPA". It means half Asian and half another race. It's actually Hawaiian slang that I picked up in college. It's meant to be slightly **derogatory** but I embrace it as a source of empowerment.

derogatory: insulting

# Consulting with a Mentor (Text)

predominantly: mostly

## My Notes

6   Hawaii is one of the country's most multiracial states and when I studied there, I was viewed as a local because some of my racial features fit the Hawaiian template. I have almond-shaped eyes, fine dark hair and olive skin that turns butterscotch in the sun. I was a confident and proud HAPA in Hawaii, but when I came back to Michigan, my **predominantly** white peers still saw me as a model minority statistic, exotic foreigner, and a token Asian in the classroom.

7   My style is not as simple as those stereotypes. No, I don't clunk around in Swedish clogs, and no, I don't speak a Chinese dialect. And that can be a problem for Asian people who pressure me to prove the legitimacy of my Chinese heritage.

8   Still, I feel like I benefited from white privilege because of my lighter skin. I've avoided most racial discrimination, but I do face a different kind of prejudice when walking around with my black boyfriend, like the occasional hard stare or intimidating remark. I feel like a society that focuses on black and white doesn't recognize my unique multicultural experience. So how do I explain who I am and what being HAPA means to me?

9   I use the universal language of food, and particularly my Swedish mother's dessert dish: rice pudding. Just as the white rice is baked into the yellow pudding, I, too, am mixed into the U.S. melting pot. Yet, as the pudding bakes, the rice retains its consistency, like I keep my own unique HAPA identity.

10   And yeah, I'm tasty, too.

11   NEARY: Kristen Lee with Tell Me More summer interns. She recently graduated from Michigan State University majoring in journalism. That's our program for today. I'm Lynn Neary and this is Tell Me More from NPR News. Let's talk more tomorrow.

## Second Read

- Reread the interview/essay to answer these text-dependent questions.
- Write any additional questions you have about the text in your Reader/Writer Notebook.

1. **Craft and Structure:** How does the writer use a hook for her statement about her heritage?

2. **Craft and Structure:** How does the writer define her cultural identity?

3. **Key Ideas and Details:** What is the main idea of this selection?

4. **Craft and Structure:** In the first sentence of paragraph 5, how would the meaning be affected if the author had used *display* instead of *flaunt*?

## Working from the Text

5. How does the writer contrast internal and external elements of her identity? Give examples from the text.

6. Lee's essay provides a real-world model for the kind of essay you will be writing for Embedded Assessment 1. Conduct a SOAPSTone analysis to explore the context for Lee's essay and purpose. You may need to infer answers to some of these elements, but cite textual clues to do so.

| | |
|---|---|
| **Speaker**<br>What does the reader know about the writer? | |
| **Occasion**<br>What are the circumstances surrounding this text? | |
| **Audience**<br>Who is the target audience? | |
| **Purpose**<br>Why did the author write this text? | |
| **Subject**<br>What is the topic? | |

**My Notes**

| Tone | |
|------|--|
| What is the author's tone, or attitude? | |

7. Revisit the mentor text, and number each paragraph to help you analyze the organizational structure of the essay. Work with a partner to discuss the purpose of each paragraph, and note your thoughts in the My Notes section.

8. Although SOAPSTone can be used to analyze texts written to respond to particular contexts, it can also be used as a planning tool to construct such texts. To help you plan for your upcoming cultural identity essay, try to generate a real-world context for your essay. As with Lee, try to use a real-world incident to help you focus your text as a way to engage or challenge readers. Revisit your work in Activity 1.7 to consider what specific aspects of your culture you may want to include as part of your subject.

| Speaker | |
|---------|--|
| Occasion | |
| Audience | |
| Purpose | |
| Subject | |
| Tone | |

## Check Your Understanding

What besides race and ethnicity help define or characterize a culture?

 **Independent Reading Checkpoint**

Review the independent reading you have completed for this unit. Connect the authors' understanding of cultural identity with the readings in this unit. What do their viewpoints have in common?

# Writing About My Cultural Identity

## ASSIGNMENT
Your assignment is to write a reflective essay explaining your cultural identity.

| | |
|---|---|
| **Planning/Prewriting: Take time to make a plan for your essay.** | ▪ How will you generate ideas about aspects of your culture that might help convey your sense of identity? |
| | ▪ How does your sense of cultural identity compare to that of your parents, your peers, or even strangers? |
| | ▪ How can a cultural conflict—either internal or external—clarify how your cultural identity influences your perspective? |
| | ▪ How might you use a particular cultural element (food, language, clothing, etc.) as a metaphor or central idea to focus your essay? |
| | ▪ What will you include in a preliminary outline of an organizational structure? |
| **Drafting and Revising: Compose your reflective essay.** | ▪ How will you use your prewriting and outline to be sure you include all the components identified in your organizational structure, including an effective introduction and conclusion? |
| | ▪ How can you and your writing group peers use the Scoring Guide to help you note areas in need of improvement such as cohesion of ideas, organizational structure, or use of language? |
| | ▪ How will you ensure that you make necessary changes to the draft as you refine your ideas? |
| | ▪ How can you revise for purposeful and clear use of language, including syntax patterns such as parallel structure and phrases? |
| **Editing and Publishing: Prepare a final draft for publication.** | ▪ Which resources will you consult (dictionary, thesaurus, spell-check, grammar handbook, style guide) to ensure grammatically correct sentences, appropriate punctuation, correct spelling, and proper text citation? |

## Reflection
After completing this Embedded Assessment, think about how you went about accomplishing this task, and respond to the following:

- Which aspects of your cultural identity were you already aware of before you began this unit, and which did you discover through your study?

- What are some of the different cultural heritages represented in your class that you became aware of through class discussions or shared writing?

# Writing About My Cultural Identity

## SCORING GUIDE

| Scoring Criteria | Exemplary | Proficient | Emerging | Incomplete |
|---|---|---|---|---|
| **Ideas** | The essay<br>• has a clear and strongly maintained central idea (e.g., internal/external conflict or central metaphor/concept) to focus the essay<br>• uses a range of well-chosen, relevant, and sufficient evidence to create a vivid sense of personal cultural identity. | The essay<br>• has an adequately maintained central idea to focus the topic<br>• uses a sufficient range of evidence to develop the explanation of cultural identity. | The essay<br>• has an unclear or insufficiently maintained central idea and lacks focus<br>• uses vague, irrelevant, or insufficient evidence to develop the explanation of cultural identity. | The essay<br>• is not coherent and does not clearly maintain a central focus<br>• provides little or no evidence to support or develop an explanation of cultural identity. |
| **Structure** | The writer<br>• uses an effective organizational strategy that creates clarity and cohesion<br>• introduces ideas smoothly, links them logically, and provides a satisfying conclusion<br>• uses appropriate and varied transitions. | The writer<br>• uses an adequate organizational strategy that creates a sense of completeness<br>• introduces ideas, links them adequately, and provides a conclusion<br>• uses some varied transitions. | The writer<br>• uses an inconsistent or confusing organization<br>• does not introduce, link, and/or conclude ideas<br>• uses weak, repetitive, or insufficient transitions. | The writer<br>• does not organize ideas clearly<br>• does not link ideas<br>• uses weak or no transitions. |
| **Use of Language** | The writer<br>• uses precise language and appropriate vocabulary to create a distinctive tone or voice<br>• uses parallel structure and various types of phrases to convey meaning or add variety and interest<br>• demonstrates strong command of conventions of grammar, usage, capitalization, punctuation, and spelling. | The writer<br>• uses appropriate vocabulary and generally maintains an appropriate tone/voice<br>• uses parallel structure and various types of phrases correctly<br>• demonstrates adequate command of conventions; some minor errors in grammar, usage, capitalization, or spelling do not interfere with meaning. | The writer<br>• uses simple or inappropriate vocabulary that does not maintain consistent tone/voice<br>• does not use parallel structure and/or varied types of phrases correctly<br>• demonstrates partial or insufficient command of conventions; errors in grammar, usage, capitalization, punctuation, and/or spelling interfere with meaning. | The writer<br>• uses vague, imprecise vocabulary and does not maintain consistent or appropriate tone/voice<br>• uses no parallel structure or phrases, or uses them incorrectly<br>• demonstrates little command of conventions; numerous errors in grammar, usage, capitalization, punctuation, and/or spelling interfere with meaning. |

## Learning Targets
- Identify the knowledge and skills needed to complete Embedded Assessment 2 successfully.
- Deconstruct a writing prompt.

LEARNING STRATEGIES:
Quickwrite, Predicting, graphic organizer, QHT

## Making Connections
In the first part of this unit, you have been exploring ideas about cultural identity. In this next part, you will extend your understanding of cultural identity and will read and synthesize information to help you take a position about the extent to which one's culture influences one's view of the world.

## Vocabulary Development
Return to the Contents page at the beginning of this unit and note the Academic Vocabulary and Literary Terms you have studied so far. Which words and terms can you now move to a new category on a QHT chart? Which could you now teach to others that you were unfamiliar with at the beginning of the unit?

## Essential Questions
How would you answer these questions now?

1. What is my cultural identity?

2. How do cultural experiences shape, impact, or influence our identity and perceptions?

## Unpacking Embedded Assessment 2
Read the assignment for Embedded Assessment 2: Writing a Synthesis Paper.

Your assignment is to collaborate with your peers to write an essay that responds to the following synthesis prompt:

To what extent does one's culture inform the way one views others and the world?

Be sure to support your claim with evidence from at least three different texts you have read, viewed, or listened to in this unit, as well as with personal experience and insights.

In your own words, summarize what you will need to know to complete this assessment successfully. With your class, create a graphic organizer to represent the skills and knowledge you will need to complete the tasks identified in the Embedded Assessment.

My Notes

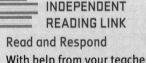

INDEPENDENT
READING LINK

Read and Respond

With help from your teacher, librarian, and peers, find a novel or memoir that explores a cultural perspective different from your own.

# Previewing Embedded Assessment 2 and Preparing for a Writing Prompt

## Deconstructing a Writing Prompt

Writing prompts often contain many details but little direction. It is easy to get caught up in the details and forget the main task. You may write an excellent response with flawless syntax, but if you do not respond to the prompt, you will not receive a high score.

## Five Parts of Every Writing Prompt

When considering any prompt, look for five basic parts. Most, if not all, of the parts will be present. Finding as many as you can will help you determine what you need to do and how to respond to the prompt correctly.

1. **Subject:** What is the subject you need to write about? A well-written prompt will identify the subject, but it may be vague. For example, a prompt might tell you to think of a childhood experience. What common themes or ideas (either implicit or explicit) are associated with the subject?

2. **Speaker:** Who is writing the answer? (You are, but are you writing it as a student, a citizen, an authority?) Use your inferencing skills to determine what perspective you should take as the writer.

3. **Type of Essay:** What kind of response are you writing—explanation, argument, synthesis, narrative? An effective prompt indicates the type of writing you need to do. It may give you a choice. Choose wisely.

4. **Task:** What is the prompt asking you to do? For example, your task may be to take a stand on an issue and write a five-paragraph persuasive essay. Read the details carefully to identify exactly what you need to do.

5. **Hints:** Does the prompt give you suggestions to get started? The prompt may suggest ideas to think about or literary devices to identify and analyze.

After deconstructing the first prompt on the following page as a class, identify all five parts of your assigned prompt with your group. You may use different colored markers to highlight different parts in each prompt or write responses to each component of the prompt in My Notes. Be prepared to share your deconstructed prompt with the other groups.

**Prompt 1:** Think of something at your school that you would like to change in order to create a more positive learning environment. The change could affect anything from a policy or procedure to an attitude or tradition. In a well-organized persuasive letter, write to an adult at your school presenting the problem, your solution to that problem, and why the environment would change.

*Subject:*

*Speaker:*

*Type of Essay:*

*Task:*

Hints:

**Prompt 2:** Contemporary life is marked by controversy. Choose a controversial local, national, or global issue with which you are familiar. Then, using appropriate evidence, write an essay that carefully considers opposing positions on this issue and proposes a solution or compromise.

**Prompt 3:** The following is a mock press release from *The Onion*, a publication devoted to humor and satire. Read the article carefully. Then write an essay in which you analyze the strategies used in the article to satirize how products are marketed to consumers.

**Prompt 4:** Your assignment is to write an analytical essay about the effect of character interaction in the play *Antigone*. Choose a character whose words, actions, or ideas contrast with Creon's character. Explain how these conflicting motivations contribute to Creon's development as a tragic hero, and how the character interactions advance the plot or develop the themes of the play.

## Check Your Understanding

Work independently to deconstruct the following prompt. Complete your work on a separate piece of paper.

**Prompt 5:** Your assignment is to collaborate with your peers to write an essay that responds to the following synthesis prompt: To what extent does one's culture inform the way one views others and the world? Be sure to support your claim with evidence from at least three different texts you have read, viewed, or listened to in this unit, as well as with personal experience and insights.

**My Notes**

ACADEMIC VOCABULARY
**Synthesis** refers to the act of combining ideas from different sources to create, express, or support a new idea.

**My Notes**

## Synthesis

Now that you understand the expectations of Embedded Assessment 2, you will need to begin working on gathering evidence from the multiple texts in the second half of the unit. These texts will serve as your resources in answering the **synthesis** writing prompt. In order to successfully answer the writing prompt, you will need to incorporate information from multiple sources with your existing ideas into one central idea.

When synthesizing information, you need a focusing idea or question for which you gather ideas from multiple texts or sources of information. For example, what if you were asked to respond to one of the following questions:

- How do parents influence our perspectives on our culture?
- How do writers/artists use conflict to convey theme?

How would you approach this task? In the space below, write down a plan for how you would do so.

Working with a partner, choose one of the questions above that you think you can best answer. Revisit the texts that you read in the first half of the unit, and choose at least two texts that would serve as good evidence to support a response to the question. Be sure to:

- Write a thesis statement for your essay responding to the question.
- Write an outline for your response.
- Explain why you chose the structure you outlined.

Possible outlines/organizations:

# Colliding Worlds

## Learning Target
- Analyze the structure of a text to explain how the author unfolds a series of ideas for effect.

## Preview
In this activity, you will read an essay and analyze the author's use of allusion.

## Allusion
Read the definition of the term **allusion** in the Literary Terms box. Writers use this literary device to draw connections between their work and the alluded reference for the purpose of evoking similar themes, tone, or to establish context. When reading a text, some allusions may not be familiar to you. Use reference materials, such as an online encyclopedia, to build your understanding of the allusions so that you comprehend the writer's full meaning of their work.

## Setting a Purpose for Reading
- Read the essay entitled "Where Worlds Collide" by Pico Iyer. In this 1995 essay, Iyer describes what people experience as they enter a new environment. As you read, mark the text for allusions and details that suggest the perspective of the new arrivals.
- Circle unknown words and phrases. Try to determine the meaning of the words by using context clues, word parts, or a dictionary.

> **ABOUT THE AUTHOR**
> Pico Iyer is a British-born journalist, novelist, and travel writer of Indian descent who grew up in Britain and California. Unlike typical travel writing, Iyer's works explore unusual or unexpected aspects of the places he visits. His book *Video Night in Kathmandu: And Other Reports from the Not-So-Far East* (1988) focuses on the West's influence on Asian culture and daily life. Critics describe his writing style as both ironic and culturally sensitive.

### LEARNING STRATEGIES:
Quickwrite, Predicting, Sketching, Marking the Text, Discussion Groups, Think-Pair-Share

### Literary Terms
An **allusion** is a reference to a well-known person, event, or place from history, music, art, or another literary work.

**My Notes**

## Essay

# Where Worlds Collide

*by* Pico Iyer

1  They come out, blinking, into the bleached, forgetful sunshine, in Dodgers caps and Rodeo Drive T-shirts, with the maps their cousins have drawn for them and the images they've brought over from *Cops* and *Terminator 2*; they come out, dazed, disoriented, heads still partly in the clouds, bodies still several time zones—or centuries—away, and they step into the Promised Land.

2  In front of them is a Van Stop, a Bus Stop, a Courtesy Tram Stop, and a Shuttle Bus Stop (the shuttles themselves tracing circuits A, B, and C). At the Shuttle Bus Stop, they see the All American Shuttle, the Apollo Shuttle, Celebrity Airport Livery, the Great American Stageline, the Movie Shuttle, the Transport, Ride-4-You, and forty-two other magic buses waiting to **whisk** them everywhere from Bakersfield to Disneyland.

**whisk:** to move or take quickly

# Colliding Worlds

**jive:** a type of fast music that may include slang and informal language

**incomprehensible:** impossible to understand

**promiscuously:** in an indiscriminate or loose manner

### My Notes

_____

_____

_____

_____

**unintelligible:** difficult to understand

**cordoning:** blocking off; barricading

## WORD CONNECTIONS

### Multiple-Meaning Words

The word *solicitor* is defined as "someone who seeks business." In England, a solicitor is a type of lawyer who represents people in the lower courts. The word also has a negative connotation as someone who may harass people on the street to sell them something or cheat them.

**intoning:** speaking or reciting in a singing voice; changing or singing in monotone

**tarmac:** a paved area at an airport where airplanes are often parked

**quarantine:** to keep people away from an area where a person or animal has a disease to prevent it from spreading

**cacophony:** loud, unpleasant sounds

They see Koreans piling into the Taeguk Airport Shuttle and the Seoul Shuttle, which will take them to Koreatown without their ever feeling they've left home; they see newcomers from the Middle East disappearing under the Arabic script of the Sahara Shuttle. They see fast-talking, finger-snapping, palm-slapping **jive** artists straight from their TV screens shouting **incomprehensible** slogans about deals, destinations, and drugs. Over there is a block-long white limo, a Lincoln Continental, and, over there, a black Chevy Blazer with Mexican stickers all over its windows, being towed. They have arrived in the Land of Opportunity, and the opportunities are swirling dizzily, **promiscuously**, around them.

3   They have already braved the ranks of Asian officials, the criminal-looking security men in jackets that say "Elsinore Airport Services," the men shaking tins that say "Helping America's Hopeless." They have already seen the tilting mugs that say "California: a new slant on life" and the portable fruit machines in the gift shop.

4   They have already, perhaps, visited the rest room where someone has written, "Yes on Proposition 187. Mexicans go home," the snack bar where a slice of pizza costs $3.19 (18 quetzals, they think in horror, or 35,000 dong), and the sign that urges them to try the Cockatoo Inn Grand Hotel. The latest arrivals at Los Angeles International Airport are ready now to claim their new lives.

5   Above them in the terminal, voices are repeating, over and over, in Japanese, Spanish, and **unintelligible** English, "Maintain visual contact with your personal property at all times." Out on the sidewalk, a man's voice and a woman's voice are alternating an unending refrain: "The white zone is for loading and unloading of passengers only. No parking." There are "Do Not Cross" yellow lines **cordoning** off parts of the sidewalk and "Wells Fargo Alarm Services" stickers on the windows; there are "Aviation Safeguard" signs on the baggage carts and "Beware of Solicitors" signs on the columns; there are even special phones "To Report Trouble." More male and female voices are **intoning** continuously, "Do not leave your car unattended" and "Unattended cars are subject to immediate tow-away." There are no military planes on the **tarmac** here, the newcomers notice, no khaki soldiers in fatigues, no instructions not to take photographs, as at home; but there are civilian restrictions every bit as strict as in many a police state.

6   "This Terminal Is in a Medfly **Quarantine** Area," says the sign between the terminals. "Stop the Spread of Medfly!" If, by chance, the new Americans have to enter a parking lot on their way out, they will be faced with "Cars left over 30 days may be impounded at Owner's Expense" and "Do not enter without a ticket." It will cost them $16 if they lose their parking ticket, they read, and $56 if they park in the wrong zone. Around them is an unending **cacophony** of antitheft devices, sirens, beepers, and car-door openers; lights are flashing everywhere, and the man who fines them $16 for losing their parking ticket has the tribal scars of Tigre across his forehead.

7   The blue skies and palm trees they saw on TV are scarcely visible from here: just an undifferentiated smoggy haze, billboards advertising Nissan and Panasonic and Canon, and beyond those an endlessly receding mess of gray streets. Overhead, they can see the all-too-familiar signs of Hilton and Hyatt and Holiday Inn; in the distance, a sea of tract houses, mini-malls, and high rises. The City of Angels awaits them.

## Second Read

- Reread the essay to answer these text-dependent questions.
- Write any additional questions you have about the text in your Reader/Writer Notebook.

1. **Key Ideas and Details:** Examine the first sentence. How does the structure of the sentence reinforce the meaning?

2. **Craft and Structure:** What does "Promised Land" mean as it is used in paragraph 1?

3. **Craft and Structure:** In paragraphs 3–5, how does Iyer develop the contrast between the American Dream and reality?

4. **Craft and Structure:** What is the author's purpose for writing this essay? What evidence supports your answer?

## Working from the Text

5. Reread the passage to see the allusions you marked in the text. Write them in the My Notes space. What do you know about the origin of these specific references in history, in literature, or in art? If some of the allusions are unfamiliar, work with your group to uncover their meaning using reference materials, and/or an online encyclopedia.

6. How does your understanding of the origin of these allusions affect your understanding of this passage? What is the overall effect of those allusions on the meaning of the essay?

**My Notes**

# Colliding Worlds

## Check Your Understanding

Summarize your understanding of the literary term *allusion*. Provide support from Iyer's essay in your summary.

### Language and Writer's Craft: Colon and Semicolon

Writers use colons and semicolons to vary sentence structure and to add emphasis.

Use a **colon** to introduce a series in a list after an independent main clause.

> **Example:** "The blue skies and palm trees they saw on TV are scarcely visible from here: just an undifferentiated smoggy haze, billboards advertising Nissan and Panasonic and Canon, and beyond those an endlessly receding mess of gray streets."

Use a **semicolon** to connect two closely related independent clauses or to connect two clauses when one is preceded by a conjunctive adverb (*however, consequently*).

> **Example:** "There are no military planes on the tarmac here, the newcomers notice, no khaki soldiers in fatigues, no instructions not to take photographs, as at home; but there are civilian restrictions every bit as strict as in many a police state."

**PRACTICE** Create a sentence using a colon and another using a semicolon and record them below.

Colon:

Semicolon:

### ACADEMIC VOCABULARY

An **argument** is a set of statements, each supporting the other, that presents a position or viewpoint. A **claim** is a position taken on an arguable viewpoint.

## Argument

In order to be successful on Embedded Assessment 2, you will need to craft an argumentative response to a writing prompt. To be valid, your **argument** must have a debatable **claim**, evidence in support of that claim, and it must address the opposition to its claim by acknowledging counterclaims. You will learn more about counterclaims in the next activity, for now we are going to focus on the first two requirements of an argument: the claim and its supporting evidence.

For a claim to be debatable, people should be able to hold differing opinions about it. If your claim is something that is generally agreed upon or accepted as fact, then there is no reason to try to convince people. An example of a debatable claim is *At least twenty-five percent of the federal budget should be spent on funding limiting air pollution*. This claim is debatable because reasonable people could disagree with it. Some people might think that this is how we should spend the nation's money. Others might argue that corporations, not the government, should be paying to limit air pollution. If you tried to argue *Air pollution is bad for the environment*, you would just be restating a fact and therefore, would not have a debatable claim.

Consider the debatable claim just mentioned, what types of evidence should be included in the argument to support the claim? There are several types of evidence, such as facts, statistics, examples, observations, quotes, and expert opinions. A successful argument for the claim might include statistics about the reduction of air pollution related to the money spent in previous national budgets, or experts explaining the correlation between air pollution and health risks causing a national emergency.

In the argument writing prompt below, you are asked to answer a question. Your answer will be your claim. Use the essay you just read as your resource to find evidence that supports your claim.

## Writing to Sources: Argument

To what extent does one's background affect his or her perception of a given situation? Write a paragraph that answers this question using "Where Worlds Collide" as your primary source. Be sure to:

- Start with a TAG (title, author, genre) statement that presents your claim.
- Support your claim by referencing multiple pieces of textual evidence from the essay, including juxtaposed images and allusions.
- Emulate the complex syntactic structure that Iyer uses by using a semicolon to combine two related sentences and using a colon to introduce a series in a list.

**Group Discussion:** Have you ever found yourself in a completely new environment? Though you may have viewed pictures or a brochure depicting the location, suddenly you are taking it all in—in person! What was that experience like? Were you comfortable or uncomfortable? Overwhelmed or pleasantly surprised? Disappointed or overjoyed? Explain your experience in a group discussion.

**INDEPENDENT READING LINK**

**Read and Respond**

Think about how the author of your independent reading succeeds in helping you experience his or her cultural perspective. Provide examples to discuss with your peers. Consider how different the world can appear through someone else's viewpoint.

**My Notes**

# Perspectives on Heritage: Poetry and Fiction

**LEARNING STRATEGIES:**
Think-Pair-Share, Predicting, graphic organizer, SIFT, Group Discussion

## Literary Terms

**Imagery** is the verbal expression of sensory experience. It is created by details that appeal to one or more of the five senses.

**Figurative language** is imaginative language not meaning to be taken literally, such as similes and metaphors.

## My Notes

ripened: ready or finished

## Learning Targets

- Analyze a poem and a short story for the authors' use of literary devices to explain how specific stylistic choices support the development of tone and theme.
- Compare and contrast how two different authors explore similar subjects and themes.

## Preview

In this activity, you will read a poem and a short story to compare and contrast their treatment of similar subjects and themes.

## Setting a Purpose for Reading

- Writers use symbols, **imagery**, and **figurative language** to help develop meaning in a story. As you read, underline lines that you think are particularly important in establishing the meaning of the quilts to the speaker.
- Circle unknown words and phrases. Try to determine the meaning of the words by using context clues, word parts, or a dictionary.

**ABOUT THE AUTHOR**

Born in 1949 in McGregor, Texas, poet Teresa Paloma Acosta grew up listening to family stories about working in and living near cotton fields. She came from a family of hardworking men and women. The women were known particularly for their sewing skills. Paloma Acosta combines her love for her Mexican heritage and her family's quilting and storytelling abilities in her poem "My Mother Pieced Quilts."

## Poetry

### my mother pieced quilts

*by* Teresa Palomo Acosta

> they were just meant as covers
> in winters
> as weapons
> against pounding january winds
> 5 but it was just that every morning I awoke to these
> october **ripened** canvases
> passed my hand across their cloth faces
> and began to wonder how you pieced
> all these together

10  these strips of gentle communion cotton and flannel
     nightgowns
   wedding **organdies**
   dime store velvets

   how you shaped patterns square and oblong and round
15  positioned
   balanced
   then cemented them
   with your thread
   a steel needle
20  a thimble
   how the thread darted in and out
   galloping along the frayed edges, tucking them in
   as you did us at night
   oh how you stretched and turned and rearranged
25  your michigan spring faded curtain pieces
   my father's santa fe work shirt
   the summer denims, the tweeds of fall

   in the evening you sat at your canvas
   —our cracked linoleum floor the drawing board
30  me lounging on your arm
   and you staking out the plan:
   whether to put the lilac purple of easter against the red
     plaid of winter-going-
   into-spring
35  whether to mix a yellow with blue and white and paint the
   corpus christi noon when my father held your hand
   whether to shape a five-point star from the
   somber black silk you wore to grandmother's funeral

   You were the river current
40  carrying the roaring notes …
   forming them into pictures of a little boy reclining
   a swallow flying
   You were the caravan master at the reins
   driving your thread needle **artillery** across the mosaic cloth bridges
45  delivering yourself in separate testimonies

**organdies:** fine cotton or silk fabric that is sewn into clothing or curtains to make them stronger

**My Notes**

**artillery:** large guns used to shoot over great distances

# Perspectives on Heritage: Poetry and Fiction

## My Notes

_____

_____

**tuberculosis:** a lung disease that causes fever, cough, and difficulty in breathing

**taut:** tight; stiff

oh mother you plunged me sobbing and laughing

into our past

into the river crossing at five

into the spinach fields

50 into the plainview cotton rows

into **tuberculosis** wards

into braids and muslin dresses

sewn hard and **taut** to withstand the thrashings of twenty-five years

stretched out they lay

55 armed/ready/shouting/celebrating

knotted with love

the quilts sing on

## Second Read

- Reread the poem to answer these text-dependent questions.
- Write any additional questions you have about the text in your Reader/Writer Notebook.

1. **Key Ideas and Details:** How do the pieces of the quilt embody cultural heritage?

2. **Craft and Structure:** Which words does the speaker use to compare her mother to a painter? Why do you think she makes this comparison?

## Working from the Text

3. Use the following graphic organizer to analyze the poem using the SIFT strategy. As you closely read the poem for examples of symbolism, imagery, figurative language, tone, and theme, be sure to write the actual words from the poem and your interpretation of their significance.

| SIFT | Textual Detail | Analysis or Interpretation | My Notes |
|---|---|---|---|
| **Symbols** | | | |
| **Images** | | | |
| **Figures of Speech** | | | |
| **Tone/ Theme** | Tone: | Theme: | |

## Check Your Understanding

How does Teresa Palomo Acosta use literary devices in "My Mother Pieced Quilts" to convey the importance of quilting in her heritage?

# Perspectives on Heritage: Poetry and Fiction

## My Notes

## Setting a Purpose for Reading

- As you read the story, apply the skills you used in your analysis of the poem to analyze the author's development of tone and theme. Annotate the text for symbols, images, figurative language, and tone.
- Circle unknown words and phrases. Try to determine the meaning of the words by using context clues, word parts, or a dictionary.

### ABOUT THE AUTHOR

Alice Walker (b. 1944) is a novelist, poet, and essayist who has published numerous works, including *Living By the Word*, a collection of essays, and *Horses Make a Landscape More Beautiful*, a book of poems. Walker established her reputation with the publication of *The Color Purple* (1982), which won the Pulitzer Prize and the American Book Award. The novel tells of a young woman's efforts to overcome the obstacles posed by racism, sexism, and poverty. Critics have praised Walker's sensitivity to the points of view and problems of characters from different walks of life.

## Short Story

# Everyday Use

*by* Alice Walker

1   I will wait for her in the yard that Maggie and I made so clean and wavy yesterday afternoon. A yard like this is more comfortable than most people know. It is not just a yard. It is like an extended living room. When the hard clay is swept clean as a floor and the fine sand around the edges lined with tiny, irregular grooves, anyone can come and sit and look up into the elm tree and wait for the breezes that never come inside the house.

2   Maggie will be nervous until after her sister goes: She will stand hopelessly in corners, **homely** and ashamed of the burn scars down her arms and legs, eyeing her sister with a mixture of envy and awe. She thinks her sister had held life always in the palm of one hand, that "no" is a word the world never learned to say to her.

3   You've no doubt seen those TV shows where the child who has "made it" is **confronted**, as a surprise, by her own mother and father, **tottering** in weakly from backstage. (A pleasant surprise, of course: What would they do if parent and child came on the show only to curse out and insult each other?) On TV mother and child embrace and smile into each other's faces. Sometimes the mother and father weep; the child wraps them in her arms and leans across the table to tell how she would not have made it without their help. I have seen these programs.

**homely:** plain and simple

**confronted:** faced or forced to see
**tottering:** moving slowly and weakly

**My Notes**

4  Sometimes I dream a dream in which Dee and I are suddenly brought together on a TV program of this sort. Out of a dark and soft-seated limousine I am ushered into a bright room filled with many people. There I meet a smiling, gray, sporty man like Johnny Carson and he shakes my hand and tells me what a fine girl I have. Then we are on the stage, and Dee is embracing me with tears in her eyes. She pins on my dress a large orchid, even though she had told me once that she thinks orchids are **tacky** flowers.

5  In real life I am a large, big-boned woman with rough, man-working hands. In the winter I wear flannel nightgowns to bed and overalls during the day. I can kill and clean a hog as mercilessly as a man. My fat keeps me hot in zero weather. I can work outside all day, breaking ice to get water for washing; I can eat pork liver cooked over the open fire minutes after it comes steaming from the hog. One winter I knocked a bull calf straight in the brain between the eyes with a sledgehammer and had the meat hung up to chill before nightfall. But of course all this does not show on television. I am the way my daughter would want me to be: a hundred pounds lighter, my skin like an uncooked **barley** pancake. My hair glistens in the hot bright lights. Johnny Carson has much to do to keep up with my quick and witty tongue.

6  But that is a mistake. I know even before I wake up. Who ever knew a Johnson with a quick tongue? Who can even imagine me looking a strange white man in the eye? It seems to me I have talked to them always with one foot raised in flight, with my head turned in whichever way is farthest from them. Dee, though. She would always look anyone in the eye. Hesitation was no part of her nature.

7  "How do I look, Mama?" Maggie says, showing just enough of her thin body enveloped in pink skirt and red blouse for me to know she's there, almost hidden by the door.

8  "Come out into the yard," I say.

9  Have you ever seen a lame animal, perhaps a dog run over by some careless person rich enough to own a car, **sidle** up to someone who is ignorant enough to be kind to him? That is the way my Maggie walks. She has been like this, chin on chest, eyes on ground, feet in shuffle, ever since the fire that burned the other house to the ground.

10  Dee is lighter than Maggie, with nicer hair and a fuller figure. She's a woman now, though sometimes I forget. How long ago was it that the other house burned? Ten, twelve years? Sometimes I can still hear the flames and feel Maggie's arms sticking to me, her hair smoking and her dress falling off her in little black papery flakes. Her eyes seemed stretched open, blazed open by the flames reflected in them. And Dee. I see her standing off under the sweet gum tree she used to dig gum out of, a look of

**tacky:** cheap or not stylish

**barley:** a kind of grain

**sidle:** creep up

# Perspectives on Heritage: Poetry and Fiction

**dingy:** shabby

## My Notes

_____

_____

**dimwit:** a person who does not display intelligence

_____

_____

_____

_____

_____

_____

_____

_____

_____

_____

_____

_____

**rawhide:** cow's skin before it is crafted into leather

_____

_____

_____

_____

_____

**furtive:** quiet and secretive

_____

_____

_____

_____

_____

_____

_____

_____

_____

_____

_____

concentration on her face as she watched the last **dingy** gray board of the house fall in toward the red-hot brick chimney. Why don't you do a dance around the ashes? I'd wanted to ask her. She had hated the house that much.

11  I used to think she hated Maggie, too. But that was before we raised the money, the church and me, to send her to Augusta to school. She used to read to us without pity, forcing words, lies, other folks' habits, whole lives upon us two, sitting trapped and ignorant underneath her voice. She washed us in a river of make-believe, burned us with a lot of knowledge we didn't necessarily need to know. Pressed us to her with the serious ways she read, to shove us away at just the moment, like **dimwits**, we seemed about to understand.

12  Dee wanted nice things. A yellow organdy dress to wear to her graduation from high school; black pumps to match a green suit she'd made from an old suit somebody gave me. She was determined to stare down any disaster in her efforts. Her eyelids would not flicker for minutes at a time. Often I fought off the temptation to shake her. At sixteen she had a style of her own: and knew what style was.

13  I never had an education myself. After second grade the school closed down. Don't ask me why: In 1927 colored asked fewer questions than they do now. Sometimes Maggie reads to me. She stumbles along good-naturedly but can't see well. She knows she is not bright. Like good looks and money, quickness passed her by. She will marry John Thomas (who has mossy teeth in an earnest face), and then I'll be free to sit here and I guess just sing church songs to myself. Although I never was a good singer. Never could carry a tune. I was always better at a man's job. I used to love to milk till I was hooked in the side in '49. Cows are soothing and slow and don't bother you, unless you try to milk them the wrong way.

14  I have deliberately turned my back on the house. It is three rooms, just like the one that burned, except the roof is tin; they don't make shingle roofs anymore. There are no real windows, just some holes cut in the sides, like the portholes in a ship, but not round and not square, with **rawhide** holding the shutters up on the outside. This house is in a pasture, too, like the other one. No doubt when Dee sees it she will want to tear it down. She wrote me once that no matter where we "choose" to live, she will manage to come see us. But she will never bring her friends. Maggie and I thought about this and Maggie asked me, "Mama, when did Dee ever *have* any friends?"

15  She had a few. **Furtive** boys in pink shirts hanging about on washday after school. Nervous girls who never laughed. Impressed with her, they worshiped the well-turned phrase, the cute shape, the scalding humor that erupted like bubbles in lye. She read to them.

16  When she was courting Jimmy T, she didn't have much time to pay to us but turned all her faultfinding power on him. He *flew* to marry a cheap city girl from a family of ignorant, flashy people. She hardly had time to recompose herself.

17  When she comes, I will meet—but there they are!

18  Maggie attempts to make a dash for the house, in her shuffling way, but I stay her with my hand. "Come back here," I say. And she stops and tries to dig a well in the sand with her toe.

19  It is hard to see them clearly through the strong sun. But even the first glimpse of leg out of the car tells me it is Dee. Her feet were always neat looking, as if God himself shaped them with a certain style. From the other side of the car comes a short, stocky man. Hair is all over his head a foot long and hanging from his chin like a kinky mule tail. I hear Maggie suck in her breath. "Uhnnnh" is what it sounds like. Like when you see the wriggling end of a snake just in front of your foot on the road. "Uhnnnh."

20  Dee next. A dress down to the ground, in this hot weather. A dress so loud it hurts my eyes. There are yellows and oranges enough to throw back the light of the sun. I feel my whole face warming from the heat waves it throws out. Earrings gold, too, and hanging down to her shoulders. Bracelets dangling and making noises when she moves her arm up to shake the folds of the dress out of her armpits. The dress is loose and flows, and as she walks closer, I like it. I hear Maggie go "Uhnnnh" again. It is her sister's hair. It stands straight up like the wool on a sheep. It is black as night and around the edges are two long pigtails that rope about like small lizards disappearing behind her ears.

21  "Wa-su-zo-Tean-o!" she says, coming on in that gliding way the dress makes her move. The short, stocky fellow with the hair to his navel is all grinning, and he follows up with "Asalamalakim, my mother and sister!" He moves to hug Maggie but she falls back, right up against the back of my chair. I feel her trembling there, and when I look up I see the perspiration falling off her chin.

22  "Don't get up," says Dee. Since I am stout, it takes something of a push. You can see me trying to move a second or two before I make it. She turns, showing white heels through her sandals, and goes back to the car. Out she peeks next with a Polaroid. She stoops down quickly and lines up picture after picture of me sitting there in front of the house with Maggie cowering behind me. She never takes a shot without making sure the house is included. When a cow comes nibbling around in the edge of the yard, she snaps it and me and Maggie and the house. Then she puts the Polaroid in the back seat of the car and comes up and kisses me on the forehead.

23  Meanwhile, Asalamalakim is going through motions with Maggie's hand. Maggie's hand is as limp as a fish, and probably as cold, despite the sweat, and she keeps trying to pull it back. It looks like Asalamalakim wants to shake hands but wants to do it fancy. Or maybe he don't know how people shake hands. Anyhow, he soon gives up on Maggie.

24  "Well," I say. "Dee."

25  "No, Mama," she says. "Not 'Dee,' Wangero Leewanika Kemanjo!"

26  "What happened to 'Dee'?" I wanted to know.

27  "She's dead," Wangero said. "I couldn't bear it any longer, being named after the people who **oppress** me."

28  "You know as well as me you was named after your aunt Dicie," I said. Dicie is my sister. She named Dee. We called her "Big Dee" after Dee was born.

**My Notes**

oppress: keep down; control through domination

# Perspectives on Heritage: Poetry and Fiction

29  "But who was *she* named after?" asked Wangero.

30  "I guess after Grandma Dee," I said.

31  "And who was she named after?" asked Wangero.

32  "Her mother," I said, and saw Wangero was getting tired. "That's about as far back as I can trace it," I said. Though, in fact, I probably could have carried it back beyond the Civil War through the branches.

33  "Well," said Asalamalakim, "there you are."

34  "Uhnnnh," I heard Maggie say.

35  "There I was not," I said, "before 'Dicie' cropped up in our family, so why should I try to trace it that far back?"

36  He just stood there grinning, looking down on me like somebody inspecting a Model A car. Every once in a while he and Wangero sent eye signals over my head.

37  "How do you pronounce this name?" I asked.

38  "You don't have to call me by it if you don't want to," said Wangero.

39  "Why shouldn't I?" I asked. "If that's what you want us to call you, we'll call you."

40  "I know it might sound awkward at first," said Wangero.

41  "I'll get used to it," I said. "Ream it out again."

42  Well, soon we got the name out of the way. Asalamalakim had a name twice as long and three times as hard. After I tripped over it two or three times, he told me to just call him Hakim-a-barber. I wanted to ask him was he a barber, but I didn't really think he was, so I didn't ask.

43  "You must belong to those beef-cattle peoples down the road," I said. They said "Asalamalakim" when they met you, too, but they didn't shake hands. Always too busy: feeding the cattle, fixing the fences, putting up salt-lick shelters, throwing down hay. When the white folks poisoned some of the herd, the men stayed up all night with rifles in their hands. I walked a mile and a half just to see the sight.

44  Hakim-a-barber said, "I accept some of their **doctrines**, but farming and raising cattle is not my style." (They didn't tell me, and I didn't ask, whether Wangero—Dee—had really gone and married him.)

## My Notes

**doctrine:** idea or belief

45　We sat down to eat and right away he said he didn't eat collards, and pork was unclean. Wangero, though, went on through the chitlins and corn bread, the greens, and everything else. She talked a blue streak over the sweet potatoes. Everything delighted her. Even the fact that we still used the benches her daddy made for the table when we couldn't afford to buy chairs.

46　"Oh, Mama!" she cried. Then turned to Hakim-a-barber. "I never knew how lovely these benches are. You can feel the rump prints," she said, running her hands underneath her and along the bench. Then she gave a sigh, and her hand closed over Grandma Dee's butter dish. "That's it!" she said. "I knew there was something I wanted to ask you if I could have." She jumped up from the table and went over in the corner where the churn stood, the milk in it **clabber** by now. She looked at the churn and looked at it.

47　"This churn top is what I need," she said. "Didn't Uncle Buddy whittle it out of a tree you all used to have?"

48　"Yes," I said.

49　"Uh huh," she said happily. "And I want the dasher, too."

50　"Uncle Buddy whittle that, too?" asked the barber.

51　Dee (Wangero) looked up at me.

52　"Aunt Dee's first husband whittled the dash," said Maggie so low you almost couldn't hear her. "His name was Henry, but they called him Stash."

53　"Maggie's brain is like an elephant's," Wangero said, laughing. "I can use the churn top as a centerpiece for the alcove table," she said, sliding a plate over the churn, "and I'll think of something artistic to do with the dasher."

54　When she finished wrapping the dasher, the handle stuck out. I took it for a moment in my hands. You didn't even have to look close to see where hands pushing the dasher up and down to make butter had left a kind of sink in the wood. In fact, there were a lot of small sinks; you could see where thumbs and fingers had sunk into the wood. It was beautiful light-yellow wood, from a tree that grew in the yard where Big Dee and Stash had lived.

55　After dinner Dee (Wangero) went to the trunk at the foot of my bed and started rifling through it. Maggie hung back in the kitchen over the dishpan. Out came Wangero with two quilts. They had been pieced by Grandma Dee, and then Big Dee and me had hung them on the quilt frames on the front porch and quilted them. One was in the Lone Star pattern. The other was Walk Around the Mountain. In both of them were scraps of dresses Grandma Dee had worn fifty and more years ago. Bits and pieces of Grandpa Jarrell's paisley shirts. And one teeny faded blue piece, about the size of a penny matchbox, that was from Great Grandpa Ezra's uniform that he wore in the Civil War.

56　"Mama," Wangero said sweet as a bird. "Can I have these old quilts?"

57　I heard something fall in the kitchen, and a minute later the kitchen door slammed.

58　"Why don't you take one or two of the others?" I asked. "These old things was just done by me and Big Dee from some tops your grandma pieced before she died."

59　"No," said Wangero. "I don't want those. They are stitched around the borders by machine."

60　"That'll make them last better," I said.

**My Notes**

**clabber:** sour milk

61 "That's not the point," said Wangero. "These are all pieces of dresses Grandma used to wear. She did all this stitching by hand. Imagine!" She held the quilts securely in her arms, stroking them.

62 "Some of the pieces, like those lavender ones, come from old clothes her mother handed down to her," I said, moving up to touch the quilts. Dee (Wangero) moved back just enough so that I couldn't reach the quilts. They already belonged to her.

63 "Imagine!" she breathed again, clutching them closely to her bosom.

64 "The truth is," I said, "I promised to give them quilts to Maggie, for when she marries John Thomas."

65 She gasped like a bee had stung her.

66 "Maggie can't appreciate these quilts!" she said. "She'd probably be backward enough to put them to everyday use."

67 "I reckon she would," I said. "God knows I been saving 'em for long enough with nobody using 'em. I hope she will!" I didn't want to bring up how I had offered Dee (Wangero) a quilt when she went away to college. Then she had told me they were old-fashioned, out of style.

68 "But they're *priceless*!" she was saying now, furiously; for she has a temper. "Maggie would put them on the bed and in five years they'd be in rags. Less than that!"

69 "She can always make some more," I said. "Maggie knows how to quilt."

70 Dee (Wangero) looked at me with hatred. "You just will not understand. The point is *these* quilts, these quilts!"

71 "Well," I said, stumped. "What would you do with them?"

72 "Hang them," she said. As if that was the only thing you *could* do with quilts.

73 Maggie by now was standing in the door. I could almost hear the sound her feet made as they scraped over each other.

74 "She can have them, Mama," she said, like somebody used to never winning anything or having anything reserved for her. "I can 'member Grandma Dee without the quilts."

**snuff:** chewing tobacco

75 I looked at her hard. She had filled her bottom lip with checkerberry **snuff**, and it gave her face a kind of dopey, hangdog look. It was Grandma Dee and Big Dee who taught her how to quilt herself. She stood there with her scarred hands hidden in the folds of her skirt. She looked at her sister with something like fear, but she wasn't mad at her. This was Maggie's portion. This was the way she knew God to work.

76 When I looked at her like that, something hit me in the top of my head and ran down to the soles of my feet. Just like when I'm in church and the spirit of God touches me and I get happy and shout. I did something I never had done before: hugged Maggie to me, then dragged her on into the room, snatched the quilts out of Miss Wangero's hands, and dumped them into Maggie's lap. Maggie just sat there on my bed with her mouth open.

77 "Take one or two of the others," I said to Dee. But she turned without a word and went out to Hakim-a-barber.

78 "You just don't understand," she said, as Maggie and I came out to the car.

79 "What don't I understand?" I wanted to know.

80 "Your heritage," she said. And then she turned to Maggie, kissed her, and said, "You ought to try to make something of yourself, too, Maggie. It's really a new day for us. But from the way you and Mama still live, you'd never know it."

81 She put on some sunglasses that hid everything above the tip of her nose and her chin.

82 Maggie smiled, maybe at the sunglasses. But a real smile, not scared. After we watched the car dust settle, I asked Maggie to bring me a dip of snuff. And then the two of us sat there just enjoying, until it was time to go in the house and go to bed.

## Second Read

- Reread the short story to answer these text-dependent questions.
- Write any additional questions you have about the text in your Reader/Writer Notebook.

4. **Craft and Structure:** What is the purpose of beginning the selection with Mama's recollections and then moving to Dee's arrival?

5. **Key Ideas and Details:** Based on paragraphs 4–6, what can be inferred about Mama's character?

# Perspectives on Heritage: Poetry and Fiction

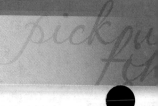

**My Notes**

6. **Key Ideas and Details:** What theme or central idea is suggested by the conversation about Dee's name in paragraphs 25–36?

7. **Key Ideas and Details:** In paragraphs 61–72, how does the conversation between Dee and Mama about the quilts develop the theme?

8. **Craft and Structure:** What does the word *priceless* mean, based on the way it is used in paragraph 68?

## Working from the Text

9. Complete the SIFT chart with your group members.

| SIFT | Textual Detail | Analysis or Interpretation |
|---|---|---|
| **Symbols** | | |
| **Images** | | |
| **Figures of Speech** | | |
| **Tone/Theme** | | |

## Check Your Understanding

Explain the meaning of the title, "Everyday Use" in the context of the short story.

**My Notes**

_____

_____

_____

_____

# Perspectives on Heritage: Poetry and Fiction

**My Notes**

## Comparing Texts

10. The quilts in "Everyday Use" and "My Mother Pieced Quilts" take on symbolic significance. What does the quilt in each story represent? How does each quilt convey the family's heritage? Use the Venn diagram to compare and contrast how the two texts explore a similar theme.

"Everyday Use"   "My Mother Pieced Quilts"

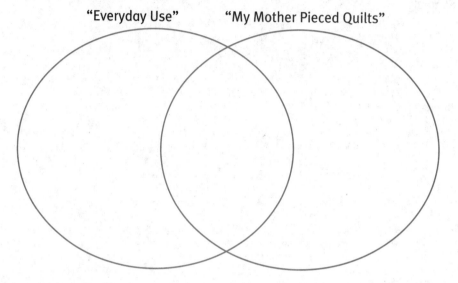

## Comparing Claims

For Embedded Assessment 2, you will be constructing an argument. One key element of argumentation that differentiates it from mere persuasion is that, in addition to presenting claims, arguments present **counterclaims**. A counterclaim asserts a different—sometimes conflicting—interpretation, explanation, or position. Both should be supportable with evidence, although you might use evidence to refute the counterclaim.

Consider the topic for Embedded Assessment 2: To what extent does one's culture influence the way one views others and the world? Study the sample claim and counterclaim below, and then create your own claim and counterclaim, using "Everyday Use" or "My Mother Pieced Quilts."

> **Potential Claim:** In Harper Lee's novel *To Kill a Mockingbird*, most of the characters in the novel are afflicted with Maycomb's "usual disease," racism, showing that culture strongly influences a person's views of what is right or wrong in the world.

> **Possible Counterclaim:** While racism may be widespread, Scout's character shows that a person's family more strongly influences a person's views of others than the broader culture does.

**ACADEMIC VOCABULARY**
A **counterclaim** is an opposing viewpoint.

## Language and Writer's Craft: Phrases and Clauses

As you continue to refine your writing skills, keep in mind that using phrases and clauses to achieve specific effects will contribute to your command of language—whether you are speaking or writing.

You have used different types of phrases in your past writing, such as noun, verb, and prepositional phrases. Some other types of phrases include adverbial, adjectival, and absolute phrases.

An **adverbial phrase** functions as an adverb and modifies a verb, adjective, or another adverb.

> **Example:** "She will stand hopelessly in corners, homely and ashamed of the burn scars down her arms and legs, eyeing her sister with a mixture of envy and awe." (modifies the verb *stand*)

An **adjectival phrase** functions as an adjective, modifying either a noun or a pronoun.

> **Example:** "these strips of gentle communion cotton and flannel nightgowns" (modifies the noun *strips*)

An **absolute phrase** consists of a noun and its modifiers. An absolute phrase may precede, follow, or interrupt the main clause and modifies or adds information to an entire sentence.

> **Example:** "Sometimes I can still hear the flames and feel Maggie's arms sticking to me, her hair smoking and her dress falling off her in little black papery flakes."

**PRACTICE** Using the My Notes space, write three original sentences, each containing an example of one phrase type: adverbial, adjectival, and absolute.

## Writing to Sources: Argument

Write an argument that contains a claim and a counterclaim and that analyzes both "Everyday Use" and "My Mother Pieced Quilts" in light of the Embedded Assessment 2. Draw on both selections as you explore the issue of the influence of culture on perception. In your writing, be sure to do the following:

- Write a clear thesis that connects the two works to the issue of the influence of culture on perception.
- Use a TAG statement (title, author, genre) to introduce new claims and texts.
- Fully develop your claim with supporting evidence and commentary. Address counterclaims fully.
- Effectively incorporate multiple direct quotations from both texts, introducing and punctuating them correctly.
- Include various types of phrases in your essay.

**My Notes**

### INDEPENDENT READING LINK

**Read and Respond**

In your independent reading, compare a character's awareness and view of heritage to the views of heritage in this unit's readings. In your Reader/Writer Notebook, write your opinion of how cultural heritage should be valued.

# Perspectives on Heritage: Nonfiction

**LEARNING STRATEGIES:**
Close Reading

**My Notes**

## Learning Targets
- Compare and contrast characters in a nonfiction text.
- Draw conclusions about individuals' responses to culture and explain conclusions in an essay.

## Preview
In this activity, you will read a personal essay and draw conclusions about the characters' perspectives on culture.

## Setting a Purpose for Reading
- As you read Mukherjee's "Two Ways to Belong in America" with your collaborative discussion team, you will take on the alternating roles of reader, responder, and listener. After one individual reads, the next will respond to the reading by summarizing, questioning, clarifying, or connecting with the text. The responder will then become the reader, the reader will become the listener, and so on until the essay is read in its entirety.
- Circle unknown words and phrases. Try to determine the meaning of the words by using context clues, word parts, or a dictionary.

**ABOUT THE AUTHOR**

Bharati Mukherjee was born in India in 1940 to wealthy parents. Reading and writing by the age of three, she knew she wanted to write professionally by the age of 10. Mukherjee attended the University of Calcutta, the University of Baroda, and the University of Iowa, where she met her husband. Both writers, they reside in California where Bharati Mukherjee is a professor at the University of California, Berkeley.

**Personal Essay**

# Two Ways to Belong in America

*by* Bharati Mukherjee

1   IOWA CITY—This is a tale of two sisters from Calcutta, Mira and Bharati, who have lived in the United States for some 35 years, but who find themselves on different sides in the current debate over the status of immigrants.

2   I am an American citizen and she is not. I am moved that thousands of long-term residents are finally taking the oath of citizenship. She is not.

3   Mira arrived in Detroit in 1960 to study child psychology and pre-school education. I followed her a year later to study creative writing at the University of Iowa. When we left India, we were almost identical in appearance and attitude. We dressed alike, in **saris**; we expressed identical views on politics, social issues, love and marriage in the same Calcutta convent-school accent. We would endure our two years in America, secure our degrees, then return to India to marry the grooms of our father's choosing.

4   Instead, Mira married an Indian student in 1962 who was getting his business administration degree at Wayne State University. They soon acquired the labor certifications necessary for the green card of hassle-free residence and employment.

5   Mira still lives in Detroit, works in the Southfield, Mich., school system, and has become nationally recognized for her contributions in the fields of pre-school education and parent-teacher relationships. After 36 years as a legal immigrant in this country, she clings passionately to her Indian citizenship and hopes to go home to India when she retires.

6   In Iowa City in 1963, I married a fellow student, an American of Canadian parentage. Because of the accident of his North Dakota birth, I bypassed labor-certification requirements and the race-related "quota" system that favored the applicant's country of origin over his or her merit. I was prepared for (and even welcomed) the emotional strain that came with marrying outside my ethnic community. In 33 years of marriage, we have lived in every part of North America. By choosing a husband who was not my father's selection, I was opting for **fluidity**, self-invention, blue jeans and T-shirts, and renouncing 3,000 years (at least) of **caste**-observant, "pure culture" marriage in the Mukherjee family. My books have often been read as unapologetic (and in some quarters overenthusiastic) texts for cultural and psychological "mongrelization." It's a word I celebrate.

7   Mira and I have stayed sisterly close by phone. In our regular Sunday morning conversations, we are **unguardedly** affectionate. I am her only blood relative on this continent. We expect to see each other through the looming crises of aging and ill health without being asked. Long before Vice President Gore's "Citizenship U.S.A." drive, we'd had our polite arguments over the ethics of retaining an overseas citizenship while expecting the permanent protection and economic benefits that come with living and working in America.

## My Notes

**sari:** an Indian garment for women

**fluidity:** changing often or easily
**caste:** class into which a Hindu person is born

**unguardedly:** speaking honestly

**superficial:** not deep or without substance

**scapegoating:** unfairly blaming someone for something done by others

**scrutiny:** study; examination

**discretion:** judgment

**manipulated:** controlled

**curtailing:** restricting; limiting

**subtext:** an underlying meaning or message

**divergence:** difference

**demotion:** lower position or rank

**referendum:** the practice of voting for or against a law on a specific issue

## GRAMMAR & USAGE

### Syntax

Commas, which separate words and phrases in a passage, can play an important role in syntax. Notice the use of commas in the paragraphs beginning with "Mira's voice." In just three sentences, Mukherjee uses fourteen commas and hardly any conjunctions. This speeds up the pacing of the writing, focusing attention on the issue of immigrant status.

Mukherjee's use of commas—often to separate items in a list—helps to express her tone. What adjectives would you use to describe the author's tone after rereading this paragraph?

8 Like well-raised sisters, we never said what was really on our minds, but we probably pitied one another. She, for the lack of structure in my life, the erasure of Indianness, the absence of an unvarying daily core. I, for the narrowness of her perspective, her uninvolvement with the mythic depths or the **superficial** pop culture of this society. But, now, with the **scapegoating** of "aliens" (documented or illegal) on the increase, and the targeting of long-term legal immigrants like Mira for new **scrutiny** and new self-consciousness, she and I find ourselves unable to maintain the same polite **discretion**. We were always unacknowledged adversaries, and we are now, more than ever, sisters.

9 "I feel used," Mira raged on the phone the other night. "I feel **manipulated** and discarded. This is such an unfair way to treat a person who was invited to stay and work here because of her talent. My employer went to the I.N.S. and petitioned for the labor certification. For over 30 years, I've invested my creativity and professional skills into the improvement of this country's pre-school system. I've obeyed all the rules, I've paid my taxes, I love my work, I love my students, I love the friends I've made. How dare America now change its rules in midstream? If America wants to make new rules **curtailing** benefits of legal immigrants, they should apply only to immigrants who arrive after those rules are already in place." To my ears, it sounded like the description of a long-enduring, comfortable yet loveless marriage, without risk or recklessness. Have we the right to demand, and to expect, that we be loved? (That, to me, is the **subtext** of the arguments by immigration advocates.) My sister is an expatriate, professionally generous and creative, socially courteous and gracious, and that's as far as her Americanization can go. She is here to maintain an identity, not to transform it.

10 I asked her if she would follow the example of others who have decided to become citizens because of the anti-immigration bills in Congress. And here, she surprised me. "If America wants to play the manipulative game, I'll play it too," she snapped. "I'll become a U.S. citizen for now, then change back to Indian when I'm ready to go home. I feel some kind of irrational attachment to India that I don't to America. Until all this hysteria against legal immigrants, I was totally happy. Having my green card meant I could visit any place in the world I wanted to and then come back to a job that's satisfying and that I do very well."

11 In one family, from two sisters alike as peas in a pod, there could not be a wider **divergence** of immigrant experience. America spoke to me—I *married* it—I embraced the **demotion** from expatriate aristocrat to immigrant nobody, surrendering those thousands of years of "pure culture," the saris, the delightfully accented English. She retained them all. Which of us is the freak?

12 Mira's voice, I realize, is the voice not just of the immigrant South Asian community but of an immigrant community of the millions who have stayed rooted in one job, one city, one house, one ancestral culture, one cuisine, for the entirety of their productive years. She speaks for greater numbers than I possibly can. Only the fluency of her English and the anger, rather than fear, born of confidence from her education, differentiate her from the seamstresses, the domestics, the technicians, the shop owners, the millions of hard-working but effectively silenced documented immigrants as well as their less fortunate "illegal" brothers and sisters.

13 Nearly 20 years ago, when I was living in my husband's ancestral homeland of Canada, I was always well-employed but never allowed to feel part of the local Quebec or larger Canadian society. Then, through a Green Paper that invited a national **referendum** on the unwanted side effects of "nontraditional" immigration, the Government officially turned against its immigrant communities, particularly those from South Asia.

14   I felt then the same sense of betrayal that Mira feels now. I will never forget the pain of that sudden turning, and the casual racist outbursts the Green Paper elicited. That sense of betrayal had its desired effect and drove me, and thousands like me, from the country.

15   Mira and I differ, however, in the ways in which we hope to interact with the country that we have chosen to live in. She is happier to live in America as an expatriate Indian than as an immigrant American. I need to feel like a part of the community I have adopted (as I tried to feel in Canada as well). I need to put roots down, to vote and make the difference that I can. The price that the immigrant willingly pays, and that the exile avoids, is the trauma of self-transformation.

## Second Read

- Reread the personal essay to answer these text-dependent questions.
- Write any additional questions you have about the text in your Reader/Writer Notebook.

1. **Key Ideas and Details:** Based on paragraph 5, what inferences can you draw about Mira's attitude to the United States?

2. **Craft and Structure:** What is the meaning of *mongrelization* as it is used in paragraph 6? What connotations does the word have?

3. **Craft and Structure:** Explain the meaning and significance of the sentence beginning "We were always unacknowledged..." in paragraph 8.

4. **Key Ideas and Details:** How does the final paragraph reflect the central idea of the selection?

5. **Craft and Structure:** What is the author's purpose in writing this piece?

**WORD CONNECTIONS**

**Etymology**

The word *expatriate* comes from the French word *expatrier*, which means "to banish." The prefix *ex-* means "out of," and the root *patrie* means "native land." *Patrie* can be traced back to Latin *pater*, meaning "father." In 1818, *expatriate* meant "one who has been banished." Today it refers to someone who chooses to live in another country.

**My Notes**

_____

_____

_____

_____

_____

_____

_____

_____

_____

_____

_____

**INDEPENDENT READING LINK**

**Read and Respond**

Look for evidence in your independent reading of how the experience of living in a different culture can change people's perspective of their own cultural identity. List examples of how this new perspective clashes with family members who resist change.

# Perspectives on Heritage: Nonfiction

## Working from the Text

6. With your group, revisit the text to complete the chart below to help you analyze the two different approaches to belonging in America.

|  | Bharati | Mira |
|---|---|---|
| Birthplace | | |
| Citizenship | | |
| Dress | | |
| Area of Study | | |
| Marriage | | |
| Views on Heritage | | |
| Attitudes Toward "Citizenship U.S.A." Drive | | |
| Attitude Toward Living in America | | |

## Check Your Understanding

Beyond comparing the two sisters in "Two Ways to Belong in America," compare the sisters in this nonfiction text with those you met in "Everyday Use." What, if any, similarities do you observe in the way the sisters view their heritage? How many parallels can your discussion group discover between these fiction and nonfiction texts?

## Writing to Sources: Explanatory

The two sets of sisters you have encountered in the last two texts include one sister who embraces her background and another who assimilates to a new culture. Choose one pair of girls (those who embrace their background, those who assimilate, or one of each), and write an essay in which you explain their attitudes to a culture. Be sure to:

- Choose an organizational structure suitable to your subject.
- Write a clear thesis that identifies your chosen set of characters and their similarities or differences.
- Include textual quotations to support your explanations.
- Cite the author of the work you are quoting in parentheses following the quotation.

**Group Discussion:** Respond to the following quotation from Mukherjee's "Two Ways to Belong in America": "The price that the immigrant willingly pays, and that the exile avoids, is the trauma of self-transformation."

# Argumentation in "An Indian Father's Plea"

**LEARNING STRATEGIES:**
Think-Pair-Share, Marking the Text, graphic organizer, Discussion

**My Notes**

## Learning Targets
- Analyze the structure of an argument.
- Explain how an argument persuades.

## Preview
In this activity, you will read an essay and analyze its structure.

## The Structure of an Argument
Although arguments are varied in their structure, content, and context, five key elements are almost always found in an effective argument.

### The Hook
- The hook grabs the reader's attention.
- It often establishes a connection between reader and writer and provides background information.
- It can be, but is not limited to, an anecdote, an image, a definition, or a quotation.

### The Claim
- The claim comes in the opening section of your paper.
- It states your belief and what you wish to argue.
- It can be straightforward and clear, for example, "I believe that…"

### Support: Reasons and Evidence
- Your support is the reasoning behind your argument.
- You provide supporting evidence for your claim (data, quotes, anecdotes, and so on) and use support to create logical appeals.

### Counterclaims: Concessions and Refutations
- A **concession** recognizes the arguments made by the other side.
- A concession builds your credibility by objectively discussing the other side and granting that the other side has some validity.
- Following the concession, a **refutation** argues at length against the opposing viewpoint by proving your side has MORE validity.

### Concluding Statement
- A concluding statement draws your argument to a close, restates your claim, and makes a final appeal.
- Avoid repeating information, but sum up your argument with a few final facts and appeals.

**ACADEMIC VOCABULARY**
A **concession** is accepting something as true. A **refutation** is proof that an opinion is wrong or false.

## Setting a Purpose for Reading

- As you read "An Indian Father's Plea" by Robert Lake, mark the text and write the elements of argumentation in the My Notes section of your text.
- Circle unknown words and phrases. Try to determine the meaning of the words by using context clues, word parts, or a dictionary.

**ABOUT THE AUTHOR**

A member of the Seneca and Cherokee Indian tribes, Robert Lake is an associate professor at Gonzaga University's School of Education in Spokane, Washington. His tribal name is Medicine Grizzlybear.

### Essay

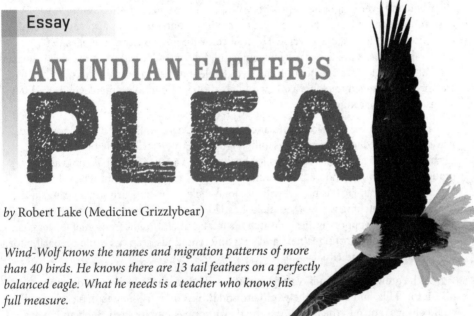

# AN INDIAN FATHER'S PLEA

*by* Robert Lake (Medicine Grizzlybear)

*Wind-Wolf knows the names and migration patterns of more than 40 birds. He knows there are 13 tail feathers on a perfectly balanced eagle. What he needs is a teacher who knows his full measure.*

1  **Dear teacher,** I would like to introduce you to my son, Wind-Wolf. He is probably what you would consider a typical Indian kid. He was born and raised on the **reservation**. He has black hair, dark brown eyes, and an olive complexion. And like so many Indian children his age, he is shy and quiet in the classroom. He is 5 years old, in kindergarten, and I can't understand why you have already labeled him a "slow learner."

2  At the age of 5, he has already been through quite an education compared with his peers in Western society. As his first introduction into this world, he was bonded to his mother and to the Mother Earth in a traditional native childbirth ceremony. And he has been continuously cared for by his mother, father, sisters, cousins, aunts, uncles, grandparents, and extended tribal family since this ceremony.

3  From his mother's warm and loving arms, Wind-Wolf was placed in a secure and specially designed Indian baby basket. His father and the medicine elders conducted another ceremony with him that served to bond him with the essence of his genetic father, the Great Spirit, the Grandfather Sun, and the Grandmother Moon. This was all done in order to introduce him properly into the new and natural world, not the world of artificiality, and to protect his sensitive and delicate soul. It is our people's way of showing the newborn respect, ensuring that he starts his life on the path of spirituality.

**My Notes**

reservation: an area of land Native Americans manage and live in, under their own tribal government

# Argumentation in "An Indian Father's Plea"

## WORD CONNECTIONS

### Content Connections

The word *culture* has different meanings in the arts, social studies, business, and science. In the arts, culture refers to a developed appreciation of such art forms as dance, opera, classical and jazz music, and the fine arts. In social studies, culture refers to the beliefs, customs, forms of communication, and artistic products of a particular country, ethnic group, or time period. In business, culture refers to a shared set of goals and values in a company or institution. In science, a culture is a living organism, such as bacteria or mold, grown in nutrients in a lab.

**intuitive:** sensitive and insightful
**faculties:** talents or abilities
**regalia:** special cultural dress

## My Notes

**integrated:** well put together

4  The traditional Indian baby basket became his "turtle's shell" and served as the first seat for his classroom. He was strapped in for safety, protected from injury by the willow roots and hazel wood construction. The basket was made by a tribal elder who had gathered her materials with prayer and in a ceremonial way. It is the same kind of basket that our people have used for thousands of years. It is specially designed to provide the child with the kind of knowledge and experience he will need in order to survive in his culture and environment.

5  Wind-Wolf was strapped in snugly with a deliberate restriction upon his arms and legs. Although you in Western society may argue that such a method serves to hinder motor-skill development and abstract reasoning, we believe it forces the child to first develop his **intuitive faculties**, rational intellect, symbolic thinking, and five senses. Wind-Wolf was with his mother constantly, closely bonded physically, as she carried him on her back or held him in front while breast-feeding. She carried him everywhere she went, and every night he slept with both parents. Because of this, Wind-Wolf's educational setting was not only a "secure" environment, but it was also very colorful, complicated, sensitive, and diverse. He has been with his mother at the ocean at daybreak when she made her prayers and gathered fresh seaweed from the rocks, he has sat with his uncles in a rowboat on the river while they fished with gill nets, and he has watched and listened to elders as they told creation stories and animal legends and sang songs around the campfires.

6  He has attended the sacred and ancient White Deerskin Dance of his people and is well-acquainted with the cultures and languages of other tribes. He has been with his mother when she gathered herbs for healing and watched his tribal aunts and grandmothers gather and prepare traditional foods such as acorn, smoked salmon, eel, and deer meat. He has played with abalone shells, pine nuts, iris grass string, and leather while watching the women make beaded jewelry and traditional native **regalia**. He has had many opportunities to watch his father, uncles, and ceremonial leaders use different kinds of colorful feathers and sing different kinds of songs while preparing for the sacred dances and rituals.

7  As he grew older, Wind-Wolf began to crawl out of the baby basket, develop his motor skills, and explore the world around him. When frightened or sleepy, he could always return to the basket, as a turtle withdraws into its shell. Such an inward journey allows one to reflect in privacy on what he has learned and to carry the new knowledge deeply into the unconscious and the soul. Shapes, sizes, colors, texture, sound, smell, feeling, taste, and the learning process are therefore functionally **integrated**—the physical and spiritual, matter and energy, conscious and unconscious, individual and social.

8  This kind of learning goes beyond the basics of distinguishing the difference between rough and smooth, square and round, hard and soft, black and white, similarities and extremes.

9  For example, Wind-Wolf was with his mother in South Dakota while she danced for seven days straight in the hot sun, fasting, and piercing herself in the sacred Sun Dance Ceremony of a distant tribe. He has been doctored in a number of different healing ceremonies by medicine men and women from diverse places ranging from Alaska and Arizona to New York and California. He has been in more than 20 different sacred sweat-lodge rituals—used by native tribes to purify mind, body, and soul—since he was 3 years old, and he has already been exposed to many different religions of his racial brothers: Protestant, Catholic, Asian Buddhist, and Tibetan Lamaist.

**My Notes**

10   <u>It takes a long time to absorb and reflect on these kinds of experiences, so maybe that is why you think my Indian child is a slow learner.</u> His aunts and grandmothers taught him to count and know his numbers while they sorted out the complex materials used to make the abstract designs in the native baskets. He listened to his mother count each and every bead and sort out numerically according to color while she **painstakingly** made complex beaded belts and necklaces. He learned his basic numbers by helping his father count and sort the rocks to be used in the sweat lodge—seven rocks for a medicine sweat, say, or 13 for the summer solstice ceremony. (The rocks are later heated and doused with water to create purifying steam.) And he was taught to learn mathematics by counting the sticks we use in our traditional native hand game. <u>So I realize he may be slow in grasping the methods and tools that you are now using in your classroom, ones quite familiar to his white peers, but I hope you will be patient with him. It takes time to adjust to a new cultural system and learn new things.</u>

**painstakingly:** thoroughly

11   He is not culturally "disadvantaged," but he is culturally "different." If you ask him how many months there are in a year, he will probably tell you 13. He will respond this way not because he doesn't know how to count properly, but because he has been taught by our traditional people that there are 13 full moons in a year according to the native tribal calendar and that there are really 13 planets in our solar system and 13 tail feathers on a perfectly balanced eagle, the most powerful kind of bird to use in ceremony and healing.

12   But he also knows that some eagles may only have 12 tail feathers, or seven, that they do not all have the same number. He knows that the flicker has exactly 10 tail feathers; that they are red and black, representing the directions of east and west, life and death; and that this bird is considered a "fire" bird, a power used in native doctoring and healing. He can probably count more than 40 different kinds of birds, tell you and his peers what kind of bird each is and where it lives, the seasons in which it appears, and how it is used in a sacred ceremony. He may have trouble writing his name on a piece of paper, but he knows how to say it and many other things in several different Indian languages. He is not fluent yet because he is only 5 years old and required by law to attend your educational system, learn your language, your values, your ways of thinking, and your methods of teaching and learning. So you see, all of these influences together make him somewhat shy and quiet—and perhaps "slow" according to your standards. But if Wind-Wolf was not prepared for his first **tentative foray** into your world, neither were you appreciative of his culture. On the first day of class, you had difficulty with his name. You wanted to call him Wind, insisting that Wolf somehow must be his middle name. The students in the class laughed at him, causing further embarrassment.

**tentative:** cautious
**foray:** journey

13   While you are trying to teach him your new methods, helping him learn new tools for self-discovery and adapt to his new learning environment, he may be looking out the window as if daydreaming. Why? Because he has been taught to watch and study the changes in nature. It is hard for him to make the appropriate psychic switch from the right to the left **hemisphere** of the brain when he sees the leaves turning bright colors, the geese heading south, and the squirrels scurrying around for nuts to get ready for a harsh winter. In his heart, in his young mind, and almost by instinct, he knows that this

**hemisphere:** one half of the brain

# Argumentation in "An Indian Father's Plea"

**My Notes**

powwow: a North American Indian ceremony that often includes singing, dancing, food, and wearing of traditional clothing

delinquent: a youth prone to trouble and lawlessness

is the time of year he is supposed to be with his people gathering and preparing fish, deer meat, and native plants and herbs, and learning his assigned tasks in this role. He is caught between two worlds, torn by two distinct cultural systems.

14  Yesterday, for the third time in two weeks, he came home crying and said he wanted to have his hair cut. He said he doesn't have any friends at school because they make fun of his long hair. I tried to explain to him that in our culture, long hair is a sign of masculinity and balance and is a source of power. But he remained adamant in his position.

15  To make matters worse, he recently encountered his first harsh case of racism. Wind-Wolf had managed to adopt at least one good school friend. On the way home from school one day, he asked his new pal if he wanted to come home to play with him until supper. That was OK with Wind-Wolf's mother, who was walking with them. When they all got to the little friend's house, the two boys ran inside to ask permission while Wind-Wolf's mother waited. But the other boy's mother lashed out: "It is OK if you have to play with him at school, but we don't allow those kind of people in our house!" When my wife asked why not, the other boy's mother answered, "Because you are Indians and we are white, and I don't want my kids growing up with your kind of people."

16  So now my young Indian child does not want to go to school anymore (even though we cut his hair). He feels that he does not belong. He is the only Indian child in your class, and he is well-aware of this fact. Instead of being proud of his race, heritage, and culture, he feels ashamed. When he watches television, he asks why the white people hate us so much and always kill our people in the movies and why they take everything away from us. He asks why the other kids in school are not taught about the power, beauty, and essence of nature or provided with an opportunity to experience the world around them firsthand. He says he hates living in the city and that he misses his Indian cousins and friends. He asks why one young white girl at school who is his friend always tells him, "I like you, Wind-Wolf, because you are a good Indian."

17  Now he refuses to sing his native songs, play with his Indian artifacts, learn his language, or participate in his sacred ceremonies. When I ask him to go to an urban **powwow** or help me with a sacred sweat-lodge ritual, he says no because "that's weird" and he doesn't want his friends at school to think he doesn't believe in God.

18  So, dear teacher, I want to introduce you to my son, Wind-Wolf, who is not really a "typical" little Indian kid after all. He stems from a long line of hereditary chiefs, medicine men and women, and ceremonial leaders whose accomplishments and unique forms of knowledge are still being studied and recorded in contemporary books. He has seven different tribal systems flowing through his blood; he is even part white. I want my child to succeed in school and in life. I don't want him to be a dropout or juvenile **delinquent** or to end up on drugs and alcohol because he is made to feel inferior or because of discrimination. I want him to be proud of his rich heritage and culture, and I would like him to develop the necessary capabilities to adapt to, and succeed in, both cultures. But I need your help.

19  What you say and what you do in the classroom, what you teach and how you teach it, and what you don't say and don't teach will have a significant effect on the potential success or failure of my child. Please remember that this is the primary year of his education and development. All I ask is that you work with me, not against me, to help educate my child in the best way. If you don't have the knowledge, preparation, experience, or training to effectively deal with culturally different children, I am willing to help you with the few resources I have available or direct you to such resources.

20 Millions of dollars have been **appropriated** by Congress and are being spent each year for "Indian Education." All you have to do is take advantage of it and encourage your school to make an effort to use it in the name of "equal education." My Indian child has a constitutional right to learn, retain, and maintain his heritage and culture. By the same token, I strongly believe that non-Indian children also have a constitutional right to learn about our Native American heritage and culture, because Indians play a significant part in the history of Western society. Until this reality is equally understood and applied in education as a whole, there will be a lot more schoolchildren in grades K–2 identified as "slow learners."

21 My son, Wind-Wolf, is not an empty glass coming into your class to be filled. He is a full basket coming into a different environment and society with something special to share. Please let him share his knowledge, heritage, and culture with you and his peers.

appropriated: taken

**My Notes**

# Argumentation in "An Indian Father's Plea"

**My Notes**

## Second Read

- Reread the essay to answer these text-dependent questions.
- Write any additional questions you have about the text in your Reader/Writer Notebook.

1. **Craft and Structure:** What is the author's purpose in paragraphs 2–10, where he describes and explains the kinds of things Wind-Wolf has been taught outside school?

2. **Key Ideas and Details:** What element of argument is displayed in the sentence beginning "Although you in Western society..." in paragraph 5?

3. **Knowledge and Ideas:** What element of an argument is displayed in the underlined sentences in paragraph 10? How do they improve the effectiveness of the speakers claim?

4. **Craft and Structure:** In paragraph 11, what is the author's claim? How does he support this claim?

5. **Craft and Structure:** How does the tone shift in paragraph 13? How does the author achieve this shift? In terms of argumentative structure, what is the author trying to achieve?

6. **Key Ideas and Details:** Summarize what the father is asking the teacher to do.

7. **Knowledge and Ideas:** What is the author's argument? Is it effective?

## Working from the Text

8. In the graphic organizer below, identify examples of the five elements of argument that appear in "An Indian Father's Plea."

| Element of Argument | Example from the Text |
|---|---|
| Hook | |
| Claim | |
| Support | |
| Concessions/ Refutations | |
| Call to Action | |

## Check Your Understanding

Discuss the effectiveness of the writer's organization of ideas with your group members. How does the organization help or hinder the argument?

### My Notes

# Argumentation in "An Indian Father's Plea"

**INDEPENDENT READING LINK**

**Read and Recommend**

In your independent reading of both fiction and nonfiction, select one reading that you would recommend to your peers as an example of a successful effort to break through cultural labeling. Write or tell your peers why you are recommending your selection.

**My Notes**

## Writing to Sources: Explain How an Argument Persuades

Explain how the writer structures the argument in "An Indian Father's Plea." In your writing, be sure to do the following:

- Identify the claim made by the writer and analyze how clear and direct it is.
- Explain what reasons and supporting evidence the writer uses and how counterclaims are addressed.
- Think about the audience for the essay and evaluate the effectiveness of the reasons, evidence, and refutations of counterclaims.
- Effectively incorporate multiple direct quotations from the text introducing and punctuating them correctly.
- Explain how the writer concludes the essay and how effective that ending is.
- Incorporate varied syntactic structures in your writing.

# Synthesis: Drafting Your Position

## Learning Targets
- Collaborate with group members to reach a consensus in response to a synthesis prompt.
- Synthesize various sources to formulate a position and state it in a thesis statement.

## Choosing a Position

Throughout the last few activities you have focused on individuals' attitudes and perspectives about cultures that have affected or influenced their own. You have analyzed perspectives through a close look at rhetorical devices and elements of argument.

In order to write a proficient synthesis essay, you need to (1) present a clear position on an issue and (2) synthesize perspectives from multiple sources, including your own experiences, in support of that position.

1. For this activity, you will work in a group to create a group synthesis essay. What are the benefits and barriers to writing a group synthesis essay? Pass a single pen and paper from person to person to write your thoughts.

2. Look at your group list. What do you need to do to be successful in this assessment? How will you turn your negatives into positives? Conduct a small group discussion by hearing from each member.

3. Read the prompt below. Consider your personal point of view based on experience and on texts you have read in response to the prompt. Write your response below the prompt.

**Writing Prompt:** To what extent does a person's culture inform the way he or she views others and the world?

> **LEARNING STRATEGIES:**
> Quickwrite, Brainstorming, Group Discussion

**My Notes**

# Synthesis: Drafting Your Position

**My Notes**

4. Working with your group, brainstorm three different ways one could respond to this type of prompt—by defending, challenging, or qualifying it.

Response #1 (Defend):

Response #2 (Challenge):

Response #3 (Qualify):

5. Share your personal responses to the prompt so everyone has a chance to hear perspectives that he or she may not have considered. Reach a consensus by asking each team member to vote for his or her position. Give 3 points to the first choice, 2 to the second, and 1 to the third. Total the points of the group to determine the most popular position.

Write your group position here:

6. Now that you have a position, brainstorm stories, essays, poems, or real-life incidents that support your position. Make a list of the texts you might use, and then pass a pen and paper around the table while each member writes one supporting idea. Each member needs to add a new piece of evidence or support.

## Check Your Understanding

After reaching a consensus and brainstorming support for your position, construct a well-crafted thesis statement that asserts your group's position. Write it below.

## Learning Target

- Collaborate to plan a synthesis essay by revising a thesis statement and mapping out an organizational strategy.

**LEARNING STRATEGIES:**
Quickwrite, Rereading, graphic organizer, Sharing and Responding, Drafting

## Creating an Argument

1. Look at the thesis statement you constructed in the previous activity. Which works that you read in this unit will help you support that thesis statement? Quickwrite your answer and reason in My Notes.

2. Each member of your group will select one author from the unit who is relevant to the conversation about how culture informs perspective. Your task is to reread the text and fill in the graphic organizer below. When you have finished, be prepared to report your findings to your group.

| | |
|---|---|
| What is your group's position? | |
| Which author is relevant to the conversation? Why? | |
| Would he/she agree, disagree, or qualify your position? | |
| What specific examples could we use to support/refute our claim? (Include at least three.) | |

**My Notes**

# Synthesis: Presenting Your Position

## My Notes

3. Report your findings to your group, and listen as they share their works and ideas. After discussing your answers, write your revised thesis in the My Notes.

4. Revisit the components of an argumentative essay in Activity 1.13, Argumentation in "An Indian Father's Plea." How will your group organize the different elements of an argumentative essay to make the strongest possible case in support of your claim? Work together to create your organizational framework. Consider the following questions as you plan your essay:

   • How will we organize our supporting ideas: by idea or by source? Consider how you may offset the challenges of a group essay as you answer this question.

   • Will our concessions and refutations be a separate paragraph from the supporting paragraphs? Or will concessions and refutations be incorporated into the paragraphs that offer explicit support for our claim?

   • Keep in mind as you make your plan that you will each be writing a separate "chunk" of your argumentative essay. How will you create cohesion between paragraphs?

## Check Your Understanding

Write your organizational plan below by creating an outline for a synthesis paper and describing how your group will complete the task.

## Independent Reading Checkpoint

Review your independent reading and select examples that you can use as evidence in your argumentative essay to support the position that culture has a strong or weak influence on how people view others and the world.

# Writing a Synthesis Paper

## ASSIGNMENT

Your assignment is to collaborate with your peers to write an essay that responds to the following synthesis prompt:

> To what extent does one's culture inform the way one views others and the world?

Be sure to support your claim with evidence from at least three different texts you have read, viewed, or listened to in this unit, as well as with personal experience and insights.

| | |
|---|---|
| **Planning and Prewriting: Take time to make a plan for your essay.** | ■ In the texts you have studied, how have the attitudes and actions of the authors or characters been influenced by their cultural backgrounds?<br>■ How will your group reach a consensus to write a preliminary thesis (claim) on the extent to which culture shapes perspective?<br>■ How will you select an organizational structure that addresses the key elements of an argument—hook, claim, support, concessions/refutations, and call to action?<br>■ Once your organizational framework is clear to all members of your group, how will you assign each individual a section to compose? For example, do you plan to write the body paragraphs separately and then synthesize your information in order to compose your opening and conclusion as a group? |
| **Drafting and Revising: Compose your synthesis paper.** | ■ How will you ensure that each group member contributes a section that supports the thesis with evidence identifying cultural influences?<br>■ How will you incorporate textual evidence from your readings into the section you will contribute to the essay?<br>■ How can you work with your group to share and respond to the individual sections in order to revise and synthesize a cohesive draft?<br>■ How can you and your group use the Scoring Guide to develop questions that will focus your discussion and revision? |
| **Editing and Publishing: Prepare your essay in final form.** | ■ How can you work collaboratively as well as individually to improve sentence variety with parallel structure, phrases, or semicolons?<br>■ How will you check that you have embedded source material using correct punctuation and in-text parenthetical citations?<br>■ Which resources (including peer editing) can help you edit for correct grammar, appropriate punctuation and capitalization, and correct spelling? |

## Reflection

After completing this Embedded Assessment, respond to the following:

- What were the benefits and challenges of writing collaboratively, and what would you do differently if faced with a similar task in the future?

- Of the texts you studied in this unit, which author or character's perspective could you relate to or understand best? Did that person have a cultural heritage similar to yours? Explain.

# Writing a Synthesis Paper

## SCORING GUIDE

| Scoring Criteria | Exemplary | Proficient | Emerging | Incomplete |
|---|---|---|---|---|
| **Ideas** | The essay<br>• has a clearly stated and strongly maintained claim that takes a specific position<br>• develops the argument effectively by integrating relevant evidence from a variety of texts and personal insights. | The essay<br>• makes an effective claim with a specific position<br>• develops an argument sufficiently by integrating evidence from a variety of texts and personal experiences. | The essay<br>• has an unclear or insufficiently maintained claim, lacks focus, or does not take a position<br>• uses vague, irrelevant, or insufficient evidence to develop the argument. | The essay<br>• is not coherent and does not make a clear claim or state a position<br>• provides little or no evidence to develop an argument. |
| **Structure** | The essay<br>• uses an effective organization that establishes clear relationships among claims, counterclaims, reasons, and evidence<br>• introduces ideas smoothly, develops claims and counterclaims fairly, and provides a satisfying conclusion<br>• uses appropriate and varied transitions. | The essay<br>• uses an adequate organization that establishes relationships among claims, counterclaims, reasons, and evidence<br>• introduces ideas, develops claims and counterclaims, and provides a conclusion<br>• uses some varied transitions. | The essay<br>• uses an inconsistent or confusing organization<br>• does not develop claims and counterclaims and/or conclude ideas<br>• uses weak, repetitive, or insufficient transitions. | The essay<br>• uses a confusing organization and/or does not link ideas<br>• does not develop claims and counterclaims or provide a conclusion<br>• uses weak or no transitions. |
| **Use of Language** | The essay<br>• uses diction and syntax that convey a formal, authoritative voice<br>• correctly embeds and punctuates parenthetical citations<br>• demonstrates strong command of conventions for grammar, usage, capitalization, punctuation, and spelling. | The essay<br>• uses diction and syntax that convey a formal voice<br>• uses generally correct parenthetical citations, with appropriate punctuation<br>• demonstrates adequate command of conventions for grammar, usage, capitalization, punctuation, and spelling. | The essay<br>• does not use appropriate diction or formal voice<br>• omits parenthetical citations<br>• demonstrates partial or insufficient command of conventions; errors in grammar, usage, capitalization, punctuation, and/or spelling interfere with meaning. | The essay<br>• uses inappropriate diction and informal voice<br>• omits parenthetical citations<br>• demonstrates little command of conventions; numerous errors in grammar, usage, capitalization, punctuation, and/or spelling interfere with meaning. |

# Cultural Perspectives

**Visual Prompt:** Thousands of athletes and spectators from many different countries and cultures participate in the Olympic Games. What are some ways that participants might show their individual cultures?

## Unit Overview

In the first half of this unit, you will read and analyze a variety of narratives by authors of various cultural backgrounds. Each author uses the narrative form to express his or her cultural perspective. As you read, you will focus on one or more of the elements of narrative writing and analyze how they are used to convey that perspective. Finally, you will use the narrative techniques that you have learned and write a narrative about an incident, either real or imagined, that communicates a cultural perspective.

In the second half of the unit, you will consider issues of justice that are commonly shared among very different cultures. Though justice is a shared issue, it doesn't mean that people agree when it comes to how it is enacted. You will read a variety of texts that argue for or against issues of justice. Evaluating each argument's claims and evidence will give you the support to craft your own argument about an issue that resonates across cultures.

# Cultural Perspectives

**GOALS:**

- To construct a narrative that expresses a cultural perspective
- To analyze narrative techniques and use them in writing
- To examine perspectives of justice across cultures and over time
- To understand and apply the elements of argument
- To develop an argument on an issue for a specific audience, using an effective genre

---

**ACADEMIC VOCABULARY**
evidence
empirical evidence
logical evidence
anecdotal evidence
fallacy

---

**Literary Terms**
anaphora
memoir
dialogue tags
narrative pacing
persona

## Contents

**Activities**

**Language & Writer's Craft**
- Introducing Dialogue (2.4)
- Sentence Variety (2.5)
- Clauses (2.6)
- Varying Sentence Beginnings (2.9)
- Outlining and Organizing an Argument (2.13)

MY INDEPENDENT READING LIST

_____
_____
_____
_____
_____
_____
_____
_____
_____
_____
_____
_____
_____
_____
_____
_____
_____

# Previewing the Unit

**LEARNING STRATEGIES:**
Predicting, Skimming/
Scanning, Graphic Organizer

**INDEPENDENT READING LINK**

**Read and Discuss**

In the first part of this unit, you will read nonfiction narratives by writers who share aspects of their lives and cultures. For outside reading, choose fiction or nonfiction narratives that explore an aspect of culture (food, dance, art, subgroups) of interest. Discuss an independent reading selection with peers, focusing on the similarities and differences in the description of a particular aspect to your own culture.

**My Notes**

## Learning Targets

- Preview the big ideas and vocabulary for the unit.
- Identify and analyze the skills and knowledge needed to complete Embedded Assessment 1 successfully.

## Making Connections

In Unit 1, you learned that all of us have a cultural identity. Writers express their cultural experiences through multiple narrative genres in both fiction and nonfiction. In this unit, you will further examine cultural influences by reading narratives expressing elements of culture. You will also look at issues of justice and how culture influences perceptions of justice. Finally, you will write an argument about an issue of justice.

## Essential Questions

1. How can cultural experiences and perspectives be conveyed through memorable narratives?

2. What issues resonate across cultures, and how are arguments developed in response?

## Developing Vocabulary

Predict what you think this unit is about. Use the words or phrases that stood out to you when you read the Unit Overview and the Key Terms on the Contents page.

## Unpacking Embedded Assessment 1

Read the following assignment for Embedded Assessment 1:

> Your assignment is to write a narrative about an incident, either real or imagined, that conveys a cultural perspective. Throughout this unit, you have studied narratives in multiple genres, and you have explored a variety of cultural perspectives. You will now select the genre you feel is most appropriate to convey a real or fictional experience that includes one or more elements of culture.

Summarize in your own words what you will need to know for this assessment. With your class, create a graphic organizer to identify the skills and knowledge needed to complete the assessment successfully. Strategize how to complete the assignment. To help you and your classmates complete the graphic organizer, review the criteria in the Scoring Guide on page 165.

# Images of Cultural Identity

## Learning Targets
- Analyze poetry to identify sensory language, structure, and technique.
- Write an explanatory text citing evidence from a poem.

LEARNING STRATEGIES:
Graphic Organizer, Think-Pair-Share, Marking the Text

## Preview
In this activity, you will read and analyze a poem about cultural identity.

## Setting a Purpose for Reading
- Writers of fiction and nonfiction use imagery and other sensory language to add color and depth to their writing. As you read the poem on the next page, mark the text for details that appeal to your sight, hearing, touch, taste, and smell.
- Circle unknown words and phrases. Try to determine the meaning of the words by using context clues, word parts, or a dictionary.

**My Notes**

### ABOUT THE AUTHOR
George Ella Lyon (1949–) is the author of award-winning children's books, including *Catalpa*, a book of poetry that won the Appalachian Book of the Year award, and the novel *With a Hammer for My Heart*. Lyon is often asked about her unusual first name. On her website, she explains that she was named after her uncle George and her aunt Ella.

## Poetry

# Where I'm From

*by* George Ella Lyon

I am from clothes-pins
from Clorox and carbon-tetrachloride.
I am from the dirt under the back porch.
(Black, glistening,
5  it tasted like beets.)
I am from the forsythia bush,
the Dutch Elm
whose long gone limbs I remember
as if they were my own.

**WORD CONNECTIONS**

**Content Connections**

*Carbon tetrachloride* is a poisonous chemical produced from the chemical compound methane. It was formerly used in dry cleaning, as a refrigerant, and in fire extinguishers, among other uses. Lyon is probably remembering its sweet smell.

# Images of Cultural Identity

## My Notes

auger: tool for boring holes

drift: be carried along by a current

### GRAMMAR & USAGE
**Sentences and Fragments**

A complete sentence includes at least one independent clause. In academic writing, it is important to make sure all of your sentences are complete. In narrative writing and in poems, however, sentence fragments can sometimes be used for effect. Notice that George Ella Lyon uses the sentence fragment "From the finger my grandfather lost to the auger, the eye my father shut to keep his sight." How does this this fragment affect the pace of the poem? What does it leave out?

10  I'm from fudge and eyeglasses,
        from Imogene and Alafair.
    I'm from the know-it-alls
        and the pass-it-ons,
    from Perk up! and Pipe down!
15  I'm from He restoreth my soul
        with a cottonball lamb
        and ten verses I can say myself.

    I'm from Artemus and Billie's Branch,
    fried corn and strong coffee.
20  From the finger my grandfather lost
        to the **auger**,
    the eye my father shut to keep his sight.

    Under my bed was a dress box
    spilling old pictures,
25  a sift of lost faces
    to **drift** beneath my dreams.
    I am from those moments—
    snapped before I budded—
    leaf-fall from the family tree.

## Second Read

- Reread the poem to answer these text-dependent questions.
- Write any additional questions you have about the text in your Reader/Writer Notebook.

1. **Craft and Structure:** How does the speaker use sensory language in lines 3–5 to show her memories of her family culture?

2. **Key Ideas and Details:** What is the central idea of the poem? What details does the speaker use to help readers understand the central idea?

## Working from the Text

3. Record textual evidence of the speaker's use of sensory details in the poem using the table below.

| Sight | Hearing | Touch | Taste | Smell |
|-------|---------|-------|-------|-------|
|       |         |       |       |       |

4. With a partner, discuss the textual evidence that you recorded in the table. How did the inclusion of sensory language help convey the speaker's culture?

My Notes

5. Notice the speaker's use of **anaphora**–the repetition of a word or phrase at the beginning of a line. The speaker repeats "I am from" (or "I'm from") in each stanza. What does each use of the phrase reveal about her identity? How does the repetition provide structure to the free verse?

### Literary Terms

**Anaphora** is the repetition of the same word or group of words at the beginning of two or more clauses or lines.

## Check Your Understanding

How would you describe the culture reflected in Lyon's poem? What clues from the poem helped you to form your description?

# Images of Cultural Identity

## My Notes

## Writing to Sources: Explanatory Text

Write an essay to explain how the author uses imagery and specific words and phrases to convey a sense of family culture and identity. How do these images reflect a particular aspect of culture? Be sure to:

- Begin with a clear thesis that states an aspect of culture explored in the poem.
- Include direct quotations and specific examples from the text. Introduce and punctuate all quotations correctly.
- Use a coherent organizational structure and make connections between specific words or images and the ideas conveyed.

# Cultural Narrative

## Learning Targets

- Analyze a narrative and identify key narrative components.
- Identify and analyze aspects of culture presented in literature.

## Elements of Narrative

You have most likely written several narratives by now in your various courses. As you recall, writers use the narrative writing mode for personal narrative—in which the writer shares something from his or her own experience—as well as fictional narrative, which is a made-up story. Whether fiction or nonfiction, writers use some common narrative techniques in telling their stories, such as creating a setting, a sequence of events, a point of view, a theme, and, of course, characters—real or imagined—who populate the narrative.

## Preview

In this activity, you will read a **memoir** and analyze the narrative techniques that the author uses to tell her story.

## Setting a Purpose for Reading

- The following text is a memoir, which is a type of personal narrative. In her memoir, Dumas writes about her experience as a newcomer to the United States and how she and her family adjust to a different culture. As you read the text, annotate it and make notes in the My Notes space as you find important narrative elements.
- Circle unknown words and phrases. Try to determine the meaning of the words by using context clues, word parts, or a dictionary.

### ABOUT THE AUTHOR

Born in Abadan, Iran, writer Firoozeh Dumas spent much of her childhood living in California. She credits her father—a Fulbright scholar and engineer who attended Texas A&M University—and his fondness for humorous storytelling with inspiring her to write stories of her own. After the events of September 11, 2001, friends urged Dumas to publish her stories as a way to remind readers of the humor and humanity of Middle Eastern cultures.

---

**LEARNING STRATEGIES:**
Marking the Text, Graphic Organizer

**My Notes**

### Literary Terms
A **memoir** is an account of the personal experiences of the author. It is also an autobiographical account.

**WORD CONNECTIONS**

### Multiple Meaning Words

The word *account* has different meanings. As a noun, *account* can mean a narrative of events, which is its use in describing a memoir as an account. It may also mean a financial record, such as a bank account or a credit card account. As a verb, *account* means to give an explanation, as in this sentence: "How would you account for the missing footballs?"

# Cultural Narrative

## GRAMMAR & USAGE
### Syntax

Syntax is the way a writer organizes the words, phrases, and clauses of sentences. The use of subordinate structures, such as subordinate clauses and appositives, lengthens a sentence, allowing more details to be packed into it. Notice that the opening sentence contains an introductory adverbial clause and an appositive. What details do these sentence parts add? Notice also that in the opening complex sentence, the main clause comes last, requiring the reader to complete the whole sentence to understand the meaning.

As you read, identify the author's syntactical choices, and consider their effects on the flow, rhythm, and content of the memoir.

**facilitate:** make easier

**prestigious:** high status

## My Notes

---

**Memoir**

from # Funny in Farsi

*by* Firoozeh Dumas

1   When I was seven, my parents, my fourteen-year-old brother, Farshid, and I moved from Abadan, Iran, to Whittier, California. Farid, the older of my two brothers, had been sent to Philadelphia the year before to attend high school. Like most Iranian youths, he had always dreamed of attending college abroad and, despite my mother's tears, had left us to live with my uncle and his American wife. I, too, had been sad at Farid's departure, but my sorrow soon faded—not coincidentally, with the receipt of a package from him. Suddenly, having my brother on a different continent seemed like a small price to pay for owning a Barbie complete with a carrying case and four outfits, including the rain gear and mini umbrella.

2   Our move to Whittier was temporary. My father, Kazem, an engineer with the National Iranian Oil Company, had been assigned to consult for an American firm for about two years. Having spent several years in Texas and California as a graduate student, my father often spoke about America with the eloquence and wonder normally reserved for a first love. To him, America was a place where anyone, no matter how humble his background, could become an important person. It was a kind and orderly nation full of clean bathrooms, a land where traffic laws were obeyed and where whales jumped through hoops. It was the Promised Land. For me, it was where I could buy more outfits for Barbie.

3   We arrived in Whittier shortly after the start of second grade; my father enrolled me in Leffingwell Elementary School. To **facilitate** my adjustment, the principal arranged for us to meet my new teacher, Mrs. Sandberg, a few days before I started school. Since my mother and I did not speak English, the meeting consisted of a dialogue between my father and Mrs. Sandberg. My father carefully explained that I had attended a **prestigious** kindergarten where all the children were taught English. Eager to impress Mrs. Sandherg, he asked me to demonstrate my knowledge of the English language. I stood up straight and proudly recited all that I knew: "White, yellow, orange, red, purple, blue, green."

4   The following Monday, my father drove my mother and me to school. He had decided that it would be a good idea for my mother to attend school with me for a few weeks. I could not understand why two people not speaking English would be better than one, but I was seven, and my opinion didn't matter much.

5   Until my first day at Leffingwell Elementary School, I had never thought of my mother as an embarrassment, but the sight of all the kids in the school staring at us before the bell rang was enough to make me pretend I didn't know her. The bell finally rang and Mrs. Sandberg came and escorted us to class. Fortunately, she had figured out that we were precisely the kind of people who would need help finding the right classroom.

**6** My mother and I sat in the back while all the children took their assigned seats. Everyone continued to stare at us. Mrs. Sandberg wrote my name on the board: F-l-R-O-O-Z-E-H. Under my name, she wrote "I-R-A-N." She then pulled down a map of the world and said something to my mom. My mom looked at me and asked me what she had said. I told her that the teachers probably wanted her to find Iran on the map.

**7** The problem was that my mother, like most women of her generation, had been only briefly educated. In her era, a girl's **sole** purpose in life was to find a husband. Having an education ranked far below more desirable **attributes** such as the ability to serve tea or prepare baklava. Before her marriage, my mother, Nazireh, had dreamed of becoming a midwife. Her father, a fairly **progressive** man, had even refused the two earlier suitors who had come for her so that his daughter could pursue her dream. My mother planned to obtain her diploma, then go to Tabriz to learn midwifery from a teacher whom my grandfather knew. Sadly, the teacher died unexpectedly, and my mother's dreams had to be buried as well.

**8** Bachelor No. 3 was my father. Like the other suitors, he had never spoken to my mother, but one of his cousins knew someone who knew my mother's sister, so that was enough. More important, my mother fit my father's physical requirements for a wife. Like most Iranians, my father preferred a fair-skinned woman with straight, light-colored hair. Having spent a year in America as a Fulbright scholar, he had returned with a photo of a woman he found attractive and asked his older sister, Sedigeh, to find someone who resembled her. Sedigeh had asked around, and that is how at age seventeen my mother officially gave up her dreams, married my father, and had a child by the end of the year.

**9** As the students continued staring at us, Mrs. Sandberg gestured to my mother to come up to the board. My mother reluctantly obeyed. I cringed. Mrs. Sandberg, using a combination of hand gestures, started pointing to the map and saying, "Iran? Iran? Iran?" Clearly, Mrs. Sandberg had planned on incorporating us into the day's lesson. I only wished she had told us that earlier so we could have stayed home.

**10** After a few awkward attempts by my mother to find Iran on the map, Mrs. Sandberg finally understood that it wasn't my mother's lack of English that was causing a problem, but rather her lack of world geography. Smiling graciously, she pointed my mother back to her seat. Mrs. Sandberg then showed everyone, including my mother and me, where Iran was on the map. My mother nodded her head, acting as if she had known the location all along but had preferred to keep it a secret. Now all the students stared at us, not just because I had come to school with my mother, not because we couldn't speak their language, but because we were stupid. I was especially mad at my mother, because she had **negated** the positive impression I had made previously by reciting the color wheel. I decided that starting the next day, she would have to stay home.

**11** The bell finally rang and it was time for us to leave. Leffingwell Elementary was just a few blocks from our house and my father, grossly underestimating our ability to get lost, had assumed that my mother and I would be able to find our way home. She and I wandered aimlessly, perhaps hoping for a shooting star or a talking animal to help guide us back. None of the streets or houses looked familiar. As we stood pondering our predicament, an enthusiastic young girl came leaping out of her house and said something. Unable to understand her, we did what we had done all day: we smiled. The girl's mother joined us, then gestured for us to follow her inside. I assumed that the girl, who appeared to be the same age as I, was a student at Leffingwell Elementary; having us inside her house was probably akin to having the circus make a personal visit.

**My Notes**

sole: only
attributes: qualities

progressive: liberal

negated: canceled out

**My Notes**

**12** Her mother handed us a telephone, and my mother, who had, thankfully, memorized my father's work number, called him and explained our situation. My father then spoke to the American woman and gave her our address. This kind stranger agreed to take us back to our house.

**13** Perhaps fearing that we might show up at their doorstep again, the woman and her daughter walked us all the way to our front porch and even helped my mother unlock the unfamiliar door. Alter making one last futile attempt at communication, they waved good-bye. Unable to thank them in words, we smiled even more broadly.

**14** After spending an entire day in America, surrounded by Americans, I realized that my father's description of America had been correct. The bathrooms were clean and the people were very, very kind.

## Second Read

- Reread the memoir to answer these text-dependent questions.
- Write any additional questions you have about the text in your Reader/Writer Notebook.

1. **Key Ideas and Details:** In paragraph 3, the narrator visits her new school for the first time. What does the narrator's first encounter with the school setting indicate about her?

2. **Craft and Structure:** In paragraph 7, Dumas tells us that her "mother's dreams had to be buried as well." Why do you think the author chooses to use this figure of speech to describe the event?

3. **Key Ideas and Details:** How does Dumas feel on her first day of school in America? What evidence in the text supports this idea?

4. **Craft and Structure:** Why does Dumas use an adult narrator to reflect on her experiences as a 7-year-old?

5. **Key Ideas and Details:** Reread the last sentence of the text. How could you use the descriptions of Dumas's emotions and her statement that "the people were very, very kind" to state the theme of the text?

## Working from the Text

6. Use this graphic organizer to record specific details from the text.

| Narrative Elements | Details from the Narrative |
|---|---|
| Setting(s) | |
| Character(s) | |
| Point of View | |
| Sequence of Events | |
| Theme | |

## Check Your Understanding

Reread the description of Dumas's mother's lack of education. Discuss with a partner: How can adding background information about a character add depth to a character in a narrative?

### Writing to Sources: Explanatory Text

Write an essay to explain how the incidents portrayed in the narrative make a point about a particular aspect of culture. Which aspect of culture is the focus of the narrative? What narrative elements does the author incorporate, and how do they contribute to the overall purpose of the memoir? Be sure to:

- Begin with a clear thesis statement that states the author's point.
- Include direct quotations and specific examples and other relevant evidence from the text. Introduce and punctuate all quotations correctly.
- Organize your ideas and information in a way that highlights important connections and distinctions.

# Author's Stylebook: Dialogue

**LEARNING STRATEGIES:**
Marking the Text, Paraphrasing, Graphic Organizer, Think-Pair-Share, Discussion Groups

**My Notes**

## Literary Terms

**Dialogue tags** are the phrases that attribute the quotation to the speaker; for example, *she said* or *he bellowed*.

## Learning Targets

- Analyze the narrative technique of dialogue in an autobiography.
- Write a narrative using direct and indirect dialogue.

## Dialogue

Authors use a variety of techniques to create narratives that make their stories come alive on the page. Authors use dialogue to provide the reader with information about a character, to provide background information, and to advance the plot. You may have noticed that the previous narrative contained almost no dialogue, which served to emphasize the confusion and embarrassment, as well as the humor, of the situation.

Dialogue may be either direct or indirect. Indirect dialogue is a paraphrase of what is said by a character or narrator. This dialogue does not need quotation marks.

**Example:** When my mother began dropping hints that I would soon be going to school, I vowed never to go to school because it was a waste of time.

Direct dialogue is the exact words spoken by a person. This dialogue uses quotation marks and **dialogue tags**.

**Example:** "This time next fall, you will be in school," hinted my mother. "Why would I go to school? You'll never see me wasting my time at school!" I vowed.

Take a moment and think about a person you know who tells great stories. What is it about their storytelling that makes it so good? One thing that they probably do is change the *way* that they say things as they tell the story. With a partner, quickly generate a list of dialogue tags other than "said" that good storytellers use.

## Preview

In this activity, you will read an excerpt from an autobiography to analyze the author's use of dialogue and then use dialogue when writing your own narrative.

## Setting a Purpose for Reading

- As you read the excerpt for the elements of a narrative, also annotate the text, noting the impact of the dialogue and dialogue tags on the story and the characters.
- Circle unknown words and phrases. Try to determine the meaning of the words by using context clues, word parts, or a dictionary.

**ABOUT THE AUTHOR**

Mark Mathabane (1960–) was born in South Africa just outside Johannesburg. He spent his childhood in an unheated shack with no electricity and no running water. Mathabane and his family lived in fear of the police who enforced the law of apartheid—sometimes violently. In 1978, Mathabane secured a tennis scholarship to a college in South Carolina. He later graduated from Dowling College in New York. During his writing career, Mathabane has produced several works of nonfiction as well as three recent novels. *Kaffir Boy* is Mathabane's story of his childhood living under apartheid.

### Autobiography

# from Kaffir Boy

*by* Mark Mathabane

1   When my mother began dropping hints that I would soon be going to school, I vowed never to go because school was a waste of time. She laughed and said, "We'll see. You don't know what you're talking about." My philosophy on school was that of a gang of ten-eleven-and twelve-year-olds whom I so revered that their every word seemed that of an oracle.

2   These boys had long left their homes and were now living in various neighborhood junkyards, making it on their own. They slept in abandoned cars, smoked glue and benzene, ate pilchards and brown bread, sneaked into the white world to caddy and, if unsuccessful, came back to the township to steal beer and soda bottles from shebeens, or goods from the Indian traders on First Avenue. Their lifestyle was exciting, adventurous and full of surprises; and I was attracted to it.  My mother told me that they were no-gooders, that they would amount to nothing, that I should not associate with them, but I paid no heed. What does she know? I used to tell myself. One thing she did not know was that the gang's way of life had captivated me wholly, particularly their philosophy on school: they hated it and considered an education a waste of time.

3   They, like myself, had grown up in an environment where the value of an education was never emphasized, where the first thing a child learned was not how to read and write and spell, but how to fight and steal and rebel; where the money to send children to school was grossly lacking, for survival was first priority. I kept my membership in the gang, knowing that for as long as I was under its influence, I would never go to school.

4   One day my mother woke me up at four in the morning.

5   "Are they here? I didn't hear any noises," I asked in the usual way.

6   "No," my mother said. "I want you to get into that washtub over there."

7   "What!" I balked, upon hearing the word *washtub*. I feared taking baths like one feared the plague. Throughout seven years of hectic living the number of baths I had taken could be counted on one hand with several fingers missing. I simply had no natural inclination for water; cleanliness was a trait I still had to acquire. Besides, we had only one bathtub in the house, and it constantly sprung a leak.

**My Notes**

**INDEPENDENT READING LINK**

**Read and Discuss**

Discuss with peers how the texts you have read in class and independently depict the role of education in different cultures. Compare and contrast this with your own views and perspectives on education. How does reading other perspectives help you understand the role of education in society? Discuss how your reading contributes to an understanding of the Essential Question, "How can cultural experiences and perspectives be conveyed through memorable narratives?"

# Author's Stylebook: Dialogue

## GRAMMAR & USAGE
### Punctuation

Quotation marks enclose direct dialogue. Punctuating dialogue correctly allows readers to easily understand when characters in a story are speaking. Ending punctuation marks generally are placed inside the quotation marks. Notice the placement of quotation marks and other punctuation in the following sentences from *Kaffir Boy*:

"Are you ready?" Granny asked my mother.

**My Notes**

**lavishly:** richly

8  "I said get into that tub!" My mother shook her finger in my face.

9  Reluctantly, I obeyed, yet wondered why all of a sudden I had to take a bath. My mother, armed with a scrobrush and a piece if Lifebouy soap, purged me of years and years of grime till I ached and bled. As I howled, feeling pain shoot through my limbs as the thistles of the brush encountered stubborn callouses, there was a loud knock at the door.

10  Instantly my mother leaped away from the tub and headed, on tiptoe, toward the bedroom. Fear seized me as I, too, thought of the police. I sat frozen in the bathtub, not knowing what to do.

11  "Open up, Mujaji [my mother's maiden name]," Granny's voice came shrilling through the door. "It's me."

12  My mother heaved a sigh of relief; her tense limbs relaxed. She turned and headed to the kitchen door, unlatched it and in came Granny and Aunt Bushy.

13  "You scared me half to death," my mother said to Granny. "I had forgotten all about your coming."

14  "Are you ready?" Granny asked my mother.

15  "Yes—just about," my mother said, beckoning me to get out of the washtub.

16  She handed me a piece of cloth to dry myself. As I dried myself, questions raced through my mind: What's going on? What's Granny doing at our house this ungodly hour of the morning? And why did she ask my mother, "Are you ready?" While I stood debating, my mother went into the bedroom and came out with a stained white shirt and a pair of faded black shorts.

17  "Here," she said, handing me the togs, "put these on."

18  "Why?" I asked.

19  "Put them on I said!"

20  I put the shirt on; it was grossly loose-fitting. It reached all the way down to my ankles. Then I saw the reason why: it was my father's shirt!

21  "But this is Papa's shirt," I complained. "It don't fit me."

22  "Put it on," my mother insisted. "I'll make it fit."

23  "The pants don't fit me either," I said. "Whose are they anyway?"

24  "Put them on," my mother said. "I'll make them fit."

25  Moments later I had the garments on; I looked ridiculous. My mother started working on the pants and shirt to make them fit. She folded the short in so many intricate ways and stashed it inside the pants, they too having been folded several times at the waist. She then chocked the pants at the waist with a piece of sisal rope to hold them up. She then **lavishly** smeared my face, arms and legs with a mixture of pig's fat and Vaseline. "This will insulate you from the cold," she said. My skin gleamed like the morning star and I felt as hot as the centre of the sun and smelled God knows like what. After embalming me, she headed to the bedroom.

26　"Where are we going, Gran'ma?" I said, hoping that she would tell me what my mother refused to tell me. I still had no idea I was about to be taken to school.

27　"Didn't your mother tell you?" Granny said with a smile. "You're going to start school."

28　"What!" I gasped, leaping from the chair where I was sitting as if it were made of hot lead. "I am not going to school!" I blurted out and raced toward the kitchen door.

29　My mother had just reappeared from the bedroom and guessing what I was up to, she yelled, "Someone get the door!"

30　Aunt Bushy immediately barred the door. I turned and headed for the window. As I leaped for the windowsill, my mother lunged at me and brought me down. I tussled, "Let go of me! I don't want to go to school! Let me go!" but my mother held fast onto me.

31　"It's no use now," she said, grinning triumphantly as she pinned me down. Turning her head in Granny's direction, she shouted, "Granny! Get a rope quickly!"

32　Granny grabbed a piece of rope nearby and came to my mother's aid. I bit and clawed every hand that grabbed me, and howled protestations against going to school; however, I was no match for the two determined **matriarchs**. In a jiffy they had me **bound**, hand and feet.

33　"What's the matter with him?" Granny, bewildered, asked my mother. "Why did he suddenly turn into an imp when I told him you're taking him to school?"

34　"You shouldn't have told him that he's being taken to school," my mother said. "He doesn't want to go there. That's why I requested you come today, to help me take him there. Those boys in the streets have been a bad influence on him."

35　As the two matriarchs hauled me through the door, they told Aunt Bushy not to go to school but stay behind and mind the house and the children.

## Second Read

- Reread the autobiography to answer these text-dependent questions.
- Write any additional questions you have about the text in your Reader/Writer Notebook.

1. **Key Ideas and Details:** How does Mathabane hint that his life is about to change on the day in which this scene takes place? Name three events from the text and explain how you know they signal something unusual is going to happen.

**My Notes**

**matriarchs:** ruling women of the family
**bound:** tied up

# Author's Stylebook: Dialogue

2. **Key Ideas and Details:** What details from Mathabane's life explain why he is so determined not to go to school?

3. **Craft and Structure:** Mathabane chooses to use mostly indirect dialogue in the beginning of the story and mostly direct dialogue at the end. What effect do his choices have on the pacing of the story? Why do you think he makes these choices?

4. **Craft and Structure:** Describe how the author uses active verbs to develop his characters in the part of the scene after the narrator is told he will be going to school.

5. **Craft and Structure:** The word *protestations* on page 119 means nearly the same as the simpler word *protests*. Why might the author have chosen to use a more formal and elaborate version of the word in this scene?

## Working from the Text

6. Use this graphic organizer to record specific details from the text.

| Narrative Elements | Details from the Narrative |
|---|---|
| Setting(s) | |
| Character(s) | |
| Point of View | |
| Sequence of Events | |
| Theme | |

### Language and Writer's Craft: Dialogue

Writers may begin a sentence with dialogue, or they may use a comma or a colon to introduce direct dialogue that comes later in a sentence. Commas are used to introduce shorter quotations, and colons are sometimes used for longer quotations.

Dialogue beginning a sentence:

"You scared me half to death," my mother said to Granny. "I had forgotten all about your coming."

Dialogue introduced using a comma:

And why did she ask my mother, "Are you ready?"

Dialogue introduced using a colon:

I stood up straight and proudly recited all that I knew: "White, yellow, orange, red, purple, blue, green."

**PRACTICE** Consider the following excerpt from *Kaffir Boy*:

As I dried myself, questions raced through my mind: What's going on? What's Granny doing at our house this ungodly hour of the morning?

Notice that a colon is used to introduce the narrator's thoughts, but quotation marks are not used. Authors differ in their treatment of a narrator's thoughts. This author chooses not to punctuate them as quoted words. Other authors might use italics or quotation marks to set these thoughts apart from the rest of the text. Add quotation marks to punctuate these quoted questions as direct quotes introduced by a colon.

My Notes

# Author's Stylebook: Dialogue

**My Notes**

7. Look back through the text you just read and find examples of direct and indirect dialogue. List and label them in the chart that follows. Practice the two methods of writing dialogue by paraphrasing the examples of direct dialogue and rewriting indirect dialogue as direct dialogue, being sure to punctuate it correctly.

| Dialogue | Practice Writing Dialogue |
|---|---|
| When my mother began dropping hints that I would soon be going to school, I vowed never to go to school because it was a waste of time. | "This time next fall, you will be in school," hinted my mother.<br><br>"Why would I go to school? You'll never see me wasting my time at school!" I vowed. |
|  |  |
|  |  |
|  |  |

8. **Collaborative Discussion:** Return to the excerpt and review the dialogue between Mathabane and his mother. Discuss with your group the impact of the dialogue on the development of the characters and the narrative. How does the author use dialogue to create the relationship between mother and son? Support your thinking with details from the story that illustrate the culture of family.

## Narrative Writing Prompt

Write a personal narrative about a memorable experience from your own childhood that illustrates one perspective or attitude from your culture. Consider the impact your family and culture had on your experience. Be sure to:

• Introduce the character(s) and setting for the narrative.

• Provide a well-structured sequence of events and a conclusion that reflects on the impact of the experience.

• Incorporate direct and indirect dialogue to aid in the development of your narrative, and punctuate dialogue correctly.

• Use precise words and phrases and sensory language.

## Learning Targets
- Analyze the narrative techniques writers use to create a sense of pacing in a narrative.
- Apply pacing to my own writing.

## Pacing
**Narrative pacing** is an important part of telling a good story. A writer controls the rhythm of a narrative with specific choices in sentence length, word choice, and details. For example, a series of short sentences can heighten suspense and increase the pace, while a series of long sentences may slow the pace.

## Preview
In this activity, you will read an essay and analyze its pacing. In addition, you will write your own narrative using the techniques you have learned so far in this unit.

## Setting a Purpose for Reading
- As you read the following essay, mark the text and write notes about where the pacing or rhythm of the narrative changes and how these changes in pacing affect you as a reader.
- Circle unknown words and phrases. Try to determine the meaning of the words by using context clues, word parts, or a dictionary.

**ABOUT THE AUTHOR**
David Matthews is the author of the memoir *Ace of Spades* published in 2007 by Henry Holt and Co. He is the son of an African American father and a Jewish mother. In his memoir, Matthews tells of growing up racially mixed in Baltimore, Maryland during the 1970s and '80s. The following essay was adapted from his memoir and printed in *The New York Times Magazine* on January 21, 2007.

### Essay

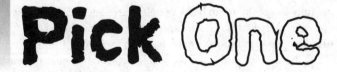

*by* David Matthews
*The New York Times*

1  In 1977, when I was nine, my father and I moved away from the protected Maryland suburbs of Washington—and away from his latest wife, my latest stepmother—to my grandmother's apartment in inner-city Baltimore. I had never seen so many houses connected to one another, block after block, nor so many people on streets, marble stoops and corners. Many of those people, I could not help noticing, were black. I had never seen so many black people in all my life.

---

**LEARNING STRATEGIES:**
Graphic Organizer, Think-Pair-Share, Marking the Text

**Literary Terms**
**Narrative pacing** refers to the speed at which a narrative moves. A writer slows pacing with more details and longer sentences. Fewer details and shorter sentences have the effect of increasing the pace.

**GRAMMAR & USAGE**
**Semicolon**
Writers use a semicolon to join independent clauses when two or more clauses are of equal importance. In paragraph 2, notice the sentence "I was black, too, though I didn't look it; and I was white, though I wasn't quite." In this sentence, the two independent clauses are about two aspects of the same problem. In paragraph 7, notice the sentence "I didn't contemplate the segregation; it was simply part of the new physical geography, and I was no explorer; I was a weak-kneed outsider, a yellowed freak." How do the independent clauses relate to one another?

**My Notes**

_____

_____

_____

# Author's Stylebook: Pacing

## GRAMMAR&USAGE
Dashes

Dashes can provide emphasis. Notice the dash used in this sentence: "I froze, and said nothing—for the time being." Here, the phrase "for the time being" is emphasized. Dashes can also set off parenthetical information, as in this sentence: "And though I was used to some measure of instability—various apartments, sundry stepmothers and girlfriends—I had always gone to the same redbrick single-level school." With this usage, the dash places more emphasis on the set-off content than parentheses would do.

**render:** pronounce
**equine:** horselike
**stumped:** baffled
**partisan:** of one belief
**avidity:** eagerness
**clause:** part of a legal document

## My Notes

_____

_____

_____

_____

**vicarious:** lived through another person

_____

_____

_____

2   I was black, too, though I didn't look it; and I was white, though I wasn't quite. My mother, a woman I'd never really met, was white and Jewish, and my father was a black man who, though outwardly hued like weak coffee, was—as I grew to learn—stridently black nationalist in his views and counted Malcolm X[1] and James Baldwin[2] among his friends. I was neither blessed nor cursed, depending on how you looked at it, with skin milky enough to classify me as white or swarthy enough to **render** me black. But before moving from our integrated and idyllic neighborhood, I really knew nothing of "race." I was pretty much just a kid, my full-time gig. And though I was used to some measure of instability—various apartments, sundry stepmothers and girlfriends—I had always gone to the same redbrick single-level school. Nothing prepared me for walking into that public-school classroom, already three weeks into fourth grade. I had never felt so utterly on my own.

3   Mrs. Eberhard, my new homeroom teacher, made an introduction of sorts, and every student turned around to study me. The black kids, who made up more than 80 percent of the school's population, ranged in shades from butterscotch to Belgian chocolate, but none had my sallow complexion, nor my fine, limp hair. And the white kids, a salting of red and alabaster faces, had noses that were tapered and blunted, free of the slightly **equine** flare of my own, and lips that unobtrusively parted their mouths, in contrast to the thickened slabs I sucked between my teeth.

4   In the hallway, on the way to class, black and white kids alike herded around me. Then the question came: "What are you?"

5   I was **stumped**. No one had ever asked what I was before. It came buzzing at me again, like a hornet shaken from its hive. The kids surrounded me, pressing me into a wall of lockers. What are you? Hey, he won't answer us. Look at me. What are you? He's black. He looks white! No way, he's too dark. Maybe he's Chinese!

6   They were rigidly **partisan**. The only thing that unified them was their inquisitiveness. And I had a hunch, based on their **avidity**, that the question had a wrong answer. There was black or white. Pick one. Nowhere in their ringing questions was the elastic **clause**, mixed. The choice was both necessary and impossible: identify myself or have it done for me. I froze, and said nothing—for the time being.

7   At lunchtime that first day, teetering on the edge of the cafeteria, my eyes scanned the room and saw an island of white kids in a sea of black faces. I didn't contemplate the segregation; it was simply part of the new physical geography, and I was no explorer; I was a weak-kneed outsider, a yellowed freak.

8   In some way I wasn't fully aware of, urban black people scared me. I didn't know how to play the dozens or do double Dutch. I didn't know the one about how your mama's so dumb she failed her pap test. I didn't know that with the wrong intonation, or the wrong addressee, any mention of one's mama could lead to a table-clearing brawl. The black kids at school carried a loose, effortless charge that crackled through their interactions. They were alive and cool. The only experience I had with cool had been **vicarious**, watching my father and his bebop-era revolutionary friends, and feeling their vague sense of disappointment when I couldn't mimic their behavior. The black kids reminded me of home, but the white kids reminded me of myself, the me I saw staring back in the mirror. On that day, I came to believe that if I had said I was black, I would have had to spend the rest of my life convincing my own people.

---

[1] **Malcolm X** (1925–1965) was an African American minister and civil rights activist who was assassinated in 1965.
[2] **James Baldwin** (1924–1987) was an African American writer and social critic.

9 Lunch tray in hand, I made a final and (at least I like to tell myself) psychologically logical choice, one I would live with, and wrestle with, for a full decade to come: I headed toward the kids who looked most like me. Goofy bell-bottoms and matching Garanimals? Check. Seventies mop-top? Check. Then a ruddy boy with blond bangs lopped off at the eyebrows looked up from his Fantastic Four comic book, caught my eye across the cafeteria, scooched over in his seat and nodded me over.

10 That was it. By the code of the cafeteria table, which was just as binding in that time and place as the laws of Jim Crow[3] or Soweto[4], I was white.

## Second Read

- Reread the essay to answer these text-dependent questions.
- Write any additional questions you have about the text in your Reader/Writer Notebook.

1. **Key Ideas and Details:** What contrast does Matthews make between his old neighborhood and his new one?

2. **Craft and Structure:** Identify Matthews's purpose in telling this story from his childhood. How does his use of narrative elements in the essay help him to achieve his purpose?

3. **Knowledge and Ideas:** Matthews makes the point that the "code of the cafeteria table ... was just as binding in that time and place as the laws of Jim Crow or Soweto." During the 20th century, the laws Matthews refers to enforced segration of black and white people in the United States and South Africa. Does his essay prove that his comparison is valid?

---

[3] **Jim Crow** is a name given to laws that enforced racial segregation in the United States from after the Civil War until 1965.
[4] **Soweto** is a part of a city in South Africa where black Africans lived under the policy of apartheid.

**My Notes**

# Author's Stylebook: Pacing

## Working from the Text

### Language and Writer's Craft: Sentence Variety

A variety of sentence types gives prose a natural rhythm. Simple sentences consist of one independent clause. Compound sentences consist of two independent clauses joined by a coordinating conjunction. Complex sentences consist of an independent clause and one or more subordinate clauses. Compound-complex sentences have two or more independent clauses as well as at least one subordinate clause.

Consider these examples from the essay:

**Simple Sentence:** "I had never felt so utterly on my own."

**Compound Sentence:** "Mrs. Eberhard, my new homeroom teacher, made an introduction of sorts, and every student turned around to study me."

**Complex Sentence:** "I was neither blessed nor cursed, depending on how you looked at it, with skin milky enough to classify me as white or swarthy enough to render me black."

**Compound-Complex Sentence:** "I was black, too, though I didn't look it; and I was white, though I wasn't quite."

**PRACTICE** With a partner, reread the essay looking for at least one example of each of these sentence types. Then write your own examples.

| Sentence Type | Example from Text | Original Example |
|---|---|---|
| Simple (one independent clause) | | |
| Compound (two or more independent clauses) | | |
| Complex (one independent clause and at least one dependent clause) | | |
| Compound-complex (two or more independent clauses and at least one dependent clause) | | |

4. What is the overall impact of sentence variety on the pacing of the essay? Provide details from the text to support your answer.

## Narrative Writing Prompt

Write a narrative about a time when you made an important decision about yourself. Vary the pacing in your narrative by working in simple, compound, complex, and compound-complex sentences. Be sure to:

- Use descriptive details to help the reader understand your story.
- Provide a smooth progression of experiences or events, using transitions to move through the story.
- Vary the pacing through the use of details and sentence types and lengths.

## Check Your Understanding

After completing your narrative, work with a partner and share your stories. Identify the change in pacing and the sentence types each of you used in your stories.

# Author's Stylebook: Description

**LEARNING STRATEGIES:**
Think-Pair-Share, Marking the Text, Rereading

## INDEPENDENT READING LINK

**Read and Research**

Examine the texts you have read independently to analyze how they present particular aspects of different cultures. What recurring themes and issues do you notice? How does an author's use of sensory details and other descriptive language convey elements and reflections of the author's culture?

**tacit:** unstated

## GRAMMAR & USAGE
**Colons**

You can use a colon after an independent clause when it is followed by a list, a quotation, an appositive, or another idea directly related to the independent clause. In this sentence, the colon helps to introduce a list: "I want to eat what the kids at school eat: bologna, hot dogs, salami—foods my parents find repugnant because they contain pork and meat by-products, crushed bone and hair glued together by chemicals and fat."

As you read this essay, find another colon, and identify its use in the sentence.

## Learning Targets
- Identify and evaluate the use of sensory details and figurative language.
- Use clauses to add variety to writing as well as convey meaning.

## Preview

In this activity, you will read an essay and evaluate the author's use of sensory details and figurative language.

## Setting a Purpose for Reading

- In the following excerpt from "If You Are What You Eat, Then What Am I?" author Geeta Kothari creates an image of a can of tuna with vivid language and telling details. As you read the passage for sensory details, highlight the descriptions that speak to your senses.
- Circle unknown words and phrases. Try to determine the meaning of the words by using context clues, word parts, or a dictionary.

## Essay

# from If You Are What You Eat, Then What Am I?

*by* Geeta Kothari

1   *"To belong is to understand the **tacit** codes of the people you live with."*—Michael Ignatieff

2   The first time my mother and I open a can of tuna, I am nine years old. We stand in the doorway of the kitchen, in semi-darkness, the can tilted toward daylight. I want to eat what the kids at school eat: bologna, hot dogs, salami—foods my parents find repugnant because they contain pork and meat by-products, crushed bone and hair glued together by chemicals and fat. Although she has never been able to tolerate the smell of fish, my mother buys the tuna, hoping to satisfy my longing for American food.

3   Indians, of course, do not eat such things.

4   The tuna smells fishy, which surprises me because I can't remember anyone's tuna sandwich actually smelling like fish. And the tuna in those sandwiches doesn't look like this, pink and shiny, like an internal organ. In fact, this looks similar to the bad foods my mother doesn't want me to eat. She is silent, holding her face away from the can while peering into it like a half-blind bird.

5   "What's wrong with it?" I ask.

6   She has no idea. My mother does not know that the tuna everyone else's mothers made for them was tuna salad.

7   "Do you think it's botulism[1]?"

---

[1] Botulism is a serious illness caused by eating improperly preserved food.

8  I have never seen botulism, but I have read about it, just as I have read about but never eaten steak and kidney pie.

9  There is so much my parents don't know. They are not like other parents, and they disappoint me and my sister. They are supposed to help us negotiate the world outside, teach us the signs, the clues to proper behavior: what to eat and how to eat it.

10  We have expectations, and my parents fail to meet them, especially my mother, who works full time. I don't understand what it means, to have a mother who works outside and inside the home; I notice only the ways in which she disappoints me. She doesn't show up for school plays. She doesn't make chocolate-frosted cupcakes for my class. At night, if I want her attention, I have to sit in the kitchen and talk to her while she cooks the evening meal, attentive to every third or fourth word I say.

11  We throw the tuna away. This time my mother is disappointed. I go to school with tuna eaters. I see their sandwiches, yet cannot explain the discrepancy between them and the stinking, oily fish in my mother's hand. We do not understand so many things, my mother and I.

## Second Read

- Reread the essay to answer these text-dependent questions.
- Write any additional questions you have about the text in your Reader/Writer Notebook.

1. **Key Ideas and Details:** Use evidence from the essay to explain why Kothari says her mother disappoints her.

2. **Craft and Structure:** What senses does Kothari appeal to in her descriptions of the can of tuna? Give examples for each. Then explain how these descriptions help to support Kothari's conclusion, "We do not understand so many things, my mother and I."

## My Notes

# Author's Stylebook: Description

## Working from the Text

3. How does this writer share elements of her culture through her descriptive details? Give examples.

4. Use the table below to record and evaluate the writer's use of sensory details. Write at least four examples of sensory details in the table. Then analyze each example to understand the effect the writer is trying to create. Finally, evaluate each detail's effectiveness in conveying the writer's experience.

| Sensory Detail | Analyze the Effect | Evaluate How Effective It Is |
|---|---|---|
|  |  |  |
|  |  |  |
|  |  |  |
|  |  |  |

## Language and Writer's Craft: Clauses

Clauses add variety to writing as well as help to convey meaning. Writers use a variety of clauses to enhance their writing.

**Adverbial clauses** (often beginning with *after*, *as far as*, *before*, *even though*, *if*, *no matter how*, *that*, *while*, or *where*) describe a verb in the sentence's main clause. An adverbial clause answers questions such as *when*?, *why*?, *how*?, or *to what degree*?

> **Example:** At night, if I want her attention, I have to sit in the kitchen and talk to her <u>while she cooks the evening meal</u>, attentive to every third or fourth word I say.

**Noun clauses** perform the same functions in a sentence as nouns. A noun clause answers such questions as *who*?, *whom*?, or *what*?

> **Example:** I don't understand <u>what it means</u>, to have a mother who works outside and inside the home; I notice only the ways in which she disappoints me.

**Adjectival clauses** (often beginning with *that*, *which*, *who*, *whom*, or *whose*) describe a noun in the sentence's main clause. An adjectival clause answers questions such as *which one*? or *what kind*?

> **Example:** I don't understand what it means, to have a mother <u>who works outside and inside the home</u>; I notice only the ways in which she disappoints me.

**PRACTICE** Think about the purpose of each of the above underlined clauses on the narrative, and note these purposes in the space provided.

## Writing to Sources: Explanatory Text

Write an essay that explains the author's use of a can of tuna as a symbol of a cultural difference. Discuss the author's use of specific words and figurative language to describe the characters' ideas about the tuna. How does this narrative technique engage readers and help them to interact with the story? Be sure to:

- Begin with a clear thesis statement that introduces the topic of the symbol and your view on how the writer uses it to engage readers.
- Include direct quotations and specific examples and details from the text to support your thesis statement. Introduce and punctuate all quotations correctly.
- Use a coherent organizational structure that shows how your ideas are connected and provide a concluding statement that follows from and supports the information.

# Elements of a Graphic Novel

**LEARNING STRATEGIES:**
Graphic Organizer,
Summarizing, Note-taking

My Notes

## Learning Targets

- Examine the narrative elements of a graphic novel.
- Relate aspects of cultural perspective to literature.
- Create a graphic panel with dialogue.

## Preview

In this activity, you will read a graphic novel and compare its presentation of historical events to an informational text.

## Features of a Graphic Novel

Graphic novels are cartoon drawings that tell a story and are published as a book. As you explore *Persepolis*, you should note the distinct features that characterize the genre. Following is a list of terms to use when referring to the novel both in your writing and speaking.

**Panel**-squares or rectangles that contain a single image

**Gutters**-space between panels

**Dialogue Balloons**-contain communication between/among characters

**Thought Bubbles**-contain a character's thoughts shared only with the reader

**Captions**-provide information about the scene or character

**Sound Effects**-visual clues about sounds in the scene

Preview the excerpt of the graphic novel to identify its features. Then label the following image using the terms provided.

## Setting a Purpose for Reading

- As you read a chapter from *Persepolis*, record details of the key narrative elements of the story in the My Notes space. Also generate a list of the characteristics of a graphic novel that the author uses to create the narrative.
- Circle unknown words and phrases. Try to determine the meaning of the words by using context clues, word parts, or a dictionary.

## ABOUT THE AUTHOR

Marjane Satrapi grew up in Tehran, Iran. As a child, she observed the increasing loss of civil liberties in her country. At the age of 14, her parents sent her to Austria to escape the turmoil in Iran. After returning to Iran for a brief period as an adult, Satrapi moved to France, where she works as an illustrator and author of children's books.

## Graphic Novel

PERSEPOLIS by Marjane Satrapi

**My Notes**

**shah:** a king of Iran

# Elements of a Graphic Novel

## My Notes

dynasties: families of rulers
succeeded: ruled after

Aryans: Caucasians

**My Notes**

**frivolities:** trivial things

# Elements of a Graphic Novel

**My Notes**

My Notes

# Elements of a Graphic Novel

**My Notes**

**royalist:** person who supports a king

My Notes

# Elements of a Graphic Novel

## Second Read

- Reread the graphic novel excerpt to answer these text-dependent questions.
- Write any additional questions you have about the text in your Reader/Writer Notebook.

1. **Craft and Structure:** What is the purpose of the graphic novel? How do the words and format of the graphic novel relate to that purpose?

2. **Key Ideas and Details:** Look at the panel on page 136 in which the narrator is pressed between her mother and grandmother. What can you infer from the art that is not stated directly in the text? What clues can you use to make this inference?

3. **Craft and Structure:** Why does the narrator compare the wait for her father to come home to "the same silence as before a storm"?

4. **Craft and Structure:** What do you notice about the dominance of black or white in each illustration on page 137? How do the illustrations support the text of the story?

5. **Craft and Structure:** Why does the grandmother say, "If I die now at least I'll be a martyr! Grandma martyr!"

6. **Craft and Structure:** At one point in the excerpt, the author switches from showing what is happening in the narrator's house to showing the historical events that the grandmother is describing. Why do you think she chooses to show this flashback?

7. **Craft and Structure:** At the end of the excerpt, we see the narrator reading a book called *The Reasons for the Revolution* and saying that she decided to read all the books she could. How does this help to bring this part of the story to a satisfying close?

## Working from the Text

8. Use the following graphic organizer to sort your annotations.

| Narrative Elements | Details from the Narrative | Characteristics of the Graphic Novel |
| --- | --- | --- |
| Setting | | |
| Character | | |
| Point of View | | |
| Sequence of Events | | |
| Theme | | |

**My Notes**

# Elements of a Graphic Novel

9. Read the informational text about the Iranian Revolution that your teacher provides. Create a Venn diagram to compare and contrast the effect of presenting this piece of history in a graphic novel form and in prose.

## Narrative Writing Prompt

Take the narrative that you wrote for Activity 2.5 and create a series of panel drawings that include dialogue. Be sure to:

- Include narrative elements of setting, character, point of view, sequence of events, and theme throughout the graphic panels.
- Use dialogue balloons and narrator blocks effectively.

# Telling a Story with Poetry

## Learning Targets
- Analyze a poem for the author's use of details, diction, and imagery to convey a cultural perspective.
- Write an explanatory text that analyzes the use of narrative elements in poetry.

## Preview
In this activity, you will read two narrative poems and then compare how each writer uses narrative elements.

LEARNING STRATEGIES:
TP-CASTT, Marking the Text, Close Reading, Drafting, Sharing and Responding

**My Notes**

## Setting a Purpose for Reading
- As you read the following poems, look for narrative elements. Make connections to the memoirs and excerpts you have read.
- Circle unknown words and phrases. Try to determine the meaning of the words by using context clues, word parts, or a dictionary.

### ABOUT THE AUTHOR
Chitra Banerjee Divakaruni (1956–) was born in India, but she has spent much of her life in the United States. Her writing has won numerous awards, including the American Book Award for her short story collection *Arranged Marriage*. Divakaruni sets her works primarily in India and the United States. Divakaruni began her writing career as a poet, but she has branched out into other genres such as short stories and novels.

### ABOUT THE AUTHOR
Rita Dove (1952–) was born in Akron, Ohio. She is a gifted poet and writer who has won numerous prestigious awards. In 1976, she won the Pulitzer Prize for Poetry for her collection of poems *Thomas and Beulah*, which are roughly based on her grandparents' lives. Ms. Dove has served as the nation's Poet Laureate, read her poetry at the White House under different presidents, and appeared on several television programs. She taught creative writing for many years and currently is a professor of English at the University of Virginia.

## My Notes

**querulous:** complaining
**disgruntled:** unhappy

**translucent:** partly transparent
**resistant:** opposing

### Poetry

# Woman with kite

*by* Chitra Banerjee Divakaruni

Meadow of crabgrass, faded dandelions,
**querulous** child-voices. She takes
from her son's **disgruntled** hands the spool
of a kite that will not fly.
5  Pulls on the heavy string, ground-glass rough
between her thumb and finger. Feels the kite,
**translucent** purple square, rise in a **resistant** arc,
flapping against the wind. Kicks off her chappals[1],
tucks up her kurta[2] so she can run with it,
10  light flecking off her hair as when she was
sexless-young. Up, up

past the puff-cheeked clouds, she
follows it, her eyes slit-smiling at the sun.
She has forgotten her tugging children, their
15  *give me, give me* wails. She sprints
backwards, sure-footed, she cannot
fail, connected to the air, she
is flying, the wind blows through her, takes
her red dupatta[3], mark of marriage.
20  And she laughs like a woman should never laugh

so the two widows on the park bench
stare and huddle their white-veiled heads
to gossip-whisper. The children have fallen,
breathless, in the grass behind.

---

[1] **Chappals** are a kind of open-toed, T-strap sandal.
[2] A **kurta** is a long, loose, shirt worn by women in India.
[3] A **dupatta** is a scarf or head covering.

25 She laughs like wild water, shaking
   her braids loose, she laughs
   like a fire, the spool a blur
   between her hands,
   the string unraveling all the way
30 to release it into space, her life,
   into its bright, weightless orbit.

## Second Read

- Reread the poem to answer these text-dependent questions.
- Write any additional questions you have about the text in your Reader/Writer Notebook.

1. **Key Ideas and Details:** What words and images does Divakaruni use to describe the woman's children and to describe the woman as she runs with the kite? Why do you think she chooses this language to describe the characters?

2. **Craft and Structure:** At the end of the poem, Divakaruni says that the string unravels all the way to release the woman's life "into its bright, weightless orbit." What metaphor is the writer using here, and what is its effect?

Poetry

# Grape Sherbet

*by* Rita Dove

The day? Memorial.
After the grill
Dad appears with his masterpiece—
swirled snow, **gelled** light.
5  We cheer. The recipe's
a secret, and he fights
a smile, his cap turned up
so the bib resembles a duck.
That morning we galloped
10  through the grassed-over mounds
and named each stone
for a lost milk tooth. Each **dollop**
of sherbet, later,
is a miracle,
15  like salt on a melon that makes it sweeter.

Everyone agrees—it's wonderful!
It's just how we imagined lavender
would taste. The diabetic grandmother
stares from the porch, a torch
20  of pure refusal.

We thought no one was lying
there under our feet,
we thought it
was a joke. I've been trying
25  to remember the taste,
but it doesn't exist.
Now I see why
you bothered,
father.

**gelled:** jelly-like

**dollop:** a scoop

## Second Read

- Reread the poem to answer these text-dependent questions.
- Write any additional questions you have about the text in your Reader/Writer Notebook.

3. **Craft and Structure:** Cite the details that Dove uses to describe her father's homemade grape sherbet. Why does she say the taste "doesn't exist"?

4. **Key Ideas and Details:** Dove closes the poem by saying, "Now I see why you bothered, father." What shift is conveyed at the end of the poem?

## Working from the Text

5. With your teacher and classmates, use TP-CASTT to analyze "Woman with Kite." As you have learned, the acronym TP-CASTT stands for title, paraphrase, connotation, attitude, shifts, title, and theme.

- **Title:** Make a prediction about what you think the title means before you read the poem.
- **Paraphrase:** Restate the poem in your own words. What is the poem about? Rephrase difficult sections word for word.
- **Connotation:** Look beyond the literal meanings of key words and images to their associations.
- **Attitude:** What is the speaker's attitude? What is the author's attitude? How does the author feel about the speaker, the characters, and the subject?
- **Title:** Reexamine the title. What do you think it means now within the context of the poem?
- **Theme:** Think of the literal and metaphorical layers of the poem, and then determine the overall theme.

**My Notes**

# Telling a Story with Poetry

6. Create a graphic organizer that identifies the narrative elements in "Woman with Kite." Focus on how the narrative elements are addressed in the format of a poem.

7. With a partner, analyze "Grape Sherbet" using TP-CASTT. Be sure to annotate the text for the elements of a narrative, cultural references, and perspective.

## Writing to Sources: Explanatory Text

Explain how the author of each poem uses narrative elements to convey a cultural perspective. How does each author use details and imagery? What specific words and phrases or figurative language are used to show the narrator's perspective? Be sure to:

- Begin with a clear thesis that introduces the title, the author, and the narrator's cultural perspective of each poem.
- Include specific examples and relevant details to show how the authors use narrative elements effectively in their poetry.
- Use a coherent organizational structure and employ transitions effectively to highlight similarities and differences in the way each author uses narrative elements.
- Include direct quotations if appropriate; punctuate all quotations correctly.
- Use an appropriate voice and a variety of phrases to add interest to your writing.
- Provide a concluding statement that supports your main point.

# Struggling with Identity: Rethinking Persona

## Learning Targets
- Analyze how an author's persona relates to audience and purpose.
- Identify allusions and connect them to the writer's purpose.
- Practice effective speaking and listening in a Socratic Seminar discussion.

LEARNING STRATEGIES:
Marking the Text, Rereading, Socratic Seminar, Discussion Groups

## Persona
**Persona** is a literary device that writers create in their stories. A **persona** allows an author to express ideas and attitudes that may not reflect his or her own. Think about your own personas. What is your persona with your family versus your persona with friends and at school?

**Literary Terms**
**Persona** is the voice assumed by a writer. It is not necessarily his or her own voice.

## Preview
In this activity, you will read an excerpt from a memoir and analyze the author's persona.

## Setting a Purpose for Reading
- Mark the text for allusions, and use metacognitive markers by placing a ? when you have a question, a ! when you have a strong reaction, and a * when you have a comment.
- Circle unknown words and phrases. Try to determine the meaning of the words by using context clues, word parts, or a dictionary.

**My Notes**

### ABOUT THE AUTHOR
Richard Rodriguez has written extensively about his own life and his struggles to reconcile his origins as the son of Mexican immigrants and his rise through American academia. In his memoir, *The Hunger of Memory*, written in English, his second language, Rodriguez examines how his assimilation into American culture affected his relationship to his Mexican roots.

## Memoir

# Excerpt from
# The Hunger of Memory

*by* Richard Rodriguez

1　I have taken Caliban's[1] advice. I have stolen their books. I will have some run of this isle.

2　Once upon a time, I was a "socially **disadvantaged**" child. An enchantedly happy child. Mine was a childhood of intense family closeness. And extreme public **alienation**.

**disadvantaged:** lacking resources such as education and money
**alienation:** separation

---

[1] Caliban is a monstrous character in Shakespeare's play *The Tempest* who wants to steal the books and magic of another character to gain power.

# Struggling with Identity: Rethinking Persona

**assimilated:** a part of a cultural group

## GRAMMAR & USAGE
### Punctuation for Effect

Writers may place quotation marks around a word to suggest irony or sarcasm. In Paragraph 2, Rodriguez places the term "socially disadvantaged" in quotation marks. This suggests that he finds the euphemism incongruous with his idea of himself—a term others applied to him. As you read, consider why he places "use" in quotation marks in this sentence: "... wasn't it a shame that I wasn't able to 'use' my Spanish ... ."

## GRAMMAR & USAGE
### Sentence Types

An effective way to create rhythm and emphasis in prose is to vary sentence types and lengths. Notice the variety in the first four sentences of paragraph 8. This paragraph begins with a sentence fragment that refers back to the previous sentence. A longer sentence then emphasizes the "year of continuous silence" it describes. Two short sentences then describe the abrupt end of the money. Find another section that includes a variety of sentences types. How does the variety reflect the author's flow of thoughts and his meaning?

**dupe:** a person who has been fooled

**pieties:** religious statements

3 Thirty years later I write this book as a middle-class American man. **Assimilated**.

4 Dark-skinned. To be seen at a Belgravia dinner party. Or in New York. Exotic in a tuxedo. My face is drawn to severe Indian features which would pass notice on the page of a *National Geographic*, but at a cocktail party in Bel Air somebody wonders: "Have you ever thought of doing any high-fashion modeling? Take this card." (In Beverly Hills will this monster make a man.)

5 A lady in a green dress asks, "Didn't we meet at the Thompsons' party last month in Malibu?"

6 And, "What do you do, Mr. Rodriguez?"

7 I write: I am a writer.

8 A part-time writer. When I began this book, five years ago, a fellowship bought me a year of continuous silence in my San Francisco apartment. But the words wouldn't come. The money ran out. So I was forced to take temporary jobs. (I have friends who, with a phone call, can find me well-paying work.) In past months I have found myself in New York. In Los Angeles. Working. With money. Among people with money. And at leisure—a weekend guest in Connecticut; at a cocktail party in Bel Air.

9 Perhaps because I have always, accidentally, been a classmate to children of rich parents, I long ago came to assume my association with their world; came to assume that I could have money, if it was money I wanted. But money, big money, has never been the goal of my life. My story is not a version of Sammy Glick's. I work to support my habit of writing. The great luxury of my life is the freedom to sit at this desk.

10 "Mr? ... "

11 Rodriguez. The name on the door. The name on my passport. The name I carry from my parents—who are no longer my parents, in a cultural sense. This is how I pronounce it: Rich-heard Road-re-guess. This is how I hear it most often.

12 The voice through the microphone says, "Ladies and gentlemen, it is with pleasure that I introduce Mr. Richard Rodriguez."

13 I am invited very often these days to speak about modern education in college auditoriums and in Holiday Inn ballrooms. I go, still feel a calling to act the teacher, though not licensed by the degree. One time my audience is a convention of university administrators; another time high school teachers of English; another time a women's alumnae group.

14 "Mr. Rodriguez has written extensively about contemporary education."

15 Several essays. I have argued particularly against two government programs—affirmative action and bilingual education.

16 "He is a provocative speaker."

17 I have become notorious among certain leaders of America's Ethnic Left. I am considered a **dupe**, an ass, the fool—Tom Brown, the brown Uncle Tom, interpreting the writing on the wall to a bunch of cigar-smoking pharaohs.

18 A dainty white lady at the women's club luncheon approaches the podium after my speech to say, after all, wasn't it a shame that I wasn't able to "use" my Spanish in school. What a shame. But how dare her lady-fingered **pieties** extend to my life!

19  There are those in White America who would anoint me to play out for them some drama of ancestral **reconciliation**. Perhaps because I am marked by indelible color they easily suppose that I am unchanged by social **mobility**, that I can claim unbroken ties with my past. The possibility! At a time when many middle-class children and parents grow distant, apart, no longer speak, romantic solutions appeal.

20  But I reject the role. (Caliban won't ferry a TV crew back to his island, there to recover his roots.)

21  Aztec ruins hold no special interest for me. I do not search Mexican graveyards for ties to unnamable ancestors. I assume I retain certain features of gesture and mood derived from buried lives. I also speak Spanish today. And read Garcia Lorca and García Márquez at my leisure. But what consolation can that fact bring against the knowledge that my mother and father have never heard of Garcia Lorca or García Márquez?

22  What preoccupies me is immediate; the separation I endure with my parents is loss. This is what matters to me; the story of the scholarship boy who returns home one summer from college to discover bewildering silence, facing his parents. This is my story. An American story. Consider me, if you choose, a comic victim of two cultures. This is my situation; writing these pages, surrounded in the room I am in by volumes of Montaigne and Shakespeare and Lawrence. They are mine now.

23  A Mexican woman passes in a black dress. She wears a white apron; she carries a tray of hors d'oeuvres. She must only be asking if there are any I want as she proffers the tray like a wheel of good fortune. I shake my head. No. Does she wonder how I am here? In Bel Air.

24  It is education that has altered my life. Carried me far.

**reconciliation:** rejoining
**mobility:** easy movement

## My Notes

## Second Read
- Reread the excerpt from the memoir to answer these text-dependent questions.
- Write any additional questions you have about the text in your Reader/Writer Notebook.

1. **Craft and Structure:** Reread the footnote about the character Caliban. Rodriguez returns to this literary allusion several times in the essay: when he says he "has stolen their books," when he quotes Shakespeare in saying a monster can "make a man," and when he refers to Caliban "ferrying a TV crew back to his island," a modern updating of a scene in *The Tempest*. Why might Rodriguez identify with this character?

2. **Key Ideas and Details:** Rodriguez says that his parents "are no longer [his] parents, in a cultural sense." What details does he use to develop this idea in the text?

3. **Craft and Structure:** Rodriguez controls the pacing of this narrative text through the use of varied sentence lengths and occasional dialogue. How does the pacing affect us as readers?

## Working from the Text

4. Reread the text, using the guiding questions below to deepen your understanding of Rodriguez's purpose. In groups of four, divide the questions among yourselves. Jot down answers to the questions, and then share your notes with each other.

   • **Allusions:** What allusions are made? How does Rodriguez draw on Shakespeare's *The Tempest*, as well as other literary works, to add depth and meaning to his text (who are Caliban, Uncle Tom, and García Márquez)?

   • **Conflicts:** What forces (either internal or external) are pulling Rodriguez in different directions?

   • **Diction:** What words have strong connotations and which images paint a vivid picture?

   • **Syntax:** Note the use of abrupt, choppy sentence fragments. What effect do they have on your reading?

   • What universal ideas about life and society does Rodriguez convey in this text?

## Introducing the Strategy: Socratic Seminar

A **Socratic Seminar** is a focused discussion that is tied to an essential question, topic, or selected text. You participate by asking questions to initiate a conversation that continues with a series of responses and additional questions. In a Socratic Seminar, you must support your opinions and responses using specific textual evidence.

## Socratic Seminar

Your teacher will lead you in a Socratic Seminar in which you discuss this piece more fully. As you participate in the discussion, keep in mind the norms for group discussions:

- Be prepared—read the texts, complete any research needed, and make notes about points to be discussed.
- Be polite—follow rules for cordial discussions, listen to all ideas, take votes to settle differences on ideas, and set timelines and goals for the discussion.
- Be inquisitive—ask questions to keep the discussion moving, to clarify your understanding of others' ideas, and to challenge ideas and conclusions.
- Be thoughtful—respond to different perspectives in your group, summarize points when needed, and adjust your own thinking in response to evidence and ideas presented within the group.

## Check Your Understanding

Reflect on how the discussion in a Socratic Seminar adds to your understanding of your reading. Also reflect on how the group applied the discussion norms. What worked well? What did not work as well?

### Language and Writer's Craft: Varying Sentence Beginnings

Sentences need not always begin with the subject. Beginning with other structures not only provides variety and interest, but can also give emphasis to an important detail or point. Sentences can begin with a word, a phrase, or a clause:

**Beginning with a word:** <u>Stunned</u>, Gretchen burst into tears.

**Beginning with a phrase:** <u>Unable to believe her eyes</u>, Gretchen burst into tears.

**Beginning with a clause:** <u>Because she was not expecting a surprise party</u>, Gretchen burst into tears.

**PRACTICE** With a partner, review the three examples of sentence beginnings and find examples of each in the texts from the unit.

| Sentence Beginnings | Example from Texts |
|---|---|
| Beginning with a word | |
| Beginning with a phrase | |
| Beginning with a clause | |

Writers who use varied syntax effectively incorporate multiple sentence types in their writing. Select one piece of writing you have completed in this unit to revise for syntactical variety. Be sure to:

- Use at least three different types of sentences.
- Incorporate a variety of sentence beginnings, including beginning with a word, beginning with a phrase, and beginning with a clause.

**My Notes**

# Changes in Perspective

**LEARNING STRATEGIES:**
Brainstorming, Graphic
Organizer, Marking the Text,
Think-Pair-Share, Close Reading

**My Notes**

## Learning Targets

- Analyze tone and diction to track changes in narrative perspective.
- Examine how both internal changes and external changes can affect perspective on experiences.

## Preview

In this activity, you will read an essay and think about changes in the narrator's perspective.

## Setting a Purpose for Reading

- As you read the following essay, use close reading and mark the text for changes in the author's perspective about Thanksgiving.
- Circle unknown words and phrases. Try to determine the meaning of the words by using context clues, word parts, or a dictionary.

**ABOUT THE AUTHOR**

Jennifer New lives in Iowa City, Iowa, and writes regularly for online and other publications. She describes herself as a dedicated writer whose "mind is forever on the page, playing with language and new ideas for books or articles."

Essay

# Thanksgiving:
## A Personal History

*by* Jennifer New

**mesmerizing:** fascinating

*From the mythic Midwest of my childhood to the* **mesmerizing** *Chicago of later years, this holiday has always evoked a place.*

1  In trying to explain what was missing from her life, how it felt hollow, a friend recently described to me a Thanksgiving she'd once had. It was just two friends and her. They had made dinner and had a wonderful time. "Nothing special happened," she explained, "But we were all funny and vibrant. I thought life would always be like that."

2  This is the holiday mind game: the too-sweet memory of that one shining moment coupled with the painful certainty that the rest of the world must be sitting at a Norman Rockwell[1] table feeling loved. It only gets worse when you begin deconstructing the purpose of such holidays. Pondering the true origins of Thanksgiving, for example, always leaves me feeling more than a bit ashamed and not the least bit festive. Don't even get me started on Christmas.

---

[1] **Norman Rockwell** was a painter whose subject was small-town life.

**3** Every year, I think more and more of divorcing myself from these blockbuster holidays. I want to be free from both the material **glut** and the Pandora's box[2] of emotions that opens every November and doesn't safely close until Jan. 2. Chief among these is the longing for that perfect day that my friend described, the wishful balance of tradition, meaning and belonging. But as an only child in a family that has never been long on tradition, I've usually felt my nose pressed against the glass, never part of the long, lively table and yet not quite able to scrap it all to spend a month in Zanzibar[3].

**glut:** excessive amount

**My Notes**

**4** When I was a kid, of course, there was none of this philosophizing. I was too thrilled by the way the day so perfectly matched the song we'd sung in school. You know the one: "Over the river and through the woods. …" Across the gray Midwestern landscape, ·driving up and down rolling hills, my parents and I would go to my grandmother's house. From the back seat, I'd peer out at the endless fields of corn, any stray stalks now standing brittle and bleached against the frostbitten black soil. Billboards and gas stations occasionally punctuated the landscape. Everything seemed unusually still, sucked dry of life by winter and the odd quiet of a holiday weekend.

**5** In less than an hour, we'd turn off the interstate, entering more familiar territory. My child's mind had created mythic markers for the approach to my grandparents'. First came the sign for a summer campground with its wooden cartoon characters, now caught alone and cold in their faded swimsuits. Farther up the road, a sentry-like boulder stood atop a hill, the final signpost before we pulled into my grandparents' lane. Suddenly, the sky was obscured by the long, reaching branches of old-growth oak and elm trees. A thick underbrush, a collage of grays and browns, extended from the road and beyond to the 13 acres of Iowa woodland on which their house was situated. A frozen creek bisected the property at the bottom of a large hill. The whole kingdom was enchanted by deer, a long orange fox, battalions of squirrels and birds of every hue.

**6** Waiting at the end of the lane was not the house from the song, that home to which the sleigh knew the way. A few years earlier my grandparents had built a new house, all rough-hewn, untreated wood and exposed beams, in lieu of the white clapboard farmhouse where they had raised their children. I vaguely understood that this piece of contemporary architecture, circa 1974, was a twist on that traditional tune, but to me it was better: a magical soaring place full of open spaces, surprises and light.

**7** Upon entering the house, I'd stand and look up. Floating above were windows that seemed impossibly high, their curtains controlled by an electric switch. On another wall was an Oriental rug so vast it seemed to have come from a palace. Hidden doors, a glass fireplace that warmed rooms on both sides and faucets sprouting water in high arcs fascinated me during each visit. In the basement, I'd roam through a virtual labyrinth of

### WORD CONNECTIONS

**Roots and Affixes**

*Philosophizing* contains two roots. The root *soph* comes from the Greek word *sophos*, meaning "wise." This root also appears in *sophistry*, *sophisticated*, and *sophomore*. The root *phil* comes from the Greek *philos*, which means "love of something." It also appears in *philology*, *philanthropy*, *philately*, and *philharmonic*.

*Empathy* contains the root *path*, from the Greek word *pathos*, meaning "feeling, suffering, or disease." This root also appears in *pathology*, *pathetic*, and *sympathy*. The suffix *-y* indicates that the word is a noun. The prefix *em-* means "with."

---

[2] In Greek mythology, **Pandora's box** was a jar that contained all the evils of the world. Pandora, the first woman created by the gods, opened the jar out of curiosity and let all the evils out.

[3] **Zanzibar** is a group of islands in Tanzania in East Africa. It represents a place that is exotic and hard to reach.

## My Notes

rooms filled with the possessions of relatives now gone. Butter urns, antique dolls and photo albums of stern-faced people competed fantastically with the intercoms and other gadgetry of the house.

8  I see now that it would have been a great setting for gaggles of cousins: having pillow fights, trudging through the snowy woods, dressing up in my grandmother's old gowns and coonskin hat. Instead, I recall holidays as having a museum-like hush. Alone with the friends I'd created in my mind and the belongings of deceased generations, I was content. Upstairs, a football game hummed from the TV, a mixer whirred in the kitchen and the stereo piped one of my grandmother's classical music 8-tracks from room to room. But the house, with its carpeting and wallpaper, absorbed it all. As I'd seen in an illustration from one of my books, I could picture the house as a cross-section, looking into each room where, alone, my family members, read, cooked, watched TV and napped. Pulling the camera farther away, the great house glowed in the violet of early nightfall, as smoke from the chimney wafted through the woodland and then over the endless dark fields, a scattering of tiny, precise stars overhead.

9  The moment that brought us there together—my grandparents, mom and dad, my uncle and his partner, and my great-grandmother—was perhaps the most quiet moment of all. Thanksgiving supper, held in the dim light of late afternoon, was a restrained meal, as though it were a play and we had all lost our scripts. Only the clank of silverware, the passing of dishes and the sharing of small talk seemed to carry us around and through it.

10  If I could go back in time and enter the minds of everyone at that table, I would not be surprised if only my great-grandmother and I were really happy to be there. My grandfather: walking in his fields, calculating numbers from stocks and commodities, fixing a piece of machinery. My parents: with friends in a warmer climate, "The White Album" on the stereo and some unexpected cash in their wallets. My uncle and his partner Bob: willing themselves back home and beyond this annual homage. (Bob himself was a mystery to me, a barrel-chested man who laughed a lot and wore—at least in the one mental snapshot I have of him—a wild patterned smock top and a gold medallion. No one had explained Bob's relationship to our family, so I assigned him a role in my own universe, much like the cartoon characters at the campground or the sentinel rock. I made sense of him and marveled at his ebullience.) And then my grandmother: thinking she should enjoy this, but tired from the cooking and management of the meal, more looking forward to a game later in the evening.

niches: ornamental recesses in a wall for displaying objects

## WORD CONNECTIONS

**Multiple Meaning Words**

*Niche* is a French word. It means both "ornamental recesses in a wall for displaying objects," as it is used in Jennifer New's essay, and "a special market for one's skills."

11  That left my great-grandmother and me. Both of us were happy to have this time with family, this mythic meal in which we both believed. And, really, everyone else was there for us: to instill tradition in me, to uphold it for her. Isn't that what most holidays are about? Everyone in the middle gets left holding the bag, squirming in their seats, while the young and old enjoy it. Within a few years, though, by the time I hit adolescence, I'd had my fill of tradition. Not the boulder, the huge house with its secret **niches** nor even the golden turkey served on an antique platter that my grandmother unearthed every year from the depths of a buffet held any appeal. Gone was my ability to see the world through the almost psychedelic rose-colored glasses of childhood. I also hadn't gained any of the empathy that comes with age. Instead, I was stuck with one foot in cynicism and the other in hypersensitivity. The beloved, magical house now looked to me like a looming example of misspent money and greed. My great-grandmother, so tiny and helpless at this point, now struck me as macabre and frightening, her papery white skin on the verge of tearing.

**My Notes**

12 Perhaps my parents took my behavior, moody and unkind as it was, as a sign that traditions are sometimes meant to be broken. I'm not sure whether they were using me to save themselves from the repetition of the annual holiday, or if they were saving the rest of the family from me. Either way, we stopped pulling into the wooded lane that fourth Thursday in November. For the next few years, we'd drive instead to Chicago. My mind managed to create similar mythic land markers: the rounded pyramids near Dekalb, Ill., which I've since realized are storage buildings; the office parks of the western suburbs where I imagined myself working as a young, single woman, à la Mary Tyler Moore; the large neon sign of a pair of lips that seemed to be a greeting especially for us, rather than the advertising for a dry cleaner that they actually were. About this point, at the neon lips, the buildings around us grew older and darker, and on the horizon the skyscrapers blinked to life in the cold twilight air. The slow enveloping by these mammoth structures was as heady as the approach down my grandparents' lane had been years earlier.

13 We would stay at a friend's apartment, or better yet, in a downtown hotel. I was mesmerized by the clip of urban life. On the wide boulevard of Michigan Avenue, I'd follow women in their fat fur coats, amazed and **appalled**. The wisps of hairs from the coat closed tight around their necks, hugging brightly made-up faces. Leather boots tapped along city streets, entering the dance of a revolving door or stepping smartly into the back of a yellow cab. The mezzanines[4] of department stores—Lord & Taylor, Marshall Fields—dazzled me; the glint of light reflected on makeup-counter mirrors, the intoxicating waft of perfume on a **cacophony** of voices. And my parents, freed of their familiar roles, seemed young and bright. They negotiated maître d's and complex museum maps; they ordered wine from long lists and knew what to tip.

14 Of course, like that adolescent hero, Holden Caulfield, I was that thing we hated most: a hypocrite. I couldn't see the irony in my fascination with the urban splendor vs. my disdain for my grandparents' hard-earned home. Or that my parents possessed the same qualities and talents no matter where we were. I definitely couldn't pan out far enough to see that I was just a teenager yearning for a bigger world, a change of pace.

**appalled:** disgusted

**cacophony:** harsh sound

---

[4] A **mezzanine** is a partial story between two floors of a building.

# Changes in Perspective

GRAMMAR & USAGE
Dashes

Remember that when you want to emphasize parenthetical information, you may use dashes rather than commas or parentheses. Jennifer New uses this technique in her sentence "This family—suburban, Jewish, bursting with noise and stories—so unlike my own … ." The parenthetical information is crucial to understanding the specific ways the families are different. Look back at the sentence "The mezzanines of department stores—Lord & Taylor, Marshall Fields—dazzled me … ." Why does New want to emphasize the names of the stores?

**eccentricities:** strange behaviors
**neuroses:** emotional illnesses

## My Notes

15 During these city trips, my sense of Thanksgiving shifted. No longer was it a wishbone drying on the kitchen windowsill, or foil-wrapped leftovers in the refrigerator. Instead, late November connoted the moneyed swirl of holiday lights flickering on the Magnificent Mile as an "El" train clamored over the Loop. It was the bellows of drivers and the urbane banter of pedestrians, weighted down with packages. The soft glow of restaurants—the darker the better—cut me so far adrift from my day-to-day world that I might as well have traveled to another continent. Far away from the immense quietude of the house in the woods, the bellhops now served as my uncles, shop clerks and waiters my cousins, and the patrons in theater lobbies and museums became my extended family. Late at night, I'd creep out of my bed to the window and watch with amazement as the city below continued to move to the beat of an all-night rumba. Without having to be invited or born into it, I was suddenly, automatically, part of something bigger and noisier than my small family.

16 In years since, I've cobbled together whatever Thanksgiving is available to me. After college, friends and I, waylaid on the West Coast without family, would whip up green-bean casserole and cranberries, reinventing the tastes of childhood with varying success. There were always broken hearts and pining for home at these occasions, but they were full of warmth and camaraderie. Then, for several years, my husband and I battled a sea of crowds in various airports, piecing together flights from one coast to the other in order to share the day with his family.

17 On my first visit, I was startled by the table set for more than 20 people. This was a family in which relatives existed in heaps, all appearing in boldface and underlined with their various **eccentricities**. **Neuroses** and guarded secrets, petty jealousies and unpaid debts were all placed on the back burner for this one day while people reacquainted themselves, hugging away any uneasiness. This family—suburban, Jewish, bursting with noise and stories—so unlike my own, made me teeter between a thrilling sense of finally having a place at a long table, and a claustrophobic yearning for a quiet spot in a dark café. Or, better yet, in a dark and quiet woodland.

**18** This year for Thanksgiving, I will rent movies, walk with the dog down still streets and have a meal with my parents and husband. Throughout the day, I'll imagine myself moving through the big house in the woods that my grandparents sold years ago. Padding down carpeted hallways, I'll rediscover hidden doorways and unpack that platter from the buffet. A bag of antique marbles will open its contents to me as the grandfather clock chimes. Counting "12," I'll look outside onto the lawn and watch a family of deer make their nightly crossing through the now barren vegetable garden, jumping over the fence that my husband and I put in their path, and into the neighbor's yard. I'll press my nose against the cold glass and wish myself outside and beyond the still of the house.

## Second Read

- Reread the essay to answer these text-dependent questions.
- Write any additional questions you have about the text in your Reader/Writer Notebook.

1. **Craft and Structure:** What clues can you use to determine the meaning of *deconstructing* in the sentence, "It only gets worse when you begin deconstructing the purpose of such holidays"? Consider both your knowledge of roots and prefixes and the context.

2. **Craft and Structure:** Use a dictionary to determine the meanings of the words *sentry* and *gaggles*. What is the effect of the writer's choice of words to describe a "sentry-like" boulder and "gaggles" of cousins?

3. **Key Ideas and Details:** Reread the author's description of what she thinks Thanksgiving should be in the third paragraph. What does the author struggle with as her perspective of Thanksgiving changes? Give evidence from the text to support your answer.

**My Notes**

4. **Craft and Structure:** Reread the footnote about Pandora's box in Greek mythology. The author uses an allusion to Pandora's box as a metaphor for the emotions she feels between Thanksgiving and New Year's. Why do you think she chooses to use this allusion?

5. **Knowledge and Ideas:** The author states that most holidays are about instilling tradition in younger family members and upholding it for older ones. She writes, "Isn't that what most holidays are about? Everyone in the middle gets left holding the bag, squirming in their seats, while the young and old enjoy it." Do you think that she gives enough evidence to prove this point valid for her readers?

6. **Craft and Structure:** How would you describe Jennifer New's purpose in writing this essay? What effect might she want to have on readers by sharing her own experiences with Thanksgivings through the years?

7. **Key Ideas and Details:** How does the author's last sentence, "I'll press my nose against the cold glass and wish myself outside and beyond the still of the house," build on her earlier image of being a child with her "nose pressed against the glass, never part of the long, lively table and not yet quite able to scrap it all"?

## Working from the Text

8. Use the following graphic organizer to record the author's changing perspective about Thanksgiving:

| Time Period | Tone toward the Thanksgiving Holiday with Textual Evidence | Words or Phrases Used to Indicate a Transition to This Time Period |
|---|---|---|
| Childhood | | "When I was a kid …" |
| | | |
| | | |
| | | |
| | | |

# Changes in Perspective

## My Notes

9. In pairs, review the narrative and share the following topics, assigning each person to one aspect of narrative writing to report and share findings to the rest of the group.

**Student 1:** Review the narrative and identify each of the narrative techniques (dialogue, pacing, and description) from this unit. For each of the identified techniques, evaluate the effectiveness of the technique in the narrative.

**Student 2:** Review the narrative and describe each of the narrative elements of the story (setting, a sequence of events, a point of view, a theme, and characters).

10. Choose a holiday or celebration and describe how your perspective on or attitude toward the holiday may have changed over time, from childhood to adolescence. Then describe how you think it might change as you get older.

**Holiday/Celebration:**

**Childhood Perspective:**

**Adolescent Perspective:**

**Future Perspective:**

## Check Your Understanding

Scan the text "Thanksgiving: A Personal History." Then write a summary of the major time periods in the author's life and how her attitude changed in each time period.

My Notes

## Drafting the Embedded Assessment

Draft a narrative about an incident, either real or imagined, that conveys a cultural perspective. You can use your notes from the Perspectives brainstorming activity you completed earlier to consider how cultural perspectives change over time. Which experience(s) will effectively demonstrate a specific cultural perspective? Which narrative techniques will you use to develop your narrative? Be sure to:

- Introduce the characters and situation and establish an effective point of view.
- Use appropriate narrative techniques to develop the incident and your cultural perspective.
- Use a logical sequence of events to develop the events in your narrative.
- Incorporate precise words and phrases and sensory and figurative language to convey a vivid picture of the experience.
- Provide a conclusion that reflects on the experience and related cultural perspective.

 **Independent Reading Checkpoint**

Review your independent reading. Analyze how one or more selections reflect a particular aspect of culture. Which narrative techniques do the authors use to effectively convey their cultural perspective? How can you use your observations and what you have learned as you write a narrative reflecting your own cultural perspective?

# Writing a Narrative

## ASSIGNMENT

Your assignment is to write a narrative about an incident, either real or imagined, that conveys a cultural perspective. Throughout this unit, you have studied narratives in multiple genres, and you have explored a variety of cultural perspectives. You will now select the genre you feel is most appropriate to convey a real or fictional experience that includes one or more elements of culture.

| | |
|---|---|
| **Prewriting/Planning:** Take time to plan your narrative. | ▪ Have you reviewed your notes about your culture and the groups (subcultures) to which you belong, in order to focus on cultural perspectives? |
| | ▪ How will you select personal experiences related to culture that you could classify as stories worth telling? |
| | ▪ What strategies will you use to help create a sequence of events, specific details, and images to convey your experience? |
| | ▪ How will you choose a narrative genre that will best suit your writing needs? |
| | ▪ How can you use your writing group to help you select a genre type and story idea that would be worth telling? |
| **Drafting:** Choose the structure of your narrative and create a draft. | ▪ How will you include important narrative techniques, such as sequencing of events, dialogue, pacing, and description to develop experiences and characters? |
| | ▪ How can you use the mentor texts of your narrative genre to help guide your drafting? |
| **Evaluating and Revising:** Create opportunities to review and incorporate changes to make your narrative better. | ▪ How can you use the Scoring Guide to ensure your narrative reflects the expectations for narrative techniques and use of language? |
| | ▪ How can you use your writing groups to solicit helpful feedback and suggestions for revision? |
| **Editing/Publishing:** Confirm that your final draft is ready for publication. | ▪ What resources can you consult to correct mistakes and produce a technically sound document? |

## Reflection

After completing this Embedded Assessment, think about how you completed the assignment. Write a reflection responding to the following questions:

1. What have you learned about how an author controls the way an audience responds to his or her writing?

2. What new narrative techniques did you include in your narrative to create an effect in your reader's response to the narrative?

# SCORING GUIDE

| Scoring Criteria | Exemplary | Proficient | Emerging | Incomplete |
| --- | --- | --- | --- | --- |
| **Ideas** | The narrative<br>• engages the reader through interesting lead-in and details<br>• uses narrative techniques (dialogue, pacing, description) to develop experiences and characters<br>• provides a conclusion that resolves issues and draws the story to a close. | The narrative<br>• describes an incident and orients the reader<br>• uses narrative techniques effectively to develop characters and experiences<br>• provides a clear conclusion to the story. | The narrative<br>• does not describe a cultural perspective or lacks essential details to orient the reader<br>• includes few narrative techniques to develop characters<br>• provides an unsatisfying conclusion that does not resolve the story. | The narrative<br>• does not contain essential details to establish a cultural perspective<br>• does not effectively use narrative techniques to develop the story<br>• does not provide a conclusion. |
| **Structure** | The narrative<br>• follows the structure of the genre with well-sequenced events<br>• clearly orients the reader and uses effective transitions to link ideas and events<br>• demonstrates a consistent point of view. | The narrative<br>• follows the structure of the genre and includes a sequence of events<br>• orients the reader and uses transitions to create a coherent whole<br>• uses a mostly consistent point of view. | The narrative<br>• may follow only parts of the structure of the genre<br>• presents disconnected events and limited coherence<br>• contains a point of view that is not appropriate for the focus of the narrative. | The narrative<br>• does not follow the structure of the genre<br>• includes few if any events and no coherence<br>• contains inconsistent and confusing points of view. |
| **Use of Language** | The narrative<br>• purposefully uses descriptive language, telling details, and vivid imagery<br>• uses meaningful dialogue when appropriate to advance the narrative<br>• demonstrates error-free spelling and use of standard English conventions. | The narrative<br>• uses descriptive language and telling details<br>• uses direct and/or indirect dialogue when appropriate<br>• demonstrates general command of conventions and spelling; minor errors do not interfere with meaning. | The narrative<br>• uses limited descriptive language or details<br>• contains little or no dialogue<br>• demonstrates limited command of conventions and spelling; errors interfere with meaning. | The narrative<br>• uses no descriptive language or details<br>• contains no effective use of dialogue<br>• contains numerous errors in grammar and conventions that interfere with meaning. |

# Previewing Embedded Assessment 2 and Thinking About Argument

## My Notes

## Learning Targets

- Identify the knowledge and skills needed to complete Embedded Assessment 2 successfully and reflect on prior learning that supports the knowledge and skills needed.
- Explore the issue of justice as a potential topic of an argument.

## Making Connections

In the first part of this unit, you explored a variety of narratives and told a memorable story that conveyed a cultural perspective. In this part of the unit, you will expand on your writing skills by writing an argumentative essay to persuade an audience to agree with your position on an issue.

## Essential Questions

Based on your learning from the first part of this unit, how would you respond to the Essential Questions now?

1. How can cultural experiences and perspectives be conveyed through memorable narratives?

2. What issues resonate across cultures, and how are arguments developed in response?

## Developing Vocabulary

Look at your Reader/Writer Notebook and review the new vocabulary you learned in the first part of this unit. Which words do you know in depth, and which words do you need to learn more about?

## Unpacking Embedded Assessment 2

Read the assignment for Embedded Assessment 2: Writing an Argumentative Essay.

> Your assignment is to develop an argument about an issue that resonates across cultures. You will choose a position, target audience, and effective genre to convey your argument to a wide audience.

In your own words, summarize what you will need to know to complete this assessment successfully. With your class, create a graphic organizer to represent the skills and knowledge you will need to complete the tasks identified in the Embedded Assessment.

## Arguing for Justice

An argument usually focuses on a topic that is of interest to many people. The topic may be one with many different sides, or it may be one with two sides: for and against. In this last part of the unit, you will explore issues of justice as an example of a topic on which people take definite positions.

### INDEPENDENT READING LINK

**Read and Research**

In this part of the unit, you will be reading informational texts as well as some well-known speeches. Speeches are often made to persuade an audience about a topic. Brainstorm and make a list of issues about which you have a definite position. Research to locate famous speeches or informational texts that present one or both sides of one or more of the issues on your list.

Societies create systems of justice to maintain order by establishing rules and laws that reasonable people understand and abide by. Even in well-organized systems, though, there are differences of opinion about what is just, what is fair, and what is right. Instances of injustice often provoke strong emotional reactions that give rise to conflicts. Examining important social issues relating to justice demands that you examine multiple perspectives and evaluate arguments for all sides of an issue.

1. Think about the following terms and write associations you have with them.

My Notes

| Term | What words come to mind when you see or hear these terms? | What has influenced your opinion of these terms? |
|---|---|---|
| Justice, justice system | | |
| Laws, rules, codes, constitution | | |
| Judge, jury, lawyers, witnesses, prosecutor, defendant, victim | | |
| Ethics, morality | | |
| Punishment, rehabilitation | | |

2. Now, using the ideas you have recorded, write a personal definition of the word *justice*. What does justice mean to you? How does your culture affect your views on justice? You can develop your definition of justice with a series of brief examples or with a narrative that illustrates your point.

# Justice and Culture

**LEARNING STRATEGIES:**
Think-Pair-Share, Close Reading, Marking the Text, Note-taking, Graphic Organizer

**My Notes**

## Learning Targets

- Analyze and synthesize details from two texts about justice.
- Explain how an argument persuades.

## Persuasion

When presenting their support for a particular point of view, writers use persuasive language to make their cases about unjust treatment or situations. A powerful argument is crafted using emotional, logical, and ethical appeals to those who have the power to take action on an issue. To take a stand against an injustice and provide a passionate and persuasive argument that convinces others of your point of view is the responsibility and right of every effective communicator.

## Preview

In this activity, you will read two texts about the same issue and analyze their claims.

## Setting a Purpose for Reading

- When presenting an argument, writers use evidence to support their positions. Of the types of **evidence**—**empirical, logical,** and **anecdotal**—anecdotal is the least reliable because it may have been passed from one person to another to another. As you read the following two texts, look for the evidence presented to support the arguments. Mark each text to identify each type of evidence, and discuss with peers the effect of that persuasive technique on the text as a whole as well as its impact on the reader.

- Circle unknown words and phrases. Try to determine the meaning of the words by using context clues, word parts, or a dictionary.

**ACADEMIC VOCABULARY**
**Evidence** is information that supports a position in an argument. **Empirical evidence** is based on experiences and direct observation through research. **Logical evidence** is based on facts and a clear rationale. **Anecdotal evidence** is based on personal accounts of incidents.

**ABOUT THE ISSUE**
**BACKGROUND INFORMATION ON MICHAEL FAY CONTROVERSY**
Michael Fay, an American teenager living in Singapore, was arrested in 1994 for possession of stolen street signs and for vandalism of automobiles. The criminal justice system in Singapore sentenced Fay to a series of "canings," in which the accused is struck several times on the buttocks with a long rattan cane. Amnesty International has declared this punishment "torture."

Before the punishment was carried out, Fay's father publicized his case all over America, hoping that people would be so horrified by the act that they would protest. What the case touched off instead was a huge debate over the effectiveness of such punishments on criminals. Proponents of caning pointed out that Singapore has very little crime, while America provides its criminals with cable TV. The case dominated much of talk radio in the months leading up to the scheduled caning.

The Clinton Administration did intervene somewhat and was able to get the number of strokes reduced. In the end, Fay was struck four times with the cane, and the case—and Fay—slipped out of the public's mind.

The Michael Fay case generated a lot of publicity. Newspaper reporters and editorial writers expressed different points of view on whether the punishment was justified.

## Editorial

# Time to Assert American Values

*from* The New York Times

**My Notes**

1   Singapore's founding leader, Lee Kuan Yew, returned to a favorite theme yesterday in defending the threatened caning of Michael Fay, an 18-year-old American found guilty of vandalism. Western countries value the individual above society; in Asia, he said, the good of society is deemed more important than individual liberties. This comfortable bit of **sophistry** helps governments from China to Indonesia **rationalize** abuses and **marginalize** courageous people who campaign for causes like due process and freedom from torture. Western nations, it is asserted, have no right to impose their values on countries that govern themselves successfully according to their own values.

2   So, the argument goes, when Americans express outrage over a punishment that causes permanent scarring—in this case, caning—they are committing an act of cultural arrogance, assuming that American values are intrinsically superior to those of another culture.

3   There is a clear problem with this argument. It assumes that dissidents, democrats and reformers in these countries are somehow less authentic representatives of their cultures than the members of the political elite who enforce oppressive punishments and suppress individual rights.

4   At times like this, Americans need to remember that this country was also founded by dissidents—by people who were misfits in their own society because they believed, among other things, that it was wrong to punish pilferage with hanging or crimes of any sort with torture.

5   These are values worth asserting around the world. Americans concerned with the **propagation** of traditional values at home should be equally energetic in asserting constitutional principles in the international contest of ideas. There are millions of acts of brutality that cannot be exposed and combated. A case like Michael Fay's is important because it provides a chance to challenge an **inhumane** practice that ought not to exist anywhere.

6   While this country cannot dictate to the government of Singapore, no one should fail to exhort it to behave mercifully. President Clinton provided a sound example when he called for a pardon. Principled private citizens ought now to call for American companies doing business in Singapore to bring their influence to bear.

7   Our colleague William Safire is right to call upon American corporations with subsidiaries in Singapore to press President Ong Teng Cheong to cancel Mr. Fay's punishment. According to Dun & Bradstreet and the U.S.-Asean Business Council, some CEOs and companies in this category are: Riley P. Bechtel of the Bechtel Group Inc.; John S. Reed of Citicorp; Roberto C. Goizueta of the Coca-Cola Company Inc.; Edgar S. Woolard Jr. of E. I. du Pont de Nemours & Company; Lee R. Raymond of Exxon Corporation; John F. Welch Jr. of the General Electric Company; Michael R. Bonsignore of Honeywell Inc.; Louis V. Gerstner Jr. of the International Business Machines Corporation; and Ralph S. Larsen of Johnson & Johnson Inc.

**sophistry:** false argument
**rationalize:** give excuses for
**marginalize:** make less important

**propagation:** the spreading of something

**inhumane:** not kind to humans

# Justice and Culture

8 Singapore needs such people as friends. Now is the time for them to make their voices heard. The Fay case provides a legitimate opening for American citizens and companies to bring political and economic pressure to bear in the propagation of freedom and basic rights. Former President Bush can lead the effort by using his speech at a Citibank seminar in Singapore Thursday to call for clemency for Michael Fay.

## Second Read

- Reread the editorial to answer these text-dependent questions.
- Write any additional questions you have about the text in your Reader/Writer Notebook.

1. **Craft and Structure:** What is the most compelling claim that the author makes in the first paragraph about the cultural conflict in values illustrated by this case of vandalism? How does it support the author's argument?

2. **Craft and Structure:** The author states, "While this country cannot dictate to the government of Singapore, no one should fail to exhort it to behave mercifully." Both *dictate* and *exhort* have to do with telling another person or group what to do. What shades of meaning distinguish the two words as used in this sentence? Look the words up in a dictionary if you need to clarify their meanings.

3. **Key Ideas and Details:** How does the author connect his statement that America should tell other countries to behave mercifully with the list of American corporations with branches in Singapore?

## Article

# Rough Justice

### A Caning in Singapore Stirs Up a Fierce Debate About Crime and Punishment

*by* Alejandro Reyes

1  The Vandalism Act of 1966 was originally **conceived** as a legal weapon to combat the spread of mainly political graffiti common during the heady days of Singapore's struggle for independence. Enacted a year after the republic left the Malaysian Federation, the law explicitly mandates between three and eight strokes of the cane for each count, though a provision allows first offenders to escape caning "if the writing, drawing, mark or inscription is done with pencil, crayon, chalk or other delible substances and not with paint, tar or other indelible substances. ..."

2  Responding to reporters' questions, U.S. chargé d'affaires Ralph Boyce said: "We see a large discrepancy between the offense and the punishment. The cars were not permanently damaged; the paint was removed with thinner. Caning leaves permanent scars. In addition, the accused is a teenager and this is his first offense."

3  By evening, the Singapore government had its reply: "Unlike some other societies which may tolerate acts of vandalism, Singapore has its own standards of social order as reflected in our laws. It is because of our tough laws against anti-social crimes that we are able to keep Singapore orderly and relatively crime-free." The statement noted that in the past five years, fourteen young men aged 18 to 21, twelve of whom were Singaporean, had been sentenced to caning for vandalism. Fay's arrest and sentencing shook the American community in Singapore. Schools advised parents to warn their children not to get into trouble. The American Chamber of Commerce said "We simply do not understand how the government can condone the permanent scarring of any 18-year-old boy—American or Singaporean—by caning for such an offense." Two dozen American senators signed a letter to Ong on Fay's behalf.

4  But according to a string of polls, Fay's caning sentence struck a chord in the U.S. Many Americans fed up with rising crime in their cities actually supported the tough punishment. Singapore's embassy in Washington said that the mail it had received was overwhelmingly approving of the tough sentence. And a radio call-in survey in Fay's hometown of Dayton, Ohio, was strongly pro-caning.

5  It wasn't long before Singapore **patriarch** Lee Kuan Yew weighed in. He reckoned the whole affair revealed America's moral decay. "The U.S. government, the U.S. Senate and the U.S. media took the opportunity to ridicule us, saying the sentence was too severe," he said in a television interview. "[The U.S.] does not restrain or punish individuals, forgiving them for whatever they have done. That's why the whole country is in chaos: drugs, violence, unemployment and homelessness. The American society is the richest and most prosperous in the world but it is hardly safe and peaceful."

6  The debate over caning put a spotlight on Singapore's legal system. Lee and the city-state's other leaders are committed to harsh punishments. Preventive detention laws allow authorities to lock up suspected criminals without trial. While caning is

GRAMMAR&USAGE
Semicolons and Colons
Colons and semicolons serve many purposes in informational writing.

When introducing a quotation after an independent clause, a colon may be used. For example, note the use of the colon in this sentence: "By evening, the Singapore government had its reply: 'Unlike some other societies which may tolerate acts of vandalism, Singapore has its own standards of social order as reflected in our laws.'"

A semicolon can be used to join two independent clauses. This implies that the two clauses are related and/or equal or perhaps that one restates the other. Consider this sentence: "The cars were not permanently damaged; the paint was removed with thinner." How are the two independent clauses related?

**conceived:** created
**patriarch:** father figure

# Justice and Culture

**mandatory:** required by law

## My Notes

**dichotomy:** division into two opposites

**accord:** agree

**mesmerized:** hypnotized

**mandatory** in cases of vandalism, rape and weapons offenses, it is also prescribed for immigration violations such as overstaying visas and hiring of illegal workers. The death penalty is automatic for drug trafficking and firing a weapon while committing a crime. At dawn on May 13, six Malaysians were hanged for drug trafficking, bringing to seventeen the number executed for such offenses so far this year, ten more than the total number of prisoners executed in all of 1993.

7  Most Singaporeans accept their brand of rough justice. Older folk readily speak of the way things were in the 1950s and 1960s when secret societies and gangs operated freely. Singapore has succeeded in keeping crime low. Since 1988, government statistics show there has been a steady decline in the crime rate from 223 per 10,000 residents to 175 per 10,000 last year. Authorities are quick to credit their tough laws and harsh penalties for much of that. …

8  "If there is a single fundamental difference between the Western and Asian worldview, it is the **dichotomy** between individual freedom and collective welfare," said Singapore businessman and former journalist Ho Kwon Ping in an address to lawyers on May 5, the day Fay was caned. "The Western cliché that it would be better for a guilty person to go free than to convict an innocent person is testimony to the importance of the individual. But an Asian perspective may well be that it is better that an innocent person be convicted if the common welfare is protected than for a guilty person to be free to inflict further harm on the community."

9  There is a basic difference too in the way the law treats a suspect. "In Britain and in America, they keep very strongly to the presumption of innocence," says Walter Woon, associate professor of law at the National University of Singapore and a nominated MP. "The prosecution must prove that you are guilty. And even if the judge may feel that you are guilty, he cannot convict you unless the prosecution has proven it. So in some cases it becomes a game between the defense and the prosecuting counsel. We would rather convict even if it doesn't **accord** with the purist's traditions of the presumption of innocence."

10  Singapore's legal system may be based on English common law, but it has developed its own legal traditions and philosophy since independence. The recent severance of all appeals to the Privy Council in London is part of that process. In fundamental ways, Singapore has departed from its British legal roots. The city-state eliminated jury trials years ago—the authorities regard them as error-prone. Acquittals can be appealed and are sometimes overturned. And judges have increased sentences on review. Recently an acquittal was overturned and a bus driver was sentenced to death for murder based only on circumstantial evidence. "Toughness is considered a virtue here," says Woon. "The system is stacked against criminals. The theory is that a person shouldn't get off on fancy argument."

11  Woon opposes caning to punish non-violent offenses. But he is not an admirer of the American system. Last year, Woon and his family were robbed at gunpoint at a bus stop near Disney World in Orlando, Florida. The experience shook him. America's legal system, he argues, "has gone completely berserk. They're so **mesmerized** by the rights of the individual that they forget that other people have rights too. There's all this focus on the perpetrator and his rights, and they forget the fellow is a criminal." Fay is no more than that, Woon says. "His mother and father have no sense of shame. Do they not feel any shame for not having brought him up properly to respect other people's property? Instead they consider themselves victims."

12 Yet harsh punishments alone are clearly not the salvation of Singapore society. The predominantly Chinese city-state also has a cohesive value system that emphasizes such Confucian virtues as respect for authority. "No matter how harsh your punishments, you're not going to get an orderly society unless the culture is in favor of order," says Woon. "In Britain and America, they seem to have lost the feeling that people are responsible for their own behavior. Here, there is still a sense of personal responsibility. If you do something against the law, you bring shame not only to yourself but to your family."

13 That "sense of shame," Woon reckons, is more powerful than **draconian** laws. "Loosening up won't mean there will be chaos," he says. "But the law must be seen to work. The punishment is not the main thing. It's the enforcement of the law. The law has to be enforced effectively and fairly."

## Second Read

- Reread the article to answer these text-dependent questions.
- Write any additional questions you have about the text in your Reader/Writer Notebook.

4. **Craft and Structure:** The author states: "Recently an acquittal was overturned and a bus driver was sentenced to death for murder based only on circumstantial evidence." Use context and the definitions of the words *circumstance* and *evidence* to explain the meaning of "circumstantial evidence" in this sentence.

5. **Knowledge and Ideas:** Both selections in this activity are about Singapore's punishment for Michael Fay, an American found guilty of vandalism. How is the author's purpose different in "Time to Assert American Values" and "Rough Justice"?

## Working from the Text

6. Return to each of the texts and locate examples of evidence in the texts that you marked and identify whether it is empirical, logical, or anecdotal. With your group, discuss the impact of the evidence on the text and the reader, using examples from the text to support your answers.

### My Notes

**draconian:** harsh

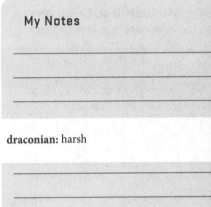

## WORD CONNECTIONS

### Etymology

*Draconian* comes from the Greek name *Draco*, a lawyer from ancient Athens who created a tough code of laws. The word *dragon* comes from a similar but unrelated Greek word, *drakon*, meaning "serpent."

# Justice and Culture

ACADEMIC VOCABULARY
A **fallacy** is a mistaken belief or a false or misleading statement based on unsound evidence. Fallacious reasoning is illogical because it relies on a fallacy.

## Reasoning and Evidence

When evaluating claims made about a topic, it is important to determine whether a writer's reasoning is valid and if the evidence provided sufficiently supports a claim. Writers may make false statements that are not fully supported by logic or evidence.

**Fallacies** are common errors in reasoning that undermine the logic of an argument. Fallacies may be based on irrelevant points and are often identified because they lack evidence to support their claim. Some common fallacies are given below.

## Examples of Common Fallacies

| | | |
|---|---|---|
| Hasty Generalization | A conclusion that is based on insufficient or biased evidence: in other words, rushing to a conclusion before all the relevant facts are available. | **Example:** Even though it's only the first day, I can tell this is going to be a boring course. |
| Either/Or | A conclusion that oversimplifies the argument by reducing it to only two sides or choices. | **Example:** We can either stop using cars or destroy the earth. |
| Ad Populum | An emotional appeal that speaks to positive (such as patriotism, religion, democracy) or negative (such as terrorism or fascism) feelings rather than the real issue at hand. | **Example:** If you were a true American, you would support the rights of people to choose whatever vehicle they want. |
| Moral Equivalence | A comparison of minor misdeeds with major atrocities. | **Example:** That parking attendant who gave me a ticket is as bad as Hitler. |
| Red Herring | A diversionary tactic that avoids the key issues, often by avoiding opposing arguments rather than addressing them. | **Example:** The level of mercury in seafood may be unsafe, but what will fishers do to support their families? |

7. With a partner, reread the previous texts about Michael Fay and look for evidence of fallacious reasoning. Provide evidence for why you think the reasoning is fallacious, and discuss how the writers could have changed their text to avoid these problems.

**My Notes**

_____

_____

_____

_____

_____

_____

_____

## Check Your Understanding

What fallacies are commonly used in arguments? Explain how anecdotal evidence could be an example of false or fallacious reasoning.

### Explain How an Argument Persuades

Describe and evaluate the arguments for and against the punishment prescribed in the Michael Fay case as they are presented in the editorial and the article. Assess the validity of the arguments and identify the one that, in your opinion, has the most relevant and sufficient evidence to support it. Be sure to:

- Start with a statement that identifies both arguments you will discuss, including the titles and authors of the passages you reference. Then state your claim about which article is best supported by evidence.

- Explain how the author builds an argument for or against the issue to persuade an audience, providing relevant evidence from the passage.

- Identify any false statements and faulty reasoning.

- Use words, phrases, and clauses to show how your ideas are related.

- Provide a concluding statement that follows from the argument you have presented.

# Taking a Stand on Justice

**LEARNING STRATEGIES:**
Discussion Groups, Think-Pair-Share, Marking the Text

**My Notes**

**INDEPENDENT READING LINK**

**Read and Recommend**
Review the notes you have been taking in your Reader/Writer Notebook about your independent reading. Which selections address the issue of justice or another issue related to culture? Choose one of the selections to recommend to your classmates. Write a one-paragraph review that explains how the work addresses an issue. Be specific. Include one or more reasons why the work might be helpful for peers to read as they consider argument in the context of culture.

**ill-conceived:** poorly thought out
**belligerents:** participants in a war

## Learning Targets
- Identify the author's purpose and analyze the argument presented.
- Analyze and evaluate the organization of ideas.
- Evaluate rhetorical appeals and their effectiveness in argument.

## Preview
In this activity, you will read a speech about civil disobedience and analyze its argument.

## Setting a Purpose for Reading
- As you read "On Civil Disobedience," highlight words and take notes on Gandhi's claim and supporting evidence.
- Circle unknown words and phrases. Try to determine the meaning of the words by using context clues, word parts, or a dictionary.

**ABOUT THE AUTHOR**
Born in 1869, Mohandas Karamchand Gandhi was a great believer in the power of using civil disobedience against governments that oppressed the poor and the disenfranchised. He spent seven years in South Africa leading and defending Indians born and living there without legal rights. It was there that he began practicing *satyagraha*, or passive resistence. Later, he returned to his homeland of India where he helped the country gain its independence from the British in 1947. He became known there as Mahatma, or "Great Soul." India, though free from Britain, suffered from internal turmoil as religious factions fought for power. Gandhi was assassinated by a fanatic in 1948.

**Speech**

Excerpt from
# On Civil Disobedience

*by* Mohandas K. Gandhi

July 27, 1916

1   There are two ways of countering injustice. One way is to smash the head of the man who perpetrates injustice and to get your own head smashed in the process. All strong people in the world adopt this course. Everywhere wars are fought and millions of people are killed. The consequence is not the progress of a nation but its decline. … No country has ever become, or will ever become, happy through victory in war. A nation does not rise that way; it only falls further. In fact, what comes to it is defeat, not victory. And if, perchance, either our act or our purpose was **ill-conceived**, it brings disaster to both **belligerents**.

**2** But through the other method of combating injustice, we alone suffer the consequences of our mistakes, and the other side is wholly spared. This other method is *satyagraha*.[1] One who resorts to it does not have to break another's head; he may merely have his own head broken. He has to be prepared to die himself suffering all the pain. In opposing the atrocious laws of the Government of South Africa, it was this method that we adopted. We made it clear to the said Government that we would never bow to its outrageous laws. No clapping is possible without two hands to do it, and no quarrel without two persons to make it. Similarly, no State is possible without two entities, the rulers and the ruled. You are our **sovereign**, our Government, only so long as we consider ourselves your subjects. When we are not subjects, you are not the sovereign either. So long as it is your endeavour to control us with justice and love, we will let you to do so. But if you wish to strike at us from behind, we cannot permit it. Whatever you do in other matters, you will have to ask our opinion about the laws that concern us. If you make laws to keep us **suppressed** in a wrongful manner and without taking us into confidence, these laws will merely adorn the statute books. We will never obey them. Award us for it what punishment you like; we will put up with it. Send us to prison and we will live there as in a paradise. Ask us to mount the **scaffold** and we will do so laughing. Shower what sufferings you like upon us; we will calmly endure all and not hurt a hair of your body. We will gladly die and will not so much as touch you. But so long as there is yet life in these our bones, we will never comply with your **arbitrary** laws.

**WORD CONNECTIONS**

**Multiple Meaning Words**

A *statute* is a written law. *Statute books* is a term that refers to the entire body of written laws used by a particular government. It doesn't refer to books in the sense of individual volumes.

**sovereign:** holding supreme power, like a king
**suppressed:** put down by force

**scaffold:** a platform on which people are executed by hanging

**arbitrary:** random and illogical

## Second Read

- Reread the speech to answer these text-dependent questions.
- Write any additional questions you have about the text in your Reader/Writer Notebook.

1. **Craft and Structure:** How does Gandhi show that the method of *satyagraha* could succeed in changing a country's unjust laws where violence could not?

2. **Key Ideas and Details:** How might Gandhi advise you to respond to an unjust law? Use evidence from the text to support your reasons.

**My Notes**

---

[1] **satyagraha:** (Sanskrit) insistence on truth; a term used by Gandhi to describe his policy of seeking reform by means of nonviolent resistance

# Taking a Stand on Justice

## Working from the Text

3. Many writers publish stories about civil strife in their countries. Compare and contrast the portrayal of reactions to civil strife in *Persepolis* and "On Civil Disobedience."

4. What do you think was the author's purpose for this text?

5. Look at how the author moves from idea to idea. How does Gandhi use cause and effect to organize his ideas? Create a graphic organizer in your Reader/Writer Notebook that shows the cause-and-effect patterns you identify in the speech.

## Language and Writer's Craft: Outlining and Organizing an Argument

To be effective, an argument should clearly state a claim and provide sound reasoning and evidence to support it. In addition, an argument should use effective transitions to guide the reader from one idea to the next. For example, in this sentence from "On Civil Disobedience," Gandhi uses the transition word *similarly* to show how two things are alike: "**Similarly**, no State is possible without two entities, the rulers and the ruled."

An argument might be organized as follows:

I. Claim (the thesis for the writer's argument)

II. Evidence (support for the claim) and explanation (description/details about why and how the evidence connects to and supports the claim)

III. Reasoning (additional logic that may be needed to support the evidence and explain why it is valid)

IV. Counterclaims (acknowledgment of other viewpoints or evidence that disagrees with your claim/thesis)

V. Refutations (evidence/reasoning that negates the counterclaims)

VI. Conclusion (concluding statement pulling the claim and the evidence together to create a call for action)

PRACTICE Consider the following statements from "On Civil Disobedience" and decide which is a claim, which is an explanation, and which is a conclusion.

No country has ever become, or will ever become, happy through victory in war.

No clapping is possible without two hands to do it, and no quarrel without two persons to make it.

But so long as there is yet life in these our bones, we will never comply with your arbitrary laws.

You may wish to use the outline structure above to outline your own argument in response to the writing prompt.

## Argument Writing Prompt

Is civil disobedience a moral responsibility of a citizen? Write an essay that addresses the question and support your position with evidence from texts in this part of the unit and real-life examples to illustrate or clarify your position. Be sure to:

- Write a precise claim and support it with valid reasoning and relevant evidence (avoid false statements and fallacious reasoning).
- Acknowledge counterclaims that anticipate the audience's knowledge level, concerns, values, and possible biases while also refuting the evidence for those claims.
- Create an organizational plan that logically sequences claims, counterclaims, reasons, and evidence.
- Maintain a formal tone, vary sentence types, and use effective transitions.

**My Notes**

# Taking a Stand on Legal Issues

**My Notes**

## Learning Targets
- Analyze the use of rhetorical appeals in argument.
- Compare and contrast how different writers approach a subject or an issue.

## Using Rhetorical Appeals

You have learned how writers use ethos, pathos, and logos to appeal to readers. In argumentative texts, reasoning should primarily be based on ethos and logos. However, pathos can be a strong appeal as part of an argument.

## Preview

In this activity, you will read two speeches about justice and analyze the speakers' use of rhetorical appeals.

## Setting a Purpose for Reading
- As you read each speech, think about the rhetorical appeals the authors use to persuade their audiences.
- Circle unknown words and phrases. Try to determine the meaning of the words by using context clues, word parts, or a dictionary.

### ABOUT THE AUTHOR

Chief Joseph (1840–1904) was the leader of a band of the Nez Percé people, originally living in the Wallowa Valley in what is now Oregon. During years of stuggle against whites who wanted their lands and broken promises from the federal government, Chief Joseph led his people in many battles to preserve their lands. On a desperate retreat toward Canada, Chief Joseph and his band were fighting the Army and the weather, and he finally surrendered in the Bear Paw Mountains of Montana.

Speech

# ON SURRENDER
## AT BEAR PAW MOUNTAIN, 1877

*by* Chief Joseph

1   Tell General Howard that I know his heart. What he told me before I have in my heart. I am tired of fighting. Our chiefs are killed. Looking Glass is dead, Tu-hul-hil-sote is dead. The old men are all dead. It is the young men who now say yes or no. He who led the young men [Joseph's brother Alikut] is dead. It is cold and we have no blankets. The little children are freezing to death. My people—some of them have run away to the hills and have no blankets and no food. No one knows where they are—perhaps freezing to death. I want to have time to look for my children and see how many of them I can find. Maybe I shall find them among the dead. Hear me, my chiefs, my heart is sick and sad. From where the sun now stands I will fight no more forever.

## Second Read

- Reread the speech to answer these text-dependent questions.
- Write any additional questions you have about the text in your Reader/Writer Notebook.

1. **Craft and Structure:** Which rhetorical appeal does Chief Joseph primarily use to appeal to his listeners: ethos, pathos, or logos? Give examples and explain their appeal.

2. **Craft and Structure:** What tone does Chief Joseph use in this speech? Explain your answer.

**ABOUT THE AUTHOR**

Susan B. Anthony (1820–1905) became a prominent leader for women's suffrage, giving speeches in both the United States and Europe. With Elizabeth Cady Stanton, she created and produced *The Revolution*, a weekly publication that lobbied for women's rights. The newspaper's motto was "Men their rights, and nothing more; women their rights, and nothing less." After lobbying for the right to vote for many years, in 1872 Anthony took matters into her own hands and voted illegally in the presidential election. Anthony was arrested and unsuccessfully fought the charges. She was fined $100, which she never paid. Anthony delivered this address to explain her own civil disobedience.

### Speech

# On Women's Right to Vote

*by* Susan B. Anthony

Philadelphia 1872

1   Friends and fellow citizens: I stand before you tonight under indictment for the alleged crime of having voted at the last presidential election, without having a lawful right to vote. It shall be my work this evening to prove to you that in

# Taking a Stand on Legal Issues

thus voting, I not only committed no crime, but, instead, simply exercised my citizen's rights, guaranteed to me and all United States citizens by the National Constitution, beyond the power of any state to deny.

2   The preamble of the Federal Constitution says:

3   *We, the people of the United States, in order to form a more perfect union, establish justice, insure* **domestic** *tranquillity, provide for the common defense, promote the general welfare, and secure the blessings of liberty to ourselves and our* **posterity***, do ordain and establish this Constitution for the United States of America.*

4   It was we, the people; not we, the white male citizens; nor yet we, the male citizens; but we, the whole people, who formed the Union. And we formed it, not to give the blessings of liberty, but to secure them; not to the half of ourselves and the half of our posterity, but to the whole people—women as well as men. And it is a downright mockery to talk to women of their enjoyment of the blessings of liberty while they are denied the use of the only means of securing them provided by this democratic-republican government—the ballot.

5   For any state to make sex a qualification that must ever result in the **disfranchisement** of one entire half of the people, is to pass a **bill of attainder**, or, an **ex post facto** law, and is therefore a violation of the supreme law of the land. By it the blessings of liberty are forever withheld from women and their female posterity.

6   To them this government has no just powers derived from the consent of the governed. To them this government is not a democracy. It is not a republic. It is an odious aristocracy; a hateful **oligarchy** of sex; the most hateful aristocracy ever established on the face of the globe; an oligarchy of wealth, where the rich govern the poor. An oligarchy of learning, where the educated govern the ignorant, or even an oligarchy of race, where the Saxon rules the African, might be endured; but this oligarchy of sex, which makes father, brothers, husband, sons, the oligarchs over the mother and sisters, the wife and daughters, of every household—which ordains all men sovereigns, all women subjects, carries **dissension**, discord, and rebellion into every home of the nation. Webster[1], Worcester, and Bouvier all define a citizen to be a person in the United States, entitled to vote and hold office.

7   The only question left to be settled now is: Are women persons? And I hardly believe any of our opponents will have the hardihood to say they are not. Being persons, then, women are citizens; and no state has a right to make any law, or to enforce any old law, that shall abridge their privileges or immunities. Hence, every discrimination against women in the constitutions and laws of the several states is today null and void, precisely as is every one against Negroes.

**domestic:** related to the home
**posterity:** all future generations

## My Notes

**disfranchisement:** deprivation of the right to vote; modern spelling is *disenfranchisement*
**bill of attainder:** a law that punishes a person or people for a crime, often without a trial
**ex post facto:** after the fact
**oligarchy:** a small group that runs a government
**dissension:** disagreement

---

1 **Webster**, Worcester, and Bouvier were all authors of dictionaries.

## Second Read

- Reread the speech to answer these text-dependent questions.
- Write any additional questions you have about the text in your Reader/Writer Notebook.

3. **Knowledge and Ideas:** What evidence does Anthony use to support her claim that she committed no crime when she voted?

4. **Craft and Structure:** What rhetorical appeal does Anthony primarily use in this speech? What secondary appeal does she use? Give examples.

## Working from the Text

5. Explain how each of the rhetorical appeals of ethos, pathos, and logos might be used to create an effective argument.

## Writing to Sources: Explanatory Text

Compare and contrast how the author of each historic speech uses argument to take a stand on a legal issue. Identify the issue in each speech and the arguments for and against as presented by the speaker. Which type of rhetorical appeals are used, and what are the similarities and differences in how the authors use them? Be sure to:

- Identify the title, author, and issue presented in each speech.
- Begin with a thesis statement that provides your main idea about how each author approaches the issue.
- Include relevant textual evidence and examples to support your thesis.
- Link main points with effective transitions to clearly identify similarities and differences in the way the speeches address the issue at hand.
- Provide a concluding section that supports your main point.

My Notes

# Taking a Stand Against Hunger

**LEARNING STRATEGIES:**
Brainstorming, Paraphrasing,
Previewing, Think-Pair-Share,
Note-taking, Discussion Groups,
Marking the Text

## My Notes

whereas: because it is true that

## Learning Targets

- Identify an author's purpose and analyze an argument presented.
- Synthesize information from print and nonprint persuasive texts.
- Conduct research and present findings in a brief presentation to peers.

## Preview

In this activity, you will read various print and nonprint persuasive texts in order to analyze the arguments presented.

## Setting a Purpose for Reading

- As you read the next two texts ("Declaration of the Rights of the Child" and the World Health Organization graph and accompanying statistics), mark the texts to identify main ideas.
- Circle unknown words and phrases. Try to determine the meaning of the words by using context clues, word parts, or a dictionary.

> **ABOUT THE DOCUMENT**
> The following document is a proclamation issued by the United Nations on November 20, 1959. The United Nations is an organization that tries to determine issues of justice that transcend individual cultures and societal rules.

## Proclamation

# Declaration of the Rights of the Child

PROCLAIMED BY GENERAL ASSEMBLY RESOLUTION 1386(XIV) OF 20 NOVEMBER 1959

1 *Whereas* the peoples of the United Nations have, in the Charter, reaffirmed their faith in fundamental human rights and in the dignity and worth of the human person, and have determined to promote social progress and better standards of life in larger freedom,

2 *Whereas* the United Nations has, in the Universal Declaration of Human Rights, proclaimed that everyone is entitled to all the rights and freedoms set forth therein, without distinction of any kind, such as race, color, sex, language, religion, political or other opinion, national or social origin, property, birth or other status,

**3** *Whereas* the child, by reason of his physical and mental immaturity, needs special safeguards and care, including appropriate legal protection, before as well as after birth,

**4** *Whereas* the need for such special safeguards has been stated in the Geneva Declaration of the Rights of the Child of 1924, and recognized in the Universal Declaration of Human Rights and in the statutes of specialized agencies and international organizations concerned with the welfare of children,

**5** *Whereas* mankind owes to the child the best it has to give,

**6** *Now therefore,*

**7** *The General Assembly*

**8** *Proclaims* this Declaration of the Rights of the Child to the end that he may have a happy childhood and enjoy for his own good and for the good of society the rights and freedoms herein set forth, and calls upon parents, upon men and women as individuals, and upon voluntary organizations, local authorities and national Governments to recognize these rights and strive for their observance by legislative and other measures progressively taken in accordance with the following principles:

*Principle 1*

**9** The child shall enjoy all the rights set forth in this Declaration. Every child, without any exception whatsoever, shall be entitled to these rights, without distinction or discrimination on account of race, color, sex, language, religion, political or other opinion, national or social origin, property, birth or other status, whether of himself or of his family.

*Principle 2*

**10** The child shall enjoy special protection, and shall be given opportunities and facilities, by law and by other means, to enable him to develop physically, mentally, morally, spiritually and socially in a healthy and normal manner and in conditions of freedom and dignity. In the enactment of laws for this purpose, the best interests of the child shall be the paramount consideration.

*Principle 3*

**11** The child shall be entitled from his birth to a name and a nationality.

*Principle 4*

**12** The child shall enjoy the benefits of social security. He shall be entitled to grow and develop in health; to this end, special care and protection shall be provided both to him and to his mother, including adequate pre-natal and post-natal care. The child shall have the right to adequate nutrition, housing, recreation and medical services.

*Principle 5*

**13** The child who is physically, mentally or socially handicapped shall be given the special treatment, education and care required by his particular condition.

### GRAMMAR *&*USAGE
Verb Tenses

Verbs have **active** and **passive** voice in all six **tenses**. A passive-voice verb always contains a form of *be* followed by the past participle of the verb.

The voice of a verb (active or passive) indicates whether the subject performs (active) or receives (passive) the action.

Active voice, future tense: "The child **shall enjoy** all the rights. …"

Passive voice, future tense: "Every child **shall be entitled**. …"

Generally, it is preferable to use the active voice in your writing. The active voice is more direct and concise. However, sometimes the passive voice is more appropriate when the doer of the action is unknown or is less important than the person receiving the action. In a formal document such as this one, why is the use of passive voice appropriate?

### My Notes

_____

_____

_____

_____

_____

_____

_____

_____

_____

_____

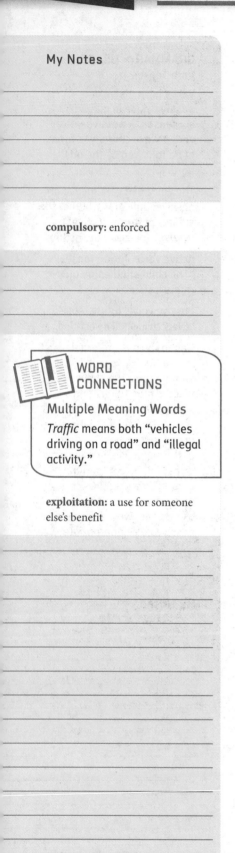

**My Notes**

compulsory: enforced

### WORD CONNECTIONS

**Multiple Meaning Words**

*Traffic* means both "vehicles driving on a road" and "illegal activity."

exploitation: a use for someone else's benefit

*Principle 6*

**14** The child, for the full and harmonious development of his personality, needs love and understanding. He shall, wherever possible, grow up in the care and under the responsibility of his parents, and, in any case, in an atmosphere of affection and of moral and material security; a child of tender years shall not, save in exceptional circumstances, be separated from his mother. Society and the public authorities shall have the duty to extend particular care to children without a family and to those without adequate means of support. Payment of State and other assistance towards the maintenance of children of large families is desirable.

*Principle 7*

**15** The child is entitled to receive education, which shall be free and **compulsory**, at least in the elementary stages. He shall be given an education which will promote his general culture and enable him, on a basis of equal opportunity, to develop his abilities, his individual judgement, and his sense of moral and social responsibility, and to become a useful member of society.

**16** The best interests of the child shall be the guiding principle of those responsible for his education and guidance; that responsibility lies in the first place with his parents.

**17** The child shall have full opportunity for play and recreation, which should be directed to the same purposes as education; society and the public authorities shall endeavour to promote the enjoyment of this right.

*Principle 8*

**18** The child shall in all circumstances be among the first to receive protection and relief.

*Principle 9*

**19** The child shall be protected against all forms of neglect, cruelty and **exploitation**. He shall not be the subject of traffic, in any form.

**20** The child shall not be admitted to employment before an appropriate minimum age; he shall in no case be caused or permitted to engage in any occupation or employment which would prejudice his health or education, or interfere with his physical, mental or moral development.

*Principle 10*

**21** The child shall be protected from practices which may foster racial, religious and any other form of discrimination. He shall be brought up in a spirit of understanding, tolerance, friendship among peoples, peace and universal brotherhood, and in full consciousness that his energy and talents should be devoted to the service of his fellow men.

## Second Read

- Reread the proclamation to answer these text-dependent questions.
- Write any additional questions you have about the text in your Reader/Writer Notebook.

1. **Key Ideas and Details:** Reread the statements at the beginning of the proclamation beginning with "Whereas." How do these statements serve to set up the principles that follow?

2. **Craft and Structure:** The word *paramount* is based in part on an Old French word, *amont*, meaning "above." How does this root, combined with the context, help you determine the meaning of the word as it is used in Principle 2?

## World Health Organization Graph

Read the following graph, and then discuss the statistics on world hunger from the World Health Organization.

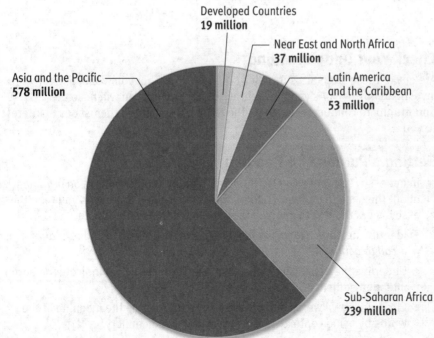

**Number of Hungry People in the World**
**925 Million Hungry People in 2010**

Developed Countries
**19 million**

Near East and North Africa
**37 million**

Asia and the Pacific
**578 million**

Latin America
and the Caribbean
**53 million**

Sub-Saharan Africa
**239 million**

**Source:** World Health Organization

# Taking a Stand Against Hunger

## My Notes

### Statistic 1

"In round numbers there are 7 billion people in the world. Thus, with an estimated 925 million hungry people in the world, 13.1 percent, or almost 1 in 7 people are hungry."

### Statistic 2

"Children are the most visible victims of undernutrition. Children who are poorly nourished suffer up to 160 days of illness each year. Poor nutrition plays a role in at least half of the 10.9 million child deaths each year—five million deaths. Undernutrition magnifies the effect of every disease, including measles and malaria."

### Second Read

- Reread the graph and statistics to answer these text-dependent questions.
- Write any additional questions you have about the text in your Reader/Writer Notebook.

3. **Knowledge and Ideas:** Look back at the "Declaration of the Rights of the Child," Principle 4. Considering the World Health Organization data, how is the world upholding the promises of the Declaration?

4. **Knowledge and Ideas:** Compare the data in the graph with Statistic 1. What does the graph show you that the statistic does not? What does the statistic tell you that the graph does not show?

### Check Your Understanding

Are any of these statistics surprising? Are there any that you would like to investigate further? As you move through this activity, you will have the opportunity to conduct research on the issue of hunger or other issues of interest to you.

### Setting a Purpose for Reading

- In her essay "School's Out for Summer," Anna Quindlen makes an argument about the need to address child hunger in the United States. As you read the essay, mark the text to indicate the components of her argument:
  - Identify the *hook, claim, evidence/support, concessions* and *refutations*, and a *call to action*.
  - Underline the persuasive appeals and look for clues that indicate the author's intended audience.
  - Circle unknown words and phrases. Try to determine the meaning of the words by using context clues, word parts, or a dictionary.

**ABOUT THE AUTHOR**

Anna Quindlen is a novelist and an award-winning and popular newspaper columnist who has written for some of the nation's most prestigious newspapers, including the *New York Times*, where she was a reporter, editor, and contributor for many years. Critics suggest that her appeal as a columnist lies in her personal approach and her insights into problems experienced by ordinary readers. She won the Pulitzer Prize for commentary in 1992.

ESSAY

# School's **Out** for Summer

*by* Anna Quindlen

1  WHEN THE AD COUNCIL CONVENED focus groups not long ago to help prepare a series of public service announcements on child hunger, there was a fairly **unanimous** response from the participants about the subject. Not here. Not in America. If there was, we would know about it. We would read about it in the paper, we would see it on the news. And of course we would stop it. In America.

2  Is it any wonder that the slogan the advertising people came up with was "The Sooner You Believe It, the Sooner We Can End It"?

3  It's the beginning of summer in America's cement cities, in the deep hidden valleys of the country and the loop-de-loop sidewalkless streets of the suburbs. For many adults who are really closet kids, this means that their blood hums with a hint of freedom, the old beloved promise of long aimless days of dirt and sweat and sunshine, T-shirts stained with Kool-Aid and flip-flops gray with street grit or backyard dust.

4  But that sort of summer has given way to something more difficult, even darker, that makes you wonder whether year-round school is not a notion whose time has come. With so many households in which both parents are working, summer is often a scramble of scheduling: day camps, school programs, the Y, the community center. Some parents who can't afford or find those kinds of services park their vacationing children in front of the television, lock the door, and go to work hoping for the best, calling home on the hour. Some kids just wander in a wilder world than the one that existed when their parents had summers free.

5  And some kids don't get enough to eat, no matter what people want to tell themselves. Do the math: During the rest of the year fifteen million students get free or cut-rate lunches at school, and many of them get breakfast, too. But only three million children are getting lunches through the federal summer lunch program. And hunger in the United States, particularly since the institution of so-called welfare reform, is epidemic. The numbers are astonishing in the land of the all-you-can-eat buffet. The Agriculture Department estimated in 1999 that twelve million children were hungry

**My Notes**

**unanimous:** agreed upon by everyone involved

# Taking a Stand Against Hunger

My Notes

**bipartisan:** done with the cooperation of two political parties

**stigma:** a mark of shame

**bodega:** a small city grocery store

**snafu:** a confusing problem
**pilfer:** steal a small amount

or at risk of going hungry. A group of big-city mayors released a study showing that in 2000, requests for food assistance from families increased almost 20 percent, more than at any time in the last decade. And last Thanksgiving a food bank in Connecticut gave away four thousand more turkeys than the year before—and still ran out of birds.

6  But while the Christmas holidays make for heartrending copy, summer is really ground zero in the battle to keep kids fed. The school lunch program, begun in the 1970s as a result of **bipartisan** federal legislation, has been by most measures an enormous success. For lots of poor families it's become a way to count on getting at least one decent meal into their children, and when it disappears it's catastrophic. Those who work at America's Second Harvest, the biggest nonprofit supply source for food banks, talk of parents who go hungry themselves so their kids can eat, who put off paying utility and phone bills, who insist their children attend remedial summer school programs simply so they can get a meal. The parents themselves are loath to talk: Of all the humiliations attached to being poor in a prosperous nation, not being able to feed your kids is at the top of the list.

7  In most cases these are not parents who are homeless or out of work. The people who run food banks report that most of their clients are minimum-wage workers who can't afford enough to eat on their salaries. "Families are struggling in a way they haven't done for a long time," says Brian Loring, the executive director of Neighborhood Centers of Johnson County, Iowa, which provides lunches to more than two hundred kids at five locations during the summer months. For a significant number of Americans, the cost of an additional meal for two school-age children for the eight weeks of summer vacation seems like a small fortune. Some don't want or seek government help because of the perceived **stigma**; some are denied food stamps because of new welfare policies. Others don't know they're eligible, and none could be blamed if they despaired of the exercise. The average length of a food stamp application is twelve often impenetrable pages; a permit to sell weapons is just two.

8  The success of the school lunch program has been, of course, that the food goes where the children are. That's the key to success for summer programs, too. Washington, D.C., has done better than any other city in the country in feeding hungry kids, sending fire trucks into housing projects to distribute leaflets about lunch locations, running a referral hotline and radio announcements. One food bank in Nevada decided to send trucks to the parks for tailgate lunches. "That's where the kids are," its director told the people at Second Harvest.

9  We Americans like need that takes place far from home, so we can feel simultaneously self-congratulatory and safe from the possibility that hard times could be lurking around the corner. Maybe that's why our mothers told us to think of the children in Africa when we wouldn't clean our plates. I stopped believing in that when I found myself in a **bodega** with a distraught woman after New York City had declared a snow day; she had three kids who ate breakfast and lunch at school, her food stamps had been held up because of some bureaucratic **snafu**, and she was considering whether to **pilfer** food from the senior center where she worked as an aide. Surely there should be ways for a civilized society to see that such a thing would never happen, from providing a simpler application for food stamps to setting a decent minimum wage.

But wishing don't make it so, as they say in policy meetings, and proposals aren't peanut butter and jelly. Find a food bank and then go grocery shopping by **proxy**. Somewhere nearby there is a mother who covets a couple of boxes of spaghetti, and you could make her dream come true. That's right. In America.

**proxy:** the power to act for someone else

## Second Read

- Reread the essay to answer these text-dependent questions.
- Write any additional questions you have about the text in your Reader/Writer Notebook.

5. **Key Ideas and Details:** How does the author use the "hook" of the Ad Council's focus groups and slogan to set up her argument about hunger in America?

6. **Craft and Structure:** Why does Quindlen use the metaphor "ground zero" to describe the problem that summer creates in the battle to keep kids fed?

7. **Key Ideas and Details:** What data and anecdotal evidence does the author provide to support her thesis that America has a big hunger problem for children even though it might be hard to believe?

8. **Knowledge and Ideas:** Do you think the author would say that the United States is meeting the principles outlined in the Declaration of the Rights of the Child? Why or why not?

**My Notes**

# Taking a Stand Against Hunger

## Working from the Text

9. In a small group, critique the effect of the author's argument. Share examples of the author's arguments (logical, empirical, anecdotal) and discuss the effectiveness of the arguments presented. Can you identify whether the author uses fallacious reasoning and, if so, where?

10. **Research:** Do you support the author's arguments, or would you take a different position? Conduct research on the issue of hunger in your community.

   - First, create a question you would like to answer through your research. Then, use available resources to find answers to your question, creating new questions or revising your question as needed based on your findings.

   - Organize your evidence by form (empirical, logical, anecdotal). Provide at least one example of each form of evidence.

   - Finally, synthesize your findings into a brief, informal presentation, and present your information to a small group of your peers.

## Argument Writing Prompt

After researching the issue of hunger in your community, write an essay that identifies the problem of hunger and argues for a solution. Support your position with evidence from your research. Be sure to:

- Establish a focus with a hook and claim.
- Demonstrate valid reasoning and sufficient evidence to support your argument.
- Use linking words and phrases to show the relationships between your claim and your reasons, your reasons and evidence, and your claims and any counterclaims.
- Write a strong conclusion that follows from your claim and supports the argument you presented.
- Cite sources using an appropriate format.

# Taking a Stand on Truth and Responsibility

LEARNING STRATEGIES:
Guided Reading,
Metacognitive Markers, Note-
taking, Marking the Text, Close
Reading, Socratic Seminar

## Learning Targets

- Analyze two complex speeches by Nobel Prize winners.
- Synthesize textual evidence by participating actively in a Socratic Seminar.
- Emulate the model speeches by drafting an argumentative speech.

## Preview

In this activity, you will read two speeches on the topic of speaking the truth in the face of adversity and then participate in a Socratic Seminar.

## Setting a Purpose for Reading

- Read Solzhenitsyn's speech and use metacognitive markers and take notes as you follow your teacher's directions.
- Circle unknown words and phrases. Try to determine the meaning of the words by using context clues, word parts, or a dictionary.

### ABOUT THE AUTHOR

Aleksandr Isayevich Solzhenitsyn (1918–2008) became a worldwide figure when he was exiled from the Soviet Union in 1974 for publishing a historical account of the wretched system of Soviet prison camps known as gulags. Solzhenitsyn had been imprisoned as a young soldier during World War II for writing a letter critical of Stalin, the Soviet dictator. His experiences in a Siberian prison became the basis for his best-known work, *A Day in the Life of Ivan Denisovitch*. For years afterward, Solzhenitsyn was forced to publish his works secretly and often abroad because of the threat of further incarceration. Solzhenitsyn lived in the United States for twenty years, but when he regained his Soviet citizenship in 1990, he returned home and continued writing until his death in 2008.

**My Notes**

### Speech

## from
# One Word of Truth Outweighs the World

*by* Aleksandr Solzhenitsyn

1 **I** THINK THAT WORLD LITERATURE has the power in these frightening times to help mankind see itself accurately despite what is **advocated** by partisans and by parties. It has the power to transmit the condensed experience of one region to another, so that different scales of values are combined, and so that one people accurately and **concisely** knows the true history of another with a power of recognition and acute awareness as if it had lived through that history itself—and could thus be spared repeating old mistakes. At the same time, perhaps we ourselves may succeed in developing our own WORLD-WIDE VIEW, like any man, with the center of the eye seeing what is nearby but the **periphery** of vision taking in what is happening in the rest of the world. We will make correlations and maintain world-wide standards.

**advocated:** argued for another's cause

**concisely:** using few words

**periphery:** outside edge

# Taking a Stand on Truth and Responsibility

**onslaught:** a violent attack

**profound:** deeply important and wise

**oratory:** public speaking

## My Notes

_____

_____

_____

_____

**dispelled:** made to go away

_____

_____

_____

_____

_____

_____

_____

_____

_____

_____

_____

2  Who, if not writers, are to condemn their own unsuccessful governments (in some states this is the easiest way to make a living; everyone who is not too lazy does it) as well as society itself, whether for its cowardly humiliation or for its self-satisfied weakness, or the lightheaded escapades of the young, or the youthful pirates brandishing knives?

3  We will be told: What can literature do against the pitiless **onslaught** of naked violence?  Let us not forget that violence does not and cannot flourish by itself; it is inevitably intertwined with LYING. Between them there is the closest, the most **profound** and natural bond: nothing screens violence except lies, and the only way lies can hold out is by violence. Whoever has once announced violence as his METHOD must inexorably choose lying as his PRINCIPLE. At birth, violence behaves openly and even proudly. But as soon as it becomes stronger and firmly established, it senses the thinning of the air around it and cannot go on without befogging itself in lies, coating itself with lying's sugary **oratory**. It does not always or necessarily go straight for the gullet; usually it demands of its victims only allegiance to the lie, only complicity in the lie.

4  The simple act of an ordinary courageous man is not to take part, not to support lies! Let *that* come into the world and even reign over it, but not through me. Writers and artists can do more: they can VANQUISH LIES!  In the struggle against lies, art has always won and always will.

5  Conspicuously, incontestably for everyone. Lies can stand up against much in the world, but not against art.

6  Once lies have been **dispelled**, the repulsive nakedness of violence will be exposed—and hollow violence will collapse.

7  That, my friend, is why I think we can help the world in its red-hot hour: not by the nay-saying of having no armaments, not by abandoning oneself to the carefree life, but by going into battle!

8 In Russian, proverbs about TRUTH are favorites. They persistently express the considerable, bitter, grim experience of the people, often astonishingly:

9 ONE WORD OF TRUTH OUTWEIGHS THE WORLD.

10 On such a seemingly fantastic violation of the law of the conservation of mass and energy are based both my own activities and my appeal to the writers of the whole world.

## Second Read

- Reread the speech to answer these text-dependent questions.
- Write any additional questions you have about the text in your Reader/Writer Notebook.

1. **Craft and Structure:** What image does the author use to explain his use of "world-wide view"? What is his meaning?

2. **Key Ideas and Details:** What conclusion does the author draw about truth? What argument supports his conclusion?

3. **Craft and Structure:** How is Solzhenitsyn's statement that the "simple act of an ordinary courageous man is not to take part, not to support lies" similar to and different from the following statement from Gandhi's speech, "On Civil Disobedience": "We made it clear to the said Government that we would never bow to its outrageous laws. No clapping is possible without two hands to do it?"

## Setting a Purpose for Reading

- Follow the same close reading process you used with "One Word of Truth" to read Wiesel's "Hope, Despair, and Memory." Be sure to mark the text for evidence of his argument, counterarguments, evidence, and reasoning.
- Circle unknown words and phrases. Try to determine the meaning of the words by using context clues, word parts, or a dictionary.

**My Notes**

# Taking a Stand on Truth and Responsibility

## My Notes

_____
_____
_____
_____
_____
_____
_____
_____
_____
_____
_____
_____
_____
_____
_____
_____

**ABOUT THE AUTHOR**

Elie Wiesel (1928–) was born in the town of Sighet, now part of Romania. During World War II, he and his family were deported to the German concentration and extermination camps. His parents and little sister perished, while Wiesel and his two older sisters survived. Liberated from Buchenwald in 1945 by Allied troops, Wiesel went to Paris, where he studied at the Sorbonne and worked as a journalist. In 1958, he published his first book, *La Nuit*, a memoir of his experiences in the concentration camps. He has since authored nearly thirty books, some of which use these events as their basic material. In his many lectures, Wiesel has concerned himself with the situation of the Jews and other groups who have suffered persecution and death because of their religion, race, or national origin. Wiesel has made his home in New York City and is now a United States citizen. He was awarded the Nobel Peace Prize in 1986.

### Speech

Excerpt from

# Hope, Despair, and Memory

*by* Elie Wiesel, December 11, 1986

**incompatible:** unable to be used together

1   Just as man cannot live without dreams, he cannot live without hope. If dreams reflect the past, hope summons the future. Does this mean that our future can be built on a rejection of the past? Surely such a choice is not necessary. The two are **incompatible**. The opposite of the past is not the future but the absence of future; the opposite of the future is not the past but the absence of past. The loss of one is equivalent to the sacrifice of the other.

2   A recollection. The time: After the war. The place: Paris. A young man struggles to readjust to life. His mother, his father, his small sister are gone. He is alone. On the verge of despair. And yet he does not give up. On the contrary, he strives to find a place among the living. He acquires a new language. He makes a few friends who, like himself, believe that the memory of evil will serve as a shield against evil; that the memory of death will serve as a shield against death.

3   This he must believe in order to go on. For he has just returned from a universe where God, betrayed by His creatures, covered His face in order not to see. Mankind, jewel of his creation, had succeeded in building an inverted Tower of Babel[1], reaching not toward heaven but toward an anti-heaven, there to create a parallel society, a new "creation" with its own princes and gods, laws and principles, jailers and prisoners. A world where the past no longer counted—no longer meant anything.

4   Stripped of possessions, all human ties severed, the prisoners found themselves in a social and cultural void. "Forget," they were told. "Forget where you came from; forget who you were. Only the present matters." But the present was only a blink of the Lord's eye. The Almighty himself was a slaughterer: it was He who decided who would live and who would die; who would be tortured, and who would be rewarded. Night after

---

[1] In the Bible, the building of the Tower of Babel caused God to divide humanity into speakers of different languages.

night, seemingly endless processions vanished into the flames, lighting up the sky. Fear dominated the universe. Indeed this was another universe; the very laws of nature had been transformed. Children looked like old men, old men whimpered like children. Men and women from every corner of Europe were suddenly reduced to nameless and faceless creatures desperate for the same ration of bread or soup, dreading the same end. Even their silence was the same for it resounded with the memory of those who were gone. Life in this accursed universe was so distorted, so unnatural that a new species had evolved. Waking among the dead, one wondered if one were still alive. …

5  Of course, we could try to forget the past. Why not? Is it not natural for a human being to repress what causes him pain, what causes him shame? Like the body, memory protects its wounds. When day breaks after a sleepless night, one's ghosts must withdraw; the dead are ordered back to their graves. But for the first time in history, we could not bury our dead. We bear their graves within ourselves.

6  For us, forgetting was never an option. …

7  And yet it is surely human to forget, even to want to forget. The Ancients saw it as a divine gift. Indeed the memory helps us to survive, forgetting allows us to go on living. How could we go on with our daily lives, if we remained constantly aware of the dangers and ghosts surrounding us? The Talmud[2] tells us that without the ability to forget, man would soon cease to learn. Without the ability to forget, man would live in a permanent, paralyzing fear of death. Only God and God alone can and must remember everything.

8  How are we to reconcile our supreme duty towards memory with the need to forget that is essential to life? No generation has had to confront this **paradox** with such urgency. The survivors wanted to communicate everything to the living: the victim's solitude and sorrow, the tears of mothers driven to madness, the prayers of the doomed beneath a fiery sky.

9  They needed to tell of the child who, in hiding with his mother, asked softly, very softly: "Can I cry now?" They needed to tell of the sick beggar who, in a sealed cattle-car, began to sing as an offering to his companions. And of the little girl who, hugging her grandmother, whispered: "Don't be afraid, don't be sorry to die … I'm not." She was seven, that little girl who went to her death without fear, without regret.

10  Each one of us felt compelled to record every story, every encounter. Each one of us felt compelled to bear witness. Such were the wishes of the dying, the **testament** of the dead. Since the so-called civilized world had no use for their lives, then let it be inhabited by their deaths. …

11  After the war we reassured ourselves that it would be enough to relate a single night in Treblinka, to tell of her cruelty, the senselessness of murder, and the outrage born of indifference: it would be enough to find the right word and the **propitious** moment to say it, to shake humanity out of its indifference and keep the torturer from torturing ever again. We thought it would be enough to read the world a poem written by a child in the Theresienstadt ghetto to ensure that no child anywhere would ever again have to endure hunger or fear. It would be enough to describe a death-camp "Selection," to prevent the human right to dignity from ever being violated again.

12  We thought it would be enough to tell of the tidal wave of hatred which broke over the Jewish people for men everywhere to decide once and for all to put an end to hatred of anyone who is "different"—whether black or white, Jew or Arab, Christian

## My Notes

**paradox:** a situation in which two opposite things are true

**testament:** legal proof

**propitious:** fortunate

---

[2] The Talmud is an important scholarly text in the Jewish religion.

# Taking a Stand on Truth and Responsibility

**anemic:** weak

## My Notes

or Moslem[3]—anyone whose orientation differs politically, philosophically, sexually. A naive undertaking? Of course. But not without a certain logic.

13  We tried. It was not easy. At first, because of the language; language failed us. We would have to invent a new vocabulary, for our own words were inadequate, **anemic**. And then too, the people around us refused to listen; and even those who listened refused to believe; and even those who believed could not comprehend. Of course they could not. Nobody could. The experience of the camps defies comprehension. …

14  I remember the killers, I remember the victims, even as I struggle to invent a thousand and one reasons to hope.

15  There may be times when we are powerless to prevent injustice, but there must never be a time when we fail to protest. The Talmud tells us that by saving a single human being, man can save the world. We may be powerless to open all the jails and free all prisoners, but by declaring our solidarity with one prisoner, we indict all jailers. None of us is in a position to eliminate war, but it is our obligation to denounce it and expose it in all its hideousness. War leaves no victors, only victims. I began with the story of Besht. And, like the Besht, mankind needs to remember more than ever. Mankind needs peace more than ever, for our entire planet, threatened by nuclear war, is in danger of total destruction. A destruction only man can provoke, only man can prevent.

16  Mankind must remember that peace is not God's gift to his creatures, it is our gift to each other.

## Second Read

- Reread the speech to answer these text-dependent questions.
- Write any additional questions you have about the text in your Reader/Writer Notebook.

4. **Craft and Structure:** What is the meaning of the comparison the author makes with the simile "Like the body, memory protects its wounds"?

5. **Craft and Structure:** What experiences does Wiesel describe using narrative techniques? Which techniques does he use? Why is narration important to his argument?

6. **Key Ideas and Details:** Why do you think both Wiesel and Solzhenitsyn speak of the importance of telling the truth?

---

[3] Moslem is an older spelling for *Muslim*, a follower of Islam.

## Working from the Text

7. Review your notes and prepare for a **Socratic Seminar** about the responsibility of speaking the truth and upholding significant memories. Socratic Seminars work best when all participants come to the discussion prepared with textual evidence and possible questions. Make sure you have three or four Level 2 or 3 questions, as well as evidence to support your thoughts on this issue, when you participate in the Socratic Seminar.

Preseminar questions:

* What is the importance of speaking the truth in the face of adversity?
* To what extent are we responsible for our fellow humans?

## Participating in the Socratic Seminar

A successful seminar depends on the participants and their willingness to engage in the conversation. The following are things to keep in mind as you participate in a Socratic Seminar:

* Talk to the participants and not the teacher or seminar leader.
* Refer to the texts to support your thinking or to challenge an idea.
* Paraphrase what other students say to make sure that you understand their points before challenging their opinions and evidence.

## Postseminar Reflection

Reflect on your experience during the seminar and your learning by reviewing your responses to the preseminar questions.

* Do you feel that you have a better understanding of the texts?
* What questions do you still have about the texts?
* How would you rate your participation in the seminar? What would you do differently in your next seminar?

### Argument Writing Prompt

Write an argumentative speech supporting a deeply held belief of your own. Support your argument by including some narrative elements. Be sure to:

* Use an organizational structure for an argument that logically sequences claims, counterclaims, valid reasons, and relevant evidence.
* Use persuasive techniques and varied syntax for effect.
* Maintain a formal and objective tone.

Read your speech to a small group of your peers. Ask them to evaluate it for the elements of an argument.

# Taking a Stand on Remembrance

LEARNING STRATEGIES:
Marking the Text, Revising

## Learning Targets
- Analyze the structure and content of two argumentative essays.
- Create a revision plan to strengthen an essay's elements of argumentation.

## Preview

In this activity, you will read two sample arguments and create a plan to revise them.

## Setting a Purpose for Reading
- The two essays that you will read next were written by students during the a timed essay. As you read, mark the text to indicate elements of argumentation.

Both essays received a 6, the highest possible score. Students had 25 minutes to respond in writing to a prompt, so the essays are not expected to be free from errors. You may notice errors as well as segments in need of revision. These essays are recognized as first drafts. The students responded to the following prompt:

### Essay Prompt

Think carefully about the issue presented in the following excerpt and the assignment below.

*Many persons believe that to move up the ladder of success and achievement, they must forget the past, repress it, and relinquish it. But others have just the opposite view. They see old memories as a chance to reckon with the past and integrate past and present.*

(Adapted from Sara Lawrence-Lightfoot, *I've Known Rivers: Lives of Loss and Liberation*)

**Assignment:** Do memories hinder or help people in their effort to learn from the past and succeed in the present? Plan and write an essay in which you develop your point of view on this issue. Support your position with reasoning and examples taken from your reading, studies, experience, or observation.

**My Notes**

## Student Essay 1

Memories act as both a help and a hindrance to the success of someone. Many people advise you to learn from the past and apply those memories so that you can effectively succeed by avoiding repeating your past mistakes. On the other hand, people who get too caught up with the past are unable to move on to the future.

Elie Wiesel's memoir, *Night*, perfectly exemplifies the double nature of memories. Wiesel, a Jewish man, suffered heavily throughout the Holocaust and *Night* is rife with horrific descriptions of his experience. These memories help to spread the view of what life was like. Through recounting these memories, Wiesel is able to educate world readers about the atrocities committed in hopes that the same blatant violations of human rights are never repeated again. His poignant pleas for a peaceful future are examples of the therapeutic property that memories can have. Through reliving the Holocaust through his writing, Wiesel was inspired to become proactive in the battle for civil rights. Some would point to his peaceful actions and the sales of his book and label him a success.

Despite the importance of recounting such memories, Wiesel acknowledges the damage that memories can also cause. Following his liberation from the Auschwitz concentration camp, Wiesel was a bitter, jaded man. He could not even write *Night* until several years later. The end of the novel describes Wiesel's gradual but absolute loss of faith throughout the experience. His past experiences haunted him for several years, rendering him passive. It was not unti he set aside his past that he could even focus on the future. Had he remained so consumed with the pain and damage caused in his past, he may have never achieved the success that he has attained.

Overall, Wiesel's experiences exemplify the importance of the past as a guide. Wiesel's past experiences helped to guide him in later life, but it was not until he pushed them aside that he could move on. To me this means that you should rely on your past without letting it control you. Allow your past to act as a guide, while making sure that you are also living in the present and looking to the future.

## Student Essay 2

The subject of the human memory is a fascinating one. Memory is what keeps the years of our past from becoming meaningless blurs. For years, scientists have studied the human mind, trying to figure out exactly how memory functions. Andrew Lloyd Weber even immortalized the subject in the song "Memory" from the musical *Cats*. With barely any mental effort, memory helps us travel back in time to important events in our life; with its aid we can see our first day of high school, smell last winter's fire, or taste yesterday's lunch. But we also have the darker stories of our lives stored in our mind. Do these memories hinder our forward progress, or must we overcome them in order to grow as individuals?

**My Notes**

# Taking a Stand on Remembrance

**My Notes**

Because memory is such a mystery to us, many authors have toyed with it in literature. Lois Lowry, in *The Giver*, describes a futuristic society in which one man, the Giver, holds the memories, both good and bad, of an entire community. Jonas, his successor, can only feel complete when he has been given both the good and the bad memories, both those of color and love as well as those of war and pain. The book's ultimate moral is that perhaps these memories are painful enough that one wants to suppress them; however, their absence makes the lessons they teach all the more meaningful—and left unlearned.

They say that history repeats itself, and it is absolutely true. History teachers constantly drill the horrors of slavery and segregation into our heads, to illustrate how far our race has come. However, World War II and Hitler's Holocaust took place less than a century ago. Japanese Americans were sent into concentration camps less than a century ago. After 9/11, anti-Arab prejudice reached new peaks. Yes, history does repeat itself. Still, with the diversity of today's world, perhaps the memories of the past can teach us once and for all—never again. These horrific memories, sadly, are necessary if we are to learn that lesson.

Many of today's celebrities and world leaders have had some sort of problem growing up. Some had learning disabilities, some physical conditions, some difficult childhoods or a hard family life. Yet they rose above it to become who they are today … perhaps the memories were necessary for them to become better people. I myself never knew the real, harsh pain of losing a loved one until my uncle died from lung cancer two years ago. Though I still miss him and deeply regret his death, I believe it has made me stronger and because of him, I will never smoke.

Memories are the past—no more, no less. They are hazy recollections your mind keeps of what has happened, what cannot be changed. Good or bad, beneficial or painful, they are simply memories. What you make of them, what you get from them, is entirely up to you.

## Working from the Text

Compare your notes with a partner, and add additional notes based on your discussion. With your partner, determine a revision plan for one of the two essays. Remember that even though these were top-scoring essays, the writers had only 25 minutes to complete them.

What revisions would you recommend to strengthen the arguments? Consult your notes from throughout the unit for guidance. Work with your partner to apply your revision plan to your selected essay.

 **Independent Reading Checkpoint**

Review your independent reading and analyze examples of how authors use evidence in argumentative essays to support their claims about particular issues. Examine and take notes about how specific issues resonate across cultures to inform your writing for the Embedded Assessment.

# Creating an Argument

## ASSIGNMENT

Your assignment is to develop an argument about an issue that resonates across cultures. You will choose a position, target audience, and effective genre to convey your argument to a wide audience.

| | |
|---|---|
| **Planning and Prewriting: Take time to make a plan for your essay.** | ▓ What further research will you have to do to support your claim?<br>▓ Have you stated your claim precisely and identified your counterclaims?<br>▓ Have you found sufficient evidence to support your claim?<br>▓ Who is your audience, and what are their concerns that must be addressed as counterclaims? |
| **Drafting: Determine the structure and organization of your essay.** | ▓ How will you organize your ideas?<br>▓ What transitions will you use to connect evidence and support for your claim?<br>▓ What counterclaims will you acknowledge, and what evidence do you have to refute them? |
| **Revising: Compose your synthesis paper.** | ▓ Have you written a precise claim?<br>▓ Have you used valid and sufficient evidence to support your claim?<br>▓ Have you created an organization that shows a clear relationship among claim, counterclaim, reasons, and evidence?<br>▓ Does your conclusion follow from and support your argument?<br>▓ Have you maintained a formal style throughout? |
| **Editing for Publication: Check that your paper is ready for publication.** | ▓ Have you included transitional words, phrases, and clauses to clarify and connect ideas?<br>▓ Have you consulted style guides to ensure that you are citing evidence correctly and using correct grammar and punctuation?<br>▓ Have you checked that all words are spelled correctly? |

## Reflection

What have you learned about the importance of audience in determining the way an argument is developed? How is logic and reasoning an important part of creating an argument?

# Creating an Argument

## SCORING GUIDE

| Scoring Criteria | Exemplary | Proficient | Emerging | Incomplete |
|---|---|---|---|---|
| **Ideas** | The argument<br>• skillfully presents a claim and provides background and a clear explanation of the issue<br>• synthesizes evidence from a variety of sources that strongly support the claim<br>• summarizes and refutes counterclaims with relevant reasoning and clear evidence<br>• concludes by clearly summarizing the main points and reinforcing the claim. | The argument<br>• supports a claim that is clearly presented with appropriate background details<br>• synthesizes evidence from multiple sources that support the claim<br>• develops claims and counterclaims fairly and uses valid reasoning, relevant and sufficient evidence, and a variety of rhetorical appeals<br>• concludes by revisiting the main points and reinforcing the claim. | The argument<br>• states a claim but does not adequately explain the issue or provide background details<br>• attempts to synthesize evidence from several sources that support the claim<br>• develops some counterclaims, but reasoning may not be completely relevant or sufficient for the evidence cited<br>• concludes by listing the main points of the thesis. | The argument<br>• states a vague or unclear claim and does not explain the issue or provide background details<br>• contains no synthesis of evidence from different sources to support the claim<br>• may or may not develop counterclaims, and reasoning may not be relevant or sufficient for the evidence cited<br>• concludes without restating the main points of the claim. |
| **Structure** | The argument<br>• follows a logical progression of ideas that establish relationships between the essential elements of hook, claim, evidence, counterclaims, and conclusion<br>• links main points with effective transitions that establish coherence. | The argument<br>• establishes clear relationships between the essential elements of hook, claim, evidence, counterclaims, and conclusion<br>• uses transitions to link the major sections of the essay and create coherence. | The argument<br>• demonstrates an awkward progression of ideas, but the reader can understand them<br>• uses some elements of hook, claim, evidence, and conclusion<br>• spends too much time on some irrelevant details and uses few transitions. | The argument<br>• does not follow a logical organization<br>• includes some details and elements of an argument, but the writing lacks clear direction and uses no transitions to help readers follow the line of thought. |
| **Use of Language** | The argument<br>• uses a formal style and tone appropriate to the audience and purpose<br>• smoothly integrates textual evidence from multiple sources, with correct citations<br>• shows excellent command of standard English capitalization, punctuation, spelling, grammar, and usage. | The argument<br>• uses a formal style and tone appropriate to the audience and purpose<br>• correctly cites textual evidence from at least three sources<br>• follows conventions of standard English capitalization, punctuation, spelling, grammar, and usage. | The argument<br>• mixes informal and formal writing styles<br>• cites some textual evidence, but citations may be missing or inaccurate<br>• includes some incorrect capitalization, punctuation, spelling, grammar, or usage that interfere with meaning. | The argument<br>• uses mostly informal writing style<br>• uses some textual evidence but does not include citations<br>• includes incorrect capitalization, punctuation, spelling, grammar, or usage that interfere with meaning. |

# Cultures in Conflict

**Visual Prompt:** What do artifacts, such as the one shown above, tell you about a culture?

## Unit Overview

"Until the lion has a voice, stories of safaris will always glorify the hunter." To illustrate this African proverb, Chinua Achebe wrote the acclaimed novel *Things Fall Apart*, in which he provides a powerful voice for the Ibo, a community nearly silenced by European colonialism. In this unit, you will continue your exploration of culture by reading and studying Achebe's novel. By immersing yourself in the culture and community of the Ibo people, you will analyze a complex community, the institutions that enable it to function, the conflicting roles of its members, and the way in which it is affected by political and social change. Your opinions of the Ibo community's response to change may be positive, negative, or mixed; however, like millions of others who have read the novel, you may find that the characters and community of *Things Fall Apart* remain with you long after your study is complete.

## GOALS:

- To analyze cultural experiences reflected in a work of literature from outside the United States

- To analyze how complex characters in a novel develop and interact to advance a plot or theme

- To research to answer questions, explore complex ideas, and gather relevant information

- To present findings to an audience clearly and logically, making use of digital media

- To draw evidence from a literary text to support analysis and reflection

### ACADEMIC VOCABULARY
reliability
validity
plagiarism
annotated bibliography

### Literary Terms
proverb
folktale
archetype
epigraph
motif
foil
characterization
foreshadowing
tragic hero
hamartia
irony
dramatic irony
verbal irony
situational irony

# Contents

### Activities

*Texts not included in these materials.*

**Language and Writer's Craft**

- Active and Passive Voice (3.5)
- Compare/Contrast (3.7)
- Academic Voice (3.8)
- Using Precise Language and Domain-Specific Vocabulary (3.11)
- Word Patterns (3.15)

**MY INDEPENDENT READING LIST**

# Previewing the Unit

LEARNING STRATEGIES:
QHT, Marking the Text,
Predicting, Graphic Organizer

**My Notes**

## Learning Targets

- Preview the unit for the big ideas and new vocabulary.
- Analyze the skills and knowledge required to complete Embedded Assessment 1 successfully.

## Making Connections

In this unit, you will continue exploring culture by looking at communities in conflict. Many cultures around the world are in conflict today, with both modern and traditional influences affecting how cultures change. As you read Chinua Achebe's novel *Things Fall Apart*, you will closely examine the Ibo culture and the changes it experiences through the eyes of the novelist.

## Essential Questions

Based on your current knowledge, respond to the following Essential Questions.

1. How might a culture change when it encounters new ideas and members?

2. How can an author use a fictional character to make a statement about culture?

## Developing Vocabulary

3. Mark the Academic Vocabulary and Literary Terms using the QHT strategy. Then in your Reader/Writer Notebook, answer the following question: What strategies will you use to gather knowledge of new terms independently and to develop the ability to use them accurately?

**INDEPENDENT READING LINK**

**Read and Discuss**

The focus of this unit is the novel *Things Fall Apart*. For independent reading, you might choose informational texts about the colonization of different parts of the world. Focus on the ways that the colonists changed the native culture. Discuss one or more of your independent reading selections with peers, explaining how the information you learned helps you better understand how the Ibo culture might have been affected by colonization.

## Unpacking Embedded Assessment 1

Read the assignment for Embedded Assessment 1: Researching and Comparing Pre- and Postcolonial Ibo Culture.

Your assignment is to examine one aspect of tribal culture presented in *Things Fall Apart*, its significance to the Ibo community, and compare and contrast how that cultural aspect changed from precolonial to postcolonial Nigeria. You will create a presentation that reflects your research.

In your own words, summarize what you will need to know to complete this assessment successfully. With your class, create a graphic organizer to represent the skills and knowledge you will need to complete the tasks identified in the Embedded Assessment.

# Proverbs and Folktales

## Learning Targets
- Analyze folktales and proverbs to gain insight into the culture of a people.
- Determine an author's purpose for including proverbs and folktales in a novel.

LEARNING STRATEGIES:
Think-Pair-Share, Word
Wall, Graphic Organizer,
Discussion Groups

## Preview
In this activity, you will prepare to read the novel *Things Fall Apart* by analyzing the proverbs and folktales of the Ibo and broader African culture.

## Proverbs and Folktales
**Proverbs** and **folktales** are one part of a culture's oral tradition. People share proverbs and folktales in order to express important stories, ideas, and beliefs about their culture.

**Literary Terms**
A **proverb** is a short saying about a general truth.
A **folktale** is a story without a known author that has been preserved through oral retellings.

1. As you read the novel *Things Fall Apart*, you will encounter many proverbs and folktales that illustrate the beliefs of the Ibo people. One memorable Ibo proverb is "Proverbs are the palm oil with which words are eaten." Explain what you think this proverb means.

2. In small groups, read and discuss the following proverbs from the novel. Then explain each one in the graphic organizer.

| Proverb | Explanation |
|---|---|
| If a child washes his hands, he could eat with kings. | |
| When the moon is shining, the cripple becomes hungry for a walk. | |
| Since men have learned to shoot without missing, [the bird] has learned to fly without perching. | |
| The clan was like a lizard. If it lost its tail it soon grew another. | |
| I cannot live on the bank of a river and wash my hands with spittle. | |
| A man who pays respect to the great paves the way for his own greatness. | |

**My Notes**

## Check Your Understanding
What general truth believed by the Ibo culture is revealed through the proverb "If one finger brought oil it soiled the others"?

# Proverbs and Folktales

## My Notes

### Literary Terms

An **archetype** is a pattern, symbol, image, or idea that recurs in literature.

3. In addition to proverbs, you will also encounter a number of folktales in the novel. Use the organizer below to record details about the folktales discussed in class. Then, either copy this organizer or create your own to record details about the folktales you find in *Things Fall Apart*, especially in Chapters 7, 9, 11, and 15.

| Folktales | |
|---|---|
| **Title** | |
| **Characters** | |
| **Setting** | |
| **Plot Summary** | |
| **Symbols and Archetypes** | |
| **Meaning of the Folktale** | |
| **Significance (reason for its retelling across generations and its inclusion in the novel)** | |

## Check Your Understanding

- What connections can you make between the proverbs and the folktales?
- How can proverbs and folktales provide insight into a culture?
- How and why might an author use proverbs and folktales in a novel?

### Writing to Sources: Explanatory Text

Explain how the proverbs and folktales you analyzed in this activity provide insight into the values of the cultures from which they come. Be sure to:

- Begin with a topic sentence summarizing your understanding of how the theme of proverbs and folktales can tell us about a culture's values.
- Include specific relevant details from the proverbs and folktales that tell you about the culture.
- Cite direct quotations and specific examples from the text. Introduce and punctuate all quotations correctly.

# Researching Context

## Learning Targets
- Gather, evaluate, and cite sources to answer questions about the historical, cultural, social, and geographical context of the novel.
- Use evidence from research to present findings to the class.

LEARNING STRATEGIES:
KWHL, Brainstorming, Graphic Organizer

## Preview
In this activity, you will conduct and present research that answers questions about the context of the novel *Things Fall Apart*.

## Conducting Internet Research
1. When researching on the Internet, it is important to evaluate the **validity** and **reliability** of the information you find. Look at the authority of the information (e.g., was it written by experts?), as well as its objectivity. Refer to the following chart to evaluate Internet sources.

ACADEMIC VOCABULARY
A source has **reliability** if its information can be trusted and is of good quality.
A source that is truthful or accurate has **validity**.

| Questions to Evaluate Internet Sources | |
|---|---|
| **The URL** | What is the website's domain?<br>.com=a for-profit organization<br>.gov, .mil, .us=a government site<br>.edu=an educational institution<br>.org=a nonprofit organization |
| **Sponsor** | What organization or group sponsors the website?<br>Does the website provide information about the sponsor (often found in an "About Us" link)? If so, what information is provided? |
| **Timeliness** | When was the site created?<br>When was the site last updated (usually posted on the top or bottom of the page)? |
| **Purpose** | What is the purpose of the site?<br>Who is the target audience?<br>Does the website present information or opinion? |
| **Author/Publisher** | Who publishes the website?<br>What credentials does the author have?<br>Is the person or group considered an authority on the topic? How do you know? |
| **Links** | Does the website provide links that work?<br>Do the links go to authoritative sources?<br>Are they objective or subjective? |

2. It is also important to avoid **plagiarism**. As you research, keep good notes about your sources and direct quotations so that you can cite them accurately. Note the URL of each site you view, as you may need to revisit the site to collect further information. Use note cards or a word processing program to record information.

ACADEMIC VOCABULARY
**Plagiarism** is the act of using another person's words or ideas without giving credit.

3. With your group, brainstorm a list of possible questions about your assigned topic. Use your questions to guide your group's research. When conducting research, refer to what you have just learned about evaluating sources and avoiding plagiarism.

# Researching Context

## Presentations

4. To prepare for your group's presentation, use note cards to create an annotated outline that includes a thesis statement and key talking points to which you can refer.

5. As you listen to your classmates' presentations, fill in the following organizer with information about their topics.

| Topic | Research Notes |
|---|---|
| Chinua Achebe | |
| Nigeria: History | |
| Nigeria: Geography and Agriculture | |
| British Colonialism and Nigeria | |
| Missionary Involvement in Africa | |
| Tribal Life | |

**INDEPENDENT READING LINK**

**Read and Research**

Review the informational texts you have chosen. Use the Questions to Evaluate Sources to make sure you are using the most appropriate texts for your purpose. Replace any texts that do not seem to be reliable and valid.

## Check Your Understanding

- What are some of the key elements of a valid and reliable Internet source?
- How did your research help provide a context for the novel?
- What new predictions can you make based on the class presentations?
- Compare and contrast the class presentations: What made some more engaging, informative, or effective than others?

# Culture Wheel

## Learning Targets
- Analyze the cumulative impact of using words and phrases from the Ibo language on the tone and meaning of the novel.
- Learn domain-specific vocabulary to use when speaking and writing about the novel.

## Previewing the Novel

**ABOUT THE AUTHOR**
Chinua Achebe (1930–2013), the son of a Christian minister, was one of Nigeria's most celebrated novelists. Born an Ibo in Ogidi, Nigeria, in 1930, Achebe was educated in English. Achebe taught English at the university level at colleges in Africa and the United States. His first and best-known novel, *Things Fall Apart*, was published in 1958. Achebe wrote several novels, short story collections, and books of essays.

1. As you examine the cover and **epigraph** of *Things Fall Apart*, what predictions can you make about the novel? Consider the title. To what "things" might Achebe be referring?

2. Copy the following names and pronunciations onto a blank bookmark supplied by your teacher. *Things Fall Apart* focuses on a culture that may be unfamiliar to you. Even though the novel is written in English, the author uses words and phrases from his native Ibo language. Review the glossary at the back of the novel. Add additional words and definitions to your bookmark as you read. Consider including: *chi*, *ilo*, *nza*, and *obi*.

| | |
|---|---|
| Achebe (Ah-chay-bay) | Nwoye (Nuh-woh-yeh) |
| Chinua ( Chin-oo-ah) | Ojiubo (Oh-jee-ooh-boh) |
| Ekwefi (Eh-kweh-fee) | Okonkwo (Oh-kawn-kwoh) |
| Ezinma (Eh-zeen-mah) | Umuofia (Oo-moo-oh-fee-ah) |
| Ikemefuna (Ee-keh-meh-foo-nah) | Unoka (Ooh-no-kah) |
| Obierika (Oh-bee-air-ee-kah) | |

---

**LEARNING STRATEGIES:**
Previewing, Predicting, Graphic Organizer

 **WORD CONNECTIONS**

**Roots and Affixes**
*Prediction* contains the root *dict* from the Latin word *dicere*, meaning "to tell or see." This root also appears in *contradict*, *dictate*, and *dictionary*. The prefix *pre-* means "before." The suffix *-ion* indicates that the word is a noun.

**Literary Terms**
An **epigraph** is a phrase, quotation, or poem that is set at the beginning of a document or component. An epigraph may help direct the reader to the author's purpose or theme.

**My Notes**

---

# Culture Wheel

3. Work with a group to review the Ibo words and their definitions below, and then place the words into the appropriate section of the Culture Wheel organizer that follows.

## Glossary of Selected Ibo Words and Phrases*

| | |
|---|---|
| agbala | woman; also used for a man who has taken no title |
| ani | Earth goddess |
| chi | personal god |
| efulefu | worthless man |
| egwugwu | masquerader who impersonates one of the ancestral spirits of the village |
| ekwe | type of drum made from wood |
| foo foo | food made from yams that serves a chief role in the annual Feast of the New Yam |
| ilo | the village green where assemblies for sports, discussions, and so on take place |
| iyi-uwa | a special kind of stone that forms the link between an ogbanje and the spirit world (Only if the iyi-uwa were discovered and destroyed would the child not die.) |
| jigida | string of waist beads worn by women |
| kola nut | food used to greet visitors and guests |
| kwenu | shout of approval and greeting |
| ilo | village playground |
| Ndichie | elders |
| obi | large living quarters of the head of the family |
| ochu | murder or manslaughter |
| ogbanje | changeling; a child who repeatedly dies and returns to its mother to be reborn |
| ogene | musical instrument; a kind of gong |
| osu | outcast (Having been dedicated to a god, the osu was taboo and not allowed to mix with the freeborn in any way.) |
| oye | one of the four market days |
| palm wine | fermented palm sap used for celebration and ceremony |
| udu | musical instrument; a type of drum made from pottery |
| yam | most valuable cash crop grown in the village |

*Source: *Things Fall Apart*, Chinua Achebe (London: William Heinemann Ltd., 1958).

## Culture Wheel

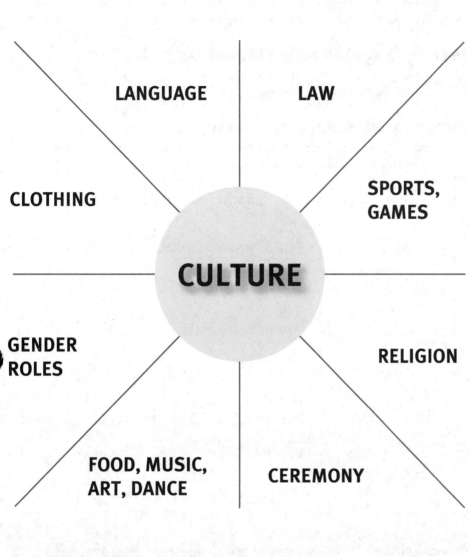

LANGUAGE

LAW

CLOTHING

SPORTS, GAMES

**CULTURE**

GENDER ROLES

RELIGION

FOOD, MUSIC, ART, DANCE

CEREMONY

4. In your Reader/Writer Notebook, write a reflection on the vocabulary work you have completed today. Why do you think Achebe included these Ibo words and phrases in his novel? What do you think the overall impact is on the novel's meaning?

**My Notes**

## Check Your Understanding

From the organizer above choose one aspect of the Ibo culture that you might want to examine further for your research presentation. Write three research questions that would help you to compare and contrast how that cultural aspect changed from precolonial to postcolonial Nigeria.

 WORD CONNECTIONS

Roots and Affixes

*Gender* contains the root *gen*, from the Greek word *genos*, meaning "race or class." This root also appears in *engender*, *generate*, and *genealogy*.

# Father and Son

**LEARNING STRATEGIES:**
Graphic Organizer, Double-Entry Journal

**My Notes**

## Learning Targets

- Analyze how a complex character interacts with other characters.
- Analyze how a complex character's motivation advances the plot.

## Reading *Things Fall Apart*, Chapters 1–4

In the following activity, you will read Chapters 1–4 and use a Double-Entry Journal to record details from the text that illustrate Okonkwo's character.

## Comparing and Contrasting Characters

1. As you read, use the organizer below or create one of your own to compare and contrast Okonkwo and his father. Record facts and details about each.

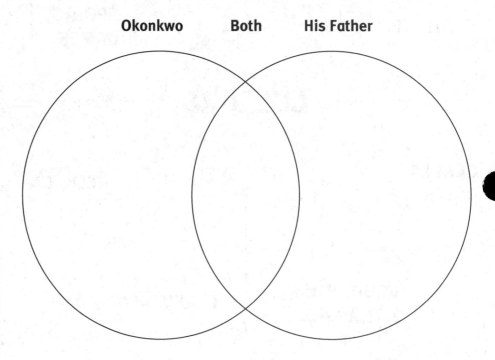

**Okonkwo   Both   His Father**

## Literary Terms

A **motif** is a recurring image, symbol, theme, character type, or subject that becomes a unifying element in an artistic work.

A **foil** is a character whose traits contrast with and therefore highlight the traits of another.

2. Authors use **motifs** for many reasons in their writing, including establishing themes and moods. Achebe uses the motif of tensions between fathers and sons in his novel. Review the facts and details about Okonkwo and his father that you recorded. How do these similarities and differences create tension between the two? Explain how Okonkwo's father serves as a **foil** to his son.

## Language and Writer's Craft: Active and Passive Voice

Sentences can be in active or passive voice. **Active voice** occurs when the subject of a sentence performs the action, so it emphasizes the person or thing that does the action. For example, in the following sentence, Okonkwo performs the action of throwing: "In the end, Okonkwo threw the Cat." Most of the time, you should use the active voice in your writing to enhance clarity and avoid wordiness. In other words, use active voice unless there is a compelling reason to use passive voice.

**Passive voice** occurs when the subject of the sentence receives the action; passive voice always uses a form of *to be* with the past participle of the verb. For example, the following sentence uses a form of *to be* (*was*) and the past participle of *throw* (*thrown*): "The Cat was thrown by Okonkwo." Only use passive voice when you want to emphasize the receiver of the action, either because the receiver of the action is more important than the doer, or because the person or thing that does the action is unknown.

PRACTICE Identify the sentences below that are in passive voice and rewrite them in active voice.

- *Things Fall Apart* was written by Chinua Achebe.
- Chinua Achebe included many proverbs in his novel.
- Showing Nigerians in stereotypical ways was avoided by Achebe.

## Writing to Sources: Explanatory Text

Write an explanatory paragraph that answers the question, how is Okonkwo's character influenced by his complex relationship with his father? Be sure to:

- Include a topic sentence that compares or contrasts the two characters.
- Use specific details and quotations from the novel as support.
- Use active voice.

**My Notes**

# Father and Son

## WORD CONNECTIONS

### Roots and Affixes

*Dominated* contains the root *dom*, from the Latin words *domus*, meaning "house," and *dominus*, meaning "master (of the house)." This root also appears in *dominant*, *predominant*, *domineer*, *dominion*, *domestic*, and *domicile*.

## My Notes

_____

_____

_____

_____

_____

## WORD CONNECTIONS

### Multiple-Meaning Words

In literature, a *foil* is a character. This word also refers to a sword used in the sport of fencing, and to aluminum foil. As a verb, to *foil* means to prevent success.

_____

_____

_____

_____

_____

_____

### Independent Practice: Double-Entry Journal

3. Look for examples of Okonkwo's feelings and fears, the reasons for those fears, and the effect they have on his actions. Also look for a **motif** or **foil**.

   • Include textual evidence from each chapter in the left-hand column.

   • Write your personal response or interpretation in the right-hand column.

   • As you read Chapters 1–4, continue the chart on a separate sheet of paper.

| Feelings and Fears: Passage from the Text | Personal Response or Interpretation |
|---|---|
| Example: "But his whole life was dominated by fear, the fear of failure and of weakness." (Ch. 2) | I wonder why Okonkwo is so afraid. How could he be a successful wrestler if he is dominated by fear? |

### Check Your Understanding

Review the notes in your Double-Entry Journal and respond to the following questions:

   • How do Okonkwo's fears influence his actions?

   • What are the reasons for his fears?

# Character in Conflict

## Learning Targets
- Cite textual evidence to support an interpretation.
- Collaborate to present your findings with visual support.

## Reading *Things Fall Apart*, Chapters 1–4

In this activity, you will revisit Chapters 1–4 and write an argument.

## Visual Interpretations

1. With your group, discuss the first four chapters of *Things Fall Apart*. In those chapters, Achebe presents Okonkwo as a man of high status in his village despite some of his less admirable traits.

   Fill in the chart below with details from Chapters 1–4 to explore the conflicting sides of Okonkwo's character.

| Okonkwo's Achievements and Status | Negative Traits and Actions |
| --- | --- |
|  |  |

2. With your group, plan a presentation using digital media that illustrates Okonkwo's dual nature. You can use a digital drawing tool like Microsoft Paint or assemble clip art in a PowerPoint to create your visual interpretation. Make strategic use of digital media to enhance your interpretation and to add interest to your presentation.

3. Present your visual interpretation to another group. Be sure to:
   - Assign talking points to all members of your group.
   - Make eye contact with your audience when speaking.
   - Refer to specific details in your visual and cite textual evidence.

**My Notes**

# Character in Conflict

## My Notes

4. In preparation for completing the Writing to Sources: Argument, work with your group to reflect on the argument stimulus below. Use a Round Table Discussion graphic organizer to take notes from your discussion.

### Writing to Sources: Argument

Take a position on the question: *Is it common for powerful leaders to have flawed characters? Why? How might this affect the community*? Write an argument essay to support your position and explain how it relates to Okonkwo's character.
Be sure to:

- State your claim in the beginning sentence.
- Use relevant evidence from the text and valid reasoning to support your claim.
- Provide a concluding statement that follows from the claim you have presented.

## Learning Targets
- Analyze how a complex character interacts with other characters.
- Write an expository essay to compare and contrast.

## Reading *Things Fall Apart*, Chapters 5–6

In this activity, you will read Chapters 5–6 and analyze the relationships between characters in the novel.

## Characterization

Writers use **characterization** to create vivid images of characters in the reader's mind.

1. Compare and contrast how Okonkwo treats his children and his wives in the chapters you have read so far. What do all of his relationships with family members have in common? How are some different from others? Choose a compare/contrast structure, such as a Venn diagram or other graphic organizer that you create.

2. Work with a partner or group to note the names and relationships of the characters. Pay special attention to Okonkwo's family. Include quotes from the novel to support your ideas. Add rows as needed to the graphic organizer below, or use your Reader/Writer Notebook.

| Character | Relationship to Okonkwo and others in the family | What do you learn about the character? | What is your reaction to the character? |
|-----------|--------------------------------------------------|----------------------------------------|------------------------------------------|
|           |                                                  |                                        |                                          |

**LEARNING STRATEGIES:**
Skimming/Scanning, Graphic Organizer

### Literary Terms
**Characterization** refers to the methods a writer uses to develop characters, including descriptions of what they say, what they do, how they act, what they think, and what others say about them.

**My Notes**

# Family Ties

## Language and Writer's Craft: Compare/Contrast

In this unit, you have been comparing and contrasting Achebe's characterization, and you will write a compare/contrast essay for Embedded Assessment 1. In a compare/contrast essay, the way you organize ideas is an important part of communicating similarities and differences.

Recall that a **thesis** is a statement of your perspective or assessment of a topic. A compare/contrast thesis, therefore, must introduce your ideas about how the subjects of your essay are similar and different. Many compare/contrast thesis statements begin with words *like, although, whereas, even though*, or *while*. These words suggest that a contrast is to follow. Here is an example:

- Although Okonkwo and Unoka both are tall men, Unoka walks with a stoop, suggesting that he is burdened by the expectations of his tribe.

Another way to write a compare/contrast thesis statement is to focus on differences and similarities. For example, consider this thesis:

- A similarity between Okonkwo and Unoka is that both are tall men. Their differences, though, are more pronounced than their similarities.

The organization of your **body paragraphs** also helps you organize your ideas logically. You may choose to discuss one subject thoroughly in one paragraph and then turn to the other subject in the next paragraph, pointing out its similarities and differences. This structure is a good choice when the first subject is more familiar or provides a lens through which to view the other subject. Alternatively, you may discuss one point of comparison at a time, explaining how the subjects compare on that point before turning to another point of comparison. In this type of organization, each point of comparison is usually discussed in its own paragraph.

**PRACTICE** Use a graphic organizer such as a Venn diagram as a prewriting tool to help you compare and contrast two of Okonkwo's family relationships in response to the writing prompt below. Using your graphic organizer, decide if you will use a subject-by-subject or a point-by-point organizational structure. Explain your choice in your Reader/Writer Notebook.

## Writing to Sources: Explanatory Text

How do Okonkwo's family relationships make him a sympathetic or an unsympathetic character? Be sure to:

- Write a thesis statement that compares and contrasts at least two relationships and explores their effect on characterization.
- Include supporting details and quotations from the novel.
- Use an effective organizational structure with transition words and phrases.

# Sacrificial Son

## Learning Targets

- Collaborate to prepare for and participate in a discussion using textual evidence to support analysis.
- Write an analytical response in a formal style and voice.

## Reading *Things Fall Apart*, Chapters 7–8

In this activity, you will read Chapters 7–8 and prepare for and participate in a Socratic Seminar.

## Foreshadowing

1. Consider how Achebe uses **foreshadowing** in the last two sentences of Chapter 1. Why do you think he tells the reader so early on that Ikemefuna is "doomed" and "ill-fated"?

## Preparing for a Socratic Seminar

2. Skim/scan Chapters 7 and 8, taking notes to answer at least one assigned question from the following graphic organizer. Include details and page numbers from the text.

3. Work with your group to create a visual and come up with talking points to present your response to the assigned question.

4. As each group presents its visual and talking points, take notes to complete the graphic organizer.

5. Write two interpretive and two universal questions related to your assigned question to use in a Socratic Seminar.

## Socratic Seminar Norms

Socratic Seminar discussions follow the norms of effective discussions, such as:

- Come to discussions prepared by having read material and collected needed evidence.
- Set rules for collegial discussions, making decisions, setting goals, assigning responsibilities, and establishing deadlines.
- Pose and respond to questions to keep discussions moving.
- Challenge and verify ideas while also adjusting conclusions based on evidence.
- Include diverse perspectives; summarize points for clarification and verify reasoning and evidence presented to support it.

> **LEARNING STRATEGIES:**
> Questioning the Text, Graphic Organizer, Note-taking, Drafting, Sharing and Responding, Discussion Groups, Socratic Seminar

> **Literary Terms**
> **Foreshadowing** refers to the use of hints or clues in a narrative to suggest future action.

**My Notes**

# Sacrificial Son

| Question | Page No. | Answer and Support |
|---|---|---|
| How has Nwoye changed, and what has caused the changes? | | |
| Describe the arrival of the locusts. What is the reaction of the people of Umuofia? | | |
| Do you think that Ikemefuna suspects that he is going to be killed? Why or why not? | | |
| How does Okonkwo feel about Ikemefuna's death? How does Nwoye feel? | | |
| Genesis 22:1–19 of the Bible presents the story of Abraham and Isaac. What similarities and differences are there in the sacrifices of Isaac and Ikemefuna? How does this incident illustrate the novel's father/son motif? | | |
| How do you think the death of Ikemefuna will affect the relationship between Okonkwo and Nwoye? | | |
| Okonkwo does not heed the advice of the old man, Ogbuefi Ezeudu. What consequences do you think there may be for his part in the death of Ikemefuna? | | |

## Language and Writer's Craft: Academic Voice

Literary analysis is typically written in **academic voice**, which uses a straightforward, formal style and avoids a conversational tone. Academic writing focuses readers on the ideas as presented in the text, rather than on the personality and voice of the author.

Academic voice uses the third-person point of view as well as **formal diction**, which avoids the use of slang, contractions, and unnecessary words such as *possibly, very, maybe,* and *really*. Academic voice sends a message to readers; it tells them that you take your writing and your readers seriously.

Consider the formal diction in this passage from *Things Fall Apart*, which helps set a tone of dignity and sorrow:

> As soon as his father walked in, that night, Nwoye knew that Ikemefuna had been killed, and something seemed to give way inside him like the snapping of a tightened bow. He did not cry. He just hung limp. He had had the same feeling not long ago, during the last harvest season.

As a contrast, read this passage from Mark Twain's 1882 "Advice to Youth." Twain's style is informal and conversational, full of the writer's personality and sense of humor:

> Go to bed early, get up early—this is wise. Some authorities say get up with the sun; some say get up with one thing, others with another. But a lark is really the best thing to get up with. It gives you a splendid reputation with everybody to know that you get up with the lark; and if you get the right kind of lark, and work at him right, you can easily train him to get up at half past nine, every time—it's no trick at all.

Note that an informal style is well suited to Twain's purpose, which is to entertain with humor. In the same way, a formal academic voice is suited to the purpose of a literary analysis.

PRACTICE In the table below, compare the differences between formal (academic) and informal style and voice.

| Characteristics of Formal Style | Characteristics of Informal Style |
|---|---|
| | |

Before you begin the following writing prompt, look over your notes, which were probably written in an informal style and voice. When you respond to the prompt, you will want to use a formal style and voice to lend credibility to your academic writing. The description of formal diction above will help you make the necessary changes.

My Notes

# Sacrificial Son

## Writing to Sources: Explanatory Text

Select one of the questions from the graphic organizer on the previous page as the basis for an analytical response. Be sure to:

- Include a clear thesis statement.
- Provide details and quotations from the text with meaningful commentary.
- Use a formal style and voice.

# Cultural Change

## Learning Targets
- Analyze how the introduction of a new character affects the development of the story.
- Predict, question, and begin to research how colonization might affect an aspect of the Ibo culture.

## Reading *Things Fall Apart*, Chapter 9

In this activity, you will read Chapter 9 and analyze how the introduction of the character Ikemefuna affects the development of the story. Then you will prepare for the Embedded Assessment by developing research questions and beginning your annotated bibliography.

## Ikemefuna

1. With your group, discuss how the events of Chapter 9 are connected to Ikemefuna's death in the previous chapter. What conclusions might Okonkwo's community draw from the juxtaposition of these two events?

2. Consider the character of Ikemefuna. Choose or create an appropriate graphic organizer in which you list details about Ikemefuna. Your organizer may be a chart, a web, or another graphic. Be sure to include details about Ikemefuna's appearance and actions as well as the attitudes other people have toward him.

3. Discuss with a partner or small group Ikemefuna's influence on the community. Be sure to discuss not only how he influenced the community but also how specific characters felt about that influence.

## Check Your Understanding

Answer the following question in two or three sentences: How do Ikemefuna's arrival, presence, and death affect the community?

## Preparing for Embedded Assessment 1

4. Work in a group to choose a topic from the culture wheel graphic organizer that you completed in Activity 3.4 or from the list below. Write research questions to compare and contrast how that cultural aspect changed from precolonial to postcolonial Nigeria. **Note:** As you research, you will find "Ibo" can also be spelled "Igbo."

### Aspects of Ibo (Igbo) Culture Affected by Colonialism

| | | | |
|---|---|---|---|
| Music | Language | Justice | Sports |
| Weddings | Hospitality | Gender Roles | Housing |
| War | Food | Clothing | Medicine |
| Festivals/ Holidays | Funeral Rites | Business Dealings | Farming |
| View of Nature | Status | Family | Religion |

LEARNING STRATEGIES:
Rereading, Marking the Text, Graphic Organizer, Drafting

My Notes

# Cultural Change

If you have access to a computer, you may want to capture researched information electronically. It will be available for reference and also to copy and paste quotations directly into your final document.

**ACADEMIC VOCABULARY**

Creating a bibliography or a Works Cited page is an important part of any research project. An **annotated bibliography** takes this process one step further by creating not only a list of sources used in research but also comments about each source.

**My Notes**

**Research Questions:**

5. After writing research questions, assign a different question to each person in your group. As you research, create note cards to record the information that you will need to cite and evaluate your sources in an **annotated bibliography**. Include the following:

   • citation: title, author, publisher, source type, date of publication or access
   • information: quotes, paraphrases, and summaries that answer your questions
   • evaluation: validity, reliability, and usefulness of the source

## Narrative Writing Prompt

Consider the impact of Ikemefuna's time in Umuofia. On a separate sheet of paper, write a short narrative from the point of view of either Okonkwo or Nwoye that reveals Ikemefuna's influence on the community (his arrival, presence, death). Be sure to:

• Convey the character's voice and point of view.
• Include specific details from the novel.
• Reflect on the impact his character had on the community.

 **Independent Reading Checkpoint**

Review your independent reading. What have you learned and observed about the ways in which colonists changed aspects of native cultures? Review any notes you made. How can you use what you have learned as you research and compare pre- and postcolonial Ibo culture? What comparisons and/or contrasts can you make between the colonization of other cultures and that of the Ibo culture?

# Researching and Comparing Pre- and Postcolonial Ibo Culture

## ASSIGNMENT

Your assignment is to examine one aspect of tribal culture presented in *Things Fall Apart*, its significance to the Ibo community, and to compare and contrast how that cultural aspect changed from precolonial to postcolonial Nigeria. You will create a presentation that reflects your research.

| | |
|---|---|
| **Planning: Take time to plan, conduct, and record your research.** | ▦ What research questions will help you compare and contrast one aspect of pre- and postcolonial Ibo culture?<br><br>▦ How will you find and incorporate textual evidence of your cultural aspect from the novel *Things Fall Apart*?<br><br>▦ How will you record your research in an annotated bibliography? |
| **Creating and Rehearsing: Collaborate with your group to create and prepare a presentation with visual support.** | ▦ How will you select the most interesting and relevant facts and details to include in your presentation?<br><br>▦ How will you organize your presentation to compare and contrast Ibo culture before and after the colonial period?<br><br>▦ How could you use a presentation tool such as PowerPoint or Prezi to incorporate audio and visual components into your presentation?<br><br>▦ How will you choose relevant images and write appropriate captions to engage your audience?<br><br>▦ How will you divide the speaking responsibilities and transition between speakers?<br><br>▦ How will you use the scoring guide to revise and provide feedback on your own and others' presentations as you rehearse? |
| **Presenting and Listening: Rehearse to deliver a smooth presentation; prepare to listen and respond to other presentations.** | ▦ What are the effective speaking and listening techniques you will need to use to engage your audience?<br><br>▦ During your peers' presentations, how will you organize your notes on the subject of each presentation? |

## Reflection

As you read the rest of *Things Fall Apart*, consider the following:

• What generalizations can you make about the impact of colonialism on native cultures?

• Which aspects of Ibo culture do you think were negatively affected by colonialism? Positively?

# Researching and Comparing Pre- and Postcolonial Ibo Culture

## SCORING GUIDE

| Scoring Criteria | Exemplary | Proficient | Emerging | Incomplete |
|---|---|---|---|---|
| **Ideas** | The presentation<br>• communicates findings and evidence clearly, concisely, and logically<br>• uses well-researched, accurate, and relevant facts, details, and examples<br>• demonstrates a deep understanding of the subject. | The presentation<br>• communicates findings and evidence<br>• uses mostly accurate and relevant facts details, and examples<br>• demonstrates an adequate understanding of the subject. | The presentation<br>• communicates insufficient findings and evidence<br>• uses inaccurate, irrelevant, or insufficient facts, details, and examples<br>• demonstrates lack of understanding of the subject. | The presentation<br>• communicates insufficient findings and/or no evidence<br>• uses few or no facts, details, and examples<br>• demonstrates lack of understanding of the subject. |
| **Structure** | The presentation<br>• introduces the topic in an engaging manner, uses smooth transitions, and provides a thoughtful conclusion<br>• thoroughly analyzes the topic through compare/contrast<br>• makes strategic use of digital media to integrate multiple sources of information. | The presentation<br>• introduces the topic, uses transitions, and provides a conclusion<br>• analyzes the topic through compare/contrast<br>• makes use of digital media to integrate multiple sources of information. | The presentation<br>• lacks an introduction, transitions, and/or a conclusion<br>• does not analyze the topic through compare/contrast<br>• makes some use of digital media but may not effectively integrate multiple sources of information. | The presentation<br>• lacks an introduction, transitions, and/or a conclusion<br>• does not analyze the topic through compare/contrast<br>• does not use digital media and/or multiple sources of information. |
| **Use of Language** | The presentation<br>• demonstrates effective oral communication skills (eye contact, pacing, command of formal English)<br>• uses precise language and domain-specific vocabulary to manage the complexity of the topic<br>• includes a complete annotated bibliography with correct citations, summaries, and source evaluations. | The presentation<br>• demonstrates adequate oral communication skills (eye contact, pacing, command of formal English)<br>• uses some precise language and domain-specific vocabulary to manage the topic<br>• includes an annotated bibliography with citations, summaries, and source evaluations. | The presentation<br>• lacks effective oral communication skills (eye contact, pacing, command of formal English)<br>• uses inappropriate language and/or vocabulary for the topic<br>• lacks an annotated bibliography and/or provides incorrect citations, summaries, and source evaluations. | The presentation<br>• lacks effective oral communication skills (eye contact, pacing, command of formal English)<br>• uses inappropriate language and no domain-specific vocabulary<br>• lacks any type of bibliography and does not provide citations, summaries, or source evaluations. |

# Previewing Embedded Assessment 2 and Creating a Tableau

## Learning Targets

- Identify and analyze the knowledge and skills needed to complete Embedded Assessment 2 successfully.
- Reflect on concepts, Essential Questions, and vocabulary.
- Analyze the roles and relationships of characters.

## Making Connections

In the first part of this unit, you have been reading the novel *Things Fall Apart* and analyzing how a writer develops a story and its characters. In this last half of the unit, you will continue reading the novel and will also read informational texts to help you set the context for the novel and learn more about its author in preparation for writing a literary analysis essay.

## Essential Questions

Based on your understanding from the first part of the unit, how would you answer the Essential Questions now?

1. How might a culture change when it encounters new ideas and members?


2. How can an author use a fictional character to make a statement about culture?


## Developing Vocabulary

Think about the Academic Vocabulary and Literary Terms you have studied so far in this unit. Which words or terms can you now move to a new category on a QHT chart? Which could you now teach to others that you were unfamiliar with at the beginning of the unit?

## Unpacking Embedded Assessment 2

Read the assignment for Embedded Assessment 2: Writing a Literary Analysis of a Novel.

> Your assignment is to write an analytical essay about *Things Fall Apart* in which you examine a character's response to the cultural collision caused by the introduction of Western ideas into Ibo culture. In your essay, analyze how the collision challenges the character's sense of identity and explain how his response shapes the meaning of the work as a whole.

In your own words, summarize what you will need to know to complete this assessment successfully. With your class, create a graphic organizer to represent the skills and knowledge you will need to complete the tasks identified in the Embedded Assessment.

---

### LEARNING STRATEGIES:
Skimming/Scanning, Summarizing, Close Reading, Role Playing

### My Notes

---

### INDEPENDENT READING LINK

**Read and Connect**

In this part of the unit, you will continue reading *Things Fall Apart* with a focus on the ways that Ibo culture changes. For your independent reading, you might choose novels, plays, or poetry from colonial or postcolonial nations (for example, India, Southeast Asian nations, South American nations, or African nations). Establish if the text was written during or after colonization. Look for ways in which the characters respond to colonization or to life after colonization.

# Previewing Embedded Assessment 2 and Creating a Tableau

## WORD CONNECTIONS

### Etymology

*Tableau* is a French word meaning "a graphic description or representation." Unlike English words that usually form a plural by adding an "s" or "es," the plural of tableau is *tableaux*.

## GRAMMAR & USAGE

### Reciprocal Pronouns

Note the reciprocal pronoun *one another* in the next-to-last line of the second bullet point. There are two reciprocal pronouns: *one another* and *each other*. Use *each other* with two people or comparisons; use *one another* with three or more.

## My Notes

## Reflecting on Character Relationships

3. Use the following graphic organizer to begin Okonkwo's family tree. Write in the names of three of his relatives, adding details about each.

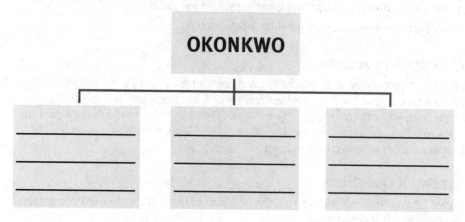

**OKONKWO**

4. Meet with a small group to compare notes. Add additional boxes and details to represent other relatives explored by your group.

## Creating an Ibo Tableau

5. Work with your group members to create a tableau (a freeze-frame snapshot) of characters from *Things Fall Apart*.

   • Begin by writing the name of each character on its own index card and giving each group member a character card.

   • Review the basic facts about your character. Write a short statement that your character will give. The statement should begin with "I am ..."; then state your character's name and reveal an interesting fact about that character. Just as the characters' positions in the tableau will explain their relationships with one another, try to let the lines you write and the way you deliver them reveal your character's attitude and personality.

   • Work with your group to decide where each character should stand, how he or she should pose, and where he or she should be positioned in relation to others. Be prepared to present your tableau to the class. You and fellow characters should strike the pose and then step out of the freeze-frame one at a time to deliver your lines.

## Check Your Understanding

What aspects of Ibo culture are highlighted in your family tree and tableau?

# Ibo Norms and Values

## Learning Targets
- Cite textual evidence to support analysis of what the text says explicitly and draw inferences from the text.
- Read closely to gather evidence from a text about the norms and values of a culture.

## Reading *Things Fall Apart*, Chapter 10

In this activity, you will read Chapter 10 and gather evidence from the text about the norms and values of the Ibo culture.

## Norms and Values of the Ibo Culture

1. After you complete a close read of Chapter 10, think about the norms and values of the Ibo culture that are illustrated in the text. Remember that the term *norms* refer to the attitudes and behaviors that are considered normal or typical to a group of people. For instance, think about the discussion norms that were established in your classroom during Unit 1. With your group, revisit Chapters 1–10 and use the following table to record the norms and values that you find evidence for in the text. What is important to the Ibo civilization and how does Achebe show this to the readers of the novel?

| Norms and Values of the Ibo | Textual Evidence |
|---|---|
|  |  |
|  |  |
|  |  |
|  |  |
|  |  |

LEARNING STRATEGIES:
Drafting, Graphic Organizer, Marking the Text

**My Notes**

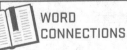

**WORD CONNECTIONS**

**Multiple-Meaning Words**

The root word of *civilization* is *civil*. *Civil* can mean "polite" or "courteous"; it also refers to anything relating to citizens or to ordinary community life.

# Ibo Norms and Values

**My Notes**

2. Work with a partner to compose several universal questions on the topic of the norms and values of the Ibo culture. Write the following questions. Use them to explore the concept of cultural norms and values in your discussion group.

## Language and Writer's Craft: Using Precise Language and Domain-Specific Vocabulary

When describing another culture, it is especially important to use **precise language** to avoid generalizing, stereotyping, or unintentionally offending your reader.

For example, consider this sentence about the Ibo people:

> They honor their elders in a way that we do not.

Framing the Ibo as *they* and the culture of the writer as *we* is a generalization that makes the Ibo seem different or "other."

Here is a better way to write the sentence, replacing the imprecise pronouns *they* and *we* with specific references to the culture or ethnic group under discussion:

> The Ibo people honor their elders in a way that may seem unusual to Americans.

Another way to make your writing stronger is to use **domain-specific vocabulary** to describe the subject. Domain-specific vocabulary words are terms associated with a narrow topic or field, rather than general terms you might see more often.

Think about how you could make the following sentence more precise using domain-specific vocabulary:

> When Okonkwo visits the clan elder at home, he brings offerings of food and drink to show his respect.

For example, you could revise the sentence this way:

> When Okonkwo visits the clan elder in his obi, he brings offerings of kola nut and palm wine to show his respect.

The words *obi*, *kola nut*, and *palm wine* refer to specific aspects of Ibo culture.

**PRACTICE** Use precise language and domain-specific vocabulary to improve the following sentences:

The case of Uzowulu is decided in a manner similar to a trial you might see in our country, including a decision made by a jury. After the trial, Uzowulu is told to bring a gift to his wife's parents and ask his wife to come back to him.

## Writing to Sources: Explanatory Text

From your notes, write a paragraph to explain the values and norms of the Ibo culture. Be sure to:

- Include a well-stated topic sentence.
- Include the best details and textual evidence that highlight the values and norms of Ibo culture and use precise or domain-specific vocabulary when possible.
- Use a logical organizational structure and employ transitions effectively to move from one key point to the next.

After you write your paragraph, share it with a discussion group.

## Check Your Understanding

Summarize why you should use precise language to speak and write about cultures.

# RAFTing with Chielo

**LEARNING STRATEGIES:**
RAFT, Oral Reading, Graphic Organizer

## My Notes

## Learning Targets
- Analyze how complex characters react to events in a plot.
- Write a narrative to explore a character's voice.

## Reading *Things Fall Apart*, Chapter 11–12

In this activity, you will read Chapters 11–12 and use the RAFT strategy to create a narrative in the voice of a character from the novel.

## Revisiting Folktales in Chapter 11

1. Go back to the graphic organizer that you used to analyze folktales in Activity 3.2. Re-create it in your Reader/Writer Notebook and add notes analyzing Ekwefi's story about the Tortoise at the beginning of Chapter 11. What do you think is the purpose of this folktale in Ibo culture: What moral or lesson does it teach?

2. What do you think is Achebe's purpose in including this story in the novel?

## Making Inferences in Chapter 12

3. As you reread the first three pages of Chapter 12, take notes in the following space to record textual evidence showing how Okonkwo, Ekwefi, and Ezinma are acting in response to the events of the previous evening. What inferences can you make from their thoughts, words, and actions?

**Okonkwo**

**Ekwefi**

**Ezinma**

**INDEPENDENT READING LINK**

**Read and Connect**
Choose two or three characters and a chunk of reading from one of your independent reading texts. Take notes to record how the characters act in response to an important event. How are their responses similar and different? Share your observations with a group.

## Introducing the Strategy: RAFT

**RAFT** stands for role, audience, format, and topic. Using this strategy, a writer can create a new text by brainstorming various roles (e.g., self, characters from other texts), audiences (e.g., a different character, a real person), formats (e.g., letter, brochure, essay, travel guide), and topics. Writers may choose a new role, audience, format, and/or topic to create a new text.

## Using the RAFT Strategy

4. Discuss your evidence and inferences in a small group. Have each group member choose the role of a different character and use the RAFT strategy to write about Chielo's abduction of Ezinma in Chapter 11. While in the role, each group member should write what his or her character is thinking, using the pronoun "I," from the time Chielo, as Priestess of Agbala, comes for Ezinma until the end of the chapter. (The character's thoughts serve as the topic.)

   **Role:** Okonkwo, Ekwefi, or Ezinma

   **Audience:** Another character, self, a god

   **Format:** Letter, monologue, diary entry, song, prayer

   **Topic:** Character's reaction to the events of Chapter 11

   Remember to:
   • Write in the first person (I, my).
   • Use diction, imagery, syntax, and tone to convey the character's voice.
   • Include specific details from the chapter.

## Check Your Understanding

As each member of your group shares his or her writing through oral reading, consider how the voices of each character are similar and different. What elements of voice (diction, imagery, syntax, or tone) are distinct to each character?

**My Notes**

# Acts of Violence

**LEARNING STRATEGIES:**
Outlining, Drafting,
Graphic Organizer

## GRAMMAR & USAGE
**Subjunctive Mood**

A verb written in subjunctive mood indicates speculations, wishes, or indirect requests rather than facts. For example, the phrase "If I were president ..." expresses a speculation or wish, so it uses *were* rather than *was*. The clause "mother asks that you be home by dark" expresses an indirect request, so it uses *be* rather than *are*.

Think about how you might use the subjunctive mood in your writing; for example, "If Okonkwo were less violent, his character would develop differently in the novel."

## My Notes

## Learning Targets
- Analyze how a theme is developed over the course of a novel.
- Write about Okonkwo's violent tendencies and their consequences.

## Reading *Things Fall Apart*, Chapter 13

In this activity, you will revisit Chapters 1–13 and consider Okonkwo's actions and how they develop the theme of Part 1.

## Revisiting Part 1: Okonkwo's Actions and Their Consequences

1. While at public gatherings, observances of rites, or festivals, Okonkwo often commits acts of violence that ruin the occasion and generate public disapproval. Review Part 1 and complete the following graphic organizer to identify Okonkwo's violent acts and their consequences.

| Violent Acts | Consequences |
|---|---|
|  |  |
|  |  |
|  |  |

2. Work with your class to construct a statement on the theme of Okonkwo's violent tendencies and their consequences.

## Writing to Sources: Explanatory Text

From your notes, write an essay to explain how Okonkwo's acts of violence throughout the course of the novel advance the plot or develop the theme. Be sure to:

- Include an introduction with a clear thesis statement.
- Provide supporting details and textual evidence from different chapters.
- Write a conclusion that explains the significance of the topic.

## Check Your Understanding

Why do you think Achebe ended Part 1 of the novel with this event? Make predictions about what might happen in Part 2.

# Gender Views

## Learning Targets
- Analyze cultural views of gender reflected in the novel.
- Make connections among different cultures' ideas about gender.

## Reading *Things Fall Apart*, Chapter 14
In this activity, you will revisit Chapters 1–13 to analyze how the Ibo culture views gender and then continue to find evidence in Chapter 14 to prepare for a group discussion.

## Revisiting Part 1: Gender Views
In your reading of *Things Fall Apart*, you may have noticed that the characters have clear ideas about how men and women should act or be. For example, in Chapter 2, Okonkwo expresses a fear of appearing to be feminine, a characteristic he equates with weakness and ineffectualness.

1. Use the following chart to record textual evidence of what it means to be a man or woman in the Ibo culture. In the second column, respond to the examples you find. Use additional paper as needed.

| Ideas About Gender in Part 1 of *Things Fall Apart* | |
|---|---|
| **Quote** | **My Comments** |
| "Even as a little boy he [Okonkwo] had resented his father's failure and weakness, and even now he still remembered how he had suffered when a playmate had told him that his father was agbala. That was how Okonkwo first came to know that agbala was not only another name for a woman, it could also mean a man who had taken no title." (Chapter 2, p. 13) | |

### WORD CONNECTIONS

**Roots and Affixes**

*Resented* contains the root *sent*, from the Latin word *sentire*, meaning "to feel." This root also appears in *sentimental, consent*, and *dissent*. The prefix *re-* means "back" or "again." The suffix *-ed* indicates that the word is a verb in the past tense.

**My Notes**

# Gender Views

## My Notes

_____
_____
_____
_____
_____
_____
_____
_____
_____
_____
_____
_____
_____
_____
_____
_____
_____
_____
_____
_____
_____
_____
_____
_____
_____
_____
_____
_____
_____
_____
_____
_____

### INDEPENDENT READING LINK

**Read and Connect**

Choose one of your independent reading selections. Identify the characters' ideas about gender in the selection. Make a chart like the one you made for the ideas about gender in *Things Fall Apart*. Record your observations about your independent reading selection.

## Gender Views in Chapter 14

2. As you reread Chapter 14, look for textual evidence that presents a different view of gender now that Okonkwo has been exiled to live with his mother's kinsmen for seven years.

| Ideas About Gender in Chapter 14 of *Things Fall Apart* | |
|---|---|
| Quote | My Comments |
| | |

## Group Discussion on Gender Views

3. Prepare to discuss the following questions with a small group by highlighting textual evidence from each chart to support your responses.

- How and why do the views of gender shift from Part 1 of the novel to the first chapter of Part 2?
- How do you feel about the attitudes toward gender that are expressed in the novel? Do you agree or disagree with them?

## Check Your Understanding

How are the ideas of gender expressed in the novel similar to and different from those in your own culture?

# A Tragic Hero?

## Learning Targets
- Understand and apply the concept of a tragic hero to Okonkwo.
- Write to explain the degree to which Okonkwo is a tragic hero.

## Reading *Things Fall Apart*, Chapter 15

In this activity, you will reread Chapters 1–15 and apply Aristotle's definition of a tragic hero to Okonkwo.

## Tragic Hero

1. A hero is not always a **tragic hero**. Read Aristotle's classical definition of a tragic hero, analyzed in the first column of the following table. Then complete the chart by providing examples from Okonkwo's life as well as the lives of other characters from literature or film.

| Aristotle's Definition of a Tragic Hero | Examples of Okonkwo's Heroic Behavior | Examples of Heroic Behavior from Books/Film |
|---|---|---|
| He has a mixture of good and bad in his personality. | | |
| He has a fatal flaw, or *hamartia*, which leads to his downfall. | | |
| He usually goes on a journey or participates in a quest. | | |
| He has a large capacity for suffering. | | |
| His downfall is often preceded by self-realization. | | |

**My Notes**

### Literary Terms
A **tragic hero** is a central character who is usually of high or noble birth and demonstrates a "fatal flaw." The tragic hero's fatal flaw is **hamartia**, an ingrained character trait that causes the hero to make decisions leading to his or her death or downfall.

# A Tragic Hero?

## My Notes

## Language and Writer's Craft: Word Patterns

Many words follow specific patterns as they change from one part of speech to another. It is important to use the correct form to make sure your writing is clear and correct. Consider these examples:

**Verb:** analyze
**Noun:** analysis
**Adjective:** analytical

**Verb:** beautify
**Noun:** beauty
**Adjective:** beautiful

Some words do not change form when they are used as different parts of speech. For example:

**Noun:** address (a residence, a speech)
**Verb:** address (speak to)

**Noun:** challenge (a dare or invitation to a contest)
**Verb:** challenge (defy or issue a call to a contest)

**PRACTICE** Using the verbs *define*, *advocate*, *indicate*, and *equate*, form a noun or an adjective for each one.

## Check Your Understanding

Look at the following word pairs and decide which is the noun and which is the adjective.

*angry, anger*          *misery, miserable*          *natural, nature*

*strong, strength*      *easy, ease*                 *zeal, zealous*

### INDEPENDENT READING LINK

**Read and Discuss**

Think about your independent reading selections. Do any of the main characters meet your criteria for being considered a tragic hero? Complete a chart like the one you completed for Okonkwo in this activity. Discuss your ideas with a group.

## Writing to Sources: Explanatory Text

To what degree does Okonkwo fit Aristotle's definition of a tragic hero? What flaws lead to his downfall? Be sure to:

- Include an introduction that defines a tragic hero.
- Provide supporting details and textual evidence from different chapters.
- Make sure to use the correct forms of nouns, verbs, and adjectives in your writing.

# Colliding Cultures

## Learning Targets
- Analyze how key plot events develop a theme related to cultural conflict.
- Cite thorough textual evidence to support analysis of what the text says explicitly and to draw evidence from the text.

LEARNING STRATEGIES:
Socratic Seminar, Graphic Organizer, Discussion Groups

## Reading *Things Fall Apart,* Chapters 16–19

In this activity, you will read Chapters 16–19 and analyze the beginning of the cultural conflict between the Ibo and the Westerners who are newly arrived.

## Predicting Cultural Conflicts

1. In Chapter 15, Uchendu says, "The world has no end, and what is good among one people is an abomination with others."

   Part 2 of *Things Fall Apart* introduces the cultural conflict when white men come into contact with the Ibo. Predict what aspects of each culture might appear as an "abomination" to the other.

**My Notes**

_____

_____

_____

_____

_____

_____

_____

_____

_____

## Key Events in Chapters 15–19

2. Chapters 15–19 span six years in the life of Okonkwo and his village. Record key events and explain their significance on the following chart.

| Key Events of Chapter | Why Events Are Important |
|---|---|
| Chapter 15–second year of exile | |
| Chapter 16–fourth year of exile | |
| Chapter 17 | |
| Chapter 18–last year of exile | |
| Chapter 19 | |

# Colliding Cultures

## Socratic Seminar

3. Work with a partner to select three to five key events. List them in the following space. For each event, write an interpretive or universal question that will help you explore the conflicting cultures in Part 2 of *Things Fall Apart*. You will use these questions as you participate in a **Socratic Seminar**.

**Event 1:**

**Event 2:**

**Event 3:**

**Event 4:**

**Event 5:**

## Writing to Sources: Explanatory Text

After you participate in a Socratic Seminar about cultural conflict in *Things Fall Apart*, choose one of the events discussed and explore its significance in a timed response. Be sure to:

- Discuss how the event develops a theme related to cultural conflict.
- Use precise vocabulary and an academic voice.
- Cite textual evidence to support your interpretation.

# Cultural Misunderstandings

## Learning Targets
- Analyze how different characters and conflicts advance the plot.
- Make connections to the cultural misunderstandings in the novel.

LEARNING STRATEGIES:
Skimming/Scanning, Graphic
Organizer, Rereading

## Reading *Things Fall Apart*, Chapters 20–22

In this activity, you will read Chapters 20–22 and make connections to the cultural misunderstandings between the Ibo and the missionaries in the novel.

## Things Fall Apart

1. Read the following excerpt from Chapter 20 of *Things Fall Apart*. Underline or highlight statements that illuminate the misunderstandings between the Ibo and the missionaries.

> Does the white man understand our customs about land?
>
> How can he when he does not even speak our tongue? But he says that our customs are bad; and our own brothers who have taken up his religion also say that our customs are bad. How do you think we can fight when our own brothers have turned against us? The white man is very clever. He came quietly and peaceably with his religion. We were amused at his foolishness and allowed him to stay. Now he has won our brothers, and our clan can no longer act like one. He has put a knife on the things that held us together and we have fallen apart.

2. With a partner, choose one of the statements and decide whether or not Obierika's assessment of the situation is accurate. Find textual evidence from the novel to support or refute the statement.

### GRAMMAR & USAGE
**Complex Sentences**

Writers use complex sentences to create an interesting style. A **complex sentence** contains an independent clause and at least one subordinate clause. Think about how clauses work in these two sentences: "He knew *that he had lost his place* (noun clause) among the nine masked spirits *who administered justice in the clan* (adjective clause)." "How do you think we can fight *when our own brothers have turned against us* (adverb clause)?" What other examples can you find from the text?

## Mr. Brown and Mr. Smith

3. Use the following chart to compare and contrast the two missionaries, Mr. Brown and Mr. Smith. Record what each says and does, along with their attitudes and beliefs. Continue on a separate page if needed.

| Mr. Brown | Mr. Smith |
|---|---|
|  |  |

**My Notes**

# Cultural Misunderstandings

## Cultural Misunderstandings

4. Work with group members to consider why someone from another culture might think the practices or beliefs listed in the following chart are strange. Add at least one more cultural aspect to the organizer along with your response.

| Cultural Practice or Belief | Why Someone from Another Culture Might Find the Practice or Belief Strange |
|---|---|
| In the novel *The Poisonwood Bible*, an African man comes to America and is shocked to find out that Americans use the bathroom *in* their house and not outside, away from the home. | |
| Many Americans adorn their bodies with different types of tattoos and piercing. | |
| | |

5. Identify Ibo beliefs and practices in *Things Fall Apart* that differ from those of modern Americans. Contrast them in the following chart.

| Ibo Belief or Practice | Modern American Belief or Practice |
|---|---|
| Twins are considered evil and abandoned in the Evil Forest. | Twins are usually welcomed and cared for by their families. |
| | |
| | |
| | |

## Check Your Understanding

- Can one culture be "right" and another culture "wrong"? Explain.
- How did the two missionaries respond differently to cultural misunderstandings?

My Notes

### INDEPENDENT READING LINK

**Read and Respond**

From the texts you have read independently, choose one main character and analyze the beliefs and practices of that character's culture. Create a chart like the one you used in this activity. Compare the beliefs or practices of the culture with those of modern Americans. Share your observations with a peer.

# Poetic Connections

## Learning Targets
- Conduct a comparative analysis between texts with similar themes.
- Present an oral interpretation of a poem.

## Reading *Things Fall Apart*, Chapter 22

1. Reread the following excerpt from Chapter 22 of *Things Fall Apart* in which the clan responds to Enoch tearing the mask from an *egwugwu*. Underline words that have strong negative connotations.

   What tone is conveyed in this passage? Why do Enoch's actions so horrify the people of Umuofia?

### WORD CONNECTIONS

**Roots and Affixes**

*Desecrated* contains the root *sacr*, from the Latin word *sacer*, meaning "holy or sacred." This root also appears in *consecrate*, *sacred*, *sacrament*, and *sacrifice*. The prefix *de-* means "from" or "away."

> The other egwugwu immediately surrounded their desecrated companion to shield him from the profane gaze of women and children, and led him away. Enoch had killed an ancestral spirit, and Umuofia was thrown into confusion.
>
> That night the Mother of the Spirits walked the length and breadth of the clan, weeping for her murdered son. It was a terrible night. Not even the oldest man in Umuofia had ever heard such a strange and fearful sound, and it was never to be heard again. It seemed as if the very soul of the tribe wept for a great evil that was coming—its own death.

## Preview

In this activity, you will work with a group to analyze a poem and present a choral reading that conveys your interpretation of its meaning.

## Setting a Purpose for Reading

- Work with your group to read and analyze one of the poems on the following pages. Consider the following:
  1. What connections can you make between the poem and the novel?
  2. What is the tone of the poem, and how is it conveyed?
  3. What is the topic and theme of the poem?

- Circle unknown words and phrases. Try to determine the meaning of the words by using context clues, word part, or a dictionary.

**My Notes**

### ABOUT THE AUTHOR
Léopold Senghor (1906–2001) was an influential poet, teacher, and politician. Educated in Senegal, a French colony at the time of his birth, and France, Senghor became one of the first black teachers in the French educational system. He cofounded the literary movement Negritude, which validated the artistic expressions of black Africans. He served for more than 20 years as Senegal's first freely elected president.

**My Notes**

## Poetry

# Prayer to the Masks

by Léopold Sédar Senghor

Masks! Masks!
Black mask red mask, you white-and-black masks
Masks of the four points from which the spirit blows
In silence I salute you!
5  Nor you the least, the Lion-headed Ancestor
You guard this place forbidden to all laughter of women, to all smiles that fade
You **distill** this air of eternity in which I breathe the air of my Fathers.
Masks of unmasked faces, stripped of the marks of illness and the lines of age
You who have **fashioned** this portrait, this my face bent over the altar of
white paper
10  In your own **image**, hear me!
The Africa of the empires is dying, see, the agony of a pitiful princess
And Europe too where we are joined by the navel.
Fix your unchanging eyes upon your children, who are given orders
Who give away their lives like the poor their last clothes.
15  Let us report present at the rebirth of the World
Like the yeast which white flour needs.
For who would teach rhythm to a dead world of machines and guns?
Who would give the cry of joy to wake the dead and the **bereaved** at dawn?
Say, who would give back the memory of life to the man whose hopes are smashed?
20  They call us men of coffee cotton oil
They call us men of death.
We are the men of the dance, whose feet draw new strength pounding the
hardened earth.

**distill:** purify

**fashioned:** created or shaped

**image:** visual representation

**bereaved:** people who have suffered the death of a loved one

## Second Read

- Reread the poem to answer these text-dependent questions.
- Write any additional questions you have about the text in your Reader/Writer Notebook.

1. **Key Ideas and Details:** What ideas do the masks represent in the poem? Why do you think the speaker greets the masks in silence?

2. **Key Ideas and Details:** What is the central idea of the poem? What details does the speaker use to help readers understand this central idea? What details convey the future role that Africa can play?

3. **Craft and Structure:** What does the speaker of the poem mean by describing Africa as "the yeast which white flour needs"? How does this point of view contrast with the point of view expressed in *Things Fall Apart*—that, in the contact between cultures, a knife has been "put on the things that held us together and we have fallen apart"?

My Notes

WORD
CONNECTIONS

**Roots and Affixes**
*Anarchy* contains the root *arch*, from the Greek word *archos*, meaning "leader." This root also appears in *architect, patriarch, archangel,* and *monarchy.* The prefix *an-* means "not" or "without."

**ABOUT THE AUTHOR**
Winner of the 1923 Nobel Prize for Literature, William Butler Yeats (1865–1939) produced some of the most enduring poems written in English in the twentieth century. Despite living in Ireland during decades of great political and religious upheaval, Yeats's poems are marked by a deep mysticism, specific symbolism, and universal emotions.

Poetry

# The Second Coming

*by* William Butler Yeats

**gyre:** spiral that expands as it goes up

**mere:** absolute
**anarchy:** lawlessness
**tide:** water-like ebb or flow of something

**intensity:** extreme feeling

**image:** mental picture

Turning and turning in the widening **gyre**
The falcon cannot hear the falconer;
Things fall apart; the center cannot hold;
**Mere anarchy** is loosed upon the world,
5   The blood-dimmed **tide** is loosed, and everywhere
The ceremony of innocence is drowned;
The best lack all conviction, while the worst
Are full of passionate **intensity**.
Surely some revelation is at hand;
10   Surely the Second Coming is at hand;
The Second Coming! Hardly are those words out
When a vast **image** out of *Spiritus Mundi*[1]
Troubles my sight: somewhere in sands of the desert
A shape with lion body and the head of a man,
15   A gaze blank and pitiless as the sun,
Is moving its slow thighs, while all about it
Reel shadows of the indignant desert birds.
The darkness drops again; but now I know
That twenty centuries of stony sleep
20   Were **vexed** to nightmare by a rocking cradle,
And what rough beast, its hour come round at last,
Slouches towards Bethlehem to be born?

## My Notes

**vexed:** agitated or troubled

[1] *Spiritus Mundi,* Latin for "world spirit," a collective, universal soul that contains the memories of all time and inspires poets.

## Second Read

- Reread the poem to answer these text-dependent questions.
- Write any additional questions you have about the text in your Reader/Writer Notebook.

4. **Craft and Structure:** What images and words does Yeats use to describe the anarchy that has overrun the world? Why do you think the poet chose this language to describe the anarchy? What is the overall effect of these choices?

5. **Craft and Structure:** An allusion is a reference to a well-known person, event, or place in history, music, art, or another literary work. The term *The Second Coming* is a biblical allusion to the return of Christ from Heaven as described in the New Testament. In lines 11–17 of the poem, what other allusion does Yeats use? Why do you think he uses it?

6. **Key Ideas and Details:** How is the final image of the beast slouching toward Bethlehem to be born linked to the poem's opening image of the circling falcon unable to hear the falconer?

## Working from the Text

7. Work with your group to prepare and present a choral reading and analysis of your poem to a group that worked on the other poem.

As you listen to the other group's presentation, take notes to compare and contrast the two poems. Which side of the cultural conflict is represented by each poem? What do they have in common?

Why did the author choose *Things Fall Apart* as a title?

### Writing to Sources: Explanatory Text

Refer to your notes to write an essay that makes connections between the poems and the novel *Things Fall Apart*. What similarities in theme or central idea did you notice?

- Include quotes or specific details from the poems and the novel to support your claims.
- Explain how specific words in the poems and the novel relate to each other and show the similarity between themes.
- Use a coherent organizational structure and employ transitions effectively to highlight similarities and difference.

**My Notes**

# A Letter to the District Commissioner

LEARNING STRATEGIES:
Discussion Groups, Drafting

## Literary Terms

**Irony** is a literary device that exploits a reader's expectations. Irony occurs when what is expected turns out to be quite different from what actually happens. **Dramatic irony** occurs when the reader or audience knows more about the circumstances or future events in a story than the characters within it. **Verbal irony** occurs when a speaker or narrator says one thing while meaning the opposite. **Situational irony** occurs when an event contradicts the expectations of the characters or the reader.

## My Notes

## Learning Targets

- Analyze the use of irony in the novel.
- Write to explain the negative effects of cultural misunderstanding.

## Reading *Things Fall Apart*, Chapter 23–25

In this activity, you will read Chapters 23–25 and analyze the author's use of **irony**.

## Irony

1. Consider the following three summarized events from the novel. What kind of irony does each represent? Explain.

**Event 1:** At the end of Chapter 15, Okonkwo tells his good friend Obierka that he doesn't know how to thank him enough for tending his yam crop while Okonkwo is in exile. Obierka tells Okonkwo to kill himself.

**Event 2:** Okonkwo's greatest fear is that he will appear weak and feminine. He appears to have little respect for women. Yet his favorite child, the one with whom he has the closest bond and understanding, is his daughter Ezinma.

**Event 3:** In Chapter 7, when Ikemefuna thinks he is journeying with the clansmen to the home of his birth, he is worried about whether his mother is alive, but otherwise feels safe. The reader knows that he is actually about to be killed.

2. With a partner, review Chapters 23–25, looking for textual evidence of different kinds of irony. List and explain at least two examples:

Example 1:

Example 2:

## Setting a Purpose for Reading

3. Reread the following two excerpts. Mark the text to show evidence of the District Commissioner's attitude toward the Ibo.

## Excerpt from Chapter 23

"We shall not do you any harm," said the District **Commissioner** to them later, "if only you agree to cooperate with us. We have brought a peaceful administration to you and your people so that you may be happy. If any man ill-treats you, we shall come to your rescue. But we will not allow you to ill-treat others. We have a court of law where we judge cases and **administer** justice just as it is done in my own country under a great queen. I have brought you here because you joined together to molest others, to burn people's houses and their place of worship. That must not happen in the **dominion** of our queen, the most powerful ruler in the world. I have decided that you will pay a fine of two hundred bags of cowries. You will be released as soon as you agree to this and undertake to collect that fine from your people. What do you say to that?"

**commissioner:** government official

**administer:** carry out or apply

**dominion:** territory of control

## Excerpt from Chapter 25

In the many years in which he had **toiled** to bring civilization to different parts of Africa he had learned a number of things. One of them was that a District Commissioner must never attend to such undignified details as cutting a hanged man from the tree. Such attention would give the natives a poor opinion of him. In the book which he planned to write he would **stress** that point. As he walked back to the court he thought about that book. Every day brought him some new **material**. The story of this man who had killed a messenger and hanged himself would make interesting reading. One could almost write a whole chapter on him. Perhaps not a whole chapter but a reasonable paragraph, at any rate. There was so much else to include, and one must be firm in cutting out details. He had already chosen the title of the book, after much thought: *The **Pacification** of the Primitive Tribes of the Lower Niger.*

**toiled:** worked long and hard

**stress:** highlight or emphasize
**material:** information, ideas, and experiences to use in a book

**pacification:** forcing peace upon

## Working from the Text

4. Discuss the types of irony used in the excerpts above. What do you think the author was trying to emphasize with his use of irony?

### Explanatory Writing Prompt

Write a letter to the District Commissioner explaining how his attitude toward the Ibo people is based on cultural misunderstanding. Suggest ways he might change to be more accommodating to the culture of the people. Be sure to:

- State your purpose for writing in the first sentence.
- Provide textual evidence of the District Commissioner's misunderstanding.
- Use an appropriate voice and tone that show respect for the Commissioner, yet asks for change.

**My Notes**

# The Author's Perspective

**LEARNING STRATEGIES:**
Discussion Groups,
Metacognitive Markers,
Note-taking

## My Notes

emergence: process of becoming known

## Learning Targets
- Make connections between the author's life and literary work.
- Analyze Achebe's purpose for writing the novel.

## Preview

In the following activity, you will read and analyze an interview with Chinua Achebe to determine the author's purpose for writing the novel.

## Setting a Purpose for Reading

- As you read the interview, use metacognitive markers as follows to mark the text:

    ! something that surprises you

    * something you can comment on: an opinion or connection

    ? something you have a question about or do not understand

- Circle unknown words and phrases. Try to determine the meaning of the words by using context clues, word part, or a dictionary.

### Interview

# AN AFRICAN VOICE

*Chinua Achebe, the author of one of the enduring works of modern African literature, sees postcolonial cultures taking shape story by story.*

*by* Katie Bacon

### Chunk 1

1  Chinua Achebe's **emergence** as "the founding father of African literature … in the English language," in the words of the Harvard University philosopher K. Anthony Appiah, could very well be traced to his encounter in the early fifties with Joyce Cary's novel *Mister Johnson*, set in Achebe's native Nigeria. Achebe read it while studying at the University College in Idaban during the last years of British colonial rule, and in a curriculum full of Shakespeare, Coleridge, and Wordsworth, *Mister Johnson* stood out as one of the few books about Africa. *Time* magazine had recently declared *Mister Johnson* the "best book ever written about Africa," but Achebe and his classmates had quite a different reaction. The students saw the Nigerian hero as an "embarrassing nitwit." *Mister Johnson*, Achebe writes, "open[ed] my eyes to the fact that my home was under attack and that my home was not merely a house or a town but, more importantly, an awakening story."

2  In 1958, Achebe responded with his own novel about Nigeria, *Things Fall Apart*, which was one of the first books to tell the story of European **colonization** from an African perspective. (It has since become a **classic**, published in fifty languages around the world.) *Things Fall Apart* marked a turning point for African authors, who in the fifties and sixties began to take back the narrative of the so-called "dark continent."

3  Achebe depicts his gradual **realization** that *Mister Johnson* was just one in a long line of books written by Westerners that presented Africans to the world in a way that Africans didn't agree with or recognize, and he examines the "process of 're-storying' peoples who had been knocked silent by all kinds of **dispossession**." He ends with a hope for the twenty-first century—that this "re-storying" will continue and will eventually result in a "balance of stories among the world's peoples."

4  Achebe encourages writers from the Third World to stay where they are and write about their own countries, as a way to help achieve this balance. Yet he himself has lived in the United States for the past ten years—a reluctant exile. In 1990, Achebe was in a car accident in Nigeria, and was paralyzed from the waist down. While recuperating in a London hospital, he received a call from Leon Botstein, the president of Bard College, offering him a teaching job and a house built for his needs. Achebe thought he would be at Bard, a small school in a quiet corner of the Hudson River Valley, for only a year or two, but the political situation in Nigeria kept worsening. During the military dictatorship of General Sani Abacha, who ruled from 1993 to 1998, much of Nigeria's wealth—the country has extensive oil fields—went into the pocket of its leader, and public infrastructure that had been quite good, like hospitals and roads, withered. In 1999, Olusegan Obasanjo became Nigeria's first democratically elected President since 1983, and the situation in Nigeria is improving, albeit slowly and shakily. Achebe is watching from afar, waiting for his country to rebuild itself enough for him to return.

5  Achebe, who is sixty-nine, has written five novels, including *Arrow of God* (1964) and *Anthills of the Savannah* (1987), five books of nonfiction, and several collections of short stories and poems. Achebe spoke recently with *Atlantic Unbound's* Katie Bacon at his home in Annandale-on-Hudson, in New York.

## QUESTION 1

**Chunk 2**

6  **You have been called the progenitor of the modern African novel, and *Things Fall Apart* has maintained its resonance in the decades since it was written. Have you been surprised by the effect the book has had?**

7  Was I surprised? Yes, at the beginning. There was no African literature as we know it today. And so I had no idea when I was writing *Things Fall Apart* whether it would even be accepted or published. All of this was new—there was nothing by which I could gauge how it was going to be received.

8  But, of course, something doesn't continue to surprise you every day. After a while I began to understand why the book had resonance. I began to understand my history even better. It wasn't as if when I wrote it I was an expert in the history of the world. I was a very young man. I knew I had a story, but how it fit into the story of the world—I really had no sense of that. Its meaning for my Igbo people was clear to me, but I didn't know how other people elsewhere would respond to it. Did it have

**colonization:** establishment of colonies

**classic:** work that is considered a masterpiece

**realization:** understanding

**dispossession:** loss of land or property

### GRAMMAR &USAGE
Dash

Writers use a dash to indicate a break in their thoughts. The dash may mean "in other words," it may be used to emphasize or clarify ideas, or it may set off parenthetical information. Notice how Bacon uses a dash in this sentence: "Yet he himself has lived in the United States for the past ten years—a reluctant exile." Bacon wants to emphasize that Achebe's choice to live in the United States is not ideal. Now consider this sentence: "[M]uch of Nigeria's wealth—the country has extensive oil fields—went into the pocket of its leader." What function do the dashes perform here?

**maintained:** continued

**resonance:** the ability to create an emotional response

### WORD CONNECTIONS
Etymology

*Progenitor* is a Latin word meaning "ancestor; the founder of a family." Today, we sometimes use it to describe someone who is the first to think of or do something.

## My Notes

any meaning or resonance for them? I realized that it did when, to give you just one example, the whole class of a girls' college in South Korea wrote to me, and each one expressed an opinion about the book. And then I learned something, which was that they had a history that was similar to the story of *Things Fall Apart*—the history of colonization. This I didn't know before. Their colonizer was Japan. So these people across the waters were able to relate to the story of dispossession in Africa. People from different parts of the world can respond to the same story, if it says something to them about their own history and their own experience.

## QUESTION 2

**9   It seems that people from places that haven't experienced colonization in the same way have also responded to the story.**

**10**   There are different forms of dispossession, many, many ways in which people are deprived or subjected to all kinds of victimization—it doesn't have to be colonization. Once you allow yourself to identify with the people in a story, then you might begin to see yourself in that story even if on the surface it's far removed from your situation. This is what I try to tell my students: this is one great thing that literature can do—it can make us identify with situations and people far away. If it does that, it's a miracle. I tell my students, it's not difficult to identify with somebody like yourself, somebody next door who looks like you. What's more difficult is to identify with someone you don't see, who's very far away, who's a different color, who eats a different kind of food. When you begin to do that then literature is really performing its wonders.

## QUESTION 3

**Chunk 3**

**11   A character in *Things Fall Apart* remarks that the white man "has put a knife on the things that held us together, and we have fallen apart." Are those things still severed, or have the wounds begun to heal?**

**severed:** split or separated

**12**   What I was referring to there, or what the speaker in the novel was thinking about, was the upsetting of a society, the disturbing of a social order. The society of Umuofia, the village in *Things Fall Apart,* was totally disrupted by the coming of the European government, missionary Christianity, and so on. That was not a temporary disturbance; it was a once and for all alteration of their society. To give you the example of Nigeria, where the novel is set, the Igbo people had organized themselves in small units, in small towns and villages, each self-governed. With the coming of the British, Igbo land as a whole was **incorporated** into a totally different **polity**, to be called Nigeria, with a whole lot of other people with whom the Igbo people had not had direct contact before. The result of that was not something from which you could recover, really. You had to learn a totally new reality, and accommodate yourself to the demands of this new reality, which is the state called Nigeria. Various nationalities, each of which had its own independent life, were forced by the British to live with people of different customs and habits and priorities and religions. And then at independence, fifty years later, they were suddenly on their own again. They began all over again to learn the rules of independence. The problems that Nigeria is having today could be seen as resulting from this effort that was **initiated** by colonial rule to create a new nation. There's nothing to indicate whether it will fail or succeed. It all depends.

**incorporated:** introduced into as part of the whole
**polity:** politically organized unit

**initiated:** started or introduced

13  One might hear someone say, How long will it take these people to get their act together? It's going to take a very, very long time, because it's really been a whole series of interruptions and disturbances, one step forward and two or three back. It has not been easy. One always wishes it had been easier. We've compounded things by our own mistakes, but it doesn't really help to pretend that we've had an easy task.

## QUESTION 4

### Chunk 4

14  In *Home and Exile*, you talk about the negative ways in which British authors such as Joseph Conrad and Joyce Cary portrayed Africans over the centuries. What purpose did that portrayal serve?

15  It was really a straightforward case of setting us up, as it were. The last four or five hundred years of European contact with Africa produced a body of literature that presented Africa in a very bad light and Africans in very **lurid** terms. The reason for this had to do with the need to **justify** the slave trade and slavery. The cruelties of this trade gradually began to trouble many people in Europe. Some people began to question it. But it was a profitable business, and so those who were engaged in it began to defend it—a **lobby** of people supporting it, justifying it, and excusing it. It was difficult to excuse and justify, and so the steps that were taken to justify it were rather extreme. You had people saying, for instance, that these people weren't really human, they're not like us. Or, that the slave trade was in fact a good thing for them, because the **alternative** to it was more brutal by far.

16  And therefore, describing this fate that the Africans would have had back home became the **motive** for the literature that was created about Africa. Even after the slave trade was abolished, in the nineteenth century, something like this literature continued, to serve the new imperialistic needs of Europe in relation to Africa. This continued until the Africans themselves, in the middle of the twentieth century, took into their own hands the telling of their story.

## QUESTION 5

17  And that's what started with *Things Fall Apart* and other books written by Africans around the 1950s.

18  Yes, that's what it turned out to be. It was not actually clear to us at the time what we were doing. We were simply writing our story. But the bigger story of how these various accounts tie in, one with the other, is only now becoming clear. We realize and recognize that it's not just colonized people whose stories have been **suppressed**, but a whole range of people across the globe who have not spoken. It's not because they don't have something to say, it simply has to do with the division of power, because storytelling has to do with power. Those who win tell the story; those who are defeated are not heard. But that has to change. It's in the interest of everybody, including the winners, to know that there's another story. If you only hear one side of the story, you have no understanding at all.

**My Notes**

**lurid:** sensational or shocking
**justify:** support or defend

**lobby:** a group that tries to influence people in authority

**alternative:** other choice

**motive:** driving purpose

**suppressed:** kept from being known or published

# The Author's Perspective

**globalization:** worldwide integration and development

**absorption:** soaking up

## My Notes

**extreme:** severe

**claim:** take ownership of

**skewed:** biased; distorted

**concentration:** focus of attention

## QUESTION 6

**Chunk 5**

**19  Do you see this balance of stories as likely to emerge in this era of globalization and the exporting of American culture?**

20   That's a real problem. The mindless **absorption** of American ideas, culture, and behavior around the world is not going to help this balance of stories, and it's not going to help the world, either. People are limiting themselves to one view of the world that comes from somewhere else. That's something that we have to battle with as we go along, both as writers and as citizens, because it's not just in the literary or artistic arena that this is going to show itself. I think one can say this limiting isn't going to be very healthy for the societies that abandon themselves.

## QUESTION 7

**21   In an *Atlantic Unbound* interview this past winter Nadine Gordimer said, "English is used by my fellow writers, blacks, who have been the most extreme victims of colonialism. They use it even though they have African languages to choose from. I think that once you've mastered a language it's your own. It can be used against you, but you can free yourself and use it as black writers do—you can claim it and use it." Do you agree with her?**

22   Yes, I definitely do. English is something you spend your lifetime acquiring, so it would be foolish not to use it. Also, in the logic of colonization and decolonization it is actually a very powerful weapon in the fight to regain what was yours. English was the language of colonization itself. It is not simply something you use because you have it anyway; it is something which you can actively claim to use as an effective weapon, as a counterargument to colonization.

## QUESTION 8

**Chunk 6**

**23   There are those who say that media coverage of Africa is one-sided—that it focuses on the famines, social unrest, and political violence, and leaves out coverage of the organizations and countries that are working. Do you agree? If so, what effect does this skewed coverage have? Is it a continuation of the anti-Africa British literature you talk about in *Home and Exile*?**

24   Yes, I do agree. I think the result has been to create a fatigue, whether it's charity fatigue or fatigue toward being good to people who are less fortunate. I think that's a pity. The reason for this **concentration** on the failings of Africans is the same as what we've been talking about—this tradition of bad news, or portraying Africa as a place that is different from the rest of the world, a place where humanity is really not recognizable. When people hear the word *Africa*, they have come to expect certain images to follow. If you see a good house in Lagos, Nigeria, it doesn't quite fit the picture you have in your head, because you are looking for the slum—that is what the world expects journalists covering a city in Africa to come back with.

25 Now, if you are covering America, you are not focusing on slums every day of your life. You see a slum once in a while, maybe you talk about it, but the rest of the time you are talking about other things. It is that ability to see the **complexity** of a place that the world doesn't seem to be able to take to Africa, because of this baggage of centuries of reporting about Africa. The result is the world doesn't really know Africa. If you are an African or you live in Africa, this stands out very clearly to you, you are constantly being bombarded with bad news, and you know that there is good news in many places. This doesn't mean that the bad news doesn't exist, that's not what I'm saying. But it exists alongside other things. Africa is not simple—people want to simplify it. Africa is very complex. Very bad things go on—they should be covered—but there are also some good things.

26 This is something that comes with this imbalance of power that we've been talking about. The people who **consume** the news that comes back from the rest of the world are probably not really interested in hearing about something that is working. Those who have the ability to send crews out to bring back the news are in a position to determine what the image of the various places should be, because they have the resources to do it. Now, an African country doesn't have a television crew coming to America, for instance, and picking up the disastrous news. So America sends out wonderful images of its success, power, energy, and politics, and the world is bombarded in a very **partial** way by good news about the powerful and bad news about the less powerful.

## QUESTION 9

27 **You mentioned that literature was used to justify slavery and imperialism. What is this negative coverage of Africa being used to justify now?**

28 It's going to be used to justify inaction, which is what this fatigue is all about. Why bother about Africa? Nothing works there, or nothing ever will work. There is a small minority of people who think that way, and they may be pushing this attitude. But even if nobody was pushing it, it would simply happen by itself. This is a case of sheer inertia, something that has been happening for a long time just goes on happening, unless something stops it. It becomes a habit of mind.

## QUESTION 10

Chunk 7

29 **Has living here changed the way you think about Nigeria?**

30 It must have, but this is not something you can weigh and measure. I've been struck, for instance, by the impressive way that political transition is managed in America. Nobody living here can miss that if you come from a place like Nigeria which is unable so far to manage political **transitions** in peace. I wish Nigeria would learn to do this. There are other things, of course, where you wish Americans would learn from Nigerians: the value of people as people, the almost complete absence of race as a factor in thought, in government. That's something that I really wish for America, because no day passes here without some racial **factor** coming up somewhere, which is a major burden on this country.

complexity: complicated nature

**My Notes**

consume: take in and use

partial: biased

### WORD CONNECTIONS

Content Connections

Achebe applies the term *inertia* to society to indicate its unwillingness to change. The term comes from science, where it relates to matter and movement. Inertia is the tendency of an object to resist any change in its state of motion unless acted upon by an outside force. For example, if at rest, an object needs a push in order to move.

transition: change from one stage to the next

factor: element

**thesis:** proposition

**by default:** automatically, as the only choice

## QUESTION 11

**31  Could you talk about your dream, expressed in *Home and Exile*, of a "universal civilization"—a civilization that some believe we've achieved and others think we haven't?**

32  What the universal civilization I dream about would be, I really don't know, but I know what it is not. It is not what is being presented today, which is clearly just European and American. A universal civilization is something that we will create. If we accept the **thesis** that it is desirable to do, then we will go and work on it and talk about it. We have not really talked about it. All those who are saying it's there are really suggesting that it's there **by default**—they are saying to us, let's stop at this point and call what we have a universal civilization. I don't think we want to swindle ourselves in that way; I think if we want a universal civilization, we should work to bring it about. And when it appears, I think we will know, because it will be different from anything we have now.

33  There may be cultures that may sadly have to go, because no one is rooting for them, but we should make the effort to prevent this. We have to hold this conversation, which is a conversation of stories, a conversation of languages, and see what happens.

## Second Read

- Reread the interview to answer these text-dependent questions.
- Write any additional questions you have about the text in your Reader/Writer Notebook.

1. **Key Ideas and Details:** What notable contrast did Achebe recognize between *Time* magazine's assessment of Joyce Cary's novel *Mister Johnson* and his own assessment of the work?

2. **Craft and Structure:** Reread the third paragraph of this interview. What is the author's purpose in discussing the book *Mister Johnson* before discussing Achebe's novel *Things Fall Apart*? How does this purpose help you understand Achebe's own purpose for writing his novel?

3. **Key Ideas and Details:** What details from the answer to Question 1 of the interview explain why Achebe's work has "fit into the story of the world"?

4. **Knowledge and Ideas:** Achebe states that literature can make us identify with situations and people far away. Based on the evidence he cites in his response to Questions 1 and 2, is this claim valid?

5. **Key Ideas and Details:** How does Achebe feel about the changes made to Igbo society? What details in the text support this idea?

6. **Craft and Structure:** Achebe claims that the problems of Nigeria today may be traced to "this effort that was initiated by colonial rule to create a new nation." What evidence does he use to support his claim? Cite particular sentences or phrases from the text.

**My Notes**

# The Author's Perspective

## My Notes

7. **Key Ideas and Details:** According to Achebe, what is the relationship between storytelling and power? How does storytelling contribute to our understanding of the world?

8. **Knowledge and Ideas:** What claim does Achebe make about mastering the English language? Do you think that he gives enough evidence to prove this claim is valid?

9. **Key Ideas and Details:** How does Achebe contrast the media coverage of Africa with the coverage of places like America? What conclusion does he draw from the contrast?

10. **Knowledge and Ideas:** Achebe states that a "universal civilization" may be possible to achieve. He asserts, "A universal civilization will be something we will create." Do you think that Achebe provides a sufficiently clear definition of "universal civilization" and how it may be achieved to prove his assertion?

## Working from the Text

11. Use metacognitive markers as you read your assigned chunk of the interview with your group. Discuss your findings. Work together to complete the following chart. Be sure each person in the group takes notes so that each of you is prepared to present your findings to a new group.

| Copy the Interviewer's Question | Summarize Achebe's Response | Add Your Commentary or Questions |
|---|---|---|
| | | |
| | | |

12. Present your chunk of the interview to a group of students who read different chunks. Include your notes from the graphic organizer, your metacognitive markers, and your responses to the key questions. Work together with your new group to compose a list of additional questions you would like to ask Mr. Achebe.

## Check Your Understanding

Reconsider the following proverb from the Unit Overview:

"Until the lion has a voice, stories of safaris will always glorify the hunter."

How can you use this proverb to explain Chinua Achebe's purpose in writing the novel *Things Fall Apart?* Do you think he was successful?

## Writing to Sources: Explanatory Text

Consider the Essential Question for this unit: "How can an author use a fictional character to make a statement about culture?" Write an essay explaining your answer to this question. Be sure to:

- Begin with a clear statement of your idea.
- Use evidence from the novel and from the interview to develop and support your response.
- Use transition words to link your main ideas and clarify the relationships between them.

## Independent Reading Checkpoint

Review your independent reading. What have you learned about the colonial or postcolonial nation(s) that were described in your texts? Did the characters respond to colonization in ways you expected or didn't expect? Review any idea notes you made. How can you use what you have learned as you read additional literature from colonial or postcolonial nations?

# Writing a Literary Analysis Essay

## ASSIGNMENT

Your assignment is to write an analytical essay about *Things Fall Apart* in which you examine a character's response to the cultural collision caused by the introduction of Western ideas into Ibo culture. In your essay, analyze how the collision challenges the character's sense of identity, and explain how his or her response shapes the meaning of the work as a whole.

| | |
|---|---|
| **Planning and Prewriting: Take time to make a plan for your essay.** | ▪ Which characters had a strong positive or negative response to the cultural collision in the novel, and which one will you choose?<br>▪ What was this character's sense of identity before encountering Western influence?<br>▪ What was this character's response to the new culture: What did he or she do, think, or say; how did he or she interact with others; how did his or her role and/or perspective shift?<br>▪ What were the consequences of this character's response and his or her willingness or unwillingness to change?<br>▪ What statement about culture is the author making through this fictional character, and how can you include this in your thesis?<br>▪ What textual support can you find for your thesis?<br>▪ How can you use an outline to plan the structure of your essay? |
| **Drafting and Revising: Compose your literary analysis essay.** | ▪ How will you introduce your topic, organize your ideas, and provide a thoughtful conclusion?<br>▪ How will you integrate textual evidence including direct quotes from the novel?<br>▪ How will you be sure to use precise language and academic voice?<br>▪ How can you experiment with syntax and use a variety of sentence structures and transitions? |
| **Editing and Publishing: Prepare a final draft for publication.** | ▪ How will you proofread and edit your essay for proper conventions of standard English capitalization, punctuation, spelling, grammar and usage?<br>▪ What tools are available for you to further polish and refine your work, such as a dictionary, thesaurus, spell-check, or grammar check?<br>▪ How can the Scoring Guide help you evaluate how well you have met the requirements of the assignment? |

## Reflection

After completing this Embedded Assessment, think about how you went about accomplishing this task, and respond to the following:

- How did your research on pre- and postcolonial Ibo culture help you understand your character's reaction to the cultural collision?

- Why is it important to read literature written from the perspective of a culture other than your own?

> 📶 **Technology Tip**
>
> To practice and improve your keyboarding skills, use a word-processing program to write your draft and prepare a final version for publication.

# Writing a Literary Analysis Essay

## SCORING GUIDE

| Scoring Criteria | Exemplary | Proficient | Emerging | Incomplete |
|---|---|---|---|---|
| **Ideas** | The essay<br>• thoroughly examines a character's response to the cultural collision in the novel<br>• clearly and accurately analyzes characterization, theme, and author's purpose<br>• develops the topic with smooth integration of relevant textual evidence, including details, quotations, and examples. | The essay<br>• examines a character's response to the cultural collision in the novel<br>• adequately analyzes characterization, theme, and author's purpose<br>• develops the topic with sufficient textual evidence, including details, quotations, and examples. | The essay<br>• incompletely examines a character's response to the cultural collision in the novel<br>• provides insufficient analysis of characterization, theme, or author's purpose<br>• provides insufficient textual evidence, including details, quotations, and examples. | The essay<br>• does not examine a character's response to the cultural collision in the novel<br>• lacks analysis of characterization, theme, or author's purpose<br>• provides little or no textual evidence, including details, quotations, and examples. |
| **Structure** | The essay<br>• uses an effective organizational strategy that follows a logical progression of ideas<br>• introduces the topic engagingly, links supporting ideas, and provides a thoughtful conclusion<br>• uses appropriate and varied transitions. | The essay<br>• uses an adequate organizational strategy that contains a logical progression of ideas<br>• introduces the topic, links supporting ideas, and provides a conclusion<br>• uses some varied transitions. | The essay<br>• uses an inconsistent or flawed organizational structure<br>• lacks an introduction to the topic, links between supporting ideas, and/or a conclusion<br>• uses weak, repetitive, or insufficient transitions. | The essay<br>• does not use an obvious organizational structure<br>• lacks an introduction to the topic, links between supporting ideas, and/or a conclusion<br>• uses no transitions. |
| **Use of Language** | The essay<br>• uses precise language and variety of sentence structures<br>• maintains an academic voice and objective tone<br>• demonstrates consistent command of conventions (grammar, usage, capitalization, punctuation, and spelling). | The essay<br>• uses some precise language and variety of sentence structures<br>• generally maintains an academic voice and objective tone<br>• demonstrates adequate command of conventions; may have some errors in grammar, usage, capitalization, punctuation, or spelling that do not interfere with meaning. | The essay<br>• uses vague or inappropriate language and flawed or simplistic sentence structures<br>• lacks an academic voice and objective tone<br>• demonstrates partial or insufficient command of conventions; errors in grammar, usage, capitalization, punctuation, or spelling interfere with meaning. | The essay<br>• uses inappropriate language and only simple sentences<br>• lacks an academic voice and objective tone<br>• demonstrates little command of conventions; significant errors in grammar, usage, capitalization, punctuation, or spelling interfere with meaning. |

# Dramatic Justice

**Visual Prompt:** Characters in dramas communicate emotions through words, actions, gestures, and facial expressions. How do masks either help or hinder the communication of emotions?

## Unit Overview

Every culture must deal with issues of justice. Great literature, beginning with the dramatic literature of ancient Greece, gives us insight into the universal theme of the human struggle with issues of justice and injustice. Different cultures may have different standards and methods for arriving at justice, but every society must explore the question of what is just and fair. In this unit, you will look at texts from around the world as you explore how cultures address the complex issues of right and wrong.

## GOALS:

- To analyze and present an oral interpretation of a monologue conveying a complex character's voice
- To evaluate and critique oral interpretations
- To analyze characterization, conflicting motivations of complex characters, and major themes in a classic Greek drama
- To analyze point of view and cultural experience reflected in literature outside the United States
- To write a literary analysis essay examining the development of a tragic hero and the development of plot and theme

### ACADEMIC VOCABULARY
justice
criteria
advance

### Literary Terms
complex character
direct/indirect characterization
character sketch
monologue
oral interpretation
stage directions
stichomythia
ode
dynamic/static character
foil

# Contents

## Activities

**Language and Writer's Craft**
- Semicolons and Colons (4.6)
- Consulting a Style Manual (4.12)

MY INDEPENDENT READING LIST

# Previewing the Unit

LEARNING STRATEGIES:
QHT, Marking the Text,
Graphic Organizer

**My Notes**

## Learning Targets

- Preview the big ideas and the vocabulary for the unit.
- Identify and analyze the skills and knowledge required to complete Embedded Assessment 1 successfully.

## Making Connections

In this unit, you will explore how literature gives us insight into people: their personalities, their motives, their choices, and their relationships with others. You will study monologues to prepare for an oral interpretation of a piece of literature. Study of the play *Antigone*, a classical dramatic work written by Sophocles, one of the great Greek tragic dramatists, ends the unit.

## Essential Questions

Based on your current knowledge, respond to the following Essential Questions.

1. How can one communicate characterization through oral interpretation?

2. How do complex characters advance the plot and develop the themes of a drama?

## Developing Vocabulary

3. Mark the Academic Vocabulary and Literary Terms using the QHT strategy. Then, in your Reader/Writer Notebook, answer the question: What strategies will you use to gather knowledge of new terms independently and to develop the ability to use them accurately?

## Unpacking Embedded Assessment 1

Preview the assignment for Embedded Assessment 1: Presenting an Oral Interpretation of Literature.

Your assignment is to research, analyze, and present an oral interpretation of a monologue. Your monologue should represent a point of view or cultural experience reflected in a work of literature from outside the United States. You will need to use vocal and visual delivery to convey a complex character's voice. You will write a character sketch of the character you are portraying. You will also evaluate your own and other students' performances and write a reflection on your oral interpretation of literature.

In your own words, summarize what you will need to know to complete this assessment successfully. With your class, create a graphic organizer to represent the skills and knowledge you will need to complete the tasks identified in the Embedded Assessment.

**INDEPENDENT READING LINK**

**Read and Recommend**
For your independent reading during this unit, consider a classic or modern play with strong, compelling characters. Choose a text from a country outside of the United States to help you prepare for the Embedded Assessment. Use a reading strategy such as note-taking, marking the text, or double-entry journals to examine the development of complex characters over the course of the play. In a group discussion, recommend your selection to peers, giving clear reasons why you are making the recommendation.

# Characterization

## Learning Targets
- Examine the methods of characterization.
- Infer an author's intended purposes and meanings for using each method.

## Direct and Indirect Characterization

Earlier you learned about characterization, which includes the methods a writer uses to describe characters and reveal their personalities. To expand on that definition, two types of characterization that help writers create **complex characters** are **direct** and **indirect characterization**.

1. Think of a memorable and complex character (one with multiple or conflicting motivations) from a book or film, one who advanced the plot or theme of the work. List three to five adjectives to describe this character. For each adjective, explain why you attribute this trait to the character and determine whether your interpretation is based on direct or indirect characterization.

2. From the information that authors share about characters, active readers make inferences to help their understanding of each character's personality and contributions to the narrative.

   Work with your group to make inferences about the character Eliza Sommers from Isabel Allende's *Daughter of Fortune*. Highlight or underline clues within each excerpt that led to your interpretation.

**LEARNING STRATEGIES:**
Marking the Text, Brainstorming, Graphic Organizer

### Literary Terms

A **complex character** is one that has multiple or conflicting motivations. **Direct characterization** is when the narrator or author provides information about the character. **Indirect characterization** is when the narrator or author shows the character interacting with others, thinking about circumstances, or speaking his or her thoughts aloud.

**My Notes**

_____

_____

_____

| Methods of Character Development | Example | What can I infer? |
|---|---|---|
| **Indirect**—The character's dialogue (what the character says, how the character speaks) | "I am eighteen, and I am not looking for gold, only my brother Joaquín," she repeated. | |
| **Indirect**—The character's thoughts (what the character thinks) | "If those women could make the voyage alone, and survive without help, she could do it, too, she resolved." | |

# Characterization

| Methods of Character Development | Example | What can I infer? |
| --- | --- | --- |
| **Indirect**—The character's actions (what the character does) | "She walked quickly, her heart thudding and her face half hidden behind her fan, sweating in the December heat. She had brought her little velvet bag with the jewels of her trousseau." | |
| **Indirect**—Comments or thoughts by other characters (what other characters say or think) | "Tao Chi'en had to admit that he felt bound to Eliza by countless fine threads, each easily cut but when twisted together forming strands like steel. They had known each other only a few years but they could look to the past and see the obstacle-filled road they had traveled together. Their similarities had erased differences of race." | |
| **Indirect**—The character's appearance (how the character dresses; physical appearance) | "Tao instructed Azucena to braid Eliza's long hair in a queue like his own while he went to look for a set of his clothes. They dressed the girl in cut-off pants, a smocked tied at the waist with a cord, and a straw hat like a Japanese parasol." | |
| **Direct**—Comments from the story's narrator (information and details the narrator or speaker shares with the readers) | "Everyone is born with some special talent, and Eliza Sommers discovered early on that she had two: a good sense of smell and a good memory. She used the first to earn a living and the second to recall her life—" | |

**My Notes**

_____

_____

_____

_____

_____

_____

_____

_____

3. When you have completed the chart, compare your interpretations with your class, and make inferences about the author's purpose for using each method of characterization. Be prepared to support your interpretation by citing textual evidence.

## Check Your Understanding

Choose a character from your independent reading and describe how the author uses both direct and indirect characterization to develop the character.

# Voices from Literature

## Learning Targets

- Analyze a scene from a play to determine how a writer develops a character through the use of direct and indirect characterization.
- Perform an oral interpretation by adapting speech to convey an analysis of a character.

## Preview

In this activity, you will read an excerpt from Shakespeare's *The Tragedy of Romeo and Juliet* and perform an oral interpretation based on your analysis of a character.

## Performance Practice

1. A requirement for effective oral performance is strong vocal delivery. Review the elements of vocal delivery and explain why each one is critical to an oral performance.

| Elements of Vocal Delivery | Explanation of Importance to an Oral Performance |
|---|---|
| Tone | |
| Pitch | |
| Volume | |
| Pace | |
| Pause | |
| Articulation | |
| Pronunciation | |

2. Your teacher will provide you with a scenario and a line of dialogue. Study your assigned scenario to decide what emotion would be appropriate in that context. During your performance, you can speak only the line of dialogue provided. In order to convey your scenario, rehearse your vocal and visual delivery (gestures, pantomime, and facial expressions).

3. As an audience member, try to make inferences about each scenario by observing the actor's vocal and visual delivery. Use the following graphic organizer to reflect on your observations and inferences.

LEARNING STRATEGIES:
Drama Game, Role Playing, Rehearsal, Discussion Groups, Visualizing, Graphic Organizer

My Notes

# Voices from Literature

| Performance Reflection | | |
|---|---|---|
| **Visual Delivery** (gestures, posture, movement, eye contact) | **Vocal Delivery** (pitch, volume, pace, rate, pauses, vocal variety, pronunciation/ articulation) | **What inferences can you make regarding this scenario?** |
| | | |
| | | |
| | | |
| | | |
| | | |

**ACADEMIC VOCABULARY**
**Justice** is the quality of being reasonable and fair in the administration of the law.

**My Notes**

## Setting a Purpose for Reading

- Two families—the Montagues and the Capulets—are enemies. Romeo, a Montague, has killed Tybalt, a Capulet, after Tybalt killed Romeo's friend, Mercutio. Both sides appeal to the Prince, who just so happens to be Mercutio's uncle, for **justice**. Benvolio pleads for the Montagues, while Lady Capulet speaks for her family. As you read, consider each character's point of view on an issue of justice that leads to the Prince's decree.

- Circle unknown words and phrases. Try to determine the meanings of the words by using context clues, word parts, or a dictionary.

**ABOUT THE AUTHOR**
William Shakespeare (1564–1616) is considered one of the most perceptive writers in the English language. He pursued a career in London as an actor but found more success as a playwright and poet, producing more than three dozen plays and many sonnets that are still performed and read today. His strength as a writer was in his ability to portray basic human emotions and situations in memorable, often heartbreaking, verse.

**Drama**

Excerpt from **The Tragedy of**
# Romeo and Juliet

*by* William Shakespeare

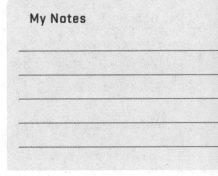

**ACT III, SCENE I:**

**PRINCE**

Where are the **vile** beginners of this **fray**?

**BENVOLIO**

O noble prince, I can discover all

The unlucky manage of this fatal brawl:

There lies the man, slain by young Romeo,

5    That slew thy kinsman, brave Mercutio.

**LADY CAPULET**

Tybalt, my cousin! O my brother's child!

O prince! O cousin! husband! O, the blood is spilt

Of my dear kinsman! Prince, as thou art true,

For blood of ours, shed blood of Montague.

10   O cousin, cousin!

**PRINCE**

Benvolio, who began this bloody fray?

**BENVOLIO**

Tybalt, here slain, whom Romeo's did slay;

Romeo that spoke him fair, bade him bethink

How nice the quarrel was, and urged **withal**

15   Your high displeasure: all this uttered

With gentle breath, calm look, knees humbly bow'd,

Could not take truce with the unruly **spleen**

Of Tybalt deaf to peace, but that he tilts

With piercing steel at bold Mercutio's breast,

20   Who all as hot, turns deadly point to point,

And, with a martial scorn, with one hand beats

Cold death aside, and with the other sends

It back to Tybalt, whose dexterity,

**Retorts** it: Romeo he cries aloud,

**My Notes**

_____
_____
_____
_____
_____

**vile:** awful
**fray:** fight

**WORD CONNECTIONS**

**Multiple-Meaning Words**

Shakespeare uses the word *fair* in line 13 of Benvolio's speech. The word *fair* has multiple meanings. When used as an adjective, it means "attractive in appearance" or "impartial." As a noun, it means "a public show." As an adverb, it means "honest" or "according to the rules." Research other meanings and use context clues to determine the meaning Shakespeare intended for the word *fair* in Benvolio's speech.

**withal:** besides

**spleen:** anger

_____
_____
_____
_____

**retorts:** returns

**My Notes**

25  'Hold, friends! friends, part!' and, swifter than

his tongue,

His agile arm beats down their fatal points,

And 'twixt them rushes; underneath whose arm

An envious thrust from Tybalt hit the life

30  Of stout Mercutio, and then Tybalt fled;

But by and by comes back to Romeo,

Who had but newly entertain'd revenge,

And to 't they go like lightning, for, ere I

Could draw to part them, was stout Tybalt slain.

35  And, as he fell, did Romeo turn and fly.

This is the truth, or let Benvolio die.

**LADY CAPULET**

He is a kinsman to the Montague;

Affection makes him false; he speaks not true:

Some twenty of them fought in this black strife,

40  And all those twenty could but kill one life.

I beg for justice, which thou, prince, must give;

Romeo slew Tybalt, Romeo must not live.

**PRINCE**

Romeo slew him, he slew Mercutio;

Who now the price of his dear blood doth owe?

**MONTAGUE**

45  Not Romeo, prince, he was Mercutio's friend;

His fault concludes but what the law should end,

The life of Tybalt.

**PRINCE**

And for that offence

Immediately we do **exile** him hence:

50  I have an interest in your hate's proceeding,

My blood for your rude brawls doth lie a-bleeding;

But I'll **amerce** you with so strong a fine

That you shall all repent the loss of mine:

I will be deaf to pleading and excuses;

55  Nor tears nor prayers shall purchase out abuses:

Therefore use none: let Romeo hence in haste,

Else, when he's found, that hour is his last.

Bear hence this body and attend our will:

Mercy but murders, pardoning those that kill.

**exile:** force to leave
**amerce:** punish

## WORD CONNECTIONS

### Etymology

In Shakespeare's time, *hence* was an adverb that was frequently used to mean "away from here" or "in the future." It comes from the Old English *heonan*, meaning "away." Here, the Prince is saying that Romeo will be immediately banned from Verona.

## Second Read

- Reread the scene to answer these text-dependent questions.
- Write any additional questions you have about the text in your Reader/Writer Notebook.

4. **Key Ideas and Details:** Explain the point of views of the Capulet and Montague families in this scene. How does each family view justice? What textual evidence supports your analysis?

5. **Key Ideas and Details:** What does Benvolio's retelling of the fight reveal about his character? Which details does he choose to emphasize, and what does that tell you about him?

6. **Key Ideas and Details:** What makes the Prince a complex character in this scene?

7. **Key Ideas and Details:** What message about life does Shakespeare's scene reveal?

**My Notes**

# Voices from Literature

## My Notes

## Working from the Text

8. Use the elements of vocal delivery to present this scene as though it's played in a TV courtroom drama. Consider the following as you rehearse.

- Who is being accused of a crime?
- What is the crime?
- Who is the judge?
- Who provides eyewitness testimony?
- What is the sentence?

## Oral Interpretation

9. Choose a character from the previous scene and write a **character sketch**. Rehearse an oral reading of your character's lines, using your character sketch as a guide for your vocal delivery. In your group, perform an oral reading of your character sketch.

As you watch and listen to the other presentations, identify the method of characterization and make inferences from the character sketch.

### Literary Terms

A **character sketch** is a brief description of a literary character. The sketch might use one or more methods of characterization to illustrate the character.

## Check Your Understanding

Reflect on the presentations you just viewed. Which were the best and which needed improvement? What made the best performances compelling? Offer suggestions to the presentations that need improvement.

### Explanatory Writing Prompt

Choose one of the characters from this scene of *Romeo and Juliet*. Write a paragraph that explains what the author reveals about that character by indirect and/or direct characterization in the events and dialogue. Refer to at least one of the indirect characterization methods from the graphic organizer in Activity 4.2 as you construct your explanation. Be sure to:

- Clearly identify the character and discuss at least two methods of characterization used by Shakespeare.
- Choose an organization for your explanation that focuses on one method of characterization at a time.
- Include text evidence from the play to illustrate each of the characterization methods discussed.

# Original Monologues

## Learning Targets
- Analyze a monologue from a work of literature outside the United States.
- Write an original monologue that conveys tone and characterization.

## Preview
In this activity, you will analyze a **monologue** using the SOAPSTone strategy and write an original monologue.

## Setting a Purpose for Reading
- As you read the monologue, annotate the text for words and phrases that evoke a strong emotion.
- Circle unknown words and phrases. Try to determine the meanings of the words by using context clues, word parts, or a dictionary.

### ABOUT THE AUTHOR
Zadie Smith was born in 1975 in northwest London. Her first novel, *White Teeth*, was the winner of the Whitbread First Novel Award, the James Tait Black Memorial Prize for fiction, and the Commonwealth Writers First Book Prize. The novel centers on the lives of two unlikely friends, the Englishman Archie Jones and the Bangladeshi Samad Iqbal.

### Novel

## Excerpt from White Teeth

*by* Zadie Smith

> *At this point in the novel, Archie and Samad are in an abandoned church in Bulgaria during World War II. They are having a discussion about destiny and consequences. Archie dismisses the thought of having children and Samad speaks the following monologue:*

1 Our children will be born of our actions. *Our accidents will become their **destinies**.* Oh, the actions will remain. It is a simple matter of what you will do when the chips are down, my friend. When the fat lady is singing. When the walls are falling in, and the sky is dark, and the ground is rumbling. In that moment our actions will define us. And it makes no difference whether you are being watched by Allah, Jesus, Buddah, or whether you are not. On cold days a man can see his breath, on a hot day he can't. On both occasions, the man *breathes*.

## Second Read
- Reread the excerpt to answer this text-dependent question.
- Write any additional questions you have about the text in your Reader/Writer Notebook.

---

### LEARNING STRATEGIES:
Quickwrite, Close Reading, Drafting, Self-Editing, SOAPSTone

### Literary Term
A **monologue** is a speech or written expression of thoughts by a character.

### My Notes
_____
_____
_____
_____
_____
_____
_____
_____
_____

destinies: future fates

### INDEPENDENT READING LINK
**Read and Connect**
Choose a compelling character from your independent reading selection. As you read about that character, look for a monologue in the text. Use the SOAPSTone strategy from this activity to analyze and annotate the monologue in your Reader/Writer Notebook. Share your findings with a group.

# Original Monologues

1. **Craft and Structure:** What point of view about how our actions define us does the narrator express?

## Working from the Text

2. Use the following SOAPSTone graphic organizer to analyze the monologue.

| SOAPSTone | Analysis | Textual Support |
|---|---|---|
| Speaker: What does the reader know about the writer? | | |
| Occasion: What are the circumstances surrounding this text? | | |
| Audience: Who is the target audience? | | |
| Purpose: Why did the author write this text? | | |
| Subject: What is the topic? | | |
| Tone: What is the author's tone or attitude? | | |

3. **Quickwrite:** What do you think the author's purpose is for including this monologue? How does it convey characterization?

4. Write an original monologue on an issue of interest to you that reveals characterization, an internal conflict, or perhaps an issue of fairness or justice. Be sure to:

   • Include a summary statement of the scenario before the monologue.

   • Describe the speaker's feelings on an internal conflict to convey theme.

   • Use diction, detail, sentence structure, and punctuation for effect.

5. Trade monologues with a partner. Rehearse and conduct an oral reading of your partner's monologue with appropriate vocal and visual delivery.

## Check Your Understanding

• To what extent did your partner interpret the monologue with the characterization and tone you intended?

• Discuss ways to refine your monologue to make your intentions clearer and revise it accordingly.

# Reflecting on Performance

**LEARNING STRATEGIES:**
Oral Interpretation,
Rehearsal, Discussion Groups

## Literary Terms

**Oral interpretation** is planned
oral reading that expresses
the meaning of a written text.

## My Notes

## Learning Targets

- Display oral interpretation skills when presenting a monologue.
- Evaluate an oral interpretation of a monologue.

## Oral Interpretation and Dramatic Monologue

1. Use the space below to describe the relationship between a monologue and an **oral interpretation**. How does one inform the other?

2. What are some of the tools actors use in a dramatic production that are not available to a performer of an oral interpretation?

3. How do performers of an oral interpretation make up for the lack of these resources?

## Evaluating Oral Interpretation

4. Use the space below to create a class rubric to evaluate oral interpretations. You may want to consult previous activities in this unit and the scoring guide for Embedded Assessment 1 for ideas.

   Be sure to include specific criteria for vocal delivery and audience engagement.

### Oral Interpretation Rubric

| Emerging | Proficient | Mastery |
|---|---|---|
|  |  |  |

## Delivering and Responding to Oral Interpretations

5. Return to the monologue that you wrote in Activity 4.4. Prepare and rehearse an oral interpretation of this monologue with appropriate vocal and visual delivery to convey characterization and tone. Include a brief introduction to establish context. Continue to rehearse until you have your monologue and introduction memorized.

6. Deliver your oral interpretation to a group of your peers. After each performance, use the rubric you created to provide feedback on strengths presented and make suggestions for improvement. Be sure to refer to specific **criteria** for vocal delivery and audience engagement.

## Check Your Understanding

In your Reader/Writer Notebook, write a reflection based on your experience performing your oral interpretation. Use feedback from your group to help you reflect on your oral interpretation of your monologue. In your reflection, explain how you prepared for and rehearsed your monologue, evaluate the strengths and challenges of your performance, and set goals to improve your performance skills.

**My Notes**

**ACADEMIC VOCABULARY**
**Criteria** are standards that can be used to evaluate or judge the success of something.

# Oral Interpretation of Literature

LEARNING STRATEGIES:
Skimming/Scanning, SMELL,
Discussion Groups

## My Notes

### WORD CONNECTIONS

**Word Relationships**

Notice in lines 7 and 8 the words *grievous* and *grievously*. *Grievous* is an adjective, while *grievously* is an adverb. The noun *grief* and the verb *grieved* are also related to these words. Writers, and particularly speakers, will often use words with similar relationships to emphasize an idea and make it easier for an audience to remember.

**interred:** buried

**grievous:** very serious

## Learning Targets
- Analyze a text using the SMELL strategy.
- Present an oral interpretation of a dramatic text.

## Preview

In this activity, you will preview four monologues and choose one to analyze and perform. Skim/scan the four monologues on the following pages. Read the scenarios and three to five lines of each. Which speaker do you think is the most interesting character, and why?

## Setting a Purpose for Reading
- As you read your monologue, use metacognitive markers by placing a ? when you have a question, an ! when you have a strong reaction, and an * when you have a comment.
- Circle unknown words and phrases. Try to determine the meanings of the words by using context clues, word parts, or a dictionary.

## Dramatic Monologue

# From ACT III, SCENE II,
## The Tragedy of Julius Caesar

*by* William Shakespeare

### Passage 1

Marc Antony, who has not been part of the plot to kill Caesar, speaks to the crowd at Caesar's funeral.

Friends, Romans, countrymen, lend me your ears.
I come to bury Caesar, not to praise him.
The evil that men do lives after them;
The good is often **interred** with their bones.
5  So let it be with Caesar. The noble Brutus
Hath told you Caesar was ambitious.
If it were so, it was a **grievous** fault,
And grievously hath Caesar answered it.
Here, under leave of Brutus and the rest—
10  For Brutus is an honorable man
So are they all, all honorable men—
Come I to speak in Caesar's funeral.
He was my friend, faithful and just to me;
But Brutus says he was ambitious,

15  And Brutus is an honorable man.

He hath brought many captives home to Rome,

Whose ransoms did the general **coffers** fill.

**coffers:** treasury

Did this in Caesar seem ambitious?

When that the poor have cried, Caesar hath wept;

20  Ambition should be made of **sterner** stuff.

**sterner:** stronger

Yet Brutus says he was ambitious,

And Brutus is an honorable man.

You all did see that on the Lupercal[1]

I thrice presented him a kingly crown,

25  Which he did thrice refuse. Was this ambition?

Yet Brutus says he was ambitious,

And sure he is an honorable man.

I speak not to disprove what Brutus spoke,

But here I am to speak what I do know.

30  You all did love him once, not without cause

What cause withholds you, then, to mourn for him?

O judgment! Thou art fled to brutish beasts,

And men have lost their reason. Bear with me;

My heart is in the coffin there with Caesar,

35  And I must pause till it come back to me.

[*He weeps.*]

## Second Read

- Reread the monologue to answer these text-dependent questions.
- Write any additional questions you have about the text in your Reader/Writer Notebook.

1. **Key Ideas and Details:** How does the opening of Antony's monologue appeal to the skeptical crowd? What specific methods does he use to appeal to them?

> **GRAMMAR & USAGE**
> **Semicolons**
> Semicolons are used to join two independent clauses that express related ideas. Notice that in lines 3 and 4, the writer uses a semicolon to join two independent clauses. The ideas expressed have a relationship of contrast: "The evil that men do lives after them; The good is often interred with their bones." What is the relationship between the ideas expressed in lines 19 and 20?

**My Notes**

---
¹ **Lupercal:** an ancient Roman festival

**My Notes**

2. **Craft and Structure:** What effect does repetition have on the speech in Passage 1? Annotate repeated words and ideas.

Dramatic Monologue

# From ACT III, SCENE II,

## The Tragedy of Julius Caesar

*by* William Shakespeare

**Passage 2**

Marc Antony continues to speak to the Romans.

> If you have tears, prepare to shed them now.
> You all do know this mantle. I remember
> The first time ever Caesar put it on;
> 'Twas on a summer's evening, in his tent,
> 5 That day he overcame the Nervii.
> Look, in this place ran Cassius' dagger through.
> See what a rent the envious Casca made.
> Through this the well-beloved Brutus stabbed,
> And as he plucked his cursed steel away,
> 10 Mark how the blood of Caesar followed it,
> As rushing out of doors to be resolved
> If Brutus so unkindly knocked or no;
> For Brutus, as you know, was Caesar's angel.
> Judge, O you gods, how dearly Caesar loved him!
> 15 This was the most unkindest cut of all.
> For when the noble Caesar saw him stab,
> Ingratitude, more strong than traitors' arms,
> Quite **vanquished** him. Then burst his mighty heart,
> And in his **mantle** muffling up his face,

**WORD CONNECTIONS**

**Roots and Affixes**

*Ingratitude* contains the root *grat*, from the Latin word *gratus*, meaning "pleasing." You might also recognize this root from the words *grateful*, *ingrate*, *gratify*, and *congratulate*. The prefix *in-* means "not," and the suffix *-tude* is used to form a noun. What do you think the noun *ingratitude*, as used in line 17, means here?

**vanquished:** defeated

**mantle:** sleeveless cloak

20 Even at the base of Pompey's statue,

Which all the while ran blood, great Caesar fell.

O, what a fall was there, my countrymen!

Then I, and you, and all of us fell down,

Whilst bloody treason flourished over us.

25 O, now you weep, and I perceive you feel

The dint of pity. These are gracious drops.

Kind souls, what weep you when you but behold

Our Caesar's vesture wounded? Look you here,

Here is himself, marr'd, as you see, with traitors.

30 [*Antony lifts Caesar's cloak.*]

## Second Read

- Reread the monologue to answer these text-dependent questions.
- Write any additional questions you have about the text in your Reader/Writer Notebook.

3. **Key Ideas and Details:** In Passage 2, Antony claims that Caesar died in more than one way. In addition to being stabbed, what else led to Caesar's death?

4. **Craft and Structure:** In Passage 2, what appeals to emotion does Antony use to win the crowd to his point of view? Explain the probable impact of those appeals.

### Dramatic Monologue

# From *Les Miserables*

*by* Victor Hugo

## Passage 3

Fantine begs for mercy and justice from Monsieur Javert, a policeman who is about to arrest her.

### WORD CONNECTIONS

**Multiple-Meaning Words**

Try to figure out what Antony meant by the word *rent* in line 7 of Passage 2. Use a dictionary to look up different meanings for the word and choose the one that best fits the words around it. Also consider what Antony meant by the word *mark* in line 10 and *fall* (with its related word *fell*) in lines 21–23. Use the connotative words surrounding these words to gain context. Then look up the different definitions of them and choose the most appropriate.

**My Notes**

**beseech:** beg

**Bourgeois:** middle-class person

### My Notes

_____

_____

_____

**vivacity:** high spirits

### GRAMMAR & USAGE
#### Colons

Colons can be used to introduce lists and dialogue. They can also be used to join independent clauses when the second clause explains, restates, gives an example, or illustrates the first clause. The colon in paragraph 1 introduces a quotation. What is the function of the colon in the sentence beginning "I will tell you..." from paragraph 2?

### GRAMMAR & USAGE
#### Sentence Variety

To keep writing interesting and engaging, writers use a wide range of sentence types. One way writers achieve sentence variety is to begin sentences in different ways. Notice these examples from *Les Miserables*:

- "If you had seen the beginning, ..." (conditional sentence, starts with *if*)
- "Perhaps I did wrong to get angry." (starts with an adverb)
- "Why did he go away?" (rhetorical question, starts with the question word *why*)

How many sentences in paragraph 2 are exclamations? Fragments? Questions? What is the shortest sentence? What is the longest?

1 **FANTINE:** Monsieur Javert, I **beseech** your mercy. I assure you that I was not in the wrong. If you had seen the beginning, you would have seen. I swear to you by the good God that I was not to blame! That gentleman, the **Bourgeois**, whom I do not know, put snow in my back. Has any one the right to put snow down our backs when we are walking along peaceably, and doing no harm to any one? I am rather ill, as you see. And then, he had been saying impertinent things to me for a long time: "You are ugly! You have no teeth!" I know well that I have no longer those teeth. I did nothing; I said to myself, "The gentleman is amusing himself." I was honest with him; I did not speak to him. It was at that moment that he put the snow down my back. Monsieur Javert, good Monsieur Inspector! is there not some person here who saw it and can tell you that this is quite true? Perhaps I did wrong to get angry. You know that one is not master of one's self at the first moment. One gives way to **vivacity**; and then, when someone puts something cold down your back just when you are not expecting it! I did wrong to spoil that gentleman's hat.

2 Why did he go away? I would ask his pardon. Oh, my God! It makes no difference to me whether I ask his pardon. Do me the favor to-day, for this once, Monsieur Javert. You know that in prison one can earn only seven sous a day; it is not the government's fault, but seven sous is one's earnings; and just fancy, I must pay one hundred francs, or my little girl will be sent to me. Oh, my God! I cannot have her with me. What I do is so vile! Oh, my Cosette! Oh, my little angel of the Holy Virgin! what will become of her, poor creature? I will tell you: it is the Thenardiers, inn-keepers, peasants; and such people are unreasonable. They want money. Don't put me in prison! You see, there is a little girl who will be turned out into the street to get along as best she may, in the very heart of the winter; and you must have pity on such a being, my good Monsieur Javert. If she were older, she might earn her living; but it cannot be done at that age. I am not a bad woman at bottom. It is not cowardliness and gluttony that have made me what I am. If I have drunk brandy, it was out of misery. I do not love it; but it benumbs the senses. When I was happy, it was only necessary to glance into my closets, and it would have been evident that I was not a coquettish and untidy woman. I had linen, a great deal of linen. Have pity on me, Monsieur Javert!

## Second Read

- Reread the monologue to answer these text-dependent questions.
- Write any additional questions you have about the text in your Reader/Writer Notebook.

5. **Key Ideas and Details:** How does Fantine appeal to Javert's sense of justice and sense of mercy?

6. **Craft and Structure:** Why do you think Fantine uses the statement *It is not cowardliness and gluttony that have made me what I am* in her appeal to Javert?

### Dramatic Monologue

# From *Oedipus Rex*

*by* Sophocles

**Passage 4**

Oedipus, the king, speaks to the citizens of Thebes. They have received news from the Oracle of Delphi that the plague on the city is a punishment from the gods for **harboring** a murderer in the city. Oedipus is unaware that he is himself the murderer.

But now, my friends,
As one who became a citizen after the murder,
I make this proclamation to Thebes:
If any man knows by whose hands Laïos,[1] son of Labdakos,
5  Met his death, I direct that man to tell me everything,
No matter what he fears for having so long withheld it.
Let it stand as promised that no further trouble
Will come to him, but he may leave the land in safety.
Moreover: If anyone knows the murderer to be foreign,
10  Let him not keep silent: he shall have his reward from me.
However, if he does conceal it; if any man
Fearing for his friend or for himself disobeys this **edict**,

Hear what I propose to do:

I solemnly forbid the people of this country,
15  Where power and throne are mind, ever to receive that man
Or speak to him, no matter who he is, or let him

**My Notes**

harboring: sheltering

edict: official order

---

[1] **Laïos:** the murdered king of Thebes

**lustration:** ceremony of purification

## GRAMMAR & USAGE
### Colons
A colon often precedes an important item of information. Notice these lines from *Oedipus Rex*: "I make this proclamation to Thebes: If any man knows by whose..." The colon introduces the proclamation and indicates a significant pause as the speaker prepares to deliver important information to his audience. How does the way the colon is used in lines 13 and 19 compare?

### My Notes

Join in sacrifice, **lustration**, or in prayer.

I decree that he be driven from every house,

Being, as he is, corruption itself to us: the Delphic[2]

20 Voice of Apollo has pronounced this revelation.

Thus I associate myself with the oracle

And take the side of the murdered king.

As for the criminal, I pray to God—

Whether it be a lurking thief, or one of a number—

25 I pray that that man's life be consumed in evil and wretchedness.

And as for me, this curse applies no less

If it should turn out that the culprit is my guest here,

Sharing my hearth.

## Second Read
- Reread the monologue to answer these text-dependent questions.
- Write any additional questions you have about the text in your Reader/Writer Notebook.

7. **Key Ideas and Details:** What does the decree that Oedipus gives the city of Thebes reveal about him as a ruler? Is he strict or lenient? What words from his speech support that conclusion?

8. **Craft and Structure:** What are the effects of the colon and dashes used in Oedipus's speech?

## Working from the Text
9. Use the SMELL strategy to help you analyze your monologue.

[2] **Delphic:** prophets who received sacred messages

| Close analysis | Response and textual evidence |
|---|---|
| **Sender-Receiver Relationship**—Who are the senders and receivers of the message, and what is their relationship (consider what different audiences the text may be addressing)? | |
| **Message**—What is a literal summary of the content? What is the meaning or significance of this information? | |
| **Emotional Strategies**—What emotional appeals (pathos) are included? What seems to be their desired effects? | |
| **Logical Strategies**—What logical arguments/appeals (logos) are included? What is their effect? | |
| **Language**—What specific language is used to support the message? How does it affect the text's effectiveness? Consider both images and actual words. | |

10. Review the effective practices for vocal delivery that you studied in Activity 4.3: pitch, volume, pace, pause, articulation, and pronunciation. Mark the text of your monologue to prepare for oral interpretation:
    - Write phonetic pronunciations of new names or words in the margin.
    - Circle key punctuation marks that indicate pacing and pauses.
    - Highlight sentences or phrases that need increase in volume.
    - Underline sentences or phrases that need decrease in volume.

11. Write an introduction that will establish a context for your monologue. In your introduction, cite the source and the author. Place the monologue in context of the text as a whole. Conduct research as needed to establish context for the audience.

**My Notes**

_____
_____
_____
_____
_____
_____
_____

**INDEPENDENT READING LINK**

**Read and Respond**

As you read about your chosen character, look for another monologue—not the one you used for Activity 4.4. Analyze the monologue using the SMELL strategy from Activity 4.6. Record your notes in your Reader/Writer Notebook. Then write a brief paragraph explaining how the analysis helped you better understand the character.

**My Notes**

_____

_____

_____

_____

_____

_____

_____

_____

_____

_____

_____

_____

_____

_____

_____

_____

_____

_____

_____

_____

_____

_____

12. Practice reading aloud your monologue frequently enough that you know it by heart. Review the evaluation you established in the last activity. Be sure to practice your pronunciation, volume, pace, and accuracy.

13. Present your oral interpretation to a group, and provide feedback to your group, members on their oral interpretations.

## Language and Writer's Craft: Semicolons and Colons

Writers often use a *semicolon* to join two independent clauses that express closely related ideas. The semicolon is a clue that the writer includes to point to a relationship between the ideas. Consider the relationship between the two clauses in the following example:

> Send me a reminder tomorrow; I will pick up the necessary items when I go shopping.

A semicolon is also preferred before introductory words (*for example, however, namely,* etc.) that introduce complete sentences, as in the following sentence:

You will need to pack several things for your trip; for example, the trip will be more comfortable with hiking boots, bottled water, a windbreaker, and sunscreen.

Use a semicolon to separate items in a series when one or more of the items contains a comma. This reduces confusion. In the following sentence, think about how confusing it might be if all the semicolons were commas:

> My family and I visited four cities this summer: Cincinnati, Ohio; Lexington, Kentucky; Charlotte, North Carolina; and Charleston, South Carolina.

Notice also the *colon* in the preceding sentence. A colon often precedes an important item of information or a list of items, including a list in bulleted form. A colon can also signal a slight pause during an oral presentation.

**PRACTICE** Revisit the explanation of characterization you wrote in Activity 4.3. Identify a place where you could use at least one semicolon to show related ideas or a colon to introduce an important item of information. As you continue to Embedded Assessment 1, find ways to incorporate colons and semicolons into your writing.

## Check Your Understanding

How does preparing an oral interpretation help you understand a text?

 **Independent Reading Checkpoint**

You have read a play with strong, compelling characters. Consider how the information you have learned about these characters will assist you as you prepare for the Embedded Assessment. Take notes about your ideas in your Reader/Writer Notebook, and use them to give a brief oral presentation to a small group of your peers.

# Presenting an Oral Interpretation of Literature

## ASSIGNMENT

Your assignment is to research, analyze, and present an oral interpretation of a monologue. Your monologue should represent a point of view or cultural experience reflected in a work of literature from outside the United States. You will need to use vocal and visual delivery to convey a complex character's voice. You will write a character sketch of the character you are portraying. You will also evaluate your own and other students' performances and write a reflection on your oral interpretation.

| | |
|---|---|
| **Planning: Take time to make a plan for your oral interpretation.** | ▨ How will you select a monologue from your independent readings, research, or class readings that conveys a complex character?<br>▨ What strategies will you use (such as SMELL) to analyze the speaker's character, tone, and motivations?<br>▨ How will you mark the text to indicate vocal and visual delivery? |
| **Drafting: Write an introduction to your monologue.** | ▨ What research will you need to do to find more information about your source text, such as the title and author?<br>▨ How will your introduction place this monologue in context of the play as a whole?<br>▨ How will you describe the motivations and complexities of your character in your character sketch? |
| **Rehearsing: Practice the delivery of your oral interpretation.** | ▨ How many times do you need to read your monologue aloud to grow comfortable with the pacing, volume, and pronunciation?<br>▨ How can you record your reading or use peer responding to help you revise your oral interpretation? |
| **Presenting and Listening: Deliver your oral interpretations within a group.** | ▨ How will you engage with your audience during the oral interpretation by using eye contact as well as vocal and visual delivery?<br>▨ What note-taking strategy will you use to respond to other students' oral interpretation skills and to record notes about the characters and texts? |

## Reflection

Write a reflection evaluating your overall performance.

- What steps did you take to help yourself understand the text and plan your delivery?

- What were the strengths and challenges of your overall performance?

- What did you learn about oral interpretation and characterization from your own and your peers' performances?

# Presenting an Oral Interpretation of Literature

## SCORING GUIDE

| Scoring Criteria | Exemplary | Proficient | Emerging | Incomplete |
|---|---|---|---|---|
| **Ideas** | The performer<br>• provides a thorough written explanation of steps taken to plan the interpretation<br>• writes a reflection that accurately evaluates strengths and weaknesses of the performance<br>• includes an insightful analysis of what has been learned about characterization and oral interpretation. | The performer<br>• provides a written explanation of steps taken to plan the oral interpretation<br>• writes a reflection that evaluates strengths and weaknesses of the performance<br>• includes an analysis of what has been learned about characterization and oral interpretation. | The performer<br>• provides some explanation of steps taken to plan the oral interpretation<br>• writes an inadequate reflection that does not evaluate strengths and weaknesses of the performance<br>• provides an insufficient analysis of what has been learned about characterization and oral interpretation. | The performer<br>• provides no written explanation of steps taken to plan the oral interpretation<br>• does not write a reflection on strengths and weaknesses of the performance<br>• provides a confused analysis of what has been learned about characterization and oral interpretation. |
| **Structure** | The performer<br>• selects a passage of strong literary merit that conveys a complex character<br>• introduces the oral interpretation in an engaging manner<br>• provides well-researched information to place the passage in the context of the work. | The performer<br>• selects a passage that conveys a complex character<br>• introduces the oral interpretation by citing source and author<br>• provides sufficient information in the introduction to place the passage in the context of the work. | The performer<br>• selects a passage for interpretation that does not convey a complex character<br>• does not cite the source and/or author of the passage<br>• provides insufficient information in the introduction to place the passage in the context of the work. | The performer<br>• selects a passage with a simple character<br>• does not cite the source and/or author of the passage<br>• provides no information in the introduction to place the passage in the context of the work. |
| **Use of Language** | The performer<br>• uses effective vocal and visual delivery strategies to orally interpret a text<br>• engages the audience with eye contact, rarely referring to notes<br>• demonstrates active listening by taking detailed notes and responding thoughtfully to other performances. | The performer<br>• uses adequate vocal and visual delivery strategies to interpret a text orally<br>• engages the audience with eye contact while referring to notes as needed<br>• demonstrates active listening by taking notes and responding to other performances. | The performer<br>• uses inadequate vocal and visual delivery strategies to interpret the text<br>• mostly reads directly from notes and rarely makes eye contact with the audience<br>• listens to other performances but takes no notes. | The performer<br>• uses inadequate vocal and visual delivery strategies to interpret the text<br>• reads directly from notes without making eye contact with the audience<br>• disrupts or distracts from other performances and takes no notes. |

# Previewing Embedded Assessment 2 and Introducing Greek Drama

## Learning Targets
- Identify the knowledge and skills necessary to complete Embedded Assessment 2 successfully.
- Reflect on understanding of vocabulary, essential questions, and character relationships.

## Making Connections

In this part of the unit, you will learn about Greek drama by reading *Antigone* (pronounced "An-T-o-knee"). As you read the play, you will examine the major characters and analyze their interactions with one another. You will also explore the concept of the tragic hero and how the play develops this theme.

## Essential Questions

Based on your study of the first part of this unit, how would you answer the questions now?

1. How can one communicate a speaker's voice through oral interpretation?

2. How do complex characters **advance** the plot and develop the themes of a drama?

## Developing Vocabulary

Think about the Academic Vocabulary and Literary Terms you have studied so far in this unit. Which words/terms can you now move to a new category on a QHT chart? Which could you now teach to others that you were unfamiliar with at the beginning of the unit? What strategies will you use to gather knowledge of new terms independently and to develop the ability to use them accurately?

## Unpacking Embedded Assessment 2

Read the assignment for Embedded Assessment 2: Writing a Literary Analysis Essay on Characterization and Theme.

Your assignment is to write an analytical essay about the effect of character interaction in the play *Antigone*. Choose a character whose words, actions, or ideas contrast with Creon's character. Explain how these conflicting motivations contibute to Creon's development as a tragic hero and how the character interactions advance the plot or develop themes of the play.

In your own words, summarize what you will need to know to complete this assessment successfully. With your class, create a graphic organizer to represent the skills and knowledge you will need to complete the tasks identified in the Embedded Assessment.

---

**LEARNING STRATEGIES:**
QHT, Graphic Organizer, Predicting

**My Notes**

_____

_____

_____

_____

_____

_____

_____

**ACADEMIC VOCABULARY**
The verb **advance** means to move or push forward and can be used in reference to an idea or, as in this case, the plot of a story.

**INDEPENDENT READING LINK**

**Read and Recommend**

For independent reading during this part of the unit, consider another classic play with strong, compelling characters. This time, focus on Greek plays and theater. As you did previously, use a reading strategy such as note-taking, marking the text, or double-entry journals to examine the development of complex characters over the course of the play. In a group discussion, recommend your selection to peers, giving clear reasons why you are making the recommendation.

# Previewing Embedded Assessment 2 and Introducing Greek Drama

© 2017 College Board. All rights reserved.

## WORD CONNECTIONS

### Word Meanings

Does the Greek word for actor—*hypokrites*—remind you of an English word? It is close to our modern word *hypocrite*, which is someone who claims certain beliefs but acts in a way that is contrary to those beliefs. In playing a role, an actor might say or do things that he or she does not actually believe.

### My Notes

## Introduction to Greek Drama

3. With your group, mark the text of one of the following topics by highlighting key information.

### Greek Theater

- Tragedies were produced as part of a religious festival every year in Athens.
- Awards were given to the playwright who presented the best series of three dramas.
- Plays were performed in vast outdoor amphitheaters that could seat 40,000.
- All actors were men. The Greek word for actor is *hypokrites*. They wore masks with built-in megaphones so they could be heard; they also wore platform shoes for added height.
- The stage was a slightly raised platform. Actors' movements were bold and definite.
- The Chorus—a group of actors who moved and sang together—acted as one character and spoke in unison during the Choral Odes, which separated the scenes of the drama.
- The Chorus set the mood, summarized the action, represented a point of view, sided with various characters, or warned of disaster.
- Greek theater incorporated unities of time, place, and action, which meant that there were no scene changes, and no complicated subplots; the plays took place in one day and in one place and focused on one event.
- Violent action took place offstage; messengers told the audience what happened.
- The audience knew the story ahead of time. The emotion of the characters is what they came to see.

### Sophocles

- Was one of three great Greek tragic playwrights (with Aeschylus and Euripides); wrote during the "golden age" of ancient Greece
- Born in 496 BC—lived for 90 years
- Wrote over 100 plays—only seven remain
- Served his city of Colonus, near Athens, in various capacities
- Entered his plays in contests—won his first at age 28; defeated Aeschylus in that competition
- Awarded first prize about 20 times and second-place prizes all other times
- Added the third actor to the cast of his plays—before this, all dramas played with only two characters other than the Chorus

4. After completing your research, work with your group to prepare a presentation. Your presentation should summarize what you have learned and highlight key details about your topic. When viewing the presentations of others, make sure to take notes. These notes will be helpful in the next activity.

# A Tragic Family

## Learning Targets

- Make inferences and predictions about how characters, conflicting motivations, and character relationships will advance a plot.
- Preview the play by learning background information about tragedy and Sophocles's Theban plays.

## Analyzing Character Motivations

1. Read the brief character sketches from the plot of the tragedy *Antigone*. Work with a small group to analyze the motivations of three different characters by filling out the corresponding rows in the chart on the next page. Then join with another group to analyze the remaining characters and complete the chart.

### Creon (kree-on)

Your nephews have killed each other in a battle over who should be king. You are now king and decree that one brother can be buried according to the customs of your land but the other cannot. You find out that someone has defied your rule.

### Antigone (an-tig-o-knee)

You are the niece of Creon, the new king. Your brother has been killed in battle. The king has decreed that no one should bury him. You refuse to follow Creon's decree and bury your brother.

### Ismene (Is-may-nay)

You are Antigone's sister. Your sister has committed a serious offense against the new king, something you would never do. One of your brothers has been buried lawfully; the other has not.

### Haemon (Hay-mon)

You are engaged to marry Antigone. Your fiancée has buried her brother, which she has been forbidden to do by your father, King Creon.

### The Chorus

The king has made a law. Someone you respect has broken that law for reasons you think are justifiable.

### The Guard

Your job is to guard a corpse to make sure no one buries it. Someone buries the body, and you must report it to the king. Later, during a dust storm, you catch someone burying the body again. You take the person to the king.

---

**LEARNING STRATEGIES:**
Discussion Groups, Graphic Organizer, Marking the Text

**My Notes**

**INDEPENDENT READING LINK**

Read and Discuss
Complete a character chart like the one in Activity 4.8 for three of the characters from your independent reading text. Share your insights with a small group.

# A Tragic Family

| Character | Three adjectives to describe how you feel | Why do you feel this way? | What will you do? | Why do you think this is a *just* response? |
|-----------|-------------------------------------------|---------------------------|-------------------|---------------------------------------------|
| Creon | | | | |
| Antigone | | | | |
| Ismene | | | | |
| Haemon | | | | |
| The Chorus | | | | |
| The Guard | | | | |

**My Notes**

## Writing to Sources: Explanatory Text

Select one of the characters from the chart on the previous page and consider his or her point of view. Based on the information in the scenarios, write an introduction to your character. Be sure to:

- Include background information from the character's scenario.
- Provide an explanation that describes the character.
- Predict how the character's motivations might conflict with those of other characters.

## Meet the Family

2. Mark the text of the following topics to build your background knowledge of the Cadmus family and their tragic past. Review this information and the information about Greek Theater and Sophocles from the previous activity in preparation for a trivia game.

## Tragedy and the Tragic Hero

- Tragedy is a difficult and rewarding form of drama, which was made into an art by the Greeks.
- Tragedy involves the downfall of a hero, usually ending with his or her destruction or death.
- From *Aristotle's Poetics:*
  ➤ Tragedy arouses the emotions of pity and fear, wonder and awe.
  ➤ The main character is a tragic hero who must be a man or woman capable of great suffering.
  ➤ The downfall of the hero usually ends with his or her destruction or death.
  ➤ The plot involves intense emotion, with a horrible truth that leads to release or *catharsis*, or purification.
  ➤ The drama does not leave the audience in depression, but with a deeper understanding of life.
- *Aristotle's Poetics* on the tragic hero:
  ➤ The tragic hero is a man [or woman] of noble stature.
  ➤ The tragic hero is a good person who is brought down by an "act of injustice" (hamartia) because he [she] knows no better or believes that a greater good will be served by his [her] actions.
  ➤ The hero has a weakness, a tragic flaw such as pride, quickness to anger, or misjudgment.
  ➤ The hero has free choice that makes his [her] downfall his [her] own fault, but experiences misfortune that is not entirely deserved.
  ➤ The hero gains self-knowledge or understanding before the downfall, and therefore experiences redemption.

**My Notes**

# A Tragic Family

## Antigone and Her Family Background

- *Antigone* is a complete play, but it is part of a cycle of three plays, including *Oedipus Rex* and *Oedipus at Colonus*, written by Sophocles about the generations of the Cadmus family.

- The plays deal with the curse placed upon the family for a crime committed against the gods. The curse begins with a prophecy to King Laius and Queen Jocasta of Thebes that their son, Oedipus, will kill his father and marry his own mother.

- To avoid fulfillment of the prophecy, the baby Oedipus is left in the mountains to die of exposure, but was found and raised by the king and queen of Corinth, not knowing his birth parents.

- Later Oedipus unknowingly kills his father and wins the hand of Jocasta, the widowed queen, thus fulfilling the prophecy. They have four children, Antigone, Ismene, Eteocles, and Polyneices.

- When Jocasta discovers the truth, she hangs herself. When Oedipus discovers the truth, he blinds and exiles himself. He leaves his brother-in-law, Creon, to look after his children.

- Before he dies, Oedipus leaves orders that his two sons share the kingship; however, Eteocles, the first to reign, refuses to step down. Polyneices, his brother, attacks the city and his brother. They kill each other in battle.

- Creon becomes king and orders Eteocles buried with religious rites and honors. He orders that Polyneices be left unburied and uncovered for birds and animals to feed on his body. According to Greek beliefs, his soul could thus never rest. Antigone buries her brother against the order of her uncle. Thus begins the play's action.

## Pronunciation Guide

Refer to online resources for explanations and examples of correct pronunciation of Greek names, such as the following helpful instructions:

- Final *e* is always pronounced: Athene = a-THEE-neh.
- *Ch* is pronounced like *k*, never as in *church*.
- *C* is pronounced soft (like *s*) before *e* and *i* sounds: otherwise it is pronounced hard (like *k*): Polyneices = poly-NI-ses.
- The same applies to *g*; soft (as in *giant*) before *e* and *i* sounds, hard (as in *gate*) otherwise.
- *Th* is always smooth, as in *thigh*, never rough, as in *they*: Athene = a-THEE-neh.
- You can pronounce the vowels as in English, but you will be a little closer to the ancient pronunciation if you pronounce them as in Romance languages (Italian, Spanish, etc.).
- *Ae* and *oe* can be pronounced like *e*.
- General rules of accent:
  > If a name has two syllables, accent the first.
  > If a name has three or more syllables, then accent the second-to-last syllable. If a name is long, accent the third-to-last syllable.
  Examples: Aeschylus = ES-kih-lus or EE-skih-lus, Aphrodite = ah-froh-DI-tee, Herodotus = heh-RAH-do-tus, Thermopylae = ther-MO-pih-lee, Thucydides = thoo-SIH-di-des

### INDEPENDENT READING LINK

**Read and Connect**

Find one or more peers who are reading an independent work by the same Greek author as you are. Together, create a trivia game like the one in Activity 4.8. Play the game with a small group.

## Trivia Game

| About the Author | It's a Tragedy | Greek Theater | Antigone and Her Family |
|---|---|---|---|
| **$200**<br>He was the author of *Oedipus Rex*, *Oedipus at Colonus*, and *Antigone*. | **$200**<br>This civilization made tragedy into an art. | **$200**<br>This city was where tragedies were produced as part of a religious festival. | **$200**<br>The other two plays in the series with *Antigone* |
| **$400**<br>This is the number of Sophocles's plays that exist today out of a total of more than 100. | **$400**<br>Downfall, usually ending with destruction or death | **$400**<br>The part of a Greek play usually chanted (or sung) in unison | **$400**<br>The King and Queen of Thebes |
| **$600**<br>It was the golden age in ancient Greece. | **$600**<br>Pity and fear, wonder and awe | **$600**<br>Masks with built-in megaphones and platform shoes | **$600**<br>"Your son will kill his father and marry his own mother." |
| **$800**<br>This was Sophocles's age when he won his first drama competition. | **$800**<br>A single flaw in character, or hamartia | **$800**<br>A group of actors that moved and sang together, acting as one character | **$800**<br>Both mother and wife of Oedipus |
| **$1,000**<br>This was the number of actors Sophocles had in the cast of his plays. | **$1,000**<br>Horrible truth that leads to release | **$1,000**<br>The Greek word for *actor* | **$1,000**<br>The decree of Creon that begins the action of the play |

**My Notes**

# Soul Sisters

LEARNING STRATEGIES:
Discussion Groups, Graphic
Organizer, Marking the
Text, Oral Reading

## Literary Terms

**Stage directions** are
instructions written into the
script of a play that indicate
stage actions, movements
of performers, or production
requirements.

## My Notes

## Learning Targets

- Infer character motive and compare characters from *Antigone*.
- Analyze a classic Greek drama and examine its text features.

## Stage Directions

**Stage directions** are often placed within parentheses and printed in italics. When reading a play script, use this text feature to help you visualize the story's setting and characters' movement. Note: "left" and "right" directions are from the actor's point of view as he or she faces the audience. Skim/scan the text of the opening scene of *Antigone*. What key information is provided by the stage directions?

## Preview

In this activity, you will read the opening scene and complete a character analysis.

## Setting a Purpose for Reading

- Read the opening scene between Antigone and Ismene. As you read, focus on the dramatic, emotional nature of the dialogue and each character's motivation or intent.
- Circle unknown words and phrases. Try to determine the meanings of the words by using context clues, word parts, or a dictionary.

**ABOUT THE AUTHOR**

Few records exist that can tell the story of the life of Sophocles (c. 496 B.C.–406 B.C.), one of the great playwrights of the golden age of ancient Greece. He spent his life in the historically and politically important city-state of Athens, where he benefited from family wealth, good social connections, an excellent education, a winning personality, and a talent for writing plays that perfectly captured the spirit of his time and place. He wrote over 100 plays, but only seven remain. Sophocles, along with Aeschylus and Euripides, is considered a master of Greek tragedy. During his time, ancient Greece was known to be in its golden age of art and forward thinking. Sophocles is credited with several innovations to the dramatic form. Increasing the number of characters in a play, for example, allowed him to make the plots more complex and interesting to audiences. By focusing on characters' fatal flaws, poor decisions, and moral dilemmas, he created suspenseful plays that also evoked audiences' sympathies.

## Drama

# Antigone

*by* Sophocles

**ANTIGONE:** daughter of Oedipus
**ISMENE:** daughter of Oedipus, sister of Antigone
**CREON:** king of Thebes
**EURYDICE:** wife of Creon

HAEMON: son of Creon and Eurydice, engaged to Antigone

TEIRESIAS: an old blind prophet

BOY: a young lad guiding Teiresias

GUARD: a soldier serving Creon

MESSENGER

CHORUS: Theban Elders

ATTENDANTS

*[Thebes,[1] in front of the palace, which stands in the background, its main doors facing the audience. Enter Antigone leading Ismene away from the palace]*

ANTIGONE     Now, dear Ismene, my own blood sister,
do you have any sense of all the troubles
Zeus keeps bringing on the two of us,
as long as we're alive? All that misery
which stems from Oedipus? There's no suffering,
no shame, no ruin—not one dishonour—
which I have not seen in all the troubles
you and I go through. What's this they're saying now,
something our general has had proclaimed
10    throughout the city? Do you know of it?
Have you heard? Or have you just missed the news?
Dishonours which better fit our enemies
are now being piled up on the ones we love.

ISMENE     I've had no word at all, Antigone,
nothing good or bad about our family,
not since we two lost both our brothers,
killed on the same day by a double blow.
And since the Argive[2] army, just last night,
has gone away, I don't know any more
20    if I've been lucky or face total ruin.

ANTIGONE     I know that. That's why I brought you here,
outside the gates, so only you can hear.

ISMENE     What is it? The way you look makes it seem
you're thinking of some dark and gloomy news.

ANTIGONE     Look—what's Creon doing with our two brothers?
He's honouring one with a full funeral
and treating the other one disgracefully!
Eteocles, they say, has had his burial
according to our customary rites,
30    to win him honour with the dead below.
But as for Polyneices, who perished
so miserably, an order has gone out
throughout the city—that's what people say.
He's to have no funeral or **lament**,
but to be left unburied and unwept,

**GRAMMAR & USAGE**
Parallel Structure

**Parallel structure** is the use of similar word patterns to express ideas of equal importance. It creates rhythm that can serve to create emphasis. Notice this example from lines 5 and 6: "There's no suffering, no shame, no ruin...." Here, Sophocles uses the repeated word pattern of "no" followed by a noun in each listed item. What does this structure emphasize about Antigone's experience?

**lament:** expression of grief

---

[1] **Thebes:** an influential city in ancient Greece
[2] **Argive army:** refers to the city of Argos, where Polyneices raised an army to fight his brother Eteocles for the throne

**My Notes**

a sweet treasure[3] for the birds to look at,
for them to feed on to their heart's content.
That's what people say the noble Creon
40    has announced to you and me—I mean to me—
and now he's coming to proclaim the fact,
to state it clearly to those who have not heard.
For Creon this matter's really serious.
Anyone who acts against the order
will be stoned to death before the city.
Now you know, and you'll quickly demonstrate
whether you are nobly born, or else
a girl unworthy of her splendid ancestors.

ISMENE    Oh my poor sister, if that's what's happening,
what can I say that would be any help
50    to ease the situation or resolve it?

ANTIGONE    Think whether you will work with me in this
and act together.

ISMENE    In what kind of work?
What do you mean?

ANTIGONE    Will you help these hands
take up Polyneices' corpse and bury it?

ISMENE    What? You're going to bury Polyneices,
when that's been made a crime for all in Thebes?

ANTIGONE    Yes. I'll do my duty to my brother—
and yours as well, if you're not prepared to.
I won't be caught betraying him.

**rash:** impulsive

ISMENE    You're too **rash**.
60    Has Creon not expressly banned that act?

ANTIGONE    Yes. But he's no right to keep me from what's mine.

ISMENE    O dear. Think, Antigone. Consider
how our father died, hated and disgraced,
when those mistakes which his own search revealed
forced him to turn his hand against himself
and stab out both his eyes. Then that woman,
his mother and his wife—her double role—
destroyed her own life in a twisted noose.
Then there's our own two brothers, both butchered
70    in a single day—that ill-fated pair
with their own hands slaughtered one another
and brought about their common doom.
Now, the two of us are left here quite alone.
Think how we'll die far worse than all the rest,
if we defy the law and move against
the king's decree,[4] against his royal power.
We must remember that by birth we're women,

---

[3] **sweet treasure:** refers to Polyneices' body left unburied, which birds and other creatures will
gorge on
[4] **king's decree:** a rule or edict issued by the king

80                  and, as such, we shouldn't fight with men.
Since those who rule are much more powerful,
we must obey in this and in events
which bring us even harsher agonies.
So I'll ask those underground for pardon—
since I'm being compelled, I will obey
those in control. That's what I'm forced to do.
It makes no sense to try to do too much.

**ANTIGONE**    I wouldn't urge you to. No. Not even
if you were **keen** to act. Doing this with you
would bring me no joy. So be what you want.
I'll still bury him. It would be fine to die

90               while doing that. I'll lie there with him,
with a man I love, pure and innocent,
for all my crime. My honours for the dead
must last much longer than for those up here.
I'll lie down there forever. As for you,
well, if you wish, you can show contempt
for those laws the gods all hold in honour.

**ISMENE**     I'm not disrespecting them. But I can't act
against the state. That's not in my nature.

**ANTIGONE**    Let that be your excuse. I'm going now

100             to make a burial mound for my dear brother.

**ISMENE**     Oh poor Antigone, I'm so afraid for you.

**ANTIGONE**    Don't fear for me. Set your own fate in order.

**ISMENE**     Make sure you don't reveal to anyone
what you intend. Keep it closely hidden.
I'll do the same.

**ANTIGONE**    No, no. Announce the fact— if you don't let everybody know,
I'll despise your silence even more.

**ISMENE**     Your heart is hot to do cold deeds.

**ANTIGONE**    But I know, I'll please the ones I'm duty bound to please.

110 **ISMENE**     Yes, if you can. But you're after something
which you're incapable of carrying out.

**ANTIGONE**    Well, when my strength is gone, then I'll give up.

**ISMENE**     A vain attempt should not be made at all.

**ANTIGONE**    I'll hate you if you're going to talk that way.
And you'll rightly earn the loathing of the dead.
So leave me and my foolishness alone—
we'll get through this fearful thing. I won't suffer
anything as bad as a disgraceful death.

**ISMENE**     All right then, go, if that's what you think right.

120             But remember this—even though your mission
makes no sense, your friends do truly love you.

*[Exit Antigone and Ismene. Enter the Chorus of Theban elders]*

## My Notes

keen: eager

## Literary Terms

In drama, **stichomythia** is the delivery of dialogue in a rapid, fast-paced manner, with actors speaking emotionally and leaving very little time between speakers.

# Soul Sisters

**My Notes**

## Second Read

- Reread the scene to answer these text-dependent questions.
- Write any additional questions you have about the text in your Reader/Writer Notebook.

1. **Key Ideas and Details:** Read lines 25–47 carefully. How does Antigone summarize Creon's proclamation? How will this ruling affect her family?

2. **Key Ideas and Details:** In lines 62–72, why does Ismene recount their family's history to her sister? What purpose might she have for this reminder?

3. **Key Ideas and Details:** The conflict between Antigone and Ismene becomes clearly stated in lines 92–98. Explain this conflict and how it advances the plot.

4. **Craft and Structure:** What effect is created by the juxtaposition of the terms *hate* and *love* in lines 114 and 121? What does the use of these terms reveal about each sister?

5. **Key Ideas and Details:** How does the play build tension and conflict between the two sisters?

My Notes

_____

_____

_____

_____

_____

_____

_____

_____

## Working from the Text

6. Reread the opening scene between Antigone and Ismene. Take notes on the two sisters in the graphic organizer. Be sure to cite line numbers when noting textual evidence.

## Character Analysis in the Opening Scene

| Character | Indirect Characterization That Defines Each Character | Quotations that Show Character Intent or Emotion | Adjectives to Describe the Character (include textual evidence) |
|---|---|---|---|
| Antigone | | "You're too rash. Has Creon not expressly banned that act?" (lines 59–60) | |
| Ismene | | | |

7. With a partner, choose a section of the text and rehearse with appropriate vocal delivery. In this opening scene, Antigone and Ismene quickly build tension and conflict between their characters with their rapid speech, or **stichomythia**. Practice this convention as you read and incorporate appropriate gestures.

## Check Your Understanding

- What key information about the Cadmus family is revealed in the opening scene?
- What are the sisters' conflicting motivations?
- How does Sophocles use the sisters' interaction to advance the plot?

**INDEPENDENT READING LINK**

**Read and Connect**

Ask a partner to work with you. Choose a dialogue from your independent reading text. If possible, use a dialogue that includes **stichomythia**, or rapid speech. Practice reading the conversation with your partner, and then read it to a small group. Repeat the activity with your partner's independent reading text.

# Chorus Lines

**LEARNING STRATEGIES:**
Discussion Groups, Oral Reading, Paraphrasing

**Literary Terms**

An **ode** is a lyric poem expressing the feelings or thoughts of a speaker, often celebrating a person, an event, or a thing.

**My Notes**

## Learning Targets

- Analyze the organization of ideas, meanings of images, and details in a text.
- Demonstrate understanding of an ode by paraphrasing succinctly.

## The Greek Chorus

In Greek drama, the choral **odes** have many purposes. Even though the Chorus is composed of a number of individuals, it functions as one character.

One member of the Chorus serves as the Chorus Leader. That person participates in a dialogue between himself/herself and the rest of the Chorus, or represents the Chorus when speaking to another character.

1. Review the information regarding the Chorus in Activity 4.7. Compare and contrast the purpose of a Chorus in Greek theater with the purpose of a Chorus in other contexts, such as in a song, a musical, or a Shakespearean play. Create a Venn diagram or another graphic organizer for your comparison.

## Preview

In this activity, you will read the first ode of the play and analyze its organization of ideas, meanings of images, and details in the text.

## Setting a Purpose for Reading

- In the First Ode, the Chorus comments on events that happened before the play opens and that set the events of the play in motion. As you read the First Ode with your group, have one person act as the Chorus Leader while the rest of the group reads the Chorus lines. After you have read the text through once, add stage movement to your second reading. In a Greek play, the Chorus moves from right to left while chanting a strophe and from left to right while chanting the antistrophe as they dance across the stage. (Since the choral odes in Greek theater were usually accompanied by soft music, you may choose to have group members hum or beat out a soft rhythm with their hands as well.)

**FIRST ODE**[1]

CHORUS—**Strophe 1**[2]

O ray of sunlight,
most beautiful that ever shone
on Thebes, city of the seven gates,
you've appeared at last,
you glowing eye of golden day,
moving above the streams of Dirce,[3]
driving into headlong flight
the white-shield warrior from Argos,
130      who marched here fully armed,
now forced back by your sharper power.

CHORUS LEADER

Against our land he marched,
sent here by the warring claims
of Polyneices, with piercing screams,
an eagle flying above our land,
covered wings as white as snow,
and **hordes** of warriors in arms,
helmets topped with horsehair crests.

CHORUS—**Antistrophe 1**[4]

140      Standing above our homes,
he ranged around our seven gates,
with threats to swallow us
and spears thirsting to kill.
Before his jaws had had their fill
and gorged themselves on Theban blood,
before Hephaistos'[5] pine-torch flames
had seized our towers, our fortress crown,
he went back, driven in retreat.
Behind him rings the din of war—
his enemy, the Theban dragon-snake,
150      too difficult for him to overcome.

CHORUS LEADER

Zeus hates an arrogant boasting tongue.
Seeing them march here in a mighty stream,
in all their clanging golden pride,
he hurled his fire and struck the man,
up there, on our battlements, as he began
to scream aloud his victory.

CHORUS—**Strophe 2**

The man swung down, torch still in hand,
and smashed into **unyielding** earth—
the one who not so long ago attacked,
160      who launched his furious, enraged assault,
to blast us, breathing raging storms.
But things turned out not as he'd hoped.

---

[1] **First Ode:** odes are choral songs chanted by the Chorus in a Greek tragedy
[2] **Strophe 1:** part of the ode the Chorus chants while moving right to left across the stage
[3] **streams of Dirce:** stream near Thebes
[4] **Antistrophe 1:** part of the ode the Chorus chants while moving back across the stage from left to right
[5] **Hephaistos:** blacksmith of the gods; he hammered out lightning bolts for Zeus

My Notes

# Chorus Lines

Great war god Ares[6] assisted us—
he smashed them down and doomed them all
to a very different fate.

CHORUS LEADER      Seven captains at seven gates
matched against seven equal warriors
paid Zeus[7] their full bronze tribute,
the god who turns the battle tide,

170      all but that pair of wretched men,
born of one father and one mother, too—
who set their conquering spears against each other
and then both shared a common death.

CHORUS—**Antistrophe 2**

Now victory with her glorious name
has come, bringing joy to well-armed Thebes.
The battle's done—let's strive now to forget
with songs and dancing all night long,
with Bacchus[8] leading us to make Thebes shake.

## Second Read

- Reread the scene to answer these text-dependent questions.
- Write any additional questions you have about the text in your Reader/Writer Notebook.

2. **Craft and Structure:** Contrast the imagery used by the Chorus and the Chorus Leader in Strophe 1. How do these images show the different tones, or attitudes, that the speakers have?

3. **Craft and Structure:** In lines 164–165, what does the Chorus mean by saying "he ... doomed them all to a very different fate"? Include pertinent details from preceding lines in your answer.

---

[6] **Ares:** god of war
[7] **Zeus:** supreme ruler of all the gods on Mount Olympus; also known as the weather god who controlled thunder, lightning, and rain
[8] **Bacchus:** Roman god of wine; equated to Dionysius, the Greek god of wine

## Working from the Text

4. Have each group member analyze a different section of the text for organization of ideas, meanings of images, and inclusion of details. Beginning with the person assigned Strophe 1, share your analysis.

5. Select either the Chorus's or the Chorus Leader's dialogue for Strophe 1, Antistrophe 1, Strophe 2, or Antistrophe 2 and write a paraphrase of the section.

## Check Your Understanding

Compare your paraphrase with someone who rewrote the same passage. If you notice significant differences and agree with them, revise your work for accuracy and completeness.

# Enter the King

**LEARNING STRATEGIES:**
Marking the Text, Visualizing, Graphic Organizer, Summarizing

## Literary Terms

A **dynamic character** in literature is one who changes in response to the events of a narrative. A **static character** remains the same throughout the narrative.

**My Notes**

## Learning Targets

- Analyze a literary text to examine changes in a dynamic character.
- Write a compare/contrast response to a literary text.

## Dynamic and Static Characters

Remember that one of the elements of Greek drama is the use of masks to portray a character's attitude or emotions. Characters who change and show different emotions throughout a narrative are **dynamic characters**. In contrast, **static characters** do not show significant changes in a narrative.

## Setting a Purpose for Reading

- As you continue reading *Antigone*, mark the text by highlighting evidence of Creon's attitude or emotions, especially as they change throughout the scene.
- Circle unknown words and phrases. Try to determine the meanings of the words by using context clues, word parts, or a dictionary.

*[The palace doors are thrown open and guards appear at the doors]*

|  | CHORUS LEADER | But here comes Creon, new king of our land, |
| 180 |  | son of Menoikeos. Thanks to the gods, |
|  |  | who've brought about our new good fortune. |
|  |  | What plan of action does he have in mind? |
|  |  | What's made him hold this special meeting, |
|  |  | with elders summoned by a general call? |

*[Enter Creon from the palace]*

|  | CREON | Men, after much tossing of our ship of state, |
|  |  | the gods have safely set things right again. |
|  |  | Of all the citizens I've summoned you, |
|  |  | because I know how well you showed respect |
|  |  | for the eternal power of the throne, |
| 190 |  | first with Laius and again with Oedipus, |
|  |  | once he restored our city. When he died, |
|  |  | you stood by his children, firm in loyalty. |
|  |  | Now his sons have perished in a single day, |
|  |  | killing each other with their own two hands, |
|  |  | a double slaughter, stained with brother's blood. |
|  |  | And so I have the throne, all royal power, |
|  |  | for I'm the one most closely linked by blood |
|  |  | to those who have been killed. It's impossible |
|  |  | to really know a man, to know his soul, |
| 200 |  | his mind and will, before one witnesses |
|  |  | his skill in governing and making laws. |
|  |  | For me, a man who rules the entire state |
|  |  | and does not take the best advice there is, |
|  |  | but through fear keeps his mouth forever shut, |
|  |  | such a man is the very worst of men— |
|  |  | and always will be. And a man who thinks |
|  |  | more highly of a friend than of his country, |
|  |  | well, he means nothing to me. Let Zeus know, |
|  |  | the god who always watches everything, |

| | | |
|---|---|---|
| 210 | | I would not stay silent if I saw disaster<br>moving here against the citizens,<br>a threat to their security. For anyone<br>who acts against the state, its enemy,<br>I'd never make my friend. For I know well<br>our country is a ship which keeps us safe,<br>and only when it sails its proper course<br>do we make friends. These are the principles<br>I'll use in order to protect our state.<br>That's why I've announced to all citizens |
| 220 | | my orders for the sons of Oedipus—<br>Eteocles, who perished in the fight<br>to save our city, the best and bravest<br>of our spearmen, will have his burial,<br>with all those purifying rituals<br>which accompany the noblest corpses,<br>as they move below. As for his brother—<br>that Polyneices, who returned from exile,<br>eager to wipe out in all-consuming fire<br>his ancestral city and its native gods, |
| 230 | | keen to seize upon his family's blood<br>and lead men into slavery—for him,<br>the proclamation in the state declares<br>he'll have no burial mound, no funeral rites,<br>and no lament. He'll be left unburied,<br>his body there for birds and dogs to eat,<br>a clear reminder of his shameful fate.<br>That's my decision. For I'll never act<br>to respect an evil man with honours<br>in preference to a man who's acted well. |
| 240 | | Anyone who's well **disposed** towards our state,<br>alive or dead, that man I will respect. |
| | CHORUS LEADER | Son of Menoikeos, if that's your will<br>for this city's friends and enemies,<br>it seems to me you now control all laws<br>concerning those who've died and us as well—<br>the ones who are still living. |
| | CREON | See to it then, and act as guardians of what's been proclaimed. |
| | CHORUS | Give that task to younger men to deal with. |
| | CREON | There are men assigned to oversee the corpse. |
| 250 | CHORUS LEADER | Then what remains that you would have us do? |
| | CREON | Don't yield to those who **contravene** my orders. |
| | CHORUS LEADER | No one is such a fool that he loves death. |
| | CREON | Yes, that will be his full reward, indeed.<br>And yet men have often been destroyed<br>because they hoped to profit in some way. |

My Notes

_____

**disposed:** inclined

**contravene:** oppose, or act contrary to

# Enter the King

**My Notes**

*[Enter a guard, coming toward the palace]*

| | | |
|---|---|---|
| | GUARD | My lord, I can't say I've come out of breath |
| | | by running here, making my feet move fast. |
| | | Many times I stopped to think things over— |
| | | and then I'd turn around, retrace my steps. |
| 260 | | My mind was saying many things to me, |
| | | "You fool, why go to where you know for sure |
| | | your punishment awaits?"—"And now, poor man, |
| | | why are you hesitating yet again? |
| | | If Creon finds this out from someone else, |
| | | how will you escape being hurt?" Such matters |
| | | kept my mind preoccupied. And so I went, |
| | | slowly and reluctantly, and thus made |
| | | a short road turn into a lengthy one. |
| | | But then the view that I should come to you |
| 270 | | won out. If what I have to say is nothing, |
| | | I'll say it nonetheless. For I've come here |
| | | clinging to the hope that I'll not suffer |
| | | anything that's not part of my destiny. |
| | CREON | What's happening that's made you so upset? |
| | GUARD | I want to tell you first about myself. |
| | | I did not do it. And I didn't see |
| | | the one who did. So it would be unjust |
| | | if I should come to grief. |
| | CREON | You **hedge** so much. Clearly you have news of |
| | | something ominous. |
| 280 | GUARD | Yes. Strange things that make me pause a lot. |
| | CREON | Why not say it and then go—just leave. |
| | GUARD | All right, I'll tell you. It's about the corpse. |
| | | Someone has buried it and disappeared, |
| | | after spreading thirsty dust onto the flesh |
| | | and undertaking all appropriate rites. |
| | CREON | What are you saying? What man would dare this? |
| | GUARD | I don't know. There was no sign of digging, |
| | | no marks of any pick axe or a mattock. |
| | | The ground was dry and hard and very smooth, |
| 290 | | without a wheel track. Whoever did it |
| | | left no trace. When the first man on day watch |
| | | revealed it to us, we were all amazed. |
| | | The corpse was hidden, but not in a tomb. |
| | | It was lightly covered up with dirt, |
| | | as if someone wanted to **avert** a curse. |
| | | There was no trace of a wild animal |
| | | or dogs who'd come to rip the corpse apart. |
| | | Then the words flew round among us all, |
| | | with every guard accusing someone else. |
| 300 | | We were about to fight, to come to blows— |
| | | no one was there to put a stop to it. |
| | | Every one of us was responsible, |

**hedge:** avoid giving a clear response

**avert:** prevent

but none of us was clearly in the wrong.
In our defence we pleaded ignorance.
Then we each stated we were quite prepared
to pick up red-hot iron, walk through flames,
or swear by all the gods that we'd not done it,
we'd no idea how the act was planned,
or how it had been carried out. At last,

310     when all our searching had proved useless,
one man spoke up, and his words forced us all
to drop our faces to the ground in fear.
We couldn't see things working out for us,
whether we agreed or disagreed with him.
He said we must report this act to you—
we must not hide it. And his view **prevailed**.
I was the unlucky man who won the prize,
the luck of the draw. That's why I'm now here,
not of my own free will or by your choice.

320     I know that—for no one likes a messenger
who comes bearing unwelcome news with him.

**CHORUS LEADER**     My lord, I've been wondering for some time now—
could this act not be something from the gods?

**CREON**     Stop now—before what you're about to say
enrages me completely and reveals
that you're not only old but stupid, too.
No one can tolerate what you've just said,
when you claim gods might care about this corpse.
Would they pay extraordinary honours

330     and bury as a man who'd served them well,
someone who came to burn their offerings,
their pillared temples, to torch their lands
and scatter all its laws? Or do you see
gods paying respect to evil men? No, no.
For quite a while some people in the town
have secretly been muttering against me.
They don't agree with what I have decreed.
They shake their heads and have not kept their necks
under my yoke, as they are duty bound to do

340     if they were men who are content with me.
I well know that these guards were led astray—
such men urged them to carry out this act
for money. To foster evil actions,
to make them commonplace among all men,
nothing is as powerful as money.
It destroys cities, driving men from home.
Money trains and twists the minds in worthy men,
so they then undertake disgraceful acts.
Money teaches men to live as scoundrels,

350     familiar with every **profane** enterprise.
But those who carry out such acts for cash
sooner or later see how for their crimes
they pay the penalty. For if great Zeus

**My Notes**

_____
_____
_____
_____
_____
_____

**prevailed:** won out

_____
_____
_____
_____
_____
_____
_____
_____
_____
_____
_____
_____
_____
_____
_____

**profane:** vulgar or improper

**My Notes**

still has my respect, then understand this—
I swear to you on oath—unless you find
the one whose hands really buried him,
unless you bring him here before my eyes,
then death for you will never be enough.
No, not before you're hung up still alive
360 and you confess to this gross, violent act.
That way you'll understand in future days,
when there's a profit to be gained from theft,
you'll learn that it's not good to be in love
with every kind of monetary gain.
You'll know more men are ruined than are saved
when they earn profits from dishonest schemes.

GUARD        Do I have your permission to speak now,
             or do I just turn around and go away?

CREON        But I find your voice so irritating—
             don't you realize that?

370 GUARD    Where does it hurt? Is it in your ears or in your mind?

CREON        Why try to question where I feel my pain?

GUARD        The man who did it—he upsets your mind.
             I offend your ears.

CREON        My, my, it's clear to see
             it's natural for you to chatter on.

GUARD        Perhaps. But I never did this.

CREON        This and more—you sold your life for silver.

GUARD        How strange and sad when the one who sorts this
             out gets it all wrong.

CREON        Well, enjoy your sophisticated views.
380          But if you don't reveal to me who did this,
             you'll just confirm how much your treasonous gains
             have made you suffer.

*[Exit Creon back into the palace. The doors close behind him]*

GUARD        Well, I hope he's found. That would be best. But
             whether caught or not—
             and that's something sheer chance will bring about—
             you won't see me coming here again.
             This time, against all hope and expectation,
             I'm still unhurt. I owe the gods great thanks.

*[Exit the Guard away from the palace]*

**SECOND ODE**

CHORUS—**Strophe 1**

There are many strange and wonderful things,
but nothing more strangely wonderful than man.
390 He moves across the white-capped ocean seas
blasted by winter storms, carving his way
under the surging waves engulfing him.

With his teams of horses he wears down
the unwearied and immortal earth,
the oldest of the gods, harassing her,
as year by year his ploughs move back and forth.

**Antistrophe 1**

He snares the light-winged flocks of birds,
herds of wild beasts, creatures from deep seas,
trapped in the fine mesh of his hunting nets.

400  O resourceful man, whose skill can overcome
ferocious beasts roaming mountain heights.
He curbs the rough-haired horses with his bit
and tames the inexhaustible mountain bulls,
setting their savage necks beneath his yoke.

**Strophe 2**

He's taught himself speech and wind-swift thought,
trained his feelings for communal civic life,
learning to escape the icy shafts of frost,
volleys of pelting rain in winter storms,
the harsh life lived under the open sky.

410  That's man—so resourceful in all he does.
There's no event his skill cannot confront—
other than death—that alone he cannot shun,
although for many baffling sicknesses
he has discovered his own remedies.

**Antistrophe 2**

The qualities of his inventive skills
bring arts beyond his dreams and lead him on,
sometimes to evil and sometimes to good.
If he treats his country's laws with due respect
and honours justice by swearing on the gods,

420  he wins high honours in his city.
But when he grows bold and turns to evil,
then he has no city. A man like that—
let him not share my home or know my mind.

## Second Read

- Reread the scene to answer these text-dependent questions.
- Write any additional questions you have about the text in your Reader/Writer Notebook.

1. **Craft and Structure:** In line 185, what does Creon mean by the metaphorical phrase "after much tossing of our ship of state"?

2. **Key Ideas and Details:** What is Creon's definition of an effective ruler? Cite evidence from the text to support your analysis.

**My Notes**

**My Notes**

3. **Key Ideas and Details:** Review lines 219–239. How does Creon justify treating the brothers so differently after their deaths? Do you think his different treatment of them is justified? Find evidence from the text to support your answer.

4. **Key Ideas and Details:** Reread lines 242–248. Using evidence from the text, discuss how the Chorus's view of Creon's control seems to have changed from the beginning of the scene.

5. **Craft and Structure:** Explain the hyperbole in lines 305–306. What emotion does this exaggerated imagery imply?

6. **Key Ideas and Details:** In line 323, why does the Chorus Leader wonder if this act could "not be something from the gods"?

7. **Key Ideas and Details:** Compare and contrast Creon's attitude toward the Chorus in lines 324–340 to his previous speech at the start of this scene (lines 189–192). How has his tone shifted?

8. **Key Ideas and Details:** What does Creon say in his speech about money (lines 341–366)? How does this speech help develop his character?

9. **Key Ideas and Details:** Has the guard's character changed at all since the beginning of the play? How would you describe his character using evidence from the text?

10. **Craft and Structure:** Why does the Chorus use the metaphor of moving "across the white-capped ocean seas" (line 390) to describe man?

## Working from the Text

11. Complete the following graphic organizer using the evidence of Creon's attitude or emotions that you highlighted in the text.

### Lines 184–321

| Emotions, Actions | What Creon Says |
|---|---|
| **What Creon Does** | **What Others Say About Creon** |

# Enter the King

## Lines 322–382 (and following stage directions)

| Emotions, Actions | What Creon Says |
|---|---|
| **What Creon Does** | **What Others Say About Creon** |

12. Summarize the main idea for each part of the Second Ode.

13. Consider how Creon portrays two sides of his character at the beginning and at the end of this scene. Describe Creon's character, and cite textual evidence for your interpretation.

### Writing to Sources: Explanatory Text

Write an explanatory paragraph that compares and contrasts the development of Creon's character from the beginning to the end of this scene. Explain whether he is a dynamic or a static character, and why you think so. Explain whether there is a static character. Be sure to:

- Begin with a clear thesis that states your position.
- Include textual evidence and commentary in a well-organized manner.
- Use comparison/contrast transitions to link ideas and details.

## Learning Targets

- Analyze different characters' conflicting motivations.
- Evaluate how the interaction of complex characters advances a plot or develops a theme.

## Preview

In this activity, you will begin by reviewing what you have already learned about the motivations of Antigone and Creon, and then you will continue reading the play and analyze how their interaction advances the plot.

## Character Motivations

1. Before you read the next section, use the following graphic organizer to review Antigone's and Creon's underlying motivations.

| Antigone | Creon |
|---|---|
| **Concern about the burial of Polyneices:** | |
| | |
| **Attitude about the power of the gods:** | |
| | |

**My Notes**

2. Up to this point in the play, the drama's two main characters have not been on stage at the same time. What is the effect of Sophocles's choice to not have the two main characters interact on the stage at this point in the plot? Predict how you think the plot will unfold when Antigone and Creon are together on the stage.

3. Use your notes to draft a statement about how the conflict between Antigone and Creon conveys a theme related to justice.

4. Predict how the interaction of these two characters will advance the plot of the play.

# Conflicting Motivations

**My Notes**

## Setting a Purpose for Reading

- As you read the following scene, mark the text for evidence of each character's motivations and beliefs.
- Circle unknown words and phrases. Try to determine the meanings of the words by using context clues, word parts, or a dictionary.

*[Enter the Guard, with Antigone]*

| | |
|---|---|
| CHORUS LEADER | What's this? I fear some omen from the gods. I can't deny what I see here so clearly— that young girl there—it's Antigone. Oh you poor girl, daughter of Oedipus, child of a such a father, so unfortunate, what's going on? Surely they've not brought you here |
| 430 | because you've disobeyed the royal laws, because they've caught you acting foolishly? |
| GUARD | This here's the one who carried out the act. We caught her as she was burying the corpse. Where's Creon? |

*[The palace doors open. Enter Creon with attendants]*

| | |
|---|---|
| CHORUS LEADER | He's coming from the house—and just in time. |
| CREON | Why have I come "just in time"? What's happening? What is it? |
| GUARD | My lord, human beings should never take an oath there's something they'll not do—for later thoughts contradict what they first meant. I'd have sworn I'd not soon venture here again. Back then, the threats you made brought me a lot of grief. But there's no joy as great as what we pray for against all hope. And so I have come back, breaking that oath I swore. I bring this girl, captured while she was honouring the grave. This time we did not draw lots. No. This time I was the lucky man, not someone else. And now, my lord, take her for questioning. Convict her. Do as you wish. As for me, by rights I'm free and clear of all this trouble. |
| CREON | This girl here—how did you catch her? And where? |
| GUARD | She was burying that man. Now you know all there is to know. |
| CREON | Do you understand just what you're saying? Are your words the truth? |
| GUARD | We saw this girl giving that dead man's corpse full burial rites—an act you'd made illegal. Is what I say simple and clear enough? |
| CREON | How did you see her, catch her in the act? |

The line numbers 440 and 450 appear in the left margin alongside the GUARD's long speech.

| | GUARD | It happened this way. When we got there, |
|---|---|---|

**460**  GUARD
It happened this way. When we got there,
after hearing those awful threats from you,
we swept off all the dust covering the corpse,
so the damp body was completely bare.
Then we sat down on rising ground up wind,
to escape the body's putrid rotting stench.
We traded insults just to stay awake,
in case someone was careless on the job.
That's how we spent the time right up 'til noon,
when the sun's bright circle in the sky
had moved half way and it was burning hot.

**470**
Then suddenly a swirling windstorm came,
whipping clouds of dust up from the ground,
filling the plain—some heaven-sent trouble.
In that level place the dirt storm damaged
all the forest growth, and the air around
was filled with dust for miles. We shut our mouths
and just endured this **scourge** sent from the gods.
A long time passed. The storm came to an end.
That's when we saw the girl. She was shrieking—
a distressing painful cry, just like a bird

**480**
who's seen an empty nest, its fledglings gone.
That's how she was when she saw the naked corpse.
She screamed out a lament, and then she swore,
calling evil curses down upon the ones
who'd done this. Then right away her hands
threw on the thirsty dust. She lifted up
a finely made bronze jug and then three times
poured out her tributes to the dead.
When we saw that, we rushed up right away
and grabbed her. She was not afraid at all.

**490**
We charged her with her previous offence
as well as this one. She just kept standing there,
denying nothing. That made me happy—
though it was painful, too. For it's a joy
escaping troubles which affect oneself,
but painful to bring evil on one's friends.
But all that is of less concern to me
than my own safety.

CREON
You there—you with your face
bent down towards the ground, what do you say?
Do you deny you did this or admit it?

**500**  ANTIGONE
I admit I did it. I won't deny that.

CREON  [to the Guard]

You're dismissed—go where you want. You're free—
no serious charges made against you.

[Exit the Guard. Creon turns to interrogate Antigone]

Tell me briefly—not in some lengthy speech—
were you aware there was a proclamation
forbidding what you did?

**scourge:** instrument of suffering

# Conflicting Motivations

**My Notes**

## WORD CONNECTIONS

### Multiple Meanings

The word ***passionate*** has several meanings related to one idea: having or showing strong emotions. Can you figure out the variations in tone or meaning of this word? Which meaning is most accurate for the context used in line 535?

**obdurate:** hardhearted or inflexible
**tempered:** hardened
**insolent:** disrespectful

## WORD CONNECTIONS

### Roots and Affixes

*Contra-* is a commonly used prefix, meaning "against." A common root word is *venire* or *vene*, meaning "to come." Knowing these two word parts, what is the meaning of "contravening" in line 545?

---

ANTIGONE     I'd heard of it. How could I not? It was public knowledge.

CREON     And yet you dared to break those very laws?

ANTIGONE     Yes. Zeus did not announce those laws to me.
510 And Justice living with the gods below
sent no such laws for men. I did not think
anything which you proclaimed strong enough
to let a mortal override the gods
and their unwritten and unchanging laws.
They're not just for today or yesterday,
but exist forever, and no one knows
where they first appeared. So I did not mean
to let a fear of any human will
lead to my punishment among the gods.
I know all too well I'm going to die—
520 how could I not?—it makes no difference
what you decree. And if I have to die
before my time, well, I count that a gain.
When someone has to live the way I do,
surrounded by so many evil things,
how can she fail to find a benefit
in death? And so for me meeting this fate
won't bring any pain. But if I'd allowed
my own mother's dead son to just lie there,
an unburied corpse, then I'd feel distress.
530 What's going on here does not hurt me at all.
If you think what I'm doing now is stupid,
perhaps I'm being charged with foolishness
by someone who's a fool.

CHORUS LEADER     It's clear enough the spirit in this girl is passionate—
her father was the same. She has no sense
of compromise in times of trouble.

CREON [*to the Chorus Leader*]

But you should know the most **obdurate** wills
are those most prone to break. The strongest iron
**tempered** in the fire to make it really hard—
540 that's the kind you see most often shatter.
I'm well aware the most tempestuous horses
are tamed by one small bit. Pride has no place
in anyone who is his neighbour's slave.
This girl here was already very **insolent**
in contravening laws we had proclaimed.
Here she again displays her proud contempt—
having done the act, she now boasts of it.
She laughs at what she's done. Well, in this case,
if she gets her way and goes unpunished,
550 then she's the man here, not me. No. She may be
my sister's child, closer to me by blood
than anyone belonging to my house

**My Notes**

who worships Zeus Herkeios[1] in my home,
but she'll not escape my harshest punishment—
her sister, too, whom I accuse as well.
She had an equal part in all their plans
to do this burial. Go summon her here.
I saw her just now inside the palace,
her mind out of control, some kind of fit.

*[Exit attendants into the palace to fetch Ismene]*

560      When people hatch their mischief in the dark
their minds often convict them in advance,
betraying their treachery. How I despise
a person caught committing evil acts
who then desires to glorify the crime.

ANTIGONE      Take me and kill me—what more do you want?

CREON      Me? Nothing. With that I have everything.

ANTIGONE      Then why delay? There's nothing in your words
that I enjoy—may that always be the case!
And what I say displeases you as much.
570      But where could I gain greater glory
than setting my own brother in his grave?
All those here would confirm this pleases them
if their lips weren't sealed by fear—being king,
which offers all sorts of various benefits,
means you can talk and act just as you wish.

CREON      In all of Thebes, you're the only one
who looks at things that way.

ANTIGONE      They share my views, but they keep their mouths
shut just for you.

CREON      These views of yours—so different from the rest—
580      don't they bring you any sense of shame?

ANTIGONE      No—there's nothing shameful in honouring
my mother's children.

CREON      You had a brother killed fighting for the other side.

ANTIGONE      Yes—from the same mother and father, too.

CREON      Why then give tributes which insult his name?

ANTIGONE      But his dead corpse won't back up what you say.

CREON      Yes, he will, if you give equal honours to a wicked man.

ANTIGONE      But the one who died was not some slave—it was
his own brother.

590   CREON      Who was destroying this country—the other one
went to his death defending it.

---

[1] **Zeus Herkeios:** refers to an altar where sacrifices and libations were offered to Zeus; Zeus was
the Divine protector of the house and the fence surrounding it; *herkos* means "fence" in Greek

# Conflicting Motivations

| | | |
|---|---|---|
| | ANTIGONE | That may be, but Hades[2] still desires equal rites for both. |
| | CREON | A good man does not wish what we give him to be the same an evil man receives. |
| | ANTIGONE | Who knows? In the world below perhaps such actions are no crime. |
| | CREON | An enemy can never be a friend, not even in death. |
| | ANTIGONE | But my nature is to love. I cannot hate. |
| 600 | CREON | Then go down to the dead. If you must love, love them. No woman's going to govern me— no, no—not while I'm still alive. |

[Enter two attendants from the house bringing Ismene to Creon]

| | | |
|---|---|---|
| | CHORUS LEADER | Ismene's coming. There—right by the door. She's crying. How she must love her sister! From her forehead a cloud casts its shadow down across her darkly flushing face— and drops its rain onto her lovely cheeks. |
| 610 | CREON | You there—you snake lurking in my house, sucking out my life's blood so secretly. I'd no idea I was nurturing two pests, who aimed to rise against my throne. Come here. Tell me this—do you admit you played your part in this burial, or will you swear an oath you had no knowledge of it? |
| | ISMENE | I did it—I admit it, and she'll back me up. So I bear the guilt as well. |
| | ANTIGONE | No, no—justice will not allow you to say that. You didn't want to. I didn't work with you. |
| | ISMENE | But now you're in trouble, I'm not ashamed of suffering, too, as your companion. |
| 620 | ANTIGONE | Hades and the dead can say who did it— I don't love a friend whose love is only words. |
| | ISMENE | You're my sister. Don't dishonour me. Let me respect the dead and die with you. |
| | ANTIGONE | Don't try to share my death or make a claim to actions which you did not do. I'll die— and that will be enough. |
| | ISMENE | But if you're gone, what is there in life for me to love? |
| | ANTIGONE | Ask Creon. He's the one you care about. |
| | ISMENE | Why hurt me like this? It doesn't help you. |

[2] **Hades:** King of the Underworld and god of the dead

| | | |
|---|---|---|
| 630 | ANTIGONE | If I am mocking you, it pains me, too. |
| | ISMENE | Even now is there some way I can help? |
| | ANTIGONE | Save yourself. I won't envy your escape. |
| | ISMENE | I feel so wretched leaving you to die. |
| | ANTIGONE | But you chose life—it was my choice to die. |
| | ISMENE | But not before I'd said those words just now. |
| | ANTIGONE | Some people may approve of how you think—others will believe my judgment's good. |
| | ISMENE | But the mistake's the same for both of us. |
| 640 | ANTIGONE | Be brave. You're alive. But my spirit died some time ago so I might help the dead. |
| | CREON | I'd say one of these girls has just revealed how mad she is—the other's been that way since she was born. |
| | ISMENE | My lord, whatever good sense people have by birth no longer stays with them once their lives go wrong—it abandons them. |
| | CREON | In your case, that's true, once you made your choice to act in evil ways with wicked people. |
| | ISMENE | How could I live alone, without her here? |
| | CREON | Don't speak of her being here. Her life is over. |
| 650 | ISMENE | You're going to kill your own son's bride? |
| | CREON | Why not? There are other fields for him to plough. |
| | ISMENE | No one will make him a more loving wife than she will. |
| | CREON | I have no desire my son should have an evil wife. |
| | ANTIGONE | Dearest Haemon, how your father wrongs you. |
| | CREON | I've had enough of this—you and your marriage. |
| | ISMENE | You really want that? You're going to take her from him? |
| | CREON | No, not me. Hades is the one who'll stop the marriage. |
| | CHORUS LEADER | So she must die—that seems decided on. |
| 660 | CREON | Yes—for you and me the matter's closed. |

[Creon turns to address his attendants]

My Notes

# Conflicting Motivations

## My Notes

**inevitable:** sure to happen

**sovereign:** king

No more delay. You slaves, take them inside.
From this point on they must act like women
and have no liberty to wander off.
Even bold men run when they see Hades
coming close to them to snatch their lives.

*[The attendants take Antigone and Ismene into the palace, leaving Creon and the Chorus on stage]*

### THIRD ODE

**CHORUS—Strophe 1**

Those who live without tasting evil
have happy lives—for when the gods
shake a house to its foundations,
670  then **inevitable** disasters strike,
falling upon whole families,
just as a surging ocean swell
running before cruel Thracian winds
across the dark trench of the sea
churns up the deep black sand
and crashes headlong on the cliffs,
which scream in pain against the wind.

**Antistrophe 1**

I see this house's age-old sorrows,
the house of Labdakos'[3] children,
sorrows falling on the sorrows of the dead,
680  one generation bringing no relief
to generations after it—some god
strikes at them—on and on without an end.
For now the light which has been shining
over the last roots of Oedipus' house
is being cut down with a bloody knife
belonging to the gods below—
for foolish talk and frenzy in the soul.

**Strophe 2**

Oh Zeus, what human trespasses
can check your power? Even Sleep,
690  who casts his nets on everything,
cannot master that—nor can the months,
the tireless months the gods control.
A **sovereign** who cannot grow old,
you hold Olympus as your own,
in all its glittering magnificence.
From now on into all future time,
as in the past, your law holds firm.
It never enters lives of human beings
in its full force without disaster.

---

[3] **Labdakos:** father to Laius, grandfather to Oedipus

700     **Antistrophe 2**

Hope ranging far and wide brings comfort
to many men—but then hope can deceive,
delusions born of volatile desire.
It comes upon the man who's ignorant
until his foot is seared in burning fire.
Someone's wisdom has revealed to us
this famous saying—sometimes the gods
lure a man's mind forward to disaster, and he
thinks evil's something good. But then he
lives only the briefest time free of catastrophe.

## Second Read

- Reread the scene to answer these text-dependent questions.
- Write any additional questions you have about the text in your Reader/Writer Notebook.

5. **Key Ideas and Details:** In lines 437–450, what are the guard's feelings about returning to speak to Creon? Why does he refer to himself as "the lucky man" in line 447?

6. **Craft and Structure:** Why is the windstorm significant in the development of the plot? What explanation does the guard give for its cause?

7. **Key Ideas and Details:** In lines 508–518, Antigone clearly states her rationale for acting against Creon's proclamation. How can you connect her reasoning to the play's themes so far?

# Conflicting Motivations

8. **Key Ideas and Details:** Why does Antigone admit what she has done even though she knows Creon will punish her? Provide evidence from the text to support your inference.

9. **Craft and Structure:** What is the meaning of the metaphors Creon uses in lines 538–542? What do they imply about how he will treat Antigone?

10. **Key Ideas and Details:** In lines 570–577, what key point do Creon and Antigone disagree on?

11. **Key Ideas and Details:** Consider the juxtaposition of lines 597–598. What do these brief statements by Antigone and Creon reveal about why these two characters disagree?

12. **Key Ideas and Details:** How and why has Ismene's attitude changed since the beginning of the play?

13. **Craft and Structure:** What key information does Ismene reveal in line 650, and how does Creon respond? Why?

14. **Craft and Structure:** In Strophe 1, what extended metaphor does the Chorus use to portray a family punished by the gods?

## Working from the Text

15. Work with your group to record and analyze your textual evidence in the following graphic organizer.

| Textual Evidence: What the Character Says | Analysis: What Motivates the Character |
|---|---|
| **Guard:** She just kept standing there, denying nothing. That made me happy—though it was painful, too. For it's a joy escaping troubles which affect oneself, but painful to bring evil on one's friends. But all that is of less concern to me than my own safety. (lines 491–497) | |
| **Creon:** | |
| **Antigone:** | |
| **Ismene:** | |

16. Revisit your prediction about how the plot would unfold as Creon and Antigone confronted each other on stage. Describe the interaction between the two of them and their differing motivations.

# Conflicting Motivations

**My Notes**

## Language and Writer's Craft: Consulting a Style Manual

Careful writers not only learn the art of writing; they also learn the mechanics. One way to do that is to consult style manuals about questions of usage. Many different manuals exist. Following are a few that you may find helpful. Check with your teacher to see whether she or he has a preference for the style manual that you use.

- *Chicago Manual of Style*
- *Elements of Style*
- *MLA Handbook*
- *MLA Style Manual*
- *New York Times Manual*
- *Oxford Guide to Style/New Hart's Rules*
- *Turabian*

In addition to this list, there are many online resources that are useful, including Purdue University's Online Writing Lab. Research other possible online sources and bookmark them for future reference.

**PRACTICE** The underlined words and phrases in the following paragraph contain usage errors. Use a style manual—either online or print—to identify and correct the usage errors.

In the drama of Sophocles, characters try to change fate, but find they're efforts have no affect. They learn that, in a battle between an individual and fate, the individual will loose; any attempt to avoid the events prophesied by the Oracle prove to be no better then doing nothing at all.

## Check Your Understanding

### Writing to Sources: Explanatory Text

Write an explanatory paragraph about two characters of your choice from the scene you have just read. Identify their conflicting motivations. Explain how the characters' interactions advance the plot or develop a theme. Be sure to:

- Write a topic sentence that identifies two characters and briefly describes their conflicting motivations.
- Comment on the conflict between the characters and clearly explain how it advances the plot or develops the theme. Make sure to briefly summarize the theme.
- Use a coherent organization structure. Make connections between specific words and images, and the ideas they convey.
- Refer to a style manual to ensure that your writing and editing follow accepted guidelines.

# An Epic Foil

## Learning Targets
- Analyze how a minor character can serve as a foil to a major character.
- Create a working outline for an essay analyzing a character foil.

LEARNING STRATEGIES:
Outlining, Marking the Text,
Drafting

## Preview
In this activity, you will read lines 710–893 of *Antigone* and create an outline for an essay analyzing a character foil.

## Foil Characters
1. Consider the three characters who have interacted with Creon so far. How was each one different from Creon?

**Guard:**

**Antigone:**

**Ismene:**

2. Which of these characters do you think has served as the strongest **foil** for Creon? How did this foil help develop and highlight Creon's character?

## Setting a Purpose for Reading
- Use two different colors to mark the text as follows:
  - ➤ Use one color to highlight evidence of Haemon's character as it is revealed by his words, thoughts, and actions.
  - ➤ Use another color to highlight Creon's character traits that are revealed or emphasized through his interactions with Haemon.
- Circle unknown words and phrases. Try to determine the meanings of the words by using context clues, word parts, or a dictionary.

**My Notes**

### Literary Terms
A **foil** is a minor character whose actions or thoughts are juxtaposed with those of a major character in order to highlight key attributes of the major character.

*[The palace doors open]*

| 710 | CHORUS LEADER | Here comes Haemon, your only living son. Is he grieving the fate of Antigone, his bride, bitter that his marriage hopes are gone? |
| | CREON | We'll soon find out—more accurately than any prophet here could indicate. |

*[Enter Haemon from the palace]*

My son, have you heard the sentence that's been passed
upon your bride? And have you now come here
angry at your father? Or are you loyal to me,
on my side no matter what I do?

| 720 | HAEMON | Father, I'm yours. For me your judgments and the ways you act on them are good— I shall follow them. I'll not consider |

**My Notes**

culprit: person who has
committed a crime
perjure: make a liar of

any marriage a greater benefit
than your fine leadership.

CREON      Indeed, my son,
that's how your heart should always be resolved,
to stand behind your father's judgmen on every
issue. That's what men pray for—
obedient children growing up at home
who will pay back their father's enemies,
730    evil to them for evil done to him,
while honouring his friends as much as he does.
A man who fathers useless children—
what can one say of him except he's bred
troubles for himself, and much to laugh at
for those who fight against him? So, my son,
don't ever throw good sense aside for pleasure,
for some woman's sake. You understand
how such embraces can turn freezing cold
when an evil woman shares your life at home.
740    What greater wound is there than a false friend?
So spit this girl out—she's your enemy.
Let her marry someone else in Hades.
Since I caught her clearly disobeying,
the only **culprit** in the entire city,
I won't **perjure** myself before the state.
No—I'll kill her. And so let her appeal
to Zeus, the god of blood relationships.
If I foster any lack of full respect
in my own family, I surely do the same
750    with those who are not linked to me by blood.
The man who acts well with his household
will be found a just man in the city.
I'd trust such a man to govern wisely
or to be content with someone ruling him.
And in the thick of battle at his post
he'll stand firm beside his fellow soldier,
a loyal, brave man. But anyone who's proud
and violates our laws or thinks he'll tell
our leaders what to do, a man like that
760    wins no praise from me. No. We must obey
whatever man the city puts in charge,
no matter what the issue—great or small,
just or unjust. For there's no greater evil
than a lack of leadership. That destroys
whole cities, turns households into ruins,
and in war makes soldiers break and run away.
When men succeed, what keeps their lives secure
in almost every case is their obedience.
That's why they must support those in control,
770    and never let some woman beat us down.
If we must fall from power, let that come
at some man's hand—at least, we won't be called
inferior to any woman.

| | | |
|---|---|---|
| | CHORUS LEADER | Unless we're being deceived by our old age, |
| | | what you've just said seems reasonable to us. |
| | HAEMON | Father, the gods instill good sense in men— |
| | | the greatest of all the things which we possess. |
| | | I could not find your words somehow not right— |
| | | I hope that's something I never learn to do. |
| 780 | | But other words might be good, as well. |
| | | Because of who you are, you can't perceive |
| | | all the things men say or do—or their complaints. |
| | | Your gaze makes citizens afraid—they can't |
| | | say anything you would not like to hear |
| | | But in the darkness I can hear them talk—. |
| | | the city is upset about the girl. |
| | | They say of all women here she least deserves |
| | | the worst of deaths for her most glorious act. |
| | | When in the slaughter her own brother died, |
| 790 | | she did not just leave him there unburied, |
| | | to be ripped apart by carrion dogs or birds. |
| | | Surely she deserves some golden honour? |
| | | That's the dark secret rumour people speak. |
| | | For me, father, nothing is more valuable |
| | | than your well being. For any children, |
| | | what could be a greater honour to them |
| | | than their father's thriving reputation? |
| | | A father feels the same about his sons. |
| | | So don't let your mind dwell on just one thought, |
| 800 | | that what you say is right and nothing else. |
| | | A man who thinks that only he is wise, |
| | | that he can speak and think like no one else, |
| | | when such men are exposed, then all can see |
| | | their emptiness inside. For any man, |
| | | even if he's wise, there's nothing shameful |
| | | in learning many things, staying flexible. |
| | | You notice how in winter floods the trees |
| | | which bend before the storm preserve their twigs. |
| | | The ones who stand against it are destroyed, |
| 810 | | root and branch. In the same way, those sailors |
| | | who keep their sails stretched tight, never easing off, |
| | | make their ship capsize—and from that point on |
| | | sail with their rowing benches all submerged. |
| | | So end your anger. Permit yourself to change. |
| | | For if I, as a younger man, may state |
| | | my views, I'd say it would be for the best |
| | | if men by nature understood all things— |
| | | if not, and that is usually the case, |
| | | when men speak well, it good to learn from them. |
| 820 | CHORUS LEADER | My lord, if what he's said is relevant, |
| | | it seems appropriate to learn from him, |
| | | and you too, Haemon, listen to the king. |
| | | The things which you both said were excellent. |

**My Notes**

# An Epic Foil

**My Notes**

| | CREON | And men my age—are we then going to school to learn what's wise from men as young as him? |
| | HAEMON | There's nothing wrong in that. And if I'm young, don't think about my age—look at what I do. |
| | CREON | And what you do—does that include this, honouring those who act against our laws? |
| 830 | HAEMON | I would not encourage anyone to show respect to evil men. |
| | CREON | And her— is she not suffering from the same disease? |
| | HAEMON | The people here in Thebes all say the same— they deny she is. |
| | CREON | So the city now will instruct me how I am to govern? |
| | HAEMON | Now you're talking like someone far too young. Don't you see that? |
| | CREON | Am I to rule this land at someone else's whim or by myself? |
| | HAEMON | A city which belongs to just one man is no true city. |
| 840 | CREON | According to our laws, does not the ruler own the city? |
| | HAEMON | By yourself you'd make an excellent king but in a desert. |
| | CREON | It seems as if this boy is fighting on the woman's side. |
| | HAEMON | That's true— if you're the woman. I'm concerned for you. |
| | CREON | You're the worst there is—you set your judgment up against your father. |
| | HAEMON | No, not when I see you making a mistake and being unjust. |
| | CREON | Is it a mistake to honour my own rule? |
| 850 | HAEMON | You're not honouring that by trampling on the gods' **prerogatives**. |
| | CREON | You foul creature— you're worse than any woman. |
| | HAEMON | You'll not catch me giving way to some disgrace. |
| | CREON | But your words all speak on her behalf. |

**prerogatives:** exclusive rights or privileges

| | | |
|---|---|---|
| HAEMON | And yours and mine— and for the gods below. | |
| CREON | You woman's slave— don't try to win me over. | |
| HAEMON | What do you want— to speak and never hear someone reply? | |
| CREON | You'll never marry her while she's alive. | |
| HAEMON | Then she'll die—and in her death kill someone else. | |
| 860 CREON | Are you so insolent you threaten me? | |
| HAEMON | Where's the threat in challenging a bad decree? | |
| CREON | You'll regret parading what you think like this— you—a person with an empty brain! | |
| HAEMON | If you were not my father, I might say you were not thinking straight. | |
| CREON | Would you, indeed? Well, then, by Olympus, I'll have you know you'll be sorry for demeaning me with all these insults. | |

*[Creon turns to his attendants]*

Go bring her out—
870     that hateful creature, so she can die right here,
with him present, before her bridegroom's eyes.

HAEMON     No. Don't ever hope for that. She'll not die
with me just standing there. And as for you—
your eyes will never see my face again.
So let your rage charge on among your friends
who want to stand by you in this.

*[Exit Haemon, running back into the palace]*

CHORUS LEADER     My lord, Haemon left in such a hurry.
He's angry—in a young man at his age
the mind turns bitter when he's feeling hurt.

CREON     Let him dream up or carry out great deeds
880     beyond the power of man, he'll not save these girls—
their fate is sealed.

CHORUS LEADER     Are you going to kill them both?

CREON     No—not the one whose hands are clean. You're right.

CHORUS LEADER     How do you plan to kill Antigone?

CREON     I'll take her on a path no people use,
and hide her in a cavern in the rocks,
while still alive. I'll set out provisions,
as much as **piety** requires, to make sure
the city is not totally corrupted.

**My Notes**

**piety:** devotion to religion; fulfillment of religious obligations

# An Epic Foil

**My Notes**

890
Then she can speak her prayers to Hades,
the only god she worships, for success
avoiding death—or else, at least, she'll learn,
although too late, how it's a waste of time
to work to honour those whom Hades holds.

## Second Read

- Reread the scene to answer these text-dependent questions.
- Write any additional questions you have about the text in your Reader/Writer Notebook.

3. **Key Ideas and Details:** Reread lines 727–731. How does this statement help you to understand what Creon expects from his son in this situation?

4. **Craft and Structure:** Haemon delivers a well-organized and moving argument to Creon in defense of Antigone in lines 776–819. Identify the different rhetorical appeals you can find in it: ethos, logos, and pathos.

5. **Key Ideas and Details:** In lines 840–850, what are Creon and Haemon arguing about? What prejudices does Creon reveal, and what do they tell you about Creon's character?

6. **Craft and Structure:** Whose death (besides Antigone's) do you think is foreshadowed in line 859: "Then she'll die—and in her death kill someone else"?

7. **Key Ideas and Details:** One of the characteristics of a tragic hero is "a good person who is brought down by an 'act of injustice.'" Explain why Creon's choice of death for Antigone is an "act of injustice."

## Working from the Text

8. Write a thesis statement about how Haemon acts as a character foil for Creon. Which of Creon's character traits are highlighted by his interactions with Haemon in this scene?

9. Use an outline to organize your ideas for an essay by identifying supporting ideas for your thesis. Draft an outline of an essay to support your thesis statement. Include the following in your outline:

- Write topic sentences that support your thesis.
- For each topic sentence, cite multiple pieces of textual evidence with quotation marks and line numbers.
- Include commentary that shows how the evidence supports the topic sentence.

## Outline of an Essay Analyzing Character Interaction

I. Thesis:

II. Topic Sentence 1:

Textual Evidence with Commentary:

III. Topic Sentence 2:

Textual Evidence with Commentary:

Textual Evidence with Commentary:

**My Notes**

# An Epic Foil

**My Notes**

Textual Evidence with Commentary:

IV. Topic Sentence 3:

Textual Evidence with Commentary:

Textual Evidence with Commentary:

Textual Evidence with Commentary:

V. Concluding Statement:

# Odes to Love and Death

## Learning Targets
- Analyze choral odes for author's purpose, literary elements, and theme.
- Present well-reasoned ideas supported with textual evidence in discussion groups.

LEARNING STRATEGIES:
Oral Reading, Summarize,
Marking the Text, Graphic
Organizer

## Preview
In this activity, you will review the purpose of choral odes in Greek drama and analyze their function in *Antigone*.

## Analyzing Choral Odes

1. Review the Introduction to Greek Drama notes in Activity 4.7. List the various purposes of the choral odes.

2. Reflect on the first three odes that you have read previously. Complete the graphic organizer later in this activity to analyze the purpose of each ode.

## Setting a Purpose for Reading

- In this section of the play, the power of love (Eros) is juxtaposed against Antigone's impending death. As you read the following passage, mark the text for the literary elements below and annotate in the margins with inferences exploring the ancient Greeks' beliefs about love and death:
  - ➤ diction
  - ➤ allusions
  - ➤ figurative language
- Circle unknown words and phrases. Try to determine the meanings of the words by using context clues, word parts, or a dictionary.

**My Notes**

### FOURTH ODE

CHORUS—**Strophe**

O Eros,[1] the conqueror in every fight,
Eros, who **squanders** all men's wealth,
who sleeps at night on girls' soft cheeks,
and roams across the ocean seas
and through the shepherd's hut—
no immortal god escapes from you,
nor any man, who lives but for a day.
And the one whom you possess goes mad.

900

**squanders:** wastes

[1] **Eros:** god of love and son of Aphrodite

# Odes to Love and Death

**Antistrophe**

perverting: corrupting

Even in good men you twist their minds,
**perverting** them to their own ruin.
You provoke these men to family strife.
The bride's desire seen glittering in her eyes—
that conquers everything, its power
enthroned beside eternal laws, for there
the goddess Aphrodite works her will,
whose ways are irresistible.

*[Antigone enters from the palace with attendants who are taking her away to her execution]*

> **WORD CONNECTIONS**
>
> **Word Relationships**
>
> The Choral Leader says that Antigone is "going to her bridal room" (line 912). He uses this as a *euphemism*, a word or phrase used in place of another word or phrase that is considered too harsh. In this context, the phrase *bridal room* refers to the place where Antigone is going to die. What is the effect of the Choral Leader using this euphemism?

910    CHORAL LEADER

When I look at her I forget my place.
I lose restraint and can't hold back my tears—
Antigone going to her bridal room
where all are laid to rest in death.

**COMMOS**

ANTIGONE—**Strophe 1**

Look at me, my native citizens,
as I go on my final journey,
as I gaze upon the sunlight one last time,
which I'll never see again—for Hades,
who brings all people to their final sleep,
leads me on, while I'm still living,
920    down to the shores of Acheron.[2]
I've not yet had my bridal chant,
nor has any wedding song been sung—
for my marriage is to Acheron.

CHORUS

Surely you carry fame with you and praise,
as you move to the deep home of the dead.
You were not stricken by lethal disease
or paid your wages with a sword.
No. You were in charge of your own fate.
So of all living human beings, you alone
930    make your way down to Hades still alive.

ANTIGONE—**Antistrophe 1**

I've heard about a guest of ours,
daughter of Tantalus,[3] from Phrygia—
she went to an excruciating death
in Sipylus,[4] right on the mountain peak.
The stone there, just like clinging ivy,
wore her down, and now, so people say,
the snow and rain never leave her there,

**My Notes**

_____
_____
_____
_____
_____
_____
_____
_____
_____
_____
_____
_____
_____
_____
_____
_____
_____
_____
_____

---

[2] **Acheron:** a river in Hades across which the dead were ferried
[3] **Tantalus:** son of Zeus who was punished by being "tantalized" by food and drink that were always just out of his reach
[4] **Sipylus:** mountain ruled by Tantalus; location of the weeping stone formation of Niobe

940   as she laments. Below her weeping eyes
her neck is wet with tears. God brings me
to a final rest which most resembles hers.

CHORUS   But Niobe[5] was a goddess, born divine—
and we are human beings, a race which dies.
But still, it's a fine thing for a woman,
once she's dead, to have it said she shared,
in life and death, the fate of demi-gods.

ANTIGONE—**Strophe 2**

Oh, you are mocking me! Why me—
by our fathers' gods—why do you all,
my own city and the richest men of Thebes,
insult me now right to my face,
950   without waiting for my death?
Well at least I have Dirce's springs,
the holy grounds of Thebes,
a city full of splendid chariots,
to witness how no friends lament for me
as I move on—you see the laws
which lead me to my rock-bound prison,
a tomb made just for me. Alas!
In my wretchedness I have no home,
not with human beings or corpses,
960   not with the living or the dead.

CHORUS   You pushed your daring to the limit, my child,
and tripped against Justice's high altar—
perhaps your agonies are paying back.
some compensation for your father.

ANTIGONE—**Antistrophe 2**

Now there you touch on my most painful thought—
my father's destiny—always on my mind,
along with that whole fate which sticks to us,
the splendid house of Labdakos—the curse
arising from a mother's marriage bed,
when she had sex with her own son, my father.
970   From what kind of parents was I born,
their wretched daughter? I go to them,
unmarried and accursed, an outcast.
Alas, too, for my brother Polyneices,
who made a fatal marriage and then died—
and with that death killed me while still alive.

CHORUS   To be piously **devout** shows reverence,
but powerful men, who in their persons
incorporate authority, cannot bear
anyone to break their rules. Hence, you die
980   because of your own selfish will.

**devout:** religious

---

[5] **Niobe:** daughter of Tantalus; all her children were killed and she was turned to stone; her rock
formation appears to weep tears for her children as it rains

My Notes

# Odes to Love and Death

epode: final stanza of the
ode; follows the strophe and
antistrophe

**My Notes**

ANTIGONE—**Epode**

Without lament, without a friend,
and with no marriage song, I'm being led
in this miserable state, along my final road.
So wretched that I no longer have the right
to look upon the sun, that sacred eye.
But my fate prompts no tears, and no
friend mourns.

CREON

990

Don't you know that no one faced with death
would ever stop the singing and the groans,
if that would help? Take her and shut her up,
as I have ordered, in her tomb's embrace.
And get it done as quickly as you can.
Then leave her there alone, all by herself—
she can sort out whether she wants suicide
or remains alive, buried in a place like that.
As far as she's concerned, we bear no guilt.
But she's lost her place living here with us.

ANTIGONE

1000

Oh my tomb and bridal chamber—
my eternal hollow dwelling place,
where I go to join my people. Most of them
have perished—Persephone[6] has welcomed them
among the dead. I'm the last one, dying here
the most evil death by far, as I move down
before the time allotted for my life is done.
But I go nourishing the vital hope
my father will be pleased to see me come,
and you, too, my mother, will welcome me,
as well as you, my own dear brother.
When you died, with my own hands I washed you.
I arranged your corpse and at the grave mound

libations: liquid gifts to a god

1010

poured out **libations**. But now, Polyneices,
this is my reward for covering your corpse.
However, for wise people I was right
to honour you. I'd never have done it
for children of my own, not as their mother,
nor for a dead husband lying in decay—
no, not in defiance of the citizens.
What law do I appeal to, claiming this?
If my husband died, there'd be another one,

1020

and if I were to lose a child of mine
I'd have another with some other man.
But since my father and my mother, too,
are hidden away in Hades' house,
I'll never have another living brother.
That was the law I used to honour you.
But Creon thought that I was in the wrong

---

[6] **Persephone:** goddess of the underworld; she was abducted by Hades and forced to spend one
third of each year there, which is the winter during which nothing blooms or grows

and acting recklessly for you, my brother.
Now he seizes me by force and leads me here—
no wedding and no bridal song, no share
1030        in married life or raising children.
Instead I go in sorrow to my grave,
without my friends, to die while still alive.
What holy justice have I violated?
In my wretchedness, why should I still look
up to the gods? Which one can I invoke
to bring me help, when for my reverence
they charge me with impiety? Well, then,
if this is something fine among the gods,
I'll come to recognize that I've done wrong.
1040        But if these people here are being unjust
may they endure no greater punishment
than the injustices they're doing to me.

CHORUS LEADER        The same storm blasts continue to attack
the mind in this young girl.

CREON        Then those escorting her
will be sorry they're so slow.

ANTIGONE        Alas, then,
those words mean death is very near at hand.

CREON        I won't encourage you or cheer you up,
by saying the sentence won't be carried out.

ANTIGONE        O city of my fathers
1050        in this land of Thebes—
and my ancestral gods,
I am being led away.
No more delaying for me.
Look on me, you lords of Thebes,
the last survivor of your royal house,
see what I have to undergo,
the kind of men who do this to me,
for paying **reverence** to true piety.

*[Antigone is led away under escort]*

**FIFTH ODE**

CHORUS—**Strophe 1**

In her brass-bound room fair Danae[7] as well
1060        endured her separation from the heaven's light,
a prisoner hidden in a chamber like a tomb,
although she, too, came from a noble line.
And she, my child, had in her care
the liquid streaming golden seed of Zeus.

**My Notes**

reverence: respect or honor

---

[7] **Danae:** daughter of a king; Zeus fell in love with her and they had a son, Perseus

**My Notes**

**Antistrophe 1**

1070

But the power of fate is full of mystery.
There's no evading it, no, not with wealth,
or war, or walls, or black sea-beaten ships.
And the hot-tempered child of Dryas,[8]
king of the Edonians, was put in prison,
closed up in the rocks by Dionysus,[9]
for his angry mocking of the god.
There the dreadful flower of his rage
slowly withered, and he came to know
the god who in his frenzy he had mocked
with his own tongue. For he had tried
to hold in check women in that frenzy
inspired by the god, the Bacchanalian fire.
More than that—he'd made the Muses angry,
challenging the gods who love the flute.

1080 **Strophe 2**

Beside the black rocks where the twin seas meet,
by Thracian Salmydessos at the Bosphorus,
close to the place where Ares dwells,
the war god witnessed the unholy wounds
which blinded the two sons of Phineus,[10]
inflicted by his savage wife—the sightless holes
cried out for someone to avenge those blows
made with her sharpened comb in blood-stained
hands.

**Antistrophe 2**

1090

In their misery they wept, lamenting
their wretched suffering, sons of a mother
whose marriage had gone wrong. And yet,
she was an offspring of an ancient family,
the race of Erechtheus, raised far away,
in caves surrounded by her father's winds,
Boreas' child, a girl who raced with horses
across steep hills—child of the gods.
But she, too, my child, suffered much
from the immortal Fates.

---

[8] **child of Dryas:** Dryas' son, who objected to the worship of Dionysus, was imprisoned and driven mad; later he was blinded by Zeus as additional punishment.

[9] **Dionysus:** Greek god of wine and son of Zeus

[10] **Phineus:** King of Thrace, who imprisoned his first wife Cleopatra; his new wife blinded Cleopatra's two sons out of jealousy.

## Second Read

- Reread the scene to answer these text-dependent questions.
- Write any additional questions you have about the text in your Reader/Writer Notebook.

3. **Key Ideas and Details:** Reread lines 915–960. How does Antigone think the public views her fate? Why does she have this impression? Is it accurate? Back up your answers with textual evidence.

4. **Key Ideas and Details:** Reread lines 1010–1025. What justification does Antigone give for burying Polyneices even though she says she would not have done it for other members of her family?

5. **Key Ideas and Details:** A martyr is someone who willingly suffers or dies rather than give up his or her cause or beliefs. Do you think that Antigone goes to her death as a martyr? Support your claims with textual evidence.

6. **Key Ideas and Details:** How do Creon and Antigone ultimately see themselves and their roles in this scene? Provide evidence from the text to support your answer.

# Odes to Love and Death

7. **Craft and Structure:** Several times in the scene, Antigone's tomb is referred to as her bridal chamber. How does this affect the mood of the audience or reader?

8. **Craft and Structure:** In lines 1072–1073, what does the Chorus mean by "the dreadful flower of his rage slowly withered"?

9. **Key Ideas and Details:** How do gods and fate play a role in this scene?

## Working from the Text

10. After reading the fourth and fifth odes, refer to the following graphic organizer to analyze the purpose of each ode.

11. Use the following questions to guide a group discussion of the ideas in this passage. Provide textual support for your opinions.

  • What attitudes and ideas about love and death are conveyed in this scene?

  • How are these ideas similar to or different from your culture's attitude toward love or death?

  • How do the different characters and their interactions help develop themes related to love and death?

| | Purposes of the Choral Odes | | |
|---|---|---|---|
| Ode | Summary of Content | Connection to the Previous Scene | Functional Purpose of the Ode |
| 1 | Polyneices and his army tried to defeat Thebes at its seven gates; Etocles and Thebans defended it along with Zeus's power, with brother killing brother. | The ode provides a description of troubles that preceded the play's beginning and adds explanation of Antigone's and Ismene's descriptions of war. | The scene serves as a bridge between Scene I, in which Antigone and Ismene are introduced and leads to the entrance of Creon. |
| 2 | | | |
| 3 | | | |
| 4 | | | |
| 5 | | | |
| 6 | | | |

**LEARNING STRATEGIES:**
Graphic Organizer, Discussion Groups, Drafting

### INDEPENDENT READING LINK
**Read and Discuss**
After you identify the tragic hero in the play *Antigone*, think about your independent reading selection. Use the characteristics of a tragic hero to identify the character in your independent reading who might be considered a tragic hero. Share your thoughts with a small group of peers.

**GRAMMAR & USAGE**
**Syntax**
The way that clauses and phrases are arranged into sentences—a writer's **syntax**—greatly affects the pacing of a text. Study the sentence structure of lines 1140–1149. Notice that the first sentence in this chunk is a four-line complex sentence. The next two sentences are each two lines long; they are followed by a rhetorical question. What is the structure of the two sentences in line 1149? How would you describe the general pattern of sentence structures here? How does this overall pattern affect the pace of Teiresias's argument and help him make his point?

## Learning Targets
- Analyze the development of a tragic hero over the course of a play.
- Write a character analysis incorporating textual support.

## Preview
In this activity, you will read and analyze the development of Creon as a tragic hero over the course of the play.

## Setting a Purpose for Reading
- Work with your group to mark the text for evidence of the following:
  ➤ Creon's further development as a tragic hero
  ➤ Traits and actions that portray Teiresias as a foil for Creon
  ➤ Content and purpose of the Sixth Choral Ode
- Circle unknown words and phrases. Try to determine the meanings of the words by using context clues, word parts, or a dictionary.

*[Enter Teiresias, led by a young boy]*

|   |   |   |
|---|---|---|
| | TEIRESIAS | Lords of Thebes, we two have walked a common path, one person's vision serving both of us. |
| 1100 | | The blind require a guide to find their way. |
| | CREON | What news do you have, old Teiresias? |
| | TEIRESIAS | I'll tell you—and you obey the prophet. |
| | CREON | I've not rejected your advice before. |
| | TEIRESIAS | That's the reason why you've steered the city on its proper course. |
| | CREON | From my experience I can confirm the help you give. |
| | TEIRESIAS | Then know this— your luck is once more on fate's razor edge. |
| 1110 | CREON | What? What you've just said makes me nervous. |
| | TEIRESIAS | You'll know—once you hear the tokens of my art. As I was sitting in my ancient place receiving omens from the flights of birds who all come there where I can hear them, I note among those birds an unknown cry— evil, unintelligible, angry screaming. I knew that they were tearing at each other with murderous claws. The noisy wings revealed that all too well. I was afraid. So right away up on the blazing altar I set up burnt offerings. But Hephaestus failed to shine out from the sacrifice— dark slime poured out onto the embers, oozing from the thighs, which smoked and spat, bile was sprayed high up into the air, and the melting thighs lost all the fat |
| 1120 | | |

which they'd been wrapped in. The rites had failed—
there was no prophecy revealed in them.
I learned that from this boy, who is my guide,
as I guide other men. Our state is sick—
your policies have done this. In the city

1130   our altars and our hearths have been **defiled**,
all of them, with rotting flesh brought there
by birds and dogs from Oedipus' son,
who lies there miserably dead. The gods
no longer will accept our sacrifice,
our prayers, our thigh bones burned in fire.
No bird will shriek out a clear sign to us,
for they have gorged themselves on fat and blood
from a man who's dead. Consider this, my son.
All men make mistakes—that's not uncommon.

1140   But when they do, they're no longer foolish
or subject to bad luck if they try to fix
the evil into which they've fallen,
once they give up their **intransigence**.
Men who put their stubbornness on show
invite accusations of stupidity.
Make concessions to the dead—don't ever stab
a man who's just been killed. What's the glory
in killing a dead person one more time?
I've been concerned for you. It's good advice.

1150   Learning can be pleasant when a man speaks well,
especially when he seeks your benefit.

CREON          Old man, you're all like archers shooting at me—
For you all I've now become your target—
even prophets have been aiming at me.
I've long been bought and sold as merchandise
among that tribe. Well, go make your profits.
If it's what you want, then trade with Sardis
for their golden-silver alloy—or for gold
from India, but you'll never hide that corpse

1160   in any grave. Even if Zeus' eagles
should choose to seize his festering body
and take it up, right to the throne of Zeus,
not even then would I, in trembling fear
of some defilement, permit that corpse
a burial. For I know well that no man
has the power to pollute the gods.
But, old Teiresias, among human beings
the wisest suffer a disgraceful fall
when, to promote themselves, they use fine words

1170   to spread around abusive insults.

TEIRESIAS          Alas, does any man know or think about …

CREON [*interrupting*]          Think what? What sort of **pithy** common thought
                                 are you about to utter?

TEIRESIAS [*ignoring the interruption*] … how good advice
                           is valuable—worth more than all possessions.

**defiled:** made unclean

**My Notes**

**intransigence:** unwillingness to compromise

**pithy:** short and clever

denigrate: slander

| | CREON | I think that's true, as much as foolishness is what harms us most. |
| | TEIRESIAS | Yet that's the sickness now infecting you. |
| | CREON | I have no desire to **denigrate** a prophet when I speak. |
| | TEIRESIAS | But that's what you are doing, when you claim my oracles are false. |
| 1180 | CREON | The tribe of prophets— all of them—are fond of money. |
| | TEIRESIAS | And kings? Their tribe loves to benefit dishonestly. |
| | CREON | You know you're speaking of the man who rules you. |
| | TEIRESIAS | I know—thanks to me you saved the city and now are in control. |
| | CREON | You're a wise prophet, but you love doing wrong. |
| | TEIRESIAS | You'll force me to speak of secrets locked inside my heart. |
| | CREON | Do it—just don't speak to benefit yourself. |
| | TEIRESIAS | I don't think that I'll be doing that— not as far as you're concerned. |
| 1190 | CREON | You can be sure you won't change my mind to make yourself more rich. |

TEIRESIAS    Then understand this well—you will not see
the sun race through its cycle many times
before you lose a child of your own loins,
a corpse in payment for these corpses.
You've thrown down to those below someone
from up above—in your arrogance
you've moved a living soul into a grave,
leaving here a body owned by gods below—

1200    unburied, dispossessed, unsanctified.
That's no concern of yours or gods above.
In this you violate the ones below.
And so destroying avengers wait for you,
Furies of Hades and the gods, who'll see
you caught up in this very wickedness.
Now see if I speak as someone who's been bribed.
It won't be long before in your own house
the men and women all cry out in sorrow,
and cities rise in hate against you—all those

1210    whose mangled soldiers have had burial rites
from dogs, wild animals, or flying birds
who carry the unholy stench back home,

to every city hearth. Like an archer,
I shoot these arrows now into your heart
because you have provoked me. I'm angry—
so my aim is good. You'll not escape their pain.
Boy, lead us home so he can vent his rage
on younger men and keep a quieter tongue
and a more temperate mind than he has now.

*[Exit Teiresias, led by the young boy]*

1220 CHORUS LEADER    My lord, my lord, such dreadful prophecies—
and now he's gone. Since my hair changed colour
from black to white, I know here in the city
he's never uttered a false prophecy.

CREON    I know that, too—and it disturbs my mind.
It's dreadful to give way, but to resist
and let destruction hammer down my spirit—
that's a fearful option, too.

CHORUS LEADER    Son of Menoikeos,
you need to listen to some good advice.

CREON    Tell me what to do. Speak up. I'll do it.

1230 CHORUS LEADER    Go and release the girl from her rock tomb.
Then prepare a grave for that unburied corpse.

CREON    This is your advice? You think I should concede?

CHORUS LEADER    Yes, my lord, as fast as possible.
Swift footed injuries sent from the gods
hack down those who act imprudently.

CREON    Alas—it's difficult. But I'll give up.
I'll not do what I'd set my heart upon.
It's not right to fight against necessity.

CHORUS LEADER    Go now and get this done. Don't give the work
to other men to do.

1240 CREON    I'll go just as I am.
Come, you servants, each and every one of you.
Come on. Bring axes with you. Go there quickly—
up to the higher ground. I've changed my mind.
Since I'm the one who tied her up, I'll go
and set her free myself. Now I'm afraid.
Until one dies the best thing well may be
to follow our established laws.

*[Creon and his attendants hurry off stage]*

**SIXTH ODE**

CHORUS—**Strophe 1**

1250    Oh you with many names,
you glory of that Theban bride,
and child of thundering Zeus,
you who cherish famous Italy,
and rule the welcoming valley lands

## WORD CONNECTIONS

### Content Connections

Besides being the god of wine and parties, Bacchus—a son of Zeus—was in charge of communication between the dead and the living. He was also the grandson of Cadmus, the founder of Thebes. In the Sixth Ode, the Chorus invokes Bacchus because of his connection to Thebes and also because the city is currently dealing with the issue of how to treat the dead. They are asking him to come "on healing feet" to help their city.

**My Notes**

of Eleusian Deo—
O Bacchus—you who dwell
in the bacchants' mother city Thebes,
beside Ismenus'[1] flowing streams,
on land sown with the teeth
of that fierce dragon.

**Antistrophe 1**

1260     Above the double mountain peaks,
the torches flashing through the murky smoke
have seen you where Corcyian nymphs
move on as they worship you

by the Kastalian stream.
And from the ivy-covered slopes
of Nysa's hills, from the green shore
so rich in vines, you come to us,
visiting our Theban ways,
while deathless voices all cry out
in honour of your name, "Evoe."[2]

1270    **Strophe 2**

You honour Thebes, our city,
above all others, you and your mother
blasted by that lightning strike.
And now when all our people here
are captive to a foul disease,
on your healing feet you come
across the moaning strait
or over the Parnassian hill.

**Antistrophe 2**

You who lead the dance,
among the fire-breathing stars,
1280    who guard the voices in the night,
child born of Zeus, oh my lord,
appear with your attendant Thyiads,
who dance in frenzy all night long,
for you their patron, Iacchus.[3]

*[Enter a Messenger]*
MESSENGER    All you here who live beside the home
of Amphion and Cadmus—in human life
there's no set place which I would praise or blame.
The lucky and unlucky rise or fall
by chance day after day—and how these things
1290    are fixed for men no one can prophesy.
For Creon, in my view, was once a man
we all looked up to. For he saved the state,
this land of Cadmus, from its enemies.
He took control and reigned as its sole king—
and prospered with the birth of noble children.

Now all is gone. For when a man has lost
what gives him pleasure, I don't include him
among the living—he's a breathing corpse.

---

[1] **Ismenus:** river near Thebes, sacred to Apollo
[2] **Evoe:** similar to hallelujah, a cry of joy shouted by worshipers at festivals
[3] **Iacchus:** another name for Dionysus

1300    Pile up a massive fortune in your home,
        if that's what you want—live like a king.
        If there's no pleasure in it, I'd not give
        to any man a vapour's shadow for it,
        not compared to human joy.

CHORUS LEADER    Have you come with news of some fresh trouble
                 in our house of kings?

MESSENGER    They're dead—
             and those alive bear the responsibility
             for those who've died.

CHORUS LEADER    Who did the killing?
                 Who's lying dead? Tell us.

MESSENGER    Haemon has been killed.
             No stranger shed his blood.

CHORUS LEADER    At his father's hand?
                 Or did he kill himself?

MESSENGER    By his own hand—
1310         angry at his father for the murder.

CHORUS LEADER    Teiresias, how your words have proven true!

MESSENGER    That's how things stand. Consider what comes
             next.

CHORUS LEADER    I see Creon's wife, poor Eurydice—
                 she's coming from the house—either by chance,
                 or else she's heard there's news about her son.

*[Enter Eurydice from the palace with some attendants]*

EURYDICE    Citizens of Thebes, I heard you talking,
            as I was walking out, going off to pray,
            to ask for help from goddess Pallas.
            While I was unfastening the gate,
1320        I heard someone speaking of bad news
            about my family. I was terrified.
            I collapsed, fainting back into the arms
            of my attendants. So tell the news again—
            I'll listen. I'm no stranger to misfortune.

MESSENGER    Dear lady, I'll speak of what I saw,
             omitting not one detail of the truth.
             Why should I ease your mind with a report
             which turns out later to be incorrect?
             The truth is always best. I went to the plain,
1330         accompanying your husband as his guide.
             Polyneices' corpse, still unlamented,
             was lying there, the greatest distance off,
             torn apart by dogs. We prayed to Pluto
             and to Hecate, goddess of the road,
             for their good will and to restrain their rage.
             We gave the corpse a ritual wash, and burned
             what was left of it on fresh-cut branches.

**My Notes**

_____

_____

_____

_____

_____

_____

_____

_____

_____

**My Notes**

We piled up a high tomb of his native earth.
Then we moved to the young girl's rocky cave,
1340    the hollow cavern of that bride of death.
From far away one man heard a voice
coming from the chamber where we'd put her
without a funeral—a piercing cry.
He went to tell our master Creon,
who, as he approached the place, heard the sound,
an unintelligible scream of sorrow.
He groaned and then spoke out these bitter words,
"Has misery made me a prophet now?
And am I travelling along a road
1350    that takes me to the worst of all disasters?
I've just heard the voice of my own son.
You servants, go ahead—get up there fast.
Remove the stones piled in the entrance way,
then stand beside the tomb and look in there
to see if that was Haemon's voice I heard,
or if the gods have been deceiving me."
Following what our desperate master asked,
we looked. In the furthest corner of the tomb
we saw Antigone hanging by the neck,
1360    held up in a noose—fine woven linen.
Haemon had his arms around her waist—
he was embracing her and crying out
in sorrow for the loss of his own bride,
now among the dead, his father's work,
and for his horrifying marriage bed.
Creon saw him, let out a fearful groan,
then went inside and called out anxiously,
"You unhappy boy, what have you done?
What are you thinking? Have you lost your mind?
1370    Come out, my child—I'm begging you—please come."
But the boy just stared at him with savage eyes,
spat in his face and, without saying a word,
drew his two-edged sword. Creon moved away,
so the boy's blow failed to strike his father.
Angry at himself, the ill-fated lad
right then and there leaned into his own sword,
driving half the blade between his ribs.
While still conscious he embraced the girl
in his weak arms, and, as he breathed his last,
1380    he coughed up streams of blood on her fair cheek.
Now he lies there, corpse on corpse, his marriage
has been fulfilled in chambers of the dead.
The unfortunate boy has shown all men
how, of all the evils which afflict mankind,
the most disastrous one is thoughtlessness.

*[Eurydice turns and slowly returns into the palace]*

| | CHORUS LEADER | What do you make of that? The queen's gone back. She left without a word, good or bad. |
|---|---|---|
| 1390 | MESSENGER | I'm surprised myself. It's about her son— she heard that terrible report. I hope she's gone because she doesn't think it right to mourn for him in public. In the home, surrounded by her servants, she'll arrange a period of mourning for the house. She's discreet and has experience— she won't make mistakes. |
| | CHORUS LEADER | I'm not sure of that. To me her staying silent was extreme— it seems to point to something **ominous**, just like a vain excess of grief. |
| 1400 | MESSENGER | I'll go in. We'll find out if she's hiding something secret, deep within her passionate heart. You're right— excessive silence can be dangerous. |

*[The Messenger goes up the stairs into the palace. Enter Creon from the side, with attendants. Creon is holding the body of Haemon.]*

| | CHORUS LEADER | Here comes the king in person—carrying in his arms, if it's right to speak of this, a clear reminder that this evil comes not from some stranger, but his own mistakes. |
|---|---|---|
| 1410 | CREON—**Strophe 1** | Aaiii—mistakes made by a foolish mind, cruel mistakes that bring on death. You see us here, all in one family— the killer and the killed. Oh the **profanity** of what I planned. Alas, my son, you died so young— a death before your time. Aaiii … aaiii … you're dead … gone— not your own foolishness but mine. |
| | CHORUS LEADER | Alas, it seems you've learned to see what's right— but far too late. |
| 1420 | CREON | Aaiiii … I've learned it in my pain. Some god clutching a great weight struck my head, then hurled me onto paths in wilderness, throwing down and casting underfoot what brought me joy. So sad … so sad … the wretched agony of human life. |

*[The Messenger reappears from the palace]*

| | MESSENGER | My lord, you come like one who stores up evil, what you hold in your arms and what you'll see before too long inside the house. |
|---|---|---|

**My Notes**

**ominous:** threatening

**profanity:** offensive deed

### WORD CONNECTIONS

**Multiple-Meaning Words**

The word *vain* has several meanings. Look up the different meanings in a dictionary and then decide which meaning best fits the context on line 1399, "Just like a vain excess of grief." *Vain* is also a homonym, or a word that sounds the same as another word or words. What are the differences among *vain*, *vein*, and *vane*? Consider their meanings and their parts of speech.

# Tragic Hero

| | | |
|---|---|---|
| | CREON | What's that?<br>Is there something still more evil than all this? |
| | MESSENGER | Your wife is dead—blood mother of that corpse—<br>slaughtered with a sword—her wounds are very new,<br>poor lady. |
| 1430 | CREON—**Antistrophe 1** | Aaiiii … a gathering place for death …<br>no sacrifice can bring this to an end.<br>Why are you destroying me? You there—<br>you bringer of this dreadful news, this agony,<br>what are you saying now? Aaiii …<br>You kill a man then kill him once again.<br>What are you saying, boy? What news?<br>A slaughter heaped on slaughter—<br>my wife, alas … she's dead? |
| | MESSENGER | [*Opening the palace doors, revealing the body of Eurydice*]<br>Look here. No longer is she concealed inside. |
| 1440 | CREON | Alas, how miserable I feel—to look upon<br>this second horror. What remains for me,<br>what's fate still got in store? I've just held<br>my own son in my arms, and now I see<br>right here in front of me another corpse.<br>Alas for this suffering mother.<br>Alas, my son. |
| 1450 | MESSENGER | Stabbed with a sharp sword at the altar,<br>she let her darkening eyesight fail,<br>once she had cried out in sorrow<br>for the glorious fate of Megareos,[4]<br>who died some time ago, and then again<br>for Haemon, and then, with her last breath,<br>she called out evil things against you,<br>the killer of your sons. |
| | CREON—**Strophe 2** | Aaaii … My fear now makes me tremble.<br>Why won't someone now strike out at me,<br>pierce my heart with a double bladed sword?<br>How miserable I am … aaiii …<br>how full of misery and pain … |
| | MESSENGER | By this woman who lies dead you stand charged<br>with the deaths of both your sons. |
| | CREON | What about her?<br>How did she die so violently? |
| 1460 | MESSENGER | She killed herself,<br>with her own hands she stabbed her belly,<br>once she heard her son's unhappy fate. |
| | CREON | Alas for me … the guilt for all of this is mine—<br>it can never be removed from me or passed |

[4] **Megareos:** youngest son of Creon and Eurydice; an inexperienced solder who died in battle

**My Notes**

to any other mortal man. I, and I alone …
I murdered you … I speak the truth.
Servants—hurry and lead me off,
get me away from here, for now
what I am in life is nothing.

1470    CHORUS LEADER    What you advise is good—if good can come
with all these evils. When we face such things
the less we say the better.

CREON—**Antistrophe 2**

Let that day come, oh let it come,
the fairest of all destinies for me,
the one which brings on my last day.
Oh, let it come, so that I never see
another dawn.

CHORUS LEADER    That's something for the times ahead.
Now we need to deal with what confronts us here.
1480    What's yet to come is the concern of those
whose task it is to deal with it.

CREON    In that prayer
I included everything I most desire.

CHORUS    Pray for nothing.
There's no release for mortal human beings,
not from events which destiny has set.

CREON    Then take this foolish man away from here.
I killed you, my son, without intending to,
and you, as well, my wife. How useless I am now.
I don't know where to look or find support.
Everything I touch goes wrong, and on my head
1490    fate climbs up with its overwhelming load.

[The Attendants help Creon move up the stairs into the palace, taking Haemon's body with them]

CHORUS    The most important part of true success
is wisdom—not to act impiously
towards the gods, for boasts of arrogant men
bring on great blows of punishment—
so in old age men can discover wisdom.

# Tragic Hero

## Second Read

- Reread the scene to answer these text-dependent questions.
- Write any additional questions you have about the text in your Reader/Writer Notebook.

1. **Craft and Structure:** In line 1109, Teiresias tells Creon that his "luck is once more on fate's razor edge." What does this metaphor mean? How should Creon react?

2. **Key Ideas and Details:** Reread lines 1111–1138. What indications do you have that Teiresias is truly a prophet? What do you think the signs he has interpreted mean? Annotate any clues that point to his being a true prophet.

3. **Key Ideas and Details:** Reread lines 1152–1192 and annotate any patterns you see in Creon's language. What excuse does Creon give for refusing to listen to Teiresias's advice? When has he made this accusation before, and what does this pattern of behavior say about his character?

4. **Craft and Structure:** Creon introduces the metaphor of the archer and the target in line 1152. How does Teiresias turn this metaphor against Creon, starting in line 1213?

5. **Key Ideas and Details:** The turning point for Creon begins in lines 1224–1227. Trace the development of this change in his conversation with the Chorus Leader. What characteristic of the tragic hero do these lines illustrate?

6. **Key Ideas and Details:** How does the Messenger describe Creon in lines 1291–1303? Does this description sound like that of a tragic hero? Explain.

7. **Key Ideas and Details:** Beginning with line 1325, what are the key events that the Messenger shares with Eurydice, Creon's wife?

8. **Craft and Structure:** What does Creon mean when he asks in line 1440, "What remains for me, what's fate still got in store?"

9. **Craft and Structure:** How does the Chorus's line "there's no release for mortal human beings, not from events which destiny has set" (lines 1485–1486) relate to Creon's question about fate in line 1440?

My Notes

10. **Key Ideas and Details:** In lines 1415–1416, the Chorus Leader tells Creon, "Alas, it seems you've learned to see what's right—but far too late." What chances was Creon given throughout the play to "see what's right," and how did he respond? How does this relate to the unfolding of the tragedy?

11. **Key Ideas and Details** What final message does the Chorus deliver, and how could you interpret this as the theme of the play?

12. **Key Ideas and Details** What does the role of the Chorus seem to be throughout the play?

13. **Key Ideas and Details** What does the end of the play imply about the conflict between fate versus free will? How do both Creon and Antigone grapple with seemingly limited free will?

## After Reading

14. Review the characteristics of a tragic hero listed in Activity 4.8. Explain which character in the play so far could be considered a tragic hero. List at least three reasons why the character meets the definition.

15. Work with a partner or small group to complete the graphic organizer. Find textual evidence to support your analysis of Creon as a tragic hero.

| Creon as a Tragic Hero | |
|---|---|
| Characteristics of the Tragic Hero | Where/when has creon demonstrated these qualities? |
| • A person of noble stature | |
| • A good person who is brought down by an "act of injustice" (hamartia) because he knows no better or believes that a greater good will be served by his actions | |
| • Has a weakness, a tragic flaw such as pride, quickness to anger, or misjudgment | |
| • Has free choice that makes his downfall his own fault | |
| • Experiences misfortune that is not entirely deserved | |
| • Gains self-knowledge or understanding before his downfall, and therefore experiences redemption | |

My Notes

# Tragic Hero

16. Return to the graphic organizer analyzing odes from Activity 4.14 and complete the last row for the sixth ode.

## Writing to Sources: Explanatory Text

Write a paragraph that explains how Teiresias contributes to Creon's development as a tragic hero. Include details about how Teiresias acts as a foil to highlight Creon's tragic flaws and how he helps Creon gain the self-knowledge necessary for redemption. Be sure to:

- Include specific relevant details about Creon's tragic flaws and Teiresias's actions as he helps Creon.
- Cite direct quotations and specific examples from both characters to show their interaction. Introduce and punctuate all quotations correctly.
- Include transitions between points and a statement that provides a conclusion.

 **Independent Reading Checkpoint**

You have read a Greek play whose characters had conflicting motivations and strong interactions. You have identified one character as a tragic hero. With a small group, discuss how to best use the information you have learned about these characters to help you prepare for the Embedded Assessment.

# Writing a Literary Analysis Essay on Characterization and Theme

## ASSIGNMENT

Your assignment is to write an analytical essay about the effect of character interaction in the play *Antigone*. Choose a character whose words, actions, or ideas contrast with Creon's character. Explain how these conflicting motivations contribute to Creon's development as a tragic hero and how the character interactions advance the plot or develop themes of the play.

| | |
|---|---|
| **Planning and Prewriting:** Take time to make a plan for your essay. | ▪ Which character will you choose to contrast with Creon? <br> ▪ Which of Creon's character traits were highlighted by his interactions with this character? <br> ▪ How did this character help develop Creon as a tragic hero? <br> ▪ How did Creon's interactions with this character advance the plot or develop a theme? <br> ▪ How can you draft a thesis that explains the significance of this character's interactions with Creon? <br> ▪ What textual support can you find for your thesis? <br> ▪ How can you use an outline to plan the structure of your essay? |
| **Drafting and Revising:** Compose your analytical essay. | ▪ How will you introduce your topic, organize your ideas, and provide a thoughtful concluding statement? <br> ▪ How will you integrate textual evidence from the play with commentary about how the evidence supports your thesis and topic sentences? <br> ▪ How will you demonstrate your understanding of literary terms such as **foil** and **tragic hero**? <br> ▪ How can you use strategies such as peer response to improve your draft? |
| **Editing and Publishing:** Prepare a final draft for publication. | ▪ How will you proofread and edit your essay for proper conventions of standard English capitalization, punctuation, spelling, grammar, and usage? <br> ▪ What tools are available for you to further polish and refine your work, such as a style guide, dictionary, thesaurus, spell-check, or grammar check? <br> ▪ How can the Scoring Guide help you evaluate how well you have met the requirements of the assignment? |

## Reflection

After completing this Embedded Assessment, think about how you went about accomplishing this task, and respond to the following question:

- How can you apply the themes of *Antigone* to today's world? Are there any laws today that you think citizens should feel justified in breaking? Why?

- Why are character interactions important in literature? In real life, what can you learn about yourself from other people?

# Writing a Literary Analysis Essay on Characterization and Theme

## SCORING GUIDE

| Scoring Criteria | Exemplary | Proficient | Emerging | Incomplete |
|---|---|---|---|---|
| **Ideas** | The essay<br>• thoroughly examines the effect of character interaction on plot or theme<br>• accurately analyzes characterization, including another character's role (such as foil) in the development of a tragic hero<br>• smoothly integrates relevant textual evidence, including details, quotations, and examples. | The essay<br>• examines the effect of character interaction on plot or theme<br>• adequately analyzes characterization, including another character's role (such as foil) in the development of a tragic hero<br>• includes sufficient textual evidence, including details, quotations, and examples. | The essay<br>• confuses the effect of character interaction on plot or theme<br>• provides some analysis of characterization and other characters' roles in the development of a tragic hero<br>• provides insufficient textual evidence (e.g., details, quotations, examples). | The essay<br>• does not examine the effect of character interaction on plot or theme<br>• lacks analysis of characterization and other characters' roles in the development of a tragic hero<br>• provides inaccurate or no textual evidence (e.g., details, quotations, examples). |
| **Structure** | The essay<br>• uses an effective organizational structure with a logical progression of ideas<br>• introduces the topic engagingly, links supporting ideas, and provides a thoughtful conclusion<br>• uses appropriate and varied transitions. | The essay<br>• uses an adequate organizational structure with a logical progression of ideas<br>• introduces the topic, links supporting ideas, and provides a conclusion<br>• uses effective transitions. | The essay<br>• uses an inconsistent organizational structure<br>• does not introduce the topic, link supporting ideas, and/or provide a conclusion<br>• uses weak, repetitive, or insufficient transitions. | The essay<br>• does not follow an obvious organizational structure<br>• does not introduce the topic, link supporting ideas, and/or provide a conclusion<br>• uses few, if any, transitions. |
| **Use of Language** | The essay<br>• uses precise language and a variety of sentence structures<br>• maintains an academic voice and objective tone<br>• demonstrates command of conventions with few errors in grammar, usage, capitalization, punctuation, and spelling. | The essay<br>• uses some precise language and different sentence structures<br>• generally maintains an academic voice and objective tone<br>• demonstrates adequate command of conventions; few errors in grammar, capitalization, punctuation, or spelling. | The essay<br>• uses vague language and simple sentences<br>• does not establish or maintain an academic voice<br>• demonstrates partial command of conventions; errors in grammar, usage, capitalization, punctuation, and/or spelling interfere with meaning. | The essay<br>• uses inappropriate language and simple or incomplete sentences<br>• does not use academic voice<br>• demonstrates little command of conventions; serious errors in grammar, usage, capitalization, punctuation, and/or spelling confuse meaning. |

# Building Cultural Bridges

**Visual Prompt:** How might people with many different cultural backgrounds support different approaches to solving the world's major issues?

## Unit Overview

In previous units of this book, you have learned that literature can bring together people from different cultures. Yet one viewing of the nightly news proves that cultural harmony is far from a reality. Cultural clashes continue to afflict the world, and conflicts over environmental resources are increasingly a source of such clashes. In this unit, you will examine one issue in depth: global warming, or climate change, and the controversy that surrounds it. You will study this issue with two purposes in mind: one, to understand the issue and the conflicts to which it contributes, and two, as a model for a research project that you will present to your classmates. You will use your study of nonfiction film to design a short film to present your project.

# Building Cultural Bridges

**GOALS:**

- To examine how nonfiction texts (print and nonprint) influence our perceptions of what is true
- To analyze how writers and speakers use evidence and appeals to support a claim
- To examine the credibility of a text or its author
- To explore a complex issue or problem from multiple perspectives and work with peers to present a solution
- To use media strategically to enhance a presentation

**ACADEMIC VOCABULARY**

controversy
documentary film
objective
subjective
imperative
fallacies
refutation
stakeholder
advocate
advocating

**Literary Terms**

dialogue
narration
diegetic sound
non-diegetic sound
logos
pathos
ethos
tone
storyboard

# Contents

## Activities

*Texts not included in these materials.*

**Language and Writer's Craft**
- Embedding Quotations (5.10)
- Punctuating Relative Clauses (5.11)
- Citation Styles (5.14)

**MY INDEPENDENT READING LIST**

# Previewing the Unit

**LEARNING STRATEGIES:**
Think-Pair-Share, QHT, Close Reading, Marking the Text, Paraphrasing

**ACADEMIC VOCABULARY**
A **controversy** is a public dispute about a topic that is debatable or arguable because it concerns an issue about which there is strong disagreement.

**My Notes**

_____

_____

_____

_____

_____

**INDEPENDENT READING LINK**

**Read and Recommend**

For your independent reading during this unit, explore nonfiction in both print and nonprint texts to enhance your understanding of how authors and directors use various techniques to engage and influence an audience. Find a variety of news articles, books, and/ or documentaries about controversial issues that interest you and expand your knowledge of the topics under study. Discuss your selections with a small group. Explain whether you recommend your choices to them and why.

## Learning Targets

- Preview the big ideas and vocabulary for the unit.
- Identify and analyze the skills and knowledge required for success in Embedded Assessment 1.

## Making Connections

In this unit, you will view the documentary film *The 11th Hour*, a film about climate change. This unit focuses on issues that cause cultural conflict. The **controversy** over climate change is an ongoing conflict, and you will study claims from both sides as well as the reasons and evidence that both offer to support their positions. You will learn several lenses through which to look at both sides of an issue to decide what is objective information and what is not.

## Essential Questions

Based on your current knowledge, how would you answer these questions?

1. How do cultural differences contribute to conflicts over environmental issues?

2. In what ways do nonfiction texts influence perceptions of their subject?

## Developing Vocabulary

Use the QHT chart to sort the Academic Vocabulary and Literary Terms. One academic goal is to move all words to the "T" column by the end of the unit. What strategies will you use to gather knowledge of new terms independently and to develop the ability to use them accurately?

## Unpacking Embedded Assessment 1

Closely read the assignment for Embedded Assessment 1: Presenting a Solution to an Environmental Conflict.

> Your assignment is to present a solution to the environmental conflict your group has researched. You will deliver a group presentation designed to contextualize the conflict for your classmates and justify your approach to resolving it.

Work with your class to paraphrase the expectations and create a graphic organizer to use as a visual reminder of the required concepts (what you need to know) and skills (what you need to do).

After each activity, use this graphic organizer to guide reflection about what you have learned and what you still need to learn in order to complete the Embedded Assessment successfully.

# The Call to Act

## Learning Targets
- Analyze the representation of a subject in the lyrics of a song and its music video.
- Analyze how various film elements contribute to theme and perspective.

## Preview

Music videos have become an art form and a great source of entertainment, but they always start with the lyrics of the song. Often, it is surprising to see how much our interpretation of a song's meaning may differ from the story or message established by its video version. Think of a song whose meaning changed for you after watching its video.

In this activity, you will read the lyrics of a song and then view its music video to analyze how various film elements contribute to theme and perspective.

## Setting a Purpose for Reading
- Read the following lyrics once. Make a prediction in the margin of what images you would expect to see based on your interpretation of the text.
- Circle unknown words and phrases. Try to determine the meaning of the words by using context clues, word parts, or a dictionary.

> **Song**
>
> # I Need to Wake Up
>
> *by* Melissa Etheridge
>
> Have I been sleeping?
> I've been so still
> Afraid of crumbling
> Have I been careless?
> 5 Dismissing all the distant rumblings
> Take me where I am supposed to be
> To comprehend the things that I can't see
>
> 'Cause I need to move
> I need to wake up
> 10 I need to change
> I need to shake up
> I need to speak out
> Something's got to break up
> I've been asleep
> 15 And I need to wake up
> Now

### LEARNING STRATEGIES:
Brainstorming, Rereading, Graphic Organizer, Marking the Text

### My Notes

### WORD CONNECTIONS

**Roots and Affixes**

*Comprehend* contains the root *prehend* from the Latin word *prehendere*, meaning "to seize." This root also appears in *reprehend, apprehend,* and *misapprehension.* The prefix *com-* means "with or together." In the context of this sentence, *comprehend* means "understand."

**My Notes**

And as a child

I danced like it was 1999

My dreams were wild

20  The promise of this new world

Would be mine

Now I am throwing off the carelessness of youth

To listen to an inconvenient truth[1]

That I need to move

25  I need to wake up

I need to change

I need to shake up

I need to speak out

Something's got to break up

30  I've been asleep

And I need to wake up

Now

I am not an island

I am not alone

35  I am my intentions

Trapped here in this flesh and bone

And I need to move

I need to wake up

I need to change

40  I need to shake up

I need to speak out

Something's got to break up

I've been asleep

And I need to wake up

45  Now

I want to change

I need to shake up

I need to speak out

Oh, something's got to break up

50  I've been asleep

And I need to wake up

Now

---

[1] The phrase *an inconvenient truth* is also the title of the documentary about climate change for which this song was written.

## Second Read

- Reread the song to answer these text-dependent questions.
- Write any additional questions you have about the text in your Reader/Writer Notebook.

1. **Key Ideas and Details:** What do you infer about the speaker's state of mind in the opening stanza? What are some words that clue you in?

2. **Craft and Structure:** How does Etheridge's use of anaphora (repetition at the beginnings of lines) affect her message? What feeling does this repetition develop?

3. **Craft and Structure:** What might Etheridge mean by the lines "Now I am throwing off the carelessness of youth / To listen to an inconvenient truth" (lines 22–23)? What is the impact of these lines? How do they connect to her overall message?

## Working from the Text

4. What do the terms *climate change* and *global warming* mean to you? Which one seems to be a more controversial term? How do you respond to hearing the terms in the media or at school? Why do these terms provoke such strong reactions from some people?

**My Notes**

# The Call to Act

## My Notes

5. Etheridge's song won the 2007 Academy Award for Best Original Song for its use in the film *An Inconvenient Truth*, which argues that climate change poses a threat to humankind so severe that immediate action is needed. With that in mind, reread the text, looking for words or phrases that take on a more specific meaning relevant to this context. List some of these below—as well as your interpretations of what their new meaning might be.

| Text | Meaning Based on Context |
|---|---|
|  |  |

## Literary Terms

**Dialogue** is the spoken words of characters or participants in a film.

**Narration** are the words that are heard as part of a film, television show, etc., and that describe what is being seen.

**Diegetic sound** is actual noises associated with the shooting of a scene, such as voices and background sounds.

**Non-diegetic sound** refers to voice-overs and commentary, sounds that do not come from the action on screen.

## Setting a Purpose for Viewing

As you watch the video of the song, consider how the video's images affect your understanding of the lyrics. In particular, observe how the video uses these documentary film elements to help support the video's message:

- **primary footage** (scenes shot by the director specifically for the film, including interviews or footage of the performer/filmmaker)
- **archival footage** (scenes taken from other sources, such as news broadcasts or home video)
- **still images** (photographs as opposed to video footage, although the camera may pan or zoom on the photo)
- **text** (subtitles, labels, graphics, etc.)

## Working from the Film

6. As you watch the video a second time, fill out the following graphic organizer, being as specific and detailed as possible with your descriptions of the video's elements.

**Nonfiction Film Viewing Guide**

**Director:**             **Title:**             **Year:**

**What Do You See** (primary or archival footage, interviews, still images, the filmmaker)?

**What Do You Hear** (dialogue, narration, diegetic, and non-diegetic sound)?

**What Do You Read** (subtitles, graphics, labels, etc.)?

**How Is It Put Together** (editing sequence, transition devices, etc.)?

**What Is the Effect** (what is the theme/message of the video, what "truth" does it convey)?

## Check Your Understanding

Describe one example of each of the four types of images listed (primary, archival, still, text) and explain its effect in the video.

## Writing to Sources: Explanatory Text

Write a paragraph that compares and contrasts the lyrics of "I Need to Wake Up" with the video of the song. Include relevant words and phrases from the song as well as examples of film techniques used in the music video. Be sure to:

- Include detailed descriptions of the various film techniques used.
- Cite direct quotations from the song. Introduce and punctuate all quotations correctly.
- Provide a conclusion that summarizes your explanation.

## Learning Targets
- Distinguish between objective and subjective points of view in a nonprint text.
- Write to establish and transform objective or subjective point of view.

## Preview
In this activity, you will view a film to distinguish between objective and subjective points of view.

## Viewing a Film

1. You are about to witness a confrontation. As with any confrontation, not everyone agrees about the facts of what has occurred. Your job will be to take a particular point of view and record the facts of the confrontation. Choose one of the following perspectives as you watch the clip.
   - You are a "fly on the wall" merely trying to report the details of the confrontation.
   - You believe Jes is in the right and that her parents are being unreasonable.
   - You believe Jes's parents have a right to be concerned and Jes is being unreasonable.

2. As you watch the film clip, take notes on what you see and hear, trying to capture specific lines of dialogue.

3. Next, write a paragraph explaining the truth of what happened from your point of view. Whichever perspective you chose, try to include specific details from the scene (dialogue, actions, etc.). Be prepared to share these details with your peers.

**My Notes**

# Throwing Light on the Subject

## WORD CONNECTIONS

### Roots and Affixes

*Objectivity* and *subjectivity* contain the root *ject*, from the Latin word *jacere*, meaning "to throw." This root also appears in *reject, injection, project,* and *ejection.* The prefix *ob-* means "toward," and *sub-* means "under or from beneath." Considering the prefixes of these words can help you understand the ways in which they are opposite.

## My Notes

_____

_____

_____

_____

_____

_____

_____

_____

## INDEPENDENT READING LINK

### Read and Discuss

Use the definitions of *objectivity* and *subjectivity* that you created for this activity to evaluate one or more of the nonfiction texts you have explored in your independent reading. Decide if your texts present information objectively or subjectively. Explain your evaluations to a small group of peers, pointing to textual evidence to support your view.

4. After discussing the best examples from each perspective, decide what distinguishes the examples that are in the second and third perspectives from those in the first perspective.

5. Based on your observations, define *objectivity* and *subjectivity*.

| | |
|---|---|
| **Objectivity** (fly on the wall) | |
| **Subjectivity** (Jes/Parents) | |

6. Share your paragraph with peers. After listening to the paragraphs of your peers, underline or highlight the words, phrases, or details you included in your paragraph that might be considered subjective.

7. Rewrite your paragraph to transform it from objective to subjective or vice versa. Be sure to:
   • Include or remove details that express an opinion rather than merely record.
   • Start with a topic sentence that indicates an appropriate point of view.
   • Select diction that denotes or connotes appropriately.

## Check Your Understanding

Annotate your paragraph to explain the choices you made to transform it.

# That's Just the Way It Is

## Learning Targets

- Compare and contrast two documentary treatments of the same subject.
- Evaluate how a director uses rhetoric and details to advance a subjective point of view.

## Preview

In this activity, you will compare and contrast two **documentary films** while evaluating their use of rhetoric and details to advance a subjective point.

## Comparing Films

1. You will next watch two film clips that cover very similar content in very different ways. Although both are considered to be documentary texts, a close reading of each reveals that some documentaries present a strongly subjective point of view toward their subject despite being nonfiction.

2. As you view the two clips, complete the viewing guides that follow. Note specific details, not just generalizations, so that you can use the details to support claims about the level of subjectivity.

3. Both of these clips come from films classified as documentary films. After watching both, complete a Venn diagram like the one below in your Reader/Writer Notebook to compare the films. Focus in particular on how the two films talk about the same subject in different ways. Is one more subjective than the other?

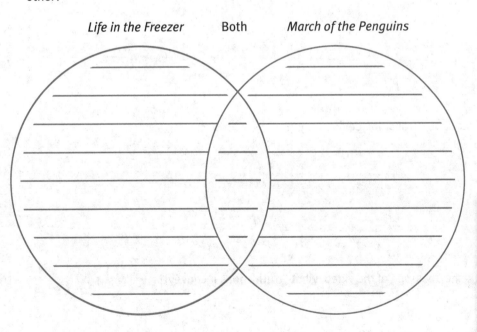

*Life in the Freezer*     Both     *March of the Penguins*

4. Now revisit your definitions of **subjective** and **objective** from the previous activity. Check their accuracy using the Academic Vocabulary feature in the margin. Based on these definitions and the clips you just watched, how might documentary films blur the distinction between objectivity and subjectivity that we associate with the label *nonfiction*? How do they sometimes "teach" something more than just the facts?

---

**LEARNING STRATEGIES:**
Close Reading, Viewing Guide

---

**ACADEMIC VOCABULARY**
A **documentary film** is a nonfiction film that provides a visual record of actual events using photographs, video footage, and interviews. Documentaries are used in many professional situations to convey information about a specific subject.

---

**WORD CONNECTIONS**

Roots and Affixes

The word *documentary* contains the root *doc*, from the Latin word *docere*, meaning "to teach." This root also appears in *document, docent,* and *doctorate.* The suffix *-ary* indicates that the word is a noun. How have the documentary clips you've watched taught you things about the subjects they contain?

---

**ACADEMIC VOCABULARY**
**Subjective** and **objective** are commonly used terms to describe the point of view or perspective adopted when presenting information. It is important to understand that if something is subjective, it is informed by opinion, bias, and feelings; whereas an objective point of view tries to be impartial, balanced, and factual in its presentation.

---

# That's Just the Way It Is

## Nonfiction Film Viewing Guide

**Director:**                    **Title:**                              **Year:**

**What Do You See** (primary or archival footage, interviews, still images, the filmmaker)?

**What Do You Hear** (dialogue, narration, diegetic, and non-diegetic sound)?

**What Do You Read** (subtitles, graphics, labels, etc.)?

**How Is It Put Together** (editing sequence, transition devices, etc.)?

**What Is the Effect** (what is the theme/message of the video, what "truth" does it convey)?

## Nonfiction Film Viewing Guide

**Director:**                        **Title:**                        **Year:**

**What Do You See** (primary or archival footage, interviews, still images, the filmmaker)?

**What Do You Hear** (dialogue, narration, diegetic, and non-diegetic sound)?

**What Do You Read** (subtitles, graphics, labels, etc.)?

**How Is It Put Together** (editing sequence, transition devices, etc.)?

**What Is the Effect** (what is the theme/message of the video, what "truth" does it convey)?

# That's Just the Way It Is

## Writing to Sources: Argument Text

Write a critique of the clip from the documentary film *March of the Penguins* that you just watched. Use valid reasoning to analyze the level of subjectivity in the film. Support your analysis with relevant descriptive details and evidence from the clip. Be sure to:

- Begin with a topic sentence that clearly states your opinion and identifies the purpose of the text's subjectivity.
- Quote or vividly describe images and sounds from the clip as evidence.
- Incorporate appropriate terminology to discuss subjective points of view and film techniques.

## Check Your Understanding

In a single sentence, explain how documentaries can be both nonfiction and subjective.

# Previewing *The 11th Hour*

## Learning Targets
- Explain how filmmakers use juxtaposition for effect in documentary films.
- Analyze how a documentary establishes point of view and ethos.

## Preview
In this activity, you will view Chapter 1 of *The 11th Hour* and analyze its point of view.

## Viewing a Documentary

1. Now you will tell a story in three sentences. Your teacher will give you three note cards. Arrange them in every possible order of events, and write each variation in the following space (there are six, but not all make sense). Then, identify the specific connotations or relationships suggested for each sequence of statements.

2. As you watch the sequence of images in the first two minutes of the film *The 11th Hour*, write down each of the images you see. Then, working with classmates, write an explanation of what relationships are suggested between the juxtaposition of each image and the one that follows it. What does the meaning of the sequence as a whole seem to be?

3. As you watch the opening scenes of *The 11th Hour*, take notes in the graphic organizer on the next page. Be sure to cite *specific* textual details. SMELL is a strategy for analyzing how a speaker constructs his or her text to connect with the target audience, building trust and appealing to them in the process.

4. Also take notes on the rhetorical appeals of **ethos, logos,** and **pathos**. Notice how these three types of appeals are embedded within the SMELL chart.

---

**LEARNING STRATEGIES:**
Manipulatives, Note-taking, SMELL, Fishbowl, Graphic Organizer

**My Notes**

**WORD CONNECTIONS**

**Roots and Affixes**

*Juxtaposition* contains the Latin prefix *justa-*, meaning "near" or "beside," and the root *pos*, meaning "to place." The root also appears in *composition* and *opposition*. In this context, *juxtaposition* means "the placement next to another."

**Literary Terms**

**Logos** is the use of factual evidence and logical thought to appeal to an audience's sense of reason. **Pathos** uses emotional language or images, while **ethos** works by establishing the writer as fair and open-minded.

# Previewing *The 11th Hour*

| SMELL |
| --- |

**Sender-Receiver Relationship:** Who are the senders and receivers of the message, and what is their relationship (consider the different audiences the film may be addressing and how the filmmakers wish us to perceive DiCaprio)? How do the filmmakers attempt to establish **ethos**?

**Message:** What is a literal summary of the content? What is the meaning or significance of this information?

**Emotional Strategies:** What emotional appeals do the directors include? What seems to be their desired effect? How do they evoke **pathos**?

**Logical Strategies:** What logical claims and evidence does the director include? What is their effect? How persuasive is this use of **logos**?

**Language:** What specific language is used in the clip to support the message? How does it affect the film's effectiveness? Consider both visual language (images) and actual words (text).

5. Consider the following issues connected to the clip you have just watched. Write a well-developed response to each prompt, and be prepared to discuss your response in front of your classmates.

A. *The 11th Hour* is a documentary film, but is it merely informational in its approach, or does it seem to be presenting some form of argument? In other words, how objective or subjective is its perspective on the issue of climate change? How does the level of subjectivity affect you as a viewer?

B. Now consider the impact of the opening scenes on your perceptions of DiCaprio's ethos—the sense that he is trustworthy, credible, fair, and open-minded. How effectively does the juxtaposition of images and scenes, in conjunction with the music, dialogue, and other sounds in the opening chapter, establish his (and the film's) ethos?

C. Some critics attack *The 11th Hour* as being alarmist, using dire projections and visual images that amount to scare tactics. Make a list of details (images, claims made by DiCaprio, the music used, etc.) that could be considered sensationalistic, and consider the effect of how they are juxtaposed within the sequence. With these points in mind, how do you respond to the critiques of the film?

## Check Your Understanding

How does juxtaposition affect meaning in a visual text?

**My Notes**

# The Nature of the Problem: Evaluating Causal Claims

LEARNING STRATEGIES:
Graphic Organizer, Note-taking

**My Notes**

## Learning Targets

* Analyze the relationship between cause-effect claims and the use of supporting evidence.
* Evaluate how filmmakers use evidence and rhetorical appeals to support a claim.

## Preview

In this activity, you will view Chapters 2–6 of *The 11th Hour* and evaluate the evidence provided to support cause-effect claims.

## What Is Evidence?

1. With a partner, review what you know about the different types of evidence and how they can be used to support a debatable or controversial claim. Which types of evidence would you expect to see used to support a causal claim? Why? Which would not be used? Why not?

| Type of Evidence/Support | Description | Used to ... |
|---|---|---|
| Facts and Statistics | | |
| Analogy (figurative or literal) | | |
| Personal Experience/ Anecdote | | |
| Illustrative Example (brief or extended) | | |
| Expert/Personal Testimony | | |
| Hypothetical Case | | |
| Visual Aid | | |

2. As you view the film, record comments about the film, questions about its
   function as a text, and a summary of the effectiveness of the argument it makes.

| Questions/Commentary | Notes |
|---|---|
| | |

**Summary Section**

# The Nature of the Problem: Evaluating Causal Claims

3. Using your notes on this section of the film, fill in the chart by identifying the various cause-effect claims made thus far.

**CAUSES**

**EFFECTS**

**Climate Change**

4. With your group, choose three of the cause-effect links to analyze. How is each causal claim supported in the film (statistics, expert testimony, hypothetical scenario, visual aid, etc.)? How persuasive is the claim as a result?

## Explain How an Argument Persuades

Evaluate how the filmmakers use evidence and rhetorical appeals to support the claim that climate change poses a real threat to human society. Identify the logical connections used to link the claim to reasons and the reasons to evidence. Cite examples of specific evidence and how they affect persuasiveness. Be sure to:

- Start with a statement that identifies the title of the film and the names of the filmmakers you are evaluating. Then state your claim about how they use evidence and rhetorical appeals in the film.

- Use words, phrases, and clauses that objectively present information from the film and show how your ideas are related.

- Provide a concluding statement that follows from the argument you have presented.

## Check Your Understanding

What types of evidence are most and least persuasive when used to support a causal claim? Why?

**My Notes**

# The Art of Objectivity: Writing an Effective Summary

## Learning Targets
- Write and revise an effective objective summary.
- Collaborate with a peer using effective speaking and listening skills.

## Preview
In this activity, you will view Chapters 7–11 of *The 11th Hour* and work collaboratively to write an objective summary of the evidence provided by the film.

## Looking for Evidence
1. You will be assigned one of the following focus areas. With your group, discuss what the evidence relevant to your topic has looked like in previous viewings.

**Ethos and Credibility:** This film relies on the testimony of experts to make its argument regarding sustainable development. Keep track of each person interviewed in this segment.
- Which ones seem most/least credible and why?
- What types of evidence do the most credible speakers use?
- How does their appearance and their delivery affect their credibility?
- Based on your responses, what can you conclude about how a speaker can make him/herself credible to an audience?

**Evidence and Persuasion:** A number of negative effects of environmental development are identified in this segment. Make a list of these as they are presented.
- How persuasive is each of these as evidence that current approaches to development must end or be changed?
- How are visual information and sound used to support the claims speakers are making?
- What kinds of evidence and appeals (logical explanations, emotional appeals, the ethos of the speakers) make these claims persuasive?
- Based on your responses, what can you conclude about how to use visuals, documented evidence, and emotional appeals to support a claim?

**Values and Perspectives:** Look at the values the film supports.
- What does the film seem to support as the right way to feel about the issues?
- What perspectives does it criticize?
- What does it say, for example, about corporate and political attitudes in our culture?
- Is growth a means to an end or an end in itself?
- What perspectives are *not* presented except through the filter of others who disagree with them?
- Based on your responses, what biases dominate in the film? Does the film effectively speak to audience members who do not share those biases? Why or why not?

**LEARNING STRATEGIES:**
Graphic Organizer, Discussion Groups, Marking the Text

**My Notes**

**WORD CONNECTIONS**

Roots and Affixes

*Persuasion* contains the root *suad*, from the Latin word *suadere*, meaning "to advise or urge." This root also appears in *dissuade* and *persuadable*.

# The Art of Objectivity: Writing an Effective Summary

2. As you watch today's segment from *The 11th Hour*, fill out the viewing guide, looking specifically for details connected to your focus area. After finishing the segment, summarize your findings for your focus area in the space below the graphic organizer.

## Nonfiction Film Viewing Guide

**Director:**                                    **Title:**                                    **Year:**

**What Do You See** (primary or archival footage, interviews, still images, the filmmaker)?

**What Do You Hear** (dialogue, narration, diegetic, and non-diegetic sound)?

**What Do You Read** (subtitles, graphics, labels, etc.)?

**How Is It Put Together** (editing sequence, transition devices, etc.)?

**What Is the Effect** (what is the theme/message of the video, what "truth" does it convey)?

**Summary:**

3. As you share information within your new groups, take notes on what one of your peers says so that you can write a summary and later report on the information. Each group member should summarize a different group member so that only one summary is being written of each presentation.

## Explanatory Writing Prompt

Write a summary of the information presented by your peer. Answer the key questions for that person's topic (see previous page). Be sure to:

- Record the central claim and major reasons provided in the source text without recording too much of the specific evidence.
- Include all major points.
- Use enough author/speaker tags (such as "DiCaprio claims ..." or "The writer argues ...") to make it clear that the ideas in the summary are those of the speaker/source.
- Report what the original speaker/text said in an objective way, rather than showing judgment of the information.

Exchange summaries with the person on whose presentation you focused. Read through the summary you receive and mark the draft with feedback on these criteria:

- How effectively has the person captured the central ideas without covering specific evidence?
- Has any key information been omitted?
- Is the summary objective or too subjective?
- Does the summary contain a sufficient number of source (author/speaker) tags?

Based on these areas, how should the person revise his/her summary to make it more comprehensive, accurate, and representative? Make notes on the paper to offer specific suggestions for how the person can revise the draft.

## Check Your Understanding

Revise your own paragraph to reflect the feedback you receive. Annotate it to show how you have made it a better summary.

**My Notes**

**INDEPENDENT READING LINK**

**Read and Respond**

Choose one of your nonfiction independent reading texts. Following the procedure you learned in this activity, write an objective summary of the text. Then share your summary with a peer.

# Questioning Appeals

**My Notes**

## Learning Targets

- Analyze how rhetorical appeals are used to support a persuasive claim in a documentary film.
- Write a review evaluating the purpose and effectiveness of the film's evidence and appeals.

## Preview

In this activity, you will view Chapters 12–16 of *The 11th Hour* and write a review of the film.

## Viewing the Final Segment

1. You will watch the final segment of the film today. Before doing so, consider the three viewing strategies you have previously used as you watched the film. Evaluate each strategy below. In the space provided, consider its purpose, its strengths, and its limitations. Based on your analysis, choose which approach to use for this final segment.

| SMELL | Questions/Commentary and Notes | Viewing Guide |
| --- | --- | --- |
| | | |

**ACADEMIC VOCABULARY**
An **imperative** is something of vital or essential importance; for example, "It is imperative that you get to school on time." A *moral imperative* is based on a person's beliefs or principles that guide one to take an action.

2. This closing chunk of the film presents the argument that taking action against climate change is a moral **imperative**. To support this position, the film attempts to use logos, ethos, and pathos to appeal to viewers and to call them to action. But how effective is this effort? As you watch the scenes in this chunk, be sure to record specific details regarding the people, images, text, sounds (including narration/quotes), and sequence of what is shown.

3. In what ways are the filmmakers trying to motivate viewers here: through logic, evidence, and reasoning? Through the credibility of experts and DiCaprio's charisma? Through provocative images that provoke a wide range of emotions? Focus closely on which elements in this remaining chunk most strongly provoke a response (whether positive or negative) for you as a viewer.

4. **Levels of Questions:** After viewing the last segment of the film, use your notes and write some Level 1 questions to review the key contents of the chunk. Follow those with Level 2 questions that analyze the contents' purpose and evaluate their effectiveness. Finally, craft some Level 3 questions that ask classmates to consider the implications of the issues in the scenes and their relevance in their own lives. An example of each is provided as a model.

| Level 1 Literal | **Example:** Who are the final three speakers featured? |
|---|---|
| Level 2 Interpretative | **Example:** Which of these three is most/least credible and persuasive? Why? |
| Level 3 Universal | **Example:** How do you respond to the discussion of such things as love and "healing power" in connection with environmentalism? |

5. Working with classmates, identify several questions that effectively guide analysis of details in the segment you viewed. Be prepared to ask your classmates to respond to these questions.

## Argument Writing Prompt

For your school newspaper, write a review of *The 11th Hour*. Take a position on whether or not it is effective as a documentary. Identify the criteria that are relevant to your target audience. Defend your position with relevant and sufficient evidence. Write a precise claim and support it with valid reasoning and relevant evidence. Be sure to:

- Acknowledge counterclaims that anticipate the audience's knowledge level, concerns, values, and possible biases while also refuting the evidence for those claims.
- Maintain a formal tone, vary sentence types, and use effective transitions.
- End with a call to action to your target audience.

## Check Your Understanding

What makes a call to action effective?

# The Ethics of Persuasion

**LEARNING STRATEGIES:**
Close Reading, Marking the Text, Graphic Organizer, SMELL, Discussion Groups, Fishbowl

## My Notes

## Learning Targets
- Analyze an interview to evaluate the impact of subjectivity on a text.
- Identify fallacies in order to evaluate a text's credibility.

## Preview

In this activity, you will read an interview with Leonardo DiCaprio and revisit *The 11th Hour* to identify any fallacies in the film.

## Persuasion

When planning a persuasive text, such as the one you and your group members will construct for Embedded Assessment 1, it is necessary to consider how to convince an audience to accept your conclusions. What information should you include or omit? What perspectives will be voiced or left silent? How much should you appeal to your audience's emotions, and how? What is the relationship between these choices and constructing a positive ethos in the text?

In this activity, you will consider the choices of DiCaprio and the directors of *The 11th Hour*, specifically examining their deliberate choice to silence certain voices and to use ethos and pathos to influence their target audience. To do so, you need to step back from your personal beliefs about the film's message for the moment and to focus only on how it is presented.

## Setting a Purpose for Reading
- As you read the following interview with Leonardo DiCaprio, mark the text for any statements he makes that might be considered controversial to those who are critics of his message. In particular, look for lines that reveal the choices he and the directors made about how to use logos, ethos, and pathos as persuasive tools in the film.
- Circle unknown words and phrases. Try to determine the meaning of the words by using context clues, word parts, or a dictionary.

**barrage:** rapid outpouring

### Article

# DICAPRIO
## Sheds Light on 11th Hour

*by* Scott Roxborough

May 20, 2007

1   Leonardo DiCaprio sat down with *The Hollywood Reporter* and a handful of select film publications at the Hotel du Cap in Cannes on Saturday to discuss his upcoming environmental documentary "The 11th Hour." The film, which premiered in a special Out of Competition screening Saturday at the Festival de Cannes, uses a **barrage** of images and reams of interviews with the world's top environmental scientists to paint a bleak but still optimistic picture of the fate of our planet. "Hour" was directed by sisters Nadia Conners and Leila Conners Petersen, who wrote the script with DiCaprio.

2  Q: What was the most difficult thing for you in making this film?

3  DiCaprio: Trying to **condense** the vision of what these scientific experts are saying (about global warming) and trying to make it as clear and as emotionally moving as possible. Trying to condense a world of issues into an hour-and-a-half format in this film was the biggest challenge. But it was about giving them a platform where they didn't have to argue about the science. Because, and I keep stressing this, this is the overwhelming majority of the scientific community that believes in this. Not to have to be challenged about the science, about if their opinions were correct or if their opinions were valid. It was about them being able to express ideas and being able to give us, the public. Listen to the scientists and give us, the public, solutions for the future.

4  Q: With "The 11th Hour" are you hoping to reach a different audience than Al Gore's "An Inconvenient Truth" just because of who you are and the kind of attention this film will get because of your involvement with it?

5  A: Yes, I guess you could call it a different audience. I mean, I didn't want to make this an overly political film, where just because of your political **affiliation**, you think you are somehow responsible for this and are somehow to blame. There are political overtones in the movie, we do point the finger. But ultimately, it is not about preaching to the choir, about reaching an audience that already gets it and already wants to become active. It's about, I suppose—and this is just about me following the lead of what the scientists and the experts have been saying—it's the cultural transformation that needs to happen. It's a swelling up from the ground level from people that are going to have to demand action. It goes beyond whether you are a Democrat or Republican in the United States. It goes beyond that. It goes into the realm of every politician having to be responsible because there is such a cultural awareness about global warming and environmental issues that they have to deal with it.

6  Q: Are you worried that, because you are a celebrity, people could dismiss this movie simply because of who you are?

7  A: I am completely aware of the fact that being someone from quote-unquote Hollywood will garner [a] certain amount of skepticism and criticism as [to] why should we listen to this person? I wanted to pose myself as a concerned citizen, not as an expert. I ask the questions and allow these people (the scientists) to give the answers. But you can also talk about the Hollywood community and about how they have traditionally been a part of a lot of great movements in the United States, going back to the civil rights movement or the peace movement. I don't think there's nothing wrong with that. As long as I don't pretend to be somebody who does have a degree, you know what I mean? But rather as a concerned citizen. Hopefully a larger audience will watch the film as opposed to if I wasn't involved with it.

8  Q: The film doesn't pander to a **populist** level. You get into a lot of pretty complicated detail in the film.

9  A: Well, that comes down to the fact that these are extremely complicated issues and can't be put into a format of predigested baby food that is spoon-fed (to the audience). These are complicated issues to wrap your head around, and we knew that. But ultimately the most important thing to us was whether you were emotionally moved at the end of the movie. And on a personal level, I believe that has been accomplished. Yes, a lot of the science is very hard to wrap your head around. But I was very clear in the movie. I want the public to be very scared by what they see. I want them to see a very bleak future. I want them to feel disillusioned halfway through and feel hopeless. And then when we get into the entire section in the second half when we talk about cultural transformation

condense: briefly summarize

**My Notes**

affiliation: membership

populist: common or mainstream

# The Ethics of Persuasion

and a new way of looking at things and the alternatives or green technology and all these things, you realize there is great hope and there are options on the table. And hopefully the audience is moved and **galvanized** to do something about it. Hopefully.

**galvanized:** moved to take action

## My Notes

## Second Read

- Reread the article to answer these text-dependent questions.
- Write any additional questions you have about the text in your Reader/Writer Notebook.

1. **Key Ideas and Details:** Why does DiCaprio believe that it was difficult to condense "the vision" and "world of issues" in making the film? What specific details does he refer to?

2. **Key Ideas and Details:** In the second question, what issue of ethos (or credibility) does the interviewer bring up? How does DiCaprio explain himself? What supporting details does he offer?

## Working from the Text

3. After reading the article, use the space below to write down the three most controversial things DiCaprio says in the interview—statements that could be used against him by someone trying to attack his credibility.

# Understanding Fallacies

**Fallacies** are ubiquitous in advertising, political discourse, and everyday conversations—and they will continue to be as long as they work as ways to persuade. However, by learning to recognize them when you see them, you can strip away their power. There are many different ways to categorize fallacies and many different names for the various types. The following fallacies (adapted from Brooke Noel Moore and Richard Parker's *Critical Thinking*, 8th ed., 2007) are some of the frequent offenders. Learn these and you'll be ready to see through many of the rhetorical scams that come your way each day.

ACADEMIC VOCABULARY
**Fallacies** are false or misleading arguments. Fallacies typically result from errors in reasoning but can also come from replacing reasoning with emotional appeals or manipulative language.

- **Post Hoc:** Literally meaning "after this," *post hoc* is a causal fallacy in which a person assumes one thing caused another simply because it happened prior to the other. For instance, the high school soccer team loses an important game the day after they start wearing new uniforms. The coach blames the loss on the new uniforms.

- **Slippery Slope:** Half an appeal to fear and half a causal fallacy, a slippery slope occurs when someone suggests that one action will lead to an inevitable and undesirable outcome. To say that allowing murals to be painted on the sides of public walls and buildings means that graffiti will soon cover an entire city is a slippery slope argument.

- **Appeal to Pity:** If you have ever asked a teacher to give you a better grade or a second chance because things have been tough recently or because you worked so hard, you're guilty of this one. It refers to an attempt to use compassion or pity to replace a logical argument.

- **Inappropriate Appeal to Authority:** We often rely on experts when we lack our own expertise in a field. But expert testimony can be fallacious in several ways: if the "authority" is not an expert in the field being discussed, if the expert is not disinterested but is biased and/or stands to profit from the testimony, if the expert's opinion is not representative of other experts in the field. For example, Linus Pauling, who won Nobel prizes in chemistry and for peace, once said taking vitamin C daily could delay cancer—but his expertise is not in medicine.

- **Either/Or (or false dilemma):** This fallacy is a conclusion that oversimplifies the argument by suggesting there are only two possible sides or choices, instead of many that involve compromise or creative thinking. For example, a person might say, "Either you're an environmentalist or you hate the planet." Or a person might argue, "Either we ease up on environmental protection or we will see our economy get worse."

## Taking a Closer Look at Chapter 5

4. As you rewatch Chapter 5, "Climate Change," from *The 11th Hour*, keep in mind DiCaprio's words regarding his intentions. What does the clip illustrate about his intentional choices regarding rhetorical appeals? Does it cross the line into relying on fallacies? Use the SMELL graphic organizer to make notes.

**My Notes**

# The Ethics of Persuasion

**Sender-Receiver Relationship:** To whom are the filmmakers explicitly addressing their argument here? How do they seem to feel about that target audience?

**Message:** What is the clip's central claim? What content does it use to support that claim?

**Emotional Strategies:** What emotional appeals does the director include? What seems to be their desired effect? Are they fallacious?

**Logical Strategies:** What logical arguments/appeals does the director include? What is their effect? Are they fallacious?

**Language:** What specific language is used in the clip to support the message? How does it impact the film's effectiveness and credibility? Are they fallacious? Consider both images and actual words.

5. After viewing the film, work with your teacher and classmates to look for instances where the film may be using fallacious reasoning or appeals. Then evaluate the examples.

| | *The 11th Hour*, Chapter 5 | Fallacious or Fair? |
|---|---|---|
| **Post Hoc** | | |
| **Appeal to Pity** | | |
| **Inappropriate Appeal to Authority** | | |
| **Slippery Slope** | | |
| **Either/Or** | | |

# The Ethics of Persuasion

## My Notes

6. After analyzing the use of reasoning and evidence in the clip, respond to the following prompt using the focus questions that follow. Cite details from the scene/film to support your responses. While you discuss the questions, a partner group will evaluate your effectiveness based on your class norms for group discussions.

**Discussion Prompt:** Defend, challenge, or qualify the following statement: DiCaprio's manipulation of viewers in this scene undermines the credibility of the film's argument.

a. What cinematic techniques do the directors use to establish the dramatic tone of the chapter?

b. Does this sequence seem manipulative? If so, in what ways? Does it use fallacious reasoning or appeals? If so, which ones?

c. Is it ethical for a filmmaker to emotionally manipulate an audience in order to be persuasive? Explain.

7. Based on this analysis, craft a consensus response to the discussion prompt. Be prepared to share an outline of your response (claim, reasons, and concluding statement) with your classmates.

## Check Your Understanding

How can you tell if an appeal or the use of a particular piece of evidence is fallacious?

### INDEPENDENT READING LINK

**Read and Respond**

Look for examples of fallacious reasoning or audience manipulation in your print and nonprint independent reading selections. Use a chart similar to the one you created for this activity to record your observations. Explain to a small group of peers how the absence or presence of fallacious reasoning and appeals affects your evaluation of each source's credibility.

# Refutation and Reputation

## Learning Targets
- Compare and contrast three different approaches to refutation.
- Evaluate how refutation and ad hominem attacks affect an argument's credibility.

## Preview

The makers of *The 11th Hour* made the conscious decision to give their experts a "platform where they didn't have to argue about the science." Not all viewers share their assumptions about "the science" regarding climate change. What attitude might different viewers have toward the science of climate change?

In this activity, you will read one of three passages that present an argument about climate change and evaluate its approach to refutation.

**My Notes**

## Argument and Refutation

Consider the following two criticisms of Leonardo DiCaprio and his film by Senator James Inhofe. What is the difference between them? Which one seems like a stronger criticism?

> "Children are now the number one target of the global warming fear campaign. DiCaprio announced his goal was to recruit young eco-activists to the cause."

> "We have seen global average temperatures flat line since 1998 and the Southern Hemisphere cool in recent years."

The first statement is an example of an *ad hominem*, or "against the man," attack. It is a type of fallacy where instead of attacking an assertion, the argument attacks the person who made the assertion. Inhofe attempts to discredit DiCaprio, but personal attacks do not challenge the argument.

On the other hand, the second statement offers evidence in support of a counterclaim—that global warming is not a fact. This statement offers evidence to dispute the facts rather than attacking the person; it serves to refute the position rather than to discredit the person who holds it.

The difference between *ad hominem* attacks and **refutation** is all-important when it comes to logic. However, *ad hominem* attacks can undermine a speaker's ethos, and that can drag the person's argument down with them.

## Setting a Purpose for Reading
- You will next read one of three passages that present contrasting positions regarding the arguments made in *The 11th Hour*. Individually, read your passage and complete a SMELL chart, sniffing out (and highlighting) evidence of the values and beliefs central to the writer's position.
- Circle unknown words and phrases. Try to determine the meaning of the words by using context clues, word parts, or a dictionary.

**ACADEMIC VOCABULARY**
**Refutation** is reasoning used to disprove an opposing point. As an element of argument, it refers to logical analysis of why an argument is flawed or inaccurate, often introducing countering evidence in support of its claims.

# Refutation and Reputation

## My Notes

_____

_____

_____

_____

_____

_____

_____

_____

_____

_____

_____

_____

_____

_____

_____

_____

**elitists:** snobs

**propaganda:** misleading publicity

**dire:** disastrous

 **WORD
CONNECTIONS**

### Content Connections

A *satellite* is a machine, moon, or planet that orbits, or travels around, a star or planet. Most often, the word *satellite* refers to an object launched from Earth into orbit. Satellites orbit Earth by the thousands, taking pictures and sending communications like TV signals and phone calls. They also record data, such as temperatures, that scientists monitor to look for patterns.

**ABOUT THE AUTHOR**

Senator James Inhofe (1934–), a Republican Senator from Oklahoma, is currently the ranking member of the Senate Armed Services Committee. He is the chairman and ranking member of the Senate Environment and Public Works Committee. He has been in politics since 1967, moving from state government in Oklahoma to the U.S. House of Representatives and then to the U.S. Senate. Prior to his life in politics, Senator Inhofe was a businessman and land developer.

Speech

# from
# Global Warming Alarmism Reaches a "Tipping Point"

*by* Senator James Inhofe

1   We are currently witnessing an international awakening of scientists who are speaking out in opposition to former Vice President Al Gore, the United Nations, the Hollywood **elitists** and the media-driven "consensus" on man-made global warming.

2   We have witnessed Antarctic ice GROW to record levels since satellite monitoring began in the 1970s. We have witnessed NASA temperature data errors that have made 1934—not 1998—the hottest year on record in the U.S. We have seen global averages temperatures flat line since 1998 and the Southern Hemisphere cool in recent years.

3   These new developments in just the last six months are but a sample of the new information coming out that continues to debunk climate alarm.

4   But before we delve into these dramatic new scientific developments, it is important to take note of our pop culture **propaganda** campaign aimed at children.

**Hollywood Targets Children with Climate Fears**

5   In addition to (Al) Gore's entry last year into Hollywood fictional disaster films, other celebrity figures have attempted to jump into the game.

6   Hollywood activist Leonardo DiCaprio decided to toss objective scientific truth out the window in his new scarefest "The 11th Hour." DiCaprio refused to interview any scientists who disagreed with his **dire** vision of the future of the Earth.

7   In fact, his film reportedly features physicist Stephen Hawking making the unchallenged assertion that "the worst-case scenario is that Earth would become like its sister planet, Venus, with a temperature of 25° centigrade."

8   I guess these "worst-case scenarios" pass for science in Hollywood these days. It also fits perfectly with DiCaprio's stated purpose of the film.

9 DiCaprio said on May 20th of this year: "I want the public to be very scared by what they see. I want them to see a very bleak future."

10 While those who went to watch DiCaprio's science fiction film may see his intended "bleak future," it is DiCaprio who has been scared by the bleak box office numbers, as his film has failed to generate any significant audience interest.

### Gore's producer to kids: 'Be activists'

11 Children are now the number one target of the global warming fear campaign. DiCaprio announced his goal was to recruit young eco-activists to the cause.

12 "We need to get kids young," DiCaprio said in a September 20 interview with USA Weekend.

13 A Canadian high school student named McKenzie was shown Gore's climate horror film in four different classes.

14 "I really don't understand why they keep showing it," McKenzie said on May 19, 2007.

15 In June, a fourth grade class from Portland Maine's East End Community School issued a dire climate report: "Global warming is a huge pending global disaster" read the elementary school kids' report according to an article in the Portland Press Herald on June 14, 2007. Remember, these are fourth graders issuing a dire global warming report.

16 And this agenda of **indoctrination** and fear aimed at children is having an impact.

17 Nine year old Alyssa Luz-Ricca was quoted in the Washington Post on April 16, 2007 as saying:

18 "I worry about [global warming] because I don't want to die."

19 The same article explained: "Psychologists say they're seeing an increasing number of young patients preoccupied by a climactic Armageddon."[1]

20 I was told by the parent of an elementary school kid last spring who said her daughter was forced to watch "An Inconvenient Truth" once a month at school and had nightmares about drowning in the film's predicted scary sea level rise.

21 The Hollywood global-warming documentary "Arctic Tale" ends with a child actor telling kids: "If your mom and dad buy a hybrid car, you'll make it easier for polar bears to get around." Unfortunately, children are hearing the scientifically unfounded doomsday message loud and clear. But the message kids are receiving is not a scientific one, it is a political message designed to create fear, nervousness and ultimately recruit them to liberal activism.

22 There are a few hopeful signs. A judge in England has ruled that schools must issue a warning before they show Gore's film to children because of scientific inaccuracies and "sentimental mush."

23 In addition, there is a new kids book called "The Sky's Not Falling! Why It's OK to Chill About Global Warming." The book counters the propaganda from the pop culture.

### Objective, Evidence-based Science is Beginning to Crush Hysteria

24 My speech today and these reports reveal that recent peer-reviewed scientific studies are totally refuting the Church of Man-made Global Warming.

**My Notes**

**indoctrination:** persuasive teaching; brainwashing

---

[1] **Armageddon:** In the Bible, the final battle that takes place at the end of the world

# Refutation and Reputation

**Global warming movement "falling apart"**

25  Meteorologist Joseph Conklin who launched the skeptical website http://www.climatepolice.com/ in 2007, recently declared the "global warming movement [is] falling apart."

26  All the while, activists like former Vice President Al Gore repeatedly continue to warn of a fast approaching climate "tipping point."

27  I agree with Gore. Global warming may have reached a "tipping point."

28  The man-made global warming fear machine crossed the "tipping point" in 2007.

29  I am convinced that future climate historians will look back at 2007 as the year the global warming fears began crumbling. The situation we are in now is very similar to where we were in the late 1970's when coming ice age fears began to dismantle.

30  Remember, it was *Newsweek* magazine which in the 1970s proclaimed meteorologists were "almost unanimous" in their view that a coming Ice Age would have negative impacts. It was also *Newsweek* in 1975 which originated the eerily similar "tipping point" rhetoric of today.

31  *Newsweek* wrote on April 28, 1975 about coming ice age fears: "The longer the planners delay, the more difficult will they find it to cope with climatic change once the results become grim reality."

32  Of course *Newsweek* essentially retracted their coming ice age article 29 years later in October 2006. In addition, a 1975 National Academy of Sciences report addressed coming ice age fears and in 1971, NASA predicted the world "could be as little as 50 or 60 years away from a disastrous new ice age."

33  Today, the greatest irony is that the UN and the media's climate hysteria grow louder as the case for alarmism fades away. While the scientific case grows weaker, the political and rhetorical proponents of climate fear are ramping up to offer hefty tax and regulatory "solutions" both internationally and domestically to "solve" the so-called "crisis."

34  Skeptical climatologist Dr. Timothy Ball, formerly of the University of Winnipeg in Canada, wrote about the current state of the climate change debate earlier this month:

35  "Imagine basing a country's energy and economic policy on an incomplete, unproven theory—a theory based entirely on computer models in which one minor variable ($CO_2$) is considered the sole driver for the entire global climate system."

36  And just how minor is that man-made $CO_2$ variable in the atmosphere?

37  Meteorologist Joseph D'Aleo, the first Director of Meteorology at The Weather Channel and former chairman of the American Meteorological Society's (AMS) Committee on Weather Analysis and Forecasting, explained in August how miniscule mankind's $CO_2$ emissions are in relation to the Earth's atmosphere.

38  "If the atmosphere was a 100-story building, our annual anthropogenic $CO_2$ contribution today would be equivalent to the linoleum on the first floor," D'Aleo wrote.

## Second Read

- Reread the speech to answer these text-dependent questions.
- Write any additional questions you have about the text in your Reader/Writer Notebook.

1. **Craft and Structure:** In the section "Hollywood Targets Children with Climate Fears," how does Inhofe attack DiCaprio's use of emotional appeals in the film? What rhetorical choices does Inhofe make when constructing that attack? Is his attack effective?

2. **Craft and Structure:** Why does Inhofe focus his refutation on the claim that there is "pop culture propaganda aimed at children"? Does this focus strengthen or weaken his argument?

3. **Knowledge and Ideas:** In the section "Global Warming Movement 'Falling Apart,'" Inhofe uses a historical analogy. What two things does he compare? Is his analogy valid and relevant? Does it refute claims about current trends?

4. **Knowledge and Ideas:** Reread the "About the Author" section that precedes Inhofe's speech. Judging from this information, what ethos, or credibility, does Inhofe have to refute DiCaprio's argument?

**My Notes**

# Refutation and Reputation

**My Notes**

**ABOUT THE AUTHOR**

Patrick Michaels is an American climatologist. Michaels is a senior research fellow for Research and Economic Development at George Mason University and a senior fellow in environmental studies at the Cato Institute. He has written a number of books and papers on climate change, including *Sound and Fury: The Science and Politics of Global Warming* (1992) and *Meltdown: The Predictable Distortion of Global Warming by Scientists, Politicians, and the Media* (2004), and is the coauthor of *Climate of Extremes: Global Warming Science They Don't Want You to Know* (2009).

Article

# Global Warming:
## No Urgent Danger; No Quick Fix

*by* Patrick J. Michaels

*Atlanta Journal-Constitution*

August 21, 2007

**nonpartisan:** neutral

**portend:** predict
**unmitigated:** complete and total

1   It's summer, it's hot and global warming is on the cover of *Newsweek*. Scare stories abound. We may only have 10 years to stop this! The future survival of our species is at stake!

2   OK, the media aren't exactly **nonpartisan**, especially on global warming. So what's the real story and what do we need to know?

3   Fact: The average surface temperature of the Earth is about 0.8°C warmer than it was in 1900, and human beings have something to do with it. But does that **portend** an **unmitigated** disaster? Can we do anything meaningful about it at this time? And if we can't, what should or can we do in the future?

4   These are politically loaded questions that must be answered truthfully, especially when considering legislation designed to reduce emissions of carbon dioxide, the main global warming gas.

5   Unfortunately, they'll probably be ignored. Right now there are a slew of bills before Congress, and many in various states, that mandate massively reducing carbon dioxide emissions. Some actually propose cutting our $CO_2$ output to 80 percent or 90 percent below 1990 levels by the year 2050.

6   Let's be charitable and simply call that legislative arrogance. US emissions are up about 18 percent from 1990 as they stand. Whenever you hear about these large cuts, ask the truth: How is this realistically going to happen?

7   I did that on an international television panel two weeks ago. My opponent, who advocated these cuts, dropped his jaw and said nothing, ultimately uttering a curse word for the entire world to hear. The fact of the matter is he had no answer because there isn't one.

8   Nor would legislation in any state or Washington, DC, have any standing in Beijing. Although the final figures aren't in yet, it's beginning to look like China has just passed the United States as the world's largest emitter of carbon dioxide. Like the United States, China has oodles of coal, and the Chinese are putting in at least one new coal-fired power plant a month. (Some reports have it at an astonishing one per week.) And just as it does in the United States, when coal burns in China, it turns largely to carbon dioxide and water.

9   What we do in the United States is having less and less of an effect on the concentration of carbon dioxide in the world's atmosphere.

10   We certainly adapted to 0.8°C temperature change quite well in the 20th century, as life expectancy doubled and some crop yields quintupled. And who knows what new and miraculously efficient power sources will develop in the next hundred years.

11   The stories about the ocean rising 20 feet as massive amounts of ice slide off of Greenland by 2100 are also fiction. For the entire half century from 1915 through 1965, Greenland was significantly warmer than it has been for the last decade. There was no disaster. More important, there's a large body of evidence that for much of the period from 3,000 to 9,000 years ago, at least the Eurasian Arctic was 2.5°C to 7°C warmer than now in the summer, when ice melts. Greenland's ice didn't disappear then, either.

12   Then there is the topic of interest this time of year—hurricanes. Will hurricanes become stronger or more frequent because of warming? My own work suggests that late in the 21st century there might be an increase in strong storms, but that it will be very hard to detect because of year-to-year variability.

13   Right now, after accounting for increasing coastal population and property values, there is no increase in damages caused by these killers. The biggest of them all was the Great Miami Hurricane of 1926. If it occurred today, it would easily cause twice as much damage as 2005's vaunted Hurricane Katrina.

14   So let's get real and give the politically incorrect answers to global warming's inconvenient questions. Global warming is real, but it does not portend immediate disaster, and there's currently no suite of technologies that can do much about it. The obvious solution is to forgo costs today on ineffective attempts to stop it, and to save our money for investment in future technologies and inevitable adaptation.

*Patrick J. Michaels is a senior fellow in environmental studies at the Cato Institute and is on leave as research professor of environmental sciences at the University of Virginia.*

## Second Read

- Reread the article to answer these text-dependent questions.
- Write any additional questions you have about the text in your Reader/Writer Notebook.

5. **Craft and Structure:** What emotions does Michaels appeal to in the opening paragraph of his article? Is his appeal there an effective way to introduce the claim he makes in his second paragraph?

### GRAMMAR & USAGE
Punctuation

We often think of punctuation as having an effect on syntax—the organization of words and clauses to form different types of sentences. But punctuation can also be used to express **tone**—the attitude of a writer toward the subject or toward the audience.

Notice how, in the opening paragraph, Michaels ends two sentences in a row with **exclamation points**: "We may only have 10 years to stop this! The future survival of our species is at stake!" Exclamation points are usually used to indicate excitement or urgency. What effect do they have here? What tone do they create?

**My Notes**

# Refutation and Reputation

6. **Knowledge and Ideas:** What two claims of global warming activists does Michaels try to refute in the second half of his article? Is Michaels's use of refutation sufficient to debunk his opponents' arguments?

7. **Knowledge and Ideas:** Reread the "About the Author" section that precedes Michaels's article. What ethos, or credibility, does Michaels have in comparison to DiCaprio and Inhofe? How does this impact his argument?

8. **Key Ideas and Details:** What solution does Michaels ultimately offer in his argument? What specific passage from the text states that solution? How is it different from what DiCaprio and Inhofe had to say?

**ABOUT THE AUTHOR**

George Marshall is the founder of the Climate Outreach Information Network, a climate change communications and training charity. His 20 years of experience in environmental campaigning includes government policy consultancies and senior management positions in Greenpeace and the Rainforest Foundation. He speaks and writes widely on climate change issues, including articles for *The New Statesman, The Guardian, New Scientist,* and *The Ecologist.* He is the author of *Carbon Detox,* a popular book offering "fresh ways to think about personal action to climate change" and is the creator of a website that examines psychological responses to climate change.

### Article

# Jeremy Clarkson and Michael O'Leary Won't Listen to Green Clichés and Complaints about Polar Bears

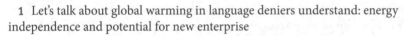

*by* George Marshall

*The Guardian* (UK)

March 9, 2009

1 Let's talk about global warming in language deniers understand: energy independence and potential for new enterprise

2 Academics meeting in Bristol at the weekend for Britain's first conference on the psychology of climate change argued that the greatest obstacles to action are not technical, economic, or political—they are the denial strategies that we adopt to protect ourselves from unwelcome information.

3 It is true that nearly 80% of people claim to be concerned about climate change. However, delve deeper and one finds that people have a remarkable tendency to define this concern in ways that keep it as far away as possible. They describe climate change as a global problem (but not a local one), as a future problem (not one for their own lifetimes) and absolve themselves of responsibility for either causing the problem or solving it.

4 Most disturbing of all, 60% of people believe that "many scientific experts still question if humans are contributing to climate change". Thirty per cent of people believe climate change is "largely down to natural causes," while 7% refuse to accept the climate is changing at all.

5 How is it possible that so many people are still unpersuaded by 40 years of research and the consensus of every major scientific institution in the world? Surely we are now long past the point at which the evidence became overwhelming?

6 If only belief formation were this simple. Having neither the time nor skills to weigh up each piece of evidence, we fall back on decision-making shortcuts formed by our education, politics, and class. In particular we measure new information against our life experience and the views of the people around us.

7 George Lakoff, of the University of California, argues that we often use metaphors to carry over experience from simple or concrete experiences into new domains. Thus, as politicians know very well, broad concepts such as freedom, independence, leadership, growth, and pride can resonate far deeper than the policies they describe.

8 None of this bodes well for a rational approach to climate change. Climate change is invariably presented as an overwhelming threat requiring unprecedented restraint, sacrifice, and government intervention. The metaphors it invokes are poisonous to people who feel rewarded by free market capitalism and distrust government interference. It is hardly surprising that political world view is by far the greatest determinant of attitudes to climate change, especially in the US where three times more Republicans than Democrats believe that "too much fuss is made about global warming."

## My Notes

### GRAMMAR & USAGE
Subjunctive Mood

One use of the subjunctive mood is to express speculation and wishful thinking about something that is unlikely to ever be real. This use of the subjunctive is often apparent by the presence of the verb *were* instead of *was* in a sentence: "I was the richest person in the world" versus "If I were the richest person in the world ..." Notice that Marshall uses the subjunctive in this statement: "If only belief formation **were** this simple." What wish or speculation is he expressing? Why is this unlikely to become true?

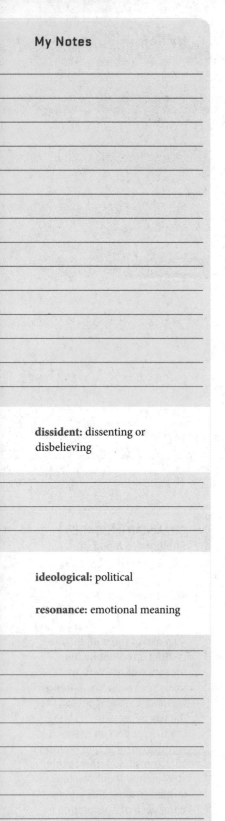

**My Notes**

**dissident:** dissenting or disbelieving

**ideological:** political

**resonance:** emotional meaning

9  An intuitive suspicion is then reinforced by a deep distrust of the key messengers: the liberal media, politicians and green campaign groups. As Jeremy Clarkson says, bundling them all together: "… everything we've been told for the past five years by the government, Al Gore, Channel 4 News, and hippies everywhere is a big bucket of nonsense." Michael O'Leary, the founder of Ryanair, likens "hairy dungaree and sandal wearing climate change alarmists" to "the CND nutters of the 1970s." These cultural prejudices, however simplistic, align belief with cultural allegiance: "People like us," they say, "do not believe in this tripe."

10  However much one distrusts environmentalists, it is harder to discount the scientists … depending, of course, on which scientists one listens to. The conservative news media continues to provide a platform for the handful of scientists who reject the scientific consensus. Of the 18 experts that appeared in Channel 4's notorious sceptic documentary "The Great Global Warming Swindle," 11 have been quoted in the past two years in the Daily and Sunday Telegraph, five of them more than five times.

11  Dr. Myanna Lahsen, a cultural anthropologist at the University of Colorado, has specialised in understanding how professional scientists, some of them with highly respected careers, turn climate sceptic. She found the largest common factor was a shared sense that they had personally lost prestige and authority as the result of campaigns by liberals and environmentalists. She concluded that their engagement in climate issues "can be understood in part as a struggle to preserve their particular culturally charged understanding of environmental reality."

12  In other words, like the general public, they form their beliefs through reference to a world view formed through politics and life experience. In order to maintain their scepticism in the face of a sustained, and sometimes heated, challenge from their peers, they have created a mutually supportive **dissident** culture around an identity as victimised speakers for the truth.

13  This individualistic romantic image is nurtured by the libertarian right think tanks that promote the sceptic arguments. One academic study of 192 sceptic books and reports found that 92% were directly associated with right-wing free-market think tanks. It concluded that the denial of climate change had been deliberately constructed "as a tactic of an elite-driven counter-movement designed to combat environmentalism."

14  So, given that scepticism is rooted in a sustained and well-funded **ideological** movement, how can sceptics be swayed? One way is to reframe climate change in a way that rejects the green cliches and creates new metaphors with a wider **resonance**. So out with the polar bears and saving the planet. Instead let's talk of energy independence, and the potential for new enterprise.

15  And then there is peer pressure, probably the most important influence of all. So, when dealing with a sceptic, don't get into a head to head with them. Just politely point out all the people they know and respect who believe that climate change is a serious problem—and they aren't sandal-wearing tree huggers, are they?

## Second Read

- Reread the article to answer these text-dependent questions.
- Write any additional questions you have about the text in your Reader/Writer Notebook.

9. **Craft and Structure:** How does Marshall refer to the people who do not believe in global warming? Why does he choose this term, and what does it imply?

10. **Craft and Structure:** Marshall uses the third person in most of his essay, in contrast to Michaels's use of first person ("we"). How does the choice of third person impact his readers?

11. **Craft and Structure:** What is Marshall trying to do in this article? What rhetorical choices does he make to accomplish that purpose?

12. **Knowledge and Ideas:** Reread the "About the Author" section that precedes Marshall's article. What ethos, or credibility, does Marshall bring to the writing of this article?

**My Notes**

# Refutation and Reputation

## GRAMMAR &USAGE
### Reciprocal Pronouns

*One another* and *each other* are **reciprocal pronouns,** which are used to describe situations in which each person in a group performs the same action toward the other person(s). Use *each other* to refer to two people and *one another* to refer to three or more people. Note the instruction to take notes as you "share your findings with one another." How would you rewrite this instruction if you were sharing with a partner, not a small group?

## My Notes

## Working from the Text

13. As you reread your assigned text, identify and evaluate the nature of the attacks made against others. Are the writers using *ad hominem* attacks, refutation, or a mixture? How do their attacks affect their own ethos—and their arguments? Keep your eyes open to other fallacies as well.

14. As you share your findings with one another, take notes on the positions and approaches in each source. Be sure to support your claims about the article's level of subjectivity by citing specfic evidence from the text.

| | |
|---|---|
| *The 11th Hour* | |
| Inhofe | |
| Michaels | |
| Marshall | |

15. As a group, rank the four pieces based on which is most/least persuasive. Come to a consensus on your ranking, and be prepared to justify your opinions, both with your group and with the class as a whole.

## Language and Writer's Craft: Embedding Quotations

When writers quote directly from other sources, they must surround the borrowed words with quotation marks. This signals to readers that the words are from another writer. For example, you could quote a fact or statistic from another writer to support a point in your own argument:

> Patrick Michaels states this compelling fact: "The average surface temperature of the Earth is about 0.8°C warmer than it was in 1900, and human beings have something to do with it."

Sometimes, however, a quotation includes words quoted from a different source or words already in quotation marks. You still use double quotation marks around the entire quote, but the quotation marks inside the quote become single quotation marks:

> Senator James Inhofe makes the point that DiCaprio's film *The 11th Hour* "features physicist Stephen Hawking making the unchallenged assertions that 'the worst-case scenario is that Earth would become like its sister planet, Venus, with a temperature of 250° centigrade.'"

**PRACTICE** Using these guidelines, use the following quotes (or parts of them) from "Jeremy Clarkson and Michael O'Leary Won't Listen to Green Clichés and Complaints about Polar Bears" in sentences, paying attention to proper punctuation:

- Most disturbing of all, 60% of people believe that "many scientific experts still question if humans are contributing to climate change." Thirty percent of people believe climate change is "largely down to natural causes," while 7% refuse to accept the climate is changing at all.

- George Lakoff, of the University of California, argues that we often use metaphors to carry over experience from simple or concrete experiences into new domains.

**My Notes**

# Refutation and Reputation

## My Notes

## Writing to Sources: Argument Text

Think about *The 11th Hour* and the three passages you just read that show different approaches to refuting the film's premise. Choose the one passage that seems to have either the most or least credible argument and refutation of the film. Draft an argument that explains and supports your claim. In your argument, examine how the passage's use of refutation or *ad hominem* attacks affects its persuasiveness. Be sure to:

- Make a clear, precise claim that includes the name and author of the passage you chose.
- Use words, phrases, and clauses to create cohesion between the claim and reasons and between reasons and evidence.
- Include quotations from both the film and the passage to support your claim. Punctuate all quotations correctly.

## Check Your Understanding

What is the relationship between how a source responds to other perspectives and its own credibility with various audiences?

# Exploring One Conflict Together

## Learning Targets
- Analyze stakeholder positions in order to understand their importance in a controversy.
- Collaborate to draft a policy proposal to resolve a conflict.

## Preview
In this activity, you will read an article and analyze stakeholder positions.

## Stakeholders
The newspaper article "A Roaring Battle Over Sea Lions" presents a range of stakeholder interests. **Stakeholders** are those motivated by various concerns. Use the explanations below to help you analyze the interests, impact, and involvement of stakeholders as you read the article.

- *Stakeholder values and interests* refers to concerns such as what values motivate the stakeholder, the project's benefit(s) to the stakeholder, the changes that the project might require the stakeholder to make, and the project activities that might cause damage or conflict for the stakeholder.

- *Stakeholder impact* refers to how important the stakeholder's participation is to the success of the proposed project. Consider:
  - ➢ The role the key stakeholder must play for the project to be successful and the likelihood that the stakeholder will play this role
  - ➢ The likelihood and impact of a stakeholder's negative response to the project

  Assign *A* for extremely important, *B* for fairly important, and *C* for not very important. You will record these letters in the graphic organizer column "Assessment of impact" after reading the article.

- *Stakeholder involvement* refers to the kinds of things that you could do to enlist stakeholder support and reduce opposition. Consider how you might approach each of the stakeholders. What kind of information will they need? Is there a limit to what changes they would support? Are there other groups or individuals that might influence the stakeholder to support your initiative? Record your strategies for obtaining support or reducing obstacles to your project in the last column in the matrix.

## Setting a Purpose for Reading
- The article "A Roaring Battle Over Sea Lions" presents perspectives on a conflict involving how to manage sea lions that are feeding on endangered salmon at the Bonneville Dam in Oregon. As you read, use the My Notes section to identify as many stakeholder groups as you can—both those that are obvious and those that may be involved even if they don't seem to have a specific agenda.

- Circle unknown words and phrases. Try to determine the meaning of the words by using context clues, word parts, or a dictionary.

LEARNING STRATEGIES:
Brainstorming, Marking the Text, Quickwrite

### ACADEMIC VOCABULARY
A **stakeholder** is a person or group that holds an interest in a particular issue. Such stakeholders may be directly or indirectly affected by the issue.

**My Notes**

# Exploring One Conflict Together

## My Notes

_____
_____
_____
_____
_____
_____
_____
_____

**rancorous:** bitter
**vigilantes:** people who take action
without authority
**euthanized:** killed

### GRAMMAR&USAGE
Clauses

A **relative clause** is a
dependent clause beginning
with a relative pronoun—
*who, whom, that, which,* or
*whose.* Relative clauses are
also called adjective clauses
because they modify nouns.

A **nonrestrictive** relative
clause, often set off by
commas, gives nonessential
information: "For Andrea Kozil,
who regularly hikes along the
river, the creatures ..."

A **restrictive** relative clause
gives essential information:
"Because they prey on
endangered wild salmon that
also inhabit the Columbia,
many ..."

Find another sentence that
includes a restrictive clause.
What is its relative pronoun?
Is the relative clause
restrictive or nonrestrictive?
What does this tell you about
the information?

**Article**

# A Roaring Battle Over
# Sea Lions

*by* Bill Hewitt
*People Magazine,* June 9, 2008

From the pages of **PEOPLE**

**At a dam outside Portland, Oregon, a controversy heats up over whether the
animals should be removed—and even killed—in order to save the salmon.**

1   Along the Columbia River, between Oregon and Washington, the sea lion stirs
strong emotions. For Andrea Kozil, who regularly hikes along the river, the creatures,
sleek and playful, are more like old friends than ordinary animals. "You can recognize
them," say Kozil. "Thousands of people come to see them; the kids name them." But for
fishermen and tribal members of the region, the sea lions, protected by federal law, are
anything but cuddly. Because they prey on endangered wild salmon that also inhabit the
Columbia, many locals see them as a threat to their way of life. "The sea lions are pretty
much out of control," complains Dennis Richey, executive director of Oregon Anglers.
"Something has to be done."

2   Feelings, already running high, have lately hit a new and more **rancorous** phase.
Earlier this year, after winning approval from the federal government, wildlife officials
in the area began a five-year program to remove as many as 85 of the California sea
lions each year—by killing them if need be—from the waters around the Bonneville
Dam, 40 miles east of Portland, where the creatures gorge on fish swimming upstream
to spawn. Animal rights activists, including the Humane Society of the United States,
have filed suit to stop the program, which was just getting under way when, on May 4,
six sea lions were found dead in traps near the dam. Authorities said on May 14 that the
animals had apparently died of heatstroke, but how the gates slammed closed remained
a mystery. "Whether it was **vigilantes** or negligence, humans killed them," says Sharon
Young of the Humane Society.

3   Those in favor of ousting the sea lions insist that their measures are a modest
response to a critical problem: The number of wild salmon are in sharp decline.
Meanwhile, the California sea lion, hunted nearly to extinction in the last century, has
made a remarkable recovery since being protected in 1972, now numbering 240,000.
Sea lions have been drawn to the Bonneville Dam because the salmon must congregate
around the fish ladders—a series of pools arranged like ascending steps—in order to
proceed upriver, making them an easy lunch. The plan to remove the sea lions included
the stipulation that efforts be made to find zoos or aquariums to take as many of the
animals as possible. Only those left over could be **euthanized**—or shot if they eluded
capture. "No one's suggesting a scorched-earth policy," says Charles Hudson, of the
Columbia River Inter-Tribal Fish Commission. "There was no bloodlust."

4   But animal rights activists maintain that the government's own statistics, based on
limited observation, suggest that the sea lions consume a relatively small percentage of
the salmon. (State officials contend that the real percentage is far higher—and growing.)
"The salmon are not going extinct because of the sea lions, but because of pollution,
dams and overfishing," says Kozil, who works for a great-ape rescue organization in
Portland and is one of the plaintiffs in the pending lawsuit to block the removal. "The
sea lions have been demonized."

**5** Hudson argues that it is the activists who have let their emotions get away from them, favoring the cute sea lions over the less attractive fish. "There seems to be a picking and choosing of one species over another," he says. "It's maddening." After the six sea lion deaths, officials agreed to suspend the removal program for this season. But that will not lay to rest the strong emotions on either side. Says Young of the Humane Society: "This issue is not going to go away."

©2008 Time Inc. All rights reserved. Reprinted/Translated from PEOPLE and published with permission of Time Inc. Reproduction in any manner in any language in whole or in part without written permission is prohibited.

## Second Read

- Reread the article to answer these text-dependent questions.
- Write any additional questions you have about the text in your Reader/Writer Notebook.

1. **Key Ideas and Details:** What different perspectives on sea lions are introduced in the first paragraph, and in what order? In what ways do these perspectives contain "strong emotions"? What impact does the order of the perspectives have, if any?

2. **Knowledge and Ideas:** Does the article's coverage seem to favor one side over the other, or does it seem fairly objective in how it presents the different perspectives? What evidence from the text supports your conclusion?

**My Notes**

# Exploring One Conflict Together

## My Notes

### Working from the Text

3. Using the chart below and the information from the beginning of the activity, choose three key stakeholders with very different positions and analyze their interests, impact, and involvement.

| Stakeholder | Stakeholder's Values and Interest(s) in the Project | Assessment of Impact | Stakeholder Involvement |
|---|---|---|---|
|  |  |  |  |
|  |  |  |  |
|  |  |  |  |

4. Based on the concerns of the stakeholders you and your classmates have chosen, what are some possible steps that could be taken to solve the conflict at Bonneville Dam?

## Argument Writing Prompt

Consider the different perspectives on the conflict at Bonneville Dam. Then collaborate with a peer to draft a policy proposal on how to resolve the conflict. As you work, think about the problem that is being addressed, as well as the stakeholders who are participating in establishing the proposal. Keep in mind what you want your proposal to accomplish as well as why your proposal is needed. Explain the procedures for translating the proposal into action. Include specific actions with suggestions on when and where to implement them. Be sure to:

- Address the proposal to members of the stakeholder groups who ideally would act based on the proposal.
- Use an appropriately formal voice.
- End with a closing statement that predicts the benefits of resolving the conflict.

## Language and Writer's Craft: Punctuating Relative Clauses

Relative clauses are often called adjective clauses because they modify nouns in the same way that an adjective does. They contain a subject and a verb. Often, relative clauses begin with a relative pronoun (*who, whom, whose, that, which*). For example: *The man who lives next door has two dogs*. Sometimes, they begin with a relative adverb (*when, why, where*). For example: *The place where we met is still our favorite destination*.

Relative adjective clauses can be restrictive (essential) or nonrestrictive (nonessential). Examine the use and punctuation of the relative clauses in the following examples from "A Roaring Battle Over Sea Lions":

**Nonrestrictive:** "... from the waters around the Bonneville Dam, 40 miles east of Portland, where the creatures gorge on fish swimming upstream to spawn." Notice that the nonrestrictive clause beginning with *where* modifies the noun *Bonneville Dam*. The comma before the clause shows that the information is not considered essential.

**Restrictive:** "Because they prey on endangered wild salmon that also inhabit the Columbia, many locals see them as a threat." Notice that the restrictive clause beginning with *that* modifies the noun *salmon*.

**PRACTICE** Return to your policy proposal on the Bonneville Dam that you wrote in this activity. Revise two sentences to use relative clauses: one restrictive and one nonrestrictive. In your writing, consider whether your relative clauses need commas (nonrestrictive) or not (restrictive).

## Check Your Understanding

What sort of difficulties are encountered when trying to resolve a complex issue such as an environmental conflict? How can a stakeholder analysis help you to evaluate potential solutions to the problem? What kinds of limitations do you have to accept when working toward a solution acceptable to people with very different cultural perspectives?

My Notes

# A World of Conflicts

LEARNING STRATEGIES:
Quickwrite, Graphic Organizer,
Note-taking, Discussion Groups

My Notes

### Learning Targets

- Collaborate to select an environmental issue for a research topic.
- Identify stakeholders in order to focus research and draft a preliminary topic proposal.

### Preview

In this activity, you will collaborate with your peers to select your research topic for Embedded Assessment 1.

### Identifying Environmental Issues

1. Using the chart below, brainstorm some environmental issues that you know of in the world. Then make a poster with a partner, charting the ideas you come up with. You may want to consult Opposing Viewpoints in Context or some other online database to expand your list of ideas.

## Environmental Issues That Link to Cultural Conflicts

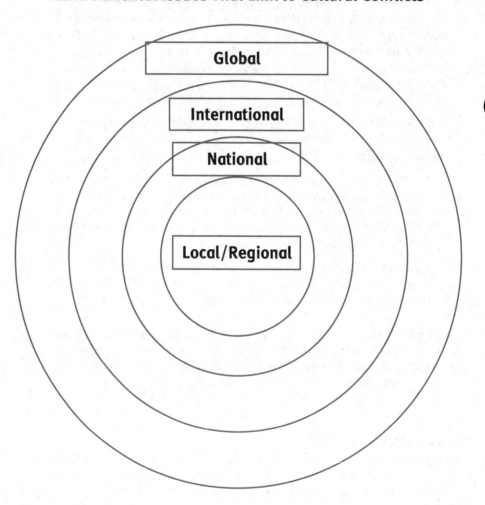

2. After viewing other posters, work with your group members to identify a few topics in each category that might be worth choosing as the topic for your project. As a group, generate some notes on what you already know and would like to learn about each topic.

| Regional | Notes | National | Notes |
|---|---|---|---|
|  |  |  |  |

| International | Notes | Global | Notes |
|---|---|---|---|
|  |  |  |  |

# A World of Conflicts

3. As you look over the list of issues, which ones do you think you might be interested in examining closely? Share your opinions with your group members.

## Planning for Research

4. As a group, choose one of the issues you have brainstormed and establish a preliminary list of stakeholders that may be involved in the conflict. Each group member can then conduct research with that stakeholder's position in mind, although your list may change as you research the conflict. With your group, fill out the chart below and submit it to your teacher for approval.

| Preliminary Topic Proposal Form |
| --- |
| • **Topic:** What is the problem being addressed? |
| • **Rationale:** Why is your proposal needed? |
| • **Stakeholders:** What groups can you initially identify as involved in the conflict? |
| • **Research Assignments:** |

• **Deadlines:**

| | | | |
| --- | --- | --- | --- |
| Source Evaluation Sheets: | _____ | Presentation Draft: | _____ |
| Annotated Bibliography: | _____ | Formal Presentation: | _____ |
| Individual Position Papers: | _____ | Personal Reflections: | _____ |
| Structured Discussion: | _____ | | |

## Learning Targets
- Apply criteria for evaluating potential sources to different articles on the same topic.
- Evaluate the use of evidence in support of a potential solution to a conflict.

LEARNING STRATEGIES:
Marking the Text, Graphic Organizer

## Preview
In this activity, you will read two articles and analyze them for bias.

## Bias
While some news sources strive hard to present objective coverage of events of the day, other sources present a more subjective point of view, controlling what information is presented even if the article avoids being blatantly opinionated. When considering such articles—or any published or online text—as potential sources to support a claim, it's important to first evaluate those sources for their level of bias/credibility. The use of a heavily biased source without acknowledgement (or at least awareness) of their bias can greatly undermine your own ethos—especially if someone else challenges your source on the basis of its bias. Can you think of examples of news reporting that you thought might be biased? Why did you think that?

**My Notes**

## Setting a Purpose for Reading
- Look for evidence of a subjective perspective in the two texts that follow. In the My Notes space, note how the writers use diction and selective information to create a relatively one-sided perspective on the issue.
- Circle unknown words and phrases. Try to determine the meaning of the words by using context clues, word parts, or a dictionary.

### Press Release

# The HSUS and Wild Fish
## Conservancy File Suit
## to Stop Sea Lion Killing
## at Bonneville Dam

*by* The Humane Society of the United Stated and the Wild Fish Conservancy

1  WASHINGTON (May 20, 2011) — The Humane Society of the United States, the Wild Fish Conservancy, and two individual citizens filed suit today in federal court, seeking to stop the National Marine Fisheries Service from authorizing the killing of as many as 255 sea lions at Bonneville Dam over the next three years.

# What's at Stake?

**My Notes**

2  In November 2010, the Court of Appeals for the Ninth Circuit overturned a prior attempt by the agency to authorize the killing of sea lions, finding that NMFS had not properly justified its decision and that salmon populations are at greater risk from overfishing and dam operations than they are from native sea lion **predation**. Sea lions have been consuming an average of 2.5 percent of the salmon over the past 3 years at the same time that permitted fisheries in the Columbia River have harvested as much as 17 percent of the record high salmon returns.

3  "Federal law allows the killing of sea lions only in very limited circumstances, when the agency proves they are having a significant negative impact on salmon," said Jonathan R. Lovvorn, senior vice president and chief counsel for animal protection litigation for the HSUS. "The National Marine Fisheries Service's decision to kill hundreds of native marine mammals to reduce salmon losses by a couple of percentage points, while simultaneously authorizing much larger man-made sources of endangered salmon mortality, is both outrageous and patently illegal."

4  While blaming sea lions for eating salmon, the states and NMFS have largely ignored recommendations of government scientists to stop stocking non-native fish like bass and walleye and adopting angler regulations that **perpetuate** their high levels of predation on salmon. Experts have warned that curbing the impact of these non-native fish is **imperative** for salmon recovery.

5  "Blaming sea lions is nothing but a distraction," said Kurt Beardslee, executive director of Wild Fish Conservancy. "The National Marine Fisheries Service needs to look objectively at dam operation and over-harvest, hatchery practices and the stocking of non-native fish which together kill significantly more salmon and prevent them from reaching high-quality spawning habitat."

**FACTS:**

- While birds, other fish, sea lions and fishermen all kill salmon, the primary threats are from loss of quality spawning habitat and dams blocking their normal migratory routes up and down river.

- The plan to shoot sea lions coincides with estimates that this spring's Columbia River salmon run is likely to be the among the largest in almost 30 years while, as of May 2011, the daily number of sea lions at the dam is the lowest since 2003 and the time each animal spends at the dam has been steadily declining.

- The major causes of salmon losses are:

*Dams:** NMFS estimates the Federal Columbia River Power System kills 16.8 percent of adult Snake River Basin Steelhead and 59.9 percent of juveniles.

*Hatcheries:** In 2010, a Congressionally-mandated science panel found that current fish hatchery practices interfere with recovery and are in urgent need of reform.

*Fishing:** The states annually authorize the incidental take of between 4.5 and 17 percent of the Upper Columbia spring Chinook and Upper Snake River spring/summer Chinook. Additional salmon are killed in ocean fisheries.

*Other Predators:** NMFS estimated that bird predators consumed 18 percent of juvenile salmonids reaching the Columbia River estuary in 1998. NMFS scientists also estimate that non-native walleye eat up to 3 million juvenile salmon in the Columbia.

*The Humane Society of the United States is the nation's largest animal protection organization—backed by 11 million Americans, or one of every 28. For more than a half-*

century, the HSUS has been fighting for the protection of all animals through advocacy, education and hands-on programs. Celebrating animals and confronting cruelty—On the Web at humanesociety.org.

Wild Fish Conservancy is a non-profit organization dedicated to the recovery and conservation of the Northwest region's wild-fish ecosystems, with about 2,400 members. Wild Fish Conservancy's staff of over 20 professional scientists, advocates, and educators work to promote technically and socially responsible habitat, hatchery, and harvest management to better sustain the region's wild fish heritage.

## Second Read

- Reread the press release to answer these text-dependent questions.
- Write any additional questions you have about the text in your Reader/Writer Notebook.

1. **Craft and Structure:** Review paragraphs 3 and 4. How does the use of words like *outrageous* and *blaming* affect the tone of the article? What kind of appeal would most likely include the use of words like these?

2. **Knowledge and Ideas:** What might be the author's purpose in introducing the list of facts? What kind of evidence does this list provide? Is it sufficient to support the central claim of the article? Is it reliable?

**My Notes**

**My Notes**

### Editorial

# Sea lions vs. salmon:
## Restore balance
## and common sense

*by* Fidelia Andy (chairwoman of the Columbia River Inter-Tribal Fish Commission and vice chairwoman of the Yakama Nation's Fish and Wildlife Committee) February 15, 2008, *Seattle Times* (Opinion)

1   "The one that got away" is a bittersweet fisherman's story. The one that "got away with it" is the bitter end—if we fail to deal with an exploding California sea lion population that is threatening endangered Columbia River salmon.

2   Our tribes strongly support the recent recommendation by NOAA Fisheries to allow limited lethal removal of problem California sea lions. The recommendation takes a significant step toward reconciling two conservation laws—the Marine Mammal Protection Act and the Endangered Species Act—that are increasingly at odds with one another.

3   Thirty-six years of unencumbered federal protection of California sea lions has produced profound success yet unanticipated consequences. The sea lions are at optimal sustainable population, according to NOAA estimates, but have gotten there at the direct expense of some endangered species.

4   Marine-mammal experts have warned that a particularly aggressive subpopulation of California sea lions will continue to exploit unnatural conditions—in this case, the fish ladder and its entrance at Bonneville Dam. They also warn that these behaviors will only get worse if left unmanaged.

5   We, as river people, remember a time when balance existed among all beings in a healthy and functioning ecosystem.

6   Dams have upset that balance. Tribal people were promised that while society reaped the benefits of dams, there would be a parallel acceptance of responsibility to **mitigate** and manage their impacts.

7   Survival, balance, integrity and dignity are cultural **mandates** for our tribes as we work to bring the wolf back to Idaho, eagles and other raptors to the Yakama Basin, and lamprey and freshwater mussels to the Columbia River. To that end, our tribes insist that all impacts to threatened and endangered salmon runs, throughout their life cycle, be addressed in their recovery.

8   A comprehensive recovery plan includes hydropower and habitat improvements, hatchery reforms, predator management and the most closely regulated fishery in the world.

9   On the Columbia River, tribal, state and federal biologists have done everything allowable under current law to give the salmon a chance. However, between 2002 and 2007, there has been a 382-percent increase in salmon being eaten by sea lions.

**mitigate:** lessen

**mandates:** commands

10  A joint request by Oregon, Washington and Idaho to lethally remove sea lions led to a legally required convening of diverse interests—independent scientists, conservationists, nonprofit leaders, and tribal, state and federal officials—to weigh evidence and make recommendations.

11  They concluded that California sea lions are having a "significant negative impact" on endangered fish and, by an overwhelming majority, recommended approval of the states' application and developed two lethal removal scenarios as part of their package.

12  According to NOAA Fisheries' environmental assessment, the most-aggressive 2008 management option could take 48,000 salmon out of the jaws of sea lions and pass them safely above Bonneville Dam. A total of only 66,646 chinook made it safely above Bonneville during the 2007 run.

13  Northwest salmon lovers can be pardoned for any sense of déjà vu. Last decade's tragedy at Ballard Locks began with similar circumstances. Regrettably in that case, **myopic** interests impeded desperately needed management, resulting in the functional extinction of the Lake Washington winter steelhead.

14  It's a heart-wrenching scene at Bonneville Dam for those who are devoting their lives to building sustainable fish populations. River watchers have reported schools of ancient sturgeon huddling in shallow water, looking for refuge from marauding sea lions. Sea lions patrol the entrance to, and even inside, the Bonneville fish ladder, thereby eliminating any normative predator-prey relationship.

15  In our view, this situation puts the integrity of both species in jeopardy.

16  Quasi-domesticated sea lions may be acceptable to the Pier 39 tourists in San Francisco, but not on the Columbia River. There is no nobility in one species squatting in a fish ladder and eating another into extinction.

17  Our Creator gave us the responsibility to protect the balance among all creatures in the ecosystem. Traditionally, we accept responsibility for the survival and prosperity of the resources that surround us.

18  Failure to accept this responsibility threatens a tragic loss of a cultural resource that is the symbol of the Northwest.

## Second Read

- Reread the editorial to answer these text-dependent questions.
- Write any additional questions you have about the text in your Reader/Writer Notebook.

3. **Craft and Structure:** Andy's piece is an editorial (opinion) written to address a broad audience. How do you think that affects the way she uses evidence and chooses words? Cite specific examples.

**My Notes**

myopic: narrow-minded

# What's at Stake?

4. **Knowledge and Ideas:** How would you define Andy's ethos, or credibility, in this editorial? How does it affect the persuasiveness of her argument?

5. **Knowledge and Ideas:** How does Andy's use of statistics and sources contrast with the way they were presented in the HSUS press release? Which article presents its support more persuasively? Explain.

6. **Knowledge and Ideas:** How does Andy use pathos in the last section of the editorial? What words and images contribute to her emotional appeals? How relevant are these words and images to her argument?

## Working from the Text

7. As you investigate the issue of your choice, it will be important to monitor the sources you use for both the level of subjectivity and the types of appeals they use. Unlike most printed sources, information posted on websites does not have to go through a process of review to check for factual accuracy. Use the following template to practice evaluating a website.

My Notes

| Topics and Questions | Responses |
|---|---|
| **The URL:** What is its domain?<br><br>.com = a for-profit organization<br><br>.gov, .mil, .us (or other country code) = a government site<br><br>.edu = an educational institution<br><br>.org = a nonprofit organization<br><br>• Is this URL someone's personal page? Why might using information from a personal page be a problem?<br><br>• Do you recognize who is publishing this page? If not, you may need to investigate to determine whether the publisher is an expert on the topic. | List website (title and URL):<br><br>What can you tell from the URL? |
| **Sponsor:**<br><br>• Does the website easily give information about the organization or group that sponsors it?<br><br>• Does it have a link (often called "About Us") that leads you to that information?<br><br>• What do you learn? | What can you learn about the page's sponsor? |
| **Timeliness:**<br><br>• When was the page last updated (usually this is posted at the top or bottom of the page)?<br><br>• How current a page is may indicate how accurate or useful the information in it will be. | What can you learn about the page's timeliness? |
| **Purpose:**<br><br>• What is the purpose of the page?<br><br>• What is its target audience? Does it present information or opinion?<br><br>• Is it primarily objective or subjective?<br><br>• How do you know? | What can you tell about the page's purpose? |
| **Author:**<br><br>• What credentials does the author have?<br><br>• Is this person or group considered an authority on the topic? | What else can you learn about the author? |
| **Links:**<br><br>• Does the page provide links?<br><br>• Do they work?<br><br>• Are they authoritative?<br><br>• Are they helpful?<br><br>• Are they objective or subjective? | What can you tell from the links provided? |

# What's at Stake? Part Two

**LEARNING STRATEGIES:**
Marking the Text

**My Notes**

## Learning Targets

- Prepare an annotated bibliography.
- Understand the link between careful documentation and ethos as a researcher.

## Preview

In this activity, you will work to create an annotated bibliography.

## Preparing for Research

1. The HSUS press release and Fidelia Andy's editorial present stakeholder positions on the Columbia River sea lion controversy. How do they achieve similar goals (though with very different agendas) in very different ways? How are their goals related to the genre of text being used (a press release compared to an editorial)? In your opinion, which more effectively advocates for its position, and how?

2. What are some guidelines you should use as you select sources for use in your upcoming project?

## During Research

3. You and your group have selected a topic that you need to research in preparation for designing a presentation to your classmates. You will first each need to find at least three sources, keeping in mind that you are trying to identify a broad range of stakeholder positions relative to your topic.

- For each source you collect, you will use the MLA (Modern Language Association) format to create an annotated bibliography entry. Annotated bibliographies are tools for tracking and processing the research work you do.

- Entries typically consist of two parts: a complete bibliographic citation for the source and an annotation (a brief summary/commentary presenting your response to the source).

- For this task, the annotation part of the bibliography will (1) *summarize* the information you found in the source, (2) *assess* the degree to which the source was helpful in your research, and (3) *reflect* on how reliable the source is given the level of subjectivity, its use of evidence, or the narrowness of the perspective it presents.

- Following are sample entries. Your teacher will provide resources that have more examples.

## Sample Magazine Entry:

Author(s). "Title of Article." *Magazine Title*. Publication date or issue: page number.

Hewitt, Bill. "A Roaring Battle Over Sea Lions." *People*. 8 June 2008: 97–98.

Hewitt presents a balanced perspective on the conflict over sea lion predation on salmon at the Bonneville Dam in Oregon, as well as a little history regarding the situation there. He identifies (and quotes) at least five major stakeholders and suggests many others as well. By quoting the people he mentions, he allows their arguments to be heard without taking a particular side himself.

## Sample Website Entry:

Author(s). Name of Page. Date of Posting/Revision. Title of the website + domain. Name of Institution/Organization Affiliated with the Site. Date of access. Web. <electronic address>.

*(NOTE: MLA now considers URLs to be optional.)*

Humane Society of the United States. "The HSUS and Wild Fish Conservancy File Suit to Stop Sea Lion Killing At Bonneville Dam." 20 May 2011. Humanesociety. org. Humane Society of the United States. Web. 17 Feb. 2012. <http://www. humanesociety.org/news/press_releases/>.

This Web article presented a seemingly objective account of the status of the legal suit objecting to the elimination of sea lions that were eating salmon at Bonneville Dam. While the language of the article is fairly unbiased, the information it presents clearly shows bias by offering factual information that suggests the sea lions are not really the problem and that they are therefore victims. It reveals the Humane Society and the Wild Fish Conservancy as major stakeholders in the controversy since they are suing the National Marine Fisheries Service and the governments of Washington and Oregon. It also mentions several individuals.

### WORD CONNECTIONS

**Roots and Affixes**

The word *predation* comes from the Latin word *praedationem*, meaning "the act of attacking or taking." Related forms are the verb *praedari* ("to rob or plunder") and the noun *praeda* ("prey"). These same roots are also found in the word *predatory*. In what context have these authors been using the word *predation*?

**My Notes**

---

### Language and Writer's Craft: Citation Styles

The *MLA Handbook for Writers of Research Papers*, published by the Modern Language Association, is one of a number of style guides used in academic and professional writing. Such style guides standardize expectations and rules (called conventions) regarding writing within particular disciplines or fields. As you observe the ways different style guides format bibliographic entries, consider the following:

- When are italics used? When are quotation marks used?
- What punctuation separates the parts of the entries?
- Is the author's first or last name listed first?
- How do you format an entry for a source with no author?

Whether citing references or looking for information on formatting a research paper, consulting a style guide will help you avoid errors.

**PRACTICE** Correct the three errors in the following bibliographic entry to make it conform to MLA style:

William Ury. The Third Side: Why We Fight And How We Can Stop. New York. Penguin Books, 2000. Print.

# What's at Stake? Part Two

**My Notes**

4. Use the following template to compile annotated entry drafts for each of your required sources. Once you have completed your annotated entries, compile a complete annotated bibliography as a group. The bibliography should be in alphabetical order. You will also need to complete a source evaluation sheet for each online resource you use.

**Source 1:**

**Annotation:**

**Source 2:**

**Annotation:**

**Source 3:**

**Annotation:**

5. You will now formally evaluate your sources and acknowledge their bias or potential limitations. This further establishes your ethos as a researcher by indicating you are aware of the bias and credibility of your sources. As you did with the class model, use the following questions and response sheet to evaluate the three sources you have chosen to use for your position paper.

**The URL:**

- What is its domain?

  .com = a for-profit organization

  .gov, .mil, .us (or other country code) = a government site

  .edu = an educational institution

  .org = a nonprofit organization

- Is this URL someone's personal page?

- Why might using information from a personal page be a problem?

- Do you recognize who is publishing this page?

- If not, you may need to investigate further to determine whether the publisher is an expert on the topic.

**Sponsor:**

- Does the website easily give information about the organization or group that sponsors it?

- Does it have a link (often called "About Us") that leads you to that information?

- What do you learn?

**Timeliness:**

- When was the page last updated (usually this is posted at the top or bottom of the page)?

- How current a page is may indicate how accurate or useful the information in it will be.

**Purpose:**

- What is the purpose of the page?

- What is its target audience?

- Does it present information or opinion?

- Is it primarily objective or subjective?

- How do you know?

**Author:**

- What credentials does the author have?

- Is this person or group considered an authority on the topic?

**Links:**

- Does the page provide links?

- Do they work?

- Are they helpful?

- Are they objective or subjective?

# What's at Stake? Part Two

6. Use the response sheet below as a template to create a similar sheet for each of your sources. Respond to the questions on the previous page.

| Evaluating Your Sources — Response Sheet |
| --- |
| **List website (title and URL):**<br><br>**What can you tell from the URL?** |
| **What can you learn about the page's sponsor?** |
| **What can you learn about the page's timeliness?** |
| **What can you tell about the page's purpose?** |
| **What else can you learn about the author?** |
| **What can you tell from the links provided?** |

## Check for Understanding

Based on your evaluation, explain the potential impact of using this source on your credibility.

# Crafting Your Position Paper

## Learning Targets
- Analyze a model position paper for rhetorical appeals and the elements of an effective argument.
- Construct a position paper by incorporating research on a stakeholder position.

## Preview
In this activity, you will analyze a model position paper and begin drafting your Embedded Assessment 1.

## Preparing to Write
1. As you prepare to write a position paper, it is important to put yourself in the position of the stakeholder you plan to represent. Begin by generating a list of major points in support of your stakeholder position. In particular, look for evidence to establish/refute key causal claims. Consider what information you may wish to quote in your paper (remember: you must cite three sources) and be sure to document each piece of information you plan to use.

LEARNING STRATEGIES:
Graphic Organizer, Discussion Groups, Drafting, Marking the Text, Revising, Adding

**My Notes**

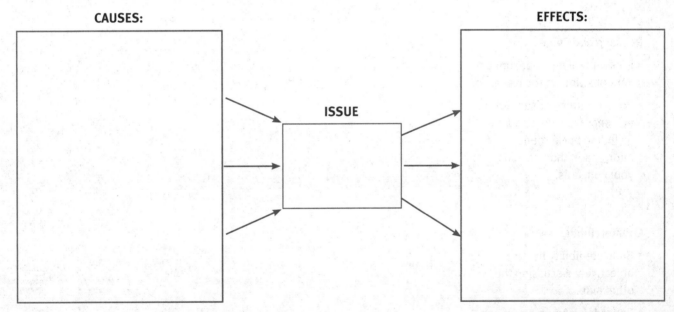

CAUSES:          ISSUE          EFFECTS:

2. Now revisit Fidelia Andy's position paper in Activity 5.13. Her piece provides a real-world example of the type of paper you need to produce. Read through her piece and annotate it for the elements of argument and her use of logos, ethos, and pathos. Use the graphic organizer on the next page to analyze Andy's argument. Then recreate it in your Reader/Writer Notebook to plan your own argument.

# Crafting Your Position Paper

**Components of My Argument**

| Element of Argument | Key Points/Information to Include |
|---|---|
| **Hook:** Grab your audience's attention and establish your subject. | |
| **Claim:** State your basic position. | |
| **Reasons and Evidence:**<br>• Present reasons that support your position on the issue.<br>• Provide sufficient supporting evidence from your sources, including background information that explains your concerns. | |
| **Counterclaims:**<br>• Build credibility by objectively discussing the other side.<br>• Concede common ground on which you can agree.<br>• Refute central claims held by the other side. | |
| **Call to Action:** Propose the solutions you support and suggest what the benefits of adopting them might be—or the consequences of failing to do so. | |

## Drafting the Embedded Assessment

Write a position paper representing your stakeholder's position regarding your group's conflict. Choose an appropriate structure for your paper. Gather multiple sources to support your claim. Write in first person, since you will be role-playing a representative of this stakeholder position in your collaboration with your group. Be sure to:

- Organize your points to present a clear argument, using the components of argumentation as a general outline.
- Cite quotes and details from your sources to develop your claims. Punctuate all quotations correctly.
- Include transitions to link main points and a final statement that restates your claim.

## Check Your Understanding

Annotate your draft, labeling the elements of argument in your paper. Also mark edits for corrections in grammar and other conventions.

My Notes

_____

_____

_____

_____

_____

_____

_____

_____

_____

_____

_____

_____

_____

_____

_____

_____

_____

_____

_____

**INDEPENDENT READING LINK**

Read and Respond
Identify the elements of an argument in one of your independent reading texts. Give an oral summary to a small group of peers that explains how the author used at least three different elements.

# Language and Writer's Craft: Documenting Your Claims

**LEARNING STRATEGIES:**
Marking the Text, Revising

**My Notes**

## Learning Targets

- Avoid plagiarism and maintain accuracy by properly citing research in writing and speech.
- Use a variety of source integration strategies to maintain the flow of ideas.

## Preview

In this activity, you will learn how to avoid plagiarism and use a variety of source integration strategies in your writing.

## Working with Sources in an Academic Essay

To build credibility for their claims, writers need to document their supporting evidence, whether they're using statistics, expert testimony, or even ideas taken from other sources. While different publications and professions use their own style guides for how to do this, the Modern Language Association (MLA) guidelines are typically used in language arts classes. MLA style also provides writers with a system for referencing their sources through parenthetical citation in their essays and in works cited pages.

Most importantly, the use of MLA style can protect writers from accusations of *plagiarism,* which is the purposeful or accidental use of source material by other writers without giving credit. Consider the following excerpt from page 10 of a U.S. Army Corps of Engineers report.

> Total estimated salmonid catch has ranged from about 4,000 to 6,000 per year since 2008. The relative impact on the 1 January to 31 May run has varied with the number of fish passing each spring, which has risen each year from 2008 to 267,194 in 2010. An estimated 4,466 adult salmonids (2.9% of the run) were consumed by pinnipeds in the tailrace of Bonneville Dam during the 2008 1 January to 31 May period. An estimated 4,489 adult salmonids (2.4% of the run) were consumed in 2009, and an estimated 6,081 adult salmonids (2.2% of the run) were consumed in 2010. Presence and predation by CSL [California sea lions] was first observed in the fall of 2008 and has been noted each fall since. Additional salmonids were caught by pinnipeds but escaped and swam away with unknown injuries (3.3%, 2.3%, and 2.6% of total salmonid catch escaped in 2008, 2009, and 2010, respectively). (Stansell 10)

Stansell, Robert J.; Karrie M. Gibbons and William T. Nagy. "Evaluation of Pinniped Predation on Adult Salmonids and other Fish in the Bonneville Dam Tailrace, 2008-2010." U.S. Army Corps of Engineers. 14 Oct. 2010. Web 2 Aug. 2012.

1. Which of the following would be considered plagiarism if it did not include a source citation? Why or why not?

   - An estimated 4,466 adult salmonids (2.9% of the run) were consumed by pinnipeds in the tailrace of Bonneville Dam during the 2008 1 January to 31 May period.

   - About 4500 salmon were eaten by sea lions at Bonneville Dam during the spring of 2008.

   - Sea lions eat thousands of salmon each spring at the Bonneville Dam.

## Options for Citing Sources

If you determine that a source citation is needed, you have options for how to document the source. Be sure to vary your source integration to maintain good flow in your writing.

**Option A:** Use the parenthetical citation to cover the source information.

**Example:** About 4,500 salmon were eaten by sea lions at Bonneville Dam during the spring of 2008 (Stansell 10).

**Option B:** Use either footnotes or endnotes to provide source information.

**Example:** About 4,500 salmon were eaten by sea lions at Bonneville Dam during the spring of 2008.[1]

**Option C:** Start with some of the source information.

**Example:** A study by Robert Stansell *et al.* found that about 4,500 salmon were eaten by sea lions at Bonneville Dam during the spring of 2008 (10).

**Option D:** End with some of the source information.

**Example:** About 4,500 salmon were eaten by sea lions at Bonneville Dam during the spring of 2008, according to the US Army Corps of Engineers (Stansell 10).

**Option E:** Insert some of the source information somewhere midsentence.

**Example:** About 4,500 salmon, a US Army Corps of Engineers report found, were eaten by sea lions at Bonneville Dam during the spring of 2008 (Stansell 10).

**Option F:** Insert an appositive or adjectival phrase to add credentials or clarify information.

**Example:** Robert Stansell, chief biologist of the US Army Corps of Engineers, found that approximately 4,500 salmon—roughly 2.4% of the total population—were eaten by sea lions in 2009 (10).

2. Revise the following sentence to incorporate appropriate source information using at least two different options.

    **Original text:** An estimated 4,489 adult salmonids (2.4% of the run) were consumed in 2009, and an estimated 6,081 adult salmonids (2.2% of the run) were consumed in 2010.

    **Paraphrased text:**

    **Version 1:**

    **Version 2:**

### WORD CONNECTIONS

**Etymology**

You may see the words *ibid.* and *et al.* in some source citations. *Ibid.* is the abbreviation for the Latin word *ibidem*, which means "in the same place." It is used to cite the same source as the previous citation. *Et al.* is the abbreviation for *et alia*, which means "and others." *Et al.* is commonly used to refer to multiple authors of the same source. These words will be useful for you to use in bibliographies.

**My Notes**

# Language and Writer's Craft: Documenting Your Claims

## My Notes

## Citing Sources Accurately

Another key ethical issue when using sources is the accuracy of the information being presented. Consider the information in the following table.

**Annual Salmonid Passage and Estimated Consumption by Pinnipeds, Bonneville Dam**

| Year | Bonneville Dam salmonid passage | Expanded salmonid estimated consumption | % of run (Jan 1– May 31) | Adjusted salmonid estimated consumption | % of run (Jan 1– May 31) |
|------|------|------|------|------|------|
| 2002 | 284,733 | 1,010 | 0.4% | — | — |
| 2003 | 217,185 | 2,329 | 1.1% | — | — |
| 2004 | 186,804 | 3,533 | 1.9% | — | — |
| 2005 | 82,006 | 2,920 | 3.4% | — | — |
| 2006 | 105,063 | 3,023 | 2.8% | 3,401 | 3.1% |
| 2007 | 88,474 | 3,859 | 4.2% | 4,355 | 4.7% |
| 2008 | 147,543 | 4,446 | 2.9% | 4,927 | 3.2% |
| 2009 | 186,060 | 4,489 | 2.4% | 4,960 | 2.7% |
| 2010 | 267,194 | 6,081 | 2.2 % | 6,321 | 2.4 |

*Source:* Stansell, Robert A. and Karrie M. Gibbons. "Pinniped Predation in the Bonneville Dam Tailrace, 2002-2010." US Army Corps of Engineers. 2010. Web. 8 Aug. 2012. PDF file.

3. Using texts you have read in this unit and the information in the table, how ethical is each of the following references?

   **Example:** "However, between 2002 and 2007, there has been a 382-percent increase in salmon being eaten by sea lions" (Andy).

   **Example:** Sea lions have been consuming an average of 2.5 percent of the salmon over the past 3 years. ...

   **Example:** The impact of sea lions on the salmon run has decreased over the past three years from 2.9% to 2.2%.

   Revise each of these examples and add a source citation. Paraphrase or use direct quotations to ensure you are ethically crediting your source.

## Working with Sources in an Oral Presentation

While using evidence in an argument is crucial to its effectiveness, the information has to be cited so that the source is evident. In speaking, this tends to take a different form than in writing. Since you do not include parenthetical citations when speaking, what information should you include to indicate that your information is reliable?

As a speaker, it is particularly important that you give a *thorough* citation of your source. Audience members may want to find the source for further investigation, and they have no way to do so except by using information offered in your speech.

**General tips on citing sources within your speech or oral presentation:**

- Do not say "quote, unquote" when you offer a direct quotation. Use brief pauses to frame the quote, instead. You may say "quote" if you are trying to emphasize the quote.
- Provide enough information about each source so that your audience could, with a little effort, find it.
- If your source is unknown to your audience, provide enough information about the source for the audience to perceive it as credible. Typically, you would provide this credentialing of the source by stating the source's expertise and qualifications to discuss the topic.

## EXAMPLES

**From a book with one author:**

Typically include: Author, brief credentials, date, and title

*"Dr. Derek Bok, President Emeritus of Harvard University, in his 2005 book, "Our Underachieving Colleges," wrote. ..."*

**From a website:**

Typically include: Site title, credentials, and date last updated (some websites may not be updated on a regular basis)

*"One of the most active developers of neurotechnology, Cyberkinetics, claims on their website last updated on March 24, 2006, that. ..."*

**From a TV or radio Show:**

Typically include: Name of show, date it aired, title of story, and name of reporter

*"On March 24, 2006, National Public Radio's Morning Edition aired a story by reporter Christopher Joyce entitled, 'Greenland glaciers moving more quickly to the ocean.' In the story, experts claimed. ..."*

# Language and Writer's Craft: Documenting Your Claims

**My Notes**

**From an interview you performed:**

Typically include: Name, date, credentials

*"In a personal interview conducted on February 12, 2006, with Charlotte Maddux, director of the local chapter of the American Cancer Society, she told me. ..."*

**From a print magazine:**

Typically include: Name of publication, name of reporter, and date

*"According to a feature article written by reporter Kelli Brown about the rising costs of medicine in the March 27, 2006, issue of Time magazine. ..."*

**From a newspaper:**

Typically include: Name of reporter, name of publication, date, and version (i.e., print or electronic version). Providing additional information may give credibility to the source.

*"In a front page article in the January 17, 2006, edition of the Washington Post which looked ahead to President Bush's second term, reporter Dana Milbank quoted White House Chief of Staff, Andrew H. Card, Jr., who said, 'President Bush. ...' "*

**From a reference work:**

Typically include: Title, credentials, and date of publication

*"The 2005 edition of Simmons Market Research, considered by most to be the nation's leading authority on the behavior of the American consumer, notes. ..."*

4. With your group members, identify specific pieces of evidence you are taking from sources in your research. For each, decide which type of source citation is most appropriate to establishing credibility and reliability. Revise to cite each source, using the models above.

## Check Your Understanding

Exchange position papers with a partner and highlight all references to specific evidence, quotes, or ideas from sources. Add editing suggestions for accurate citation of sources, where needed. Be sure to vary the use of direct and indirect quotations, and vary your syntax to enhance the flow of the writing.

Select key evidence that you will use to present your stakeholder's concerns to your group. Make a plan for how you will integrate oral source citations for this evidence.

 **Independent Reading Checkpoint**

Review your independent reading. Think about the ways the print and nonprint texts enhanced your understanding of how authors and directors use various techniques to engage and influence an audience. Which text stood out for you as being especially effective? Why? Was there a text that you thought was ineffective? Why?

# Presenting a Solution to an Environmental Conflict

## ASSIGNMENT

Your assignment is to present a solution to the environmental conflict your group has researched. You will deliver a group presentation designed to contextualize the conflict for your classmates and justify your approach to resolving it.

| | |
|---|---|
| **Planning: Collaborate with your group to evaluate stakeholder positions and potential solutions.** | ▪ How will you use logic, evidence, and rhetorical appeals to advocate your stakeholder's concerns? <br> ▪ How will you integrate oral source citations to cite your research? <br> ▪ How will your group identify common ground, significant obstacles, and potential solutions—and evaluate which solutions might actually work? |
| **Drafting and Organizing: Draft a policy proposal and organize a collaborative presentation.** | ▪ How will you work cooperatively to bridge gaps and meld arguments together into a policy proposal? (Use the policy proposal modeled in Activity 5.13.) <br> ▪ How will your group create a joint presentation that explains the process and the resulting conclusions to the rest of the class? <br> ▪ What background information will you provide to give a context for the conflict? <br> ▪ How will you engage your audience with a hook and provide an effective conclusion with a clear call to action? <br> ▪ What organizational structure will you select? <br> ▪ Which stakeholder positions will you present to the class (use at least three)? <br> ▪ What evidence and citations will you include to develop claims, counterclaims, and reasons? <br> ▪ How will you argue for a proposed solution to the problem, one that respects the wishes of all stakeholders as completely as possible and that has a positive impact? |
| **Rehearsing and Presenting: Use effective speaking and listening to prepare, present, and observe.** | ▪ How can you apply the speaking skills you practiced in Unit 3 to rehearse effective delivery? <br> ▪ How will you involve all group members in the presentation? <br> ▪ How can you use maps, visual aids, or other media to engage your audience? <br> ▪ How will you take notes to demonstrate your understanding, questioning, and evaluating of your peers' presentations? |

## Reflection

After completing this Embedded Assessment, think about how you went about accomplishing this task, and respond to the following:

- What conflicting cultural values or beliefs contribute to the debate surrounding your topic—and how much did these play into your own reaction to it?

- How persuasive was your own proposal compared to others? What content, organization, delivery, or media enhanced their persuasiveness or credibility?

 **Technology Tip**

You might use PowerPoint, Prezi, or another media tool to engage your audience, using principles you learned through your study of documentary film.

# Presenting a Solution to an Environmental Conflict

## SCORING GUIDE

| Scoring Criteria | Exemplary | Proficient | Emerging | Incomplete |
|---|---|---|---|---|
| **Ideas** | The presentation<br>• supports a strong policy proposal with a clear explanation of a variety of stakeholder positions<br>• argues persuasively for an insightful potential solution<br>• develops claims, counterclaims, and reasons with evidence and citations from a variety of credible sources. | The presentation<br>• supports a policy proposal with an adequate explanation of several stakeholder positions<br>• argues persuasively, for the most part, for a logical potential solution<br>• develops claims, counterclaims, and reasons with sufficient evidence and citations from reliable sources. | The presentation<br>• has an inadequate policy proposal; includes partial explanation of stakeholder positions<br>• uses an inconsistently persuasive argument; solution is illogical<br>• develops claims, counterclaims, and reasons insufficiently; may use limited or unreliable sources. | The presentation<br>• has no policy proposal and/or lacks stakeholder positions<br>• does not propose a potential solution<br>• does not develop an argument and/or provides little or no evidence of research. |
| **Structure** | The presentation<br>• demonstrates extensive evidence of collaboration and preparation<br>• has an engaging introduction that thoroughly explains the conflict<br>• follows a smooth and effective organizational structure<br>• concludes with a clear call to action. | The presentation<br>• demonstrates adequate evidence of collaboration and preparation<br>• has an introduction that explains the conflict<br>• follows a logical organizational structure<br>• includes an adequate conclusion. | The presentation<br>• demonstrates insufficient or uneven collaboration and/or preparation<br>• has a weak introduction<br>• uses a flawed or illogical organizational structure<br>• includes a weak or partial conclusion. | The presentation<br>• demonstrates a lack of collaboration or preparation<br>• lacks an introduction<br>• has little or no organizational structure<br>• lacks a conclusion. |
| **Use of Language** | The presentation<br>• uses persuasive language and precise diction<br>• demonstrates command of the conventions of standard English grammar, usage, and language<br>• cites and evaluates sources thoroughly in an annotated bibliography<br>• integrates oral citations smoothly. | The presentation<br>• uses appropriate language and some precise diction<br>• demonstrates adequate command of the conventions of standard English<br>• cites and evaluates sources in an annotated bibliography<br>• includes adequate oral citations. | The presentation<br>• uses inappropriate language; may use basic diction<br>• demonstrates partial command of the conventions of standard English<br>• begins to cite and/or evaluate sources in an annotated bibliography; may use improper format<br>• includes inadequate oral citations. | The presentation<br>• does not communicate; vague or confusing<br>• has frequent errors in standard English grammar, usage, and language<br>• lacks an annotated bibliography<br>• lacks oral citations. |

# Previewing Embedded Assessment 2 and Documentary Film

## Learning Targets

- Identify the knowledge and skills needed to complete Embedded Assessment 2 successfully.
- Revise, refine, and reflect on an understanding of vocabulary words and the essential questions.

## Making Connections

In the first part of this unit, you have looked at claims and evidence surrounding a controversial issue. You have learned that it is essential to evaluate evidence for its objectivity or subjectivity and to consider the source of information and how a stakeholder's position may affect how an issue is presented. In the next part of this unit, you will continue exploring argumentative techniques presented in documentary film as you prepare to choose an issue and create your own documentary **advocating** for your position on the issue.

## Essential Questions

Based on your study of the first part of this unit, how would you answer the questions now? Which activities in the first half of the unit helped inform your response?

1. How do cultural differences contribute to conflicts over environmental issues?

2. In what ways do nonfiction texts influence perceptions of their subject?

## Developing Vocabulary

Review the Academic Vocabulary and Literary Terms you have studied so far in this unit. Which words/terms can you now move to a new category on a QHT chart? Which could you now teach to others that you were unfamiliar with at the beginning of the unit?

## Unpacking Embedded Assessment 2

Closely read the assignment and examine the Scoring Guide criteria for Embedded Assessment 2: Representing an Argument in a Documentary Film.

> Your assignment is to transform your presentation from the first Embedded Assessment into a documentary film advocating for a particular solution to the issue. Use research-based evidence, persuasive appeals, and documentary film techniques to engage an audience and convince them of your argument.

In your own words, summarize what you will need to know to complete this assessment successfully. With your class, create a graphic organizer to represent the skills and knowledge you will need to complete the tasks identified in the Embedded Assessment.

---

**LEARNING STRATEGIES:**
QHT, Close Reading, Metacognitive Markers, Close Reading, Marking the Text

---

**ACADEMIC VOCABULARY**
To **advocate** for something is to speak or write in favor of it by publicly recommending or supporting it through some action. In an argument, you are **advocating** for a specific claim.

---

**My Notes**

_____

_____

_____

_____

_____

_____

_____

_____

---

**INDEPENDENT READING LINK**

**Read and Respond**

Research and find a variety of documentary films. You may want to ask your teacher, media specialist, or peers for suggestions. Or you might want to conduct a web search. Identify any of the documentaries that you can view online for free. Analyze and evaluate several of these films so you can become familiar with the film styles and conventions. Share your findings with peers.

# Previewing Embedded Assessment 2 and Documentary Film

## My Notes

## So You Want to Be a Director

During the first part of this unit, you explored the techniques through which filmmakers and writers explore their subjects and present their positions, sometimes seemingly objectively, in the form of an informational text, but sometimes very subjectively, with the intent of making an explicit argument.

Put your knowledge of film to work representing an argument in favor of one position on the issue you explored during Embedded Assessment 1. Instead of mediating, your group will advocate in favor of one solution. You will use the content (images, text, narration, music) and the appeals (the use of logos, ethos, and pathos) to support a message in a documentary film.

## Previewing Documentary Modes and Styles

When we watch films and televisions shows that are fictional, we are aware that the creators/writers are not showing us reality. However, when we watch nonfiction films and television shows, we tend to assume that what we see is absolute reality and truth. Yet nonfiction films and television shows, as well as nonfiction books and articles, are shaped by their creators.

One way to analyze nonfiction films and television shows is to look at the documentary modes, or methods, that the creators use to shape their creation. One critic has identified four modes—expository, observational, interactive, and reflexive—that the creators of nonfiction films and television shows use. Read the explanation of each mode that follows and consider the questions that follow each explanation. (Adapted from *Reading in the Reel World*, by John Golden, NCTE, 2006)

3. Have each group member read about a different mode before defining it for the group. Work together to create a poster that defines and includes the key elements of each mode.

   **Expository Mode:** The film explains a subject to the viewer. Think of a historical documentary or nature show. In direct address, a voice-over narrative tells us information about the subject. In indirect address, no central narrator talks directly to the audience, but we are shown (or hear) other people talking about the subject as we look at images of it. With either form of address, the filmmaker/creator is making choices about what to explain and how to explain it, but the viewer is not necessarily aware of those choices.

   - How does the speaker's tone influence perception of the subject?
   - What do you notice when comparing what is heard with what is being shown at the same time?

## WORD CONNECTIONS

### Multiple Meaning Words

*Mode* is a word that has many academic uses. Here it refers to the method by which something is done. *Mode* is also a word used in mathematics, where it refers to the most frequent number in a data set. Look up a few other definitions for the word *mode* and practice using different versions in different sentences.

**Observational Mode:** This is a "fly on the wall" mode, in which the camera seems to follow the subject without commenting on it. This mode features minimal editing or cutting, little or no use of non-diegetic sound, and no voice-over or interaction between the filmmaker and what is being filmed. It comes across as exclusively "showing," rather than "telling," which suggests extreme objectivity. The camera is merely recording reality instead of constructing it. Nevertheless, the filmmaker/creator chooses what reality the camera will record.

- What is not shown?
- How do framing, angle, and lighting potentially influence our perceptions of the subject?

**Interactive Mode:** The filmmaker/creator's presence is evident; we may hear the questions being asked or see the filmmakers engaging with the subjects. We also get the sense that those on film are aware of being filmed and are perhaps modifying how they present themselves as a result of this awareness. Think of reality TV: The situations themselves only exist because the film/show is provoking them into existence. Again, the filmmaker/creator is making the choices, though the viewer may be a little more aware that those choices are being made.

- Is the filmmaker provoking reactions for the sake of entertainment or to make a persuasive point? Or both?
- How much does the filmmaker's presence affect our sense of reality?

**Reflexive Mode:** The text calls attention to itself as a constructed text through deliberate editing or sound effects or satirical self-examination. It may expose its own apparatus via shots of the film crew at work. When using this mode, the filmmaker/creator is saying "Look, I'm creating this film/show. Watch me." The viewer is aware of some, if not all, of the choices being made.

- How does the text's reflection on itself impact our willingness to consider the film's message?
- Can a text be reflexive and still claim to be objective? Truthful?

## Check Your Understanding

Which mode do you think you will want to use in your own documentary film script, and why?

**My Notes**

**WORD CONNECTIONS**

Multiple Meaning Words

The word *reflexive* has somewhat different meanings depending on how it is used. Using a dictionary, look up the multiple meanings of *reflexive* and record them in your Reader/Writer Notebook. Use context to determine the correct meaning of the word as it is used in the term *reflexive mode*. Then, try using the word *reflexive* in a new sentence.

# Setting the Mode and Tone

## My Notes

## Learning Targets

- Identify and distinguish between different modes used by documentary filmmakers.
- Write to explain how a director's mode influences the film's tone and subjectivity.

## Preview

In this activity, you will view multiple film clips and identify the modes used by documentary filmmakers to create point of view.

## Documentary Versus Fiction Film

1. As you may have noticed throughout this unit, documentary films break a lot of rules that fiction films usually follow. Most importantly, perhaps, in fiction films—with few exceptions—the camera represents a silent observer of the lives of people who do not know they're being watched. Think back on the various types of film texts you have watched in this unit. What are somes ways in which the line between director and subject is crossed?

## Literary Terms

**Tone** is a writer's or speaker's (or filmmaker's) attitude toward a subject.

2. Review the posters you made to explore the documentary modes and styles in the previous activity. While a single film may move in and out of various modes, a director's choice to break into a more obviously biased mode will have a big impact on **tone**, as these modes more openly reveal the director's perspective on the subject. It is similar to how an essay that breaks into highly subjective descriptions and the use of first person takes on a more transparent tone than does one that sticks to more objective language and third person.

## Viewing the Film

3. As you watch the four film clips, take notes on how the narrative point of view is constructed. Once you have identified the mode used in the clip, consider how the narration, editing, and sound help create the tone. Use the graphic organizer on the next page.

**Text:** *Life in the Freezer*          **Director:**          **Mode:**

**Text:** *March of the Penguins*          **Director:**          **Mode:**

**Text:** *The 11th Hour*          **Director:**          **Mode:**

**Text:** "I Need to Wake Up"          **Director:**          **Mode:**

# Setting the Mode and Tone

## INDEPENDENT READING LINK

**Read and Respond**

Choose clips from three or four of the documentary films you researched. Use the graphic organizer from this activity to identify the mode used in each clip, and evaluate how the narration, editing, and sound help create the tone. Share your work with a small group.

## Writing to Sources: Argument Text

Choose one of the clips you have just watched. Write a critique that analyzes how the mode of one of the clips affects the tone. State your opinion about the effectiveness of the tone. Include commentary that explains the connotation and tone created by the images or sounds. Be sure to:

- Begin with a topic sentence that clearly states the tone and your claim about the tone.
- Support your claim by including specific details from the clip regarding narration, image, sound, sequence, and other related evidence.
- Incorporate appropriate terminology to discuss documentary modes and styles.

## Independent Practice

Watch at least four documentary film trailers. Use the following graphic organizer to take notes as you make predictions about each film and reflect on the effectiveness of the trailer.

| Documentary Film Title | Predict the Mode: Does it appear subjective or objective? Explain. | Rate your interest level from 1 to 10 (low to high). Explain. |
|---|---|---|
| | | |
| | | |
| | | |
| | | |

## Check Your Understanding

Rank the four modes from most objective to most subjective, and then explain your rankings.

# Documentary Film Techniques

## Learning Targets

- Analyze documentary film techniques in short films.
- Collaborate to storyboard the exposition for a documentary film.

## Preview

In this activity, you will learn and analyze documentary film techniques in short films.

## Previewing Film Techniques

1. Read the text that follows, which explains the various film techniques used to create documentary films. Mark the text as follows:

   - Put a *Q* next to terms that you have questions about (unfamiliar).
   - Put an *H* next to terms that you have heard of (somewhat familiar).
   - Put a *T* next to terms you could teach (very familiar).

2. Make a display card for one of the terms. Include the name of the technique, a brief description, and at least two of the following:

   - one purpose or possible effect of the technique
   - a visual representation of the technique
   - an example of how the technique was used in a documentary film

3. Post your display card in the correct category on a bulletin board. Find the cards for terms that you marked with a *Q* in Step 1. Use the cards to become familiar enough to at least change your *Q*s to *H*s.

## Documentary Film Techniques

### Framing and Angles

**Shot:** A single piece of film uninterrupted by cuts.

**Establishing Shot:** Often a long shot or a series of shots that sets the scene, it is used to establish setting and to show transitions between locations.

**Long Shot (LS):** A shot from some distance; if filming a person, the full body is shown (also called a full shot).

**Medium Shot (MS):** The most common shot; the camera seems to be a medium distance from the object being filmed.

**Close Up (CU):** The object or subject takes up most of the frame, and so the viewer is forced to look at what the director intends the viewer look at.

**Two Shot:** A scene between two people shot exclusively from an angle that includes both characters more or less equally.

**Eye Level:** A shot taken from a normal height; most shots seen are eye level because it is the most natural angle.

**High Angle:** The camera is above the subject, making the subject look small, weak, powerless, and trapped.

**Low Angle:** The camera films the subject from below, making the subject look larger, strong, powerful, and threatening.

**My Notes**

# Documentary Film Techniques

**My Notes**

## Movement and Transitions

**Pan:** A stationary camera moves from side to side along a horizontal axis.

**Tilt:** A stationary camera moves up or down along a vertical axis.

**Zoom:** A stationary camera where the lens moves to make an object seem to move closer to or further away from the camera.

**"Ken Burns" Effect:** A technique in which the camera slowly zooms in on a still photograph and pans from one image to another.

**Montage:** Transitional sequences of rapidly edited images, used to suggest the lapse of time or the passing of events.

**Dolly/Tracking:** The camera is on a track that allows it to move with the action. The term also refers to any camera mounted on a vehicle.

**Cut:** The most common editing technique; two pieces of film are spliced together to "cut" to another image.

**Fade:** A scene that can begin in darkness and gradually assume full brightness (fade-in) or where the image may gradually get darker (fade-out).

**Dissolve:** A kind of fade in which one image is slowly replaced by another. It can create a connection between images.

**Wipe:** A new image wipes off the previous image. A wipe is more fluid than a cut and quicker than a dissolve.

**Shot-Reverse-Shot:** A shot of one subject, then another, then back to the first. It is often used for conversation or reaction shots.

## Visual Elements

**Color/Black and White/Sepia:** A film can be shot partly or entirely in color, black and white, or sepia tones (a brownish pigment.)

**Charts and Graphs:** A pie chart, bar graph, or line graph to emphasize a statistic or help the audience visualize data.

**Photographs:** Still images used to emphasize a point or illustrate a time in history before video was available.

**Interview:** Expert or celebrity interviews can be used to enhance a film's ethos or present opposing views.

**Real People:** "Man on the street" polls and reactions can illustrate a commonly held belief.

**Reconstruction/Reenactment:** Filming actors as they recreate a true event. This technique is controversial and should be clearly labeled.

**Animation:** Hand-drawn, computer-generated, or three-dimensional objects (such as clay figures) can be animated for part or all of a film.

**Archival/Stock Footage:** Many websites offer downloads of clips such as wildlife images and historical footage that you can use in your film.

**Logos/Symbols:** A graphic or emblem representing a company, organization, or idea.

**Captions/Subtitles/Text:** Text can identify a setting as a caption, clarify spoken words as a subtitle, or appear on screen to make a point.

## Vocals and Sound

**Diegetic:** Sound that could logically be heard by the people in the film, such as dialogue.

**Non-diegetic:** Sound that is designed for audience reaction only, such as the score or sound effects.

**Film Score:** Background music that is composed specifically to accompany a film.

**Soundtrack:** Recorded music accompanying and synchronized to the images of a film; may include significant lyrics.

**Narration (Voice-Over):** Commentary provided by an off-camera speaker whose voice is placed over the video imagery.

**Sound Effects:** Artificially created or enhanced sounds used for emphasis or artistic effect.

**Talking Heads:** A medium or close up shot of a person talking, usually in response to an interview question.

**Walk and Talk:** A storytelling technique in which two people have a conversation on their way to or as they are exploring a setting.

## Analyzing the Techniques

4. As you watch a variety of short films, work with a small group to take turns analyzing different categories of documentary film techniques in the following graphic organizer. Before each film, assign a different category (row) for each group member to focus on. After each film, share your observations and discuss the effect of the filmmaker's choices.

# Documentary Film Techniques

**Category 1: Framing and Angles**

Film Title:

Film Techniques Observed:

**Category 2: Movement and Transitions**

Film Title:

Film Techniques Observed:

**Category 3: Visual Elements**

Film Title:

Film Techniques Observed:

**Category 4: Vocals and Sound**

Film Title:

Film Techniques Observed:

## Storyboard Your Exposition

5. Work with your group to plan how you will transform the introduction from your presentation into film using a variety of techniques. You might use the following graphic organizer or an online storyboard to plan your film. Several storyboard tools are available online. If you decide to use one, search until you find one that you like.

**Literary Terms**

A **storyboard** shows images and sequencing for the purpose of visualizing a film.

| Shot, Framing, Angle (describe or sketch) | Movement and Transitions | Visual Elements | Vocals and Sound |
|---|---|---|---|
| | | | |
| | | | |
| | | | |
| | | | |

## Check Your Understanding

Explain how storyboarding can help writers and directors create a plan for filming. Why might it be difficult to storyboard an entire documentary film in advance?

# Arguments with Film

**LEARNING STRATEGIES:**
Graphic Organizer, Sharing and
Responding, Outlining, Drafting

**My Notes**

## Learning Targets

- Analyze the elements of arguments and appeals in film.
- Collaborate to draft a documentary film proposal.

## Preview

In this activity, you will analyze the elements of arguments and appeals in film and draft your documentary film proposal.

## Elements of an Argument in Film

1. Review the elements of an argument that you analyzed in Activity 5.15. In the first column of the graphic organizer below, paraphrase each of the elements listed.

2. As you view the film, take notes on how each of the elements is represented in a short documentary film.

| Elements of Argument | Film Title: |
|---|---|
| **Hook:** | |
| **Claim:** | |
| **Support:** | |
| **Concessions/Refutations:** | |
| **Call to Action:** | |

3. Use the SMELL strategy to independently analyze the argument in another documentary film.

**Sender-Receiver Relationship:** To whom are the filmmakers explicitly addressing their argument here? How do they seem to feel about that target audience?

**Message:** What is the clip's central claim? What content does it use to support that claim?

**Emotional Strategies:** What emotional appeals does the director include? What seems to be their desired effect? Are they fallacious?

**Logical Strategies:** What logical arguments/appeals does the director include? What is their effect? Are they fallacious?

**Language:** What specific language is used to support the message? How does it impact the film's effectiveness and credibility? Are they fallacious? Consider both images and actual words.

## Check Your Understanding

Compare notes with a student who analyzed a different documentary. Which film had the most persuasive and effective argument? How can you use similar strategies to represent your own argument in a documentary film?

# Arguments with Film

**My Notes**

## Planning a Documentary Film

Documentary films, by their very nature, rarely begin with a script. Part of the process of making this kind of film is the unpredictability of capturing what happens when you are out in the field. However, that does not mean that you go out and film without a plan.

To get funding to make a documentary, filmmakers begin with a proposal outlining the topic of the film, where and how it will be made, who will be in the film, and perhaps an estimated cost. Although there is no one correct way to organize a documentary, there are key elements you will need to include.

- **Title and Logline:** Brainstorm a creative title and engaging logline for your documentary film. Think of the logline as the one sentence that would appear on your film's poster. It should tell a prospective audience what the film is about and make them want to see it.

- **Overview:** Write a brief summary of your film, including the issue or conflict and the solution your group has chosen. Identify a specific audience and goal and explain how your documentary film will use logical, emotional, and ethical appeals to persuade the audience.

- **Outline:** Draft an outline to represent the film's sequencing. Include an introduction and all of the elements of an argument, as well as estimates for how much you will spend on each section. Note that your outline may change later when you actually shoot and edit your film.

- **Production Elements:** Make a list of the materials you will need to gather, and assign preliminary tasks to different group members. Include a variety of interviews, archival footage, photographs, animation, music, and charts/graphs. Locate needed supplies such as a camera and editing software.

4. Collaborate with your group to create a documentary film proposal.

## Check Your Understanding

When you have finished writing your documentary proposal, pitch (sell) your ideas to another group. As you listen to the other group's ideas, give them feedback about the following questions:

- What elements of the film sound the most engaging, and why?

- What parts of their plan sound the most difficult or troublesome? How might they overcome these challenges?

- What questions do you have about the issue that weren't answered in their documentary film proposal?

 **Independent Reading Checkpoint**

Review your independent documentary film selections. Think about how can you use your own observations and what you have learned about the techniques of argumentation to evaluate each film. Make a list of the ways that each film might help you as you create your own documentary.

# Representing an Argument in a Documentary Film

## ASSIGNMENT

Your assignment is to transform your presentation from the first Embedded Assessment into a documentary film advocating for a particular solution to the issue. Use research-based evidence, persuasive appeals, and documentary film techniques to engage an audience and convince them of your argument.

| | |
|---|---|
| **Planning and Preparing:** Take time to make a plan for transforming your presentation into a documentary film. | ▨ Which proposed solutions in your presentation were the most engaging and/or persuasive?<br>▨ How will your film present the problem or conflict and advocate for a solution?<br>▨ How will your film seek to fairly and objectively present opposing or diverse points of view?<br>▨ Who is your target audience, and what do you want your target audience to think or do after viewing your film?<br>▨ How can you use your documentary film proposal and introduction storyboard to aid your planning? |
| **Creating and Editing:** Use a variety of documentary film techniques and appeals to present your argument. | ▨ What documentary film mode or style will you use, and how subjective will your film be as a result?<br>▨ How will you organize your film to include exposition, research-based evidence, and the elements of an argument?<br>▨ How can you use logical, emotional, and ethical appeals (logos, pathos, and ethos) to persuade your audience?<br>▨ How will you integrate a variety of documentary film techniques for specific effects?<br>▨ How will you use the Scoring Guide criteria to guide you in refining your documentary film? |
| **Screening and Viewing:** Share your film with an audience and evaluate other students' documentary films. | ▨ How will you share your film with an audience?<br>▨ How will you evaluate the effective use of documentary and persuasive techniques in other student films? |

## Reflection

After completing this Embedded Assessment, think about how you went about accomplishing this task, and respond to the following:

- How was the process of creating a documentary film different from planning a class presentation? Which did you prefer, and why?
- Compare and contrast your film to another documentary you've seen, such as *The 11th Hour*. Which elements did you have in common? Which did you avoid, and why?

 **Technology Tip**

To produce your film, you will need to access a video, slideshow, or animation program such as MovieMaker, PhotoStory, iMovie, Animoto, or Adobe Flash. When your film is complete, consider publishing it online at a website such as Vimeo, YouTube, or TeacherTube.

# Representing an Argument in a Documentary Film

## SCORING GUIDE

| Scoring Criteria | Exemplary | Proficient | Emerging | Incomplete |
|---|---|---|---|---|
| **Ideas** | The film<br>• establishes the conflict clearly in an engaging manner<br>• advocates persuasively for a solution<br>• presents an opposing point of view fairly and objectively<br>• incorporates a variety of documentary film techniques purposefully<br>• includes an effective call for action. | The film<br>• establishes the nature of the conflict adequately<br>• advocates for a logical solution<br>• presents an opposing point of view fairly and objectively for the most part<br>• includes sufficient documentary film techniques<br>• includes a call for action. | The film<br>• establishes the nature of the conflict inadequately<br>• advocates for an illogical or undeveloped solution or solutions<br>• presents an opposing point of view unfairly or subjectively<br>• includes insufficient documentary film techniques<br>• has an ineffective call for action. | The film<br>• does not establish the nature of the conflict<br>• does not advocate for a solution<br>• presents no opposing points of view<br>• includes minimal documentary film techniques<br>• lacks a call for action. |
| **Structure** | The film<br>• demonstrates extensive evidence of collaboration and preparation<br>• has an engaging and effective introduction and conclusion<br>• follows a smooth and effective organizational structure<br>• uses transitions and juxtaposition of ideas and images for effect. | The film<br>• demonstrates adequate evidence of collaboration and preparation<br>• has an adequate introduction and conclusion<br>• follows a logical organizational structure<br>• uses transitions between ideas and images for clarity and cohesion. | The film<br>• demonstrates insufficient or uneven collaboration and/or preparation<br>• has a weak introduction and/or conclusion<br>• uses a flawed or illogical organizational structure<br>• uses inadequate or awkward transitions. | The film<br>• demonstrates a failure to collaborate or prepare<br>• lacks an introduction and/or conclusion<br>• has little or no organizational structure<br>• lacks transitions. |
| **Use of Language** | The film<br>• communicates to a target audience clearly with a strong sense of purpose<br>• demonstrates command of the conventions of standard English grammar, usage, and language<br>• uses logical, ethical, and emotional appeals effectively. | The film<br>• communicates to a target audience with a sense of purpose<br>• demonstrates adequate command of the conventions of standard English grammar, usage, and language<br>• uses sufficient logical, ethical, and emotional appeals. | The film<br>• communicates inappropriately; may use basic diction<br>• demonstrates partial command of the conventions of standard English grammar, usage, and language<br>• uses insufficient logical, ethical, and emotional appeals. | The film<br>• does not communicate clearly; may use vague or confusing language<br>• has frequent errors in standard English grammar, usage, and language<br>• does not include persuasive appeals. |

# Resources

# Unit 1 Independent Reading List

## Suggestions for Independent Reading

The Independent Reading Lists for each unit are divided into the categories of Literature and Nonfiction/Informational Text. Each list comprises titles related to the theme and content of the unit. For your independent reading, you can select from this wide array of titles, which have been chosen based on complexity and interest. You can also do your own research for other titles that captivate your interest and relate to the unit of study.

### Unit 1: Cultural Conversations

#### Literature

| Author | Title | Lexile |
|---|---|---|
| Bernier-Grand, Carmen T. | *Frida: Viva la Vida! Long Live Life!* | 750L |
| Garcia, Cristina | *The Aguero Sisters* | 1000L |
| Jin, Ha | *Ocean of Words Army Stories* | 790L |
| McCunn, Ruthanne Lum | *Thousand Pieces of Gold* | 940L |
| Porter, Connie | *Imani All Mine* | 580L |
| Walker, Alice | *Meridian* | 1010L |
| Whitaker, Alecia | *Wildflower* | 830L |
| Wright, Richard | *Black Boy* | 950L |
| Smith, Zadie | *White Teeth* | 960L |

#### Nonfiction/Informational Text

| Author | Title | Lexile |
|---|---|---|
| Beal, Merrill D. | *"I Will Fight No More Forever": Chief Joseph and the Nez Perce War* | 1130L |
| Carrick Hill, Laban | *America Dreaming: How Youth Changed America in the 60's* | 1190L |
| Cunxin, Li | *Mao's Last Dancer* | 810L |
| Le Guin, Ursula K. | *Always Coming Home* | N/A |
| Nabhan, Gary Paul | *Why Some Like It Hot: Food, Genes, and Cultural Diversity* | N/A |
| Nerburn, Kent | *Chief Joseph & the Flight of the Nez Perce: The Untold Story of an American Tragedy* | N/A |
| Santiago, Esmeralda | *When I Was Puerto Rican: A Memoir* | 1029L |
| Sherr, Lynn | *Failure Is Impossible: Susan B. Anthony in Her Own Words* | N/A |
| Stone, Tanya Lee | *The Good, the Bad, and the Barbie: A Doll's History and Her Impact on Us* | 1120L |
| Tobin, Jacqueline L. & Dobard, Raymond G. | *Hidden in Plain View: A Secret Story of Quilts and the Underground Railroad* | N/A |
| Ward, Geoffrey C. & Burns, Ken | *Not for Ourselves Alone: The Story of Elizabeth Cady Stanton and Susan B. Anthony* | N/A |

# Unit 2 Independent Reading List

## Unit 2: Cultural Perspectives

### Literature

| Author | Title | Lexile |
|---|---|---|
| Aronson, Marc & Budhos, Marina | *Sugar Changed the World* | 1130L |
| Achebe, Chinua | *Arrow of God* | 880L |
| Abdel-Fattah, Randa | *Does My Head Look Big in This?* | 850L |
| Alexie, Sherman | *The Absolutely True Diary of a Part-Time Indian* | 600L |
| Alvarez, Julia | *How the Garcia Girls Lost Their Accents* | 950L |
| Anaya, Rudolfo | *Bless Me, Ultima* | 840L |
| Barakat, Ibtisam | *Tasting the Sky* | 870L |
| Buck, Pearl S. | *The Good Earth* | 1530L |
| Carmi, Daniella | *Samir and Yonatan* | 810L |
| Díaz, Junot | *The Brief and Wondrous Life of Oscar Wao* | 1010L |
| Esquivel, Laura | *Like Water for Chocolate* | 1030L |
| Ferris, Timothy | *The Whole Shebang* | N/A |
| Jin, Ha | *Waiting* | N/A |
| Hudson, Jan | *Sweetgrass* | 640L |
| Kidd, Sue Monk | *The Secret Life of Bees* | 840L |
| Na, An | *The Fold* | 700L |
| Oates, Joyce Carol | *Big Mouth and Ugly Girl* | 720L |
| Park, Linda Sue | *A Single Shard* | 920L |
| Tan, Amy | *The Bonesetter's Daughter* | 800L |

### Nonfiction/Informational Text

| Author | Title | Lexile |
|---|---|---|
| Alvarez, Julia | *Something to Declare* | 1100L |
| Coates, Ta-Nehisi | *Between the World and Me* | 1090L |
| Kurlansky, Mark | *The Story of Salt* | 1100L |
| Laure, Jason et al. | *South Africa* | 1020L |
| O'Brien, Anne Silby & O'Brien, Perry Edmond | *After Gandhi: One Hundred Years of Nonviolent Resistance* | 1080L |
| Pham, Andrew X. | *Catfish and Mandala: A Two-Wheeled Voyage Through the Landscape and Memory of Vietnam* | N/A |
| Reef, Catherine | *Frida & Diego: Art, Love, Life* | 1080L |
| Seierstad, Asne | *The Bookseller of Kabul* | N/A |
| Sherr, Lynn | *America the Beautiful: The Stirring True Story Behind Our Nation's Favorite Song* | 1210L |
| Shetterly, Robert | *Americans Who Tell the Truth* | N/A |
| Thoreau, Henry David | *The Higher Law: Thoreau on Civil Disobedience and Reform* | N/A |
| Yousafzai, Malala | *I Am Malala* | 1000L |

# Unit 3 Independent Reading List

## Unit 3: Cultures in Conflict

### Literature

| Author | Title | Lexile |
|---|---|---|
| Abani, Chris | *Graceland* | N/A |
| Achebe, Chinua | *Anthills of the Savannah* | 1030L |
| Alvarez, Julia | *In the Time of the Butterflies* | 910L |
| Cheng, Nien | *Life and Death in Shanghai* | N/A |
| Coetzee, J. M. | *Life and Times of Michael K* | 940L |
| Dayrell, Elphinstone | *The King And The Ju Ju Tree: Forty Amazing Folk Tales from Southern Nigeria* | N/A |
| Eggers, Dave | *What Is the What?* | N/A |
| Emecheta, Buchi | *The Bride Price* | 1060L |
| Gordimer, Nadine | *Jump and Other Stories* | 1030L |
| Jhabvala, Ruth Prawer | *Heat and Dust* | N/A |
| Kincaid, Jamaica | *A Small Place* | N/A |
| Lahiri, Jhumpa | *The Namesake* | 1210L |
| Lake, Nick | *In Darkness* | 800L |
| Naidoo, Beverley | *Chain of Fire* | 910L |
| Temple, Frances | *Taste of Salt: A Story of Modern Haiti* | 650L |
| Winter, Jeanette | *The Librarian of Basra* | 640L |

### Nonfiction/Informational Text

| Author | Title | Lexile |
|---|---|---|
| Ali, Nujood & Minoui, Delphine | *I Am Nujood: Age 10 and Divorced* | N/A |
| al-Windawi, Thura | *Thura's Diary: My Life in Wartime Iraq* | 990L |
| Bhutto, Benazir | *Daughter of Destiny: An Autobiography* | N/A |
| Freedman, Russell | *Because They Marched: The People's Campaign for Voting Rights That Changed America* | 1160L |
| Freedman, Russell | *We Will Not Be Silent: The White Rose Student Resistance Movement That Defied Adolf Hitler* | 630L |
| Hogan, Linda | *The Woman Who Watches Over the World: A Native Memoir* | N/A |

# Unit 4 Independent Reading List

| Unit 4: Dramatic Justice | | |
|---|---|---|
| **Literature** | | |
| **Author** | **Title** | **Lexile** |
| Aristophanes | *The Birds* | NP |
| Doctorow, Cory | *Little Brother* | N/A |
| Golding, William | *Lord of the Flies* | 770L |
| Hansberry, Lorraine | *A Raisin in the Sun* | NP |
| Kaufman, Moisés | *The Laramie Project* | N/A |
| Mann, Abby | *Judgment at Nuremberg: A Play* | N/A |
| Miller, Frank | *The Dark Knight* | N/A |
| Morrison, Toni | *The Bluest Eye* | 920L |
| Wein, Elizabeth | *Code Name Verity* | 1020L |
| **Nonfiction/Informational Text** | | |
| **Author** | **Title** | **Lexile** |
| Bryson, Bill | *Notes from a Small Island* | N/A |
| Hakim, Joy | *The Story of Science: Aristotle Leads the Way* | 950L |
| McKissack, Patricia C. & McKissack, Fredrick L. | *Young, Black, and Determined: A Biography of Lorraine Hansberry* | 1160L |
| Mlodinow, Leonard | *Euclid's Window: The Story of Geometry from Parallel Lines to Hyperspace* | N/A |
| Sotomayor, Sonia | *My Beloved World* | N/A |

# Unit 5 Independent Reading List

## Unit 5: Building Cultural Bridges

### Literature

| Author | Title | Lexile |
|--------|-------|--------|
| Alvarez, Julia | *Before We Were Free* | 890L |
| Beatty, Patricia | *Lupita Mañana* | 760L |
| Choi, Sook Nyul | *Gathering of Pearls* | N/A |
| Danticat, Edwidge | *Behind the Mountains* | 940L |
| Jen, Gish | *Typical American* | N/A |
| Klass, David | *California Blue* | 820L |
| Knowles, John | *A Separate Peace* | 1110L |
| Stockett, Kathryn | *The Help* | 930L |

### Nonfiction/Informational Text

| Author | Title | Lexile |
|--------|-------|--------|
| Gonick, Larry & Alice Outwater | *Cartoon Guide to the Environment* | N/A |
| Hickam, Jr., Homer H. | *Rocket Boys* | N/A |
| Jacquet, Luc & Maison, Jerome | *March of the Penguins* | N/A |
| Kurlansky, Mark | *World Without Fish* | 1230L |
| Laskin, David | *Braving the Elements* | N/A |
| Pollan, Michael | *The Omnivore's Dilemma* | 930L |
| Silverstein, Ken | *The Radioactive Boy Scout: The Frightening True Story of a Whiz Kid and His Homemade Nuclear Reactor* | 1300L |
| Simon, Seymour | *Penguins* | 1030L |
| Stevens, William K. | *Change in the Weather: People, Weather, and the Science of Climate Change* | N/A |
| Stewart, Brent S., Clapham, Phillip J., & Powell, James A. | *National Audubon Society Guide to Marine Mammals of the World* | N/A |

## Suggested Documentary Films

| Director | Documentary Film Title | Release Year |
|----------|------------------------|--------------|
| Balog, James, National Geographic | *Chasing Ice* | 2012 |
| Cheney, Ian | *PBS: The City Dark* | 2012 |
| Chang, Yung | *PBS: Up the Yangtze* | 2008 |
| Cowperthwaite, Gabriela | *Black Fish* | 2013 |
| Gunn Carr, Drury and Doug Hawes-Davis | *PBS: Libby, Montana* | 2007 |
| Jaquet, Luc | *March of the Penguins* | 2005 |

# Independent Reading Log

NAME _____ DATE _____

Directions: This log is a place to record your progress and thinking about your independent reading during each unit. Add your log pages to your Reader/Writer Notebook or keep them as a separate place to record your reading insights.

Unit _____

Independent Reading Title _____

Author(s) _____ Text Type _____

Pages read: from _____ to _____

_____

_____

_____

_____

_____

Independent Reading Title _____

Author(s) _____ Text Type _____

Pages read: from _____ to _____

_____

_____

_____

_____

_____

_____

_____

Independent Reading Title _____

Author(s) _____ Text Type _____

Pages read: from _____ to _____

_____

_____

_____

_____

_____

_____

_____

Unit _____

Independent Reading Title _____

Author(s) _____ Text Type _____

Pages read: from _____ to _____

_____

_____

_____

_____

_____

Independent Reading Title _____

Author(s) _____ Text Type _____

Pages read: from _____ to _____

_____

_____

_____

_____

_____

Independent Reading Title _____

Author(s) _____ Text Type _____

Pages read: from _____ to _____

_____

_____

_____

_____

_____

_____

_____

Independent Reading Title _____

Author(s) _____ Text Type _____

Pages read: from _____ to _____

_____

_____

_____

_____

_____

_____

_____

# SpringBoard Learning Strategies

## READING STRATEGIES

| STRATEGY | DEFINITION | PURPOSE |
|---|---|---|
| **Chunking the Text** | Breaking the text into smaller, manageable units of sense (e.g., words, sentences, paragraphs, whole text) by numbering, separating phrases, drawing boxes | To reduce the intimidation factor when encountering long words, sentences, or whole texts; to increase comprehension of difficult or challenging text |
| **Close Reading** | Accessing small chunks of text to read, reread, mark, and annotate key passages, word-for-word, sentence-by-sentence, and line-by-line | To develop comprehensive understanding by engaging in one or more focused readings of a text |
| **Diffusing** | Reading a passage; noting unfamiliar words; discovering meaning of unfamiliar words using context clues, dictionaries, and/or thesauruses; and replacing unfamiliar words with familiar ones | To facilitate a close reading of text, the use of resources, an understanding of synonyms, and increased comprehension of text |
| **Double-Entry Journal** | Creating a two-column journal (also called Dialectical Journal) with a student-selected passage in one column and the student's response in the second column (e.g., asking questions of the text, forming personal responses, interpreting the text, reflecting on the process of making meaning of the text) | To assist in note-taking and organizing key textual elements and responses noted during reading in order to generate textual support that can be incorporated into a piece of writing at a later time |
| **Graphic Organizer** | Using a visual representation for the organization of information from the text | To facilitate increased comprehension and discussion |
| **KWHL Chart** | Setting up discussion that allows students to activate prior knowledge by answering "What do I know?"; sets a purpose by answering "What do I want to know?"; helps preview a task by answering "How will I learn it?"; and reflects on new knowledge by answering "What have I learned?" | To organize thinking, access prior knowledge, and reflect on learning to increase comprehension and engagement |
| **Marking the Text** | Selecting text by highlighting, underlining, and/or annotating for specific components, such as main idea, imagery, literary devices, and so on | To focus reading for specific purposes, such as author's craft, and to organize information from selections; to facilitate reexamination of a text |
| **Metacognitive Markers** | Responding to text with a system of cueing marks where students use a ? for questions about the text; a ! for reactions related to the text; a * for comments about the text; and underline to signal key ideas | To track responses to texts and use those responses as a point of departure for talking or writing about texts |
| **OPTIC** | **O** (Overview): Write notes on what the visual appears to be about. **P** (Parts): Zoom in on the parts of the visual and describe any elements or details that seem important. **T** (Title): Highlight the words of the title of the visual (if one is available). **I** (Interrelationships): Use the title as the theory and the parts of the visual as clues to detect and specify how the elements of the graphic are related. | To analyze graphic and visual images as forms of text |

| STRATEGY | DEFINITION | PURPOSE |
|---|---|---|
| **OPTIC** (continued) | **C** (Conclusion); Draw a conclusion about the visual as a whole. What does the visual mean? Summarize the message of the visual in one or two sentences. | |
| **Predicting** | Making guesses about the text by using the title and pictures and/or thinking ahead about events which may occur based on evidence in the text | To help students become actively involved, interested, and mentally prepared to understand ideas |
| **Previewing** | Examining a text's structure, features, layout, format, questions, directions, prior to reading | To gain familiarity with the text, make connections to the text, and extend prior knowledge to set a purpose for reading |
| **QHT** | Expanding prior knowledge of vocabulary words by marking words with a Q, H, or T (Q signals words students do not know; H signals words students have heard and might be able to identify; T signals words students know well enough to teach to their peers) | To allow students to build on their prior knowledge of words, to provide a forum for peer teaching and learning of new words, and to serve as a prereading exercise to aid in comprehension |
| **Questioning the Text\*** The AP Vertical Teams Guide for English (109–112) | Developing levels of questions about text; that is, literal, interpretive, and universal questions that prompt deeper thinking about a text | To engage more actively with texts, read with greater purpose and focus, and ultimately answer questions to gain greater insight into the text; helps students to comprehend and interpret |
| **Paraphrasing** | Restating in one's own words the essential information expressed in a text, whether it be narration, dialogue, or informational text | To encourage and facilitate comprehension of challenging text |
| **RAFT** | Primarily used to generate new text, this strategy can also be used to analyze a text by examining the role of the speaker (R), the intended audience (A), the format of the text (F), and the topic of the text (T). | To initiate reader response; to facilitate an analysis of a text to gain focus prior to creating a new text |
| **Rereading** | Encountering the same text with more than one reading | To identify additional details; to clarify meaning and/or reinforce comprehension of texts |
| **SIFT\*** The AP Vertical Teams Guide for English (17–20) | Analyzing a fictional text by examining stylistic elements, especially symbol, images, and figures of speech in order to show how all work together to reveal tone and theme | To focus and facilitate an analysis of a fictional text by examining the title and text for symbolism, identifying images and sensory details, analyzing figurative language and identifying how all these elements reveal tone and theme |
| **Skimming/Scanning** | Skimming by rapid or superficial reading of a text to form an overall impression or to obtain a general understanding of the material; scanning focuses on key words, phrases, or specific details and provides speedy recognition of information | To quickly form an overall impression prior to an in-depth study of a text; to answer specific questions or quickly locate targeted information or detail in a text |
| **SMELL\*** The AP Vertical Teams Guide for English (138–139) | Analyzing a persuasive speech or essay by asking five essential questions: <br><br>• Sender-receiver relationship—What is the sender-receiver relationship? Who are the images and language meant to attract? Describe the speaker of the text. <br><br>• Message—What is the message? Summarize the statement made in the text. | To analyze a persuasive speech or essay by focusing on five essential questions |

| STRATEGY | DEFINITION | PURPOSE |
|---|---|---|
| **SMELL\*** (continued) | • Emotional Strategies—What is the desired effect?<br><br>• Logical Strategies—What logic is operating? How does it (or its absence) affect the message? Consider the logic of the images as well as the words.<br><br>• Language—What does the language of the text describe? How does it affect the meaning and effectiveness of the writing? Consider the language of the images as well as the words. | |
| **SOAPSTone\*** | Analyzing text by discussing and identifying Speaker, Occasion, Audience, Purpose, Subject, and Tone | To facilitate the analysis of specific elements of nonfiction literary and informational texts and show the relationship among the elements to an understanding of the whole |
| **Summarizing** | Giving a brief statement of the main points or essential information expressed in a text, whether it be narration, dialogue, or informational text | To facilitate comprehension and recall of a text |
| **Think Aloud** | Talking through a difficult passage or task by using a form of metacognition whereby the reader expresses how he/she has made sense of the text | To reflect on how readers make meaning of challenging texts and to facilitate discussion |
| **TP-CASTT\***<br>The AP Vertical Teams Guide for English (94–99) | Analyzing a poetic text by identifying and discussing Title, Paraphrase, Connotation, Attitude, Shift, Theme, and Title again | To facilitate the analysis of specific elements of a literary text, especially poetry. To show how the elements work together to create meaning |
| **Visualizing** | Forming a picture (mentally and/or literally) while reading a text | To increase reading comprehension and promote active engagement with text |
| **Word Maps** | Using a clearly defined graphic organizer such as concept circles or word webs to identify and reinforce word meanings | To provide a visual tool for identifying and remembering multiple aspects of words and word meanings |

**\*Delineates AP strategy**

# WRITING STRATEGIES

| STRATEGY | DEFINITION | PURPOSE |
|---|---|---|
| **Adding** | Making conscious choices to enhance a text by adding additional words, phrases, sentences, or ideas | To refine and clarify the writer's thoughts during revision and/or drafting |
| **Brainstorming** | Using a flexible but deliberate process of listing multiple ideas in a short period of time without excluding any idea from the preliminary list | To generate ideas, concepts, or key words that provide a focus and/or establish organization as part of the prewriting or revision process |
| **Deleting** | Providing clarity and cohesiveness for a text by eliminating words, phrases, sentences, or ideas | To refine and clarify the writer's thoughts during revision and/or drafting |
| **Drafting** | Composing a text in its initial form | To incorporate brainstormed or initial ideas into a written format |

| STRATEGY | DEFINITION | PURPOSE |
|---|---|---|
| **Free writing** | Writing freely without constraints in order to capture thinking and convey the writer's purpose | To refine and clarify the writer's thoughts, spark new ideas, and/or generate content during revision and/or drafting |
| **Generating Questions** | Clarifying and developing ideas by asking questions of the draft. May be part of self-editing or peer editing | To clarify and develop ideas in a draft; used during drafting and as part of writer response |
| **Graphic Organizer** | Organizing ideas and information visually (e.g., Venn diagrams, flowcharts, cluster maps) | To provide a visual system for organizing multiple ideas, details, and/or textual support to be included in a piece of writing |
| **Looping** | After free writing, circling one section of a text to promote elaboration or the generation of new ideas for that section. This process is repeated to further develop ideas from the newly generated segments | To refine and clarify the writer's thoughts, spark new ideas, and/or generate new content during revision and/or drafting |
| **Mapping** | Creating a graphic organizer that serves as a visual representation of the organizational plan for a written text | To generate ideas, concepts, or key words that provide a focus and/or establish organization during the prewriting, drafting, or revision process |
| **Marking the Draft** | Interacting with the draft version of a piece of writing by highlighting, underlining, color-coding, and annotating to indicate revision ideas | To encourage focused, reflective thinking about revising drafts |
| **Note-taking** | Making notes about ideas in response to text or discussions; one form is the double-entry journal in which textual evidence is recorded on the left side and personal commentary about the meaning of the evidence on the other side. | To assist in organizing key textual elements and responses noted during reading in order to generate textual support that can be incorporated into a piece of writing at a later time. Note-taking is also a reading and listening strategy. |
| **Outlining** | Using a system of numerals and letters in order to identify topics and supporting details and ensure an appropriate balance of ideas | To generate ideas, concepts, or key words that provide a focus and/or establish organization prior to writing an initial draft and/or during the revision process |
| **Quickwrite** | Writing for a short, specific amount of time in response to a prompt provided | To generate multiple ideas in a quick fashion that could be turned into longer pieces of writing at a later time (may be considered as part of the drafting process) |
| **RAFT** | Generating a new text and/or transforming a text by identifying and manipulating its component parts of Role, Audience, Format, and Topic | To generate a new text by identifying the main elements of a text during the prewriting and drafting stages of the writing process |
| **Rearranging** | Selecting components of a text and moving them to another place within the text and/or modifying the order in which the author's ideas are presented | To refine and clarify the writer's thoughts during revision and/or drafting |
| **Self-Editing/Peer Editing** | Working individually or with a partner to examine a text closely in order to identify areas that might need to be corrected for grammar, punctuation, spelling | To provide a systematic process for editing a written text to ensure correctness of identified components such as conventions of Standard English |

| STRATEGY | DEFINITION | PURPOSE |
|---|---|---|
| **Sharing and Responding** | Communicating with another person or a small group of peers who respond to a piece of writing as focused readers (not necessarily as evaluators) | To make suggestions for improvement to the work of others and/or to receive appropriate and relevant feedback on the writer's own work, used during the drafting and revision process |
| **Sketching** | Drawing or sketching ideas or ordering ideas. Includes storyboarding, visualizing | To generate and/or clarify ideas by visualizing them. May be part of prewriting |
| **Substituting/Replacing** | Replacing original words or phrases in a text with new words or phrases that achieve the desired effect | To refine and clarify the writer's thoughts during revision and/or drafting |
| **TWIST\*** <br> The AP Vertical Teams Guide for English (167–174) | Arriving at a thesis statement that incorporates the following literary elements: tone, word choice (diction), imagery, style, and theme | To craft an interpretive thesis in response to a prompt about a text |
| **Webbing** | Developing a graphic organizer that consists of a series of circles connected with lines to indicate relationships among ideas | To generate ideas, concepts, or key words that provide a focus and/or establish organization prior to writing an initial draft and/or during the revision process |
| **Writer's Checklist** | Using a co-constructed checklist (that could be written on a bookmark and/or displayed on the wall) in order to look for specific features of a writing text and check for accuracy | To focus on key areas of the writing process so that the writer can effectively revise a draft and correct mistake |
| **Writing Groups** | A type of discussion group devoted to sharing and responding of student work | To facilitate a collaborative approach to generating ideas for and revising writing |

# SPEAKING AND LISTENING STRATEGIES

| STRATEGY | DEFINITION | PURPOSE |
|---|---|---|
| **Choral Reading** | Reading text lines aloud in student groups and/or individually to present an interpretation | To develop fluency; differentiate between the reading of statements and questions; practice phrasing, pacing, and reading dialogue; show how a character's emotions are captured through vocal stress and intonation |
| **Note-taking** | Creating a record of information while listening to a speaker or reading a text | To facilitate active listening or close reading; to record and organize ideas that assist in processing information |
| **Oral Reading** | Reading aloud one's own text or the texts of others (e.g., echo reading, choral reading, paired readings) | To share one's own work or the work of others; build fluency and increase confidence in presenting to a group |
| **Rehearsal** | Encouraging multiple practices of a piece of text prior to a performance | To provide students with an opportunity to clarify the meaning of a text prior to a performance as they refine the use of dramatic conventions (e.g., gestures, vocal interpretations, facial expressions) |
| **Role-Playing** | Assuming the role or persona of a character | To develop the voice, emotions, and mannerisms of a character to facilitate improved comprehension of a text |

# COLLABORATIVE STRATEGIES

| STRATEGY | DEFINITION | PURPOSE |
|---|---|---|
| **Discussion Groups** | Engaging in an interactive, small group discussion, often with an assigned role; to consider a topic, text, or question | To gain new understanding of or insight into a text from multiple perspectives |
| **Think-Pair-Share** | Pairing with a peer to share ideas; before sharing ideas and discussion with a larger group | To construct meaning about a topic or question; to test thinking in relation to the ideas of others; to prepare for a discussion with a larger group |

# Graphic Organizer Directory

## English Language Arts Graphic Organizers

Audience Notes and Feedback

Definition and Reflection

Editor's/Writer's Checklist

Evaluating Online Sources

Fallacies 101

OPTIC

Presenting Scoring Guide

RAFT

SMELL

SOAPSTone

TP-CASTT Analysis

TP-CASTT

Verbal & Visual Word Association

Web Organizer

Word Map

## English Language Development Graphic Organizers

Active Listening Feedback

Active Listening Notes

Cause and Effect

Character Map

Collaborative Dialogue

Conclusion Builder

Conflict Map

Conversation for Quickwrite

Idea and Argument Evaluator

Idea Connector

Key Idea and Details Chart

Narrative Analysis and Writing

Notes for Reading Independently

Opinion Builder

Paragraph Frame for Conclusions

Paragraph Frame for Sequencing

Paraphrasing and Summarizing Map

Peer Editing

Persuasive/Argument Writing Map

Roots and Affixes Brainstorm

Round Table Discussion

Sequence of Events Time Line

Text Structure Stairs

Unknown Word Solver

Venn Diagram for Writing a Comparison

Word Choice Analyzer

# Audience Notes and Feedback

| Scoring Criteria | Notes/Feedback |
|---|---|
| Introduction / Conclusion | |
| Timing | |
| Voice | |
| Eyes / Gestures | |
| Use of Media, Visuals, Props | |
| Audience Engagement | |

# Definition and Reflection

| Academic Vocabulary Word |
| --- |

| Definition in own words |
| --- |

| Graphic Representation (literal or symbolic) |
| --- |

**My experiences with this concept:**

- I haven't really thought about this concept.

  _____

- I have only thought about this concept in Language Arts class.

  _____

- I have applied this concept in other classes.

  _____

- I have applied this concept outside of school.

  _____

**My level of understanding:**

- I am still trying to understand this concept.

  _____

- I am familiar with this concept, but I am not comfortable applying it.

  _____

- I am very comfortable with this concept and I know how to apply it.

  _____

- I could teach this concept to another classmate.

  _____

# Editor's / Writer's Checklist

## Organizational Elements

| | |
|---|---|
| | Does your title express the topic and engage the reader? |
| | Do you have an engaging hook or lead to open your essay? |
| | Do you end your introductory paragraph with a thesis statement that states an opinion on a topic and suggests an organization? |
| | Do you have topic sentences that relate to the thesis statement? |
| | Do your body paragraphs contain detail and commentary to support your topic sentences? |
| | Do you include transitions to link ideas? |
| | Do your body paragraphs contain concluding sentences that also act as transitional statements to the next paragraph? |
| | Have you ended your essay with a strong conclusion that comments on the significance of your thesis ideas? |

## Sentence Elements

| | |
|---|---|
| | Have you revised to make sure all sentences are complete sentences? |
| | Do your sentences contain vivid verbs and descriptive adjectives when appropriate? |
| | Is the verb tense of your writing consistent? Do the subject and verb agree? |
| | Is pronoun use appropriate and consistent? |
| | Is parallel structure used to advantage and when appropriate? |
| | Do you vary sentence beginnings? Have you started sentences with a subordinate clause? |
| | Are your sentence types (simple, compound, complex) and lengths varied for interest and emphasis? |
| | Have you tried to include figurative and sensory language for effect? |
| | Have you used appositives when appropriate? |
| | Have you checked punctuation use for correctness, especially for appositives, complex sentences and parallel structure? |
| | Have you incorporated and punctuated quoted material correctly? |

# Evaluating Online Sources

**The URL**
- What is its domain?
    - .com = a for-profit organization
    - .gov, .mil, .us (or other country code) = a government site
    - .edu = affiliated with an educational institution
    - .org = a nonprofit organization

- Is this URL someone's personal page?
- Why might using information from a personal page be a problem?
- Do you recognize who is publishing this page?
- If not, you may need to investigate further to determine whether the publisher is an expert on the topic.

**Sponsor:**
- Does the website easily give information about the organization or group that sponsors it?
- Does it have a link (often called "About Us") that leads you to that information?
- What do you learn?

**Timeliness:**
- When was the page last updated (usually this is posted at the top or bottom of the page)?
- How current a page is may indicate how accurate or useful the information in it will be.

**Purpose:**
- What is the purpose of the page?
- What is its target audience?
- Does it present information or opinion?
- Is it primarily objective or subjective?
- How do you know?

**Author:**
- What credentials does the author have?
- Is this person or group considered an authority on the topic?

**Links**
- Does the page provide links?
- Do they work?
- Are they helpful?
- Are they objective or subjective?

# Fallacies 101

| | |
|---|---|
| **Ad Hominem (Against the Man)/ Genetic Fallacy** | "My opponent, a vicious and evil person, should absolutely never be elected to office."<br>The Volkswagen Beetle is an evil car because it was originally designed by Hitler's army. |
| **Straw Man** | People say that Mark Twain was a good author, but I disagree. If he was such a good author, why didn't he write using his own name? |
| **Appeal To Pity** | "Jonathan couldn't have cheated! He's such a nice boy and he tries so hard." |
| **Ad Baculum (Scare Tactics)** | If you don't support the party's tax plan, you and your family will be reduced to poverty.<br>Chairman of the Board: "All those opposed to my arguments for the opening of a new department, signify by saying, 'I resign.'" |
| **Slippery Slope Fallacy** | "If I don't study for the test, then I'm going to get a bad grade. If I get a bad grade on the test, I'll get a bad grade in the class, and I won't get into a good college. Getting into a good college is the most important part of getting a good job; so if I don't study for the test, I won't get a good job!" |
| **Argument from Outrage** | The airline canceled my flight an hour before takeoff and wouldn't tell me why. This is an outrage! We should all boycott the company. |
| **Red Herring** | The new dress code banning slogan t-shirts isn't fair. Students have the right to free speech just like anyone else. |
| **Hasty Generalization** | They hit two home runs in the first inning of the season. This team is going all the way to the World Series! |
| **Post Hoc** | I ate a turkey sandwich and now I feel tired, so the turkey must have made me tired. |
| **Ad Populum** | You should turn to channel 6. It's the most watched channel this year. There is always a long line at that restaurant, so the food must be really good. |
| **Either/Or** | We can either stop using cars or destroy Earth.<br>We must drill now or we'll remain dependent on foreign oil suppliers. |

# OPTIC

Title of Piece:

Artist: _____          Type of artwork: _____

| | |
|---|---|
| **O**verview | Look at the artwork for at least 10 seconds. Generate questions; e.g., What is the subject? What strikes you as interesting, odd, etc.? What is happening? |
| **P**arts | Look closely at the artwork, making note of important elements and details. Ask additional questions, such as: Who are the figures? What is the setting and time period? What symbols are present? What historical information would aid understanding of this piece? |
| **T**itle | Consider what the title and any written elements of the text suggest about meaning. How does the title relate to what is portrayed? |
| **I**nterrelationships | Look for connections between and among the title, caption, and the parts of the art. How are the different elements related? |
| **C**onclusion | Form a conclusion about the meaning/theme of the text. Remember the questions you asked when you first examined it. Be prepared to support your conclusions with evidence. |

# Presenting Scoring Guide

| Scoring Criteria | Exemplary | Proficient | Emerging | Incomplete |
|---|---|---|---|---|
| **Introduction / Conclusion** | The presentation<br>• provides a clear, engaging, and appropriate introduction to the topic or performance<br>• provides a clear, engaging, and appropriate conclusion that closes, summarizes, draws connections to broader themes, or supports the ideas presented. | The presentation<br>• provides a clear and appropriate introduction to the topic or performance<br>• provides a clear and appropriate conclusion that closes, summarizes, draws connections to broader themes, or supports the ideas presented. | The presentation<br>• provides an adequate introduction to the topic or performance<br>• provides an adequate conclusion that closes, summarizes, draws connections to broader themes, or supports the ideas presented. | The presentation<br>• does not provide an introduction to the topic or performance<br>• does not provide a conclusion that closes, summarizes, draws connections to broader themes, or supports the ideas presented. |
| **Timing** | The presentation<br>• thoroughly delivers its intended message within the allotted time<br>• is thoughtfully and appropriately paced throughout. | The presentation<br>• mostly delivers its intended message within the allotted time<br>• is appropriately paced most of the time. | The presentation<br>• delivers some of its intended message within the allotted time<br>• is sometimes not paced appropriately. | The presentation<br>• does not deliver its intended message within the allotted time<br>• is not paced appropriately. |
| **Voice (Volume, Pronunciation)** | The presentation<br>• is delivered with adequate volume enabling audience members to fully comprehend what is said<br>• is delivered with clear pronunciation. | The presentation<br>• is delivered with adequate volume enabling audience members to mostly comprehend what is said<br>• is delivered with mostly clear pronunciation. | The presentation<br>• is delivered with somewhat adequate volume enabling audience members to comprehend some of what is said<br>• is delivered with somewhat clear pronunciation. | The presentation<br>• is not delivered with adequate volume, so that audience members are unable to comprehend what is said<br>• is delivered with unclear pronunciation. |
| **Eyes/Gestures** | The presentation<br>• is delivered with appropriate eye contact that helps engage audience members<br>• makes use of thoughtfully selected gestures and/or body language to convey meaning. | The presentation<br>• is delivered with some appropriate eye contact that helps engage audience members<br>• makes use of gestures and/or body language to convey meaning. | The presentation<br>• is delivered with occasional eye contact that sometimes engages audience members<br>• makes some use of gestures and/or body language to convey meaning. | The presentation<br>• is not delivered with eye contact to engage audience members<br>• makes little or no use of gestures and/or body language to convey meaning. |
| **Use of Media, Visuals, Props** | The presentation<br>• makes use of highly engaging visuals, multimedia, and/or props that enhance delivery. | The presentation<br>• makes use of visuals, multimedia, and/or props that enhance delivery. | The presentation<br>• makes use of some visuals, multimedia, and/or props that somewhat enhance delivery. | The presentation<br>• makes use of few or no visuals, multimedia, and/or props that enhance delivery. |
| **Audience Engagement** | The presentation<br>• includes thoughtful and appropriate interactions with and responses to audience members. | The presentation<br>• includes appropriate interactions with and responses to audience members. | The presentation<br>• includes a few interactions with and responses to audience members. | The presentation<br>• does not include interactions with and responses to audience members. |

# RAFT

| | |
|---|---|
| **Role** | Who or what are you as a writer? |
| **Audience** | As a writer, to whom are you writing? |
| **Format** | As a writer, what format would be appropriate for your audience (essay, letter, speech, poem, etc.)? |
| **Topic** | As a writer, what is the subject of your writing? What points do you want to make? |

# SMELL

**Sender-Receiver Relationship**—Who are the senders and receivers of the message, and what is their relationship (consider what different audiences the text may be addressing)?

**Message**—What is a literal summary of the content? What is the meaning/significance of this information?

**Emotional Strategies**—What emotional appeals (*pathos*) are included? What seems to be their desired effect?

**Logical Strategies**—What logical arguments/appeals (*logos*) are included? What is their effect?

**Language**—What specific language is used to support the message? How does it affect the text's effectiveness? Consider both images and actual words.

# SOAPSTone

| SOAPSTone | Analysis | Textual Support |
|---|---|---|
| **S**<br>What does the reader know about the writer? | | |
| **O**<br>What are the circumstances surrounding this text? | | |
| **A**<br>Who is the target audience? | | |
| **P**<br>Why did the author write this text? | | |
| **S**<br>What is the topic? | | |
| **T**one<br>What is the author's tone, or attitude? | | |

# TP-CASTT Analysis

**Poem Title:**

**Author:**

**T**itle: Make a Prediction. What do you think the title means before you read the poem?

**P**araphrase: Translate the poem in your own words. What is the poem about? Rephrase difficult sections word for word.

**C**onnotation: Look beyond the literal meaning of key words and images to their associations.

**A**ttitude: What is the speaker's attitude? What is the author's attitude? How does the author feel about the speaker, about other characters, about the subject?

**S**hifts: Where do the shifts in tone, setting, voice, etc., occur? Look for time and place, keywords, punctuation, stanza divisions, changes in length or rhyme, and sentence structure. What is the purpose of each shift? How do they contribute to effect and meaning?

**T**itle: Reexamine the title. What do you think it means now in the context of the poem?

**T**heme: Think of the literal and metaphorical layers of the poem. Then determine the overall theme. The theme must be written in a complete sentence.

# TP-CASTT

**Poem Title:**

**Author:**

| | | |
|---|---|---|
| **T** | | |
| **P** | | |
| **C** | | |
| **A** | | |
| **S** | | |
| **T** | | |
| **T** | | |

# Verbal & Visual Word Association

| Definition in Your Own Words | Important Elements |
|---|---|
| | |

**Academic Vocabulary Word**

| Visual Representation | Personal Association |
|---|---|
| | |

# Web Organizer

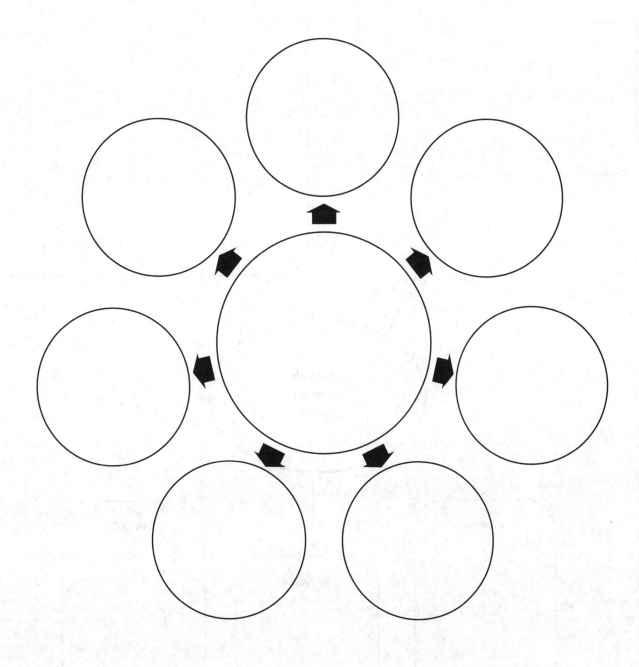

# Word Map

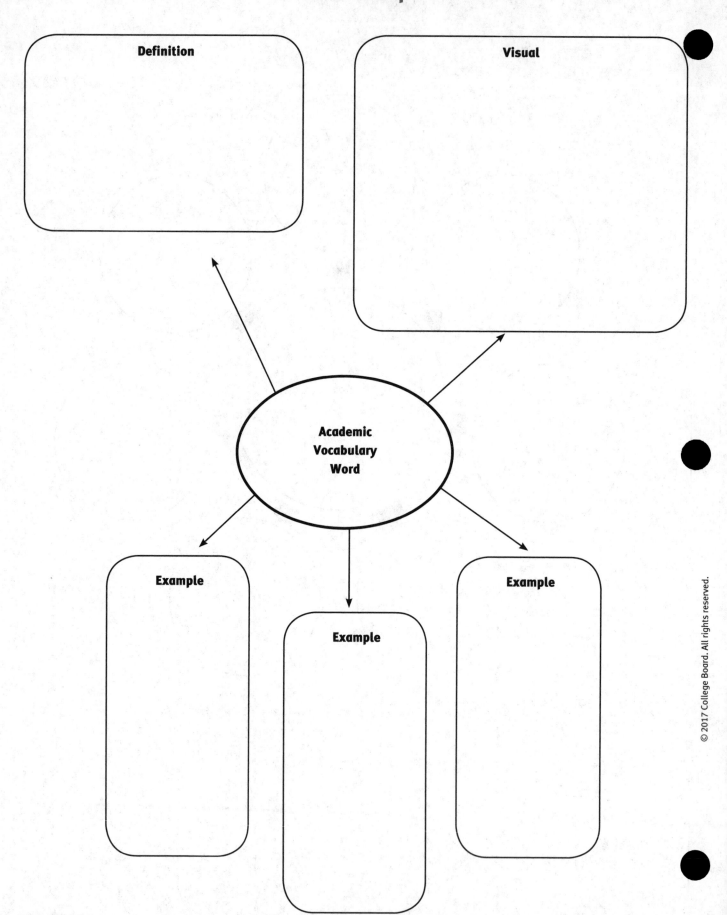

**Definition**

**Visual**

**Academic
Vocabulary
Word**

**Example**

**Example**

**Example**

# Active Listening Feedback

Presenter's name: _____

## Content

What is the presenter's purpose? _____

What is the presenter's main point? _____

Do you agree with the presenter? Why or why not? _____

_____

_____

## Form

Did the presenter use a clear, loud voice? ☐ yes ☐ no

Did the presenter make eye contact? ☐ yes ☐ no

**One thing I really liked about the presentation:**

_____

_____

_____

**One question I still have:**

_____

_____

_____

**Other comments or notes:**

# Active Listening Notes

Title: _____

**Who?**

**What?**

**Where?**

**When?**

**Why?**

**How?**

# Cause and Effect

Title: _____

**Cause:** What happened?

➤ **Effect:** An effect of this is

**Cause:** What happened?

➤ **Effect:** An effect of this is

**Cause:** What happened?

➤ **Effect:** An effect of this is

**Cause:** What happened?

➤ **Effect:** An effect of this is

# Character Map

Character name: _____

**What does the character look like?**

**How does the character act?**

**What do other characters say or think about the character?**

# Collaborative Dialogue

Topic: _____

| **"Wh-" Prompts** |
| Who?   What?   Where? |
| When?   Why? |

**Speaker 1**

**Speaker 2**

# Conclusion Builder

**Evidence**

**Evidence**

**Evidence**

**Based on this evidence, I can conclude**

# Conflict Map

Title: _____

---

**What is the main conflict in this story?**

---

**What causes this conflict?**

---

**How is the conflict resolved?**

---

**What are some other ways the conflict could have been resolved?**

# Conversation for Quickwrite

**1.** Turn to a partner and restate the quickwrite in your own words.

**2.** Brainstorm key words to use in your quickwrite response.

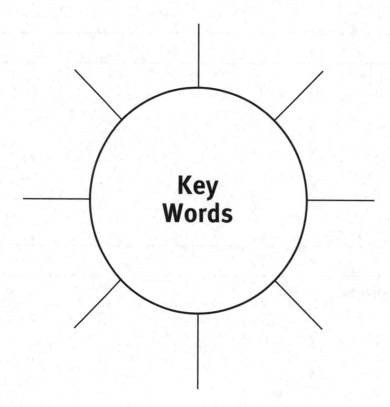

**Key Words**

**3.** Take turns explaining your quickwrite response to your partner. Try using some of the key words.

**4.** On your own, write a response to the quickwrite.

_____ DATE _____

# Idea and Argument Evaluator

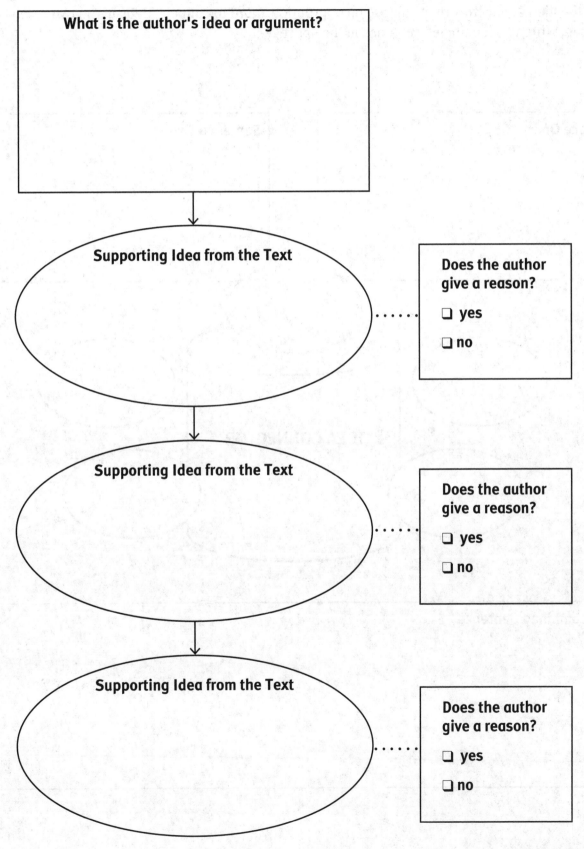

What is the author's idea or argument?

Supporting Idea from the Text

Does the author give a reason?

❏ yes

❏ no

Supporting Idea from the Text

Does the author give a reason?

❏ yes

❏ no

Supporting Idea from the Text

Does the author give a reason?

❏ yes

❏ no

# Idea Connector

**Directions:** Write two simple sentences about the same topic. Next, write transition words around the Idea Connector. Then, choose an appropriate word to connect ideas in the two sentences. Write your combined sentence in the space below.

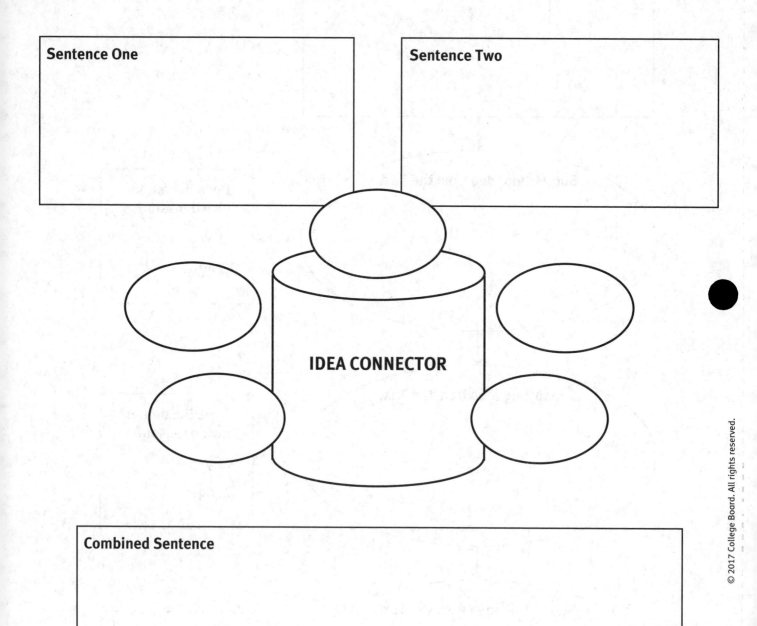

**Sentence One**

**Sentence Two**

**IDEA CONNECTOR**

**Combined Sentence**

# Key Idea and Details Chart

Title/Topic _____

Key Idea _____

_____

_____

Supporting Detail 1 _____

_____

_____

Supporting Detail 2 _____

_____

_____

Supporting Detail 3 _____

_____

_____

Supporting Detail 4 _____

_____

_____

Restate topic sentence: _____

_____

Concluding sentence: _____

_____

_____

# Narrative Analysis and Writing

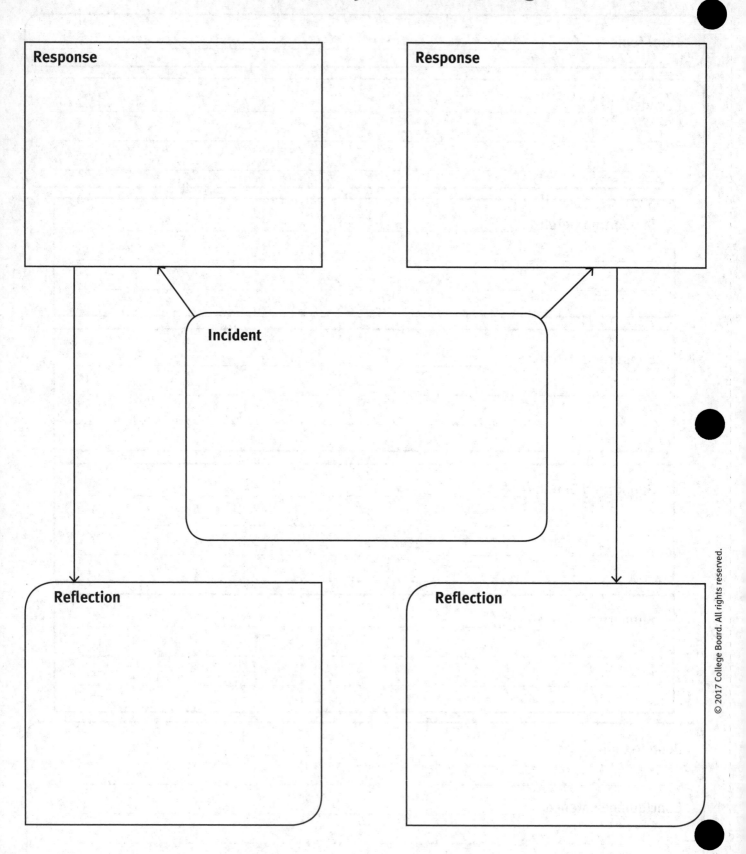

Response

Response

Incident

Reflection

Reflection

NAME _____ DATE _____

# Notes for Reading Independently

Title: _____

| The main characters are | The setting is | The main conflict is |
|---|---|---|
| | | |

| The climax happens when | The conflict is resolved when |
|---|---|
| | |

**My brief summary of** _____

# Opinion Builder

**Reason**

**Reason**

Based on these reasons, my opinion is

**Reason**

**Reason**

# Paragraph Frame for Conclusions

© 2017 College Board. All rights reserved.

**Conclusion Words and Phrases**

shows that

based on

suggests that

leads to

indicates that

influences

The _____ (story, poem, play, passage, etc.)

shows that *(helps us to conclude that)* _____

_____

_____

There are several reasons why. First, _____

_____

_____

_____

_____

A second reason is _____

_____

_____

_____

_____

Finally, _____

_____

_____

_____

In conclusion, _____

_____

_____

_____

# Paragraph Frame for Sequencing

**Sequence Words and Phrases**

at the beginning

in the first place

as a result

later

eventually

in the end

lastly

In the _____ (story, poem, play, passage, etc.)

there are three important _____

(events, steps, directions, etc.)

First, _____

_____

_____

_____

_____

Second, _____

_____

_____

_____

_____

Third, _____

_____

_____

_____

_____

Finally, _____

_____

_____

_____

_____

NAME _____ DATE _____

# Paraphrasing and Summarizing Map

| What does the text say? | How can I say it in my own words? |
| --- | --- |
|  |  |
|  |  |
|  |  |

**How can I use my own words to summarize the text?**

# Peer Editing

Writer's name: _____

Did the writer answer the prompt? ☐ yes ☐ no

Did the writer provide evidence to support his or her reasons? ☐ yes ☐ no

Is the writing organized in a way that makes sense? ☐ yes ☐ no

Did the writer vary sentence structures to make the writing more interesting? ☐ yes ☐ no

Are there any spelling or punctuation mistakes? ☐ yes ☐ no

Are there any grammar errors? ☐ yes ☐ no

**Two things I really liked about the writer's story:**

1. _____

_____

_____

2. _____

_____

_____

**One thing I think the writer could do to improve the writing:**

1. _____

_____

_____

**Other comments or notes:**

# Persuasive/Argument Writing Map

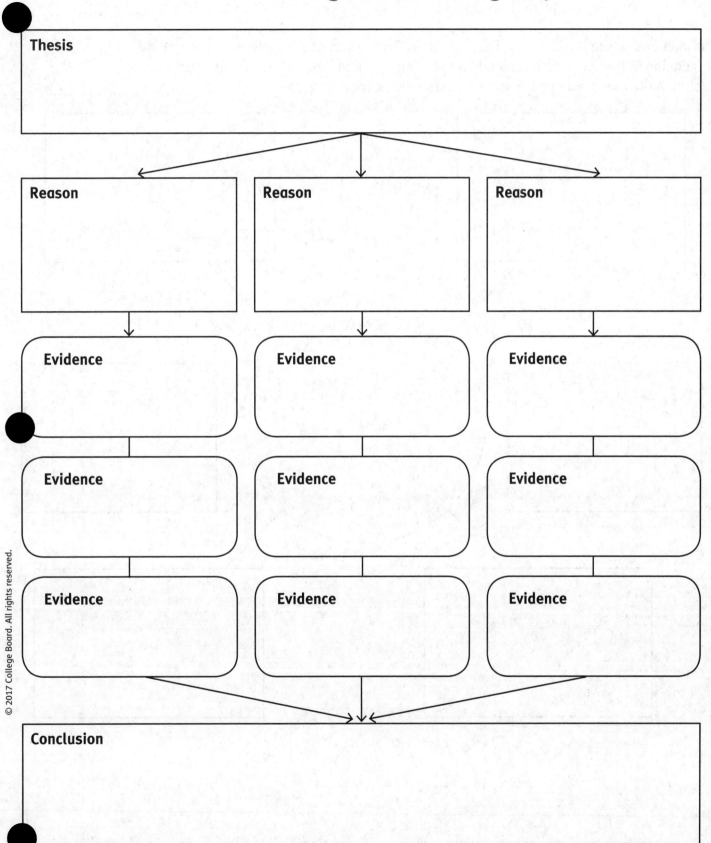

**Thesis**

**Reason**

**Reason**

**Reason**

**Evidence**

**Evidence**

**Evidence**

**Evidence**

**Evidence**

**Evidence**

**Evidence**

**Evidence**

**Evidence**

**Conclusion**

# Roots and Affixes Brainstorm

**Directions:** Write the root or affix in the circle. Brainstorm or use a dictionary to find the meaning of the root or affix and add it to the circle. Then, find words that use that root or affix. Write one word in each box. Write a sentence for each word.

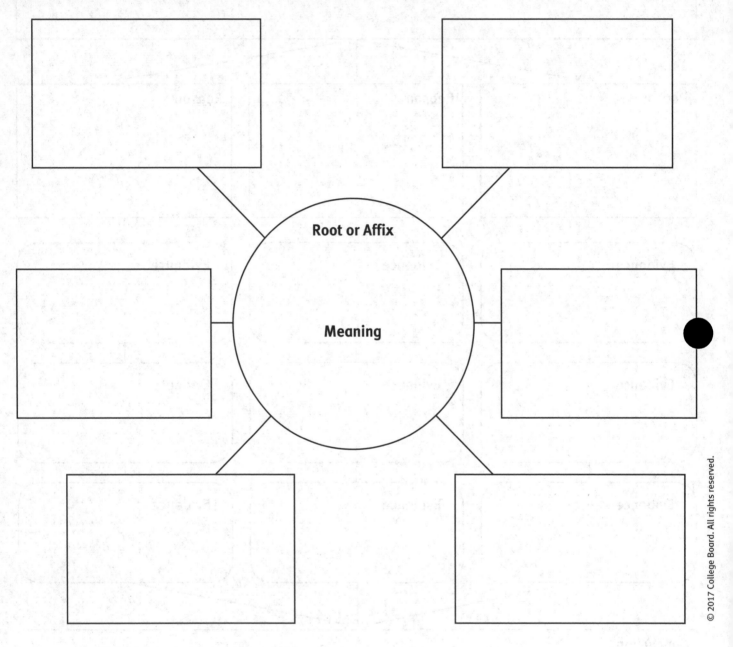

DATE _____

# Round Table Discussion

**Directions:** Write the topic in the center box. One student begins by stating his or her ideas while the student to the left takes notes. Then the next student speaks while the student to his or her left takes notes, and so on.

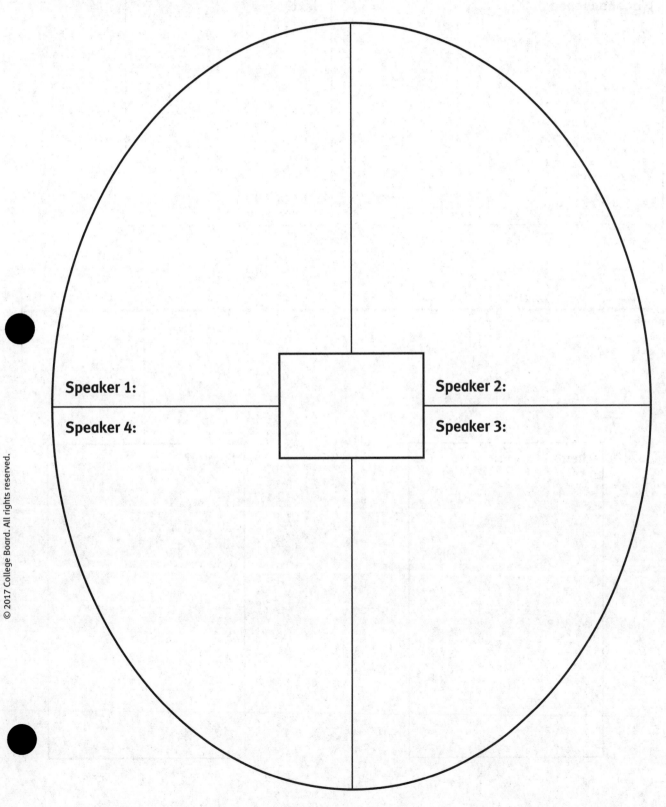

Speaker 1:

Speaker 2:

Speaker 4:

Speaker 3:

# Sequence of Events Time Line

Title: _____

**What happened first?**

**Next?**

Beginning                    Middle                    End

**Then?**

**Finally?**

# Text Structure Stairs

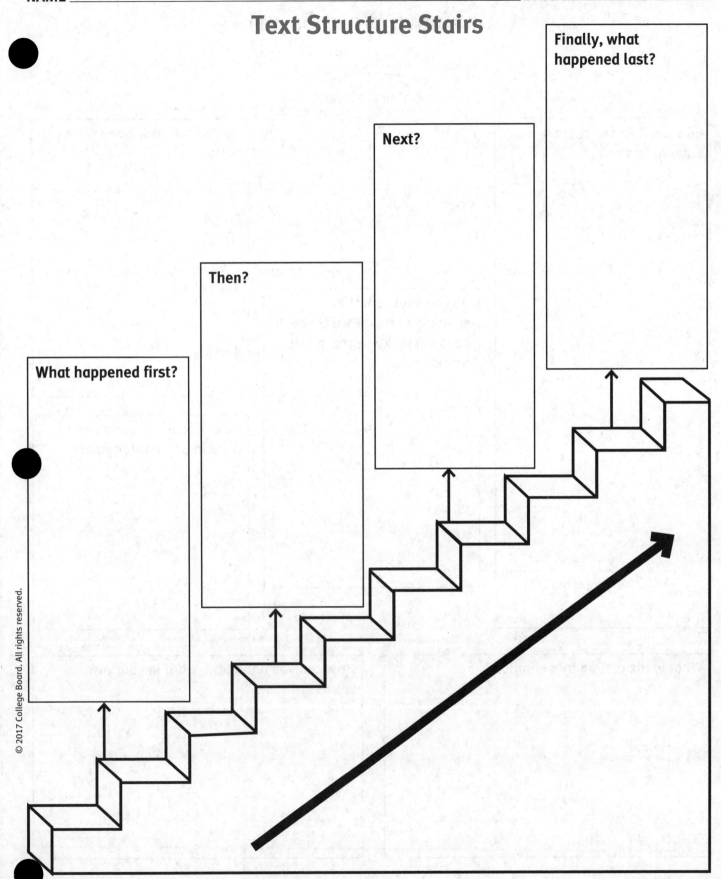

**Finally, what happened last?**

**Next?**

**Then?**

**What happened first?**

# Unknown Word Solver

**Unknown Word**

**Can you find any context clues? List them.**

**Do you recognize any word parts?**

**Prefix:**

**Root Word:**

**Suffix:**

**Do you know another meaning of this word that does not make sense in this context?**

**Does it look or sound like a word in another language?**

**What is the dictionary definition?**

**How can you define the word in your own words?**

NAME _____ DATE _____

# Venn Diagram for Writing a Comparison

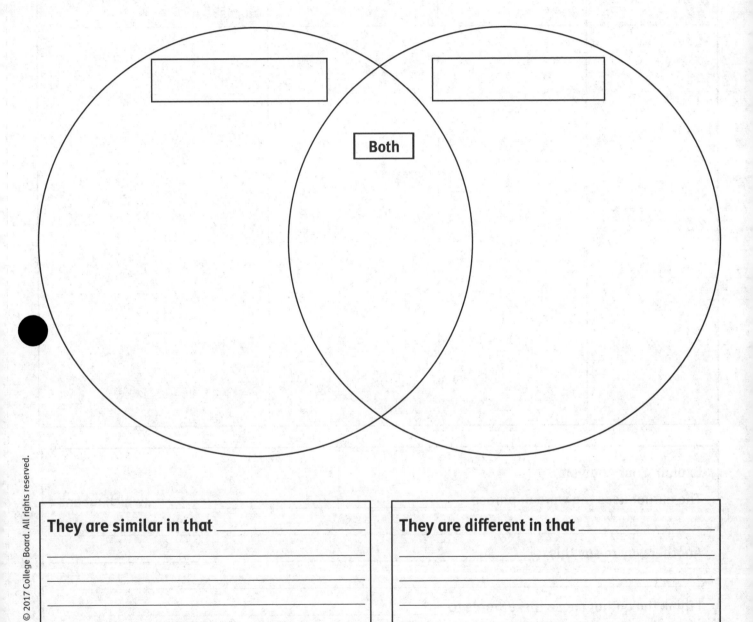

Both

**They are similar in that** _____

_____

_____

_____

_____

_____

_____

**They are different in that** _____

_____

_____

_____

_____

_____

_____

# Word Choice Analyzer

| Word or phrase from the text | What does the word or phrase mean? | What is another way to say the same thing? | What effect did the author produce by choosing these words? |
|---|---|---|---|
| | | | |

**Explain Your Analysis**

The author uses the word or phrase _____ , which means

_____

Another way to say this is _____

_____

I think the author chose these words to _____

_____

_____

One way I can modify this sentence to add detail is to _____

_____

# Glossary / Glosario

## A

**active-voice verbs:** verbs for which the subject performs the action

**verbos en voz activa:** forma verbal que indica que el sujeto realiza la acción

**advance:** to move or push forward; for example, advance the plot of a story

**avanzar:** mover hacia adelante; por ejemplo, cuando avanza el argumento de un cuento

**advertising techniques:** specific methods used in print, graphics, or videos to persuade people to buy a product or use a service

**técnicas publicitarias:** métodos específicos usados en impresos, gráfica o videos para persuadir a las personas a comprar un producto o usar un servicio

**advocate:** speak or write in favor of something by publicly recommending or supporting it through some action

**abogar por:** hablar o escribir a favor de algo recomendándolo o apoyándolo públicamente mediante alguna acción

**advocating:** in an argument, speaking or writing in favor of a specific claim

**abogar:** defender por escrito o de palabra un punto específico en un debate o discusión

**alliteration:** the repetition of initial consonant sounds in words that are close together

**aliteración:** repetición de sonidos consonánticos iniciales en palabras cercanas

**allusion:** a reference made to a well-known person, event, or place from history, music, art, or another literary work

**alusión:** referencia a una persona, evento o lugar muy conocidos de la historia, música, arte u otra obra literaria

**analogy:** a comparison between two things for the purpose of drawing conclusions about one based on its similarities to the other

**analogía:** comparación entre dos cosas con el propósito de sacar conclusiones sobre las semejanzas que una cosa tiene a otra

**anaphora:** the repetition of the same word or group of words at the beginnings of two or more clauses or lines

**anáfora:** repetición de la misma palabra o grupo de palabras al comienzo de una o más cláusulas o versos

**anecdotal evidence:** evidence based on personal accounts of incidents

**evidencia anecdótica:** evidencia basada en relatos personales de los hechos

**annotated bibliography:** a list of sources used in research along with comments or summaries about each source

**bibliografía anotada:** lista de fuentes utilizadas en la investigación, junto con comentarios o resúmenes acerca de cada fuente

**antagonist:** the character who opposes or struggles against the main character

**antagonista:** personaje que se opone o lucha contra el personaje principal

**aphorism:** a short statement expressing an opinion or general truth

**aforismo:** afirmación corta que expresa una opinión o verdad general

**archetype:** a universal symbol—images, characters, motifs, or patterns—that recurs in the myths, dreams, oral traditions, songs, literature, and other texts of peoples widely separated by time and place

**arquetipos:** símbolos universales—imágenes, personajes, motivos o patrones—reiterativos en los mitos, el arte y la literatura alrededor del mundo

**archival footage:** film footage taken from another, previously recorded, source

**cortometraje de archivo:** fragmento de película tomada de otra fuente grabada previamente

**argument:** a set of statements, each supporting the other, that presents a position or viewpoint

**argumento:** forma de redacción que presenta una opinión o idea particular y la apoya con evidencia

**argumentation:** the act or process of arguing that includes the *hook* (quotation, example, or idea that catches readers' attention), *claim* (the opinion or thesis statement), *support* (evidence in the form of facts, statistics, examples, anecdotes, or expert opinions), *concession* (the writer's admission that the other side of the argument has a valid point), *refutation* (a well-reasoned denial of an opponent's point, based on solid evidence), and *call to action* (a request of readers)

**argumentación:** la estructura de una argumentación incluye el *gancho* (cita, ejemplo o idea que capta la atención del lector), *afirmación* (declaración de opinión o tesis), *apoyo* (evidencia en forma de hechos, estadísticas, ejemplos, anécdotas u opiniones de expertos), *concesión* (admisión por parte del escritor de que la otra parte del debate tiene un punto válido), *refutación* (negación bien razonada de una opinión del oponente, basada en evidencia sólida) y *llamado a la acción* (petición inspirada de lectores)

**argument by analogy:** a comparison of two similar situations, implying that the outcome of one will resemble the outcome of the other

**argumento por analogía:** comparación de dos situaciones semejantes, infiriendo que el resultado de será parecido al resultado de la otra

**artifact:** an object made by a human being, typically an item that has cultural or historical significance
**artefacto:** objeto hecho por un ser humano, generalmente un objeto que tiene importancia cultural o histórica

**artistic license:** the practice of rewording of dialogue, alteration of language, or reordering of the plot of a text created by another artist
**licencia artística:** la costumbre de reformular un diálogo, aliteración de palabras, o arreglo de la trama de un texto creado por otro artista

**aside:** a short speech spoken by an actor directly to the audience and unheard by other actors on stage
**aparte:** alocución breve dicha por un actor directamente al público y que no escuchan los demás actores que están en el escenario

**assonance:** the repetition of similar vowel sounds in accented syllables, followed by different consonant sounds, in words that are close together
**asonancia:** repetición de sonidos vocálicos similares en sílabas acentuadas, seguida de diferentes sonidos consonánticos, en palabras que están cercanas

**audience:** the intended readers, listeners, or viewers of specific types of written, spoken, or visual texts
**público:** lectores objetivo, oyentes o espectadores de tipos específicos de textos escritos, hablados o visuales

**audience analysis:** determination of the characteristics and knowledge of the people who will read a work or hear a speech
**análisis del público:** determinar las características y conocimiento de las personas que leen una obra o escuchan un discurso

**author's purpose:** the specific reason or reasons for the writing; what the author hopes to accomplish
**propósito del autor:** razón específica para escribir; lo que el autor espera lograr

**autobiography:** an account written by a person about his or her own life
**autobiografía:** narración de una vida escrita por el propio sujeto del relato

# B

**balanced sentence:** a sentence that presents ideas of equal weight in similar grammatical forms to emphasize the similarity or difference between the ideas
**oración balanceada:** oración que representa ideas de igual peso en formas gramaticales similares para enfatizar la semejanza o diferencia entre las ideas

**bias:** an inclination or mental leaning for or against something; prevents impartial judgment
**sesgo:** inclinación o tendencia mental a favor o en contra de algo, lo que impide una opinión imparcial

**bibliography:** a list of the sources used for research
**bibliografía:** lista de fuentes primarias en la preparación de un texto

**biography:** a description or account of events from a person's life, written by another person
**biografía:** descripción o narración de la vida de una persona o los sucesos importantes de su vida escritos por otra persona

**blank verse:** unrhymed verse
**verso libre:** verso que no tiene rima

**blocking:** in drama, the way actors position themselves in relation to one another, the audience, and the objects on the stage
**bloqueo:** en drama, el modo en que los actores se sitúan entre sí, con el público y los objetos en el escenario

**book review:** a formal assessment or examination of a book
**reseña de libro:** evaluación o examinación formal de un libro

# C

**call to action:** a restatement of the claim and what the writer wants the reader to do
**llamado a la acción:** repetición de la afirmación y lo que el escritor quiere que el lector responda

**caricature:** a visual or verbal representation in which characteristics or traits are exaggerated or distorted for emphasis
**caricatura:** representación visual o verbal en la que las características o rasgos se exageran o se distorsionan para dar énfasis

**catalog poem:** a poem that uses repetition and variation in the creation of a list, or catalog, of objects or desires, plans, or memories
**lista en poema:** poema que usa repetición y variación en la creación de una lista o catálogo, de objetos o deseos o planes o memorias

**cause:** an action, event, or situation that brings about a particular result
**causa:** acción, suceso o situación que produce un resultado particular

**censor:** to examine materials for objectionable content
**censurar:** examinar materiales por contenido desagradable

**censorship:** the act of suppressing public speech or publication of materials deemed to be offensive by the censor
**censura:** acto de suprimir un discurso público o publicación de materiales considerados ofensivos por un censor

**challenge:** to oppose or refute a statement that has been made
**poner en duda:** oponerse a algo o refutar una declaración que alguien ha hecho

**characterization:** the methods a writer uses to develop characters
**caracterización:** métodos que usa un escritor para desarrollar personajes

**characters:** people, animals, or imaginary creatures that take part in the action of a story. A short story usually centers on a *main character* but may also contain one or more *minor characters*, who are not as complex, but whose thoughts, words, or actions move the plot along. A character who is *dynamic* changes in response to the events of the narrative; a character who is *static* remains the same throughout the narrative. A *round* character is fully developed—he or she shows a variety of traits; a *flat* character is one-dimensional, usually showing only one trait.

**personajes:** personas, animales o criaturas imaginarias que participan en la acción de un cuento. Un cuento corto normalmente se centra en un *personaje principal*, pero puede también contener uno o más *personajes secundarios*, que no son tan complejos, pero cuyos pensamientos, palabras o acciones hacen avanzar la trama. Un personaje que es *dinámico* cambia según los eventos del relato; un personaje que es *estático* permanece igual a lo largo del relato. Un personaje *complejo* está completamente desarrollado: muestra una diversidad de rasgos; un personaje *simple* es unidimensional, mostrando normalmente sólo un rasgo.

**character sketch:** a brief description of a literary character
**reseña del personaje:** breve descripción de un personaje literario

**chorus:** in traditional or classic drama, a group of performers who speak as one and comment on the action of the play
**coro:** en el drama tradicional o clásico, grupo de actores que hablan al unísono y comentan la acción de la obra teatral

**cinematic elements:** the features of cinema—movies, film, video—that contribute to its form and structure: *angle* (the view from which the image is shot), *framing* (how a scene is structured), *lighting* (the type of lighting used to light a scene), *mise en scène* (the composition, setting, or staging of an image, or a scene in a film), and *sound* (the sound effects and music accompanying each scene)
**elementos cinematográficos:** las características del cine—películas, filmaciones, video—que contribuyen a darle forma y estructura: *angulación* (vista desde la cual se toma la imagen), *encuadre* (cómo se estructura una escena), iluminación (tipo de *iluminación* que se usa para una escena), y *montaje* (composición, ambiente o escenificación de una imagen o escena en una película), y *sonido* (efectos sonoros y música que acompañan cada escena)

**cinematic techniques:** the methods a director uses to communicate meaning and to evoke particular emotional responses from viewers
**técnicas cinematográficas:** métodos que emplea un director para comunicar un significado y evocar cierta respuesta emocional de los videntes

**claim:** a position taken on an arguable viewpoint
**afirmación:** declaración de opinión (o tesis) que asevera una idea o establece un debate hacia una posición específica

**cliché:** an overused expression or idea
**cliché:** expresión o idea que se usa en exceso

**climax:** the point at which the action reaches its peak; the point of greatest interest or suspense in a story; the turning point at which the outcome of a conflict is decided
**clímax:** punto en el que la acción alcanza su punto culminante; punto de mayor interés en un cuento; punto de inflexión en el que se decide el resultado del conflicto

**coherence:** the quality of unity or logical connection among ideas; the clear and orderly presentation of ideas in a paragraph or essay
**coherencia:** calidad de unidad o relación lógica entre las ideas; presentación clara y ordenada de las ideas en un párrafo o ensayo

**commentary:** in an expository essay or paragraph, the explanation of the importance or relevance of supporting details and the way the details support the larger analysis
**comentario:** expresión oral o escrita de opiniones o explicaciones sobre una situación, tema o suceso

**complementary:** combined in a way that enhances all elements combined
**complementario:** combinar dos o más elementos de una manera que mejora los dos

**complex character:** a character that has multiple or conflicting motivations
**personaje complejo:** personaje que tiene motivaciones multiples o conflictivas

**complex sentence:** a sentence containing one independent clause and one or more subordinate clauses
**oración compleja:** oración que contiene una cláusula independiente y una o más cláusulas subordinadas

**complications:** the events in a plot that develop a conflict; the complications move the plot forward in its rising action
**complicaciones:** sucesos de una trama que desarrollan el conflicto; las complicaciones hacen avanzar la trama en su acción ascendente

**compound sentence:** a sentence containing two independent clauses
**oración compuesta:** oración que contiene dos cláusulas independientes

**concession:** an admission in an argument that the opposing side has valid points
**concesión:** admitir en un debate que el lado opositor tiene opiniones válidas

**concluding statement:** a statement that follows from and supports the claim made in an argument
**declaración concluyente:** declaración que sigue de la afirmación, o la apoya, en un argumento

**conflict:** a struggle or problem in a story. An *internal conflict* occurs when a character struggles between opposing needs or desires or emotions within his or her own mind. An *external conflict* occurs when a character struggles against an outside force. This force may be another character, a societal expectation, or something in the physical world.

**conflicto:** lucha o problema en un cuento. Un *conflicto interno* ocurre cuando un personaje lucha entre necesidades o deseos o emociones que se contraponen dentro de su mente. Un *conflicto externo* ocurre cuando un personaje lucha contra una fuerza externa. Esta fuerza puede ser otro personaje, una expectativa social o algo del mundo físico.

**connotation:** the associations and emotional overtones attached to a word beyond its literal definition, or denotation; a connotation may be positive, negative, or neutral
**connotación:** asociaciones y alusiones emocionales unidas a una palabra más allá de su definición literal o denotación; una connotación puede ser positiva, negativa, o neutra

**consonance:** the repetition of final consonant sounds in stressed syllables with different vowel sounds
**consonancia:** repetición de sonidos consonánticos finales en sílabas acentuadas con diferentes sonidos vocálicos

**context:** the circumstances or conditions in which something exists or takes place
**contexto:** circunstancias o condiciones en las que algo ocurre

**controversy:** a public debate or dispute about a topic that is debatable or arguable because it concerns an issue about which there is strong disagreement
**controversia:** debate o discusión pública acerca de un tema sobre el cual existen puntos de vista diferentes u opuestos

**conventions:** standard features, practices, and forms associated with the way something is usually done
**convenciones:** prácticas y formas usuales asociadas con las costumbres de hacer algo

**counterclaim:** an opposing viewpoint
**contrareclamación:** expresar un punto de vista opuesto a otro establecido

**couplet:** two consecutive lines of verse with end rhyme; a couplet usually expresses a complete unit of thought
**copla:** dos líneas de versos consecutivos con rima final; una copla normalmente expresa una unidad de pensamiento completa

**credibility:** the quality of being trusted or believed
**credibilidad:** calidad de ser confiable o creíble

**criteria:** standards that can be used to evaluate or judge the success of something
**criterios:** estándares que se usan para evaluar o juzgar el éxito de algo

**critical lens:** a particular identifiable perspective as in Reader Response Criticism, Cultural Criticism, etc., through which a text can be analyzed and interpreted
**ojo crítico:** punto de vista particular identificable como por ejemplo Teoría de la recepción, Crítica sociocultural, etc., por medio del que se puede analizar e interpretar un texto

**cultural conflict:** a struggle that occurs when people with different cultural expectations or attitudes interact
**conflicto cultural:** lucha que ocurre cuando interactúan personas con diferentes expectativas o actitudes culturales

**Cultural Criticism:** criticism that focuses on the elements of culture and how they affect one's perceptions and understanding of texts
**crítica cultural:** analizar un texto basándose en elementos culturales y como ellos afectan la percepción y lacomprensión de textos

**culture:** the shared set of arts, ideals, skills, institutions, customs, attitude, values, and achievements that characterize a group of people, and that are passed on or taught to succeeding generations
**cultura:** conjunto de artes, ideas, destrezas, instituciones, costumbres, actitud, valores y logros compartidos que caracterizan a un grupo de personas, y que se transfieren o enseñan a las generaciones siguientes

**cumulative (or loose) sentence:** a sentence in which the main clause comes first, followed by subordinate structures or clauses
**oración acumulativa (o frases sueltas):** oración cuya cláusula principal viene primero, seguida de estructuras o cláusulas subordinadas

# D

**deductive reasoning:** a process of drawing a specific conclusion from general information
**razonamiento deductivo:** proceso en que se usa información general para sacar una conclusión específica

**defend:** to support a statement that has been made
**defender:** dar apoyo a una declaración que alguien ha hecho

**denotation:** the precise meaning of a word
**denotación:** significado literal de una palabra

**detail:** a specific fact, observation, or incident; any of the small pieces or parts that make up something else
**detalle:** hecho, observación o incidente específico; cualquiera de las pequeñas piezas o partes que constituyen otra cosa

**dialect:** the distinctive language—including the sounds, spelling, grammar, and diction—of a specific group or class of people
**dialecto:** lenguaje distintivo, incluyendo sonidos, ortografía, gramática y dicción, de un grupo o clase específico de personas

**dialogue:** the spoken words of characters in a narrative or film
**diálogo:** palabras que dicen los personajes en un relato o película

**dialogue tags:** the phrases that attribute a quotation to the speaker, for example, *she said* or *he bellowed*
**marcas del diálogo:** frases que atribuyen la cita de un hablante, por ejemplo, *dijo ella* o *bramó él.*

**diction:** a writer's word choices, which often convey voice and tone
**dicción:** selección de palabras por parte del escritor; elemento estilístico que ayuda a transmitir voz y tono

**diegetic sound:** actual noises associated with the shooting of a scene, such as voices and background sounds
**sonido diegético:** sonidos lógicos que los personajes pueden oír en una escena en la pantalla

**direct characterization:** specific information about a character provided by the narrator or author
**caracterización directa:** información específica sobre un personaje creada por un narrador o autor

**discourse:** the language or speech used in a particular context or subject
**discurso:** lenguaje o habla usada en un contexto o tema en particular

**documentary film treatment:** an engaging proposal intended to sell an idea for a documentary film to an investor
**enfoque documental:** una propuesta atractiva con el propósito de vender una idea sobre un documental a un inversionista

**documentary or nonfiction film:** a genre of filmmaking that provides a visual record of actual events using photographs, video footage, and interviews
**documental o película de no-ficción:** género cinematográfico que realiza un registro visual de sucesos basados en hechos por medio del uso de fotografías, registro en videos y entrevistas

**dominant group:** a more powerful group that may perceive another group as marginalized or subordinate
**grupo dominante:** un grupo más poderoso que puede percibir a otro grupo como maginado o subordinado

**drama:** a play written for stage, radio, film, or television, usually about a serious topic or situation
**drama:** obra teatral escrita para representar en un escenario, radio, cine o televisión, normalmente sobre un tema o situación seria

**dramatic irony:** a form of irony in which the reader or audience knows more about the circumstances or future events in a story than the characters within it
**ironía dramática:** una forma de la ironía en que los lectores o el público sabe más sobre las circunstancias o sucesos futuros que los personajes en la escena

**dramaturge:** a member of an acting company who helps the director and actors make informed decisions about the performance by researching information relevant to the play and its context
**dramaturgo:** socio de una compañía teatral que ayuda al director y a los actores tomar decisiones informadas sobre la interpretación investigando información relevante a la obra teatral y su contexto

**dynamic (or round) character:** in literature, one who evolves and grows in the story and has a complex personality
**personaje dinámico:** en la literatura, un personaje que cambia debido a los sucesos de una narrativa

# E

**editorial:** an article in a newspaper or magazine expressing the opinion of its editor or publisher
**editorial:** artículo de periódico o revista, que expresa la opinión de su editor

**effect:** the result or influence of using a specific literary or cinematic device; a result produced by a cause
**efecto:** resultado o influencia de usar un recurso literario o cinematográfico específico; resultado o producto de una causa

**empirical evidence:** evidence based on experiences and direct observation through research
**evidencia empírica:** evidencia basada en experiencias y en la observación directa por medio de la investigación

**enfranchisement:** having the rights of citizenship, such as the right to vote
**emancipación:** tener los derechos de la ciudananía, tales como el derecho al voto

**epigram:** a short, witty saying
**epigrama:** dicho corto e ingenioso

**epigraph:** a phrase, quotation, or poem that is set at the beginning of a document or component
**epígrafe:** frase, cita, o poema que aparece al comienzo de un documento o componente

**epithet:** a descriptive word or phrase used in place of or along with a name
**epíteto:** palabra o frase descriptiva usada en lugar de o junto con un nombre

**ethos:** (ethical appeal) a rhetorical appeal that focuses on the character or qualifications of the speaker
**ethos:** (recurso ético) recurso retórico centrado en la ética o en el carácter o capacidades del orador

**evidence:** the information that supports a position in an argument; forms of evidence include facts, statistics (numerical facts), expert opinions, examples, and anecdotes; *see also* anecdotal, empirical, and logical evidence
**evidencia:** información que apoya o prueba una idea o afirmación; formas de evidencia incluyen hechos, estadística (datos numéricos), opiniones de expertos, ejemplos y anécdotas; *ver también* evidencia anecdótica, empírica y lógica

**exaggeration:** a statement that represents something as larger, better, or worse than it really is
**exageración:** representar algo como más grande, mejor o peor que lo que realmente es

**exemplification:** the act of defining by example by showing specific, relevant examples that fit a writer's definition of a topic or concept
**ejemplificación:** definir por ejemplo mostrando ejemplos específicos y relevantes que se ajustan a la definición de un tema o concepto del escritor

**explicit theme:** a theme that is clearly stated by the writer
**tema explícito:** tema que está claramente establecido por el escritor

**exposition:** events that give a reader background information needed to understand a story (characters are introduced, the setting is described, and the conflict begins to unfold)
**exposición:** sucesos que dan al lector los antecedentes necesarios para comprender un cuento. Durante la exposición, se presentan los personajes, se describe el ambiente y se comienza a revelar el conflicto.

**expository writing:** a form of writing whose purpose is to explain, describe, or give information about a topic in order to inform a reader
**escrito expositivo:** forma de la escritura cuyo propósito es explicar, describir o dar información sobre un tema para informar al lector

**extended metaphor:** a comparison between two unlike things that continues throughout a series of sentences in a paragraph or lines in a poem
**metáfora extendida:** metáfora que se extiende por varios versos o a través de un poema completo

**external coherence:** unity or logical connection between paragraphs with effective transitions and transitional devices
**coherencia externa:** unidad o conexión lógica entre párrafos con transiciones efectivas y recursos transitionales

# F

**fallacy:** a false or misleading argument
**falacia:** declaración falsa o engañosa sin apoyo en evidencia real

**falling action:** the events in a play, story, or novel that follow the climax, or moment of greatest suspense, and lead to the resolution
**acción descendente:** sucesos de una obra teatral, cuento o novela posteriores al clímax, o momento de mayor suspenso, y que conllevan a la resolución

**Feminist Criticism:** criticism that focuses on relationships between genders and examines a text based on the patterns of thought, behavior, values, enfranchisement, and power in relations between and within the sexes
**crítica feminista:** se enfoca en la relación entre los sexos y examina un texto basándose en el diseño de pensamiento, comportamiento, valores, emancipación, y poder en las relaciones entre los sexos

**figurative language:** imaginative language not meant to be taken literally, such as similes or metaphors
**lenguaje figurativo:** lenguaje imaginativo o figuras retóricas que no pretenden ser tomados literalmente; el lenguaje figurativo usa figuras literarias

**film techniques:** the methods a director uses to communicate meaning and to evoke particular emotional responses in viewers

**técnicas cinematográficas:** metodos que usa un director en la comunicación del significado y evocar una respuesta emocional específica en los videntes

**fixed form:** a form of poetry in which the length and pattern are determined by established usage of tradition, such as a sonnet
**forma fija:** forma de poesía en la que la longitud y el patrón están determinados por el uso de la tradición, como un soneto

**flashback:** an interruption or transition to a time before the current events in a narrative
**flashback:** interrupción en la secuencia de los sucesos para relatar sucesos ocurridos en el pasado

**flat (or static) character:** a character who is uncomplicated and stays the same without changing or growing during the story
**personaje estático:** personaje no complicado que permanence del mismo caracter y que no cambia a lo largo de una historia

**foil:** a minor character whose actions or thoughts are juxtaposed against those of a major character in order to highlight key attributes of the major character
**antagonista:** personaje cuyas acciones o pensamientos se yuxtaponen a los de un personaje principal con el fin de destacar atributos clave del personaje principal

**folktale:** a story without a known author that has been preserved through oral retellings
**cuento folclórico:** cuento sin autor conocido que se ha conservado por medio de relatos orales

**footage:** literally, a length of film; the expression is still used to refer to digital video clips
**metraje:** literalmente, la longitud de una película; la expresión aún se usa para referirse a video clips digitales

**foreshadowing:** the use of hints or clues in a narrative to suggest future action
**presagio:** uso de claves o pistas en un relato para sugerir una acción futura

**form:** the particular structure or organization of a work
**forma:** estructura o organización particular de una obra

**free verse:** poetry without a fixed pattern of meter and rhyme
**verso libre:** poesía que no sigue ningún patrón, ritmo o rima regular

# G

**genre:** a kind or style of literature or art, each with its own specific characteristics. For example, poetry, short story, and novel are literary genres. Painting and sculpture are artistic genres.
**género:** tipo o estilo de literatura o arte, cada uno con sus propias características específicas. Por ejemplo, la poesía, el cuento corto y la novela son géneros literarios. La pintura y la escultura son géneros artísticos.

**genre conventions:** the essential features and format that characterize a particular genre, or style of literature or art
**convenciones genéricas:** características básicas y el formato que caracterizan un género específico

**graphic novel:** a book-length narrative, or story, in the form of a comic strip rather than words
**novela gráfica:** narrativa o cuento del largo de un libro, en forma de tira cómica más que palabras

**graphics:** images or text used to provide information on screen
**gráfica:** imágenes o texto que se usa para dar información en pantalla

# H

**hamartia:** a tragic hero's fatal flaw; an ingrained character trait that causes a hero to make decisions leading to his or her death or downfall
**hamartia:** error fatal de un héroe trágico; característica propia de un personaje que causa que un héroe tome decisiones que finalmente llevan a su muerte o caída

**hero:** the main character or protagonist of a play, with whom audiences become emotionally invested
**héroe:** personaje principal o protagonista de una obra teatral, con el que el público se involucra emocionalmente

**historical context:** the circumstances or conditions in which something takes place
**contexto historico:** circunstancias o condiciones en las cuales algo sucede o pasa

**hook:** an opening in an argument or a piece of writing that grabs the reader's attention
**gancho:** cita, anécdota o ejemplo interesante al comienzo de un escrito, que capta la atención del lector

**Horatian satire:** satire that pokes fun at human foibles and folly with a witty, gentle, even indulgent tone
**sátira de Horacio:** sátira en que se burla de las debilidades y locuras con un tono suave, ingenioso, hasta indulgente

**humor:** the quality of being amusing
**humor:** calidad de ser divertido

**hyperbole:** exaggeration used to suggest strong emotion or create a comic effect
**hipérbole:** exageración que se usa para sugerir una emoción fuerte o crear un efecto cómico

# I

**iamb:** a metrical foot that consists of an unstressed syllable followed by a stressed syllable
**yambo:** pie métrico que consta de una sílaba átona seguida de una sílaba acentuada

**iambic pentameter:** a rhythmic pattern of five feet (or units), each consisting of one unstressed syllable followed by a stressed syllable

**pentámetro yámbico:** patrón rítmico de cinco pies (o unidades) de una sílaba átona seguida de una sílaba acentuada

**image:** a word or phrase that appeals to one of more of the five senses and creates a picture
**imagen:** palabra o frase que apela a uno o más de los cinco sentido y crea un cuadro

**imagery:** the verbal expression of sensory experience; descriptive or figurative language used to create word pictures; imagery is created by details that appeal to one or more of the five senses
**imaginería:** lenguaje descriptivo o figurativo utilizado para crear imágenes verbales; la imaginería es creada por detalles que apelan a uno o más de los cinco sentidos

**imperative:** something of vital or essential importance
**imprescindible:** algo de importancia vital o esencial

**imperialism:** a policy of extending the rule or influence of a country over other countries or colonies; the political, military, or economic domination of one country by another
**imperialismo:** política de extender el dominio o la influencia de un país sobre otros países o colonias; dominio político; militar o económico de un país sobre otro(s)

**implied theme:** a theme that is understood through the writer's diction, language construction, and use of literary devices
**tema implícito:** tema que se entiende a través de la dicción del escritor, construcción lingüística y uso de recursos literarios

**indirect characterization:** characterization that occurs when the narrator or author shows the character interacting with others, thinking about circumstances, or speaking his or her thoughts aloud
**caracterización indirecta:** el desarrollo de un personaje según un narrador o autor por las interacciones del personaje con otros, pensamientos sobre las circunstancias, o su habilidad de enunciar sus pensamientos en voz alta

**inductive reasoning:** a process of looking at individual facts to draw a general conclusion
**razonamiento inductivo:** proceso de observación de hechos individuales para sacar una conclusión general

**inference:** a conclusion about ideas or information not directly stated
**inferencia:** conclusión sobre las ideas o información no presentadas directamente

**interior monologue:** a literary device in which a character's internal emotions and thoughts are presented
**monólogo interior:** recurso literario en el que se presentan las emociones internas y pensamientos de un personaje

**interpretation:** the act of making meaning from something, such as a text
**interpretación:** acto de interpretar un significado de algo, tal como un texto

**internal coherence:** unity or logical connection within paragraphs
**coherencia interna:** unidad o conexión lógica entre párrafos

**irony:** a literary device that exploits readers' expectations; irony occurs when what happens turns out to be quite different from what was expected. *Dramatic irony* is a form of irony in which the reader or audience knows more about the circumstances or future events in a story than the characters within it; *verbal irony* occurs when a speaker or narrator says one thing while meaning the opposite; *situational irony* occurs when an event contradicts the expectations of the characters or the reader.
**ironía:** recurso literario que explota las expectativas de los lectores; la ironía ocurre cuando lo que se espera resulta ser bastante diferente de lo que realmente ocurre. La *ironía dramática* es una forma de ironía en la que el lector o la audiencia saben más acerca de las circunstancias o sucesos futuros de un cuento que los personajes del mismo; la *ironía verbal* ocurre cuando un orador o narrador dice una cosa queriendo decir lo contrario; la *ironía situacional* ocurre cuando un suceso contradice las expectativas de los personajes o del lector.

# J

**justice:** the quality of being reasonable and fair in the administration of the law; the ideal of rightness or fairness
**justicia:** calidad de ser razonable e imparcial en la administración de la ley; ideal de rectitud o equidad

**Juvenalian satire:** satire that denounces, sometimes harshly, human vice and error in dignified and solemn tones
**sátira de Juvenal:** sátira de denuncia, a veces con aspereza, los vicios y errores humanos con tonos dignos y solemnes

**juxtaposition:** the arrangement of two or more things for the purpose of comparison
**yuxtaposición:** ordenamiento de dos o más cosas con el objeto de compararlas

# L

**lining out:** the process of creating line breaks to add shape and meaning in free verse poetry
**llamada y respuesta:** proceso de crear rupturas de lineas para dar forma y significado en la poesía del verso libre

**literal language:** the exact meanings, or denotations, of words
**lenguaje literal:** los signficados y denotaciones exactos de las palabras

**literary theory:** a systematic study of literature using various methods to analyze texts
**teoría literaria:** intento de establecer principios para interpretar y evaluar textos literarios

**logical evidence:** evidence based on facts and a clear rationale
**evidencia lógica:** evidencia basada en hechos y una clara fundamentación

**logos:** (logical appeal) a rhetorical appeal that uses factual evidence and logical thought to appeal to the audience's sense of reason
**logos:** (apelación lógica) apelación retórica que usa la evidencia factual y la lógica para apelar al sentido de la razón

# M

**main idea:** a statement (often one sentence) that summarizes the key details of a text
**idea principal:** declaración (con frecuencia una oración) que resume los detalles claves de un texto

**marginalize:** to relegate or confine a person to a lower or outer limit
**marginar:** relegar o confinar a una persona a un límite bajo o ajeno

**Marxist Criticism:** criticism that asserts that economics provides the foundation for all social, political, and ideological reality
**crítica marxista:** ver un texto a través de la perspectiva en que la economía proporciona la fundación de toda realidad social, política, e ideológica

**media:** collectively refers to the organizations that communicate information to the public
**medios de comunicación:** colectivamente refiere a las organizaciones que comunican información al público

**media channel:** a method an organization uses to communicate, such as radio, television, website, newspaper, or magazine
**canales mediaticos:** método que usa una organización en la comunicación como radio, televisión, sitios de web, periódico, o revista

**memoir:** an autobiographical account of the personal experiences of the author
**memoria:** narración autobiográfica que presenta lasexperiencias personales de un autor

**metacognition:** the ability to know and be aware of one's own thought processes; self-reflection
**metacognición:** capacidad de conocer y estar consciente de los propios procesos del pensamiento; introspección

**metaphor:** a comparison between two unlike things in which one thing is spoken of as if it were another, for example, the moon was a crisp white cracker
**metáfora:** comparación entre dos cosas diferentes en la que se habla de una cosa como si fuera otra, por ejemplo, la luna era una galletita blanca crujiente

**meter:** a pattern of stressed and unstressed syllables in poetry
**métrica:** patrón de sílabas acentuadas y átonas en poesía

**mise en scène:** the composition, or setting, of a stage
**puesta en escena:** la composición o el lugar de un escenario

**monologue:** a speech or written expression of thoughts by a character

**monólogo:** discurso dramático que hace un solo personaje en una obra teatral

**montage:** a composite picture that is created by bringing together a number of images and arranging them to create a connected whole
**montaje:** cuadro compuesto que se crea al reunir un número de imágenes y que al organizarlas se crea un todo relacionado

**mood:** the atmosphere or predominant emotion in a literary work, the effect of the words on the audience
**carácter:** atmósfera o sentimiento general en una obra literaria

**motif:** a recurrent image, symbol, theme, character type, subject, or narrative detail that becomes a unifying element in an artistic work or text
**motivo:** imagen, símbolo, tema, tipo de personaje, tema o detalle narrativo recurrente que se convierte en un elemento unificador en una obra artística

**musical (or sound) device:** the use of sound to convey and reinforce the meaning or experience of poetry
**aparatos musicales:** uso del sonido para transmitir y reforzar el significado o experiencia de la poesía

**myth:** a traditional story that explains the actions of gods or heroes or the origins of the elements of nature
**mito:** cuento tradicional que explica las acciones de dioses o héroes, o los orígenes de los elementos de la naturaleza

# N

**narration:** the words that are heard as part of a film, television show, etc., and that describe what is being seen
**narración:** las palabras que leemos en un relato literario o que escuchamos en una película, show de televisión describiendo lo que vemos

**narrative:** a story about a series of events that includes character development, plot structure, and theme; can be a work of fiction or nonfiction
**narrativa:** narración sobre una serie de sucesos que incluye el desarrollo de personajes, estructora del argumento, y el tema; puede ser una obra de ficción o no ficción

**narrative pacing:** the speed at which a narrative moves
**compás de la narrativa:** la rapidez en que una narrativa pasa

**narrator:** the person telling the story
**narrador:** persona que cuenta una historia

**non-diegetic sound:** sound that cannot logically be heard by the characters on screen; examples include mood music and voice-overs
**sonido no diegético:** voces y comentarios superpuestos; sonidos que no provienen de la acción en pantalla.

# O

**objective:** based on factual information
**objetivo:** imparcial, basado en los hechos, equilibrado

**objective tone:** a tone that is more clinical and that is not influenced by emotion
**tono objetivo:** tono que es mas aséptico y que no se deja influir por la emoción

**objectivity:** the representation of facts or ideas without injecting personal feelings or biases
**objetividad:** representación de los hechos o ideas sin agregar sentimientos o prejuicios personales

**ode:** a lyric poem expressing feelings or thoughts of a speaker, often celebrating a person, event, or thing
**oda:** poema lírico que expresa sentimientos o pensamientos de un orador, que frecuentemente celebra a una persona, suceso o cosa

**onomatopoeia:** the occurrence of a word whose sound suggests its meaning
**onomatopeya:** palabras cuyo sonido sugiere su significado

**oral interpretation:** a planned oral reading that expresses the meaning of a written text
**interpretación oral:** lectura oral planeada que interpreta el signficado de un text escrito

**oral tradition:** the passing down of stories, tales, proverbs, and other culturally important ideas through oral retellings
**tradición oral:** traspaso de historias, cuentos, proverbios y otras historias de importancia cultural por medio de relatos orales

**oxymoron:** words that appear to contradict each other; for example, cold fire
**oxímoron:** palabras que parecen contradecirse mutuamente; por ejemplo, fuego frío

# P

**paradox:** a statement that contains two seemingly incompatible points
**paradoja:** declaración que contiene dos asuntos aparentemente incompatibles

**parallel structure (parallelism):** refers to a grammatical or structural similarity between sentences or parts of a sentence, so that elements of equal importance are equally developed and similarly phrased for emphasis
**estructura paralela (paralelismo):** se refiere a una similitud gramatical o estructural entre oraciones o partes de una oración, de modo que los elementos de igual importancia se desarrollen por igual y se expresen de manera similar para dar énfasis

**paraphrase:** to briefly restate ideas from another source in one's own words
**parafrasear:** volver a presentar las ideas de otra fuente en nuestras propias palabras

**parenthetical citations:** used for citing sources in an essay
**citas parentéticas:** usadas en citas de fuentes primarias en un ensayo

**parody:** a literary or artistic work that imitates the characteristic style of an author or a work for comic effect or ridicule
**parodia:** obra literaria o artística que imita el estilo característico de un autor o una obra para dar un efecto cómico o ridículo

**passive-voice verbs:** verb form in which the subject receives the action; the passive voice consists of a form of the verb *be* plus a past participle of the verb
**verbos en voz pasiva:** forma verbal en la que el sujeto recibe la acción; la voz pasiva se forma con el verbo *ser* más el participio pasado de un verbo

**pathos:** (emotional appeal) a rhetorical appeal to the reader's or listener's senses or emotions pathos: (apelación emocional) apelación retórica a los sentidos o emociones de los lectores u oyentes

**patriarchal:** having the male as head of the household and with authority over women and children
**patriarcal:** sociedad en que el varón es jefe del hogar en el cual mantiene autoridad sobre las mujeres y niños

**perception:** one person's interpretation of sensory or conceptual information
**percepción:** interpretación de una persona en cuanto a información sensorial o conceptual

**periodic sentence:** a sentence that makes sense only when the end of the sentence is reached, that is, when the main clause comes last
**oración periódica:** oración que tiene sentido sólo cuando se llega al final de la oración, es decir, cuando la cláusula principal viene al final

**persona:** the voice assumed by a writer to express ideas or beliefs that may not be his or her own
**personaje:** voz que asume un escritor para expresar ideas o creencias que pueden no ser las propias

**personification:** a figure of speech that gives human qualities to an animal, object, or idea
**personificación:** figura literaria que da características humanas a un animal, objeto o idea

**perspective:** a way of looking at the world or a mental concept about things or events, one that judges relationships within or among things or events
**perspectiva:** manera de visualizar el mundo o concepto mental de las cosas o sucesos, que juzga las relaciones dentro o entre cosas o sucesos

**persuasive argument:** an argument that convinces readers to accept or believe a writer's perspective on a topic
**argumento persuasivo:** argumento que convence a los lectores a aceptar o creer en la perspectiva de un escritor acerca de un tema

**photo essay:** a collection of photographic images that reveal the author's perspective on a subject
**ensayo fotográfico:** recolección de imágenes fotográficas que revelan la perspectiva del autor acerca de un tema

**plagiarism:** the act of using another person's words or ideas without giving credit
**plagio:** usar como propias las palabras o ideas de otro escritor

**plot:** the sequence of related events that make up a story
**trama:** secuencia de sucesos relacionados que conforman un cuento o novela

**poetic structure:** the organization of words, lines, and images as well as ideas
**estructura poética:** organización de las palabras, versos e imágenes, así como también de las ideas

**poetry:** language written in lines and stanzas
**poesía:** género literario que se concreta en un poema y está sujeto a medida o cadencia

**point of view:** the perspective from which a narrative is told, that is, first person, third-person limited, or third-person omniscient
**punto de vista:** perspectiva desde la cual se cuenta un relato, es decir, primera persona, tercera persona limitada o tercera persona omnisciente

**precept:** a rule, instruction, or principle that guides a person's actions and/or moral behavior
**precepto:** regla, instrucción o principio que guía las acciones de una persona y/o conducta moral de alguien

**primary footage:** film footage shot by the filmmaker for the text at hand
**metraje principal:** filmación hecha por el cineasta para el texto que tiene a mano

**primary source:** an original document or image created by someone who experiences an event first hand
**fuente primaria:** documento original que contiene información de primera mano acerca de un tema

**prologue:** the introduction or preface to a literary work
**prólogo:** introducción o prefacio de una obra literaria

**prose:** ordinary written or spoken language, using sentences and paragraphs, without deliberate or regular meter or rhyme; not poetry or song
**prosa:** forma común del lenguaje escrito o hablado, usando oraciones y párrafos, sin métrica o rima deliberada o regular; ni poesía ni canción

**protagonist:** the central character in a work of literature, the one who is involved in the main conflict in the plot
**protagonista:** personaje central de una obra literaria, el que participa en el conflicto principal de la trama

**proverb:** a short saying about a general truth
**proverbio:** dicho corto sobre una verdad general

# Q

**qualify:** to consider to what extent a statement is true or untrue (to what extent you agree or disagree)

**calificar:** consider hasta qué punto una declaración es verdadera o falsa

**quatrain:** a four-line stanza in a poem
**cuarteta:** en un poema, estrofa de cuatro versos

# R

**Reader Response Criticism:** criticism that focuses on a reader's active engagement with a piece of print or nonprint text; shaped by the reader's own experiences, social ethics, moral values, and general views of the world
**crítica de reacción del lector:** análisis de un texto basado en las experiencias, ética social, valores, y percepciones generales del mundo

**reasoning:** the thinking or logic used to make a claim in an argument
**razonamiento:** pensamiento o lógica que se usa para hacer una afirmación en un argumento

**refrain:** a regularly repeated line or group of lines in a poem or song, usually at the end of a stanza
**estribillo:** verso o grupo de versos que se repiten con regularidad en un poema o canción, normalmente al final de una estrofa

**refutation:** the reasoning used to disprove an opposing point
**refutación:** razonamiento que se usa para rechazar una opinión contraria

**reliability:** the extent to which a source provides quality and trustworthy information
**confiabilidad:** grado en el que una fuente da información confiable y de buena calidad

**reliable:** dependable; in research, information is reliable if it can be trusted and is of good quality
**fiable:** confiable; en la investigación, la información es fiable si es fidedigna y de buena calidad

**renaissance:** a rebirth or revival
**renacimiento:** un volver a nacer o una reanimación

**repetition:** the use of any element of language—a sound, a word, a phrase, a line, or a stanza—more than once
**repetición:** uso de cualquier elemento del lenguaje—un sonido, una palabra, una frase, un verso o una estrofa—más de una vez

**resolution (denouement):** the end of a text, in which the main conflict is finally resolved
**resolución (desenlace):** final de una obra teatral, cuento o novela, en el que el conflicto principal finalmente se resuelve

**résumé:** a document that outlines a person's skills, education, and work history
**currículum vitae:** documento que resume las destrezas, educación y experiencia laboral de una persona

**rhetoric:** the art of using words to persuade in writing or speaking

**retórica:** arte de usar las palabras para persuadir por escrito o de manera hablada

**rhetorical appeals:** emotional, ethical, and logical arguments used to persuade an audience to agree with the writer or speaker
**recursos retóricos:** uso de argumentos emocionales, éticos y lógicos para persuadir por escrito o de manera hablada

**rhetorical context:** the subject, purpose, audience, occasion, or situation in which writing or speaking occurs
**contexto retórico:** sujeto, propósito, audiencia, ocasión o situación en que ocurre el escrito

**rhetorical devices:** specific techniques used in writing or speaking to create a literary effect or enhance effectiveness
**dispositivos retóricos:** técnicas específicas que se usan al escribir o al hablar para crear un efecto literario o mejorar la efectividad

**rhetorical question:** a question that is asked for effect or one for which the answer is obvious
**pregunta retórica:** pregunta hecha para producir un efecto o cuya respuesta es obvia

**rhyme:** the repetition of sounds at the ends of words
**rima:** repetición de sonidos al final de las palabras

**rhyme scheme:** a consistent pattern of rhyme throughout a poem
**esquema de la rima:** patrón consistente de una rima a lo largo de un poema

**rhythm:** the pattern of stressed and unstressed syllables in spoken or written language, especially in poetry
**ritmo:** patrón de sílabas acentuadas y no acentuadas en lenguaje hablado o escrito, especialmente en poesía

**rising action:** the movement of a plot toward a climax or moment of greatest excitement; the rising action is fueled by the characters' responses to the conflict
**acción ascendente:** movimiento de una trama hacia el clímax o momento de mayor emoción; la acción ascendente es impulsada por las reacciones de los personajes ante el conflicto

**round (or dynamic) character:** a character who evolves and grows in the story and has a complex personality
**personaje dinámico:** personaje que evoluciona y crece en la historia y que tiene una personalidad compleja

# S

**satire:** a manner of writing that mocks social conventions, actions, or attitudes with wit and humor
**sátira:** manera de escribir en que se burla de convenciones sociales, acciones, o actitudes con ingenio y humor

**scenario:** an outline, a brief account, a script, or a synopsis of a proposed series of events

**escenario:** bosquejo, relato breve, libreto o sinopsis de una serie de sucesos propuestos

**secondary audience:** a group that may receive a message intended for a target audience
**audiencia secundaria:** grupo que puede recibir un mensaje orientado a una audiencia específica

**secondary source:** a discussion about or commentary on a primary source; the key feature of a secondary source is that it offers an interpretation of information gathered from primary sources
**fuente secundaria:** discusión o comentario acerca de una fuente primaria; la característica clave de una fuente secundaria es que ofrece una interpretación de la información recopilada en las fuentes primarias

**sensory details:** details that appeal to or evoke one or more of the five senses—sight, sound, smell, taste, and touch
**detalles sensoriales:** detalles que apelan o evocan uno o más de los cinco sentidos—vista, oído, gusto, olfato, y tacto

**sensory images:** images that appeal to the reader's senses—sight, sound, smell, taste, and touch
**imágenes sensoriales:** imágenes que apelan a los sentidos del lector—vista, oído, olfato, gusto, y tacto

**sequence of events:** the order in which things happen in a story
**secuencia de eventos:** orden en que los sucesos de una historia pasan:

**setting:** the time and place in which a story happens
**ambiente:** tiempo y lugar en el que ocurre un relato

**simile:** a comparison of two different things or ideas using the words *like* or *as*, for example, the moon was as white as milk
**símil:** comparación entre dos o más cosas o ideas diferentes usando las palabras *como* o *tan*, por ejemplo, la luna estaba tan blanca como la leche

**situational irony:** a form of irony that occurs when an event contradicts the expectations of the characters or the reader
**ironía situacional:** ocurre cuando un evento contradice las espectativas de los personajes o el lector

**slanters:** rhetorical devices used to present the subject in a biased way
**soslayo:** recursos retóricos para presentar el tema de modo sesgado

**slogan:** a short, catchy phrase used for advertising by a business, club, or political party
**eslogan:** frase corta y tendenciosa que usa como publicidad para un negocio, club o partido político

**social commentary:** an expression of an opinion with the goal of promoting change by appealing to a sense of justice
**comentario social:** expresión de una opinión con el objeto de promover el cambio al apelar a un sentido de justicia

**soliloquy:** a long speech delivered by an actor alone on the stage; represents the character's internal thoughts
**soliloquio:** discurso largo realizado por un actor sobre el escenario que representa sus pensamientos internos

**sonnet:** a 14-line lyric poem, usually written in iambic pentameter and following a strict pattern of rhyme
**soneto:** poema lírico de catorce versos, normalmente escrito en un pentámetro yámbico y que sigue un patrón de rima estricto

**speaker:** the imaginary voice or persona of the writer or author
**orador:** voz o persona imaginaria del escritor o autor

**stage directions:** instructions written into the script of a play that indicate stage actions, movements of performers, or production requirements
**direcciones escénicas:** instrucciones escritas en un guión o drama que indican acción, movimiento de actors, or requisitos de la producción

**stakeholder:** a person motivated or affected by a course of action
**participante:** persona motivada o afectada por el curso de una acción

**stanza:** a group of lines, usually similar in length and pattern, that form a unit within a poem
**estrofa:** grupo de versos, normalmente similares en longitud y patrón, que forman una unidad dentro de un poema

**static (or flat) character:** a character who is uncomplicated and remains the same without changing or growing throughout a narrative
**personaje estático:** personaje que no cambia a lo largo de una narrativa

**stereotype:** an oversimplified, generalized conception, opinion, and/or image about particular groups of people
**estereotipo:** concepto generalizado, opinión y/o imagen demasiado simplificada acerca de grupos específicos de personas

**stichomythia:** in drama, the delivery of dialogue in a rapid, fast-paced manner, with actors speaking emotionally and leaving very little time between speakers
**esticomitia:** en el drama, es la rendición del diálogo de una manera rápida con actores que hablan con emoción, dejando espacio muy breve entre los hablantes

**storyboard:** a tool to show images and sequencing for the purpose of visualizing a film or a story
**guión gráfico:** método de mostrar imágenes y secuencias con el propósito de visualizar una película o historia

**strategize:** to plan the actions one will take to complete a task
**estrategizar:** planear las acciones de uno para complir una tarea

**structure:** the way a literary work is organized; the arrangement of the parts in a literary work
**estructura:** manera en que la obra literaria está organizada; disposición de las partes en una obra literaria

**style:** the distinctive way a writer uses language, characterized by elements of diction, syntax, imagery, organization, and so on
**estilo:** manera distintiva en que un escritor usa el lenguaje, caracterizada por elementos de dicción, sintaxis, lenguaje figurado, etc.

**subculture:** a smaller subsection of a culture, for example, within the culture of a high school may be many subcultures
**subcultura:** subsección más pequeña de una cultura, por ejemplo, dentro de la cultura de una escuela secundaria puede haber muchas subculturas

**subjective:** influenced by personal opinions or ideas
**subjetivo:** influenciado por opiniones o ideas personales
**subjective tone:** a tone that is obviously influenced by the author's feelings or emotions
**tono subjetivo:** tono obviamente influído por los sentimientos o emociones del autor

**subjectivity:** judgment based on one's personal point of view, opinion, or values
**subjetividad:** en base en nuestro punto de vista, opinión o valores personales

**subordinate:** a person or group that is perceived as having a lower social or economic status
**subordinado:** persona o grupo percibido de ser de rango social o estado económico bajo

**subplot:** a secondary or side story that develops from and supports the main plot and usually involves minor characters
**argumento secundario:** una historia secundaria o periférica que apoya el argumento principal y que suele involucrar a personajes secundarios o menores

**subtext:** the underlying or implicit meaning in dialogue or the implied relationship between characters in a book, movie, play, or film; the subtext of a work is not explicitly stated
**subtexto:** significado subyacente o implícito en el diálogo o la relación implícita entre los personajes de un libro, película, u obra teatral. El subtexto de una obra no se establece de manera explícita.

**survey:** a method of collecting data from a group of people; it can be written, such as a print or online questionnaire, or oral, such as an in-person interview
**encuesta:** método para recolectar datos de un grupo de personas; puede ser escrita, como un impreso o cuestionario en línea, u oral, como en una entrevista personal

**symbol:** anything (object, animal, event, person, or place) that represents itself but also stands for something else on a figurative level
**símbolo:** cualquier cosa (objeto, animal, evento, persona o lugar) que se representa a sí misma, pero también representa otra cosa a nivel figurativo

**symbolic:** serving as a symbol; involving the use of symbols or symbolism

**simbólico:** que sirve como símbolo; que implica el uso de símbolos o simbolismo

**synecdoche:** a figure of speech in which a part is used to represent the whole or vice versa
**sinécdoque:** figura retórica en que una parte se usa para representar el todo, o vice-versa

**syntax:** the arrangement of words and the order of grammatical elements in a sentence; the way in which words are put together to make meaningful elements, such as phrases, clauses, and sentences
**sintaxis:** disposición de las palabras y orden de los elementos gramaticales en una oración; manera en que las palabras se juntan para formar elementos significativos como frases, cláusulas y oraciones

**synthesis:** the act of combining ideas from different sources to create, express, or support a new idea
**síntesis:** acto de combinar ideas de diferentes fuentes para crear, expresar o apoyar una nueva idea

# T

**target audience:** the intended group for which a work is designed to appeal or reach
**público objetivo:** grupo al que se pretende apelar o llegar con una obra

**theatrical elements:** elements used by dramatists and directors to tell a story on stage. Elements include *costumes* (the clothing worn by actors to express their characters), *makeup* (cosmetics used to change actors' appearances and express their characters), *props* (objects used to help set the scene, advance a plot, and make a story realistic), *set* (the place where the action takes place, as suggested by objects, such as furniture, placed on a stage), and *acting choices* (gestures, movements, staging, and vocal techniques actors use to convey their characters and tell a story).
**elementos teatrales:** elementos utilizados por los dramaturgos y directores para contar una historia en el escenario. Los elementos incluyen *vestuario* (ropa que usan los actores para expresar sus personajes), *maquillaje* (cosméticos que se usan para cambiar la apariencia de los actores y expresar sus personajes), *elementos* (objetos que se usan para ayudar a montar la escena, avanzar la trama y crear una historia realista), *plató* (lugar donde tiene lugar la acción, según lo sugieren los objetos, como muebles, colocados sobre un escenario), y *opciones de actuación* (gestos, movimientos, representación y técnicas vocales que se usan para transmitir sus personajes y narrar una historia).

**thematic statement:** an interpretive statement articulating the central meaning of a text
**oración temática:** afirmación interpretativa que articula el significado o mensaje central de un texto

**theme:** a writer's central idea or main message; *see also* explicit theme, implied theme

**tema:** idea central o mensaje principal acerca de la vida de un escritor; *véase también* tema explícito, tema implícito

**thesis:** the main idea or point of an essay or article; in an argumentative essay the thesis is the writer's position on an issue
**tesis:** idea o punto principal de un ensayo o artículo; en un ensayo argumentativo, la tesis es la opinión del autor acerca de un tema

**tone:** a writer's (or speaker's) attitude toward a subject, character, or audience
**tono:** actitud de un escritor u orador acerca de un tema

**topic sentence:** a sentence that states the main idea of a paragraph; in an essay, the topic sentence also makes a point that supports the thesis statement
**oración principal:** oración que establece la idea principal de un párrafo; en un ensayo, la oración principal también establece una proposición que apoya el enunciado de la tesis

**tragedy:** a dramatic play that tells the story of a character, usually of a noble class, who meets an untimely and unhappy death or downfall, often because of a specific character flaw or twist of fate
**tragedia:** obra teatral dramática que cuenta la historia de un personaje, normalmente de origen noble, que encuentra una muerte o caída imprevista o infeliz, con frecuencia debido a un defecto específico del personaje o una vuelta del destino

**tragic hero:** a central character who is usually of high or noble birth and demonstrates a "fatal flaw," or hamartia
**héroe trágico:** héroe arquetípico basado en el concepto griego de la tragedia; el héroe trágico tiene un defecto que lo hace vulnerable a la caída o a la muerte

**transcript:** a written copy or record of a conversation that takes place between two or more people
**transcripción:** copia escrita de una conversación que sucede entre dos o más personas

# U

**understatement:** the representation of something as smaller or less significant than it really is; the opposite of exaggeration or hyperbole

**subestimación:** representación de algo como más pequeño o menos importante de lo que realmente es; lo opuesto a la exageración o hipérbole

# V

**valid:** believable or truthful
**válido:** creíble o verídico

**validity:** the quality of truth or accuracy in a source
**validez:** calidad de verdad o precisión en una fuente

**verbal irony:** a form of irony that occurs when a speaker or narrator says one thing while meaning the opposite
**ironía verbal:** ocurre cuando un hablante o narrador dice una cosa mientras quiere decir lo opuesto

**verify:** to prove or confirm that something is true
**verificar:** probar o confirmar que algo es verdadero

**vignette:** a picture or visual or a brief descriptive literary piece
**viñeta:** ilustración o representación visual o pieza literaria descriptiva breve

**visual delivery:** the way a performer on stage interprets plot, character, and conflict through movement, gestures, and facial expressions
**presentación visual:** manera en que un actor en un escenario interpreta trama, carácter, y conflicto a través de movimiento, gestos, y expresiones de la cara

**visual rhetoric:** an argument or points made by visuals such as photographs or by other visual features of a text
**retórica visual:** argumentos o asuntos representados en visuales como fotos u otros rasgos visuales de un texto

**vocal delivery:** the way a performer on stage expresses the meaning of a text through volume, pitch, rate or speed of speech, pauses, pronunciation, and articulation
**presentación vocal:** manera en que se expresan las palabras en el escenario, por medio del volumen, tono, rapidez o velocidad del discurso, pausas, pronunciación y articulación

**voice:** a writer's (or speaker's) distinctive use of language to express ideas as well as his or her persona
**voz:** manera en que el escritor u orador usa las palabras y el tono para expresar ideas, así como también su personaje o personalidad

# Index of Skills

## Literary Skills

Adverbs, relative, 419
Allusions, 61, 63
Analogies, 386, 405
    historical, 405
Anaphora, 109, 373
Antistrophes, 308, 309
Appeal to pity fallacy, 397, 399
Archetypes, 210
Arguments, 64, 88, 94, 95
Author's purpose, 85, 94, 173, 178, 213,
    236, 260, 272, 281, 425
Autobiography, 111, 117–119
Background, 115
Call to action, 392, 393
Characterization, 221, 271, 272, 278,
    281, 365
    direct, 271, 272, 278
    indirect, 271, 272, 278
Characters, 227, 320
    complex, 270, 271, 277, 295
    dynamic, 312, 320
    motivation, 297, 302, 321, 322, 332,
    365, 392
    static, 312, 320
Character sketches, 232, 278,
    293, 297
Chorus, 296, 297, 308, 309–310
Concessions, 88
Conflict, 21, 30, 39, 42, 48, 49, 152, 167,
    208, 219, 271, 281, 295, 299, 306,
    307, 321, 332, 362, 364, 370, 415,
    418, 419
    cultural, 170, 243, 244, 245, 246, 251,
    370, 419, 422, 431, 437, 443,
    445, 458
    internal and external, 31, 32, 281
Context, 291
Cultural identity, 6, 7, 8, 9, 11, 12, 15,
    17, 31, 32, 36, 39, 41, 42, 50, 53,
    65, 85, 107, 110, 131
Cultural narrative, 112–114, 115, 117–
    119, 122, 123–125, 127–128, 148,
    163, 164
Culture, definition, 5
Description, 128–129
Details, 385
Dialogue, 116, 118, 121, 122, 152, 271,
    273, 278, 288, 302, 305, 307, 308,
    311, 374, 453
    balloons, 132, 142
    direct, 118, 120, 122
    indirect, 120, 122
    tags, 116

Diction (word choice), 48, 120, 152,
    225, 378
    formal, 225
Diegetic sound, 374, 453
Editorials, 169–170
Either/or fallacy (false dilemma), 397, 399
Epigraphs, 213
Essential Questions, 4, 57, 106, 166,
    208, 231, 270, 295, 370, 445
Ethos, 180, 383, 385, 389, 392, 412
Euphemisms, 150, 342
Figurative language, 66, 68, 131
Flashbacks, 140
Foils, 216, 218, 333, 339, 364
Folktales, 209, 210, 236
Foreshadowing, 223, 338
Graphic novels, 132, 133–139
Greek drama, 296, 300
    trivia game, 299, 301
Greek pronunciation, 300
Hamartia, 241
Illustrations, 132, 140
Images/imagery, 66, 107, 110
Inappropriate appeal to authority,
    397, 399
Indirect dialogue, 116
Irony, 150, 252
    dramatic, 252
    situational, 252
    verbal, 252
Juxtaposition, 41, 42, 65, 385
Logos, 383, 392
Memoirs, 43, 111, 112–114, 115,
    149–151
Metaphors, 15, 145, 160, 191, 319,
    360, 413
Monologues, 279, 281, 282
Mood, 48, 216, 238, 296, 409
Moral imperative, 392
Motifs, 216
Motivation, 297, 302, 321, 322, 332,
    365, 392
Narration, 114, 140, 141, 374
Narrative pacing, 123, 152
Narrative techniques, 107, 111, 131,
    162, 163
Non-diegetic sound, 374, 447, 453
Norms, 233
Objectivity, 378, 379, 385, 388, 390
Odes, 308, 341
Oral interpretation, 282, 283, 293, 294
Pathos, 180, 383, 392
Persona, 149
Perspective, 103, 106, 117, 123, 143,
    148, 153, 154, 159, 161, 162,

    163, 164, 166, 167, 222, 223,
    265, 371, 377, 378, 379, 385,
    389, 394, 414, 415, 417, 419,
    423, 430, 431, 448
Plot, 116, 216, 238, 243, 245, 268, 270,
    271, 295, 297, 299, 307, 321,
    331, 332
    summary, 210
Poetic license, 27
Poetry, 42, 109, 148
Point of view, 111, 142, 162, 163, 168,
    200, 225, 228, 249, 270, 274, 296,
    299, 302, 377, 379, 423, 448
    first person, 437, 448
    subjective and objective, 379
    third person, 225
Post hoc fallacy, 397, 399
Proverbs, 209
Refutations, 88
Rhetorical appeals, 176, 180, 181, 183,
    338, 383, 388, 392, 397, 443
Ridicule/sarcasm, 150
Sensory language, 107, 109, 128, 130
Setting, 111, 122, 142, 302, 451, 453
Slippery slope fallacy, 397, 399
Speeches, 166
Stage directions, 302
Stakeholders, 415, 418, 419, 422, 435
Stichomythia, 305, 307
Storyboards, 455
Strophes, 308, 309
Style, 225
Subjectivity, 378, 379, 382, 385, 423
Subplots, 296
Symbol(ism), 39, 68, 80, 131, 210,
    216, 453
Syntax, 18, 152, 153, 350
Synthesis, 60, 97, 100
Thematic statement, 32
Theme, 32, 111, 115, 128, 142, 147, 162,
    210, 213, 216, 238, 244, 247, 251,
    270, 271, 281, 295, 321, 329, 332,
    348, 365, 371, 380
Tone, 30, 68, 181, 199, 225, 237, 247,
    253, 273, 281, 283, 393, 400, 407,
    425, 446, 448, 450
Tragedy, 296, 299
Tragic hero, 241, 242, 299, 338, 362,
    364, 365
Voice, 9
    active, 185, 217
    formal (academic), 16, 17, 32, 225, 226
    informal, 16
    passive, 185, 217
    personal, 39, 42

# Reading Skills

Annotating the text, 35, 42, 111, 116, 141, 148, 149, 279, 286, 341, 360, 378, 435

Choral reading, 247, 251

Chunking the text, 21–29, 263

Close reading, 68, 154, 195, 370, 379, 397

Compare and contrast, 8, 17, 66, 86, 117, 178, 216, 225, 228, 245, 251, 310

Credibility, 389, 400

Double-entry journal, 216, 218, 219, 270

Evaluating causal claims, 387, 388

Evidence, 218, 386, 388, 389

Graphic organizers, 4, 5, 6, 17, 32, 38, 50, 53, 57, 68, 69, 79, 80, 86, 95, 106, 109, 115, 121, 122, 130, 141, 142, 148, 161, 166, 167, 178, 208, 209, 210, 215, 218, 219, 224, 227, 232, 233, 236, 238, 239, 241, 243, 245, 246, 263, 270, 271, 272, 273, 274, 280, 291, 295, 298, 307, 319–320, 321, 331, 341, 348, 349, 363, 364, 370, 374, 375, 378, 379, 380, 381, 383, 384, 386, 387, 388, 398, 399, 415, 417, 420, 429, 435, 436, 445, 449, 450, 454, 455

Group discussion, 5, 7, 8, 36, 42, 57, 82, 86, 122, 153, 173, 192, 208, 209, 214, 219, 227, 232, 234, 237, 240, 247, 251, 263, 311, 331, 348, 350, 362, 388, 389, 390, 393, 400, 413, 418, 445, 446, 453, 455

Independent Reading Checkpoint, 54, 100, 163, 202, 228, 264, 292, 364, 442, 458

Independent Reading Link, 8, 12, 17, 29, 42, 57, 65, 81, 85, 96, 106, 117, 128, 166, 176, 208, 212, 231, 236, 240, 242, 246, 292, 295, 297, 307, 350, 370, 378, 391, 400, 437, 445, 450

Inferring, 35, 49, 53, 77, 85, 236, 271, 341

Interpretation, 68, 218, 272

Interpreting graphs and tables, 187, 188

Levels of questions, 393

Marking the text, 9, 13, 21, 33, 39, 43, 51, 61, 63, 66, 70, 82, 89, 107, 111, 116, 123, 128, 132, 143, 149, 154, 168, 176, 180, 184, 188, 193, 195, 200, 245, 247, 254, 270, 271, 274, 279, 284, 291, 296, 299, 302, 312, 322, 333, 341, 347, 350, 371, 394, 401, 415, 423, 451

Metacognitive markers, 33, 149, 193, 254, 263, 284

Note-taking, 11, 15, 16, 30, 35, 41, 48, 52, 58, 62, 68, 77, 85, 94, 108, 111, 114, 119, 123, 125, 129, 131, 132, 140, 145, 147, 159, 170, 173, 176, 177, 178, 181, 183, 187, 188, 191, 193, 195, 198, 202, 208, 211, 212, 222, 223, 236, 249, 251, 260, 263, 270, 277, 283, 285, 287, 288, 290, 292, 306, 307, 310, 317, 329, 338, 360, 373, 377, 383, 391, 396, 405, 407, 411, 412, 415, 417, 423, 425, 427, 435, 448, 450, 456

OPTIC, 37, 38, 42

Oral reading, 237

Organization, 54, 95

Paraphrasing, 199, 311, 370

Play scripts, 302

Point of view, 377, 378

Predicting, 213, 227, 243, 321, 331, 371, 450

Pronunciation, 213

RAFT, 236, 237

Reflecting, 153, 278, 341, 370, 450

Rereading, 11, 15, 30, 35, 41, 48, 52, 62, 63, 68, 77, 85, 94, 99, 108, 114, 115, 119, 125, 126, 129, 140, 145, 147, 152, 159, 170, 173, 174, 177, 181, 183, 187, 188, 191, 195, 198, 236, 240, 241, 247, 249, 251, 253, 260, 277, 285, 287, 288, 290, 306, 307, 310, 317, 329, 338, 347, 360, 373, 396, 397, 405, 407, 411, 412, 417, 425, 427, 435

Reviewing notes, 32, 36, 166, 176, 199, 202, 218, 225, 228, 236, 251, 299, 321, 341, 393

Role playing, 237

Scanning, 163

Second read, 11, 15, 30, 35, 41, 48, 52, 62, 68, 77, 85, 94, 108, 114, 119, 125, 129, 140, 145, 147, 151, 159, 170, 173, 177, 181, 183, 187, 191, 195, 198, 249, 251, 260, 277, 285, 287, 288, 290, 306, 310, 317, 329, 338, 347, 360, 373, 396, 405, 407, 411, 417, 425, 427

Sharing and responding, 6, 82, 99, 162, 192, 202, 272, 311, 350, 393, 437, 453, 457

SIFT strategy, 68, 69, 79

Skimming/scanning, 284, 302

SMELL strategy, 290–291, 292, 383, 384, 392, 397–398, 401, 457

SOAPStone analysis, 53, 54, 280

Socratic Seminar, 152, 153, 199, 223, 244

Summarizing, 4, 12, 29, 57, 64, 82, 94, 106, 163, 208, 270, 320, 387, 391, 445

Synthesizing information, 42

Textual evidence, 30, 36, 53, 240, 252, 307, 320, 321, 331, 339–340, 341, 347, 363, 365

Theme, 30, 68, 238

Think-pair-share, 8, 54, 109, 115, 126, 148, 153, 162, 174, 176, 227, 234, 244, 245, 252, 307, 386, 412

Title, 79, 147, 213

Tone, 30, 49, 54, 84, 94, 225

TP-CASTT strategy, 147

Visuals, 37, 38, 223

# Writing Skills

Academic voice, 16, 17, 32, 225, 226

*Ad hominem*, 401, 412, 414

Annotated bibliographies, 228, 430, 431, 432 Annotating the text, 20, 391, 437

Argument, 64, 88, 95, 96, 99, 166, 175, 178, 179, 192, 199, 203, 220, 382, 388, 393, 401, 415, 419, 435, 436, 450, 456

Artistic Prompt, 42

Audience, 7, 96, 237, 252, 273, 283, 284, 290, 291, 296, 370, 383, 393, 394, 400, 407, 414, 427, 443, 445, 453, 458

Bias, 423, 433

Brainstorming, 98, 163, 166, 211, 237, 420, 458

Call to action, 188, 393, 436, 443, 456

Claims, 64, 65, 80, 81, 88, 94, 96, 100, 170, 174, 175, 176, 178, 179, 183, 188, 192, 199, 202, 220, 251, 370, 379, 386, 388, 389, 391, 392, 393, 401, 414, 423, 435, 437, 438, 445, 450, 456

Collaboration, 97, 98, 99, 229, 419–422, 443, 458

Compare and contrast, 42, 183, 221, 222, 227, 308, 320

Concessions, 88, 100

Concluding statements, 17, 88, 220, 419, 437

Conclusions, 96, 163, 175, 178, 183, 192, 238, 340, 376, 388

Counterclaims, 64, 80, 81, 88, 178, 393, 401, 436

Creative Writing Prompt, 42

Definitions, 167

Descriptions, 127, 376

Details, 32, 107, 112, 115, 121, 123, 127, 148, 210, 216, 219, 223, 227, 232, 235, 272, 311, 320, 364, 377, 378, 379, 383, 385, 392, 393, 437

descriptive, 127, 130, 178, 376, 382

sensory, 107, 109, 128, 130

Dialogue, 121, 122

Diction (word choice), 120, 152, 225, 378
Drafting, 55, 97, 99, 101, 163, 164, 203, 265, 293, 321, 339, 365, 419, 437, 443
Editing, 55, 101, 164, 203, 265, 365, 437, 442, 459
Embedded Assessment, 55–56, 101–102, 164–165, 203–204, 229–230, 265–266, 293–294, 365–366, 443–444, 459–460
  unpacking, 4, 57, 106, 166, 208, 231, 270, 295, 370, 445
Essays
  academic, 438
  arguments, 100, 166, 175, 179, 192, 199, 220
  compare/contrast, 222
  cultural identity, 54, 87
  explanatory, 7, 32, 42, 110, 115, 131, 148, 175, 238, 251, 264
  literary analysis, 231, 265, 295, 333, 339, 365, 366
  personal narrative, 122, 127
  persuasive, 394
  reflective, 4
  synthesis, 97
Ethical appeals, 400
Ethical use of sources, 440
Evaluating and revising, 164, 199, 202, 203, 281
Evaluating sources, 211, 212, 423, 429, 430, 432, 433, 434
Evidence, 64, 65, 81, 88, 96, 98, 168, 173, 174, 175, 179, 183, 188, 192, 220, 320, 331, 388, 435, 450
  anecdotal, 168, 175, 191
  commentary on, 320, 339
  empirical, 168
  logical, 168
  quotations as, 32, 36, 42, 87, 210, 217, 226, 251, 376, 382, 435
  textual, 219, 235, 238, 242, 339–340
Explanations, 175, 178, 332, 376
Fallacies, 174, 175, 397, 401
Graphic organizers, 99, 212, 221, 222, 308, 421, 422, 432, 433, 434, 435, 456
Group discussions, 17, 65, 87, 97, 98, 100, 211, 221, 227, 235, 421
Hooks, 52, 88, 191, 192, 456
Introductions, 238, 242, 291, 299
Letter to official, 253
Literary analysis, 225, 265, 266
Marking the text, 378, 391, 442
*MLA Handbook for Writers of Research Papers*, 430, 431, 438
Monologues, 291
Narratives, 163, 164

Organization, 42, 60, 87, 100, 163, 178, 179, 199, 222, 235, 251, 278, 332, 443, 458
Outlining, 60, 178, 212, 339, 400
Paraphrasing, 122, 147, 439
Persuasive techniques, 394, 397, 399, 414
Persuasive texts, 168, 199, 389, 394
Plagiarism, 211, 438
Planning, 54, 55, 101, 164, 203, 229, 265, 293, 365, 422, 435, 436, 443, 458, 459
Point of view, 228, 377, 378
Position paper, 435
Poster creation, 420, 446
Precise language, 234, 235
Prewriting, 55, 101, 164, 203, 222, 265, 365
Proposals, 419, 458
Publishing, 55, 101, 164, 265, 365, 459
Purpose statement, 253
Quickwrite, 176, 281, 292, 396, 419, 431
Quotations
  citing, 87, 364
  as evidence, 32, 36, 42, 87, 210, 217, 226, 251, 376, 382, 435
  integrating, 17, 36, 42, 81, 96, 210, 442
RAFT, 236, 237
Reasoning, 174, 175, 192, 400
Reflecting, 55, 101, 164, 203, 229, 265, 365, 430, 443, 459
Reflective commentary, 320
Refutations, 88, 100, 178, 188, 401, 412, 414, 456
Research, 128, 166, 188, 192, 208, 211, 215, 264, 265, 270, 291, 293, 332, 370, 420, 422, 430, 431, 433, 442, 443, 445, 459
  note cards, 212
  questions, 60, 215, 227, 228
Revising, 16, 20, 50, 55, 100, 101, 164, 192, 203, 265, 365, 378, 391, 442
Rhetorical appeals, 176, 180, 181, 183, 338, 383, 388, 392, 397, 443
Rhetorical questions, 288, 351
Role playing, 437
Scoring guide, 56, 102, 165, 204, 230, 266, 294, 366, 444, 460
Scripts, 447, 458
Sharing, 36, 60, 127, 199, 202, 212, 235, 281, 377, 378, 385, 391, 437
Sources
  annotating, 430, 432
  citing, 192, 430, 431, 432, 438, 439, 440
  evaluating, 211, 212, 423, 429, 430, 432, 433, 434

  incorporating, 439, 440, 441–442
  locating, 430
  in oral presentations, 441–442
  sample bibliographic entries, 431
  in synthesis papers, 60
  websites, 211, 429, 431, 432
Storyboards, 451, 455
Style, 20, 65, 225
Style manuals, 332
Summarizing, 12, 163, 166, 210, 231, 235, 295, 391, 430
Summary statement, 281
TAG statement, 65, 81
Technology tips, 228, 265, 443, 459
Thesis statement, 17, 36, 42, 60, 81, 87, 98, 99, 100, 115, 131, 183, 212, 222, 226, 238, 320, 339
Titles, 458
Tone, 179, 199, 225, 253, 393, 407, 450
Topic selection, 227, 421, 422
Topic sentence, 210, 217, 235, 264, 332, 339, 378, 382, 450
Transitions, 17, 36, 42, 235, 264
Visual interpretation, 219
Visual Prompt, 1, 103, 205, 267, 367
Writing prompt
  argument, 65, 81, 100, 179, 192, 199, 203, 220, 388, 393, 415, 419, 435
  compare/contrast, 222
  cultural influences, 97
  deconstructing prompts, 58, 59
  essay, 200
  explanatory text, 7, 32, 36, 42, 87, 96, 110, 115, 131, 148, 183, 210, 217, 222, 226, 235, 238, 242, 244, 251, 253, 264, 278, 320, 332, 364, 376, 388, 391
  film critique, 382, 385, 388, 450
  literary analysis essay, 339, 365, 366
  monologue, 281
  narrative, 122, 127, 142, 228
  panel drawings, 142
  poetry, 42
  responding to, 98
  synthesis paper, 57, 97, 100
Writing to Sources, 32, 36, 42, 65, 81, 87, 96, 110, 115, 131, 148, 183, 210, 217, 220, 222, 226, 235, 238, 242, 244, 251, 264, 299, 320, 332, 364, 376, 382, 414, 450

## Media Skills

Artistic Prompt, 42
Audience, 42, 383
Camera angles, 447, 451, 455
Camera movements, 452, 455

## Speaking and Listening Skills

## Language Skills

formal (academic), 16, 17, 32,
  225, 226
informal, 16
passive, 185, 217

# Vocabulary Skills

Academic Vocabulary, 2, 60, 64, 80, 88,
  104, 168, 174, 206, 211, 228, 268,
  274, 283, 295, 368, 370, 379, 392,
  397, 401, 415, 445
Cognates, 26
Connotation, 85, 147, 170
Content connections, 37, 90, 107, 259,
  354, 402
Context clues, 35, 173
Domain-specific vocabulary, 234
Etymology, 13, 85, 173, 232, 255,
  276, 439
Foreign words, 213, 214, 215
Literary terms, 2, 9, 18, 21, 32, 39, 61,
  66, 104, 109, 111, 116, 123, 149,
  206, 209, 210, 213, 216, 221, 223,
  241, 252, 268, 271, 278, 279, 282,
  302, 305, 308, 312, 333, 368, 374,
  383, 448
Multiple-meaning words, 62, 111, 156,
  177, 186, 218, 233, 275, 287, 324,
  357, 446, 447
QHT chart, 57, 208, 231, 270, 295,
  370, 445
Roots and affixes, 40, 155, 187, 213, 215,
  218, 239, 250, 286, 324, 371, 378,
  379, 383, 389, 431
Word meanings, 296
Word patterns, 242
Word relationships, 284, 342

# Index of Authors and Titles

# Credits

"Ethnic Hash" by Patricia J. Williams from *Transition* No. 73. Copyright © 1997 W.E.B. Du Bois Institute. Published by Indiana University Press on behalf of W.E.B. Du Bois Institute.

"Two Kinds" from The Joy Luck Club by Amy Tan. Copyright © 1989 by Amy Tan. Used by permission of G. P. Putnam's Sons, a division of Penguin Group (USA) Inc.

"Legal Alien" from *Chants* by Pat Mora. Copyright © 1985 Arté Publico Press—University of Houston. Reproduced with permission from the publisher.

"By Any Other Name" from *Gifts of Passage: An Informal Autobiography* by Santha Rama Rau. Copyright © 1961 by Santha Rama Rau. Originally published in *The New Yorker* (March 17, 1951).

"Multiculturalism Explained in One Word: HAPA" from National Public Radio. Copyright © 2008 NPR.

"Where Worlds Collide" by Pico Iyer. Copyright © Pico Iyer. Reproduced by permission.

"My Mother Pieced Quilts" by Teresa Palomo Acosta. Used by permission.

"Everyday Use" from *Love & Trouble: Stories of Black Women* by Alice Walker. Copyright © 1973 by Alice Walker, reproduced by permission of Houghton Mifflin Harcourt Publishing Company.

"Two Ways to Belong in America" by Bharati Mukherjee *The New York Times*, September 22, 1996. Copyright © The New York Times.

"An Indian Father's Plea" by Robert Lake, as appeared in *Teacher Magazine*, Vol. 2, No. 1, September 1990. Used by permission of the author.

"Where I'm From" by George Ella Lyon. Absey and Co., 1999. Reprinted with permission of Absey and Company.

From *Funny in Farsi* by Firoozeh Dumas, copyright © 2003 by Firoozeh Dumas. Used by permission of Villard Books, a division of Random House, Inc.

From *Kaffir Boy* by Mark Mathabane. Copyright © 1986 by Mark Mathabane. Touchstone (a registered trademark of Simon & Schuster Inc.).

"Pick One" by David Matthews *The New York Times*, January 21, 2007. Copyright © 2007 by David Matthews.

"If You Are What You Eat, Then What Am I?" by Geeta Kothari *The Kenyon Review New Series*, Vol. 21, No. 1 (Winter, A24 1999), pp. 6–14. Copyright © The Kenyon Review.

From *Persepolis: The Story of a Childhood* by Marjane Satrapi, translated by Mattias Ripa & Blake Ferris, translation copyright © 2003 by L'Association, Paris, France. Used by permission of Pantheon Books, a division of Random House, Inc.

"Woman with Kite" by Chitra Banerjee Divakaruni from *Leaving Yuba City: Poems*. Copyright © 1997 by Chitra Banerjee Divakaruni. Published by Anchor Books, a division of Random House, Inc.

"Grape Sherbet" by Rita Dove from *Selected Poems*. Published by Vintage copyright © 1993.

From *The Hunger of Memory: The Education of Richard Rodriguez* by Richard Rodriguez. Reprinted by permission of David R. Godine, Publisher, Inc. Copyright © 1982 by Richard Rodriguez.

"Thanksgiving, a Personal History" by Jennifer New. This article first appeared in Salon.com. An online version remains in the *Salon* archives. Reproduced with permission.

"Time to Assert American Values" from *The New York Times*, April 13, 1994, © 1994 the New York Times. All rights reserved. Used by permission and protected by the Copyright Laws of the United States. The printing, copying, redistribution, or retransmission of the Material without express written permission is prohibited.

"Rough Justice" by Alejandro Reyes. *Asiaweek*, May 25, 1994. www.corpun.com

From "On Civil Disobedience" by Mohandas K. Gandhi. Reprinted by permission of Navajivan Trust.

*Declaration of the Rights of the Child*, 1959. Copyright © United Nations, 1959. Reproduced with permission.

"School's Out for Summer" from *Loud and Clear* by Anna Quindlen. Copyright © 2004 by Anna Quindlen. Reprinted by permission of International Creative Management, Inc.

"One Word of Truth Outweighs the World" by Aleksandr Solzhenitsyn. Copyright © 1970, The Nobel Foundation.

From "Hope, Despair, and Memory" Nobel Lecture by Elie Wiesel, December 11, 1986. Copyright © 1986, The Nobel Foundation.

From *Things Fall Apart* by Chinua Achebe, Heinemann 1971. Used by permission of Pearson Education Limited.

"Prayer to the Masks" from *The Collected Poetry* by Léopold Sédar Senghor, translated by Melvin Dixon, pp. 13-14. Copyright © 1991 by the Rector and Visitors of the University of Virginia. Reproduced by permission of the University of Virginia Press.

"An African Voice" by Katie Bacon as appeared in *The Atlantic*, August 2, 2000. Reproduced by permission of Tribune Media Services.

*Antigone* by Sophocles, translated by Ian Johnston, Great Literature from Malaspina Great Books, Vancouver Island University. Used by permission of Ian Johnston.

"I Need to Wake Up" written by Melissa Etheridge. Copyright © 2006 Songs of Ridge Road (ASCAP). All rights reserved. Used by permission.

"DiCaprio Sheds Light on 11th Hour" from HollywoodReporter.com, May 20, 2007. The Hollywood Reporter article used with permission of Prometheus Global Media, LLC.

"Global Warming: No Urgent Danger; No Quick Fix" by Patrick J. Michaels, as appeared in *Atlanta Journal-Constitution*, August 21, 2007. Reprinted by permission of the author.

"Jeremy Clarkson and Michael O'Leary Won't Listen to Green Clichés and Complaints about Polar Bears" by George Marshall from *The Guardian* (UK) March 9, 2009. Copyright Guardian News & Media Ltd 2009. Reprinted by permission.

"A Roaring Battle Over Sea Lions" by Bill Hewitt from *People*, June 9, 2008, Vol. 69, No.22. Copyright © 2009 Time, Inc. All rights reserved. Reproduced from People Magazine with permission.

"Sea Lions vs. Salmon: Restore Balance and Common Sense" by Fidelia Andy *Seattle Times* February 15, 2008. Copyright © 2008 The Seattle Times Company.

## Image Credits

Cover: David Prince/Offset.com; 1 ARENA Creative/Shutterstock; 14 Richard M Lee/Shutterstock; 24 James Steidl/Shutterstock; 25 Mark Aplet/ Shutterstock; 27 Nadasazh/Shutterstock; 29 Horlyan/Shutterstock; 33 Apic/Contributor/ Getty Images; 37 Christie's Images/ The Bridgeman Art Library; 45 Nickolay Stanev/ Shutterstock; 48 szefei/Shutterstock; 66 true nature/ Shutterstock; 68 lev radin/Shutterstock; 71 Jill Lang/ Shutterstock; 73 kylesmith/Shutterstock; 74 George Muresan/Shutterstock; 74 VectorZilla/Shutterstock; 77 SeanPavonePhoto/Shutterstock; 89 Sergey Uryadnikov/ Shutterstock; 91 val lawless/Shutterstock; 93 Nenad.C/ Shutterstock; 103 Stanislaw Tokarski/Shutterstock; 129 bogdan ionescu/Shutterstock; 146 Rose-Marie Henriksson/Shutterstock; 155 Lerche&Johnson/ Shutterstock; 157 dibrova/Shutterstock; 158 Kurkul/ Shutterstock; 171 Byelikova Oksana/Shutterstock; 176 SNEHIT/Shutterstock; 180 Carolina K. Smith MD/ Shutterstock; 181 Scott Rothstein/Shutterstock; 182 jeff gynane/Shutterstock; 190 Carlos Horta/Shutterstock; 194 Eugene Ivanov/Shutterstock; 205 Phaitoon Sutunyawatchai/Shutterstock; 248 Elnur/Shutterstock; 250 EcoPrint/Shutterstock; 267 Elnur/Shutterstock; 275 greglith/Shutterstock; 284 Amra Pasic/Shutterstock; 355 Thumbelina/Shutterstock; 367 © KidStock/Blend Images/Corbis; 409 gillmar/Shutterstock; 416 Jorg Hackermann/Shutterstock